The *Social Psychology* of *Prosocial Behavior*

The Social Psychology of Prosocial Behavior

John F. Dovidio
University of Connecticut

Jane Allyn Piliavin
University of Wisconsin

David A. Schroeder
University of Arkansas

Louis A. Penner
Wayne State University
University of Michigan

Psychology Press
Taylor & Francis Group

New York   London

First Published by Lawrence Erlbaum Associates, Inc., Publishers
10 Industrial Avenue
Mahwah, New Jersey 07430

Reprinted 2010 by Psychology Press

Lawrence Erlbaum Associates, Inc., Publishers
10 Industrial Avenue
Mahwah, New Jersey 07430

Cover art: "Good Samaritan" bronze medal by Donal Hord, courtesy Special Collections, San Diego Public Library

Cover design by Tomai Maridou

Library of Congress Cataloging-in-Publication Data

Dovidio, John F.
 The social psychology of prosocial behavior / John F. Dovidio
 … [et al.].
  p. cm.
 Includes bibliographical references and index.
 ISBN 0-8058-4935-1 (cloth : alk. paper)
 ISBN 0-8058-4936-X (pbk. : alk. paper)
 1. Helping behavior. 2. Social psychology. I. Title.
 HM1146.D68   2006
 158'.3—dc22   2005057453
                                        CIP

This book is dedicated to our families:
Linda, Alison, and Michael
Irv, Allyn, Libby, Maasai, Isaac, and N'Dea
Susie, Lisa, and Kevin
Teri, Charles, and Ellen

To our spouses—for their patience,
support, encouragement, and love;
and to our children and grandchildren—
for being constant reminders of what is really
important in this life and why we need to
understand how to make the world a better,
more helpful place.

Contents

Preface   ix

1 *An Introduction to Prosocial Behavior*   1

2 *The Origins of Prosocial Behavior:*
       Are People Selfish or Selfless by Nature?   33

3 *The Context: When Will People Help?*   65

4 *Why Do People Help?*   106

5 *Planned and Long-Term Helping*   144

6 *The Development of Prosocial Behavior*   180

7 Being the Helper and Being Helped:
   Causes and Consequences   223

8 Prosocial Behavior in Collectives:
   Cooperation Within and Between Groups   268

9 Prosocial Behavior: The Past, Present,
   and Future   308

   References   349

   Author Index   391

   Subject Index   405

Preface

T his book did not turn out the way we expected it would. Perhaps we had listened too much to colleagues who kept asking, "Why are you writing another book on prosocial behavior? There is not much new there." So our original plan was simply to write a new, updated version of our 1995 volume, *The Psychology of Helping and Altruism: Problems and Puzzles*. However, as we started to work on the project, something we had suspected became quite evident to us—there have been many significant new developments in the area of prosocial behavior. There is indeed not much new on the traditional topic of spontaneous interpersonal helping—or bystander intervention. It is no longer the "hot topic" it was in the 1960s and 1970s, when it was one of the dominant research areas in social psychology. Although work in this area has continued to evolve, it is an empirically and conceptually mature area. It may even have reached the state in which we can say that no more work is needed! Perhaps in contrast to the rapid and profound developments of earlier times, the more recent developments on other topic areas have happened at a much slower pace, but they were happening nonetheless.

Thus, as we began the task of updating our earlier book, it became obvious that the study of prosocial behavior was not what it was 30 years ago, or even 10 years ago when our first book on helping and altruism was published. In fact, it is much more exciting today. Although once research on the topic was narrow, focusing on the particular phenomenon of one-on-one helping with strangers, it is now more multidimensional, encompassing a wide range of phenomena including volunteering, blood donation, actions to assist organizations and other people within those organizations, "whistle blowing" to prevent organizations from causing harm, and cooperation within and between groups. The field has also changed dramatically in theoretical scope. Most of the previous theoretical emphasis was on interpersonal processes (what we have labeled "meso-level processes"), but most of the new conceptual breakthroughs have involved, on the one hand, work in more "micro-level processes" related to behavioral genetics and neuroscience and, on the other hand, research in more "macro-level processes" related to planned and sustained actions for or within organizations and prosocial behavior within and between groups. Although the study of helping formerly was primarily the province of social psychologists, it is now of interest to geneticists, biologists, neuroscientists, evolutionary psychologists, economists, sociologists, and political scientists.

Thus, the current book is *not* our old book sprinkled with new references. We still have spontaneous interpersonal helping as an important focus of the volume, and we have retained and updated some sections of the coverage of the 1995 book. However, this book is significantly different from the previous volume in both style and substance. First, stylistically, the current book is more focused on the central themes, containing fewer photographs, cartoons, and boxes. The study of prosocial behavior is a fascinating story, and we let the work speak more for itself. Still, we have tried to present this story with a writing style that will appeal and be accessible to lay readers, undergraduates, graduate students, and professionals in a broad range of disciplines. Second, the research discussed in the book reflects the most recent developments in the field. Forty percent of the references were published since 1995, the year in which the previous book was published.

Third, and most fundamentally, the current book is organized differently and has a decidedly different emphasis than the 1995 volume. It builds systematically from micro-level processes through meso-level processes to macro-level processes—taking the multilevel perspective that we introduced in our recent *Annual Review of Psychology* article (Penner, Dovidio, Piliavin, & Schroeder, 2005). The traditional topic of spontaneous, interpersonal helping is still important, but it now shares the limelight much more with planned, sustained, and collective forms of prosocial behavior. Thus, the conceptual and empirical scope of the present book is much broader than our earlier efforts. And we believe it shows that the "conventional wisdom" that there is not much new to say about prosocial behavior is, quite simply, wrong.

This volume has important personal significance for us. Each of us has been a contributing scholar in this area for over 30 years. Chronologically, philosophically, and professionally, the authors of this book are all in some ways "children of the '60s." In the 1960s, Jane Piliavin had already embarked on her academic career. But it was during this time that she began a career-long program of research on prosocial behavior, including the study of helping in emergencies and long-term prosocial actions such as blood donations. The other authors were students in the 1960s who read the emerging work on helping during that period and were fascinated by it, but we approached the topic from different perspectives. Lou Penner studied prosocial behavior from an individual-difference perspective, asking questions about what personality characteristics differentiate helpers from nonhelpers. Jack Dovidio began his career studying social connections that promote helping and then used helping as a means to study racial attitudes and intergroup relations. Dave Schroeder studied how to make individuals and members of groups more cooperative and helpful even when it might be to their immediate benefit to be selfish. We did not know one another as we began our work on these issues and were literally spread from coast to coast. Despite these differences, all of us shared one very important thing in common: We all saw studying helping and other prosocial actions as a way to incorporate our social interests and concerns into the research that we conducted. It was our common research interests that brought us together, first as professional acquaintances, then as coauthors and co-investigators, then, perhaps most importantly, as friends. Over the years, we have published together in many different combinations. However, as this book illustrates, we have an enduring relationship with each other and a sustained commitment to the study of prosocial behavior as a social force.

Besides original empirical contributions, our careers, both individually and collectively, have been punctuated by authored and edited volumes and review papers summarizing the field at various stages. In addition to our previous volume, *The Psychology of Helping and Altruism: Problems and Puzzles* (1995), over the last 25 years we have written other books on various topics related to helping, altruism, and cooperation, such as *Emergency Intervention* (Piliavin, Dovidio, Gaertner, & Clark, 1981) and *Giving Blood: The Development of an Altruistic Identity* (Piliavin & Callero, 1991), and edited volumes, such as *Social Dilemmas: Perspectives on Individuals and Groups* (Schroeder, 1995), on the topic. We also published a series of review papers charting developments in the study of prosocial behavior (chronologically): Dovidio (1984), Piliavin and Charng (1990), Dovidio, Piliavin, Gaertner, Schroeder, and Clark (1991), Dovidio and Penner (2001), and Penner, Dovidio, Piliavin, and Schroeder (2005). Thus, study of prosocial actions has been part of our professional lives for a long time; we have "grown up" studying when, how, and why people are good to one another. And, as the current volume indicates, the study of prosocial behavior has grown and matured, as well, but it is still also lively, exciting, and energetic—which is how we like to think of ourselves as we have aged.

This book is primarily intended for upper level undergraduate classes and graduate courses in psychology, sociology, and related disciplines, as well as a resource for scholars in the area. Our goal was to write a book that provides a comprehensive review of the literature on prosocial behavior, highlights recent developments in the field, reflects the increasing scope of study in this area, and stimulates people, both in everyday life and in formal scholarship, to work in this area. The new title, *The Social Psychology of Prosocial Behavior*, was chosen to communicate the expanded scope of the volume. Although there are other books on this topic, this volume is distinguished by its breadth and integration. We draw on the varied expertise of four researchers to examine prosocial behavior in terms of micro-level, meso-level, and macro-level processes. Moreover, we attempt to identify common themes and processes in different types of prosocial behavior—such as helping in emergencies, sustained volunteering, prosocial behavior in organizations, and cooperation—and offer both critical analysis and synthesis. We focus not only on integration within chapters and topics but across chapters as well. Our goal is to describe an impressive body of scholarly accomplishments, recognizing the unique facets of different forms of prosocial behavior while elucidating common underlying processes. Our hope is that we not simply to inform readers, but that we also stimulate a new group of students and scholars to study the causes and consequences of prosocial behavior. Although this is perhaps an ambitious goal, we hope this book will represent something of a paradigm shift as we push the boundaries of what the field defines as "prosocial behavior."

ACKNOWLEDGMENTS

In a project of this sort, there are many people who have contributed in many ways to the success of the endeavor, and we feel that it is important to acknowledge and publicly express our sincerely thanks and deep appreciation to them. We were all helped immeasurably by the students at our respectively universities who helped track down references, sat through courses we taught that helped us (and we hope them) better understand the subtleties and nuances of different topics, stimulated our thinking with their perceptive questions and demands for answers, and kept us honest as they read early drafts of the chapters we had written. Therefore, we thank the following students: Alicia

Bembenek, Kim Kinsey, Jessica Nolan (University of Arkansas); Genevieve Cullen, James Donewald, Heather Joseph, Megan MacDonald, Diana Palombo, Allison Stewart, Brittainey Sullivan (University of Connecticut); and Erica Siegl (University of Wisconsin). We also thank our friends and colleagues who offered moral support and helped point us in the right direction to find important articles that we might have otherwise. Among these folks are Eric Knowles, Denise Beike, Jesse Bering, Craig Parks, Marc Fredette, Steve Hitlin, and Doug Behrend. Bob Kerins provided us valuable assistance with his detailed comments on earlier versions of several chapters. We also thank our reviewers: Mark Snyder, University of Minnesota; Nancy Eisenberg, Arizona State University; William Graziano, Purdue University; and Allen Omoto, Claremont State University. We express our deepest gratitude to Irv Piliavin, who started the whole process off 40 years ago with his original ideas and collaborative research in this area with Jane Piliavin. That work produced the first version of the Arousal: Cost-Reward Model, which not only yielded important studies on prosocial behavior but also stimulated collaborations among the four authors of the present volume.

It is also appropriate that each of the authors acknowledge the help received from the other authors. This book may be a prime example of the how cooperation leads to a better outcome than could be realized by the efforts of any one of the individuals involved. No doubt due to our friendships, the successes of our previous work together, and the respect that we have for one another, each of us trusted the others to do what was best for the project. No one was a free rider; all of the authors contributed more or less equally to the project. We suggested in our last book that the order of authorship on the cover should rotate every 3 months; we still have not figured out a way to make that happen. But Jack took the lead on several pieces of this project, and thus he moves to the top of the list this time. After that, Jane, Dave, and Lou just fade together into the equality of "et al."

We want to express sincere appreciation for the support we have received from Lawrence Erlbaum Associates. In particular, our editor, Debra Riegert, first had the confidence that this was a project that deserved to be pursued and then had the patience to help us see it through to completion.

Resource support for this project came from several sources. The Marie Wilson Howells Funds at the University of Arkansas provided support to Dave Schroeder. A one-semester sabbatical from the University of Wisconsin allowed Jane Piliavin to spend much of her time in the spring semester of 2005 on this new volume. A grant to her from the National Institute on Aging (1-R03-AG21526) and funds from her

Conway–Bascom Professorship from the University of Wisconsin supported the work on the health consequences of aging reported in chapter 7, as well as work on this volume. Colgate University provided funds that allowed the authors to meet for a long weekend in Hamilton, NY, to discuss the initial plans for the book and to stimulate our writing. We are grateful for the financial assistance from the Charles A. Dana Professorship to Jack Dovidio and for help with arrangements for the work session provided by Kathy Langworthy and Helen Payne. Lou Penner's efforts were greatly aided by his association with the Research Center for Group Dynamics at the University of Michigan. Irv Piliavin was gracious enough to let us gather later in the process at his and Jane's rental beach house to start the final push to the completion of the book, although we are pretty sure he had a better time visiting his son and grandson in Seattle during that time than he would have had if he had stayed at home!

Finally and most importantly, we thank those closest to us for their patience, support, encouragement, and love as we spent time with our chapter drafts and computers rather than with them; our spouses Irv, Linda, Susie, and Teri have been absolutely wonderful and supportive, perfect examples of what being prosocial and even altruistic is really all about. Although our children (Dave: Kevin and Lisa; Lou: Charlie and Ellen; Jack: Alison and Michael; Jane: Allyn and Libby) are much older than they were when we were working on our first joint book and are now off pursuing lives of their own, they—as well as Jane's grandchildren Maasai, Isaac, and N'Dea—are still constant reminders of what is important in life and why we need to understand how to make the world a better, more helpful place.

CHAPTER 1

An Introduction to Prosocial Behavior

Consider the following short vignettes as we set the stage for our consideration of prosocial behavior.

On September 11, 2001, four commercial airliners were hijacked by terrorists. Two were flown into the towers of the 110-story World Trade Center in lower Manhattan, a third was flown into the Pentagon outside of Washington, DC, and the fourth crashed into a farm field in Pennsylvania. More than 3,000 people were killed as the result of the terrorists' actions. Within this horrendous tragedy, evidence of incredibly heroic prosocial acts by hundreds of people from all walks of life can be found. Trained professionals—police officers, firefighters, paramedics—and people in the buildings attacked risked their lives as they tried to rescue survivors of these attacks. New York Policewoman Moira Smith helped people out of one of the Twin Towers, and then went back in to help more people. She was killed when the building collapsed. Other ordinary citizens simply rose to the occasion. Brian Clark, a vice-president for a brokerage firm, heard someone call for help as he struggled down the stairway and found Stanley Praimnath trapped behind a pile of heavy debris. As Praimnath jumped, Clark grabbed his collar and lifted him to safety. Together they made their way down the stairway to safety, leaving the building only five minutes before it collapsed (Murphy, 2002).

Hurricane Katrina struck the coastal areas of Alabama, Mississippi, and Louisiana on Monday morning, August 29, 2005, making landfall just east of New Orleans. Thousands of homes and businesses along the coast of the Gulf of Mexico were simply swept away when a 25-foot storm surge came ashore. Approximately 1.5 million people had left the affected area in anticipation of the storm, but over 100,000 people remained in the city of New Orleans itself when the hurricane hit. When the levees holding back the waters of the Mississippi River and Lake Pontchartrain failed, the city did not have the means to provide the basic resources of food, water, medical care, and safe housing for those in dire need. Those who had remained behind then had to be evacuated from the city and taken to relocation centers and shelters in the surrounding states and throughout the country. Although well over $1 billion in donations to charitable organizations was collected in short order and many billions more in aid from federal and state governments would be needed to address the full scope of the disaster, it was often the prosocial actions of the citizens of the communities where the shelters were located that made the most important and immediate impact on the lives of these unfortunate evacuees. After brief stays in the shelters, families were often moved to vacant apartments or rental houses made available by local owners, and some families were invited to stay in private homes. Clothing for those who had lost everything was donated and distributed free of charge. Doctors and other health professionals volunteered their time and expertise to provide care. Children who enrolled in new schools were warmly welcomed by their new classmates. Why would ordinary citizens open their homes, give so freely of their time and money, and do whatever they could to provide the necessities of life and to give such a warm reception to people whom they did not know?

Era Watson Walker was born in 1911 and grew up in the hills of rural Arkansas. When she was young, her mother would do volunteer work at their church, and Era thought that she had an "angel for a mother ... the best person I ever knew." As an adult, Era has had a full life, raising two adopted daughters while teaching fifth graders for 30 years. She also taught Sunday school and was a Girl Scout leader. When she retired from teaching in 1971 at age 60 to take care of the three children she adopted from one of her daughters, she began to fill her "free time" with some volunteer work. After the death of her husband of nearly 60 years in 1988, Era tried to volunteer somewhere each day. At age 93, she decided to cut back a little and stopped working at the Art Center of the Ozarks and the Jones Center for Families. But she still volunteers in the office of her church over the lunch hour on Wednesdays, she serves as a counselor for clients who come to the Bread of Life pantry on Thursdays, and on

Fridays she is the receptionist for the Shiloh Museum of Ozark History. For her many years of work, Era was given the "Volunteer of the Year Award" by the local United Way Foundation. She says she volunteers because she "just likes working with and for people" and that she "didn't even think about getting a prize for it." She has given thousands of hours to benefit the lives of others, continuing a family tradition of volunteering. Era says she thinks there is "a little bit of mamma in me." No one would disagree.

Louis Soto is a volunteer who literally gives of himself—he gives blood. From 1958 until 1988, Louis gave 23 gallons of blood, one pint at a time, to help people whom he did not know and would never see, and he helped them to stay alive. He began his quest toward a personal goal of giving 35 gallons of blood in 1954, when he heard about a person who suffered from hemophilia and needed many units of blood each year to survive. Soto has been recognized by the Red Cross for giving blood in every city and town in his home state of Connecticut that had held a blood drive. He is trying to donate blood in the capital of each state in the union, and he thinks nothing of driving thousands of miles from his home to make a donation. His family celebrates the 17th birthday of each child—he has 11 children—by visiting the Red Cross blood donation station, and the family forms caravans to drive around the country to give blood when a need may arise. Obviously the organizers with the Red Cross know about Louis and his commitment, and they will occasionally make specific requests for his help: "We've got a child who needs 20 pints of blood. Do you want to take a ride?" (Hopfensperger, 1988). Who can say how many more gallons he may have given by now?

On the day after Christmas, December 26, 2004, a massive tsunami raced across the Indian Ocean from the site of a tremendous underwater earthquake. The water "piled up" as it approached the shore, and the tsunami wave rose to 80–100 feet along the hardest hit areas nearest to the origin of the quake. An estimated 300,000 people were killed. The people of the world responded to this disaster in prosocial ways, with governments, relief organizations, and individuals pledging billions of dollars for aid. Military units from countries around the world took food, water, and medical supplies to those most in need and ferried out the injured for medical attention. Volunteers from nongovernmental organizations such as the Red Cross/Red Crescent and others contributed logistical expertise and person-power to the relief efforts. The massive outpouring of help and the volunteers who did their part to coordinate the relief efforts corresponded to the massive scope of the disaster.

Rwanda is a country in east-central Africa, inhabited by people from two major tribes: the Hut and the Tutsi. They speak the same language, have a history of intermarriage, and share many cultural beliefs and values, but when Belgium controlled the country, they favored the Tutsis over the more numerous Hut, who were generally seen as less sophisticated agricultural people in comparison to the cattle-owning Tutsi elite. But when Rwanda became an independent country in 1962, the Hutus took power.

In early April 1994, the plane of Rwandan President Juvenal Habyarimana was shot down; he died in the crash. Although it was not clear who was responsible, widespread ethnic violence erupted and genocide against the Tutsi people began. Encouraged by radio propaganda, Hut citizens began to murder their Tutsi neighbors. Within 100 days, 800,000 Tutsi and Tutsi sympathizers were brutally murdered. Despite credible reports of the ongoing genocide, not one country offered assistance or protection to the Tutsi. The United Nations, which had troops stationed in Rwanda when the killing began, withdrew entirely after 10 of its soldiers were killed (Gourevitch, 1999)

Paul Rusesabagina was the manager of a hotel where hundreds of people—Tutsi and moderate Hutu seeking safety from the carnage going on around them—sought safe haven. On several occasions, Hutu military authorities advised Rusesabagina that everyone in the hotel was to be turned over to the military; later there was a threat that the hotel would be attacked by the militia. Rusesabagina contacted industrial and governmental authorities and leaders of countries around the world, informing them about the situation and seeking their help to avoid a slaughter. Because of his previous connections with those in power, his guile and ability to make deals (e.g., bribery, trading liquor for the safety of his charges), and ultimately his willingness to put his own life on the line to protect the lives of those at the hotel, Rusesabagina was a true hero of this dark time in Rwanda's history, saving the lives of over 1,200 innocent men, women, and children from death. For this, he was recognized as the 2000 recipient of the Immortal Chaplains Prize for Humanity, and his story was told in the 2004 movie *Hotel Rwanda*.

In February 2005, the New England Patriots defeated the Philadelphia Eagles 24–21 in Super Bowl XXXIX to win their third NFL Championship in the past 4 years. How had a team that only 5 years before had compiled one of the worst records in the league come back to start become a sports dynasty? One of the keys to success for the Patriots was an emphasis on the *team*—a group of individuals who are willing to work and make sacrifices together to achieve something larger than what the individual pieces might suggest would be possible. As Gestalt psychologists would say, "They make the whole greater than the sum of its parts." Consider the statements of their head coach Bill Belichick (reported in Lavin, 2005): "The strength of the wolf is the pack.... On a football team, it's not the strength of the individual player but ... the strength of the unit and how they all function together." To a social psychologist, what Belichick is really saying is that success comes when the members of the team *cooperate* with one another. The players had confidence in their teammates; they trusted each other and believed that their sacrifices would be reciprocated. Cooperation as a prosocial action leads to success for the group, and everyone shares in the bounty.

You may have never done anything as heroic or dramatic as Policewoman Smith and Mr. Clark. You almost certainly have not given 20+ gallons of blood to the Red Cross or provided safety for refugees avoiding genocide, and the chances are slim that you have ever been on a NFL Championship team. However, you certainly have performed numerous helpful acts for others. You may have donated money or clothing to the relief efforts for the victims of Hurricane Katrina. You may not have volunteered to leave your job to go to a disaster area to help unfortunate victims rebuild homes or repair, but, like Era Walker, you may have distributed food at a local food pantry or homeless shelter. You may have been on a sports team that won the local league or high school conference championship, and you have probably worked on a group project that was especially good because everyone had done their fair share and made some sacrifices to make the project a success. Each of these actions is an example of a prosocial behavior: that is, "behavior that benefits others" (Hinde & Groebel, 1991, p. 5).

Our book is about people contributing to the well-being of others—how, when, and why they do it. As the vignettes demonstrate, prosocial actions may be given under many different guises, and a person may offer assistance to others for many different reasons. Our goal in this book is to explore the variety of ways that prosocial actions are performed and the many reasons why people benefit each other. Prosocial behavior involves interactions between a benefactor (or helper) and someone being helped. Thus, we also consider helping from the points of view of both the person giving assistance and the person receiving the help. In addition, we consider recipients of help as active participants in the transaction; how they behave and what they say have substantial impact on whether they will receive assistance. We do this by asking a number of questions about prosocial behaviors.

At first glance, it may appear that the questions about prosocial actions may have some pretty obvious answers, and that "common sense" is all that is needed to understand prosocial behavior. However, common sense does not always provide correct answers to questions *common sense ↳ doesnt always explain it* (margin note)

prop of 1 person helping ↓ as # of ppl present ↑ (margin note)

about helping and being helped. Consider the following situation. It is early evening, and you are walking home from class. As you round a corner, you twist your ankle on the uneven pavement. You go down in a heap on the empty sidewalk and cannot get up! You are in intense pain; your ankle is badly sprained and may even be broken. As you lie there, you hear the voices of people in an apartment building across the street. If you hope to be helped, would you rather have a single person or 20 people know about your plight? It seems so clear that when there are more people available to help there should be a better chance of being helped. After all, conventional wisdom and common sense tell us that "there's safety in numbers." Social psychologists, however, often find that such conventional wisdom sometimes lets us down; in many situations such as this one, the likelihood that any one person will help goes down as the number of people present goes up. Although you still may get help from at least one of the many people around you, the chance of any one of them helping is reduced. We examine this issue in detail in chapter 3.

Consider another situation. During the Depression of the 1930s, banks were not regulated by the federal government, so there was no insurance on people's deposits. Imagine that you lived in a small town with only one bank during the Depression, and the rumor began to spread that your bank was going to fail. The bank officers assure you and the other customers that everything will be fine; they tell you that everyone's money will be safe if everyone is just patient and allows the bank to deal with a short-term problem. For the town as a whole to survive, it is absolutely essential that the bank continue to operate. But you have your entire savings in that bank! Do you trust the bank, let your account remain, and help save the town? Do you rush to withdraw your money, even if your actions might contribute to a run on the bank and cause it to fail? In the long run, some faith in the bank would be the best course of action for everyone involved. You would have your money, the bank would remain in business, and the town would survive. But, as was seen during the Depression when thousands of banks failed, people will often do what is best for themselves personally in the short run, giving little thought to the impact on the "collective good." What would you have done?

This example represents a form of prosocial behavior that moves beyond one person helping another to situations in which many people acting together (in this case, everyone leaving their money in the bank) might provide benefits for the group (in this case, saving the bank and the town). Groups acting in concert can often accomplish what individuals acting in the pursuit of their own self interest cannot. However, groups must depend on the combined efforts and actions of each of their members; in some cases, if even a single member does not work with others in a coordinated effort, the group may fail. Many examples of cooperation in which everyone helps each other can also be found, and we consider cooperation within and between groups when we get to chapter 8.

Or how about this situation? You are a new student at a university and are having terrible difficulty with a math class. But two people who sit near you are sailing through the class and seem to know and be liked by all the other students in the course. The class is given a homework assignment that counts for 10% of your grade and you have no idea how to do it. Each of these students realizes that you are lost and decides to offer you some help. One says, "Don't worry, I'll solve the problems and then let you copy my answers." The other one says, "Don't worry, I'll show you how to solve the problems if you will help me move my new computer equipment into my room." There is no way the instructor could ever find out how either of the people helped you, and you are pretty desperate. Which offer would you accept? Well, it turns out that most people would choose the second one, even though it requires much more time and effort. We discuss why in chapters 7 and 8.

Not all of the correct answers to questions about prosocial actions are counterintuitive, but we often find that our basic assumptions about prosocial behavior will rarely be correct in all circumstances. By recognizing the limits of "common sense" and "conventional wisdom" and the value of empirical research findings, we can understand prosocial behavior more fully.

UNDERSTANDING PROSOCIAL BEHAVIOR: A COMMON CONCERN

Why should we be concerned with prosocial behavior in the first place? Are people really interested in this topic? One indirect but valid way of determining what is important to members of a society or culture is to simply look at what they talk and write about (Goldberg, 1993). Using this approach, there is abundant evidence that people have, indeed, been interested in trying to understand the nature of prosocial behavior for a long time. Furthermore, this interest has not been restricted to just one culture or to just one period in the history of humanity. The multiple perspectives that have been used by others to understand prosocial behavior may help us to recognize some common and enduring themes that can contribute to our understanding of this topic. To gain these insights, we consider stories illustrating prosocial behavior that come from various cultures, writings from diverse religions, and ideas of major philosophers.

Folktales and Parables About Prosocial Behavior

Folktales, legends, and parables can provide insights into the *themes* that are of common concern to members of a culture and the lessons of life that are considered valuable enough to be passed on from generation to generation. Because prosocial behavior may have an adaptive value increasing the chances of an individual's, group's, and culture's survival (e.g., Campbell, 1975; Dawkins, 1976; Sober & Wilson, 1998), it is not surprising that the stories and folklore of many cultures stress the value of helping one another and the trouble that results from being selfish and greedy. The following stories illustrate the fundamental importance of reciprocal helping and heroism.

One of the most explicit tales of the value of prosocial action comes from African American culture (see Box 1.1). The story of "Spreading Fingers of Friendship" (Abrahams, 1985) is intended to clearly show the tangible benefits of prosocial action. It provides a vivid contrast between the consequences of selfishness and sharing. This tale of Ba Yua and his wives also reflects the strong sense of communalism and duty to one's social group that pervades African cultures (Boykin, 1983).

Other folktales take a different approach to prosocial behavior. Rather than primarily stressing the personal benefits of commonplace and simple acts of helping, they encourage dramatic selfless behavior by providing members of a culture with stories about heroic acts, some of which may include extreme self-sacrifice. For example, Box 1.2 presents a Native American legend from the Oneida nation that describes the courage of a warrior maiden, Aliquipiso. This heroine of the Oneidas endures torture and ultimately gives her life to save her people from starvation (Erdoes & Ortiz, 1984). The actions of Aliquipiso serve as graphic examples of the lengths to which some people will go to promote the well-being of others. The fact that the sacrifices of such heroic individuals are widely reported reflects both the distinctiveness of such feats and the great value that people place on such extraordinary actions.

Although the stories of Aliquipiso and the wives of Ba Yua have been passed from generation to generation by oral tradition (until recent years), other tales with similar messages have been maintained in the written mode. The New Testament parable of the Good Samaritan (Luke 10:29–37) serves as an example of this. In this well-known tale, a man who has been beaten and robbed on his way from Jerusalem to Jericho received no assistance from two passing men of strong religious convictions, a priest and a Levite. However, a Samaritan, who was considered to be something of a religious outcast, stopped to help the victim, bandaging his wounds and taking him to an inn for further treatment. The Samaritan not only gave the innkeeper money to cover any immediate expense but also promised to re-

[handwritten annotations: → 2 wives; ↳ spread fingers, literally/figuratively ↳ husband dies + latter gets brought food.]

Box 1.1

SPREADING FINGERS OF FRIENDSHIP

Ba Yua worked on the plantation. He would bring food from the plantation to his two wives in the city. But when he gave his wives the food, he told them, "When you eat, you must spread your fingers." Now when he said this, the first wife did not understand very well what he meant. He told the second wife the same thing, and she understood what he meant. When he brought them food, they were not to eat them alone, they were to share half with others. You must share with people, not keep all for yourself.

Now the first wife, whatever she cooked, she ate. Then she went outside, and spread her fingers to the air, and said, "Ba Yua said when I eat I must spread my fingers." Ba Yua brought her much bacon and salt fish, but she always ate it alone. But when Ba Yua brought the things for the second wife, she shared with other people.

Not long afterward Ba Yua died, and nobody brought anything to the wife who spread her fingers to the air. She sat alone. But to the wife who had shared things with others, many people brought her things. One brought her a cow, one brought her sugar, one brought her coffee.

Now, one day, the first wife went to the second, and she said, "Sister, ever since Ba Yua died, I have been hungry; no one brought me anything. But look how many people have brought provisions for you!" The second wife asked her, "Well, when Ba Yua brought you things, what did you do with them?" She said, "I ate them." Then the second wife said again, "When Ba Yua said to you, 'You must spread your fingers,' what did you do?" She said, "When I ate, I spread my fingers in the air." The second wife laughed and said, "Well, then, the air must bring you things, because you spread your fingers for the air. For myself, the same people to whom I gave food now bring me things in return." [Adapted from Abrahams (1985).] Original material from Herskovits, F. J., & Herskovits, M. J. (1938/1969). Spreading fingers for friendship. From Suriname Folklore. Copyright © 1938. New York, NY: Columbia University Press. Reprinted with permission.

---

pay any other costs that might be incurred when he returned. Jesus indicated that the Samaritan was the "neighbor" of the fallen victim and admonished those listening to this parable to follow the Samaritan's model: "Go, and do likewise." Although the Samaritan's action may not have been as dramatic as Aliquipiso's heroic behavior, the message is the same: <u>We need to be concerned about the well-being of others.</u>

Telling these stories with their prosocial themes served and continues to serve as an important <u>means of instruction</u> for successive generations of a clan, tribe, society, or culture. The message of the need for prosocial behavior is timeless, and the tales are as relevant today as they were when they were first told. *[handwritten: ↳ still relevant.]*

Box 1.2

THE WARRIOR MAIDEN

Long ago, in the days before the white man came to this continent, the Oneida people were beset by their old enemies, the Mingoes. The villages of the Oneida lay deserted, their fields untended, the ruins of their homes blackened. The men had taken the women, the old people, the young boys and girls into the deep forest, hiding them in secret places among rocks, in caves, and on desolate mountains.

Thus the Oneida people were safe in their inaccessible retreats, but they were also starving. Whatever food they had been able to save was soon eaten up. They could either stay in their hideouts and starve, or leave them in search of food and be discovered by their enemies. The warrior chiefs and sachems met in council but could find no other way out.

Then a young girl stepped forward in the council and said that the good spirits had sent her a dream showing how to save the Oneida. Her name was Aliquipiso and she was not afraid to give her life for her people.

Aliquipiso told the council: "We are hiding on top of a high, sheer cliff. Above us the mountain is covered with boulders and heavy sharp rocks. You warriors wait and watch here. I will go to the Mingoes and lead them to the spot at the foot of the cliff where they all can be crushed and destroyed."

During the night the girl went down from the heights into the forest below by way of a secret path. In the morning, Mingoe scouts found her wandering through the woods as if lost. They took her to the burned and abandoned village where she had once lived, for this was now their camp. They brought her before their warrior chief. "Show us the way to the place where your people are hiding," he commanded. "If you do this, we shall adopt you into our tribe. If you refuse, you will be tortured at the stake."

"I will not show you the way," answered Aliquipiso. The Mingoes tied her to a blackened tree stump and tortured her with fire, as was their custom. Even the wild Mingoes were astonished at the courage with which the girl endured it. At last Aliquipiso pretended to weaken under the pain. "Don't hurt me any more," she cried, "I'll show you the way."

As night came again, the Mingoes bound Aliquipiso's hands behind her back and pushed her ahead of them. Soundlessly the mass of Mingoe warriors crept behind her through thickets and rough places, over winding paths and deer trails, until at last they arrived beneath the towering cliff of sheer granite. "Come closer, Mingoe warriors," she said in a low voice, "gather around me. The Oneidas above are sleeping, thinking themselves safe. I'll show you the secret passage that leads upward." The Mingoes crowded together in a dense mass with the girl in the center. Then Aliquipiso uttered a piercing cry: "Oneidas! The enemies are here! Destroy them!"

(continued on next page)

The Mingoes scarcely had time to strike her down before huge boulders and rocks rained upon them. There was no escape; it seemed as if the angry mountain itself were falling on them, crushing them, burying them. So many Mingoe warriors died that the other bands of Mingoe invaders stopped pillaging the Oneida country and retired to their own hunting grounds. They never again made war on Aliquipiso's people. "Warrior Maiden," from American Indian Myths and Legends by Richard Erdoes and Alfonso Ortiz, copyright © 1984 by Richard Erdoes and Orlando Ortiz. Used by permission of Pantheon Books, a division of Random House, Inc.

Aliquipiso → saved her tribe by luring enemies

Religion and Prosocial Behavior

The lessons that can be learned from folktales and parables are also represented and have been formalized in the major religions of the world. The tenets of these religions provide abstract ethical principles that the followers of the faith are expected to interpret and follow. In some cases, concrete rules of behavior are prescriptive and leave little room for misinterpretation or confusion. As with the folktales just presented, however, it is easy to identify common themes running through diverse religions.

One common theme is the importance of concern for others. Consider, for example, the *Talmud*, a collection of commentaries and interpretations written by Jewish scholars concerning the first five books of the Old Testament. According to this important book in Judaism, "Benevolence is one of the pillars upon which the world rests." In the religion of Islam, the Qur'anic word *Zakah* refers to charity and voluntary contributions as expressions of kindness and as a means to comfort those less fortunate; moreover, it reflects a balance of responsibilities between the individual and society. The teachings of the venerable Chinese philosopher Confucius (551–479 B.C.) express a similar sentiment: "Wisdom, *benevolence*, and fortitude, these are the universal virtues" (*Doctrine of the Mean*, 20: 8; italics added; cited in Hume, 1959, p. 122). The teachings of Lao-Tze (604–517 B.C.), which serve as the basis for Taoism, also advise that one should deal positively with others. Part of Lao-Tze's description of a good person includes the prescriptions "to help [others] in their straits; to rescue them from their perils" (*Sacred Books of the East*, 40: 237–238; cited in Hume, 1959, p. 142). Within Native American religions, Fools Crow, one of the most revered medicine men of the Sioux (or Lakota) nations, stated that tribal elders do not let the rest of the tribe forget the teachings of the "wise old ones" who were taught that inner peace and love were the greatest of Wakan

Tanka's (Lakota for Creator, meaning "Great Spirit") gifts. According to Fools Crow, "We put the *well-being* of other people and of all nature first. We cling to this like a person clings to a raft on a roaring river" (Mails, 1988, p. 8; italics added).

These beliefs of benevolence and love for others are incorporated into a common rule of social behavior that is found in many of the major religions of the world and is often referred to as the Golden Rule: Do unto others as you would have others do unto you. The Jewish version of the prescription for prosocial action may be found in the Old Testament book of Leviticus: "You should love your neighbor as yourself" (Leviticus 19:18). In Christianity, this rule is presented in the Gospel of Luke: "And as you wish that men would do to you, do so to them" (Luke 6:31, *Revised Standard Version*). Given the close relationship between Judaism and Christianity, this similarity might not be too surprising.

However, the same advice can be found in the teachings of Confucius ["What you do not want done to yourself, do not do to others" (*Analects*, 15: 23; cited in Hume, 1959, p. 277)], Taoism's Lao-Tze ["To those who are good to me, I am good. And to those who are not good to me, I am also good. And thus all get to be good" (*Tao-The-King*, 49: 2)], the Buddhist tradition ["Consider others as yourself" (*Dhammapada* 10.1)], and Hinduism ["Do naught to others which if done to thee would cause thee pain: this is the sum of duty" (*Mahabharata*, 5:1517; cited in Hume, 1959, p. 277)]. Although the wording may differ slightly, the sentiment is the same: We should treat others as we would like to be treated. It is clear that this prosocial rule of human behavior is not one that has emerged from a single culture, but rather is a more universal rule for social behavior that appears to play an adaptive function for well-being and perhaps even the survival of the individual and the group.

The notion that human beings should be concerned with the well-being of other people does seem to be at odds with their natural tendencies to "look out for number one." Therefore, it may not be surprising that the abstract "Golden Rule" has been further codified in some religions to compel to a greater or lesser extent benevolence and goodwill to others. For example, as noted above, *zakah* is one of the "Five Pillars of Islam," an annual obligation or duty to contribute a percentage of one's assets to the community for care of orphans, the indigent, and others in need. Many Christian denominations prescribe (or at least recommend) that their members tithe or give 10% of their income to support the activities of the church. Of course, the fact that such specific prescriptions for prosocial behavior are needed does reinforce the notion that there is a natural tendency for people to behave selfishly. Laws, whether civil or religious, typically emerge because there are problems that need to be solved or behaviors that need to be changed (e.g., Schroeder, Steel, Woodell, & Bembenek, 2003). Societies do not typically pass laws to rein-

woulan't have rules unless we needed them.

force and endorse appropriate behaviors that are already being displayed. When social institutions such as religions find it necessary to establish explicit rules to ensure desirable behaviors, one can reasonably surmise that people are not spontaneously conforming to the highest moral and social standards.

Even differences between kinds of help have drawn the attention of religious writers. Moses Maimonides, a 12th-century Talmudic commentator, tried to differentiate among types of helping, no doubt in response to people seeking guidance for their own behaviors. He specified an eight-step hierarchy or "ladder" of prosocial actions (see Box 1.3) in his "Golden Ladder of Charity" (Ausubel, 1948). The bottom two "rungs" of the ladder involve help that is given reluctantly or that does not correspond to the need of the sufferer. The middle rungs include help that is not given until it is requested and aid given in such a way that the recipient feels shame. At the higher levels, help is given anonymously, so that the recipient does not know the benefactor and the benefactor does not know the recipient. Finally, at the highest rung of the ladder is charity provided to prevent future need, such as teaching an individual a trade or referring business so that the person can make an honest living and not have to rely on charity. In addition to specifying the types of help that one should give, this classification scheme demonstrates a keen sensitivity to the reactions of the recipient of help, recognizing that receiving help may threaten the person's self-image and possibly lower self-esteem. Maimonides's consideration of the consequences of receiving help anticipated an issue that is of interest among social psychologists, and a recent book by Salamon (2003) applied these lessons to our modern life, including her own reactions to a homeless man in New York that followed many of the rungs of Maimonides's ladder. We return to this issue in chapter 7.

The religious writings just presented are intended to provide people with strong encouragement to be prosocial in their interactions with others (often with the promise of some "heavenly reward"). Philosophers, social theorists, and others with a more secular perspective have not been as concerned with how people *ought* to act; rather, these writers have attempted to describe how people *do* act. In doing this, they have often reached very different conclusions. As is usual in discussions of philosophy, we begin with the views of the social philosophers of ancient Greece.

Philosophers and Prosocial Behavior

In general, the Greek philosophers were somewhat equivocal about human nature. Socrates (470–399 B.C.) believed that each person pursued that which was "good"—that is, that which was in his or her own

Box 1.3

THE GOLDEN LADDER OF CHARITY

There are eight degrees or steps, says Maimonides, in the duty of charity.

The first and lowest degree is to give—but with reluctance or regret. This is the gift of the hand, but not of the heart.

The second is to give cheerfully, but not proportionately to the distress of the sufferer.

The third is to give cheerfully and proportionately, but not until we are solicited.

The fourth is to give cheerfully, proportionately, and even unsolicited; but to put it in the poor man's hand, thereby exciting in him the painful emotion of shame.

The fifth is to give charity in such a way that the distressed may receive the bounty and know the benefactor, without their being known to him. Such was the conduct of our ancestors, who used to tie up money in the hind-corners of their cloaks, so that the poor might take it unperceived.

The sixth, which rises still higher, is to know the objects of our bounty, but remain unknown to them. Such was the conduct of those of our ancestors who used to convey their charitable gifts to poor people's dwellings, taking care that their own persons and names should remain unknown.

The seventh is still more meritorious, namely, to bestow charity in such a way that the benefactor may not know the relieved person, nor they the name of their benefactor. This was done by our charitable forefathers during the existence of the Temple. For there was in that holy building a place called the Chamber of Silence or Inostentation; wherein the good deposited secretly whatever their generous hearts suggested; and from which the most respectable poor families were maintained with equal secrecy.

Lastly, the eighth and most meritorious of all, is to anticipate charity by preventing poverty; namely to assist the reduced brother, either by a considerable gift, of a loan of money, or by teaching him a trade, or by putting him in the way of business, so that he may earn an honest livelihood; and not be forced to the dreadful alternative of holding up his hand for charity. And it is to this Scripture alludes when it says, "And if thy brother be waxen poor and fallen in decay with thee, then thou shalt support him: Yea though he be a stranger or a sojourner, that he may live with thee."

This is the highest step and the summit of charity's Golden Ladder. [From A Treasury of Jewish Folklore by Nathon Ausubel, copyright © 1984, 1976 by Crown Publishers, Inc. Used by permission of Crown Publishers, a division of Random House, Inc.]

14

best interest. Plato (427–347 B.C.) was a bit more pessimistic about human nature: "Human nature will be always drawing him into avarice and selfishness, avoiding pain and pursuing pleasure without any reason, and will bring these to the front, obscuring the juster and better" (*Laws*, Book IX, p. 754). However, Plato recognized that there were means by which these base instincts could be curbed: "Mankind must have laws, and conform to them or their life would be as bad as that of the most savage beast" (*Laws*, Book IX, p. 754). Later, Aristotle (384–322 B.C.) addressed some of the same issues, but, unlike the egoistic views of Socrates and Plato, he had a more positive view of people, seeing them as basically noble, generous, and good. He believed humans were quite concerned about their social relationships and therefore, by implication, about the well-being of others. Aristotle argued that there is an asymmetry between the reactions of a helper and a person being helped, with the benefactor having a more positive feeling for the recipient than the recipient has for the benefactor.

Almost 2,000 years later, other western European philosophers also addressed the question of whether people are good or bad by nature. Like the Greek philosophers, they often disagreed in the conclusions they reached. Part of the reason for these disagreements was that often their pronouncements on the general character of human nature were, in fact, greatly influenced by the specific time and place in which they lived. For example, Niccolo Machiavelli (1469–1527) lived in 15th- and 16th-century Florence, Italy, and observed the actions of the infamous Medici family members as they connived, plotted, and even murdered to achieve political power and personal riches. Accordingly, his view of human nature was that it was not particularly benign. In *The Prince*, Machiavelli (1513/2003) described people as being "ungrateful, fickle, false" and willing to use others to their own end with little or no real concern for those they have used; in fact, Machiavelli may have written *The Prince* to curry favor for himself from the Medici family. The notion that people would do something to help others without expecting to receive an even greater benefit for themselves is certainly contrary to Machiavelli's characterization of human nature—the Prince may be generous to his subjects, but the pragmatic reason for this generosity is to avoid being hated and to avoid running the risk of being overthrown.

Thomas Hobbes (1588–1679), disturbed and frightened by the political and social upheaval he saw in 17th-century England (i.e., bitter religious and political battles between King Charles I and the House of Commons), espoused a different but equally bleak view of human nature. He believed that the natural state of human affairs was of individual versus individual, each doing what was in his or her own best interest. This selfishness might produce helping, but the motivation for

apol 8?

depends on where & when

such prosocial action would certainly be some expected benefit for the helper. In fact, Hobbes (1651/1668/1994) felt that the only thing that motivates cooperative actions among humans is fear of some outside agent who would punish the most egregious instances of harming others. In the absence of such a threat to keep "them all in awe," he claimed that people would be in almost continual conflict, with "every man against every man." Hobbes (like Plato) believed that the only solution was for people to establish social contracts in the form of governments (what Hobbes calls the "Leviathan") that force restrictions on their own inherently selfish desires. The motives that underlie the creation of the Leviathan are not concerns for others but only self-concern. Presumably, the best government in Hobbes's view would be one that provides each of us with protection from the exploitative attempts of others but imposes only minimal constraints on *our own* self-serving actions.

There is, of course, another possibility. Maybe it is society and the government that it creates that are inherently corrupt and the individual who is good. This was the position of Jean-Jacques Rousseau (1712–1778), a Swiss/French philosopher who wrote some years after Machiavelli and Hobbes. Like many intellectuals in western Europe at that time, Rousseau believed that people are basically good; he believed humans were "noble savages" (see Damrosch, 2005). In his view, human nature starts out as noble, upright, and good—people have an innate sensitivity to others that leads to mutually beneficial relations. If individuals were able to mature in a "natural" state, Rousseau claimed that they would develop a strong moral sense of their obligations to others and live a "virtuous" social existence. As things normally occur, however, this virtue is gradually eroded and corrupted by societal institutions, such as the excesses of French society that Rousseau observed and that ultimately led to the French Revolution in the 18th century. According to Rousseau, society leads people to derive their satisfaction from "being better" than others rather than from an appreciation of the natural harmony of the inner self, the natural environment, and other people. Rousseau believed that progressive educational programs that addressed the changing needs of a person would promote a genuine concern for the common good and a recognition of the need to live in harmonious relations with others.

At this point we would like to make two points clear. Questions about the essence of "human nature" are not idle exercises of the past. More recent philosophers have also grappled with the issue of the core of human nature, and many of the ideas that have been discussed have found their way into the political beliefs and economic systems of the 20th and 21st centuries. For example, Karl Marx (1818–1883) and Friedrich Engels (1820–1895) argued in the *Communist Manifesto* (Marx

& Engels, 1848/1998) for a sharing arrangement among the citizens of a state (the proletariat), and the result was the political system of communism that became the form of government for many countries, most notably in the former Union of Soviet Socialist Republics; to a certain degree, communism is still the dominant political/economic philosophy in the People's Republic of China. The prescription for communal living and the benchmark for communist ideology were captured in the phrase "From each according to his ability; to each according to his need." Although the true cooperative philosophy of Marxist theory was not well captured in the Lenin–Stalin form of communism of the Soviet Union, this ideal of everyone doing all they possibly can for the well-being of the group, secure in the knowledge that all their needs would be satisfied, is a perfect example of the potential benefits of cooperation for the common good.

At roughly the same time as Marx and Engels were introducing their views in Europe, various so-called "utopian societies" emerging in the United States during the mid-1800s strived for a truly communal lifestyle, including the Amana Colonies of Iowa, the Oneida community of New York, and New Harmony in Ohio (see Tyler, 1962, for descriptions of these communities). These groups often began as small, closed communities in which all work and production was done by the members of the group. The critical point to recognize in the charters and constitutions of these "communal living experiments" is the high value placed on cooperation and sharing (of good and bad) by the adherents of the groups, who often gave up successful careers and moved away from their families to be a part of these communities. Unfortunately, problems seemed to emerge when more self-serving motives began to arise in some individuals in the group, leading to internal rifts that often brought an end to the communities (e.g., Baden, 1998a, pp. 135–153).

The utopian societies and the "pure" form of communism were based on the assumption that the common good could be achieved and everyone would prosper if everyone pulled together and contributed their fair share to the well being of the community. A more recent social philosopher, however, proposed a very different view of what was necessary for the greater good to be achieved, reflecting a very different view of human nature. Ayn Rand, author and playwright of the middle part of the 20th century, touted the egoistic approach to life in many of her writings, including *The Virtues of Selfishness* (1964). Her "Objectivism" philosophy advocated rugged American individualism and what she called the "morality of rational egoism." In sharp contrast to the virtues of cooperation and communitarianism, she saw the pursuit of one's own self-interest as being the highest form of morality, and, conversely, selflessness as the deepest immorality. In a 1964 interview in *Playboy* maga-

OK to help if can but charity shouldn't be a duty/virtue

zine (Toffler, 1964), she conceded that there is "nothing wrong with helping other people, if and when they are worthy of the help and you can afford it" (p. 32). But she argued, "What I am fighting is the idea that charity is a moral duty and a primary virtue" (p. 33). For Rand, to pursue one's own happiness is the greatest value, and self-responsibility for one's actions was a major focus of her philosophy. In addition, this notion of self-interest is very much in line with the writings of Adam Smith (1723–1790), who believed that if each person pursued his or her own best interest, an "invisible hand" would lead to the best outcome for all. The roots of capitalism and the United States's free enterprise system can be traced back to Smith's beliefs, espoused in *The Wealth of Nations* (1776/1933). It may not be surprising to find that such influential "free-market" economists as Nobel Prize winner Milton Friedman and Alan Greenspan (retired chairman of the Federal Reserve Board, which sets interest rates and other economic policies of the United States) were among Ayn Rand's devoted followers.

Folktales, legends, religious teachings, and moral philosophies inculcate the members of a society and culture with the values that guide their lives and also provide us with a rich conceptual background for the study of prosocial behavior. However, reliance on these sources will not enable us to answer the questions that we might have about helping, altruism, and cooperation. In fact, although some common themes do emerge from these disparate sources, often they reach very different conclusions about how humans *should* act and how humans *do* act. In these cases, there is no impartial means to determine which one is correct. Thus, other strategies need to be pursued if we are to finally grasp the full complexities of the domain of prosocial behavior. The strategy we take in this book is to rely on the systematic, scientific study of prosocial behavior.

THE SCIENTIFIC STUDY OF PROSOCIAL BEHAVIOR

Among the scientific disciplines, social psychology has taken the lead in the study of prosocial behavior. William McDougall, author of one of the first social psychology text books in 1908, provided an early explanation for prosocial actions. According to McDougall, social behavior is governed by a set of primary instincts (*flight, repulsion, curiosity, pugnacity, self-abasement, self-assertion,* and *parenting*), which are capable of prompting thought and action. These instincts are inextricably linked to corresponding emotions (i.e., *fear, disgust, wonder, anger, subjection, elation,* and *tenderness,* respectively). Of particular interest for our purposes is the "parental" instinct and the associated "tender emotion" that McDougall posited as being at the root of prosocial behavior. He suggested that a mother's care of her child is the prototype of the parenting instinct, and he argued that it can be more powerful than any of the other instincts. McDougall (1908/1936) claimed that the tender emotion is not equivalent to sympathy, but he believed that the prosocial behaviors of "generosity, gratitude, love, pity, true benevolence, and altruistic conduct of every kind" (p. 61) arise from this instinct and its corresponding emotion.

McDougall's approach to understanding social behavior, in general, and prosocial behavior, in particular, sought to identify the underlying processes responsible for this facet of human action. The folktales, religions, and moral philosophies presented earlier were primarily concerned with the description and prescription of prosocial behavior, focusing on how people *do act* or *should act* rather than trying to understand *why* they act as they do. McDougall's emphasis on questions of why people act as they do represented a major shift in the study of prosocial behavior. Unfortunately, however, the methods of investigation that were available to McDougall in the early 1900s did not lend themselves well to answering the questions that he sought to answer. Moreover, the growing influence of behaviorism (e.g., Watson, 1913) during this period seriously limited the impact that any instinct-based theory could have on the field of psychology at that time. McDougall had to rely on the same procedures that the early philosophers had used in their attempts to understand helping—a critical conceptual analysis of the phenomenon of interest that ultimately relied on intuition, authority, and rationalism. Although often enlightening, the claims made by those who employed such strategies suffered from a lack of observable, objective kinds of evidence that would support them. Without *empirical*, objective data, people are forced to rely solely on logical arguments of an authority rather than on direct observations to verify the authority's conclusions.

Perhaps it was for this reason that for almost 50 years after McDougall's introduction of the topic, there was little interest among psychologists in the study of prosocial behavior. Beginning in the early 1960s, however, researchers began to recognize the important role of prosocial behavior in the ways individuals and groups functioned (Gouldner, 1960). And then things changed even more dramatically in the mid-1960s.

The event that is frequently cited as being responsible for this change was the murder of a young woman, known as the Kitty Genovese incident. As Katherine "Kitty" Genovese returned from work to her home in Queens, NY, early one morning, she was attacked and stabbed repeatedly by a lone assailant. Although at least 38 others listened or watched in silence from their apartments, no one came to her assistance. Thirty minutes after the attack had begun, one of the anonymous witnesses finally reported the incident to the police. By then, it was too late to help—Ms. Genovese had died of her wounds. Ms. Genovese's murder drew the attention of the general public and social scientists alike. The apparent callousness and indifference of people who live in big cities (especially New York City) were widely condemned in the popular press. What could possibly have caused such apathy?

Kitty Genovese's murder also attracted the interest of two social psychologists, Bibb Latané and John Darley. But rather than approaching the event from the perspective of philosophy, offering more social commentary, or using a critical conceptual analysis, they applied the contemporary methods and knowledge of social psychology to understand this unfortunate incident more fully. In particular, Latané and Darley used the experimental method to find answers to many of the questions raised by Ms. Genovese's murder. For example, why did none of her neighbors leave their apartments to give her protection? Why did the one witness who called the police wait so long to make his telephone call, and why did he wish to remain anonymous?

By using the empirical approach that is a defining feature of the scientific method, Latané and Darley were able to identify some of the situational factors that can promote or inhibit helping. As we show in chapters 3 and 4, their research program led to the development of a model of the decision-making processes that people use when deciding whether to help someone in distress. Latané and Darley opened the floodgates for empirical research work on helping behavior. In the 20 years after Ms. Genovese's murder, over 1,000 research articles were published concerning prosocial behavior (Dovidio, 1984). Moreover, in the past 20 years the study of prosocial behavior has expanded in exciting ways well beyond the study of emergency intervention and other, more everyday forms of spontaneous helping. Prosocial behavior is recognized today as a much broader phenomenon and behavior that is intertwined in the fabric of social life. We examine these emerging topics, as well as the traditional issues, in the chapters of this book.

We do not want to suggest, however, that the systematic and scientific study of prosocial behavior is the exclusive domain of social psychology. Within psychology, prosocial actions are also of interest to many developmental and personality psychologists. Outside of psychology, social scientists in sociology, anthropology, economics, organizational behavior, and political science study the causes and consequences of positive forms of interpersonal behavior, and these approaches complement the social psychological approach to helping and altruism. On the whole, psychologists tend to focus on individuals as opposed to collectives (i.e., groups, societies, cultures), and, as a result, they tend to study the factors that influence a single person to act in a prosocial manner *within* dyadic (two-person) or group (multiperson) situations. The individual therefore may be seen as the primary level of analysis. But to answer some of the important questions about prosocial behavior, we need and in fact want to also consider the broad social and societal context in which prosocial actions occur. These other "social" sciences provide this perspective.

Finally, we need to mention that the social and behavioral sciences are not the only disciplines that study prosocial behavior. As we show later (primarily in chap. 2), there is considerable interest in altruism and other prosocial actions among ethologists, geneticists, sociobiologists, and other natural scientists.

all domains – not just psych

Defining Our Terms

Thus far, we having been using words and phrases such as *prosocial behavior, altruism, helping,* and *cooperation* in a somewhat loose and informal manner. Before we proceed any further, we need to define more precisely these and other terms that we use throughout this book. As we present our definitions of the terms of interest, you can gain some sense of the kinds of problems one encounters when one tries to provide precise, "scientific" definitions of the phenomena of interest. That is, within psychology and across scientific disciplines one of the greatest problems in the systematic study of prosocial behaviors has been the lack of consensus about the meanings of these critical terms. This is reasonable, because, as we stress repeatedly throughout this book, the psychology of helping and altruism involves complex scientific, semantic, and philosophical issues. With this caveat in mind, let us proceed.

We try to understand and elucidate different kinds of *prosocial* behaviors. *Prosocial behavior* is the label for a broad category of actions that are "defined by society as generally beneficial to other people and to the ongoing political system" (J. A. Piliavin, Dovidio, Gaertner, & Clark, 1981, p. 4). There are several features of this definition that deserve comment. First, as we noted earlier, prosocial behavior is necessarily an interpersonal act: There must be a benefactor and one (or more) recipient(s) of the benefits for a prosocial act to occur. Second, the phrase *defined by society* implies that a given behavior is not inherently or universally prosocial (or antisocial for that matter). Rather, this is a social judgment that could change dramatically as the result of changes in the circumstances or historical and political context in which the behavior takes place. For instance, taking something from a store without paying for it would normally be considered an antisocial action, but many people would view taking desperately needed medical supplies from the wreckage of a neighborhood drugstore following some devastating natural disaster as a prosocial action and the person who did this might be viewed as a hero.

Conversely, consider the "Good Samaritan" laws that were enacted in Germany in the 1930s. These laws required German citizens to help the police round up and imprison criminals and enemies of the state (J. A. Piliavin et al., 1981). At first, this may appear to be a prosocial behavior. However, in the 1930s in Germany the "police" were the SS, or Shutzstaffel secret police, and the "criminals" were homosexuals, Gypsies, Jews, and other groups whose sole "crime" was to be hated by the Nazi government. Many of the people who were rounded up and imprisoned as a result of the enforcement of these laws were later killed in concentration camps. Thus today, with the benefit of historical perspective and what we now see as a different "definition by society," we see the German citizens' compliance with these so-called Good Samaritan laws as antisocial and morally reprehensible, to say the least.

Although we need to be mindful of the contextual nature of prosocial behavior, it is not this part of the definition that may cause problems for the person who wants to study prosocial behavior. Recall some of the examples presented at the beginning of this chapter: holding the door for another student, volunteering to help in a service organization, working together with team members, and assisting at the scene of an accident. There would be little disagreement among the vast majority of people in our society that these are all prosocial actions. The problem with the term *prosocial behavior* is that it may be too broad for some of our purposes. It can be used to describe an extremely wide range of actions. In many instances, the term does not capture the important distinctions between and differences among the various kinds of prosocial actions in which humans engage. To answer many of the important questions about the phenomena of interest, we must try to distinguish among three subcategories of prosocial behavior: helping, altruism, and cooperation.

Helping. The category of greatest interest to this book is *helping,* which we define as an action that has the consequence of providing some benefit to or improving the well-being of another person. The definition for helping is not particularly stringent; as long as the well-being of one or more people is improved by the actions of another (e.g., giving a gift, providing resources to accomplish a task), helping has occurred. In some cases, such as donating money to a charitable organization, the benefactor may not even come into direct contact with the recipient of aid.

In an attempt to identify categories of helping, McGuire (1994) asked college students to list the different kinds of help they had received from and given to friends, casual acquaintances, and strangers. (The most frequent helping behavior reported by the students was helping someone with a homework assignment or schoolwork.) McGuire used the students' answers to generate a classification scheme for different kinds of helping behaviors. According to her analysis, there are four kinds of helping: (a) *casual helping*—doing some small favor for a casual acquaintance, such as lending the person a pen; (b) *substantial personal helping*—expending some considerable effort to provide a friend with tangible benefit, such as helping the friend move into an apartment; (c) *emotional helping*—providing emotional or personal support to a friend, such listening to a friend's personal problems; and (d) *emergency helping*—coming to the aid of a stranger with an acute problem, such as helping the victim of an accident.

Just as college students can identify different kinds of helping, literally hundreds of different kinds of behaviors have been used by researchers studying helping behavior. These include simple tasks (such as telling a stranger what time it is, picking up dropped pencils, or contributing to a service organization) and more difficult tasks that require a significant commitment of time and/or energy (such as chaperoning a group of teenagers to the zoo, or helping a heart attack victim). Because Kitty Genovese's murder stimulated much of the work in this area, many researchers chose to use experimental methodologies and situations that would fit in McGuire's category of "emergency helping." Many of these helping studies have been conducted in laboratory settings, but many others have been field experiments conducted in naturalistic situations. For example, Piliavin and Piliavin (1972) staged "emergencies" in the subways of Philadelphia to determine if the presence of blood would affect bystanders' rate of helping a "victim" (actually a confederate of the experimenters) who had collapsed. Still other studies have used questionnaires, interviews, and naturalistic observations to study helping. There is virtually no limit to the number of the behaviors, kinds of settings, and variety of methods that have been used to study this phenomenon.

In an attempt to provide a clearer picture of what helping really is, Pearce and Amato (1980) proposed a classification scheme (or taxonomy) that categorizes helping situations along three critical dimensions (see Fig. 1.1). On the basis of their analysis, they suggested that helping situations can be rated according to the extent to which the help is *planned and formal* (e.g., volunteering to serve as a "buddy" for a person with AIDS) versus *spontaneous and informal* (e.g., telling someone they had just dropped a package). Helping can also differ according to the *seriousness* of the problem (e.g., the difference between giving

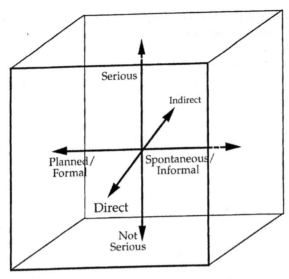

FIG. 1.1.   Pearce and Amato's three-dimensional taxonomy of helping situations.

change to make a telephone call and giving aid to a heart attack victim). Finally, helping situations can differ in terms of whether the help involves *indirect giving* of assistance, such as making a donation to a favorite charity, or *doing* something *directly* to help the person in need, such as pulling a young child from the path of a speeding car.

Although Pearce and Amato's and McGuire's taxonomies differ somewhat from one another, they both suggest to us two important conclusions about helping: Not all helping is the same, and the factors that affect helping in one set of circumstances may not have the same impact on helping in other situations. You can find examples of both these conclusions in every chapter of this book. In fact, we examine in great detail the differences that exist between the kind of emergency intervention and spontaneous helping that first spawned research in this area and more recent work that investigates the nature of long-term helping, and in the final chapter of the book we propose alternative models that capture and specify how these two categories of helping differ.

Altruism.   The concept of altruism is very closely related to helping. But if we return to the definition of helping that we just presented, we can begin to see how the two concepts differ. In our definition of helping, the *intent* of the benefactor and whether or not the benefactor also *benefits* from helping were not at issue. This is not the case for altruism. Altruism is often seen as a specific kind of helping with some additional characteristics that concern the helper's intentions and benefits. In general, helping researchers in social psychology have reserved the term *altruism* for cases in which the benefactor provides aid to another *without the anticipation of rewards from external sources for providing assistance* (Macaulay & Berkowitz, 1970). This definition is consistent with a more recent definition of altruism offered by Aronson, Wilson, and Akert (2004): "Altruism is helping purely out of the desire to benefit someone else, with no benefit (and often a cost) to oneself" (p. 382).

As the definition by Aronson et al. might suggest, some theorists would like to restrict the use of the altruism label even further and impose the additional condition that helpers must incur some cost for their action (e.g., Krebs, 1982; Wispé, 1978). The addition of the self-sacrifice criterion as a necessary condition for altruism presents some problems, primarily because it shifts the focus of the definition from the beneficial consequences received by the victim to the consequences realized by the helper (Batson, 1991). The self-sacrifice criterion does, however, make explicit the widely held belief that true altruists cannot receive any personal benefit for their actions.

In the preceding definitions that have tried to differentiate between helping and altruism, the major focus has been on the *act* of providing assistance and the consequences of the behavior *for the helper*. C. Daniel Batson (e.g., 1991, 1998), however, proposed an alternative point of view that has been quite influential among social psychologists who study prosocial actions. He argued that we should concentrate on the *motivation* for the act rather than on its consequences when trying to draw these distinctions. He claims the important contrast is between helping that is motivated by egoistic concerns (e.g., "If I help that person, it will make me feel good and look good to others") and helping that is motivated by altruistic concerns (e.g., "I want to help this victim avoid further suffering"). This distinction actually has its roots in early work by Auguste Comte (1851/1875; cited in Batson, 1991), who first coined the term "altruism" to contrast it with "egoistic" helping. For Batson (1991, 1998), altruism refers not to the prosocial act per se but to the underlying reason for the act: "Altruism is a motivational state with the ultimate goal of increasing another's welfare" (p. 6). Of course, as outsiders we cannot directly observe or measure a person's "motivational state." As a consequence, it is often very difficult to determine if an act of helping is truly "altruistic." For example, when a person races into a burning building to rescue someone trapped inside, is that person primarily motivated *altruistically*, by his or her concern for the welfare of those who might remain in the building, or *egoistically*, by his or her desire to curry favor and praise with this "heroic act" or, alternatively, to avoid a sense of guilt if nothing was done?

Batson did not deny the existence of egoistically motivated helping, but he offered significant empirical support for his argument that there are certain instances (particularly when a potential helper feels "empathic concern" for the person in need) in which the *primary motive* for providing help is to improve the state of another. Even if the helper does receive some social or material reward for providing assistance, as long as the helper's primary intention was to help the other person, Batson argued that the act should be considered altruistic. Batson conducted a number of impressive experiments, the results of which appear to support his theoretical position on the existence of altruism. However, not everyone agrees with Batson's interpretations of his findings (e.g., Cialdini, Brown, Lewis, Luce, & Neuberg, 1997). This has been the subject of a long and lively debate, to which we return in chapter 4.

Other disciplines have still other definitions of altruism. Economists, for example, define altruism in terms of the value of an act for the recipient and more specifically of the cost of the action for the donor. Biologists and ethologists view altruism in terms of the contribution that an action makes to the survival of some group's gene pool, what is sometimes referred as "inclusive fitness." More specifically, according to these scientists, an altruistic behavior is one that increases the likelihood that an altruist's close genetic relatives will survive and reproduce, and thus pass their genes on to successive generations (Dawkins, 1984). Note that for the biologist, an individual helper's motivational concerns and intentions are essentially irrelevant. Indeed, so-called "evolutionary altruism" (e.g., a bee sacrificing its life to protect the hive) occurs without any thought or awareness (Sober, 1988, 1992; Sober & Wilson, 1998; see also chap. 2).

Given the divergent views of what constitutes an altruistic action and the numerous definitions of altruism that have been offered, we are not prepared to select the *one* correct way of defining it. Others faced this problem as well. For example, Sober and Wilson (1998) simply used two different labels (i.e., psychological altruism and evolutionary altruism) as their solution to the dilemma. As a result, there may appear to be some inconsistencies across the chapters in how we use the word *altruism*, depending on the context within which we are using it. But at a minimum, when we use the word *altruism*, we are referring to a helpful act that is carried out in the absence of obvious and tangible rewards for the helper. Sometimes we go beyond this rather minimalistic definition and specifically discuss the motivations, intentions, and consequences for the helper. As we noted before, we recognize that all prosocial acts are not created equal and that the intentions and motives of helpers may be the critical criteria for distinguishing between the various forms of helping that we discuss. But there are places in the book where we are not able to make these distinctions, because we are not completely sure of how to characterize a particular prosocial action. As we just told you, in something as complex and multifaceted as helping, some amount of ambiguity and inconsistency is unavoidable. It is important to recognize, however, that we do not see "helping" and "altruism" as being synonymous; all acts of altruism are acts of helping, but all helping is not necessarily altruism.

    Cooperation. *Helping* and *altruism* refer primarily to situations in which one person (or group) provides aid to another (or others) in need, but there are times when people come together to work together toward a *common goal* that will be beneficial to all concerned. Michael Argyle (1991) defined *cooperation* in the broad perspective of social life: "acting together, in a coordinated way at work, leisure, or in social relationships, in the pursuit of shared goals, the enjoyment of the joint activity, or simply furthering the relationship" (p. 4). (This definition may be somewhat reminiscent of the philosophical discussion of utopian societies and communal living.) Argyle further identified three ways in which individuals may cooperate with one another: cooperation for material rewards, communal relationships, and coordination (p. 5). Kohn (1986), in his critical appraisal of what he sees as our competitive society, defined cooperation as "an arrangement that is not merely noncompetitive but requires us to work together in order to achieve our goals" (p. 6). Kohn (1990) saw cooperation as a "humanizing experience [that] … transcends egocentric and objectifying postures, encourages trust, sensitivity, open communication, and, ultimately, prosocial activity" (p. 93).

    Because cooperators can reasonably expect that they all will mutually benefit to some degree from their joint efforts, cooperation is a specific kind of prosocial behavior. Cooperation thus differs from the unilateral kinds of helping that we have discussed thus far. The primary difference is that, with cooperation, all those involved in the exchange contribute in one way or another to the group's outcome as partners sharing in the group's attempt to achieve some common goal. In helping relationships, the two parties are typically not equal partners, with one entity (a person or group) being in need of assistance and the other entity (a person or group) possessing the resources to respond to their needs. Indeed, in some other instances, the two parties in a helping relationship may be driven apart by the interaction and have differing and perhaps even diametrically opposing goals. For example, the benefactor may be perceived as assuming a position of power over the recipient, who may then feel a sense of indebtedness (Nadler, 1991). As a consequence, the recipient's sense of obligation to the helper may strain the relationship. In cooperative exchanges, how-ever, because of the absence of a power hierarchy and the realization of common rewards, greater group cohesiveness and more positive inter-personal relations usually occur.

Just as helping researchers have discovered that there may be both egoistic and altruistic motivations when a person decides to help an-other, the situations in which cooperation has been studied are often constructed so that different motives of the individuals involved come in conflict with one another. Consider the following situation. The hot water heater in your apartment provides just enough hot water for you and your roommates to each take a quick shower in the morning. You re-ally enjoy letting the hot water beat down on you, but you also realize that your roommates would have to take cold showers if you indulged yourself. What would you do? (For that matter, what would Machiavelli or Hobbes or Rousseau or Ayn Rand do?) The answer to this question and the study of cooperative (and competitive) strategies in this kind of situation is also part of understanding prosocial behavior. We discuss this issue in chapter 8 when we discuss *social dilemmas* in which one's personal best outcome is at odds with the best collective outcome.

OUR VIEW OF PROSOCIAL BEHAVIOR

The study of prosocial behavior remains full of unsolved problems and unanswered questions. It is interesting that Latané and Darley's (1970) book reporting the work that sparked so much interest in the area of prosocial behavior had a question as its title—*The Unresponsive By-stander: Why Doesn't He Help?* Later, Batson (1991) titled his book on this topic *The Altruism Question*. Many questions about prosocial behavior remain to be asked and remain to be answered, and our goal for the re-mainder of this book is to delve deeply into this most intriguing aspect of social relations.

For example, although Latané and Darley and the public at large were shocked, surprised, and even outraged that people were reluctant to come to the aid of Ms. Genovese, was there really any good reason why we ought to expect someone to provide aid to a perfect stranger? What would make a person willing to get involved in a potentially dangerous emergency situation or to give time or money to some charitable cause from which she will receive little or no benefit? Is there something about a person—some personal characteristic, perhaps—that makes that per-son more inclined to give help or to cooperate with others? If there is some personal characteristic related to a tendency to help, is that tendency due to some inborn, genetic endowment that makes helping a part of the human condition, or has the person simply learned to be helpful in the same way that people learn many other social behaviors? And what about the people who are in need of help? Are there certain circumstances in which people confronted with problems will try to solve their own problems instead of asking for assistance from someone else?

These kinds of questions illustrate the broad issues that confront social psychologists and other scientists in their efforts to understand more fully the nature of prosocial behavior. We use these questions and many others to guide our exploration of this intriguing field of investigation. Chapters 2 through 8 of this book begin with one or more of these questions about some aspect of prosocial action. Using the introductory question as our starting point, we then consider the research findings as they pertain to this question. Rather than simply describing a series of research studies, we present the basic concepts and principles that have been identified. We conclude each chapter with a summary and an answer to the introductory question. Here are brief synopses of each of the chapters of the book and the questions asked in each of them.

In chapter 2, we explore reasons for the seeming pervasiveness of prosocial behavior among human beings and the claim made by some (e.g., Hunt, 1990) that humans are "compassionate beasts." Specifically we consider the evidence for a genetic basis for prosocial tendencies and seek to understand the processes and mechanisms that are responsible for such tendencies. To answer questions about genetic predispositions for prosocial behavior, we present concepts from behavioral genetics and evolutionary theory, including evolutionary psychology, and neuroscience in an attempt to explain why humans seem so predisposed to be prosocial. For example, we discuss the biological mechanisms and social processes that may be responsible for humans' remarkable tendency to empathize with others in need. Although we often think of "survival of the fittest" as meaning that the strongest, fastest, and perhaps smartest will win out, our analysis and review suggest that being the "nicest" might also be included in the listing of who is "the fittest" in some cases.

The focus of interest in chapter 3 is on how bystanders react when they see a person in distress; this is the question, raised by Kitty Genovese's murder, that first generated interest in the study of helping behavior. Because the bystanders in that situation were passive, Bibb Latané and John Darley initially asked the question of why bystanders *do not* help. We ask substantially revised versions of the question: "*When* will a bystander help?" and "What conditions lead a bystander to offer help to a person in need?" More specifically, chapter 3 explores how the context or situation affects a bystander's decision of whether or not to offer short-term, spontaneous help in an emergency. To answer these questions, we introduce a model of how people make decisions about helping, and we complement this model with a discussion of how the costs and rewards associated with helping affect the actions a bystander takes.

Chapter 4 also focuses on bystander intervention and short-term helping, but chapter 3 asked *when* will people help, whereas chapter 4 asks the question "*Why* do bystanders decide to intervene on another person's behalf?" That is, we address the factors that motivate a bystander to offer help: What purpose does helping play, and what function does helping serve for the helper? Although we typically assume that benefiting the person in need drives our prosocial behavior (that is, altruistic motives), we argue that benefit for the helper (i.e., egoistic motives) can often be the major motive for helping. We review theories concerned with the roles played by learning experiences, moods and emotions, social norms, and one's personal and social identity in motivating one person to help another.

For historic reasons, social scientists began their study of prosocial behavior with bystander intervention. However, emergency intervention is a rather uncommon helping opportunity in most people's lives. In chapter 5 we turn to more recent research that focuses on long-term helping. Such long-term helping is typically more planful; that is, more thought and consideration are given not only to the question of whether to help but also to the matter of how best to help over the long run. We start our consideration of this work by discussing how community activists may first identify a helping need and thereby stimulate the development of groups and organizations to respond to those needs. We then examine in some detail the processes that lead people to volunteer—to contribute their time, money, and effort, with some particular attention paid to blood donation as a special case of volunteering. We also consider prosocial behavior within organizational and industrial settings and how organizational citizenship and, in some cases, whistle blowing about organizational problems can have beneficial results.

Chapter 6 is again concerned with the origins of prosocial behaviors in humans, but in this chapter we approach the issue from a more traditional developmental psychology perspective and much less from the biological or genetic perspective that we took in chapter 2. There are three broad questions around which the chapter is organized: How do helping and other prosocial behaviors change as people mature, what are the processes that are responsible for these developmental changes that influence a variety of prosocial behaviors, and how do these processes subsequently affect the behaviors of adults? To answer these questions, we investigate age-related changes in the factors that motivate people to help, the way people think about helping, and how people engage in helpful and altruistic behaviors. We then discuss the kinds of cognitive development and learning experiences that appear to be responsible for these changes and conclude with a brief consideration of how developmental processes affect prosocial behavior in adults; including gender differences in helping.

In chapter 7, our focus turns from prosocial actions per se to the people who perform the prosocial act and to the people who are the recipients of these actions. Human nature and situational factors play important roles in determining if and when help will be given, but important individual differences exist among people in terms of how likely a person is to be helpful. Therefore, we examine when and how certain personality traits and other personal attributes are related to different kinds of prosocial actions, and we then look at the consequences of being helpful for the person who helps. Finally, we consider helping from the perspective of the person who needs assistance. People with problems do not invariably seek help or even accept it when it is offered. Therefore, we explore the circumstances that either lead people to seek help or inhibit them from asking for assistance, and then examine the impact of receiving assistance on the recipient of help.

Chapter 8 represents something of a change in our approach to the study of prosocial behaviors. Although most of the preceding chapters have focused on prosocial actions between a single benefactor and some individual or group in need, this chapter explores prosocial actions between two or more people who have come together for mutual benefits through cooperation. We first consider the many factors that contribute to cooperative behavior among members of a group who can expect positive outcomes by sharing assets and perhaps sacrificing for one another so that everyone will "win." We see how the processes that facilitate helping and volunteering translate into prosocial acts of cooperation, and then we explore new, emergent processes that seem only to operate on prosocial behavior in group settings. We conclude by extending our consideration of cooperation *within* groups to the study of cooperative behavior *between* groups, and by so doing, we find that many of the factors that break down prejudice and discrimination between groups also serve to promote greater intergroup cooperation.

Chapter 9, the final chapter, is divided into three distinct sections, relating to the past, present, and future of research on prosocial behavior. In the first section, about the past, we review how work on prosocial behavior has developed. In the second section, about the present, we summarize the answers to many of the questions we asked in each of the chapters and propose some theoretical models that attempt to integrate what we believe we know about prosocial action. In the third section, which focuses on the future, we propose a multilevel approach to the study of prosocial behavior, suggesting that prosocial behavior would be best understood by considering it from three interrelated perspectives: intraindividual processes (micro-level processes, such as biological mechanisms), interpersonal processes (meso-level processes, such as the relationship between the helper and recipient), and intra- and intergroup processes (macro-level processes, such as helping and cooperation within and between groups). Using this multilevel perspective as a framework, we suggest promising new avenues of inquiry. In addition, throughout chapter 9 we seek "a little help from our friends" and report what other researchers in the field of prosocial behavior see as the important research areas and questions for the future. This final chapter contains what we know about helping, altruism, and cooperation, and what we do not know but believe we need to learn. The exciting prospect for us is that there seem to be so many new areas to study and questions to ask. But let us begin with what we know.

CHAPTER 2

The Origins of Prosocial Behavior: Are People Selfish or Selfless by Nature?

T he basic issue addressed in this chapter concerns whether or not humans are genetically predisposed to be prosocial and helpful. This is a question that has been of major interest to evolutionary theorists over the years. Charles Darwin (1859) originally argued that evolution is determined primarily by the principle of "survival of the fittest." Those individuals who are best adapted to their environment will be most likely to survive and reproduce, and thus their genetic characteristics will become more prevalent in the species in succeeding generations. Darwin's theory was interpreted at the time to mean that individuals who were the most selfish would be the most likely to survive.

But against this argument was the simple fact that studies of humans and other social animals produced widespread evidence of prosocial, often apparently altruistic, behavior. The evidence that helping was such a common, and seemingly fundamental, aspect of social life led evolutionary theorists to challenge the principle of survival of the fittest that traditionally directed the field. Thus, both philosophers and scientists have, over the years, come to recognize the impressive depth of selfless behavior in human and animal societies, as well as the significant capacity for selfishness. This leads us to the focus of this chapter.

THE QUESTION

The central question of this chapter is, "Are people naturally inclined to be selfless and altruistic?" In this chapter we attempt to answer this question by examining the evolutionary and genetic processes that play a role in altruistic behaviors, as well as the biologically related mechanisms that appear to be involved when people act prosocially. Evolutionary-based theories provide a general framework and rationale for *why* people might be prosocially disposed by nature. Biological structures and processes represent the mechanisms by which these genetic predispositions are manifested. They explain *how* and *when* forms of prosocial behavior will be expressed.

This chapter is thus organized into three main sections. In the first of these, we briefly outline some of the basic issues—terminology, methods, and limits—that need to be considered in evaluating the question of whether people are prosocial by nature. In the second section, we discuss traditional and contemporary evolutionary theories and supporting evidence. In the third section, we illustrate with the topic of empathy how biologically based mechanisms operate to produce prosocial behavior.

ASKING THE RIGHT QUESTION

The question of whether there is a genetic and thus biological basis to be helpful toward others is deceptively simple. It is actually a very complex question that needs to be framed in a correct and responsible way, and even then it is a question that is difficult to answer. One of the problems involves how to integrate the different ways that people from diverse disciplines look at and talk about the issue. A second problem involves understanding how biological and environmental influences are conceptually related. A third issue focuses on the methodological challenges for disentangling biological and environmental influences on behavior. And a fourth problem relates to how to interpret the data and the societal implications of research of this type.

What Do We Mean by Altruism?

As we described in chapter 1, the significance of prosocial action in the social life of humans has attracted the interest of a wide range of scholars. These scholars bring philosophical, psychological, and biological perspectives to the topic. They also bring different terminologies. One problem, therefore, is agreeing on a definition of the term *altruism*.

In chapter 1, we defined altruism in terms of people's intentions and motivations when they offered help to another person. We distinguished it from *helping*, which is defined by its consequences rather than by its intentions. Helping is an act that benefits another person. These definitions represent a social psychological perspective. For biologists and evolutionary theorists who work with a variety of different species (such as ants, bees, mice, and monkeys), however, intentions in a human sense often do not apply or are impossible to assess. Thus, these researchers use the term *altruism* to refer broadly to any action that involves some costs for the helper but increases the likelihood that other members of their species will survive, reproduce, and thus pass their genes on to successive generations. So, for these scientists, the beneficiary of altruism is not a particular individual but a particular gene pool. Because this chapter primarily examines the biological bases of prosocial actions, we adopt a biological perspective and the terminology that accompanies it.

Nature and/or Nurture

A second difficulty with answering the question about whether people are altruistic by nature involves the dynamic and complex nature of altruistic *behavior*. Evolutionary theorists and geneticists have long understood how certain physical traits are genetically determined. Eye color is inherited from parents; each of them passes on genes for eye color to a child, and the combination of their dominant and recessive genes determines what the child's eye color will be.

In addition, there have been some remarkable recent advances in our knowledge of genes and how they affect people throughout their lifetimes. For example, medical researchers have identified specific genes associated with several diseases, such as Parkinson's disease and breast cancer. In addition, the ambitious Human Genome Project, a project jointly sponsored by the National Human Genome Research Institute and the U.S. Department of Energy, has now mapped the entire human genetic structure, creating the possibility of understanding a wide range of human orientations, talents, and susceptibilities. These advances in the study of genetics also hold great promise for understanding prosocial and altruistic behavior.

In addition, psychologists studying how people develop different kinds of personalities have converged on appreciating the potentially significant contribution of genetic factors to things such as temperament. The term *temperament* refers to general behavioral tendencies, such as how active a person is, or how responsive the person is to the people and things around him or her (Clark & Watson, 1999). Developmental psychologists who study the behaviors of newborns report individual differences in their temperaments from almost the moment of birth. For example, some babies are "hard" (i.e., fussy, cranky, prone to cry), and others are "easy" (i.e., calm, quiet; Dehart, Sroufe, & Cooper, 2003). Many researchers now believe that these kinds of differences in newborns' temperaments are due to genetic or biological factors (Clark & Watson, 1999).

Nevertheless, because human behavior, including prosocial, helping, and altruistic behavior, involves complex motivations, decisions, and actions, it is unlikely that it can be traced *directly* to certain strands of DNA (deoxyribonucleic acid). Rather, these behaviors are likely to be the *indirect* product of the actions of a substantial number of genes, interacting in a complex manner. Moreover, these genetic processes are not immune to environmental, social, and cultural influences (DeKay & Buss, 1992). Instead, one of the major discoveries in contemporary behavioral genetics is that there is a constant interplay between our genes and our environment. That is, genes influence how people react to and act on the world around them. Their environment, in turn, affects which genes will be "expressed" (that is, genes that actually affect a person's physical appearance, physiology and/or behavior[1]) and when this expression will occur. Thus, even asking the question of whether some human behavior or characteristic is *solely* due to "nature" or to "nurture" is now considered to be inappropriate and passé by those who study prosocial actions and other complex social behaviors. A complex interaction between genes and the environment is responsible for most behaviors, including prosocial ones.

Disentangling Nature and Nurture

Recognizing this complexity, it is still valuable to understand how genetic and biological factors contribute to the development of prosocial

---

[1]When a gene is expressed, the observable effects are called the *phenotype*. However, not all observable characteristics are produced by genes; some could be due to environment. Hair color, for example, could be dues to a person's genes or to a bottle of hair coloring. If it is the former, then the phenotype matches the *genotype*.

dispositions and actions. How can psychologists disentangle environmental forces, which operate even from before birth, from genetic and biological influences?

A general strategy for determining whether a type of response has primarily a genetic basis involves looking for similarities in these behaviors across organisms, cultures, and individuals who are genetically similar but who have had very different learning experiences. If common outcomes and processes can be identified despite vast differences in socialization, then an inherited biological capacity is likely to be a factor. Techniques that represent this approach include cross-species, cross-cultural, and behavioral genetics studies. An alternate approach to determine the contribution of genetics is to study neonates (newborns), whose behavior has yet to be influenced by socialization. Another way of studying the link between genetics and behavior is by examining the relationship between certain types of genetic defects or hormonal deficiencies and patterns of social behavior.

In *cross-cultural studies*, researchers investigate whether certain social behaviors or personal characteristics are found in a large number of different and apparently unrelated societies. If they are, this would suggest that the common behaviors or characteristics are critical to human survival and thus have some genetic basis. In *cross-species comparative research*, demonstrating that the same pattern of behavior found in humans is also consistently present in other animals (particularly in gorillas and chimpanzees, with whom people share 98% of their DNA sequences) would provide a clue that it may be a part of "human nature."

Behavioral genetics techniques consider genetic relationships between individuals (such as family members or twins) that might produce similar talents or predispositions (Plomin & Caspi, 1999) Have you ever noticed behaviors that seem to "run in families"? For example, a large percentage of outstanding athletes have relatives who were also quite good at sports. Michael Vick, the current quarterback for professional football's Atlanta Falcons, has a brother and a first cousin who are also outstanding football players. Musical talent also "runs in families"; Johann Sebastian Bach had several sons who were also excellent composers. One technique that is commonly used in this type of work is quantifying the *heritability* of a characteristic. *Heritability* concerns the percentage of the *differences* that exist among people that is inherited or may be due to heredity. If a characteristic has 50% heritability, this means that half of the variation or differences between people on that trait can be attributed to inherited genetic factors.

Other researchers carry out *neonate (newborn baby) studies*. Infants' behavior is examined very early in life, when the influences of socialization and learning experiences are minimized. As was suggested earlier, these studies do find evidence of some innate social behaviors in humans. For example, babies less than a day old are able to imitate the facial expressions of adults (Meltzoff, 2002). This finding, along with evidence that other primates also imitate adults at an early age, strongly suggests that the tendency to imitate is innate.

Finally, there are other techniques that directly investigate the impact of genetic processes on behavior. For instance, hormones influence several forms of behavior (e.g., aggression, sexual behavior, maternal behavior). Experiments conducted with animals (e.g., by varying levels of testosterone) and studies of hormonal or genetic abnormalities in humans (e.g., a male who carries two Y chromosomes instead of the normal one) can provide evidence of genetic causes of social behaviors. Thus, there are several methods that enable us to ask whether some human behaviors are innate (see Dilalla & Gottesman, 2004).

Interpreting and Applying Biological Theories

Of course there are also significant limitations to these approaches. Each approach is fallible in its own way. For example, cross-cultural similarities could be the result of similar necessities of life that produced the development of similar cultural solutions all around the world. Modern communication and transportation advances of the past century have also tended to homogenize the experiences of people of the world, and these shared experiences provide yet another reason why similarities might be observed. Cross-species generalizations should also be made cautiously because humans clearly are unique animals, relying more heavily on higher order cognitive processes than other animals. Thus, methodologically, only a convergence of conclusions across these different techniques should be taken as strong evidence of a genetic basis of altruism or any other complex human behavior. We can provide evidence from each of these approaches pointing to the systematic influence of genetics and biology in prosocial behavior.

However, even as we make the case for genetic and biological influences on prosocial and altruistic behavior, it is important to understand what this means and what it does not. These findings need to be interpreted cautiously for several reasons. First, the impact of inherited characteristics to explain a person's or group of people's behavior is typically dependent on environmental influences. Environmental forces can increase or decrease the impact of genetic predispositions. No legitimate biologist would propose that a single gene, operating independently of other genes and environmental factors, irrevocably and irreversibly could determine whether a person will or will not engage in a complex behavior such as altruism (Ridley & Dawkins, 1984). Genes that directly affect brain activities and other physiological processes are turned on and turned off by events that happen in the environment (Ridley, 2003).

Second, environmental influences often modify genetic factors. For example, height is clearly an inherited characteristic, greatly influenced by genes. But in the United States and Canada, people born in the 20th century were, on average, substantially taller than those born in the 18th or 19th century. This was not because of differences in genes but because people's diets became more nutritious, and this environmental factor substantially influenced average height. Third, even when a substantial genetic influence is implicated by a large heritability component, heritability only enables researchers to make predictions at an aggregate or population level, not at an individual level. For example, individuals with two alcoholic parents have a greater *chance* of becoming alcoholic adults than individuals with no alcoholic parents, but this does not mean that any individual person with this heredity *must* become alcoholic. There is currently no way to identify specifically *which* children of alcoholic parents will, indeed, develop alcoholism.

Fourth, in interpreting these studies and results, it is important to be aware of some of the political implications and social controversies that have accompanied the raising of this question historically. For instance, Social Darwinism (the application of the principle of "the survival of the fittest" to social systems) was used in the late 19th century to justify colonialism and the exploitation of people of color in Africa. Racist ideologies based on claims of genetic superiority provided the bases for the Nazi holocaust and for apartheid in South Africa, and, more recently, played a role in brutal civil wars in places such as Kosovo, Rwanda, and Sudan. Because of the misapplication and abuse of biological views of human behavior, social scientists have shied away from this perspective. Nevertheless, we believe that it is appropriate for social scientists to study the genetic bases of behavior while being careful to interpret and apply these theories responsibly. Biology does not *determine* any individual's or any group's destiny.

The question still remains, however, of whether this approach will actually provide evidence of a genetic basis for altruism in humans. We now turn our attention to evolutionary theories that can suggest why people could be selfish or selfless by nature.

EVOLUTIONARY PERSPECTIVES ON ALTRUISM

Although people generally associate evolutionary theory with Charles Darwin, his theory represents just one theory of its type. It is, of course, the original theory, and it has had a profound scientific, social, and political impact on how people view the world. Subsequent theories, drawing on principles of sociobiology and modern genetics, have also been developed. We begin this section with Darwin's view of evolution, which is portrayed in his classic 1859 book *The Origin of Species by Means of Natural Selection*. We then consider alternative and more recent formulations of evolutionary theory.

Darwin's Principles of Natural Selection

From almost the date of the publication of Darwin's *Origin of Species*, there was an interesting problem for evolutionary theorists. It begins with the original version of the theory of natural selection, which was proposed by one of Darwin's close collaborators, Alfred Russel Wallace. Wallace's theory contained four simple, interrelated principles. The first of these was called the "Principle of Variation," which says that members of species vary in their physiological and behavioral traits. The second principle, "Inheritance," says that at least some portion of this variation is inherited from one's ancestors. According to the third principle, "Adaptation," there is almost always competition among members of a species for food and other scarce resources, and, because of variation, some individual members are able to compete more effectively than others. This leads to the fourth and critical principle, "Evolution," which states that those individuals who are most effective at competition are the most likely to survive, reproduce, and produce children with similar traits (Barett, Dunbar, & Lycett, 2002). This is the concept of "survival of the fittest." According to Darwin, "nature is red in tooth and claw"; it is "the struggle of all against all." The big question for altruism is, "If this is true, how could a tendency for self-sacrifice have evolved?"

Some theorists have tried to resolve the conflict by suggesting that altruistic behavior is more apparent than real:

> The economy of nature is competitive from beginning to end.... The impulses that lead one animal to sacrifice himself for another turn out to have their ultimate rationale in gaining advantage over a third.... Where it is in his own interest, every organism may reasonably be expected to aid his fellows.... Yet given a full chance to act in his own interest, nothing but expediency will restrain him from brutalizing, from maiming, from murdering—his brother, his mate, his parent, or his child. Scratch an "altruist," and watch a "hypocrite" bleed. (Ghiselin, 1974, p. 247; cited in Ridley & Dawkins, 1984)

Other people have argued that the inconsistency between the evolutionary notion of survival of the fittest and the existence of altruism demonstrates a basic fallacy in the theory of evolution. Indeed, even today, people who take a strong biblical view of the origins of humans—creationists—use altruism among humans and animals as part of their campaign against evolutionary theory. Consider this quote from the "Crystal Clear Creation" Web site:

> There are many examples of animals helping other animals, which shows that the evolutionary idea of "survival of the fittest" is flawed. We believe that the explanation for helpful animals cannot be found in a purposeless theory like evolution, but rather in understanding that God the Creator has placed the world's array of animals on earth for His glory as they fill particular roles in the planet's ecology. (Retrieved December 20, 2005 from Crystal Clear Creation, n.d.)

There were flaws in early evolutionary theory, but they were not the ones identified on this Web site. And it turns out that there is nothing inconsistent between the existence of altruistic action and the mechanisms involved in evolution. To the contrary, there is good reason to believe that altruism as we have defined it in this chapter can often *increase* the probability that a person's traits will be passed on to a subsequent generation. As scholars became more aware of this possibility, new evolutionary perspectives were developed.

alt. can ↑ prob of putting on genes.

New Evolutionary Perspectives

In the early 1960s, some prominent evolutionary theorists began to modify the original Darwinian model in some fairly substantial ways. These new ideas diverged from the Darwinian perspective in one very important respect: The focus turned away from the survival of an individual *person* to the survival of that individual's *genes* as the primary mechanism by which evolution occurs. This led to a reconsideration of the benefits of altruism for survival. *focus from ind to gene survival*

The Evolutionary Benefits of Altruism.   We begin our discussion of how altruism can produce evolutionary benefits with a personal and painful example of altruism among insects. One of the authors of this book is a gardener. One summer there was a beehive under the boards of her house near her garden. Every time she tried to weed the section of the garden near the hive, a few guard bees came out and "buzzed" her. Usually she retreated. One day she did not, and her

Bee dies for hive

nose was sore for days from the suicidal attack of one of those guards! The guard bee made the supreme sacrifice in the act of protecting the hive; stinging someone is fatal to a bee. When it embedded its stinger in the victim's nose and then withdrew, the bee died. But bees are not nature's only altruists. Observations of other animals, ranging from bats to prairie dogs to lions to baboons to humans, also find that within-species cooperative and prosocial actions are extremely common, and many of them at least *appear* to be selfless and altruistic (Clutton-Brock, 2002; Griffin & West, 2003)

Consider the bee who dies to protect the hive, the prairie dog that puts itself at risk to warn others of the presence of a dangerous predator, the baboon who challenges the leopard, or people who risk their lives to save others in the stories that appear throughout this book. These individuals clearly reduce their personal chances of survival. Members of a species who sacrifice their lives for others will, on the average, have fewer offspring than those who save themselves. (Worker bees, of course, have no children of their own, perhaps explaining their extreme altruism.) Thus, in Darwin's terms, these individuals cannot be the "fittest." Nevertheless, the more current evolutionary perspectives suggest mechanisms that might allow for the development of innate altruistic tendencies. In the next section, we consider several processes whereby altruism could lead to evolutionary success. Following that section, we examine environmental and social conditions that might foster the evolution of altruistic behavior.

Evolutionary Mechanisms: Genes, not People. How can altruistic tendencies evolve when altruists, by definition, are less likely to survive? To answer this, we must reconsider how evolution takes place. Recall that the original evolutionary view was that natural selection takes place at the level of the individual—that the fittest *people* will survive. They did not consider another possibility: that evolution takes place at the level of genes (Buss, 2004). The reason for this was that Darwin and his contemporaries were simply not aware of what genes were and the role they play in the transmission of traits across generations. (The role of genes in this process was not understood until many years after Darwin's death.) But according to contemporary evolutionary theorists, it is not the survival of the organism that is critical in evolutionary success, but rather it is the survival of the *gene*. According to Ridley and Dawkins (1984), "The animal can be regarded as a machine designed to preserve copies of the genes inside it" (p. 32).

Hamilton (1964) coined the term *inclusive fitness* to describe the successful transmission of an individual's genes to a subsequent gene pool. Inclusive fitness concerns not the number of direct descendants an individual has in a subsequent generation, but rather the number of copies of his or her genes that are present in the next generation. Individuals can increase their fitness either by directly passing their genes on to their descendants or by aiding in the reproduction of other individuals who carry the same genes. If altruistic traits increase inclusive fitness and have a genetic basis, they will be passed on across generations along with the altruistic individuals' other characteristics. This principle is fundamental to three current influential evolutionary theories: kin selection, reciprocal altruism, and group selection.

Kin Selection Theory. A common sentiment among most, if not all, parents is that whatever their children do, they will still love and care for them. This is, of course, is what good parents are *supposed* to say and do. However, genetic theories of the origins of altruism suggest that this sentiment may be more than just a self-serving refrain. Specifically, *kin selection theory* focuses on the actions of people who are genetically related. It proposes that the children of a parent who is totally indifferent to their needs are unlikely to survive; thus a "neglectful parent gene," which might have been passed on to these unfortunate offspring, is unlikely to survive. Thus, it is quite reasonable to propose that the vast majority of parents are genetically inclined to be "altruistic" toward their children. Note that we have momentarily returned to the social psychological definition of altruism: help that is primarily intended to benefit another person. Unfortunately, there are dramatic and tragic exceptions to these general tendencies. Pathologically abusive and uncaring parents are, however, very much the exception rather than the rule, and there is evidence that this behavior is substantially environmentally determined (Strauss, 1992).

What evidence is there to support the concept of kin selection? Much of the empirical work on kin selection has focused on the relationship between "relatedness" (i.e., the percentage of genes two individuals share in common) and willingness to help. Some of the most dramatic examples of altruism among other animals involve self-sacrifice by parents to benefit their offspring. Many ground-nesting birds, such as the killdeer, attempt to distract predators who threaten their young. As the predator approaches, the parent leaves the nest to attract attention to itself, limping as if its wing were injured. The predator, spying easy prey, is lured away from the nest to stalk the "injured" parent. At the last possible moment, the bird abandons all deceptive pretense and takes to the air, leaving the predator confused and hungry. The animal that threatened the nest is now disoriented and some distance away; it is unlikely that it will be able to find the nest and the helpless young birds in it. In this way, the young are saved—but only at great risk to the parent.

Studies of other animals also indicate a preference for helping relatives and other members of the social group over nonrelatives and strangers. For example, Curry (1988) observed that mockingbirds were more likely to feed hungry, closely related nestlings (other than their own) than they were to feed unrelated nestlings. Sherman (1985) found that when threatened by predators such as coyotes and weasels, ground squirrels were much more likely to warn genetically-related squirrels and squirrels with whom they lived than to warn unrelated squirrels or those from other areas. Figure 2.1 presents the results of another study on kinship and helping in animals (Sherman, 1981). In this study, Sherman recorded the percentage of female squirrels that helped another squirrel chase away animals who entered the first squirrel's territory. The figure shows that the greatest percentage of cooperative chases occurred among mothers, daughters and sisters. Note that the more closely related the animals were, the more cooperation there was between them.

Why does self-sacrifice for one's relatives make evolutionary sense? Remember that from this new evolutionary perspective, the sole purpose of reproduction is to increase the incidence of one's genes in subsequent generations (Alcock, 2001). A parent passes on approximately

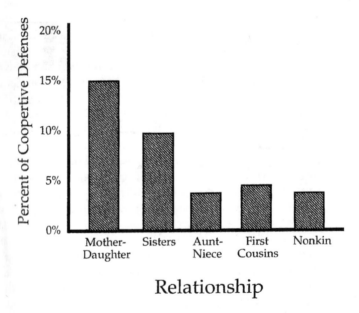

FIG. 2.1. More closely-related squirrels are more cooperative in the defense of space. Adapted from Sherman (1981), with permission.

50% of its genes to each of its offspring. Thus, if an altruistic father gives his life to insure the survival of at least two of his offspring and they are fertile, there is no net loss of his genes in the species. As described in more detail in Box 2.1, under some conditions altruists who help other relatives can substantially increase the likelihood of their own genes being passed on to successive generations. The examples presented in this box show how an altruist who gives her life to save the lives of her siblings (or even her siblings' children) can do more to pass on her genes—that is, to increase her inclusive fitness—than does a nonaltruist who saves her own life at the expense of her relative's lives. As long as relatives live near each other or can be recognized as relatives so that altruistic actions can usually be directed toward kin, an altruistic gene will survive and, in fact, out-compete a selfish gene.

The cross-cultural evidence for kin selection is also supportive. Data from 13 anthropological studies across a wide variety of cultures revealed that relatives were given more help overall than nonrelatives, with close kin receiving the most help (Essock-Vitale & McGuire, 1985). The more closely people are related genetically, the more helpful they are to one another. For example, in a study of living kidney donors, Borgida, Conner, and Manteufal (1992) found that donors were about three times as likely to do this for a relative as for a nonrelative (73% vs. 27%). However, there are other possible explanations of greater helping among relatives. For example, it may simply be that people feel more obligated to help their kin than unrelated strangers because of social pressure from one's family to help relatives.

Much more persuasive evidence for kin selection comes from studies in which predictions derived from this theory were essentially "pitted" against social norms and rules for helping. One of the most notable of these studies was conducted by Burnstein, Crandall, and Kitayama (1994). They asked students from the United States and Japan to imagine they were in a situation where they were forced to choose among three people who asked them for either an "every day" (e.g., running an errand) or a "life-or-death" form of helping (e.g., saving someone from a fire). The characteristics of the people in need were also systematically varied. Most relevant here, Burnstein et al. manipulated how closely related the person asking the favor was to the potential helper. Within both cultures, life-or-death helping was significantly more likely to be offered with closer genetic relatedness between the helper and the target. Thus, siblings were more likely to be helped than cousins, and cousins more likely to be helped than unrelated friends. Relatedness had much less effect on mundane, everyday helping, as evolutionary theory would suggest.

But remember that the theory of kin selection does *not* say we will always help close relatives; rather, it proposes that we are most likely to do

Box 2.1

THE GENETIC BENEFITS OF ALTRUISM

From a genetic perspective, the survival of a group of related individuals depends on the survival of its gene pool. Altruism is any self-sacrificing action that contributes to this goal. Geneticists also believe that altruists' genes can be maintained in a gene pool even if their actions result in their death before they have offspring. To explain this paradoxical statement, we must introduce the concept of relatedness. Relatedness represents the probability that a selected gene from one individual will be represented in a relative. For example, the probability that a parent and child will share a gene is .50, the same probability that siblings (brothers and sisters) will share a particular gene. The probability that aunts and uncles will share a selected gene with nieces and nephews is .25. If altruistic actions increase the reproductive success (i.e., the probability that an individual will have offspring) of genetic relatives of the altruist, this can also increase the genetic success (i.e., the likelihood that a specific gene will be passed on to subsequent generations) of the altruist's genes.

To illustrate this concept, we present three hypothetical cases in which a person must choose between an altruistic and a selfish action. To simplify the matter, in all three cases the reproductive success of the individuals involved is assumed to be the same—they all would have one offspring.

Case 1. Choosing between saving one's own life or the lives of three siblings. Which choice is more likely to preserve the actor's genes in the group's gene pool?

Answer: Saving the three siblings.

Explanation: The genetic benefit of saving oneself would be .5, assuming one offspring in the future. This is outweighed by the genetic benefit of saving three brothers or sisters, who each have a .5 probability of sharing a gene with the altruist. Thus, the probable genetic benefit to the altruist would be 1.5 (3 persons × .5 = 1.5). The net benefit is therefore +1.0 (1.5 − .5).

Case 2. Choosing between saving one's own life or the lives of three nieces or nephews. Which choice is more likely to preserve the actor's genes in the group's gene pool?

Answer: Saving the three nieces and nephews.

Explanation: Again the genetic benefit of saving oneself is .5 (1 person × .5). This benefit is less than the genetic benefit of saving the three nieces and nephews. The probability of each of them sharing a gene in common with the altruist is .25. Thus the probable genetic benefits of this action are .75 (3 × .25 = .75). The net benefit is +.25.

this when it benefits our own inclusive fitness. Thus, kin selection theory would predict that life-or-death helping of a close relative would decrease if, for some reason, the relative was not likely to produce offspring. Burnstein and his associates tested such ideas. For example, they varied the age and the health of the relatives who needed help to survive. With regard to age, relatives who were beyond the age when they probably could produce children were less likely to receive life-or-death helping than younger relatives. This finding also did not occur for everyday helping.

Figure 2.2 shows the results when the health of the relatives was varied. Although sick relatives received *more* everyday helping than healthy ones, they received *less* life-or-death help than healthy ones. According to the theory of kin selection, this is because the "reproductive value" of sick relatives is less than that of healthy ones—they are less likely to have children, and therefore there is less evolutionary benefit (in terms of inclusive fitness) for the helper. Thus, in this simulation, participants helped their

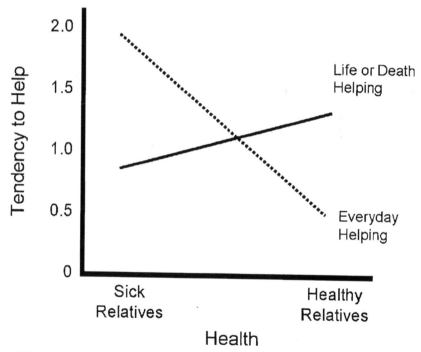

FIG. 2.2. People are more likely to help relatives with life-or-death helping when they are within the age-range for producing children. From Burnstein, Crandall, and Kitayama (1994), with permission.

kin in a manner that maximized their own inclusive fitness. Wang (2002) reported a similar set of findings.

Others have tested the theory of kin selection in another way, by looking at how grandparents treated their grandchildren. Grandmothers and grandfathers differ in "parental certainty," that is, the confidence they have that a child or a grandchild is actually related to them. A grandmother knows for certain whether or not she gave birth to her children and thus knows for sure that someone she believes is her biological child actually is related to her. If she has a daughter, she is also certain that the daughter's children are related to her. Things are a little less certain for other grandparents. For example, for a grandfather, there is always the possibility that another man has impregnated his own partner or, or if he had a son, the partner of his son. Thus, the grandmother in this example has much more parental certainty than does the grandfather. Thus kin selection theory would predict that maternal grandmothers (i.e., women who had daughters) should treat their grandchildren better than maternal grandfathers (i.e., men who had daughters) or paternal grandmothers (i.e, women who had sons). Euler and Witzel (1996) tested this idea by asking a large number of people to recall how their grandparents treated them when they were children. As predicted, the maternal grandmothers were recalled as significantly more caring than maternal grandfathers or paternal grandmothers. Maternal grandmothers are also willing to leave considerably more inheritance to their grandchildren than are paternal grandfathers (Hartung, 1985). In the same vein, maternal aunts and uncles show more interest in their nephews and nieces than do paternal aunts and uncles (Gaulin, McBurney, & Brakeman-Wartell, 1997; Laham, Gonsalkorale, & von Hippel, 2005). More generally, there is also some reason to believe that women's willingness to help may be more affected by kinship than is men's (Salmon & Daly, 1996). All of these findings support the notion that the more certain we are that someone is actually our relative, the more likely we are to help him or her.

Other research on kin selection has focused on learning more about the thoughts and feelings that are responsible for these kin preferences in helping. This work is important because it addresses how the presumed genetic tendencies are translated into behaviors. Korchmaros and Kenny (2001) had participants rate how close emotionally they felt to each of a number of relatives and then asked their willingness to offer them help in life or death situations. Korchmaros and Kenny found that emotional closeness partially explained the effects of genetic relatedness on willingness to help. That is, they reported that people were more likely to help relatives than nonrelatives because they felt closer to them. Neyer and Lang (2003) reported similar findings. However, Kruger (2003) found that feelings such as empathic concern and a sense of "oneness" with the target could not explain greater helping of kin. Thus, the search for the psychological processes that make people more likely to help relatives continues.

Comparisons of helping between fraternal and identical twins provide still further evidence for the kin selection theory of altruism (Segal, 1993). Identical twins have exactly the same genetic makeup, whereas fraternal twins share 50% of their genes on the average—the same as with other siblings. Note that in terms of inclusive fitness, identical twins would benefit much more from being altruistic to one another than would fraternal twins. In an experimental study, Nancy Segal (1984) found greater cooperation between identical than between same-sex fraternal twins. The two kinds of twins were carefully matched on overall IQ levels and on IQ similarity within a pair. Nevertheless, 94% of the identical twins but only 46% of the fraternal twins cooperated on a puzzle task. On a second task in which twins worked once for their own benefit and once for their twin's benefit, identical twins worked significantly harder for their twin than did fraternal twins. Identical twins are also more cooperative than fraternal twins on tasks in which participants make choices to compete for their personal gain or to trust the other person and cooperate for their mutual benefit (Segal, 1991).

Despite some unanswered questions about the specific mechanisms responsible for kin selection and more general criticisms of how well kin selection theory explains prosocial behavior in humans (Caporael, 2001), this theory has gained wide acceptance among evolutionary psychologists (Buss, 2004). In addition, kin selection has been used to explain why people are more likely to help others who are more similar to them (see chap. 3); people may unconsciously associate similarity with genetic closeness (Krebs, 1987). Of course, like all theories, there are limitations to the theory of kin selection. For example, it does not directly address the origins of prosocial actions that might occur among unrelated people and groups. Thus, we turn to other evolutionary processes to explain this more general altruistic orientation.

Reciprocal Altruism.   In almost every culture that has been studied, researchers have identified something called the *norm of reciprocity* (e.g., Gouldner, 1960). Within the prosocial context, the norm dictates that people should help others who have helped them. As we noted at the beginning of this chapter, cross-cultural similarities in behavior suggest that genetic influences may be involved. Robert Trivers (1971) first used the term *reciprocal altruism* to refer to a genetic tendency for mutual helping. Reciprocal altruism easily explains cooperation when mutual benefits are simultaneously received by all participants. For example, emperor penguins conserve heat by huddling together. By huddling together, each penguin benefits by exposing less body area to the winter cold. Reciprocal altruism also explains why people will tend to help others who have previously helped them. In essence, it is the genetic version of the "Golden Rule": Do good unto others under the assumption that, when they have the chance, they will reciprocate and do good unto you.

It is much harder to explain why humans may have developed a tendency to help unrelated individuals when the helping does not immediately benefit the helper. That is, helping a nonrelative creates certain risks for the helper. For example, if very few people are genetically predisposed to help unrelated individuals, those who do help will not be likely to meet others who carry this gene. Their prosocial actions may never be repaid. Rothstein and Pierotti (1988) proposed that "easy" forms of cooperation (such as the cooperative huddling of emperor penguins) may have evolved first and formed a basis for the development of more complex types or reciprocal helping across time. Because sharing, helping, and cooperation are behaviorally similar, they may be emotionally interconnected (Moore, 1984). In this way, genetic selection for sharing could lead to positive emotions being associated with all forms of helping, and the norm or ethic that favors them.

Still, this does not explain why reciprocal altruism could be an evolutionarily successful strategy. That is, although we almost always benefit genetically from helping our kin to survive and reproduce, we would only benefit from helping strangers if they return the favor. If they fail to return it for any reason, there can be a large cost for our actions and little or no benefit. Thus, reciprocal altruism only makes sense if we are reasonably good at knowing in advance who will help us in return and who will not. In addition, we have to be pretty good at identifying both potential "altruists" and potential "cheaters." In their *social contract theory*, Cosmides and Tooby (1992) suggested that humans have developed just such skills.

More specifically, Cosmides and Tooby argued that the basic problem is that in most instances when you help someone, some time goes by before the person has an opportunity to help you. Thus, most of the time you have to make correct judgments about what the person will do in the future. In order to do this, humans need five related skills or abilities: distinguishing among different people, remembering your past interactions with specific individuals, letting another person know what you want or need, understanding what that person wants or needs, and understanding the costs and benefits involved in a wide variety of human interactions. It is that last ability that is the object of the most interest and controversy.

Tooby and Cosmides (1992) did a series of experiments that appear to show that humans are actually quite good at solving problems that involve figuring out the costs and benefits of helping and who is a cheater and who is not (also see Dunbar, 1999). That is, "the human mind has evolved psychological mechanisms specifically designed to detect cheaters" (Buss, 2004, p. 264). Although this conclusion is accepted by many theorists, others (e.g., Cheng & Holyoak, 1989) question whether such sophisticated and specific thought processes could have developed as the result of evolutionary processes and suggest, instead, that they simply represent humans' ability to engage in complex forms of reasoning.

Whatever the outcome of this debate, there is evidence of a neural basis for negative reactions to violations of social contracts. For example, Valerie Stone and her associates (Stone, Cosmides, Tooby, Kroll, & Knight, 2002) gave different kinds of mental reasoning problems to people with certain kinds of brain damage and to people without such damage and compared their performance on these problems. The two groups were equally able to understand problems that involved taking precautions before engaging in risky behaviors, but the brain-damaged individuals did much worse on problems that required understanding that the benefits they receive in an interaction should be proportional to the costs they pay—the notion of reciprocity.

For reciprocal altruism to continue over time, there must also be a willingness to punish those who do cheat and to find ways of socializing people such that they will voluntarily refrain from cheating. Evolutionary theorists have considered this matter. One of the things that would facilitate this willingness is the evolution of strong emotions that will motivate swift and severe punishments for cheating, which in turn will serve to insure that cheaters do not prosper. According to Trivers, "Tendencies … to detect and punish cheaters with 'moralistic aggression' should tend to be selected for, as should guilt at failure to reciprocate" (cited by Vine, 1983, p. 4). There is very good reason to believe that such tendencies exist in humans. de Quervain et al. (2004) examined the brain processes and mechanisms associated with the punishment of people who cheat in their interactions with others. Specifically, they scanned people's brains while the people punished someone who had not been cooperative in an economic exchange. de Quervain at al. found increased activity in the region of the brain associated with experiencing personally rewarding activities. This suggests that people derive satisfaction from punishing cheaters; it is not possible to know as yet, however, whether this is an innate or a learned reaction.

Group Selection Theory. The final evolutionary theory that has been used to explain altruism is group selection theory (Boehm, 2000; Sober & Wilson, 1998). This approach proposes that natural selection can operate at the group level, and groups with altruistic members are less likely to become extinct than are groups comprised entirely of selfish individuals. In other words, group-level selection argues that if two groups are in direct competition with one another, the group with a larger proportion of altruists (i.e., people willing to sacrifice themselves for the group) will have a distinct advantage over a group comprised mainly of selfish individuals. The "altruistic group" would dominate the selfish group and derive a distinct reproductive advantage over them. Thus at a population level, the number of phenotypic (and presumably genotypic) altruists would increase relative to selfish individuals.

Although early versions of group selection theory placed it somewhat in opposition to individual-level selection theories (e.g., kin selection), more recent versions allow for selection to occur at both levels (so-called "multilevel selection theories"; McAndrew, 2002). From the perspective of psychologists, the major problem with group selection theory is the difficulty one encounters when devising ways to test it. Biologists argue that the conditions that would make group selection likely to occur (e.g., a low level of reproductive competition within a group) are almost never found in nature (Williams, 1966). As far as we are aware, the major arguments in support of the group-selection explanation are based on logic rather than empirical findings. This does not mean the explanation is wrong, but rather that it appears to have less support among psychologists and other behavioral scientists interested in evolutionary explanations of prosocial tendencies (Buss, 2003).

As we noted earlier in this chapter, environmental factors interact with biological processes in determining complex human behavior. In this vein, we cannot talk about the evolution of altruism in the absence of some consideration of other biological processes, as well as the environmental and social influences that can foster this process.

Fostering the Evolution of Altruism

The preceding material makes a reasonable argument that the growth and maintenance of "altruistic genes" may be of benefit to the survival of a species. However, it is also probably true that, in contrast to characteristics such as strength or intelligence that would likely provide survival advantages under any circumstances, altruism is more fragile and needs special circumstances if it is to be passed on across generations. What kinds of circumstances will best foster the development of innate altruistic tendencies? In general, conditions are needed that will increase the likelihood of mutual altruistic tendencies among individuals and decrease the likelihood of exploitation. There are three environmental or social factors that seem to facilitate the process: isolation, the ability to recognize other altruists, and the ability to detect cheating.

Isolation. An altruistic gene will have a better chance to develop if groups are somewhat isolated from each other. This isolation increases the probability that altruists will eventually benefit from others' altruistic behavior. This factor is particularly relevant to human evolution. Early humans lived in rather small bands of related individuals, somewhat isolated from other groups. In addition, the requirements of the hunting and gathering lifestyle should have increased the survival value of cooperative and altruistic behaviors, given that people were mating within the group.

Obviously, this theory cannot be tested in experiments using real people. However, there are alternative methods. For instance, computer programs can be written that simulate different evolutionary circumstances. The output from these simulation programs can tell us what conditions were most likely to produce altruistic tendencies in a species. Morgan (1985) used such a computer simulation to study the conditions that might best foster the emergence of altruism among humans. According to Morgan's computer simulation, reciprocity fosters the development of an altruistic gene most strongly when groups of related members remain isolated from one another. Nevertheless, even when groups become large and split into more, smaller groups, general reciprocity among members of these groups also facilitates the development of altruistic genes to some degree within the community. Thus, groups do not have to include only genetically related members and be segregated from other groups for reciprocal altruism to benefit members and enhance inclusive fitness.

From an evolutionary perspective, altruistic behavior appears to have general, long-term benefits that offset the potential short-term costs to the individual. Indeed, these computer simulations of evolutionary processes also showed that in groups that included both altruists and nonaltruists, individual altruists had lower inclusive fitness—that is, they left fewer descendants—than did nonaltruists. However, the more altruists there were in the group, the better was the collective outcome for the group members as a whole. This provides evidence of the importance of physical and social isolation for the evolution of altruism, and also some support for group selection theory.

Recognition. It is important to remember that the evolutionary benefits of altruism are not necessarily limited to members of the altruist's immediate family, who would be well known and easily recognizable to her or him. Conceivably, help that is given to any genetic relative (e.g., a cousin) could affect the incidence of the altruist's genes in subsequent generations. Thus, for kin-based altruism to be evolutionarily successful, potential altruists must be able to recognize (consciously or unconsciously) who their kin are. If altruism is directed too often at non-kin at the expense of kin, the selection mechanism presented in Box

2.1 will not work. Nevertheless, it is not always easy to identify more distant kin from non-kin. Recall the last time you attended a large social gathering, such as a wedding, that included many close and distant relatives and many nonrelatives. How many times did you need to be reintroduced to your genetic kin? How then can altruists spontaneously recognize their kin?

One possibility is that there may be biological cues. J. Phillipe Rushton and his associates (e.g., Rushton, Russell, & Wells, 1984) proposed that there is an innate basis for the ability to recognize that another individual is genetically similar, and this ability underlies both kin and reciprocity selection. Among animals, there is evidence to support the Rushton et al. claim. For example, Ligout, Sebe, and Porter (2004) found that 4-week-old lambs could distinguish between the bleats of their siblings and those of unrelated lambs. In addition, many animals can specifically recognize genetically related individuals using smell, appearance, or some other observable characteristics.

It appears that humans may also have this ability (Porter, 1987). For example, new mothers can pick out pictures of their own infants from a set of pictures within a few hours after birth, even when there has been very little contact with the infant and only portions of the infants' faces (e.g., their eyes or mouths) were shown to the mothers (Porter, Cernoch, & Balogh, 1984; Porter, Boyle, Hardister, & Balogh, 1989). Unrelated individuals presented with pictures of mothers and infants could also match them with above-chance accuracy, indicating that there is a detectable resemblance between mothers and their babies as early as the second day of life (Porter, 1987). Odors, such as those on t-shirts just worn by an infant, are also reliable recognition cues for humans (Porter, Cernoch, & McLaughlin, 1983; Porter et al., 1985).

Social Cues. Social cues may also be important for reciprocal altruism. For reciprocal altruism to work, it is important that individuals bearing the "reciprocity gene" be matched with each other. Humans and other animals must therefore be equipped with strategies and abilities for recognizing other altruists when they meet them. Similarity may provide the cue. That is, individuals may infer that others who are similar to them in appearance or personality may also be similar to them genetically (Glassman, Packel, & Brown, 1986; Segal, 1993). Thus, altruists should be more inclined to help others who are similar to them. As we shall see in the next chapter, strangers regularly exhibit this tendency. Furthermore, even within families, helping is more common among members who are more similar in personality (Leek & Smith, 1989, 1991), suggesting there may be a genetic basis for the finding that people prefer to help similar others.

Summary

To summarize, the current state of evolutionary perspectives on altruism—animal, social psychological, cross-cultural, and behavioral genetics research—provides convergent evidence for a genetic or inherited basis for altruism. Around the world, reciprocity is the norm. When people are unable to reciprocate, they experience negative emotions that minimize the likelihood that they will tolerate "cheating." Furthermore, people are more likely to offer help to others with whom they are more closely related. Consistent with the old adage, with respect to altruism, "blood is thicker than water." Also, the closer the degree of the relationship, the thicker the blood appears to be.

Although selfishness certainly has survival value, so does altruism; there are mechanisms for the genetic transmission of altruistic tendencies from one generation to another. The coexistence of both tendencies in our genetic heritage is not a logical or natural contradiction. We may want to reconsider exactly what is meant by the notion of "survival of the fittest." Contrary to how most people might define the term, *fittest* does not necessarily mean *strongest* or *toughest*. Sometimes *fittest* refers to being the "smartest" or "most sociable" or simply possessing some special physical characteristic that allows an organism to get more food, to avoid predators, or to adapt to threatening environmental conditions. As this relates to our present discussion, sometimes competition and selfishness are needed; at other times, cooperation and altruism are more beneficial. The next logical question is, "How are these genes expressed?"

FROM GENES TO ACTIONS

Unlike many other animals, humans engage in few (if any) rigidly controlled, highly stereotyped behaviors that can be directly tied to their genetic heritage. That is, we have few "instincts." Behaviors like alarm calls in birds or the suicidal altruistic responses of worker bees when their hive is threatened are simply not found in humans. So how would such a gene "for" altruism operate? How can genetic tendencies be translated into action?

As we suggested at the beginning of this chapter, genes likely influence human behavior in an indirect manner. They may affect some part of the nervous system and predispose people to be especially sensitive to certain aspects of their environment (e.g., loud, unexpected cries) or to experience certain emotions. The parts of the human brain that govern emotions—the limbic system—evolved earlier than the relatively recent neocortex, which is more involved with cognition and judgment. Thus emotion might provide a mechanism through which genes can produce altruistic actions. As we show in chapter 4, a range of emotions (such as guilt, sadness, distress, and concern) can motivate helping and altruism in humans. The capacity to experience sympathetic emotions in response to another person's problem or distress might therefore be the key element linking genetic predispositions to immediate action (Cunningham, 1985/1986; Hoffman, 1981; MacDonald, 1984). In this section of the chapter, we discuss the evidence for a genetic or biological basis of a particular emotional response—empathy—that has been shown to have important implications for helping and altruism in humans.

There are two major reasons why empathy has attracted so much interest as a possible link between genes and altruistic actions. The first and most important is that there is a substantial relationship between the ability to experience empathy and willingness to engage in prosocial behaviors. For example, Nancy Eisenberg and her associates (e.g., Eisenberg & Fabes, 1990; Eisenberg et al., 2002; Eisenberg & Miller, 1987; Eisenberg & Morris, 2001) reported that the more empathic children were, the more likely they were to act prosocially. A similar relationship is found among adults: Empathy plays a critical role in adults' decisions to offer or not to offer help (e.g., Batson, 1991; Batson & Oleson, 1991; Davis, 1994). One accepted measure of empathy is vicariously induced physiological arousal (e.g., changes in heart rate in response to another person's distress). Several studies have found that changes in heart rate predict how likely it is that people will help and the speed with which they help (Dovidio et al., 1991; Eisenberg, Fabes, & Miller, 1990). Thus, across a wide range of people and situations, empathy is a critical element in helping.

Although there does appear to be a consistent relationship between empathy and helping, this relationship, in and of itself, does not prove that biological factors are responsible for altruism. As we discuss in chapter 6, people's learning experiences as they grow up can and do dramatically affect how likely they are to experience empathy when another person is in trouble. Therefore, additional convergent evidence is needed to place empathy in a biological context.

The second reason why we illustrate this process with empathy is that, as mentioned earlier, there appears to be a specific part of the brain that gives humans the physiological or neurological capacity to empathize with other people. The portion of the brain that appears to enable a person to be emotionally involved with other people is called the *limbic system*. This brain structure was present very early in human evolutionary history (Maclean, 1973, 1985). Indeed, it may have been present among the earliest mammals over 180 million years ago, and therefore, even our most "primitive" ancestors may have had the capacity for empathy.

Empathic responses can lead to altruistic actions, and, according to modern evolutionary theory, altruistic actions may have considerable value in the survival of some gene pools or kinship groups over others. Therefore, empathy could have increased the likelihood that certain kinds of humans survived and continued to evolve into increasingly complex forms as their neocortex developed and grew (Hoffman, 2000). More recently, some theorists have argued that the neural basis for empathic and prosocial actions may not be confined to the limbic system. For example, Preston and deWaal (2002) suggested that so-called "mirror neurons" (neural cells that code the actions of other people) enable humans to understand and imitate the actions of others and also give us the ability to empathize with others' emotional state. They further argued that empathic reactions are more or less automatic responses to other people. And perhaps most interestingly, Preston and deWaal claimed that the human tendency to help others is the *result* of the evolutionary advantages conferred on those who responded to the emotions of others. That is, Preston and deWaal (2002) argued that although helping our relatives benefits our inclusive fitness, it is really a by-product of a more basic human attribute: a "highly adaptive nervous system organization" (p. 6).

A somewhat similar argument was made by Buck (2002), who suggested that the left hemisphere is more strongly associated with prosocial emotions and feelings than is the right hemisphere. He further argued that these emotions facilitate positive communication among members of a species and result in cooperative exchanges that provide an evolutionary advantage to the parties to such interactions. Buck (2002) thus proposed that "communicative genes (rather than kin selection or reciprocal altruism) underlie genuine altruism" (p. 742).

Both of these new theories of the neural bases of empathy and prosocial actions are intriguing, but at present they are theories that have numerous critics among neuroscientists, evolutionary psychologists, and developmental and social psychologists. It may be some time before we will know whether these theories can really challenge the traditional evolutionary explanations of the origins of prosocial actions. But the works of Preston and deWaal and Buck do give further strength and support to the argument that there is a neural basis for empathy.

We now consider how a predisposition to altruism might develop in humans through this mechanism. In particular, we apply two of the approaches for obtaining evidence for the genetic basis of altruism that we described earlier in this chapter, studies of behavioral genetics and early development.

The Heritability of Empathy

As discussed earlier, behavioral geneticists are often interested in assessing the heritability of characteristics. One basic tool in this approach, which has been used in the study of empathy, is the *twin study* methodology. If identical twins are more alike on some characteristic than fraternal twins even though they share the same environment, this may be taken as evidence of heritability. As explained earlier in this chapter, heritability is the percentage of the differences that exist among people (or variability) on some characteristic that may be due to heredity.

In one study using the twin methodology, 71% of the variability in empathy in response to others' distress was found to be due to genetic influences (Matthews, Batson, Horn, & Rosenman, 1981). In another study, Rushton and his colleagues administered a self-report measure of empathy to about 600 adult identical twins and 800 adult fraternal twins (Rushton, Fulker, Neale, Nias, & Eysenck, 1986). They estimated the heritability of empathy in their subjects to be about 50%; that is, about half of the *differences* between the empathic tendencies of their subjects was attributable to genetic effects.

More recent research (e.g., Davis, Luce, & Kraus, 1994; Robinson, Zahn-Waxler, & Emde, 2001) produced similar, but less dramatic estimates of the heritability of empathic tendencies. Davis and his colleagues gave 509 pairs of identical twins and 330 pairs of fraternal twins questions that measured positive affective empathy (feelings of compassion and concern for unfortunate others), negative affective empathy (feelings of personal discomfort and distress in response to distress in others), and cognitive empathy (the ability to see things from another person's perspective). For both kinds of affective empathy, Davis et al. found larger correlations between the scores of the identical twins than the fraternal twins. Again we see evidence that heredity plays a role in affective empathy. However, the Davis et al. estimates of the heritability of affective empathy were lower than those obtained in Rushton's studies (.28 for empathic concern and .32 for personal distress vs. .50). Furthermore, on the measure of cognitive empathy (or perspective taking), the differences between identical and fraternal twins were not significant, suggesting that genetic factors are not responsible for individual differences in this kind of empathy.

In an earlier study, Zahn-Waxler, Robinson, and Emde (1992) observed and recorded displays of positive and negative affective empathy in 14-month-old identical and fraternal twins, then observed them again when the twins were 20 months old. The researchers concluded that at 14 months about 30% of the differences in the children's empathic tendencies were inherited. However, Zahn-Waxler et al. found that the heritability of empathy had declined somewhat by the time the children were 20 months old. In fact, the heritability estimate for negative empathy was no longer significant (see also Zahn-Waxler, Schiro, Robinson, Emde, & Schmitz, 2001).

These findings underscore something we noted earlier in this chapter: The fact that a behavior has a genetic component does not necessarily diminish the importance of environmental and social influences. Indeed, as we pointed out, environmental influences and socialization forces can override genetic contributions—even before a child is 2 years old, as the Zahn-Waxler et al. work demonstrated.

The Development of Empathy

A second technique for assessing genetic influence on prosocial responses such as empathy involves studying the development of empathy, beginning at birth. At birth, the influence of the environment (outside the womb) and of socialization is minimal. Examining the development of empathy illuminates the interplay of genetic and environmental influences.

Precursors of Empathy. Consistent with the view that empathy is a mechanism by which people's altruistic nature is expressed, empathylike reactions have been observed in humans at very early ages. Beginning over 80 years ago, researchers found that 4-month-old babies would cry when they heard other children cry (Arlitt, 1930; Humphrey, 1923). These findings suggested an innate capacity to empathize, although one could quite reasonably argue that 4-month-old infants could have already learned to associate distress in others with distressful circumstances for themselves. However, research has found vicarious crying in infants as young as 1 day old (Martin & Clark, 1982; Sagi & Hoffman, 1976; Simner, 1971). For example, Martin and Clark exposed 1-day-old infants to tape recordings of three different sounds: another newborn crying, an 11-month-old child crying, and the child's own crying. The tape that elicited the most crying in babies was the one that contained the sound of another newborn crying. In fact, it produced more crying than the sound of the child's own crying!

Of course, these studies of newborns' crying do not conclusively prove empathy is an innate emotional process. Even children this young are capable of learning simple associations, and they may have already learned to associate distress in others with unpleasant consequences for themselves (Hoffman, 1978). Infants could also simply be reproducing a sound they have heard (Thompson, 1987). In any case, one must still be impressed with the fact that humans show at least the precursors of true empathy within a day or two after birth. This seems to suggest that, at a minimum, humans are predisposed to be empathic.

Developmental Trends in Empathy.

Developmental Trends in Empathy. Martin Hoffman is one of the foremost proponents of the idea that there is a genetic basis for human empathy in response to distress in others, which in turn can lead to attempts to help. However, Hoffman (1978, 1984, 1990) did not believe that true empathy emerges until an infant has passed through several developmental stages. The first and most primitive stage is global empathy. Hoffman used this term to describe the crying responses in newborns that were just discussed. He argued that during the first year of life, human infants do not have a sense of themselves as unique individuals separate and distinct from others; they are unable to differentiate themselves from other people. What happens to others, in essence, is happening to them.

Hoffman (1990) provided a clear example of how children respond at this stage of their development. An 11-month-old girl saw another child fall and begin to cry. The girl looked as if she was going to cry herself and "put her thumb in her mouth and buried her head in her mother's lap as she does when she herself is hurt" (Hoffman, 1990, p. 155). The child's feelings represented some degree of empathy; she understood the other child's pain. Nevertheless, Hoffman argues that this kind of self-centered emotional response (i.e., feeling personally distressed) is not likely to lead to helpful actions toward the other child.

By the time children reach about 1 year of age, they are beginning to become aware that they are physically distinct from others, and they have developed a rather rudimentary awareness that other people can be in distress or pain while they are not. But their empathy is still rather self-oriented. That is, they assume that someone in distress feels exactly the same way they would feel if they were distressed, and they also respond accordingly. A typical response for 1- or 2-year-old children who see another child in distress might be to give their own favorite toy or their "security blanket" to the other child. For example, one child brought his *own* mother to comfort a distressed playmate, despite the fact that the playmate's mother was nearby (Hoffman, 1978).

By the time children reach the age of 2 or 3, their empathic skills are more fully developed. They now understand that different things can distress different people and that different actions are needed to alleviate this distress. Furthermore, because they now have the tool of language at their disposal, they can understand rather complex feelings in others, such as disappointment, sadness over something lost, and even feeling bad about one's self (i.e., low self-esteem). The final stage in Hoffman's model of the development of empathy occurs in late childhood. At this age, children can experience empathy in response to another person's life conditions rather than just that person's immediate circumstances. Their vicarious reactions can be produced by events that happened to the person before they met or will happen after the two part company. The ability to experience such feelings may even cause children to help or comfort someone whom they do not know well.

Although Hoffman's model is widely accepted, it is based more on general theories of child development than on systematic observations of how infants actually behave. One of the more comprehensive attempts to directly examine empathy and prosocial behavior in infants and toddlers was carried out by Marion Radke-Yarrow and Carolyn Zahn-Waxler. Their work is important for two reasons. First, it provides some empirical tests of Hoffman's ideas, and second, it permits us to examine the interplay between inherited predispositions to be empathic and prosocial and the effects of parental behaviors and other learning experiences.

Naturalistic Observations of Infants and Toddlers.   Radke-Yarrow, Zahn-Waxler and their associates (e.g., Radke-Yarrow & Zahn-Waxler, 1984; Zahn-Waxler, Radke-Yarrow, Wagner, & Chapman, 1992) studied empathy and prosocial behavior as children interact in their natural environment with their parents, playmates, and others. In contrast to the typical laboratory experiment, the children were observed in their own homes. To do this, these researchers enlisted the aid of the children's mothers, who were trained to systematically observe and tape record their children's reactions to distress in other people. Sometimes the distress the children saw was real; sometimes the mothers simulated certain emotions. Within the real situations, the researchers examined those in which the children were merely innocent bystanders and those in which they themselves were responsible for the other person's distress.

Zahn-Waxler et al. (1992) studied a group of children at three different ages: 13 to 15 months, 18 to 20 months, and 23 to 25 months. The major question was whether the children's reactions to distress in others changed as they grew older. Although the researchers studied many reactions, we only discuss here empathy (which they defined as "emotional arousal that appears to reflect sympathetic concern for the [distressed person]") and prosocial behavior (e.g., offering physical or verbal comfort, providing direct help, or sharing something of value). As Fig. 2.3 shows, there were substantial changes in both empathy and prosocial behavior as the children matured.

When the children were 13 to 15 months old, distress in others was unlikely to produce an empathic response; less than 10% of the chil-

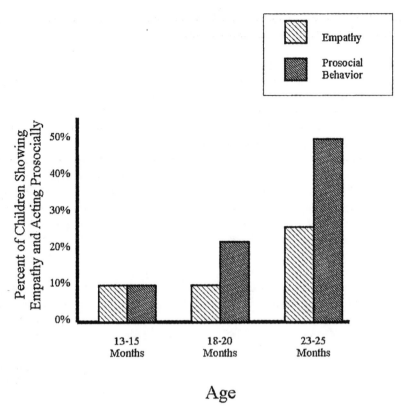

FIG. 2.3. Developmental trends in empathy and prosocial behavior both increase with age. Adapted from Zahn-Waxler et al. (1992), with permission.

dren showed empathy for a distressed person (even their mothers). Prosocial actions toward someone in distress were equally unlikely. However, by the time the children were 2 years old, about a quarter of them showed empathy for a distressed person, and almost half acted prosocially toward the person in distress (e.g., they hugged the distressed person or verbally comforted him or her). This increase in empathy and prosocial behavior occurred even when it was the child who had caused the other person's distress. We see a steady increase in empathy and helpfulness as children mature.

Zahn-Waxler and Radke-Yarrow found this pattern of changes in several different studies, but they were quick to point out that within these developmental patterns, there were substantial differences among the children they studied. Some children were much more empathic and prosocial than others. How can these individual differences be explained? Are they due to inherited differences between the children or to differences in their environments? As is true with any nature–nurture question, the answer is "probably both."

Empathy and Regulating Emotions. Nancy Eisenberg and her colleagues (e.g., Liew et al., 2003; Valiente et al., 2004) proposed a model of how innate differences and parenting practice might interact to produce individual differences in empathy. These researchers believed that individual differences in empathy may in part be due to inherited differences in children's temperaments— some children may be inherently more emotional and sensitive to the world around them than are others. These inherited differences predispose these children to react more emotionally when they see others in distress. However, the way in which parents respond to and deal with these innate emotional responses plays a critical role in the development of empathy and results in some children being more empathic than others. More specifically, these researchers believe that when more empathic children are very young, their mothers may reinforce the child's natural inclinations to experience strong emotions when they see someone else in distress. However, as the children get older, the mothers also teach them how to regulate their emotions and keep them under some control. Thus, the children's emotions do not become so overwhelming that they becomes more concerned with their own feelings than with the feelings of the person in distress. As a result, these children are predisposed to be empathic and helpful when they see someone in distress.

Readiness to Learn and Empathy. The possibility that the way one is socialized can influence the development of empathy is consistent with studies that have demonstrated that it is possible, using the principles of classical conditioning, to teach children to respond empathically (Aronfreed, 1970; Aronfreed & Paskal, 1965). But even these studies may need to be placed within a biological context. There is evidence from studies using both nonhuman and human species that show that it is easier to classically condition some responses than others. For example, it is easier to condition monkeys to fear pictures of snakes than pictures of flowers (Öhman & Mineka, 2001, 2003). Öhman and Dimberg (1978) used human subjects and found it was easier to condition a physiological response to angry faces than to happy faces. Thus, there seems to be a genetically based readiness to learn to fear specific stimuli. Perhaps because of the evolutionary advantages altruism confers, children are also genetically predisposed to learn empathic responses and thus are more responsive to experiences that lead them to be prosocial.

THE ANSWER: SUMMARY AND IMPLICATIONS

This chapter began with a simple question: Is there a biological basis for prosocial actions among humans? That is, are humans naturally inclined to respond to the distress of others with positive emotions and a willingness to help? It turns out that this simple question, like a lot of simple questions, has a very complex answer. The major reason for this complexity is that it is impossible to neatly separate genetic influences on behavior from environmental ones. This is because each source of influence affects the other and they work together to produce complex social behaviors such as altruism. But with this important qualification in mind, we must conclude there is a biological basis for prosocial actions in humans. The evidence in support of this conclusion comes from studies of cross-cultural and cross-species behaviors, research in behavioral genetics, and observations of newborn infants. Contemporary evolutionary theory, with its emphasis on genes as the key to evolutionary success, provides a very compelling argument that altruism may be essential to the survival of all animals (including humans). Processes such as kin selection in helping may have given an evolutionary advantage to those who were inclined to help close relatives, and reciprocal altruism may explain why prosocial actions directed at nonrelatives may have yielded similar benefits.

It does not appear likely that specific genes directly cause altruistic behaviors. Rather, genetic influences operate indirectly by giving people certain general propensities to act in certain ways and capacities such as the ability to respond empathically and/or the ability to effectively understand the emotional states of others people. These tendencies to respond to the behaviors of others make it much more likely that altruistic behaviors will occur. There appears to be a natural predisposition to empathize with others in distress, but the responsivity can be moderated by learning experiences. Thus, although we conclude that at least some of people's willingness to offer help to others has a biological basis, we also recognize that such tendencies are the product of both nature and nurture and that the two cannot be separated.

In the next two chapters we look at some of the specific variables that represent the environmental influences on one aspect of prosocial behavior, interpersonal helping. In chapter 3 we ask the question, "When will people help?" and in chapter 4, "Why do people help?" In exploring these questions, we focus on more traditional psychological variables: situational factors, motivations, social norms, and culture.

CHAPTER 3

The Context: When Will People Help?

I n chapter 2, we asked a fundamental question, "Are people pro-social by nature?" Then we considered how this question has been addressed across time, cultures, and disciplines. In this chapter, we first illustrate the range of human response to the needs of others, from apparent empathy to heroic action. The capacity of people to show such dramatically divergent reactions suggests the profound power of situations on helping and prosocial behavior. This chapter thus temporarily shifts the focus from the nature of humans to how the *nature of situations* can determine when people will help and when they will not. Research on this topic, which explores bystander interventions in emergencies and other forms of interpersonal helping, has been a traditional focus of psychological work on prosocial behavior (see Batson, 1998; Dovidio & Penner, 2001). It is a mature area of social psychology, with generally accepted theories and explanations. Although there has been much less activity on the topic recently than in the past, much of this research is considered classic work. The topic is important not only historically but also as a foundation for more recent conceptual advances that are discussed later in the book.

THE QUESTION

To set the stage for our discussion, we begin by describing two dramatic events that vividly illustrate the range of responses that bystanders can make when they encounter others in trouble or distress. One reflects perhaps the worst qualities of human nature, and the second exemplifies the best. The first is the assault of Kitty Genovese, mentioned briefly in chapter 1.

> On the night of Friday, March 13, 1964, in New York City, as Kitty Genovese arrived home late from work she was brutally attacked by a man with a knife in the parking lot outside her apartment. She cried out for help. Lights went on, and faces appeared in the windows of the apartments overlooking the parking lot; the assailant fled from the scene. However, nobody came to help Kitty Genovese, and the police did not come. So the assailant returned to the parking lot; he stalked, caught, and stabbed his victim again. Kitty Genovese cried out once more. Lights again went on, faces again appeared, and the attacker again escaped into the darkness. Still no one came to help. As the wounded woman staggered toward the entrance of her building, the man returned. This time he stabbed her until she died. We know so much about this event, which involved three separate incidents over a 45-minute period, because when the police arrived a short time later, they found that 38 people had witnessed the event from beginning to end. But not one of the 38 witnesses had done anything to stop the attacker or to help Kitty Genovese. Despite the widespread publicity that has been given to this incident and the sense of moral outrage it stimulated, observers of similar crimes still fail to respond in many cases. For example, in 1999, two women were abducted from busy parking lots in broad daylight in Las Vegas and then sexually assaulted in the desert. No reports of the crimes were made until the victims themselves contacted the police.

Other events seem to demonstrate the very best of human nature. Take, for example, the case of Reginald Denny.

> In 1992, South Central Los Angeles was ravaged by the worst civil disturbance in the history of the United States. On April 29, Reginald O. Denny stopped his sand-and-gravel truck at the intersection of Florence and Normandie Streets, because mobs filled the streets and he could not drive his truck any farther. Suddenly, the door of his truck opened. Four youths dragged him out and began to beat him mercilessly. They punched him; they kicked him; they hit him with makeshift clubs and bricks. He was close to death from

massive head injuries when four strangers—three men and a woman—risked their lives to come to his rescue. Watching this horrifying scene on live television in the relative safety of their homes nearby, they had rushed outside, jumped into their car, and driven to the scene. Fending off his attackers, they lifted him into the cab of his truck and drove him to the hospital. According to Denny's doctors, had his rescuers gotten him to the hospital five minutes later, he would have died. Reginald Denny was White; the four people who saved his life were African Americans. The response of the four rescuers in this case seems to reflect the ultimate in caring—the willingness to risk one's own life for the safety of another person.

These two examples illustrate extremes in how people react to the needs of others. They suggest that whatever the basic tendencies of human beings may be, they are not automatically expressed or exhibited in the same way in all situations. Thus, part of understanding prosocial behavior involves learning how the situation can influence helping and examining when people *will* help and when they *will not*.

UNDERSTANDING WHEN PEOPLE WILL HELP

Events such as these raise intriguing questions about prosocial behavior not only among the public but also among social psychologists who study helping. In fact, it was the Kitty Genovese tragedy that stimulated much of the initial research on prosocial behavior. Moreover, incidents such as these and the brief vignettes with which we started this book in chapter 1 vividly illustrate the dramatic range of human response, from deadly apathy to heroic actions and generosity of tremendous proportions. As already suggested, these events make it obvious that the question of *whether* people are selfish or selfless is overly simplistic. People are obviously capable of extreme forms of both apathy and caring. In addition, the consistent response of large numbers of people in each of these incidents also reveals that these behaviors should not be dismissed as unusual reactions by abnormal people; they represent the normal range of responses of people in these abnormal situations. As a consequence, stimulated initially by the Kitty Genovese incident and reinforced by other events showing apparent unconcern for or impressive sensitivity to others in dire need, social psychologists recognized the critical power of the situation. Researchers first focused on the conditions that seemed to lead people *not* to help, and then research interests evolved to address the more general question, "When do people help?"

In this chapter we first consider what it is about some situations that makes nonintervention the normal response. In attempting to answer this and other questions of interest in this chapter, we rely heavily on the results of laboratory and field experiments conducted by researchers interested in the phenomenon of "bystander intervention"—when a bystander observes a person in distress or in need of help and intervenes (or fails to intervene) on that person's behalf. We then examine what it is about other situations that lead people to be more helpful and generous.

The first researchers who tried systematically to explain the Kitty Genovese incident were two social psychologists, Bibb Latané and John Darley. In the mid 1960s, they began a landmark program of studies to find out why normal people might not help another person in distress (Darley & Latané, 1968; Latané & Darley, 1970; also see chap. 1). The behavior of witnesses during Kitty Genovese's attack was portrayed in the media as cold and uncaring, and frequently labeled as "bystander apathy." However, both interviews with the witnesses and observations by social psychologists who began to investigate bystander behavior in the laboratory converged on a quite different conclusion. People do care, but for a variety of reasons they often decide not to intervene. We examine these reasons, and how they affect the decision about whether to intervene, in the next section of this chapter.

A Decision Model of Bystander Intervention

Emergency situations are unusual and complex. Except for those individuals with professional training (e.g., emergency medical technicians, police, firefighters), people rarely have experience to guide their actions. Thus they need to make a number of decisions quickly and under great pressure. Latané and Darley's seminal research on this topic focused on the nature and sequence of decisions that bystanders must make when they witness emergencies.

The Latané and Darley decision model of bystander intervention proposes that whether or not a person helps depends on the outcomes of a series of sequential decisions. They represent the process as a decision tree (see Fig. 3.1). Before a person initiates a helping response, that person goes through five decision-making steps. The bystander must: (a) *notice* that something is wrong, (b) *define* it as an emergency, (c) *decide* whether to take personal responsibility, (d) *choose* what kind of help to give, and (e) *determine* to implement the chosen course of action. The decision made at any one step has important implications for the bystander's ultimate response; failing to notice, define, decide, choose, or determine as one moves along these steps means the bystander will not help the victim.

At first glance, the steps in the model seem obvious and straightforward. The contribution of this decision tree may seem to be that it explic-

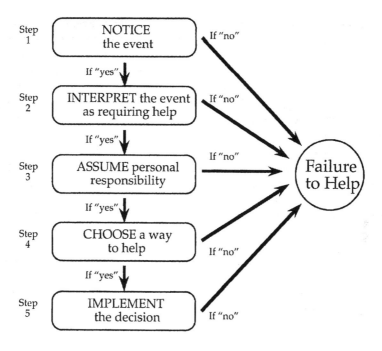

FIG. 3.1. Steps in Latané and Darley decision model of bystander intervention.

itly identifies the decisions that must be made and organizes them into a logical sequence. However, the apparent simplicity of this model should not obscure more subtle issues and influences.

Step 1: Noticing That Something Is Wrong. Obviously, a bystander must notice that something is wrong before initiating any action. A bystander who is physically separated from a victim (e.g., the bystander is in Chicago and the victim is in Timbuktu) and knows nothing about the plight or even the existence of that person cannot be expected to be helpful. When bystanders and a victim are in close enough proximity so that they *can* be aware of each other, there are a number of immediate influences that can direct people's attention so that they realize that another person is in trouble. Some of these influences are related to a person's particular state of mind at the time of the incident. A person's mood, for instance, can focus attention outwards, making them more sensitive to others, or inwards, preoccupying people with their own needs. Other factors relate to the nature of the situation of need and its capacity to "grab" bystanders' attention.

A *mood* is a transitory feeling, such as being happy or being frustrated. As we discuss more fully later in this chapter, there is considerable evidence that individuals are more likely to help when in a good mood than when not feeling particularly good or bad (Salovey, Mayer, & Rosenhan, 1991). (We consider the effects of bad moods in the next chapter.) Could the effects of good mood on helping be due, at least in part, to increased attentiveness to others? Isen (1993) proposed that being in a good mood makes people analyze situations more deeply, fully, and creatively. This enhanced sensitivity might also make people more likely to notice someone else's problem.

Two studies carried out by McMillen, Sanders, and Solomon (1977) suggest that this may be the case. In the first study, the experimenter provided students with positive or negative information about their performance on a task, which produced a good or bad mood in them. Then, while a student worked on another task, the experimenters increased the volume of white noise until he or she looked up, indicating that the noise had "registered." Students in good moods were more attentive to their environment; they noticed the noise at a significantly lower decibel level. In the second study, after the same two first steps—the mood manipulation and being assigned to another task—the students saw an overburdened, female confederate who needed assistance to open a door. The majority of students experiencing good moods noticed her plight and helped, regardless of whether the woman made a noise to attract their attention. Students experiencing bad moods, however, helped her only if she actively tried to attract their attention. Thus, good moods seem to make people generally more sensitive to others' needs.

Sometimes even incidental events that create good moods can significantly influence people' prosocial sensitivity to others. For instance, when people discovered change that was left in the coin return of a public telephone (this study was done before there were cell phones and calling cards!), they were more likely to help a stranger, someone whom they would never meet, by mailing a letter that had been forgotten and left nearby (Levin & Isen, 1975). In addition, people walking through a mall are more likely to retrieve a dropped pen for a stranger when there are pleasant aromas of cookies baking or coffee roasting, in large part because these fragrances put people in better moods (Baron, 1997). Uplifting music can also produce good moods and increase helping (North, Tarrant, & Hargreaves, 2004).

In addition to the influences of how a person feels at the time, the nature and clarity of the event itself can also critically affect whether people will notice that something is potentially wrong. Some events inherently attract more attention than others. For example, in one study (J. A. Piliavin, I. M. Piliavin, & Broll, 1976), some bystanders saw a vivid scene in which a confederate either stumbled and fell down a flight of stairs or slumped to the floor in a faint. Other bystanders witnessed only the aftermath of the accident or fainting spell (i.e., the confederate rubbing his or her ankle or regaining consciousness). Because of the motion, sound, and vividness, the action of the fall or faint is more attention-getting than the aftermath of the incident. As would be expected on the basis of the first step of the Latané and Darley model (see Fig. 3.1), bystanders helped the victim more frequently when the incident was more vivid—89% of the time in the vivid scenario conditions, but only 13% in the aftermath conditions. People are substantially more likely to help—in this case, seven times as likely—when it is clearer that something is wrong.

But even when people do notice that something is out of the ordinary, they will not always help. The next decision point in the Latané and Darley model concerns *interpreting* the situation as one in which help is needed.

Step 2: Interpreting a Need for Help. One of the important influences on whether a situation is interpreted as requiring immediate assistance also lies in the nature of the event. Situations that elicit "distress cues" in the victim are likely to be interpreted as emergencies. One distress cue is screaming, and, not surprisingly, screaming is a particularly effective way of not only getting bystanders to notice an event but also communicating the seriousness of the problem. Screams often lead people to interpret an event as an *emergency*, that is, as an unusual event in which the victim's need is serious, deteriorating rapidly, and requiring outside assistance (Shotland & Huston, 1979). Figure 3.2 summarizes the results of several experiments that manipulated the presence or absence of screams in potential emergency situations.

Note that not only is there a large difference between helping in emergencies with and without distress cues (such as screams), but there is also an extremely high level of bystander intervention in situations in which the victim's need is apparent. Victims who make their serious need clear by screaming receive help 75% to 100% of the time. Under these circumstances, there is little evidence of bystander apathy. Once participants interpret the situation as an emergency, they are very likely to help. Unfortunately, people who choose to suffer silently or are unable to make their needs known are more likely to continue to suffer.

One reason why screams increase the likelihood of helping so much is that they make it unambiguously clear to everyone within earshot that the situation requires immediate assistance. There are, of course, other ways that this same goal can be accomplished, such as presenting the situation as one in which there would be a rapid and serious deterioration of the victim's condition if no one helps. For example, Shotland and Huston (1979) found that people were much more likely to help others who asked for a ride home so they could receive an insulin injection or to get back to a roommate who had taken too many sleeping

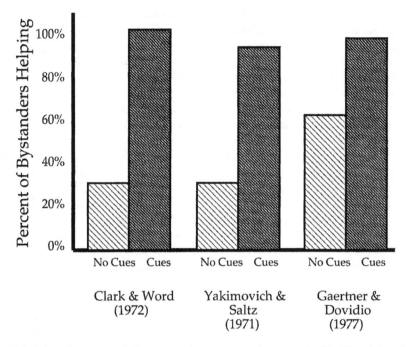

FIG. 3.2. Clear cues of distress, such as screams, increase the likelihood that the situation will be interpreted as requiring assistance and thereby facilitate helping.

pills (an average of 64% of the time) than to help people who needed a ride so they could take allergy medicine or get back to a depressed roommate (an average of 45%).

In some circumstances, people may notice that something is amiss, but because the nature of the event is unclear, they cannot readily interpret what is going on. What will bystanders do then? People have a basic need to understand their environment, and when they are confused they often look to other people for information and guidance. In such instances, informational social influence—using other people's behavior and opinions as information to interpret events and decide on the correct action to take—becomes important. People in new or unusual surroundings typically look to others in the same situation to learn about what they should be feeling, thinking, and doing. Because emergency situations are usually novel and unexpected, the behavior of others can strongly influence whether an event is understood as requiring assistance and consequently can affect the likelihood of intervention.

An experiment by Latané and Darley (1970) illustrates the profound effect that the actions of others can have in emergency situations. Male students were invited to an interview to discuss some of the problems involved in life at a large urban university. As these students were completing a questionnaire, they were exposed to a potentially dangerous situation. "Smoke" began to pour into the room through a wall vent. The smoke continued to increase until the room was so filled with smoke that a person could barely see the opposite side of the room. Nevertheless, the danger of the situation was somewhat ambiguous; because real smoke was not used, there was no smell of burning. The social context was varied by the presence and actions of other people in the room. The students were either alone, with two equally naive strangers, or with two confederates who had been instructed only to shrug their shoulders and act as if nothing was wrong. The behavior of the two confederates was designed to lead participants to interpret the situation as one that did not require action. The major question was whether these students would respond in ways that would save *their own* lives (such as leaving the room).

The results revealed the significant social influence of the behavior of others in emergency situations. People who were alone were more likely to report the smoke than were those with other bystanders. Although 75% of the students who were alone reported the smoke, only 10% of the students with the two passive confederates responded in ways that insured their safety. The passive behavior of the confederates led many of the people who did not respond to interpret the situation as something other than critical. These people came to believe that nothing was wrong and therefore no action was necessary. Participants in this study used the behaviors of others as the basis for interpreting what was happening. To make sense out of this unusual situation—a room filling with smoke while others seemed unconcerned—some came up with creative explanations that could explain both the smoky substance and the seeming lack of concern of the other people in the room. They concluded that the smoke was "truth gas" being used by the experimenters to get them to answer the questions honestly.

What about the condition with the three real participants and no confederates to influence them? Because there were three people involved, you might expect that the likelihood that *at least one* of these three people would respond would be higher than the percentage of participants who took action when there was only one person present (75%). Actually, only 38% of the time did any one of the participants take action in this condition. This is an illustration of a phenomenon known as *pluralistic ignorance*. Each participant, trying to stay "cool" but also trying to understand what was happening, probably looked calm and unconcerned to the other two people. The outward calm of the other two participants then led each person to feel and act more calm, which in turn signaled to the two other participants that nothing was wrong. The group developed a shared illusion that the situation was not an emergency at all and that there was no need to take action. Of course, if this emergency had been real, these behaviors could have created an ironic situation in which three people would have died—apparently calmly!

Although the presence of others typically inhibits intervention (Latané, Nida, & Wilson, 1981), that outcome is not inevitable. Because of informational social influence, what other people say and do are critical elements. When other bystanders act calm, they help define ambiguous situations as not emergencies; when other bystanders act alarmed, the likelihood that the situation will be interpreted as one requiring help will be increased (Wilson, 1976).

In one study by Ervin Staub (1974), for instance, pairs of bystanders heard a crash in an adjoining room, followed by a female victim's cry for help; one of the bystanders was the experimenter's confederate. His behavior was designed to influence how participants interpreted the situation. In one condition, the confederate emphasized the possible seriousness of the situation by remarking, "That sounds bad. Maybe we should do something," and then prepared to enter the adjacent room. In the other condition, the confederate suggested to the other bystander that the situation really did not require assistance: "That sounds like a tape recording. Maybe they are trying to test us." Those people who heard the confederate reinforce the severity of the situation helped 100% of the time. As expected from the social influence hypothesis, those people who heard the confederate minimize the seriousness of the situation helped only 25% of the time. By comparison, when two naive participants were placed in this situation, help was given 60% of the time. Therefore, the presence of others can either facilitate or inhibit helping, depending on whether the actions or statements of these others suggest that help is or is not needed.

In this context, let us return to the people who saved Reginald Denny's life. In the trial of the men charged with the attack, one of the rescuers testified that when she and her brother saw the beating on television, her brother looked at her said, "'We are Christians. We've got to go help him out,' and I said 'right.' Then he went and got his keys." Without this exchange, Reginald Denny might have died.

Clarity and Need. We have demonstrated that whether a bystander interprets an event as a situation requiring assistance depends on both the clarity of the situation and the actions of other bystanders. How are these factors related? One hypothesis is that when a situation is ambiguous, people's desire to understand it leads them to look to others to define the situation. Conversely, when the event is unambiguous and the need for help is clear, bystanders will have less need to look to others for information and should therefore be less influenced by the reactions of other bystanders. Support for this reasoning comes from a study by Clark and Word (1972).

In this experiment, male college students participated alone or in two-person or five-person groups. While students were filling out questionnaires, they witnessed an apparent university maintenance employee enter an adjacent room carrying a ladder and a set of Venetian blinds. After a few minutes, the students heard either an unambiguous or ambiguous emergency. In the unambiguous emergency, there was a loud crash and groans of pain; in the ambiguous emergency, there was a crash but no verbal cues indicating pain or need for assistance.

As illustrated in Fig. 3.3, the typical *bystander effect* (the inhibiting effect of the presence of others on helping) occurred for groups exposed to the ambiguous emergency. Students who were in two- and five-person groups were less likely to intervene than were those who were alone. When the situation was unambiguous, however, the presence of others had no effect; helping occurred in every case, regardless of the presence of others. For these participants, the emergency was so clear that there could be only one interpretation for what was happening: The victim

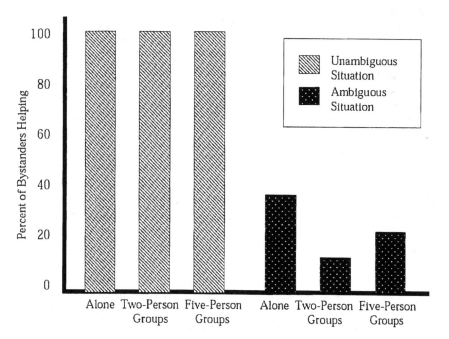

FIG. 3.3. The impact of informational social influence is stronger in ambiguous than in unambiguous situations. Adapted from Clark and Word (1972), with permission.

→ when unambiguous

was severely hurt, and assistance was needed immediately. Under these conditions, the presence of others had little impact on participants' interpretations and consequently had little effect on bystander response.

In ambiguous situations, then, people will seek social information to gain a better understanding of what is going on. And it is likely that they will be most influenced by those who are perceived to provide the most valid information. Specifically, *social comparison theory* (Festinger, 1954) suggests that people will be most influenced by the behaviors of others who are seen as similar to them. Similarity may be based on any number of dimensions that seem relevant in a given situation: similarity of attitudes, common background or preparation, comparable ability, proximity, or shared fate. Consistent with social comparison theory, Smith, Smythe, and Lien (1972) found that participants who were with another bystander (really a confederate) generally helped less often than participants who were alone, *and* the inhibiting effect of this other bystander was much greater when the participants believed the confederate was similar to them than when they believed the confederate was dissimilar. Bystanders were more likely to accept the "no-help-needed" definition implied by the confederate's passive behavior when they believed that the confederate was similar to themselves.

The first two steps in the Latané and Darley model (i.e., noticing the event and interpreting it as a situation requiring assistance) are well supported by the research evidence. But, do they explain the behavior of bystanders in the Kitty Genovese incident? Not entirely. The victim's screams brought people to their windows; they noticed the event. Many people also clearly saw the attack; they understood that she needed help. Because most people could not see the reactions of others who were in different apartments, however, it is unlikely that informational social influence distorted their perception of the victim's need for help. Although noticing the event and defining it as an emergency may increase the likelihood of intervention, there are additional decisions that must be made before people offer assistance. The next step in the Latané and Darley model involves the decision to take *personal* responsibility for helping.

Step 3: Taking Personal Responsibility. When a person believes that he or she is the only witness to an emergency, the answer to the question "Is it *my* responsibility to help?" is fairly obvious. The person bears 100% of the responsibility for helping and would bear 100% of the guilt and blame for not helping. Not surprisingly, people in these circumstances typically help (see Fig. 3.3). However, when a bystander believes that other people are also witnessing the emergency and that these other people are also capable of helping, then the answer to the question concerning accepting personal responsibility is less obvious. If you believe

[handwritten margin note: If everyone assumes someone else will do - noone will]

that someone else will take action, then that assumption may relieve you from the responsibility of intervening. But what will happen if everyone believes that someone else will do it? Unfortunately, no one will do it—and that is presumably what occurred in the Kitty Genovese case.

The Presence of Others.   Darley and Latané (1968) devised a laboratory test of the Kitty Genovese incident to examine how the *presumed* presence of others can influence intervention even when no social information about the severity of the situation can possibly be conveyed through their actions or words. College students *in separate cubicles* discussed problems associated with living in an urban environment over an intercom system that allowed only one person to talk at a time. Participants were led to believe that their discussion group consisted of either two people (the participant and the future victim), three people (the participant, future victim, and one other), or six people (the participant, future victim, and four others). All group members except the one participant were actually on tape. A confederate of the experimenter played the role of the victim. Early in the discussion, the confederate casually mentioned that he had epilepsy and that the anxiety and stress resulting from living in a large city made him prone to seizures. Later, he became increasingly loud and incoherent, choking, gasping, and crying out before lapsing into silence. The critical question was whether helping would be affected by the number of bystanders the participants *thought* also heard the seizure.

The number of other bystanders believed to be present when the victim had the seizure—just before the true participant's turn to talk—exerted a strong effect on the way the participants responded to this emergency. The more other bystanders the participants thought were present, the less likely the participants were to help. Eighty-five percent of the participants who thought they were alone with the victim left their cubicles and tried to help before the end of the seizure (which lasted 3 minutes), but only 62% of the people who believed that one other bystander was available and 31% of those who thought that four others were present helped during this time period. Within 6 minutes after the seizure began, 100% of the bystanders who were alone, 81% of the people with one other presumed bystander, and 62% of the people with four other presumed bystanders attempted to help.

Because bystanders could not see one another and therefore could not be misled by each other's inaction, social influence and pluralistic ignorance cannot account for the failure to intervene. Instead, the key factor seems to be whether bystanders would take personal responsibility. When other bystanders are present, *diffusion of responsibility* occurs. That is, people may feel less personally responsible for helping

[handwritten margin note at bottom: can't see or hear other P's so no social inf or pluralistic ignorance → personal resp.]

*less personally
resp cuz think
others will intervene*

*best
ex
for kitty*

less limited

*crowded vs
not crowd
place*

lot apathy

because they come to believe that others will intervene. This process seems to be the best explanation for the lack of action by the witnesses to the Kitty Genovese incident; the witnesses saw the lights in their neighbors' apartments and assumed that one of the other witnesses would call the police or go to Kitty Genovese's rescue.

The diffusion of responsibility effect is a fundamental process in human behavior. Merely thinking about being with others may be sufficient to make people feel less personally accountable for helping, and thus less helpful, in a subsequent situation. In a series of experiments, Garcia, Weaver, Moskowitz, and Darley (2002) asked participants to imagine being with a friend at a restaurant or movie theater or, alternatively, being with a friend at a *crowded* restaurant or movie theater. The researchers then examined the participants' subsequent responses to hypothetical and real helping situations. Participants who had been asked to imagine being in crowded social setting with a friend were less generous when later asked hypothetically how much money they would contribute to their university; those who had thought about being in the crowded situation also gave less of their time when they were actually asked to volunteer to help another experimenter. In addition, thinking about a crowded social setting made people think less about being accountable, and this effect occurred over and above any feelings of discomfort related to imagining being in a crowded room. Consistent with the original diffusion of responsibility hypothesis, imagining being with many other people relative to being with just one other person made people less sensitive to their personal responsibility and subsequently less helpful to others.

It is important to emphasize that the inhibiting effect of the presence of others through diffusion of responsibility is not bystander apathy. In many cases, people may be truly concerned about the welfare of the victim, but they sincerely believe that someone else will help. Holding this belief, they do not have to assume *personal* responsibility and therefore do not help (Otten, Penner, & Waugh, 1988). One implication of this reasoning is that bystanders may diffuse responsibility when there are other witnesses who are capable of helping but not when there are people who are incapable of helping (Korte, 1969).

Leonard Bickman (1971) conducted a direct test of this hypothesis. College students, who believed that they either were the only bystander or were one of two bystanders heard an emergency over an intercom system. Participants who believed that the other bystander was as close to a victim as they were (in the same building), and therefore equally capable of helping, diffused responsibility. They were much less likely to help than were participants who believed that they were alone. However, when participants believed that the other bystander was in another building and was unable to intervene, they helped as frequently as those who were alone. Therefore, people who diffuse responsibility are not necessarily uncaring; they may simply believe that others are more likely or perhaps better qualified to help.

One way of preventing diffusion of responsibility from occurring, besides making it clear that others are not as capable of helping, is to focus responsibility onto one person. Although others are present, the responsibility for helping is often assumed to belong to the person in charge. For instance, have you ever asked a stranger to watch your possessions while you were gone for a short time? Have you ever wondered whether these people would actually protect your belongings? An experiment provides an answer (Moriarty, 1975). Confederates either asked sunbathers on a beach to watch their possessions while they went for a walk or, in a control condition, asked them for a match as they left for their walk. Soon after, a second confederate wandered by, snatched a radio from the unoccupied blanket, and ran down the beach. For people who had agreed to accept responsibility, the response was impressive. Ninety-four percent intervened, often in dramatic and physical fashion. By contrast, only 20% of the bystanders who were not explicitly made responsible tried to prevent the theft. Thus, once people assume positions of leadership in a group, agree to accept responsibility, or publicly state their intention to help, they are likely to intervene, even though other potential helpers are available (Firestone, Lichtman, & Colamosca, 1975; Schwartz, 1977; Zuckerman & Reis, 1978).

Situational Standards. Situations bring with them a set of expectations about what behaviors are permissible and what ones are not. For instance, people are expected to behave differently in a place of worship, a library, a classroom, and a party. As people in emergency situations attempt to determine exactly what they should do, these situational standards of behavior, which are normally reasonable and functional, can significantly influence their decision to help, often in ways that appear somewhat unreasonable or irrational to outside observers.

In a 1971 study, Staub established social rules by telling seventh-grade students either that they were permitted to enter an adjacent room to take a break from the questionnaires they were completing or that they were expressly prohibited from entering the room because they might influence each other's answers on the questionnaires. Later, the students heard an apparent emergency, an accident involving a person in the next room. Would seventh graders let the rule prohibiting them from entering that room prevent them from intervening? It would seem that the potential consequences to the victim for not being helped should outweigh personal consequences to the bystander for violating the rule. (In fact, because the reason for not entering the room—sharing answers with the person in the room—would no longer be relevant if an emergency was in progress, the prohibition was actually meaningless.) Nevertheless, social rules still exerted a substantial effect. Although 91% of those who were given prior permission to enter the room offered help, only 45% of the seventh graders who were previously prohibited from entering the room offered help.

Would adults act in the same way? In a subsequent study, Staub (1971) showed that they do. Adults (ages 18 to 28 years) who were previously prohibited from entering the room (so that the person working on a timed task would not be disturbed) were less likely to help than were participants permitted to enter the room to get a cup of coffee (61% vs. 89%). Once again, the social context strongly influenced a bystander's decision to take personal responsibility for intervention, the third step in the Latané and Darley model.

Steps 4 and 5: Deciding What Kind of Help to Give and Implementing the Decision. The fourth and fifth decision steps involve deciding *what* to do and *implementing* the chosen course of action. Although the first three steps in the Latané and Darley model have received careful empirical scrutiny and support, these last two steps have not been the focus of much research. That is, most of the studies of bystanders' responses in emergencies have examined whether or not people will do *something* but not what that something is. The research that does exist, however, supports these last parts of the model.

A significant proportion of college students are trained in first-aid procedures. Shotland and Heinold (1985) considered the question of whether this knowledge would actually make people more effective helpers. In the context of the Latané and Darley model, will bystanders with first-aid training be better able to decide what to do (Step 4) and then act effectively on that decision (Step 5)? In Shotland and Heinold's experiment, bystanders who did or did not have previous first-aid training encountered an emergency in which the victim appeared to have profuse arterial bleeding. Consistent with the first two steps of the model, the clearer the emergency was at the onset, the more likely it was for a bystander to do *something*. In addition, bystanders without first-aid training were just as likely to do something as were bystanders with this background. First-aid training, however, had a significant impact on *what* these bystanders did. Consistent with the fourth and fifth steps, people with first-aid training offered help with greater medical effectiveness than did those without training. In fact, the "assistance" given by people without training would often have been medically harmful had the victim's emergency been real.

Ineffective assistance can also be harmful to the helper. Clark and Word (1974) found that people who had little experience with electricity would sometimes inadvertently jeopardize their own lives while attempting to help a victim who had apparently been severely shocked. These participants ran over and impulsively touched the victim who was still touching a "live" electrical wire. If the situation had been real, this action would have been both ineffective for the victim and deadly for the bystander. Thus, the last two steps of the Latané and Darley model are critical. Bystanders must decide what to do and know how to do it before intervention is truly helpful.

Summary

The decision tree model of bystander intervention proposes that before a bystander actually intervenes on behalf of a victim, he or she makes a set of sequential decisions: Is something wrong? Is it an emergency? Is it my responsibility to offer help? What kind of help should I give? How should I give it? These decisions are influenced by the situation in which the emergency occurs, the nature of the emergency, the presence of other bystanders and their reactions, and social norms and rules. Overall, the Latané and Darley decision model of intervention provides a valuable framework for understanding when bystanders will or will not help others in need.

The research guided by the Latané and Darley model has been important for several reasons. First, it illustrates the contribution that social psychology can make to understanding "real-world" problems. First impressions can be wrong. Public outrage portrayed the bystanders in the Kitty Genovese incident as apathetic, uncaring, and basically "abnormal," but the social psychological research revealed a very different explanation. Through careful analysis and research, Latané and Darley, and the researchers who followed their pioneering efforts, showed how behaviors that might appear so abnormal can be understood using principles of normal behavior. People in situations such as the Kitty Genovese attack are not apathetic; they are caring, involved, and aroused. The problem is that these situations are complex and confusing, and bystanders must make a series of decisions, make them quickly, and make them in a very specific way before they will intervene.

Second, although public response focused on questions of human nature, Latané and Darley emphasized the unrecognized importance of the nature of the situation. These studies illustrate the tremendous impact of situations (including the social aspects of the situation) on how people interpret an emergency and their decision about whether to respond to it personally. A consistent finding is that people are unduly influenced by the actions of others and situational standards under these circumstances. Why are people so easily influenced in these situations? One answer involves the nature of emergencies. As noted earlier, emergencies are unusual events, associated with confusion and uncertainty. As a consequence, people rely on the most readily available cues to help them understand the situation and how they should behave in it. Moreover, because of the time pressure involved and the intense emotional reactions that people often have to the distress of others, emergencies are highly arousing. As we consider more fully in the next chapter, arousal leads people to become more focused on immediate and salient aspects of their situation, such as the actions of others around them, often to the exclusion of other cues to which they would normally attend. Thus, bystanders in emergencies may appear to overreact to immediate cues and make decisions that seem irrational to detached observers. This line of research does not imply that human nature is irrelevant to understanding prosocial behavior (as we have discussed in chap. 2); instead, it convincingly demonstrates that the power of the situation should not be underestimated in explanations concerning when people help and when they do not.

Third, although the Latané and Darley model was initially developed to understand how people respond in emergencies that require immediate assistance, aspects of the model have been successfully applied to wide variety of situations, including giving someone directions (Latané et al., 1981), receiving help from Internet chat rooms (Markey, 2000), preventing someone from driving drunk (Rabow, Newcomb, Monto, & Hernandez, 1990), deciding whether to donate a kidney to a relative (Borgida, Conner, & Manteufal, 1992), reporting wrongdoing or improprieties on the job (i.e., "whistle blowing"; Dozier & Miceli, 1985; Miceli, Roach, & Near, 1988), and deciding whether to report suspected child abuse (Hoefnagels & Zwikker, 2001). The model provides an analytical framework for understanding some other general findings regarding helping behavior.

For example, one of the initial explanations for the apparent bystander apathy in the Kitty Genovese case focused on where the incident occurred—metropolitan New York City. The argument was that urban living makes people insensitive to the needs of others. Indeed, social psychological research does indicate that people are less helpful—at least to strangers—in urban than in rural environments across a range of different countries (e.g., the United States, the United Kingdom, Saudi Arabia, and Sudan; Hedge & Yousif, 1992; Steblay, 1987; Yousif & Korte, 1995). But what specifically is it about these situations that might make people in cities less likely to help than people in smaller towns? The Latané and Darley model suggests places to look for explanations.

One possible explanation, relating to the first step in the Latané and Darley model, is that because cities are busy places full of noise and activity, people in urban environments are simply less likely to notice that something is wrong than are people in quieter, rural environments. To reduce stimulation to a manageable and comfortable level, people may try to restrict their attention to only those aspects of the environment that are most *personally* important and to block out irrelevant stimulation (Milgram, 1970), which may involve the needs of other people. As a consequence, the problems of strangers may go largely unnoticed.

Indeed, consistent with this *stimulus overload* hypothesis, conditions that tax people's senses tend to reduce their prosocial responsiveness to others. For example, Levine, Martinez, Brase, and Sorenson (1994) assessed the helpfulness of people in 36 U.S. cities in terms of a variety of everyday behaviors. Three experimenters traveled to these different cities, and to various locations in each city, to stage a number of potential helping situations. For example, they accidentally dropped pens as they walked along city streets, or they wore leg braces and dropped magazines they were carrying on the sidewalk. They also dressed in dark glasses and carried a cane to portray a blind person trying to cross the street. In some cases, experimenters left "lost letters" on the street to see if they would be mailed; in others they directly asked for change for a quarter or for a donation to the United Way.

What kinds of cities are helpful, and which ones are not? The cities, listed in order of the most to the least prosocial, are presented in Table 3.1. One of the strongest predictors of helpfulness was the population density of the city: Cities that were more densely populated ranked lower in helpfulness. Also consistent with this stimulus overload explanation, Bickman et al. (1973) found that students living in high-density, high-rise dormitories were less likely to return a "lost letter" than were similar students who lived in less densely populated buildings.

Direct evidence for the role of attentiveness to others' needs, the process implicated in the second step of the Latané and Darley model, comes from a clever field study by Mathews and Canon (1975). In this experiment, a confederate wearing or not wearing a cast dropped several boxes of books a few feet in front of a person walking along the street. The key manipulation of environmental stimulation was whether or not a nearby power lawn mower was running when this event occurred. People in the control condition without the mower running were very responsive to the need of the person in the cast, spontaneously helping 80% of the time. However, those who were overstimulated by the loud noise helped only 15% of the time, the same proportion who helped a nonhandicapped person in both conditions. These findings suggest that excessive stimulation can reduce the likeli-

TABLE 3.1
Helpfulness of U.S. Cities

1. Rochester, NY	13. Canton, OH	25. Youngstown, OH
2. Houston, TX	14. Kansas City, MO	26. Sacramento, CA
3. Nashville, TN	15. Worcester, MA	27. Salt Lake City, UT
4. Memphis, TN	16. Santa Barbara, CA	28. Boston, MA
5. Knoxville, TN	17. Dallas, TX	29. Providence, RI
6. Louisville, KY	18. San Jose, CA	30. Chicago, IL
7. St. Louis, MO	19. San Diego, CA	31. Shreveport, LA
8. Detroit, MI	20. Springfield, MA	32. Philadelphia, PA
9. East Lansing, MI	21. Atlanta, GA	33. Fresno, CA
10. Chattanooga, TN	22. Bakersfield, CA	34. Los Angeles, CA
11. Indianapolis, IN	23. Buffalo, NY	35. New York City
12. Columbus, OH	24. San Francisco, CA	36. Paterson, NJ

Note. From Levine et al. (1994).

hood that people will realize that help is needed, which according to the Latané and Darley model prevents the bystander from moving on to the next decision step. If people do not notice or recognize that something is wrong, they will not help.

Another possible explanation for why people are less helpful in cities than in smaller towns involves different *social norms* about how one should behave in these different environments. This influence relates to the third step in the Latané and Darley model, that is, deciding whether to take personal responsibility for helping. Specifically, small towns and large cities are generally believed to have different norms concerning helping. At least in terms of stereotypes, residents of small communities are expected to be helpful and socially supportive, whereas urban dwellers are expected to be unhelpful and insensitive to the needs of others (Krupat & Guild, 1980). Consistent with the normative explanation, even in situations in which a person's need is made clear and potential helpers are explicitly asked for assistance, people tend to be less helpful in urban than in rural settings (Levine et al., 1994; Steblay, 1987). Similarly, Foss (1983) found that proportionately more blood was donated on smaller college campuses. Piliavin and Libby (1985/1986) found that the level of blood donation in Wisconsin communities was directly related to perceived social norms. Thus, urban and larger social environments lead to decreased helping relative to rural and smaller environments, not only as a consequence of coping with stimulus overload (i.e., not noticing events) but also because people seem less concerned about the needs of others once these needs are recognized.

The Latané and Darley model does not present a complete picture, however. There are situations in which bystanders will not intervene even though the need of a victim is apparent and the personal focus of responsibility is clear. Some of these are fairly obvious. For example, the greater the personal danger to the helper, the less likely people are to help (Shotland & Straw, 1976). To account for these additional factors influencing helping, frameworks such as the *cost–reward analysis* have been developed. The basic assumption of this perspective on helping is that when bystanders decide on what actions to take, they try to minimize costs and maximize rewards. The cost–reward analysis in some ways serves to "fine-tune" some of the processes outlined by Latané and Darley. That is, a cost–reward analysis allows a more fine-grained analysis of how the nature of the situation and characteristics of the victim influence helping. The cost–reward analysis can thus be viewed as a complementary perspective to the Latané and Darley decision model, rather than as an alternative or competing framework.

A COST–REWARD ANALYSIS

A cost-reward analysis of helping assumes an economic view of human behavior—people are motivated to maximize rewards and to minimize their costs (Epstein & Hornstein, 1969; J. A. Piliavin, Dovidio, Gaertner, & Clark, 1981). From this perspective, people are relatively rational and mainly concerned about their self-interest. In a potential helping situation, a person analyzes the circumstances, weighs the probable costs and rewards of alternative courses of action, and then arrives at a decision that will result in the best personal outcome. This is one form of "egoism," which was discussed briefly in the first chapter. There are two basic categories of costs and rewards: those for *helping*, and those for *not* helping. Costs for helping can involve lost time, effort, danger, embarrassment, and disruption of ongoing activities. However, helping can also be rewarding. Rewards for helping may include money, fame, self-praise, avoidance of guilt, thanks from the victim, and the intrinsic pleasure derived from having helped. Helping is more likely to occur when the rewards for helping outweigh the costs. Anything that lowers the costs or increases the rewards for helping enhances a person's inclination to help. Costs for *not* helping may involve feelings of guilt and the cognitive and emotional discomfort associated with knowing another person is suffering. Helping is more likely as these costs increase. One advantage of the cost–reward approach is that once potential costs and rewards have been identified, the effects of this combination of factors can readily be predicted. In the next section, we examine a variety of situational dimensions that influence costs and rewards and thus helping, typically in circumstances in which the need for help is clear.

Costs and Rewards for Helping

The negative value associated with the costs for helping and the positive value associated with rewards for helping are subjective ones. They are based on the perceptions of the bystander, not on "objective" assessments of uninvolved outsiders. Therefore, to address this issue, most researchers have attempted to set up situations in which most people's perceptions of costs and rewards will be similar. Researchers have identified several situational factors that yield similar cost estimates from different people. Table 3.2 summarizes these and how they influence helping.

Effort and Time. Earlier in this chapter, we reviewed several experiments in which people witnessed emergencies in which the victims' screams made it appear that they were seriously injured (see Fig. 3.2). Participants in these experiments were near the victim, and it was relatively easy to help. These are situations in which the personal costs for helping in terms of time and effort are outweighed by the combination of rewards for helping (praise and potential fame) and costs for *not* helping (the victim dying). As you recall, helping is very likely under these circumstances.

In other situations, however, bystanders' own concerns and time pressures may prevail over the needs of another person. Bystanders weigh the needs of the victim and their own needs and goals, and then decide whether helping is too costly in that circumstance (see Dovidio, J. A. Piliavin, Gaertner, Schroeder, & Clark, 1991; J. A. Piliavin et al., 1981). This decision is based on a relatively rational assessment of the situation, and a person who fails to help is not necessarily a "bad" person. For example, Darley and Batson (1973) conducted a study in which seminary students (presumably "good" people) were asked to make a presentation on some topic. (Half were to talk about the parable of the

TABLE 3.2
Examples of Costs and Rewards
Associated With Helping and Not Helping

Costs and Rewards for Helping	Example
Cost for helping	
Psychological aversion	Situations involving someone (e.g., a drunk) or something (e.g., blood) that people find unpleasant
Possible physical harm	High likelihood that direct intervention may be dangerous (e.g., possible personal attack) or painful (e.g., possible electric shock) to the helper
Effort and time	Helping that involves the interruption or postponement of important or desired activity (e.g., missing a scheduled appointment)
Money expended or foregone	Helping that is perceived as being more financially costly (e.g., giving $25 instead of $1)
Social disapproval	Intervention that requires breaking a social rule (e.g., going someplace that is prohibited, violating group norms to help)
Reward for helping	
Monetary compensation	Promise of higher financial reward (i.e., expectations of more money)
Social reward	Expectation that there will be social benefits to the helper (e.g., fame, gratitude, reciprocity)
Cost for the victim receiving no help	
Relating to concern for the victim	
Victim deservingness	Victim seen as innocent or not responsible for the problem
Victim need	The situation involves the serious need for the victim (e.g., severe injury or psychological problem)
Clarity of victim's need	The need of the victim is unambiguous and is unlikely to be misinterpreted (e.g., the situation involves screams for help)
Relating to personal concerns	
Guilt or blame	Anticipated negative outcomes for not helping (e.g., the possibility of being publicly identified as someone who failed to help a person in need)
Potential irresponsibility	Bystander has clear responsibility (e.g., personally identified as responsible; in position of responsibility, such as a group leader)
Unpleasant arousal	Feelings of upset and distress associated with witnessing another person suffer

"good Samaritan.") The talk was to be given in another building, and time pressure was manipulated by leading the participants to believe that they were either early, on time, or late for their presentations. On their way to give the speech, the seminarians passed a person who was slumped in a doorway. The seminarians who were early for their presentations were the most likely to help, and those who were late were least likely to help. Those who thought that they were late not only hurried past the victim but also often stepped over him. The costs of helping associated with time pressure made these otherwise "good" people less responsive to the needs of others.

Helping others can also involve the risk of direct personal harm or negative emotional reactions, or, in some situations, carry with it social stigmatization. These are all important costs that deter helping.

Potential Personal Harm. As suggested earlier, helping is sometimes dangerous, and in many real-life emergencies, the fear of being harmed may be a major deterrent to intervention. In the Kitty Genovese incident, for instance, it is possible that many of the bystanders hesitated to help because rushing to her aid might have meant putting their own lives on the line. The impact of these kinds of fears is clearly illustrated in a field experiment conducted in the New York subway (H. Allen, unpublished study, cited in Latané & Darley, 1970). In this experiment, one confederate asked a subway rider (the participant) for directions. Another confederate interrupted and gave obviously incorrect information. The behavior of interest was whether people would help the person asking for directions by providing the correct information. Fear of harm was manipulated by varying the behavior of the confederate who gave the incorrect information. Some participants had seen him physically intimidate another person (also a confederate) who had apparently tripped over him; others had heard him shout verbal abuse without physical threats; and in a control condition, the tripping incident passed with no response from him.

As you might expect, even though it was easy to help in this situation, the potential costs associated with contradicting the possibly abusive confederate strongly influenced people's behavior. Only 16% of the people who witnessed threats of physical violence helped, and 28% of those who heard the verbal abuse helped. By contrast, 50% of the people in the control condition helped by giving the correct directions. Obviously, self-interest in avoiding harm influenced whether these people behaved in a helpful manner. In addition, research has shown that less life-threatening but potentially painful risks (e.g., receiving electric shocks) can make people reluctant to help. Not surprisingly, people are less likely to help another person when helping means that they will suffer some discomfort or harm themselves (Batson, O'Quin, Fultz, Vanderplas, & Isen, 1983; McGovern, 1976; Midlarsky & Midlarsky, 1973).

Unpleasant Emotional Consequences.   Helping someone may sound like a very desirable activity, but it can often involve unpleasant experiences. Helping opportunities are unusual and unexpected events, and when people encounter them, they often experience a range of insecurities. If people are asked to do something unfamiliar, they may feel some self-doubt, potential embarrassment, and concern about failing others. These are all potential costs for helping, and the stronger these feelings, the less likely people are to offer assistance (Edelmann, Childs, Harvey, Kellock, & Strain-Clark, 1984; Ladd, Lange, & Stremmel, 1983; Midlarsky & Hannah, 1985; Staub, 1974).

In emergencies, victims are often physically injured or disfigured. Intervention may require that the bystander come in contact with blood and other bodily fluids. Clearly, this cost could make even the most well-intentioned bystander reticent to become involved. Experiments have directly examined this possibility. The setting of one study was in a train on the Philadelphia subway (J. A. Piliavin & I. M. Piliavin, 1972). The victim, a confederate of the experimenter, quietly collapsed to the floor and stared at the ceiling (thus avoiding eye contact with bystanders). For half the trials, as the victim fell, a trickle of "blood" ran down his chin; for the other half, there was no blood. Because many people have an aversion to blood, the researchers reasoned that the presence of blood would increase the unpleasantness (i.e., costs) associated with providing help. As expected, bystanders were not only slower to help the bloody than the nonbloody victim, they also helped the bloody victim less often overall (65% vs. 95%). Personal costs for helping in the form of anticipated negative experiences can readily outweigh even the serious need of a victim. This study was conducted over 30 years ago; it is very likely that visible bleeding would have an even stronger impact on helping today. The fact that AIDS can be transmitted through contact with blood would dramatically increase the potential costs for helping. Indeed, in some recent instances, even emergency medical personnel have refused to help seriously injured and bleeding people because they feared these people might carry the AIDS virus.

Stigma by Association.   Costs for helping can also involve harm to one's reputation. The mere association of people with members of stigmatized groups can lead them to be stigmatized as well. For example, heterosexual people who are seen interacting with homosexual men may be denigrated by others who have homophobic attitudes, and simply being seen near an obese person can result in a person being evaluated more negatively (Hebl & Mannix, 2003; Neuberg, Smith, Hoffman, & Russell, 1994). These types of costs for helping can strongly affect people's decisions about whether to help others. People who chose not to volunteer for an AIDS organization reported that fear of stigmatization was a primary reason, and among those who did volunteer, "burnout" was directly related to how much stigmatization they experienced for helping (Snyder, Omoto, & Crain, 1999).

Rewards for Helping. According to the cost–reward framework, rewards should increase helping. Although a considerable amount of research has focused on the effects of costs for helping, relatively few studies have examined the effects of rewards. As anyone who has received an allowance from their parents would suspect, monetary rewards increase helping (Wilson & Kahn, 1975). Also, people are more likely to help if they are led to believe that helping will enhance their mood (Gueguen & De Gail, 2003), and the promise of other forms of personal gain also increases helping. People are more likely to help when helping is framed as an opportunity for skill development (a benefit for the helper) than as an interruption (a cost for the helper; Perlow & Weeks, 2002).

Social rewards are also very important (Deutsch & Lamberti, 1986). People are more likely to donate their time and money to charity if they believe it will increase their popularity, bring them recognition from others (Fisher & Ackerman, 1998; Reddy, 1980), or help them maintain their good reputation and be rewarded by others (Johnson, Erez, Kiker, & Motowidlo, 2002). Even a simple "thank you" can be effective. In an experiment by McGovern, Ditzian, and Taylor (1975), a female confederate asked male participants to take an electrical shock for her. If the participants agreed, she said nothing in a control condition but responded with "thank you" in a reinforcement condition. After the initial shock trial, participants who had been reinforced continued to be more helpful throughout the experiment than did participants who were not reinforced.

Reinforcement from the person being helped can also come indirectly. For example, the helper may experience personal gratification when she or he sees the situation improve for the person in need; this also increases helping. People are more helpful when they can perceive that their help is actually improving the other person's condition (Smith, Keating, & Stotland, 1989; Utne & Kidd, 1980).

Rewarding Moods. When we discussed factors affecting whether or not one notices an event, we noted that being in a good mood seems to make one more attentive to the social situation, leading to a greater likelihood of helping. However, being in a good mood also leads to helping when people are made aware of another's need, such as when

→ more optimistic

they are asked directly for assistance (e.g., Baron, 1997). This latter finding suggests at least two other routes, related to costs and rewards, by which good moods may promote helping.

First, being in a good mood appears to make one think more about good things (such as rewards) than about bad things (such as punishments). Alice Isen and her colleagues have found that individuals who were in a good mood were more likely to think about positive things, to retrieve more positive thoughts from memory, and to have a more positive outlook on life (Isen, 1970; Isen, Clark, & Schwartz, 1976; Isen & Levin, 1972; Isen, Shalker, Clark, & Karp, 1978). Thus, people in good moods may think more about the rewards for helping and think less about the costs.

Second, when people are in good moods, they may compare their own circumstances to those of people around them (Clark & Isen, 1982). If they feel an imbalance between their own good fortune and the situation of less fortunate others, they will be motivated to correct this inequity. One way of doing this is by helping others, and the reward for helping is in restoring a sense of fairness and balance.

Thus far we have examined the way that the emotional states and the situational context of a potential helper influence when people help. However, as we noted in chapter 1, helping is an interpersonal act, and often there are implicit costs and rewards associated with helping different kinds of people. Therefore, in the next section, we consider how the bystander's relationship to the person in need can affect costs and rewards and, thus, helping.

Relationships to People in Need

The nature of the relationship between a potential helper and the person in need can significantly alter the balance between costs and rewards. We consider five aspects of the relationship between persons in need and potential helpers: attraction, similarity, quality of the relationship, group membership, and racial characteristics.

Attraction. Positive feelings about the person in need, or "interpersonal attraction," also increase helping. This effect occurs whether the attraction is based on physical appearance, friendly behavior, or personal qualities (Dovidio & Gaertner, 1983; Harrell, 1978; Kelley & Byrne, 1976; Kleinke, 1977). According to the cost–reward analysis, one reason why physical attractiveness promotes helping, particularly by members of the other sex, is because it increases potential rewards. For example, helping may provide an opportunity to initiate a relationship with an attractive person.

Although this explanation fits with common sense and experience, it cannot completely account for these findings. Suppose you found a job application that was left accidentally in a phone booth, and it needed to be mailed. The application included a picture of either a physically attractive or an unattractive woman. Would that person's attractiveness make a difference in whether you would mail the application, even though helping (i.e., mailing the application) would be anonymous, and it would be highly improbable that you would ever meet the applicant? For a substantial number of people, the answer is "yes" (Benson, Karabenick, & Lerner, 1976). People helped the attractive person about half of the time, but they helped the unattractive person only about a third of the time. Interpersonal attraction can thus increase helping even when the rewards are not tangible.

Similarity. We have all heard the saying, "Birds of a feather flock together." Our concern is: Will these birds be helpful? Does similarity between a potential helper and a person in need influence the probability of helping? Several experiments have examined this issue, and similarity has been manipulated in various ways, including dress style, nationality, personality, and attitudes. The results are consistent: People are more likely to help others who are similar to themselves than they are to help those who are dissimilar (see Dovidio, 1984).

Why does similarity lead to more helping? One reason is that perceived similarity leads to interpersonal attraction (Byrne, 1971), and people are likely to help others whom they like. Another reason may be a sense of connection; people are more helpful to others when those others are included within a person's conception of the self (Cialdini, Brown, Lewis, Luce, & Neuberg, 1997). Additionally, being with others who share our values, interests, and beliefs is much more pleasant than being with those who do not. People who are seen as dissimilar are typically perceived as unpredictable, holding different beliefs and values, and threatening. From a cost–reward perspective, therefore, the costs of simply being with similar others are lower, and the anticipated benefits are higher. There may also be special costs associated with *not* helping a person who is similar, such as greater shame or guilt. To summarize, the more similar the victim is to the bystander, the greater is the guilt (cost) for not helping, the less is the apprehension (cost) about how the other person will react, and perhaps the greater is the anticipated appreciation (reward) for helping. (In chap. 2, we discussed the possible biological basis for the similarity-helping relationship.) Based on cost–reward factors such as these, it is not surprising that people are particularly eager to help others who are more similar to themselves.

Quality of Relationship. The quality of a relationship that a person has with another person in need is a powerful determinant of helping. In general, people who feel stronger ties to specific others are more likely to offer them help, and people in deeper, closer, and more sustained relationships are more likely to help each other (Anderson & Williams, 1996; Bryan, Hammer, & Fisher, 2000). For instance, people who desire a communal relationship—a long-term, close relationship—with another person experience elevated positive affect when they choose or even are required to help that person. In contrast, those who do not desire a continuing relationship react with negative affect when they are required to help (Williamson & Clark, 1992).

Shared Group Membership. Although *similarity* often refers to the correspondence of attitudes and traits between two individuals and can vary by degree (e.g., 25%, 50%, or 75% similarity), shared group identity represents the all-or-none categorization of a person as a member of your own group or as a member of another group. As suggested by social identity theory (Tajfel & Turner, 1979) and self-categorization theory (Turner, Hogg, Oakes, Reicher, & Wetherell, 1987), thinking of others in terms of group membership has a profound effect on the way people think about and act toward others. People remember more detailed information about members of their own group compared to members of other groups, think of them in more positive terms, evaluate them more favorably, and, relevant to our focus, are more generous in their allocation of resources to them (see Gaertner & Dovidio, 2000).

The effects of shared group membership go beyond the influence of perceived interpersonal similarity. Hornstein and his colleagues (Flippen, Hornsteein, Siegal, & Weitzman, 1996; Hornstein, 1976) demonstrated that common identity, which may be based on shared group identity or common fate, gives rise to a sense of "we-ness," which, in turn, leads to more positive behaviors, such as helping. As a consequence, people are more helpful in groups in which people's outcomes are more interdependent and their fates are tied together more intimately (Allen, Sargeant, & Bradley, 2003). Similarly, people become more helpful to other members of their group when they feel that their group is being threatened. For instance, Americans became substantially more helpful to one other, exhibiting significant increases in volunteering, after the terrorist attacks on the United States on September 11, 2001 (Penner, Brannick, Webb, & Connell, 2005). Also, appeals for assistance are more effective when people imply that the person asking for help is from the potential helper's group rather than from another group (Vaes, Paladino, & Leyens, 2002).

In a direct test of the influence of group membership, Dovidio et al. (1997) found that inducing a common group identity between members of different laboratory groups increased helping toward others who were formerly perceived as outgroup members. The amount and kind of helping observed exceeded what could be accounted for by perceived similarity alone; there was some additional motivation to help by virtue of everyone being seen as members of the same group.

Outside of the laboratory, Levine, Prosser, Evans, and Reicher (2005) relied on existing intergroup rivalries between soccer fans in England to stage opportunities to help ingroup or outgroup members. To make group membership salient, the experimenters had participants complete a questionnaire about their team preferences. Then, as a continuing aspect of the cover story, participants were told that they would next go to a nearby building to view a videotape of a soccer match between their team and a rival team and to answer some questions about the game. On the way to the nearby building, participants encountered a jogger who had apparently slipped and injured his ankle. In one of their experiments, Levine et al. found that bystanders were willing to help the injured stranger much more often when the victim wore the ingroup team's shirt (92% of the time) than when he wore a rival team's shirt (30% of the time) or an unbranded sports shirt (33% of the time). Note that the effect is due to the increase in help given to the injured ingroup victim and not a reduction in help given to the fan of the competing team. In a second experiment, Levine et al. emphasized a different kind of group identity of participants, their common group identity as football fans, rather than the separate identities of fans of different soccer clubs. In this study, participants were more likely to help the injured jogger when he was also perceived to be a soccer fan, regardless of whether his shirt identified him as a fan of the participant's team (80% helping) or of a rival team (70% helping), than when the victim did not appear to be a soccer fan (the unbranded sports shirt condition, 22% helping). Thus, group membership has a distinct impact on helping, with the primary distinction being whether the person in need shares the group identity that is salient to the participant at the time.

Within the United States, making common group membership salient can also have substantial effects on interracial helping. In a field experiment conducted at the University of Delaware football stadium prior to a game between the University of Delaware and Westchester State University, Black and White student interviewers, wearing either a University of Delaware or Westchester State University hat, approached White fans who wore clothes associated with either team (Nier, Gaertner, Dovidio, Banker, & Ward, 2001). These fans were asked if they would be willing to be interviewed about their food preferences. White fans were signifi-

— football study → white more likely to get interviewed by Black if same team fan

helps

racism

cantly more cooperative with a Black interviewer when they shared a superordinate university identity with one another (reflected in their clothing) than when they did not (60% vs. 38%). For White interviewers, with whom the White fans already shared racial group membership, the effect was much less pronounced (43% vs. 40%) and not significant.

Group membership also alters how different forces determine helping. For instance, people are not only more helpful to ingroup than to outgroup members generally, but they are also more influenced in their decisions to help by ingroup than by outgroup members (Levine, Cassidy, Brazier, & Reicher, 2002). Levine et al. (2002) found that the "bystander effect," in which people are inhibited from helping when other bystanders are passive, occurs primarily when the other witnesses are members of the bystander's ingroup. In addition, Simon, Stürmer, and Steffens (2000) found that different factors influence homosexuals and heterosexuals to volunteer for an AIDS service organization. Homosexuals were more willing to volunteer when their collective identity in terms of sexual orientation was high—an identity shared with a substantial portion of victims of AIDS—than when their identity as a unique individual was high; the pattern for heterosexuals was reversed. The researchers concluded that "AIDS volunteerism emerged as a form of intragroup helping for homosexuals and as a form of inter-individual helping for heterosexuals" (Simon et al., 2000, p. 497). In subsequent research, Stürmer, Snyder, and Omoto (2005) further showed that when the common group identity with a person in need is salient, people develop an empathic bond with the person in need (see chap. 4) and help regardless of how much they like him or her personally; what primarily matters is that they are members of the same group. In contrast, what matters most when people are from different groups is interpersonal attraction; people are more likely to help a member of a different group if they like that person more. Thus, shared group identity not only produces high levels of helping, but the decision to help under these conditions is based on different factors than helping within *interpersonal* relationships.

Although this general tendency to help members of your own group more than members of other groups occurs cross-culturally, the effect is stronger in some societies than in others. In some cultures, such as in Japan and China, people are socialized to place a higher value on group achievement than on individual success. In these *collectivist* cultures, the interests of the individual are often subjugated to the needs of the group. In other cultures, such as in the United States, the emphasis is primarily on individual achievement. These are considered *individualist* cultures. The group membership–helping effect is stronger in collectivist cultures (see Moghaddam, Taylor, & Wright, 1993, pp. 119–121). For instance, Michael Bond and Kwok Leung (1988, as cited in Moghaddam et al., 1993) found that Chinese and Japanese participants helped members of their own groups more than did participants from the United States. American participants helped people from other groups more than did the Chinese and Japanese participants. Even across Western societies, cultures may differ. For example, Feldman (1968) examined the differential treatment of foreign and compatriot strangers by Parisians, Athenians, and Bostonians in five different social contexts. When differences occurred, the ingroup members were treated better in Paris and Boston, but the outgroup foreigners were treated better in Athens. In addition, within the United States, people with more collectivistic cultural orientation are less likely to help strangers, particularly when the helping involves greater planning (Conway, Ryder, Tweed, & Sokol, 2001).

Although much of the earlier research on when people help considered helping as an *interpersonal* behavior, more recent studies demonstrate that helping can also be an *intergroup* act. Consequently, the relationship of others to a person's social group (e.g., race or ethnicity) even within the same culture can also influence helping. We focus on race in the next section to illustrate the impact of a specific type of group membership—racial groups within the United States.

Racial Groups. The prediction concerning how racial characteristics (i.e., racial similarities and differences between the bystander and the person in need) would affect helping seems straightforward. From an intergroup perspective, Whites and Blacks in the United States would be likely to perceive themselves as members of different groups. From an interpersonal perspective, racial dissimilarity often leads to the assumption of belief dissimilarity (Rokeach & Mezei, 1966; Stein, Hardyck, & Smith, 1965). Therefore, bystanders would be expected to be less likely to help someone of a different race than someone of their own race. Also, in the United States, Blacks have been the target of prejudice, and stigmatized persons are less likely to receive help than people who are not stigmatized, which would be expected to lead to lower cross-racial helping, particularly among Whites (Edelmann, Evans, Pegg, & Tremain, 1983; Piliavin, Rodin, & Piliavin, 1969; Walton et al., 1988).

The relationship between helping and racial differences is not this simple, however. Recall that in the incident presented in the beginning of this chapter, it was four Black people who heroically rescued the White victim, Reginald Denny. Research findings suggest that racial effects in helping are quite complicated. Some experimenters have found that participants help people who they believe belong to another racial group *less* often than they help people they believe belong to their own racial group (Benson et al., 1976; Wegner & Crano, 1975; West, Whitney, & Schnedler, 1975). Other researchers have found no differences associated with the victim's race on the amount of help that White and Black bystanders offer (Bickman & Kamzan, 1973; Gaertner & Bickman, 1971; Saucier, Miller, & Doucet, 2005). Still other investigators have found that Whites are *more* likely to help Blacks than Whites (Dovidio & Gaertner, 1981; Dutton & Lake, 1973). What can account for these seemingly contradictory results?

Aversive Racism. When will Whites discriminate against Blacks in their helping behavior? Samuel Gaertner and one of the authors of this book (Dovidio & Gaertner, 2004; Gaertner & Dovidio, 1986) used research on helping and on race prejudice to develop a broad model of interracial behaviors. It uses the concept of aversive racism to understand Whites' racial attitudes and behavior. *Aversive racism* represents a modern, subtle form of racial bias. According to this perspective, many Whites who may truly believe that they are not prejudiced still harbor *unconscious* negative feelings toward Blacks. As a consequence of possessing both conscious, nonprejudiced convictions and unconscious, negative feelings, aversive racists discriminate against Blacks in some situations but not in others.

What kinds of situations are these? Gaertner and Dovidio (1986; Dovidio & Gaertner, 2004) proposed that in situations in which the social norms for appropriate behavior are clear and unambiguous, aversive racists will *not* discriminate against Blacks. Wrongdoing would be obvious under these circumstances and would threaten their self-belief that they are not prejudiced. That is, there are significant costs associated with discriminating against a black person under these conditions. However, aversive racists' negative feelings will be expressed and discrimination *will* occur when social norms are weak or ambiguous, or when a person can justify a negative response on the basis of some factor other than race (e.g., "the person caused this problem by not working hard enough"; Frey & Gaertner, 1986). For example, Whites may express support for programs like Affirmative Action *in principle*, but they may seize on excuses (e.g., concerns about maintaining traditional standards) to oppose implementing these programs *in practice* (see Dovidio, Mann, & Gaertner, 1989).

How important is aversive racism in helping situations? One study by Gaertner and Dovidio (1977) suggested that it is a critical determinant even when a Black victim has suffered a life-threatening injury. White college students overheard a very serious accident involving the person who was attempting to send them messages from a nearby cubicle. The experimenters varied two important aspects of this situation. First, some of the students believed that they were the only witness to the emergency, whereas others believed that there were two other (White) bystanders who also heard the accident. The presumed presence of others allowed participants to diffuse responsibility—if they were so inclined. Second, the experimenters led some participants to believe that the victim was White and others to believe that the victim was Black.

As the researchers expected, when White bystanders believed that they were the only witness to an emergency—when appropriate behavior was clearly defined—they did not discriminate against the Black victim. In fact, they helped Black victims slightly more often than they helped White victims (94% vs. 81%). However, when they believed that there were other people present (and the bystanders had the opportunity to diffuse responsibility), participants helped Black victims about half as often as they helped White victims (38% vs. 75%). The opportunity to diffuse responsibility offered a nonrace-related excuse for bystanders to treat victims differently but in a way that allowed them to avoid recognizing that racial bias was a factor. It was not due to a decision to intentionally let the Black victim suffer—that would be obviously racist. Instead, it was a decision to let someone *else* help. Of course, if each of the witnesses diffuses responsibility, no one will help; the consequences of subtle bias will be as deadly as the effects of blatant racism.

The aversive racism framework identifies additional cost–reward considerations that make the effects of race more complicated than the effects of similarity or attraction. In particular, there is a special cost for aversive racists associated with discriminating against Blacks: It would threaten a very important aspect of their self-image. Thus, when discrimination would be obvious (as in not helping a Black victim when you are the only witness), these cost considerations outweigh the influence of similarity. In fact, since it may be rewarding for aversive racists to reaffirm their nonprejudiced self-images (Dutton & Lennox, 1974), they are often *more* likely to help Blacks than Whites under these conditions. However, when aversive racists can rationalize not helping on the basis of some factor *other* than race (as in the belief that someone else will help), their self-image is no longer threatened, and these special costs do not apply. These Whites are then less likely to help Blacks than Whites, as the research on similarity and attraction suggests.

Recently Saucier, Miller, and Doucet (2005) reviewed the research literature on Whites' willingness to help other Whites and Blacks. Their summary provides an interesting and important overview of how prejudice affects helping. An earlier literature search by Crosby, Bromley, and Saxe (1980) found that Blacks overall were offered help less frequently than Whites, particularly when the helping did not require face-to-face help to be given. Although Crosby et al. noted that no bias was seen in the majority of studies, when bias did occur, it was consistently in the direction of less help for Blacks. Saucier and his colleagues conducted a

Blacks offered help less freq than whites

statistical analysis of the findings of more recent research (from 1987 to 2000). This analytic technique is called a *meta-analysis*, and it enabled Saucier et al. to quantify the amount of discrimination or bias found under different conditions or situations; this provided an empirical test of how aversive racism affected interracial helping. Saucier et al. rated the helping situation for each of the studies on a series of dimensions (e.g., ambiguity of the problem, time needed to help, potential harm to the helper, potential harm to the victim, cost or financial investment to help, difficulty and effort of helping, and physical distance between the participants and the person in need). They examined a total of 31 studies involving over 14,000 participants.

The results were consistent with the earlier conclusions drawn by Crosby et al. (1980) about race and helping and provided further evidence of the effects of aversive racism on helping decisions. Averaging across all of these studies, Saucier et al. found that Whites helped Blacks and Whites about the same amount. However, Whites helped other Whites more than they helped Blacks in situations where helping would take a lot of time, where the helper perceived some risk for helping, where the help needed was difficult and required significant effort, and when the distance between the helper and the victim was great. Taken together, these results suggest that, as the aversive racism theory would predict, Blacks were helped less than Whites when the situation provided the Whites with a way to rationalize and find excuses for not helping that *apparently* had nothing to do with race. Interestingly, Saucier et al. also reported that the greater the emergency, the greater were the differences in help offered to Blacks and Whites. They explained this by suggesting that in situations requiring quick and immediate action, Whites have a harder time suppressing or inhibiting discriminatory behaviors. This pattern is also completely consistent with the theory of aversive racism.

Summary

We have seen that costs and rewards have relatively straightforward effects on helping. As costs for helping increase, helping decreases; as rewards for helping increase, intervention increases. These costs and rewards may be directly related to the nature of the helping opportunity or may be associated with the potential benefactor's relationship to the person in need. As we noted earlier, this type of cost/benefit analysis fine-tunes the steps in the Latané and Darley decision model. Once people notice the event, interpret the situation as one requiring assistance, and recognize their personal responsibility, the costs and rewards associated with helping determine the level of intervention. The research on the race of the person in need, however, suggests the potential complexities of the cost–reward approach that allows predictions that go well beyond the scope of Latané and Darley's five steps. Costs and rewards come in various forms, such as threats to your self-image or opportunities to meet an attractive person. These considerations can influence how likely a bystander is to assume *personal* responsibility for helping. Thus, costs and rewards not only affect what happens *within* each step of the model but also influence how people proceed *through* these steps.

COMBINING COSTS AND REWARDS

Over 35 years ago, one of the authors of this book, Jane Piliavin, and her colleagues developed the *arousal: cost–reward model,* which considers more fully the nature of costs, the effects of different combinations of costs, and their effects on the *type* of response bystanders will make (I. M. Piliavin, Rodin, & Piliavin, 1969; J. A. Piliavin et al., 1981; Dovidio et al., 1991). This section summarizes the cost–reward component of the model; the arousal component is examined in the next chapter.

Arousal: Cost–Reward Model

In the arousal: cost–reward model, there are two basic categories of potential costs and rewards for a bystander. One category is *personal costs for helping*. These costs involve negative outcomes imposed on the helper for making a direct helping response. Injury, effort, and embarrassment are examples of such potential costs for helping, as we discussed in earlier sections of this chapter. The other category is *costs for the victim not receiving help*. It contains two subcategories. First, there are *personal costs for not helping,* which are direct negative outcomes to the bystander for failing to aid the victim. These include guilt, shame, and criticism; we alluded to these costs previously as well. Second, there are *empathic costs* for the victim receiving no help, which are based primarily on the bystander's awareness of the victim's continued distress. In particular, these empathic costs involve internalizing the victim's need and distress as well as more sympathetic and concerned feelings for the victim. These empathic costs are higher when the other person is perceived as being in more immediate or greater need (Lee & Murnighan, 2001). Empathic costs are generally higher, and thus people are more helpful, when people are in need for reasons beyond their control (e.g., because of physical disability; Taylor, 1998). These costs for not helping are lower, and thus people tend to be less helpful, when the person is seen as more responsible for his or her plight (Otten et al., 1988).

The arousal: cost–reward model makes predictions not only about whether a bystander will make a response but also about *what* that response will be. The response is a function of both the costs for helping and the costs for the victim not receiving help. As can be seen in the upper left-hand cell of Fig. 3.4, when the costs for no help to the victim are high (e.g., the person is seriously injured) and when costs for direct help are low (e.g., helping is not dangerous), direct help (e.g., rushing to the aid of the victim) is most likely. However, direct helping becomes less likely as the costs for helping increase. The literature on the effects of costs on helping, which we covered earlier in this chapter, strongly supports this hypothesis.

What happens when the helper's costs for helping and victim's costs for not receiving helping are both high? (See the upper right-hand cell of Fig. 3.4) This is when the bystander is between the proverbial rock and hard place. The Kitty Genovese incident fits this description nicely. The

Costs for Direct Help

		Low	High
Costs for No Help to the Victim	**High**	Direct Intervention	Indirect Intervention or → / Redefinition of the situation, disparagement of victim, diffusion of responsibility
	Low	Variable: A function of perceived norms in the situation	Leave the scene, ignore, deny

FIG. 3.4. Costs for direct help and costs for no help to the victim combine to determine how people will respond. Adapted from Piliavin et al. (1981), with permission.

bystander has a strong desire to do something. The cost to Kitty Genovese for not being helped is high—her death. But the high cost of direct intervention (i.e., the possibility of the bystander being killed) deters the bystander from becoming directly involved. The bystander, therefore, experiences a very strong conflict between the need to help and the fear, distaste, or, in some cases, the physical impossibility of helping. The arousal: cost–reward model's prediction is that bystanders can resolve this conflict either by offering *indirect help*, such as seeking an institutional helper (i.e., doctor, police officer), or by *cognitively reinterpreting* the situation. That is, bystanders might psychologically alter the perceived costs to the victim for not helping. They can do this by redefining the situation as not being an emergency, by concluding that someone else will intervene (i.e., diffusing responsibility), or by convincing themselves that the person is not really deserving of help. These rationalizations lower the perceived costs for not helping (e.g., "Even if I do not help, someone else will") and allow bystanders to leave the scene or return to their interrupted activity.

Research supports these predictions and suggests that some responses may be more common than others. In serious emergencies (high cost for not helping situations), indirect helping becomes more likely as costs for helping increase (J. A. Piliavin et al., 1981). Overall, however, indirect helping is relatively infrequent, perhaps because it is difficult for bystanders to pull themselves away from such involving situations to seek others who can help better than they can. Cognitive reinterpretation seems to be the most common and possibly the most efficient way of resolving the high cost for helping/high cost for not helping dilemma. For instance, bystanders are more likely to diffuse responsibility when the person in need is physically disfigured (creating a relatively high cost for helping) than when the person is not (I. M. Piliavin, Piliavin, & Rodin, 1975; Walton et al., 1988). Although the reinterpretation process occurs quickly and probably without conscious awareness, it is as if the bystander initially recognizes the need for assistance, becomes hesitant because of the costs for helping, and then searches for a reasonably justifiable excuse for not helping (Gaertner & Dovidio, 1977; Schwartz & Howard, 1982). As we have indicated before, this is not the same as apathy. People do care; ironically, it is the fact that they are very sensitive to the other person's need that initially places them in the dilemma.

Now consider the bottom right-hand cell of Fig. 3.4. In it, the costs for no help to the victim are low, and the costs for direct help are high. Imagine that you see a dangerous-looking hitchhiker while you are driving down the highway. Will you stop and offer assistance? The costs to the hitchhiker for no help seem low (i.e., he is not in any jeopardy); the potential costs to you for helping (i.e., possible attack) seem high. Under these circumstances, people are most likely to leave the scene (e.g., drive by) or deny the legitimate need of the hitchhiker for help.

The response of bystanders in situations in which both costs for help and costs for not helping are low (the bottom left-hand box of Fig. 3.4) is most difficult to predict. For instance, suppose you see someone drop her books in the hallway. In such a situation, social norms, personality differences, and relationships to the person in need (see chap. 7) are presumed to have their strongest impact (Dovidio et al., 1991; J. A. Piliavin et al., 1981). Small changes in the situation will also have noticeable effects. Helping will increase as the costs for the victim *not* receiving help (both personal and empathic) begin to increase. Among these are the following: making it more difficult for the bystander to escape the situation unnoticed or without guilt, increasing the need of the victim, having the victim make stronger and more immediate appeals for help, or making the person in need seem more deserving of help (see Dovidio et al., 1991). These changes tend to move the situation from the bottom left-hand cell to the top left-hand cell of Fig. 3.4. In summary, the arousal: cost–reward model extends earlier work by identifying various kinds of costs and illustrating how different combinations of costs lead to different types of actions.

THE ANSWER: SUMMARY AND IMPLICATIONS

We began the chapter with the broad question, "When will people help?" Stimulated by the Kitty Genovese incident, Latané and Darley (1970) developed a decision-tree model of bystander intervention. The five steps in their model offered a valuable, new perspective for understanding when people help, and evidence in support of the model is strong: The more likely bystanders are to notice an event, interpret it as a situation requiring help, and assume personal responsibility, the more likely they are to help. In addition, people who are more knowledgeable about what to do and better trained to deliver assistance are more likely to help effectively.

We further considered the situational factors and psychological processes that determine whether bystanders will notice the event, how the event will be interpreted, and whether people assume responsibility. These influences, which are presented in Table 3.3, are not confined to helping situations; they are general principles of group and individual behavior that are relevant to a broad range of social functioning.

The cost–reward analysis offers a powerful refinement to the processes described in the Latané and Darley model. The cost–reward analysis extends the Latané and Darley model in three ways. First, among bystanders

TABLE 3.3
Summary of Situational Factors and Psychological Processes
That Determine Whether a Person Will Be Helped

Decision Steps	Possible Influences	Impact
1. Notice the Event	Clarity and vividness	Clearer and more vivid events are more likely to be noticed
	Stimulus overload	Excess environmental stimulation reduces the likelihood that the event will be noticed
2. Interpret the event as requiring help	Perceptual cues	Events that involve more cues of another person's need are more likely to be interpreted as situations requiring help
	Informational social influence	Particularly in perceptually unclear (ambiguous) situations, the behavior of others will define whether help is required
	Relationship to the person in need	People are more likely to recognize the need of others with whom they are closer
	High costs for helping	People may resolve the high cost for helping–high cost for no help dilemma by reinterpreting the situation as one not requiring assistance
3. Assume personal responsibility	Immediate and general norms	Norms affect whether people will feel that they should help
	Presence of others	The opportunity to come to believe that other people can help allows a person to diffuse responsibility
	Focusing responsibility	People are more likely to take action when they are in positions of explicit responsibility
	Relationship to the person in need	People are more likely to accept responsibility for helping others with whom they are closer
	High costs for helping	People may resolve the high cost for helping–high cost for no help dilemma by diffusing personal responsibility for helping
4. Choose a way to help	Knowledge and training	People who are more knowledgeable about the situation can better evaluate alternative courses of action
5. Implement the decision	Training and experience	Bystanders who are well trained are more likely to help safely and effectively

who recognize the need for helping and accept personal responsibility, assessment of costs and rewards accounts for some of the differences in helping because of specific aspects of the situation (e.g., danger) and characteristics of the person in need (e.g., attractiveness). In one test of the arousal: cost–reward model that systematically varied costs for helping and costs for not helping and then asked participants what they would do, 76% of participants' helping intentions could be explained by sensitivity to these costs (Fritzsche, Finkelstein, & Penner, 2000). These factors also figure prominently in very consequential decisions, such as the reasons why donors decide to donate bone marrow to strangers (Switzer, Dew, Butterworth, Simmons, & Schimmel, 1997). Second, the cost–reward analysis component of the arousal: cost–reward model illustrates the dynamic and cyclical nature of the decision to help. For example, when help is badly needed but is very costly to give, bystanders in this "high-high" dilemma may actively reinterpret the situation in ways that alter perceived costs (e.g., by becoming more likely to diffuse responsibility). Third, this framework explicitly considers not only whether a bystander will do something or not but also what the response will be: direct help, indirect help, reinterpretation, or leaving the scene.

The evidence in this chapter also illustrates the general value of social psychological theory and research. What may seem to be obvious at a first glance may actually be quite different under close scientific scrutiny, and often "common sense" is wrong. Many people who hear about the Kitty Genovese incident attribute the lack of help to widespread bystander apathy and "bad" or "abnormal" people, but the research findings suggest a very different picture. When the need of the victim and the responsibility of the bystander are clear and the cost/reward considerations are favorable, people will help—very frequently and very dramatically, as was the case in the rescue of Reginald Denny. People are far from apathetic. In fact, it is remarkable that people will be so helpful to strangers. Why *do* people help others, anyway? That is the question we consider in the next chapter.

CHAPTER 4

*Why Do
People Help?*

(handwritten margin notes: "babies respond to distress <1" "1-2 → spontan. prosocial beh")

A s we saw in chapter 3, people are capable of great heroism and generosity to others in need. However, less dramatic forms of helping are integral to daily life. Helping is an everyday behavior that occurs frequently and spontaneously among people of all ages, from the very young (McGuire, 1994) to the elderly (Bergin, Bergin, & French, 1995; Midlarsky, Kahana, Corley, Nemeroff, & Schonbar, 1999). Before they are even 1 year old, infants begin to respond to distress in other children (Lamb & Zakhireh, 1997), and spontaneous prosocial behavior emerges between the ages of 1 and 2 years (see chap. 6; see also Zahn-Waxler, Radke-Yarrow, Wagner, & Chapman, 1992). In chapter 3 we focused on spontaneous helping, such as the heroic acts that followed the September 11, 2001, attacks in New York and the subway bombings in London in 2005, but people also help by donating large amounts of money (e.g., Bill Gates, has committed over $3 billion of his personal fortune to organizations working in world health), giving gallons of blood, and volunteering sometimes hundreds of hours a year to benefit schools, religious organizations, and other charities (see chap. 5). Helping is a pervasive aspect of our lives. But why? What motivates people to help others?

THE QUESTION

The central question of this chapter is, *Why* do people help? This issue returns us to the old debate among philosophers (see chap. 1): Are peo-

106

ple altruistic or egoistic, selfless or selfish? It is easy to demonstrate that people can be motivated by self-interest, but are people ever motivated primarily by concern for others? In this chapter we explore the range of possible motivations for spontaneous helping of the kind discussed in chapter 3, and we later use these motivations as a foundation for considering more deliberative, sustained, and collective forms of helping, such as volunteering time and donating money or other resources (e.g., blood), which we examine in subsequent chapters.

One challenge for understanding people's motivations for helping is that self-reports of intentions and motivations are not necessarily accurate. What people say and even what they honestly believe may not always accurately represent the actual causes of their behavior. People are often unaware if they behave in a certain way (Greenwald et al., 2002), and often come up with post hoc explanations (Ross & Nisbett, 1991; Wilson, 2002) that portray themselves in the best possible light. For example, people typically report that they volunteer because of their concern for others, and they report that helping others gives them a sense of meaning and purpose (Davis, Hall, & Meyer, 2003; Dickson-Gómez, Knowlton, & Latkin, 2004). Similarly, the most frequent reasons cited for donating blood are humanitarian or altruistic concerns (J. A. Piliavin & Callero, 1991). By contrast, the typical reason that people give for *not* donating money or volunteering is that they simply were not asked.

People's true motives are often more complex, however, and self-interest may be involved. One of the fundamental principles of human behavior is that people are motivated to do things that are personally reinforcing, things that bring them immediate gratification or have longer term personal benefits. People may engage in helping that appears to be spontaneous but actually occurs because helping will result in respect or praise from others, because it will make the helpers feel good (or better, if they are feeling bad), or because it will increase the likelihood that others may help them some day (Dovidio & Penner, 2001). Similarly, people may donate money to achieve personal recognition, to get ahead in their careers, to gain the respect of others, or even for personal gain (Reddy, 1980). In fact, Reddy found that "the most powerful single variable" in determining whether people make charitable contributions is whether the donation would reduce their taxes.

Motives for volunteering time may also involve personal benefits. One-third of the volunteers surveyed by Reddy said they donated their time because they "had an interest in the activity," "thought [they] would enjoy doing the work," or wanted to "feel needed." Snyder (1992) found similar kinds of motivations among volunteers who help people with AIDS. Thus, although people often report "altruistic" reasons for helping, personal needs and goals also appear to be very important.

Within psychology, attempts to understand what motivates people to help have focused on three possible processes or explanations: (a) learning, (b) social and personal standards, and (c) arousal and emotion (affect). The *learning* explanation applies general principles from learning theories to the acquisition of helping skills and of beliefs about why these skills should be used to benefit others. The *social and personal standards* approach considers how people's personal values can motivate helping by affecting both cognitive (what people think) and affective (what people feel) processes. Finally, the *arousal and affect* approach emphasizes how the particular emotion that a person feels can motivate helping in different ways. Some of the arousal and affect theories share a guiding principle with learning theory. They posit that people are motivated to behave in ways that bring them some kind of rewards—in this case, feeling better. However, there are some theorists who argue that under some very special circumstances people may be motivated by the primary goal of making *another person* feel better, that is, by true altruism.

LEARNED HELPFULNESS

As we observed in the first chapter, philosophers have long debated whether people are inherently good or bad. Nevertheless, philosophers who were on opposites sides of this issue have agreed on one thing: Society needs its members to be concerned about the welfare of others and to be helpful toward them. Psychologists have focused on how such values can be taught to the members of society.

A basic principle of learning theory has been Thorndike's *law of effect.* This principle is quite simple, but very important—people will be more likely to engage in actions that are rewarded and less likely to engage in actions that are punished. Building on Thorndike's law of effect, learning theorists have identified certain fundamental learning processes. One of these, *operant conditioning*, concerns the extent to which the occurrence of a behavior can be modified by the positive or negative consequences of the action. Research conducted on operant conditioning shows that people are motivated to help others because they have been positively reinforced for helping in the past. Reinforcement may occur through the presentation of positive outcomes (e.g., praise) or the relief of negative circumstances (e.g., terminating electric shock). Conversely, people may learn *not* to help others because helping has led to negative consequences (see Grusec, 1991a; Staub, 1981).

Positive or negative outcomes for helping can have a virtually immediate impact. For example, in an experiment by Moss and Page (1972), individuals were approached by a confederate on a busy street. The con-

— study→+ve/–ve comment for giving directions.
↳ 93% +ve helped
pickup wallet vs 40% –ve →immediate effect

federate asked for directions to a local department store, one for which most residents knew the location. In most cases, the person complied with the request. The consequences of helping were systematically varied. In the positive reinforcement condition, the confederate smiled and said, "Thank you very much. I really appreciate this." In the negative consequence (punishment) condition, the confederate rudely interrupted the person and remarked, "I can't understand what you're saying. Never mind, I'll ask someone else."

These consequences had a dramatic effect on subsequent helping. A short time later, participants encountered another person who had "accidentally" dropped a small bag. More than 93% of the positively reinforced participants subsequently helped this person, whereas only 40% of those who had been punished offered assistance. People in a control condition, who were neither previously rewarded nor punished, also exhibited a high level of helpfulness, about 85%, not statistically different from those who were rewarded. Thus, being punished for being helpful made the people much less likely to help. The influence of the effects of rewards and punishments helps explain how perceived costs and benefits, described in the previous chapter, affect when people help. For example, as we described in chapter 3, people are more likely to help others who are more attractive because the anticipated (or hoped for) rewards are greater, and they are less likely to help others when the expected consequence associated with helping involves a greater potential for punishment (i.e., personal harm) for intervening (H. Allen, unpublished study cited in Latané & Darley, 1970; Kelley & Byrne, 1976).

Although punishment for helping generally reduces the likelihood that a person will help again, it is not the case that punishment for *not* helping will *increase* prosocial behavior. That is, punishment for selfish actions or for choosing not to help when assistance is needed is not an effective tool for parents or peers to teach people to be helpful. In the short run, punishment arouses negative feelings, such as anger, that are incompatible with a prosocial orientation; hostile people tend not to be helpful. In the long run, these negative feelings interfere with the socialization of concern for others and intrinsic motivations for helping (Grusec, 1991b; Hoffman, 1970). Consequently, if parents punish their child for not helping, they may be sending a mixed message. Punishment in this context may therefore be particularly confusing and may inadvertently teach the child to also respond to others' needs with coldness and rejection (see chap. 6).

Besides direct experience, people can also learn to expect certain consequences for helping or not helping through information from other people, a process known as social learning. This information can come through specific instructions or by watching how other people behave.

— punishment for not helping work
↳ doesn't work
↳ mixed message
↳ –ve feelings
w/ prosocial

—learn vicariously too

As Albert Bandura (1977, p. 22) noted, "Learning would be exceedingly laborious, not to mention hazardous, if people had to rely solely on the effects of their own actions to inform them what to do." For example, trial-and-error would not be a good way to learn skydiving. Much of the initial research on social learning theory focused on how observing others (e.g., watching a person hit a large inflated doll) influenced aggression. Subsequent work has made a convincing case that social learning and modeling are also important for prosocial behavior.

Social learning commonly occurs by observing others' behavior and the consequences it produces for them (Bandura, 1977, 1986). In an experiment that illustrates the effects of social learning on helping, people walking down a street saw a person (really a confederate) return a lost wallet (Hornstein, 1970). This person either appeared pleased to be able to help or displeased at the bother of having to help. Later, in the experiment, the participants also came across a "lost" wallet. People who had previously seen the person who was pleased to help helped much more than people who had observed the unpleasant consequences for helping.

In summary, both direct reinforcement and modeling can affect an individual's desire to be helpful in a given situation. People *learn* to be helpful—in much the same way they can learn to be selfish or aggressive. There is, of course, much more to the process of learning to be helpful. These are discussed in more detail in chapter 6 when we consider the mechanisms by which children learn helpfulness. Now we turn to the other processes that may explain why people help.

— study → lost wallet → see person act +/- for having to help
→ P find wallet → + help more than -

SOCIAL AND PERSONAL NORMS

Through personal and social learning people not only come to know how they should behave in a particular situation, but they also acquire an understanding of how others expect them to behave generally (social norms) and develop their own standards and ideals for their behavior (personal norms). Social norms, which are rules for accepted and expected behavior in situations, are an important determinant of people's intentions to help (Warburton & Terry, 2000). Personal norms are an individual's expression of feelings of obligation to behave in a particular manner in a particular type of situation (Schwartz, 1977); personal norms are more specific than social norms, which are assumed to apply to most people most of the time.

Although the specific mechanisms by which norms motivate helping are rarely identified in experiments, both cognitive (learning) and affective (emotional) factors are probably involved. Personal and social norms provide standards of appropriate behavior, something to strive for. Thus, meeting these normative standards may be rewarding. Norms also define what people *ought* to do. People use personal and social standards to guide what they should do and how they should do it (Higgins & Spiegel, 2004). Failure to satisfy these obligations may make people feel bad or generate criticism from others (Archer, 1984; Williamson, Clark, Pegalis, & Behan, 1996). Norms may therefore provide both the proverbial "carrot and the stick," leading people to strive for personal and social rewards, while trying to avoid personal negative feelings and social punishments.

Social Norms

Normative theories of helping emphasize that people help others because they have expectations based on previous social learning or because the current behavior of others suggests that helping is the socially appropriate response. One of the most common reasons people give for becoming involved in volunteer work is to satisfy others' expectations of them (Reddy, 1980). Researchers have identified two classes of social norms involving helping. One class relates to feelings of fairness and involves perceptions of things such as *reciprocity* (Gouldner, 1960), *equity* (Walster, Walster, & Berscheid, 1978), and *justice* (Lerner, 1980). The other class of norms relates to very general standards and expectations of aiding, such as the *social responsibility norm* that people should help a person who is dependent on them (Berkowitz, 1972).

The Norm of Reciprocity. People learn through socialization how to coordinate their actions with others' behaviors. For example, taking turns in games and other activities is a critical social skill for children to develop (e.g., Garvey, 1990). Think back to when you were a small child. Do you remember your reaction to the playmate who would not take turns? Or, more recently, do you recall your reaction to the person who cut in line in front of you at the store? The strength of these reactions indicates how basic this unwritten rule of social behavior is in our society. As mentioned in chapter 2, the *norm of reciprocity* refers to a type of turn taking with regard to helping. According to this norm, people should help those who have helped them, and they should not help those who have denied them help for no legitimate reason (Gouldner, 1960). It is a highly internalized norm; it influences people's private and anonymous behaviors as well as their public actions. For example, Whatley, Webster, Smith, and Rhodes (1999) found that people reciprocated favors whether or not the person who did the initial favor would be aware that their prosocial act had been repaid.

—

[handwritten margin notes at top: "—imbalance motivates to reciprocate. —attempt to maintain stable/recip. relationships" "study → Xmas cards sent to random → 20% sent back"]

This principle implies that people attempt to maintain stable, reciprocal relationships with others. An imbalance in the relationship is uncomfortable and motivates a person to return the favor. For example, visits are often traded back and forth between families to keep the "social ledger" in balance. To illustrate this principle, consider this intriguing finding from a field study. Two researchers sent out Christmas greeting cards to total strangers. A surprisingly large number of these strangers (about 20%) responded with holiday greetings of their own—even though they did not know these people who had sent them the cards in the first place (Kunz & Woolcott, 1976).

Does this kind of "social ledger" exist for informal helping relationships as well? It appears so. People normally reciprocate assistance to others who have helped them. For instance, when servers at a restaurant wrote a helpful message about an upcoming dinner special on the back of their customers' checks, the size of their tips increased from 17% to 20% of the bill (Rind & Strohmetz, 1999). Reciprocity is a particularly strong influence when the person expects to see the helper again, although, as we noted earlier (Whatley et al., 1999), it also operates when there is no expectation of future interaction (Carnevale, Pruitt, & Carrington, 1982; Goranson & Berkowitz, 1966). Also, the more assistance a person receives, the more help he or she subsequently gives (Kahn & Tice, 1973). The need to reciprocate may also influence our behavior more generally. Suppose someone does you a favor but is not around to provide you an opportunity to reciprocate. Will you be more likely to do someone *else* a favor? Apparently so. In one experiment (Berkowitz & Daniels, 1964), some participants received favors, whereas others did not. Although the helper was no longer involved, students who had received favors were more likely to offer assistance to another person in need than were students who had not previously been helped. In the same vein, college alumni say that reciprocity is one of the key reasons why they continue to give substantial time and money to their college long after they have graduated (Diamond & Kashyap, 1997).

In addition, reciprocity can be a particularly effective way to obtain help when others want to avoid future social obligations associated with being "charitable" to others. People are often concerned that giving too generously to others may increase the likelihood that they will be asked again (and again) for assistance. Thus, framing a request for help in terms of reciprocity or an exchange may be particularly effective when the person or group in need has a substantial or chronic problem; it defines the relationship in a narrow way that can limit feelings of obligation to help again in the future. For example, Holmes, Miller, and Lerner (2002) found that when potential donors received a request for donations and the need was high ("over two hundred children will be damaged for life if they

[handwritten margin notes at left and bottom: "also some reasons why people give to fundraisers" "If person not avail anymore group helping diff person in need"]

— can limit giving/taking to generously by defining/
framing favours narrowly

don't get helped"), they were more likely to make donations if they were offered a small gift (a decorative candle) in exchange for their donations. According to Holmes et al. (2002), "the exchange provided psychological cover for their act of compassion" (p. 144). → *when need was high*

Reciprocity is such a fundamental principle that, as we saw in chapter 2, some researchers have proposed that it has a biological basis. Perhaps because this motive is so strong, it can also be manipulated to exploit us. Salespeople often begin their "pitch" with a "free" gift. The strategy is, people who receive something will want to give something back—possibly enough to make a significant purchase. It often works. In one study (Regan, 1971), students who were participating on a task with a confederate were given a brief rest period. During the break, the confederate performed an unexpected favor for half the students: He returned from the break carrying two soft drinks and said, "I bought one for you, too." In another condition, the confederate returned from the break empty-handed.

According to the norm of reciprocity, the students who received the drink should feel obligated to do something nice for the confederate who brought back the soda. As the confederate and the students were about to leave the room, the confederate asked them to do *him* a favor. He explained that if he sold the most tickets for a raffle, he would win a $50 prize himself. He then asked the students to buy some tickets, saying, "The more the better." Students who had received the unexpected favor were eager to satisfy their feelings of obligation; they bought twice as many tickets than those who had not received a favor. If this sounds fair, it is because we are familiar with and endorse the norm of reciprocity. What makes this situation exploitative, however, is that soft drinks cost only 10 cents at the time, but the raffle tickets cost 25 cents each. In their attempt to repay the favor, these students bought an average of two tickets each. The "free" drink they received was not free after all—it cost them almost five times as much as if they had bought the soda themselves!

→ study → bought 2x more raffle tickets if confed brought them a soda

sometimes we over reciprocate — 10¢ soda but 25¢ each ticket

Equity. The principles of fairness and balance that underlie the reciprocity norm are related to two other social needs. One is the need for *equity*. Equity exists when people in a relationship believe there is a balance or fairness between what they contribute to the relationship and what they receive from it (Adams, 1963; Walster et al., 1978). When people perceive an imbalance, they are motivated to restore equity. There is considerable evidence showing equity motives in helping. People who have unfairly received benefits—for example, those who receive too much reward based on their contribution to a group activity—often freely choose to give up some of their reward (e.g., Schmitt & Marwell, 1972). The key element here is that people *perceive* that they have been unfairly overcompensated. This does not always happen.

workers → if perceive unfair tx → contribute less

Because people tend to overestimate the value of their contributions, they typically believe they have earned—and thus deserve—what they have received. On the other hand, if people feel they been under-compensated, they will contribute less. George (1991) found, for example, that workers who felt they had been treated unfairly were less helpful to others and to their organization as a whole. That is, workers who felt they received less than they gave were less likely to go beyond what was required of them on the job.

The need to see the world as fair and just is also central to Melvin Lerner's *just-world hypothesis* (Lerner, 1980). The central aspect of the belief in a just world is that good things happen to good people, and that bad things happen to bad people. Thus, one reason why people help others may be because it is a virtuous act that makes them feel that they are deserving of good fortune. Conversely, under some circumstances, not helping may make them seem like a bad person, and consequently deserving of ill fortune. For example, in one set of studies by Zuckerman (1975), students who believed more strongly in a just world (based on their scores on the Belief in a Just World Scale) were more likely to volunteer to serve in an experiment and more likely to donate their time to read to a blind person shortly before taking an exam, but not shortly after the exam. Presumably, helping others was a way for students to establish that they deserved the good fortune of a just world when it came time to take their exam! *help the unfortunate to rebalance...*

Like equity theory, the just-world hypothesis suggests that people will be motivated to help others who have been treated unfairly—to make the world fair and just again. Moreover, because of the need to see the world as just, people, particularly those with a stronger belief in a just world, may be more likely to help those who have been injured unfairly. Bierhoff, Klein, and Kramp (1991), for instance, interviewed people who helped victims of actual traffic accidents and a sample of people (matched for age, sex, and socioeconomic status) who did not help the victims. Those who helped believed more strongly in a just world than those who did not.

However, there are other responses to another's misfortune that can also make the world *appear* just. Besides helping or compensating the victim, one could punish the perpetrator or come to believe that the victim got what he or she deserved. In fact, Lerner and his colleagues have shown that people will often devalue an innocent victim, because they are motivated to see the world as just. In general, if helping is possible and does not require undue commitment, most people will choose to help. However, if a person cannot be helped or the investment for helping is substantial, the just-world hypothesis suggests that people will not help (Miller, 1977) and instead will derogate the victim, which makes the world seem right again but in a different way. Innocent people do not suffer unfairly; thus victims must not actually be innocent, but rather are simply getting what they deserve. Illustrative of this idea, Furnham (1995) found that the more strongly English students believed in a just world, the more negative were their views of people with disabilities, and Applebaum (2002) demonstrated that German students who believed in a just world were more likely to be opposed to disadvantaged groups receiving government aid.

This tendency to blame the victim may explain why innocent victims of crimes (e.g., victims of rape) are sometimes accused of being responsible for their victimization—of "asking for it" by their dress or being in the wrong place. Ironically, the need to see the world as just leads people to make unfair judgments about what people deserve based on what they have received. For example, the recent people's courts in Rwanda are attempting to establish a collective sense of justice for past injuries in the genocide that occurred there in 1994, a step that can be instrumental for achieving reconciliation. These deliberations will require a careful framing of the causes of the genocide in a way that evokes sympathy and understanding for the victims rather than blaming them. Rationalizations that "blame the victim" could lead to retraumatization and a rekindling of hostilities among the people of Rwanda (Staub, 2004).

The Norm of Social Responsibility. According to this social norm, people are expected to help others who are dependent on them. Much of the classic work in this area was conducted by Leonard Berkowitz. In a series of experiments, students assembled paper envelopes under the supervision of another student. They were told that their work was actually a test of the other person's supervisory skill. Berkowitz and his colleagues varied how much the students believed the evaluation of the supervisor would depend on their performance. In general, the participants in this study were socially responsible. Even when there was no possible gain for themselves, students were more motivated to work when the consequences for the supervisor were greater (e.g., Berkowitz & Daniels, 1963). The norm of social responsibility also explains why, as we saw in chapter 3, people are more likely to help others who are physically handicapped and who are seen as having a significant need (Clark, 1975).

People's willingness to help others who are dependent on them has its limits, however. There are several exceptions to this rule. One involves *why* people are dependent. As we show later when Weiner's attributional model is presented, people have different reactions when a problem is caused *by the person* rather than by forces beyond the person's control. People are reluctant to help others whose own behavior caused

study more motivated to make good envelopes w/ higher dependence supervisor's score. of

their dependency (Frey & Gaertner, 1986). For example, if people believe that African Americans' disadvantaged economic status is due more to lack of effort than to social barriers, they are less likely to support social welfare programs designed to help the disadvantaged. Similarly, people are less likely to support programs to help "welfare recipients" than they are to help "the poor." Presumably, this reaction is because of stereotypes that welfare recipients are more personally responsible for their needy situation than are the poor in general (Henry, Reyna, & Weiner, 2004). Students are also less sympathetic and less likely to help a person who developed AIDS through sexual promiscuity than through a blood transfusion (Weiner, Perry, & Magnusson, 1988). In general, the perceived controllability of a person's problem is one of the major determinants of whether others will feel sympathy (when the need has an uncontrollable cause) or anger (when the need has a controllable cause), which, in turn, influences whether people respond helpfully or aggressively (Greitemeyer & Rudolph, 2003).

As we show in chapter 7, individual differences matter as well; different people respond in various ways to others' situations. Linda Skitka (1999) studied how liberals and conservatives responded to victims of a natural disaster. Telephone interviewers contacted a representative sample of over 1,000 people across the United States to assess their reaction to victims of massive flooding of the Mississippi and Ohio Rivers at the time. The interviewers described three different towns that had taken various measures in the past to control flooding. One town had increased taxes substantially to build a flood wall. A second town had voted against such action because the wall would have ruined the view of the river, which was a major tourist attraction and an important economic factor for the community. A third town did not build a flood wall because the community had voted down the increase in taxes that was needed for the construction. Thus, the towns varied in their attempts, through prior planning and commitment, to protect themselves against flooding.

In general, people were more supportive of federal assistance for the communities that had demonstrated more efforts to protect against the river flooding. However, liberals and conservatives responded differently. Liberals were less concerned about the communities' preparation than were conservatives; they supported aid for all three communities, regardless of the previous action to prepare for the flood. In contrast, conservatives were strongly influenced by prior preparation, supporting significantly more aid for the community that had already built the flood wall than for the other two towns, making their support for aid to the two other towns contingent on future reform.

There are also many differences across groups and cultures that influence reactions to dependency. As we noted in chapter 3, some cultures are more "individualistic," oriented toward individual gain and responsibility; others are more "collectivistic," directed toward the group welfare. The Americans and British tend to be individualistic, whereas the Chinese and Japanese tend to be collectivistic. As one consequence, people in these cultures may respond differently to others' dependency. Chinese psychologist Hing-Keung Ma (1985) asked people in London and in Hong Kong their reactions to a range of other people's problems. Hong Kong residents appeared more responsive to the needs of others. These feelings of social responsibility to help among collectively oriented people are particularly strong for others, even strangers, who are perceived to be part of their group (Barrett et al., 2004). There have also been traditional gender differences within the United States. Women are generally more sensitive to the dependency of others than are men (see chap. 6). In fact, men often respond to people who are very dependent on them by providing *less* rather than more help (Enzle & Harvey, 1979). Thus, the norm of social responsibility is only a *general* rule; it does not apply equally in all situations or to all people.

Personal Norms and Standards. Although general norms of social responsibility may provide only vague guides for behavior in concrete situations, the use of personal norms and standards is valuable for predicting how a particular person will behave in a specific situation. According to Schwartz and Howard (1981, 1982, 1984), *personal norms* are "feelings of moral obligation to perform or refrain from specific action" (1984, p. 234). Personal norms are generated in a specific situation by a person considering what the possible choices are and the implications of such actions for personal norms and values. The more central these personal standards are, the stronger will be the emotional arousal associated with acting or not acting in a certain way.

Personal norms do predict actual helping. For example, personal norms have been found to correlate significantly with such prosocial behaviors as giving blood or bone marrow, tutoring blind children, and working with elderly welfare recipients (Schwartz & Howard, 1982). The average correlation, however, is usually quite low (around .3). The influence of personal norms on helping behavior is greatly increased, however, if dispositional tendencies such as *awareness of consequences* (i.e., the extent to which people notice others' needs spontaneously) and *denial of responsibility* (i.e., the extent to which individuals accept excuses for inaction under circumstances that arouse personal normative standards) are also considered. For individuals who are high on awareness and low on denial, the correlations between personal norms and actions are often close to .50. The most striking finding of this kind involved asking Israeli students about their willingness to tutor blind children and then observing their actual behavior. For students high on denial, the correlation was –.03; essentially no relationship was found between their words and deeds. However, among those low in denial of responsibility, there was a correlation of .72 between their personal norms and actions. These people put their money (or, in this case, their time) where their mouths were (Schwartz & Howard, 1981).

The impact of personal norms also depends on how much people think about the normative standards. If you hold a personal norm that you should help in a particular situation, focusing on that norm should increase helping. Focusing your attention inward produces a state called *objective self-awareness* in which you are likely to compare yourself to some important standard or ideal behavior (Gibbons, 1990; Wicklund, 1975). If these standards involve helping, you will be more likely to help (Hoover, Wood, & Knowles, 1983).

The research on personal norms and standards converges to make a relatively clear picture. People who possess standards of helping in specific areas will be inclined to help. Whether they ultimately help, however, depends on whether they attend to these norms and accept personal responsibility for helping. This topic also introduces a critical issue that we consider in detail in chapter 7—differences among people in their willingness to help. Nevertheless, even though people may have different standards and norms, the nature of the motivation to help—to meet those standards and satisfy feelings of moral obligation—may be fundamentally similar.

FEELINGS AND HELPFULNESS

Although our behavior is guided by thoughts (cognitions), it is also greatly influenced by what we feel (affect). We are both logical and emotional beings. In this section we explore a third class of reasons why people help: We examine how different emotions motivate helping, often in different ways.

For over 100 years, psychologists have recognized that arousal is a fundamental element of emotions. Potential helping situations thus typically involve emotional experiences for potential helpers because they are usually arousing: People are aroused by the distress of others (see Eisenberg & Fabes, 1991). This reaction occurs even among very young children and occurs across cultures. In fact, this phenomenon is so strong and universal that some researchers have proposed that *empathic arousal*, arousal generated vicariously by another person's distress, has a biological and evolutionary basis; humans may be *inherently* empathic creatures (Cunningham, 1985/1986; Hoffman,

[handwritten margin notes at top: "perception of nature of arousal on sit = misinterpret"]

1981; see chap. 2). The role of empathic emotions in prosocial motivation is the focus of several arousal and affect models of helping.

Although many researchers agree that empathic arousal is an important and fundamental human emotion (see Dovidio, 1984), there is much less agreement about how it feels to be empathic and how this emotion actually motivates people to help. In general, the emotions that people feel are at least partially determined by how they interpret the arousal that they are experiencing; physiologically, there are few differences in the nature of the arousal between different emotions. Therefore, people may interpret unexplained arousal as fear if they are around frightened people; this same physiological arousal may be experienced as anger if they are around angry people (Schachter & Singer, 1962). For instance, male participants who walked across a narrow suspension bridge, which normally made people anxious and aroused, felt more romantically interested in a physically attractive female experimenter than did those who walked across a more stable bridge with her (Dutton & Aron, 1974). Thus, depending on the situation, arousal may sometimes be interpreted as one emotion, sometimes as a somewhat different emotion. Recall the last time you came home late and your parents were waiting up for you. How quickly did their arousal, which they had been interpreting as worry, become reinterpreted as anger? Similarly, empathic arousal may produce different emotions.

Emotions are complex experiences. In chapter 3, we explained how and why feeling *good* promotes helping. We were careful to note, however, that this does not imply that negative moods necessarily *suppress* helping. In fact, some negative emotions can lead people to be more helpful. Moreover, the emotional responses that a person can experience in a potential helping situation, which might be generally classified as negative affect, can be quite varied and can reflect very different subjective experiences. For example, research indicates that in serious emergency situations, bystanders usually become upset and distressed, but in less critical, less intense situations, observers may feel sad (Cialdini et al., 1987), tense (Hornstein, 1982), or even concerned and compassionate (Batson, 1991).

Historically, social psychologists treated motives rather broadly and compared how positive versus negative feelings affected people's behaviors. More recently, researchers have focused more of their attention on the causes and consequences of particular or specific emotions (so-called *differentiated emotions*; Mackie & Smith, 2000). They believe that the particular emotion a person experiences critically shapes a person's motivation and behavioral orientation to others. For example, some emotions, such as disgust, produce avoidance of others, whereas other emotions, such as sympathy, lead us to approach others (Fiske, Xu, Cuddy, & Glick, 1999; Keltner, Gruenfeld, &

[handwritten note at bottom: "the emo experienced shapes motv + bel to othrs"]

Anderson, 2003). Even negative emotions differ substantially in their action tendencies. Anger leads to action against another person or group, whereas fear promotes avoidance (Mackie, Devos, & Smith, 2000). We adopt this latter, more differentiated approach for understanding the role of emotion for prosocial motivation.

Emotions and Helping

People can experience a number of different emotions when they see another person's need or problem. Some, such as upset and distress, may result from intense arousal generated from an emergency that places the person in an unexpected and unfamiliar situation, in which there is great time pressure, and the possibility is high that another person may be injured or harmed in some way. Other emotions, such as discomfort (cognitive dissonance), may be based on the perception of injustice—that someone is in an unfair circumstance (Harmon-Jones, Peterson, & Vaughn, 2003). Still other emotions, such as sympathy and compassion, may reflect a primary concern for the welfare of a specific other person. Over the past 30 years, social psychologists have devoted considerable time and energy debating the different motivational properties of these emotional reactions (see Batson, 1998; Dovidio & Penner, 2001). We do not focus on the details of this debate. Instead, drawing on the more general research on differentiated emotion, we consider the factors that shape the emotion a person experiences and then consider the particular motivating properties of these different emotions for helping.

What determines the specific emotion that a person experiences in response to another's problem? There are two factors. One, obviously, is the nature of the event itself. The other, when the situation allows, is the interpretation that people may use to explain the victim's need for assistance. With respect to the nature of the situation, as we noted in the previous chapter, potential helping situations can vary substantially in vividness, seriousness, and intensity. For example, whether bystanders witnessed the aftermath of a fall (a person rubbing his or her leg) or the entire event (the person falling down the stairs and then rubbing his or her leg) affected the likelihood that they would notice the other person and recognize the other person's need (J. A. Piliavin, Piliavin, & Broll, 1976). Clear and serious situations are more arousing than situations that are ambiguous and not serious (J. A. Piliavin, Dovidio, Gaertner, & Clark, 1981). The amount of arousal that a witness experiences may then limit the types of emotions that they will experience. In addition, arousal also causes people to focus their attention more on critical, central aspects of the situation and away from less relevant, peripheral elements (Easterbrook, 1959). Thus, the intensity of arousal can reduce the opportunity people have to consider alternative explanations for the cause of a problem and instead lead them to narrow their focus of attention more on the needs of the other person.

In contrast, when situations are less critical and immediate, observers have more time and opportunity to assess the person's need more fully. There is more latitude for interpretation, and people tend to be systematic in how they search for their explanations. Bernard Weiner (1980, 1986) suggested that another's need for help stimulates a search for causes by the observer. People seek to understand *why* the person needs assistance. They consider whether the person needs help because of an internal and controllable cause (e.g., the person's lack of effort on a task) or an external and uncontrollable cause (e.g., the difficulty of the task). These explanations, or attributions, in turn create an emotional experience that may motivate action. Weiner suggested, for example, that attributing a person's problem to uncontrollable causes (e.g., bad luck) produces sympathy that motivates helping. But attributing the same problem to controllable causes (e.g., lack of effort, bad judgment) may generate anger, which may inhibit helping.

To test this idea, Schmidt and Weiner (1988) asked their participants to imagine they are walking across campus one afternoon when a male student, whom they do not know, stops them. He says that they are both in the same class and asks to borrow class notes from last week. To test their hypotheses about the role of attributions, Schmidt and Weiner varied why the student was asking for the notes. For some participants, the student's need was presented as being beyond his control. In this condition, the student asking for the notes was wearing an eye patch and dark glasses and explained that he needed the notes because eye treatments prevented him from taking his own. For other participants, the problem was the student's own fault: He needed the notes because he had gone to the beach instead of going to class.

Not surprisingly, participants were more likely to help the person who had eye trouble—the person whose problem was due to factors beyond his control. Of particular interest, however, is *why* these differences occurred. The nature of people's emotional reactions was critical. The more the requestor could be blamed for his problem, the more anger participants reported; the less responsible the requestor was seen for his problem, the more sympathy was elicited. It was the nature of these emotions that directly determined the helping decision: The more sympathy and the less anger people reported they would feel, the more they said they would help. Thus, as Weiner (1980) proposed, "Attributions guide our feelings, but emotional reactions provide the motor and direction for behavior" (p. 186).

guilt → study (broken camera)

Negative Moods

As we noted earlier, negative moods are not simply the absence or the opposite of good moods, and there are many different types of negative emotions and moods that may be associated with different consequences (Watson, Weise, Vaidya, & Tellegen, 1999). The nature of the specific emotion people experience affects the likelihood of helping and whom they are likely to help (Mitchell, Brown, Morris-Villagran, & Villagran, 2001). Although Weiner's model suggests that some negative emotions, such as anger and disgust, make people less likely to help, other unpleasant emotions can actually increase helping.

When people deviate from the standards they hold for themselves, they typically experience guilt. People who experience guilt because they feel they have harmed another person in some way are particularly likely to help (Dovidio, 1984; Salovey, Mayer, & Rosenhan, 1991). They are not only more likely to help the person they have harmed, but they are also more likely to help *anyone* who needs assistance. In one field experiment (Regan, Williams, & Sparling, 1972), a confederate stopped women at a shopping center and asked them to use his camera to take a picture of him. As a woman would attempt to take his picture, the camera would "break." In the guilt condition, women were led to believe that they were responsible for breaking the camera; in the control condition, they were told that it was not their fault. Soon after this incident, the participants had an opportunity to help a woman whose groceries were falling from her shopping bag. The results were clear: Fifty-five percent of the participants who were made to feel guilty helped, whereas only 15% of those in the control condition helped. This effect has also been found across a wide range of situations. People help more when they have previously transgressed than when they have not.

Although, as we saw in chapter 3, positive moods can also increase helping, the processes responsible for the effects of guilt on helping are quite different from those for good moods (e.g., accessibility of positive thoughts, greater sensitivity to events, more inclusive orientations toward others). So why do people help when they feel guilty? One explanation is that when people feel that they have unfairly harmed others, their self-esteem suffers. Therefore, they try to make amends. This *image-reparation hypothesis* suggests that by making a positive social response, people's self-esteem is restored, their self-image is repaired, and they can again appear to be "decent" people. Thus, guilt motivates helping for a mainly self-oriented reason—to reestablish oneself as a good and worthy person. This is why guilt can motivate helping in general—help for the person whom one has harmed or for someone else who may need help. Helping, regardless of who you help, is an effective way of reasserting your self-worth. Although the research on image reparation has focused generally on the impact of violations of a person's self-image on subsequent helping, it is possible that people might respond differently to "damage" to different aspects of their self-image, depending on how central the dimension is to their feelings of self-worth (Crocker, Luhtanen, Cooper, & Bouvrette, 2003).

Guilt is not the only negative state that motivates helping. For example, *witnessing* unjust harm to another person does not elicit guilt when one is not responsible for the harm; instead, these violations of general standards of fairness tend to produce a different emotional reaction—sadness. People experiencing sadness also become motivated to help (Cialdini, Baumann, & Kenrick, 1981; Cialdini, Darby, & Vincent, 1973). To the extent that this helping is intended to address the sadness that one is feeling and to make the world seem just, predictable, and "right" again, it might also be motivated by self-oriented concerns.

Negative State Relief Model

Robert Cialdini and his colleagues have proposed a more comprehensive model, the *negative state relief model* (Cialdini, Kenrick, & Baumann, 1982; Cialdini et al., 1987), to provide an integrated explanation of the effects of negative emotions on helping. According to this explanation for why negative moods might promote helping, *harming* another person or *witnessing* another person being harmed can produce negative feelings such as guilt or sadness. People who experience these negative states are then motivated to reduce them. Through socialization and experience, people have learned that helping can serve as a secondary reinforcer that makes them feel good (Williamson & Clark, 1989; Yinon & Landau, 1987; also see chap. 6). For instance, helping others can improve people's self-esteem and heighten their sense of integrity (Bonhote, Romano-Egan, & Cornwell, 1999; Toch, 2000). The good feelings derived from helping may therefore relieve their negative mood. Thus, negative moods may motivate people to help, because of the processes of operant conditioning. That is, helping produces the reward of making them feel better. In contrast to the image-reparation hypothesis, the negative state relief model proposes that people are motivated primarily to *feel* good rather than to *look* good. In both theories, however, the motivation for helping is essentially *egoistic* or self-centered. That is, the primary motive for helping another person is that helping improves the *helper's own* situation.

There are three fundamental assumptions in the negative state relief model. First, the negative state that motivates a person to help can origi-

① the -ve state can have a variety of sources
② other things can better their mood b4 helping →then↓ likely to help.
③ helping only if they think it will help

nate from a variety of sources. Sadness may be suffered due to one's own *even if* experiences, such as the loss of a loved one, failure to achieve a goal, or the *they* deterioration of a relationship. It may be guilt from having personally *guess* harmed a person or sadness from simply observing another person's un- *that* fortunate situation; alternatively, it could come from feelings of guilt *mood* from a transgression against an unrelated person or sadness associated *will be* with a entirely different person's problem. All of these emotions, because *improving* they are negative experiences, can motivate helping (Cialdini et al., 1973).

Of course, helping is just one way that the negative feelings can be eliminated. A second assumption of the negative state relief model is that other events besides helping may be just as effective in making a person feel better. If some other event that improves the potential helper's mood precedes the opportunity to help, the potential helper would no longer be particularly motivated to provide assistance—the negative affective state has already been eliminated. In one of the initial tests of this model, Cialdini and his colleagues (1973) created feelings of guilt by having participants accidentally ruin a graduate student's thesis data or feelings of sadness by having them witness another person ruin the data. Some of these participants later experienced a positive event (i.e., received praise for their performance on a maze-tracing task); other participants did not have such a positive experience. Both groups were then offered the chance to provide help to another person. As illustrated in Fig. 4.1, guilt and sadness increased helping compared to a neutral-mood control group, except among the participants who experienced the positive event (praise). Once these participants' negative moods were relieved by receiving praise, they were no longer highly motivated to help others. Perhaps for similar reasons, people are more helpful as they enter a Catholic church for confession (when presumably they are feeling guilty) than after they leave confession (and are presumably absolved of their sins; Harris, Benson, & Hall, 1975).

Furthermore, simply the anticipation that one's mood *will be* improved soon is enough to reduce the motivation for helping. If people believe that their mood will improve without them having to do anything, why should they go through the effort of helping someone else to improve their mood? A study by Schaller and Cialdini (1988) demonstrated this point. They found that people who felt sad helped less when they expected that they would soon be listening to a comedy tape than when they thought the tape would not be funny. Because the comedy tape would lift their spirits (i.e., relieve the negative mood state), there was no longer any personal benefit for helping another person.

A third assumption of this model is that negative moods motivate helping only if people believe that their moods can be improved by helping. Negative feelings will *not* promote helping if people believe that

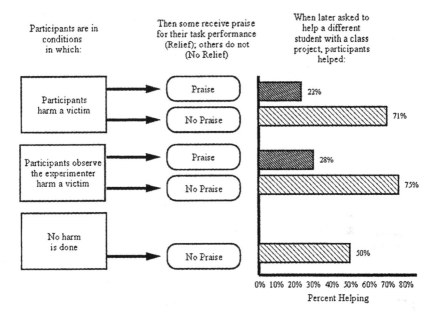

FIG. 4.1. The negative state relief model: People who cause or witness harm are more helpful, except when a positive event, such as praise, relieves these negative feelings before the helping opportunity. From Cialdini, Darby, and Vincent (1973), with permission.

these feelings cannot be relieved. Remember, according to the negative state relief model, people are acting out of self-interest.

In one study illustrating this point (Manucia, Baumann, & Cialdini, 1984), participants were administered a substance, "Mnemoxine" (actually a placebo), that they were told was a fast-acting memory drug. The experimenters informed some people that the substance had an unusual side-effect that would "take whatever mood is present and prolong it artificially. So ... [if] you are feeling sad when it takes effect, you will continue to be sad for the next 30 minutes or so, no matter what." The researchers told other people that Mnemoxine had no effects on mood. To create a sad mood, some participants were then asked to reminisce about sad experiences. Two key findings supported the negative state relief model. First, as in previous studies, when participants thought the substance had no side effects (i.e., when they believed that helping could improve their mood), those who felt sad helped more than did participants who were in neutral moods. The second finding was that when people believed that Mnemoxine had "frozen" their moods, and therefore that helping could not improve their mood, feeling sad did not motivate people to help. According to the negative state relief model, there was no reason for participants to help in the "frozen mood" condition because it could not make them feel better.

The negative state relief model continues to be generally accepted as a viable motivational framework for spontaneous helping and helping in response to direct requests (Boster et al., 1999), at least when people experience the specific negative emotions of guilt or sadness. However, depending on the nature of the event associated with a person's need for assistance, people may experience many other emotions as well. We see this in another theory of how emotions affect helping—the arousal: cost–reward framework.

Arousal: Cost–Reward Model

This theory originated from studying people's more intense emotional responses in emergency situations. Thus, it is not surprising that arousal is a central motivational concept in the Piliavin et al. (1981) arousal: cost–reward model (see also Dovidio et al., 1991), which we introduced in chapter 3. In this model, arousal motivates a bystander to take action, and the cost-reward analysis shapes the direction that action will take spurred by the arousal. Specifically, this model proposes that empathic arousal is generated by witnessing the distress of another person. When the bystander's empathic arousal is attributed to the other person's distress, it is emotionally experienced by the observer as unpleasant, and the bystander is therefore motivated to reduce it. Bystanders' emotional responses become linked with the distress of the person in need. Although bystanders do not experience the same specific emotion as the person in distress, they do feel upset, alarmed, and distressed when observing the distress of another. One efficient way of reducing this arousal is by helping to relieve the other's distress. The key elements of this model are summarized in Table 4.1. We discuss the first three, which primarily concern arousal and helping.

Proposition 1: Becoming Aroused. There is substantial evidence for the first proposition—that people are fundamentally responsive to the distress of others (see Eisenberg & Fabes, 1991). Adults and children not only report feeling empathy, but they also become physiologically aroused by the pain and suffering of others. Moreover, people sometimes do not simply feel bad *for* a person, they also feel bad *with* the person. In one study, for instance, participants saw a person show strong facial distress in response to repeated and apparently painful electric shocks. These participants reacted with

TABLE 4.1
The Five Basic Propositions of the Arousal:
Cost–Reward Model

1. Observation of another's problem or crisis arouses bystanders. The degree of arousal is directly related to the clarity, severity, and duration of need and to bystanders' psychological and physical closeness to the person in need.

2. In general, arousal occasioned by observations of a problem or crisis and attributed to that event becomes more unpleasant as it increases, and bystanders have a greater motivation to reduce it. ↑ arousal → worse event

3. Bystanders will choose responses that most rapidly and completely reduce the arousal and incur as few net costs (costs minus rewards) as possible.

4. There will be (a) special circumstances that give rise to, and (b) specific personality types who engage in, rapid, impulsive, noncalculative, "irrational" helping or escape behavior following observation of an emergency.

5. On termination of contact with the situation, arousal will decrease with time, whether or not the victim is helped.

---

physiological arousal reflecting their own distress and also with facial expressions that were similar to those of the person being shocked (Vaughan & Lanzetta, 1980). Preschool children also spontaneously show signs of facial concern and physiological arousal at the distress of others (Eisenberg & Fabes, 1991), and there is evidence that even 1- and 2-day-old infants will respond with crying to the distress of another infant (Sagi & Hoffman, 1976; Simner, 1971).

Proposition 2: The Attribution of Arousal. The evidence also supports the second proposition of the arousal: cost–reward model (see Table 4.1), namely, that empathic arousal attributed to the other person's situation motivates helping. Gaertner and Dovidio (1977), for example, measured heart rates while people were deciding whether to help in an emergency. As the arousal: cost–reward model predicted, people who were more aroused at the time of an emergency were more helpful. This relationship between arousal and helping is now well established (Dovidio, 1984). Facial, gestural, and vocal indications of empathy, as well as self-reports, are consistently positively related to helping (see Dovidio et al., 1991; Eisenberg & Miller, 1987).

Of course, people will differ in how much arousal is experienced and how that arousal is interpreted. The model recognizes this and identifies some of the characteristics of the bystander (e.g., his or her social sensitivity towards others), of the victim (e.g., attractiveness), and of the helper–victim relationship (i.e., a sense of we-ness), as well as characteristics of the situation (e.g., severity) that may influence the amount of arousal generated. A simplified view of this part of the model is illustrated in Fig. 4.2. In general, arousal is greater when the bystander is more empathic, the victim is more socially attractive, the bystander–victim relationship is closer, and the emergency situation is more serious (see Piliavin et al., 1981).

The importance of the association of arousal with the other person's distress is demonstrated by studies that manipulate how people attribute and interpret their arousal. If the arousal: cost–reward model is correct, then the primary determinant of helping is not the absolute amount of arousal experienced, but rather the amount of arousal that the potential helper believes is due to the other person's situation. If a bystander is initially aroused by another person's problem but later comes to believe that *something else* is the cause, then the arousal would not be expected to motivate intervention. Helping would not be perceived as relieving the cause of the arousal.

Gaertner and Dovidio (1977) demonstrated this effect using a "misattribution paradigm." The objective in a misattribution paradigm is to lead two groups of people who are initially aroused by the same event to *believe* that the causes of arousal are different. One way of doing this is by giving different participants different possible explanations of

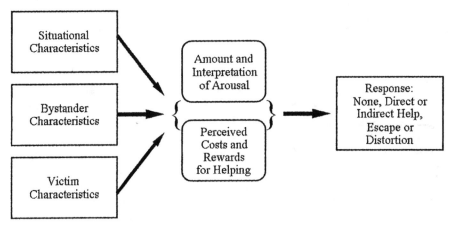

FIG. 4.2.   Simplified version of the arousal: cost–reward model.

their arousal before they experience it (Nisbett & Schachter, 1966). Gaertner and Dovidio (1977) informed participants that their study examined the effects of a pill (actually a placebo) on their ability to receive ESP (extrasensory perception) messages. Some people were told that the pill would arouse them, thus potentially confusing them about the source of any subsequent arousal. Others were informed that the pill would *not* arouse them, thus minimizing or eliminating the potential for confusion. Later, people in both groups heard an ambiguous emergency, a possible accident involving the other participant in the experiment (really a confederate). The results supported the model. People who believed that some of the arousal generated because of the accident was due to the pill were less likely to help (55% vs. 85%) and responded more slowly than did participants who could not readily attribute their arousal to the pill. Because the placebo pill in fact did not arouse people, the key element here was what people *believed* had aroused them, not differences in their overall level of arousal.

Misattribution can also make people *more* helpful. Sometimes people may experience arousal for one reason and then attribute it to a very different source. Arousal due to one source (e.g., fear or suspense) can become associated with another source (e.g., a member of the other sex). Once this misattribution is made, people respond more intensely than they normally would (Dutton & Aron, 1989; Zillman, 1983). Applying this process to helping behavior, bystanders should be more helpful than normal if prior arousal becomes associated with another person's problem. This is what occurs. Arousal from such diverse sources as exercise (Sterling & Gaertner, 1984), erotic films (Mueller & Donnerstein, 1981), and aggressive films (Mueller, Donnerstein, & Hallam, 1983) increases helpfulness when the arousal is attributed to the immediate need of another person. Consistent with the second proposition of the arousal: cost–reward model, these findings represent powerful evidence that arousal attributed to another person's need motivates helping.

Proposition 3: Assessing the Situation. The arousal: cost–reward model suggests not only that arousal motivates action, but also that the arousal can affect how people perceive costs and rewards for various potential actions. As we noted before, one effect of increased arousal is that it narrows a person's focus of attention toward important aspects of a situation and draws attention away from less central aspects (Easterbrook, 1959; Eysenck, 1977). High levels of arousal may thus alter how people perceive and weigh information in assessing potential costs and rewards (see chap. 3). Because a victim and his or her need may capture the attention of a highly aroused bystander, the bystander may not consider potential dangers associated with intervention. The costs asso-

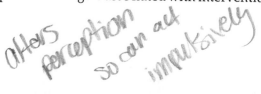

alters perception so can act impulsively

ex. live wire victim.

ex. highschool shooting

ciated with not helping the victim (e.g., that the victim might die) dominate the bystander's evaluations of the potential costs for helping by the bystander. As a consequence, highly aroused bystanders may help impulsively and possibly heroically—responding very rapidly and apparently without regard to personal costs (see Piliavin et al., 1981).

However, it is possible for bystanders to help too quickly and in ways that are dangerous. Clark and Word (1974), for instance, found in a very vivid emergency situation that all of their participants very rapidly helped a victim who was apparently being electrocuted by a "live" wire. A large proportion of these participants directly intervened and touched the victim, an action that would have electrocuted them had the situation been real. Many of these participants later realized the consequences of their action but reported, like many actual "heros," that they "just didn't think." For example, when a high school student in Springfield, Oregon, began shooting his classmates in the hallway of the school in 1998, 10 students wrestled him to the ground, took away the gun, and held him until the police arrived. One of the students who intervened so heroically was Mike Peebles. When asked about why he intervened, he said, "I really didn't have time to think." According to Proposition 3, perhaps he did think, but not about all of those possible costs associated with intervention.

Thus, there is considerable support for the major propositions of the arousal: cost–reward model that empathic arousal motivates helping. But note that the nature of this motivation is essentially egoistic. Another's distress generates empathic arousal, but the bystander's primary goal in helping is to reduce his or her own unpleasant state. Helping may typically be perceived as an efficient way to reduce this arousal, but other ways (such as leaving the scene; see Fig. 4.2) are possible, and sometimes even more attractive alternatives.

Comparing the Negative State Relief and the Arousal: Cost–Reward Models

Although these two egoistic models of what motivates people to help may appear similar, there are at least two important differences between them. First, the attribution of arousal plays a central role in the arousal: cost–reward model; only arousal *attributed to the plight of the other person* will motivate helping. In contrast, the negative state relief model posits that, *regardless of their attributed source*, negative states (particularly guilt and sadness; see Cialdini et al., 1987) can motivate helping. The second major distinction between the two models is that the arousal: cost–reward model is a tension-reduction model that assumes that the victim's need produces an arousal state in the potential benefactor and that the goal of helping is to alleviate one's own aversive state. According to the negative state relief model, people are motivated to obtain the reward that comes with helping, namely, feeling good.

Thus far, the motivations for helping that we have considered all represent some form of egoism. Although helping obviously benefits the recipient, the *primary reason* that people help others is to benefit themselves. Learning theory suggests that people are motivated to obtain rewards from others (e.g., praise) or from oneself (e.g., pride) and to avoid punishments (e.g., blame or shame). This principle also applies to the arousal and affect theories. The common theme is that people help others mainly to make themselves feel better; the primary motivation for helping is a hedonistic or selfish one. What is your reaction to this? Is selfishness *your* only motivation for helping? Is it even possible for purely selfless, altruistic helping to occur? C. Daniel Batson and his colleagues (see Batson, 1991) argued extensively that altruistic—other-oriented—helping is possible. Their work on the *empathy–altruism hypothesis* illustrates when and how this occurs.

Empathy–Altruism Hypothesis

In contrast to the egoistic models of helping, Batson (see Batson, 1991) proposed the empathy–altruism model of helping. Batson acknowledged that egoistically motivated helping occurs. In fact, he recognized that *most* helping may be egoistically motivated. But he argues that true altruism may exist as well. As we mentioned in chapter 1, Batson (1991, p. 6) defined altruism as "a motivational state with the ultimate goal of increasing another's welfare."

Of course, just believing that altruism can motivate helping is not enough. Empirical evidence that shows the existence of altruistically motivated behavior must also be found. Most of this evidence comes from the carefully controlled confines of the laboratory. That is where Batson and his colleagues began their search for altruism.

The primary mechanism in Batson's *empathy–altruism hypothesis* is the emotional reaction to another person's problem. As we have already seen in this chapter, witnessing another person in need can produce sadness or personal distress (e.g., upset, worry, alarm). Batson suggested that under some circumstances it elicits a different emotion, *empathic concern,* which he defined as "an other-oriented emotional response (e.g., sympathy, compassion) congruent with the … welfare of another person" (Batson & Oleson, 1991, p. 63). Although sadness and personal distress generate an egoistic desire to reduce *one's own* distress, Batson (1987, 1991) proposed that empathic concern produces an altruistic motivation to reduce the *other person's distress*. The challenge of demonstrating the existence of altruistic motivation is to show how empathic concern leads to helping in ways that cannot be explained by prevailing theories of egoistic motivation. That is, a clear case needs to be made that it is concern about the other person's welfare, not a desire to improve one's own welfare, that *primarily* drives one's helping behavior in a particular situation. Feelings that have been found to represent empathic concern, personal distress, and sadness are presented in Table 4.2 (Fultz, Schaller, & Cialdini, 1988).

To explain how his model of motivation for helping differs from the ones we have previously discussed, Batson (1991) identified three different "paths" to helping. A simplified version of Batson's presentation of these paths is shown in Fig. 4.3. The first two paths are egoistic. Path 1 is based on social learning and reinforcement; it corresponds to the processes proposed in the negative state relief model. Path 2 involves tension reduction and concerns the mechanisms described in the arousal: cost–reward model.

Path 3 represents altruism. In this path, perception of another person's need in conjunction with a special bond with that person (e.g., because of similarity to the person or a deliberate attempt to take that person's perspective) generates empathic concern. Empathic concern, in turn, evokes altruistic motivation. The altruistically motivated person will then help if

TABLE 4.2
Items Reflecting Empathic Concern,
Personal Distress, and Sadness

Empathic Concern	Personal Distress	Sadness
Moved	Upset	Sad
Warm	Worried	Dejected
Softhearted	Alarmed	Sorrowful
Tender	Grieved	Low-spirited
Compassionate	Disturbed	Downhearted
Sympathetic	Distressed	Downcast
Touched	Uneasy	Heavyhearted
Concerned	Troubled	Feeling low

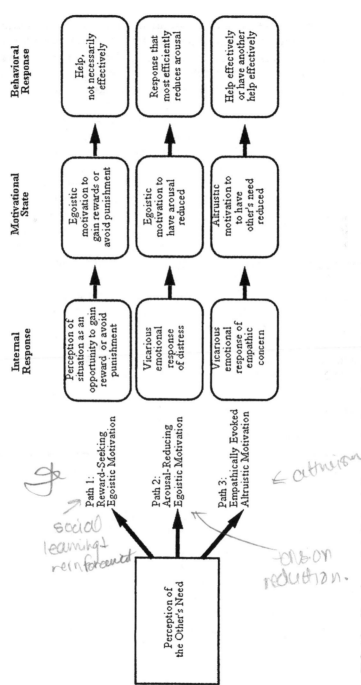

FIG. 4.3.   Key elements in Batson's three motivational paths to helping.

133

(a) helping is possible, (b) helping is perceived to be ultimately beneficial to the person in need, and (c) helping personally will provide greater benefit to the person in need than will assistance from another person who is able to offer it. Thus, empathic concern is hypothesized to produce greater sensitivity to the welfare of the other person. These different emotions all tend to increase helping but in different ways.

How can we test whether people are altruistically motivated? Because motives are not directly observable, you could ask people why they helped. But as we discussed at the beginning of this chapter, even if people say they were motivated by altruistic concerns, this would not necessarily be proof they were. People could simply be saying something that sounds good to both of you and places them in the most flattering light. Alternatively, you could systematically vary the helping situation to rule out alternative explanations, and this strategy is the one that Batson and his colleagues adopted in their experiments on why people help.

Batson and his colleagues (see Batson, 1991) began with the hypothesis that empathic concern generates an altruistic motivation for helping. They created situations in which their participants helped, and then modified these situations to rule out alternative explanations of why helping occurred. The question of the existence of altruistic motivation was therefore approached in a series of steps. It was like a mystery story in which the detective eliminates one suspect after another until only one is left. In particular, Batson and his colleagues tried sequentially to rule out various egoistic explanations and, by implication, to find support for the existence of altruistic motivation. If it is not egoism, then, Batson argued that it must be altruism.

One alternative explanation for why empathic concern leads to helping is because helping is seen as an efficient way to reduce the arousal. How can you demonstrate that under certain circumstances people are instead primarily altruistically motivated to increase the welfare of another person? One way would be to make it easy for people to reduce their arousal by leaving the scene. According to Batson, when escaping from the situation would be easy, egoistically motivated people who are concerned mainly about their own welfare should choose to leave the scene rather than help; escaping is the less costly option. Altruistically motivated people, in contrast, would help because that is the only way to improve the *other* person's welfare. That is, altruistically motivated people will do what is best for the other person even if it is not the most efficient way to reduce their own arousal. To test this possibility, Toi and Batson (1982) created a situation in which it was moderately costly to help someone (several hours of tutoring for a student named Carol, who had been in a car accident), and it was either difficult for someone not to help (they would be seeing the other person again) or easy not to help (they would

Created sits in which As helped
& modified them to rule out other explanations
WHY DO PEOPLE HELP? • **135**

never have to meet the other person again). Toi and Batson reasoned that if students were likely to meet Carol again in the future, guilt, shame, and anticipated blame would make leaving the scene *more costly* than helping. But when it was unlikely that students would see Carol again, escape from the situation would be easy and thus *less costly* than helping.

The central prediction was that egoistically motivated people would do whatever was personally less costly, that is, leave the scene when escape was easy and help when escape was more difficult. In contrast, because altruistically motivated people are primarily concerned with the other's welfare, they were predicted to help even when helping was more costly. To induce empathic concern, some students were instructed to imagine how the person in the interview felt. As the researchers predicted, these empathically concerned students helped at equivalently high levels regardless of whether it was relatively easy or difficult to leave the scene without helping (71% vs. 81%). That is, these students seemed altruistically motivated by the desire to improve the other person's welfare, because they chose to help even when it was personally more costly to help than to leave without helping. Only helping—not leaving the scene—will relieve the other person's problem. In contrast, students who were not experiencing a high degree of empathic concern but were experiencing high personal distress showed the egoistic pattern of helping. They helped very frequently (76%) when it was easier (i.e., less costly) to help than to leave. When it was easier to leave than to help, however, these students typically left; only 33% helped. They seemed to do whatever was best for themselves.

These results, and numerous subsequent studies based on this rationale (see Batson, 1991, and Batson & Oleson, 1991, for full reviews), provided initial evidence that people who were experiencing empathic concern were motivated primarily by the desire to improve the other person's welfare—altruistic motivation. However, a number of alternative, egoistic interpretations have been offered to the empathy–altruism hypothesis. In general, the debate over whether altruistic motivation exists and can be demonstrated experimentally has been a model of the scientific enterprise. Batson and his colleagues initially devised a series of clever experiments, like the one by Toi and Batson (1982), to show how high empathy (representing a preponderance of empathic concern) leads to altruistic motivation and helping even when it is easy to escape, whereas low empathy (reflecting mainly personal distress) leads to egoistic motivation and helping only when helping is less costly than leaving the scene.

Subsequent researchers then came up with alternative egoistic explanations for these findings. One interpretation was that, even under conditions that Toi and Batson described as easy escape, leaving the scene may be more costly than helping because people might believe that others would think poorly of them for not helping (Archer, Diaz-Loving, Gollwitzer, Davis, & Foushee, 1981) or because they will think badly about themselves if they do not help (Dovidio, 1984; Schaller & Cialdini, 1988). Batson and his colleagues responded with a new set of experiments supportive of the empathy–altruism hypothesis. They reported that people experiencing empathic concern when escape is easy continued to show high levels of helping even when others were unable to learn whether they help or not (Fultz, Batson, Fortenbach, McCarthy, & Varney, 1986) and when they were given a good justification for not helping (i.e., explicitly told that most people did not help the person in need under the same circumstances; Batson et al., 1988, Study 2 & 3), which would relieve any guilt or other form of self-punishment.

This exchange of ideas, with researchers reinterpreting findings, identifying alternative interpretations, and conducting new experiments in their attempts to demonstrate or refute the existence of altruistic motivation, has continued over the past 25 years. The debate is not whether empathy can motivate helping; that has been clearly demonstrated for a range of interpersonal behaviors and even for behaviors directed toward other beneficiaries, such as the environment (Lee & Holden, 1999). The issue is whether this motivation is fundamentally altruistic. Recently, for example, Maner et al. (2002) found that people experiencing high empathy develop a self–other merged identity with a victim. The researchers' key argument was that because of this merged identity, their participants' own emotional state became coordinated and overlapped with the other person's negative feelings. As a consequence, the participants were basically motivated to relieve what has become a shared *personal* negative state. We summarize the different challenges to Batson's empathy–altruism hypothesis and the evidence for and against the position in Table 4.3.

Over time, however, an impressive body of evidence has been accumulated, not only by Batson and his colleagues but also by independent researchers who make a very strong case for the existence of altruistic motivation and its implications. For example, one implication is although egoistically motivated people would not be motivated to help another person if their mood could not be improved (i.e., because it was "frozen" by a drug, as we described earlier with the Manucia et al., 1984, study), this mood freezing manipulation would not deter altruistically motivated people from helping, because they are concerned primarily with improving the other person's welfare, not their own. This is what a study by Schroeder, Dovidio, Sibicky, Matthews, and Allen (1988) found (but see also Cialdini et al., 1987, Study 2, for a different result). Contrary to the negative state relief interpretation and consistent with the view

TABLE 4.3

Alternatives to Altruism	*Source*	*Response*	*Source*
Empathy-specific punishment			
People will think particularly badly of an empathically-aroused person if he or she leaves the scene without helping.	Archer et al. (1981)	Empathically concerned people help even if others are not in a position to evaluate them.	Fultz et al. (1986)
Empathically concerned people will think particularly badly of themselves if they do not help.	Schaller and Cialdini (1988)	Empathically concerned people help even when they learn that most other people do not help in this situation, providing a good excuse not to help.	Batson et al. (1988) (studies 2 & 3)
Empathy-specific reward			
Helping is especially rewarding for empathically concerned people.	Smith, Keating, and Stotland (1989)	Empathically concerned people help even when they will not learn of the benefits of their aid.	Batson et al. (1991)
		Empathically concerned people feel just as good when they learn that others have helped as when they help.	Batson et al. (1988)

(continued on next page)

TABLE 4.3 (*continued*)

Alternatives to Altruism	Source	Response	Source
Relieving sadness			
Empathically concerned people help because they also feel greater sadness, and sadness is a negative state that motivates egoistic helping.	Cialdini et al. (1987); Schaller and Cialdini (1988)	Empathically concerned people help even when they believe their moods cannot improve.	Schroeder et al. (1988)
		Empathically concerned people help even when they believe that their mood will be enhanced another way.	Batson et al. (1989)
		Empathically concerned people help in a way that is directed at relieving the other person's specific problem, not at helping others generally.	Dovidio et al. (1990)
Self–other merging			
The conditions that lead to empathic concern create a sense of self–other merging, which then produces an egoistic motivation to help.	Cialdini et al. (1997); Maner et al. (2002)	Empathic concern, at least in some cases, motivates helping under conditions that inhibited self–other merging and predicted helping over and above merged identity.	Batson et al. (1997)

that empathic people are motivated by the other person's welfare, Schroeder et al. found that people experiencing high levels of empathic concern demonstrated high levels of helpfulness even when they believed that their own moods were unalterable.

Other findings also converge to support the basic proposition of the empathy–altruism hypothesis, which is that people experiencing relatively high levels of empathic concern are *altruistically* motivated and primarily concerned about improving the welfare of the other person in need, whereas those low in empathic concern are *egoistically* motivated. For instance, if people are concerned mainly about making another person feel better, they would be expected to be less motivated to help when their actions cannot relieve the other person's distress (compared to when it will) or when helping someone will be harmful to him or her in the long run (e.g., buying a person a package of cigarettes). In contrast, if people are egoistically motivated, they would be likely to help, regardless of the effect on other people, because they can feel better (and improve their own mood) just by trying to help. The research evidence indicates that when people are experiencing empathic concern, they attend primarily to the effects of their action on the other person. For example, they are less likely to help when this action would not improve the other person's mood even though it might improve the helper's own mood or when the immediate act of helping would be actually harmful to the other person in the longer term (e.g., because giving too much help would undermine the other person learning to solve the problem on his or her own; Dovidio, Schroeder, Allen, & Sibicky, 1989; Sibicky, Schroeder, & Dovidio, 1995).

In addition, empathic concern produces a very specific type of motivation, one aimed specifically at ameliorating the other person's condition that had aroused the emotion in the first place (Dovidio, Allen, & Schroeder, 1990). Recall from earlier in this chapter that guilt increases helping directed not only toward rectifying the harm (e.g., helping the person on the experiment that was ruined) but also in unrelated areas (e.g., helping someone pick up groceries). Do the prosocial effects of empathic concern also generalize to other situations? The answer is, no. In particular, Dovidio et al. (1990) demonstrated that empathically aroused participants helped a person in need more when helping relieved the person's main problem than when it solved an unrelated problem. This finding was inconsistent with predictions of the egoistic negative state relief model, which suggests that people will engage in any kind of helping that will improve their mood. But the findings did support the empathy–altruism hypothesis. That is, Dovidio et al. found that when people experienced empathic concern, they did not engage in just any type of helping available to them. Rather, people only engaged in helping that would alleviate the problem that produced their empathic concern. This is because they were motivated by a desire to solve the other person's main problem, not to eliminate another problem or find another way to feel better.

Psychology is dominated by principles of egoism and hedonism, however, and a persuasive demonstration of truly altruistic motivation must withstand the challenge of all alternative interpretations based on egoistic motivation. As long as other researchers can identify other plausible "suspects," the case for the existence of altruistic helping is not totally closed. Nevertheless, the empathy–altruism hypothesis has successfully withstood a range of different challenges over the past 25 years (see Batson, 1998; see also Table 4.1) and has produced a strong case for the existence of altruistic motivation, at least in a circumscribed set of situations.

Demonstrations that purely altruistic helping can take place— even those that occur in the somewhat sterile environment of a laboratory—have significant implications both within psychology and beyond. Within psychology, the existence of altruism challenges the assumption that people are inherently motivated only by self-interest. This hedonistic view of human nature has been a fundamental principle underlying approaches as disparate as Sigmund Freud's psychoanalytic theory (e.g., the pleasure principle) and B. F. Skinner's behavioristic perspective (e.g., the application of the law of effect). These approaches all propose that people's actions are determined by the actual or anticipated consequences that they will personally receive. The demonstration of altruistic motivation reveals that the perceived consequences for others can also be fundamentally important.

Although the context may be sterile and the conceptual distinctions may sometimes seem too fine, this laboratory activity is critical. Just as researchers attempt to understand the causes of diseases such as cancer and AIDS with microscopes and test tubes, behavioral researchers are attempting to understand the very essence of why people help others. Although these techniques might seem microscopic, the implications and potential applications are large and broad. If altruistic helping really exists and if we can understand the causes of other-oriented altruism, then perhaps we can make human behavior more humane.

The controversy over the existence of altruistic motivation has also focused researchers on particular forms of helping. Nevertheless, as we discussed in chapter 2, helping and other forms of prosocial action are integral even to species that are limited in their cognitive capacities and reflection. Thus, in the next section we consider altruism from other perspectives and identify different types of altruism.

TYPES OF ALTRUISM

The prosocial actions we have examined in this chapter can be compared to those discussed in chapter 2. In that chapter, we were almost exclusively concerned with altruism as behavioral geneticists would define it: behavior that increases the chances of another's survival at some cost to the helper. Conscious motivation had nothing to do with this kind of altruism. We can see this when we consider the actions of animals such as ants, bees, and birds. They display behaviors that are "hard-wired" into the organism and performed without any apparent hesitation or thought. The ground squirrel sees a hawk and gives the alarm; the ant smells the intruder and attacks. Sober (2002) called this *evolutionary altruism.* However, with higher mammals, and in particular primates, this is not the way things usually work. In this chapter we saw that among humans there is thought and deliberation before a helpful act occurs, and, of course, sometimes it may not occur. Sober (1992) called this *psychological altruism*—a conscious action specifically intended to benefit another person at some cost to the actor, taken with an understanding of what is to be gained and lost. Psychological altruism is relatively rare in nonhuman species. But what about humans? Do they display both kinds of altruism? If so, could there be two different mechanisms affecting humans' altruistic behavior, both with innate components?

We have seen in this chapter that it is easy to make the case that some form of psychological altruism occurs among humans. It is based on conscious, rational decision making and involves intentions to benefit another person. Because intentions are involved, the social psychological distinction between altruism (with the goal of improving another person's welfare) and helping (with the goal of improving one's own welfare) is relevant. The capacities for empathy and emotional communication are two mechanisms that can contribute to the processes involved in this type of helping. But do humans also display evidence of evolutionary altruism? This more "primitive" form might be triggered under very specific conditions and would lead to rapid, perhaps unthinking, altruistic action. Evolutionary altruism would be less subject to environmental variables and higher order mental processes than would the more sophisticated psychological altruism.

Although humans are more rational and reflective than other animals, we still share a biological heritage with other species. As a consequence, many vestiges of our evolutionary past—including evolutionary altruism—may remain. As we have described before, we know that people in some circumstances may engage in very rapid, almost reflexive helping (see also chap. 3). Piliavin et al. (1981) reviewed a large number of experiments involving apparently real emergencies and found considerable evidence of impulsive helping. This type of helping resembles evolutionary altruism in other species—it is also rapid and is generally unaffected by the social context (e.g., as the opportunity to diffuse responsibility onto others) and potential costs for intervening (e.g., personal danger).

Piliavin et al. (1981) proposed that clear, realistic situations involving friends or acquaintances produce high levels of arousal and focus attention on the victim's plight. As a consequence, the bystander is most concerned with "the costs for the victim receiving no help. Personal costs of helping (to the bystander) become peripheral and are not attended to. Therefore, the impulsive helping behavior that may appear irrational to an uninvolved observer ... may be a quite 'rational' response for a bystander attending primarily to the costs for the victim receiving no help" (p. 174).

This description comes very close to Sober's definition of evolutionary altruism. The response is rapid, relatively unthinking, and without consideration of concerns for personal safety. Piliavin et al. also pointed out, "One of the factors that seems to be predictive of impulsive helping is prior acquaintance between the observer and the victim" (p. 174). In the case of a strong friendship or a love relationship, it is even more likely that impulsive helping will occur, because of increased arousal as well as greater sensitivity to the other's problem (Clark, Mills, & Corcoran, 1989). Thus, both sophisticated reasoning and more primitive, noncognitive biological mechanisms may permit humans to perform a range of altruistic behaviors well beyond those of other organisms.

THE ANSWER: SUMMARY AND IMPLICATIONS

In conclusion, the answer to the question concerning why people help involves both their thoughts and their feelings (i.e., cognitions and emotions). With regard to cognitions, people can learn through their direct experience or from observing others that helping is a positively valued social behavior. The other important cognitions involve social and personal norms. Norms establish standards for when people should help, and they lead people to expect certain social and personal rewards and punishments. Personal norms, for example, motivate helping because people have developed ideals about how they should act in certain situations and also experience feelings of personal responsibility and obligation to help.

Turning to feelings, the way people interpret empathic arousal shapes their motivation to help. The nature of the emotion that is experienced determines the nature of the motivation it generates. If the emotion is anger or disgust, people are motivated *not* to help. If the emotion is personal distress, sadness, or tension, they are egoistically or selfishly motivated to improve their own welfare by helping others. If, however, there is a special bond to the person in need that leads people to interpret their arousal as empathic concern, they may be altruistically motivated to help. That is, their primary goal is to reduce the other person's distress.

The use of terms such as *egoistic* or even *selfish* to describe why people sometimes help may make us lose sight of a very important point: Even egoistic motivations to help others are essentially prosocial. If I am motivated to help you because I am distressed or saddened by your situation, I am still motivated to help you. In fact, it is quite remarkable how the fates of people who have never met can be so intertwined and complementary. Your benefit is mine; mine is yours.

CHAPTER 5

Planned and Long-Term Helping

I n the preceding two chapters, we focused our attention on the short-term kinds of helping that occur spontaneously between two people—a person in immediate need of assistance and someone in a position to provide that needed help. In this chapter we shift our consideration to other kinds of helping that occur among people who are part of larger groups. Our primary focus is not on help that is spontaneously given in response to an immediate need, but rather on help that occurs after the helper has had time to think about the costs and benefits of the act and takes place over an extended period of time. The behaviors we discuss include things like organizing a collective effort to address some local or national problem or spending 10 hours a week as an unpaid volunteer at some local charity. Helping others based on formal obligations, such as caring for relatives, is excluded.

There are many kinds of planned and long-term helping behavior. We divide them here into three sets. The first set includes community activism and volunteering. *Volunteering* is long-term helping that takes place in existing organizations, such as a shelter for the homeless, a rape crisis hotline, or a program for tutoring children who need help in school. *Community activism*, in contrast, often involves identifying a helping need when there is little in place to address the problem, and activists often initiate the development of organizations to address these needs on a continuing basis. We begin our discussion by examining *community activism*; then we look at *volunteering*. Specifically, we address the reasons why people volunteer their time, money, and effort to organizations designed to help others, or begin such organizations from scratch.

Community activism and volunteering both involve continuing contributions that people not formally employed by an organization make to benefit others. There is a second category of planned and long-term helping that occurs among paid employees of large organizations. We look at two of these behaviors. The first is called *organizational citizenship behavior*—prosocial actions of the paid employees of a large company who go out of their way to help a coworker or the company itself; the second is called *principled organizational dissent* and concerns people who decide the organization they work for is doing something wrong or unethical and "blow the whistle" on it.

Finally, in this chapter, we consider a third kind of informal helping that probably falls somewhere in between the spontaneous kinds of helping discussed in the previous two chapters and the planned, long-term helping that is the focus of most of this chapter. It is help given by people whose occupations place them in unique positions to extend assistance to others. Informal helpers include the neighborhood bartender who provides people advice and the hair stylist who spends a good part of the day listening to the problems of their customers and offering support. This is an important and interesting phenomenon that may account for many everyday prosocial actions.

THE QUESTION

Although these types of planned, long-term helping are different in many ways from the spontaneous, short-term helping we have discussed in the previous chapters, the two main questions that we ask will have a familiar ring to them. First, what factors initially lead people to engage in long-term planned helping? We need to ask this kind of question again because planned, long-term helping differs from spontaneous interpersonal helping in several important ways. Chief among these is that although interpersonal helping almost always involves a face-to-face encounter between the helper and the recipient, planned helping is often intended to benefit people whom the helper has never met and may well never meet. Planned, long-term helping is also often intended to help an organization or some other large entity, not a specific individual. Because of these differences, explaining what instigates planned, long-term prosocial behavior requires that in addition to examining the situation in which the helping occurs (as was the case with interpersonal helping) we must also consider how variables outside the immediate situation affect helpers' behaviors. These include things such as their personal and demographic characteristics and their relationships with large organizations.

The second general question we ask applies in a unique way to planned and long-term helping. The question is, Why do people continue to perform these behaviors over long periods of time? That is, what sustains these behaviors sometimes in the face of considerable costs and effort? Again, this will require that we extend our search for the answer to variables we have not considered before. Finally, in this chapter, we also try to differentiate among the various classes of planned prosocial actions, answering the questions about what initiates and what sustains these actions, by examining not only the different circumstances in which they occur but also the different forms that help takes within these settings.

COMMUNITY ACTIVISM

Community activism is prosocial because the goal is to benefit others through one's actions. It involves recognizing a need that exceeds a single person's resources and then taking action to mobilize others to address the problem. Often, community activism means challenging conventional beliefs or traditional ways of doing things. Community activists often "rock the boat." But why take these risks?

The study of community activism typically focuses on the nature of the specific crisis or event that causes community activism and the personal attributes of the community activist. For example, Kayal (1993) provides a case study of community activism in his book *Bearing Witness: Gay Men's Health Crisis and the Politics of AIDS*. The Gay Men's Health Crisis (GMHC) group was initially founded to make people more aware of the AIDS epidemic and to raise money for research. What was the motivation behind this prosocial effort? The organization was *other-oriented*, in the sense that most of those who were initially active in the organization did not have AIDS. Yet, in the sense of identification with those afflicted in the gay community, personal interests were involved. As the GMHC grew, the focus of the group shifted to the care and support of persons with AIDS, and its impact reached far beyond the gay community. The ranks of volunteers to support these gay men included many heterosexual women (but relatively few heterosexual men) and lesbians. The motives of these people were varied. Some said that their motives were essentially altruistic, but most mentioned personal rewards. The great majority of the GMHC volunteers claimed that they got more from their participation than they gave.

Although people may report a wide range of reasons for becoming involved in these large-scale, community-oriented helping activities, there may be some commonalities in the types of motivations and the kinds of people involved. In 1987, William Berkowitz wrote a collection of brief biographies of people who became prosocial activists in their communities. Berkowitz called these people *local heroes*. For example, Homer Fahrner, a retired engineer, deplored the fact that elderly people were starving while produce rotted in the California fields; therefore, he started the Senior Gleaners, who collected the produce and distributed this food to needy people. Among the other heroes were Bill and Helen Sample, who wanted to make the last days of dying children's lives a little happier, so they started the Sunshine Foundation; Curtis Sliwa, the founder of the Guardian Angels, a group that fights urban crime; and Candy Lightner, who started Mothers Against Drunk Driving (MADD).

Some of these people seemed to be motivated solely by altruistic concerns, and some seemed to be motivated by self-interest. For example, Homer Fahrner was not poor, and the Samples had no sick children. But Curtis Sliwa did live in a dangerous urban area, and Candy Lightner's daughter had been killed by a drunk driver. Whatever their reasons for starting these groups, many other people have been helped by the organizations initiated by these local heroes. It is clear that the drive that kept all of these heroes going was not based solely on self-interest but also on a determination to solve problems that caused other people to suffer or to accomplish goals that would improve the life of the collectivity. In other words, all of these individuals were focused on some community—either an actual local community or some community of shared interests, such as sick children or hungry people.

What kind of people become local heroes? There are more differences between Berkowitz's heroes than there are similarities. Some are affluent, whereas others are poverty-stricken; there are men and women, rural and urban residents, and elderly and young people. Berkowitz suggested, however, that these people do have several characteristics in common: few familial obligations, strong parental influence, a spiritual background, and the political ethic of the 1960s. Personality similarities included naiveté (not realizing what they were getting themselves into!), high energy coupled with the ability to pace themselves, and a boundless capacity for humor. Two additional characteristics struck Berkowitz, however. First, these local heroes displayed strong emotions: They had experienced excitement about the issue that made them want to "jump out of their seats" and anger that made them want to really "kick butt."

Second, the heroes had a strong belief in and reliance on traditional virtue, that is, commitment, tolerance for criticism, hard work, optimism, persistence, and the willingness to take a risk for a good cause.

In general, paralleling the findings for spontaneous helping, the factors that lead a person to become a social activist involve both affective and cognitive elements. The emotional element (e.g., excitement or anger) stimulates initial action. However, because the required actions involved are complex and long-term, the ability to formulate solutions, skill in executing a plan, and a willingness to take risks and persevere weigh much more heavily in community activism than in spontaneous interpersonal helping.

Community activists start their prosocial work in something of a void, often working outside the conventional bounds of the community to find solutions to the new problems they see. For this reason, the qualities of hard work and persistence serve the local heroes well. If successful, the results of their efforts set the stage for the establishment of organizations that will eventually take over the task at hand, move the work of the group into the mainstream (e.g., MADD), and continue to provide the prosocial services the community activists who started the movement originally conceived.

Once helping organizations are established, often as the result of community activism, they need to be staffed. Volunteers, people who give freely of their time and resources, are often essential to the functioning of these organizations.

VOLUNTEERING

Volunteering is unpaid service given freely to a nonprofit organization that directly or indirectly delivers goods and services to individuals, groups of individuals, or a cause (Wilson, 2000). There are, of course, people who volunteer on their own rather than as part of an organizational effort, usually referred to as *informal helpers*, and there are some individuals who are called "stipended volunteers" (e.g., members of the Peace Corps or Americorps; Clotfelter, 1999) who receive modest compensation for their services. But the most common kind of volunteering is performed by people who are giving their time and effort freely to a charity, religious organization, or other kinds of service organizations.

Volunteerism is an extremely common and widespread kind of prosocial behavior. About 45% of all Americans over the age of 18 years report that they spend at least some time each week working as a volunteer. Independent Sector (2002) estimated that Americans spend 19 billion hours per year volunteering and put the value of these efforts at $226 billion. This amount represents the equivalent of 2.5% of the U.S. gross domestic product (GDP) and is greater than the GDP of 85% of the countries in the world (U.S. Department of Energy, August, 2003). Widespread volunteering is not confined to the United States. In the United Kingdom, 48% of adults volunteer for service organizations. Between 30% and 35% of the adult populations in Australia, Germany, and Ireland report having volunteered, and in Canada and Japan the numbers are approximately 25% of the adult population (National Centre for Volunteering Research, 2002; Reed & Selbee, 2002; Volunteering Australia, 2005). Thus, volunteering is an extremely common form of prosocial behavior.

In addition, in contrast to the types of interpersonal helping described in chapter 3 and chapter 4, volunteering involves something Allen Omoto and Mark Snyder (1995) called *"nonobligated helping."* That is, in most interpersonal helping, there is some implicit or explicit sense on the part of the potential helpers that they *ought* to offer aid to the potential recipient due to normative expectations. These feelings of obligation may be elicited by the verbal and nonverbal behaviors of a distressed stranger, as in the classic bystander intervention paradigm (Dovidio et al., 1991). The sense of obligation also often comes from some long-term personal association between the helper and recipient or familial or kinship ties (see chap. 2). The most dramatic example of obligated helping would be the relatively high percentage of organ donors who come to the aid of their relatives, but a more common form of obligated helping is the provision of social support among close friends and relatives (Albrecht & Adelman, 1987; Borgida, Conner, & Mantteufel, 1992). In contrast, with volunteering there are rarely personal ties or associations between helpers and the ultimate recipients of their help. In fact, in many instances the helpers and those who benefit from their help never even meet. If people do not feel obligated to help, why then do they volunteer?

Initial Decision to Volunteer

The decision to volunteer, like many other social behaviors, is often strongly influenced by the actions of other people. There is good reason to believe that many people who volunteer are subjected to some direct or indirect form of social pressure to engage in this action. In their study of blood donors, which will be discussed in more detail later in the chapter, Piliavin and Callero (1991) found that perceived expectations of others (and sometimes direct pressure from them) led to initial donations. Approximately 40% of the people who volunteer in the United States reported that they were directly asked to become a volunteer (U.S. Department of Labor, 2002). Remember that "defining the situation" was one of the critical steps to help to be given in emergency intervention situations, and being asked to volunteer may make the need of the organization clear to the potential helper as well.

Penner (2004) proposed that there are also nonsocial stimuli that can activate the desire to volunteer. These could range from some personal circumstance in a person's life (e.g., the loss of a loved one to some disease) to a particular feeling or thought that becomes salient to the potential volunteer. Jonas, Schimel, Greenberg, and Pyszczynski (2002) looked at how the salience of certain thoughts could affect willingness to make donations to a charity. The thought they studied was *mortality salience*, becoming aware of and concerned about one's own mortality. Based on terror management theory (e.g., Greenberg, Solomon, & Pyszczynski 1997), Jonas et al. proposed that making people aware of their own mortality makes them more strongly endorse a "cultural worldview" that encourages helping others, and it is this endorsement that increases their willingness to help others. They tested this idea by increasing mortality salience in one group of participants but not another, and members of the former group were significantly more inclined to think and act prosocially, as evidenced in part by increased donations to charities.

Extraordinary events of historic proportions can also create conditions that make volunteering more likely. One kind of historical event that has been studied in relation to volunteering is natural or person-caused disasters. As you read in some of the earlier chapters, incredible acts of personal courage, in which people risk their lives to save a friend, relative, and even total strangers, are often seen in response to disasters. The aftermath of disasters also results in an increase in people's willingness to volunteer after the immediate danger has passed. As a case study, let us look at how the terrorist attacks of September 11, 2001, affected volunteering in the United States. But first, a little background for the study that examined this question (Penner, Brannick, Webb, & Connell, 2005) may be helpful.

Since August 1998, an organization named Volunteermatch has operated a Web site designed to increase volunteerism in the United States (http://www.volunteermatch.org/). When entering this Web site, users are presented with a list of 27 different categories of charities that address a wide variety of issues or target groups (e.g., Advocacy and Human Rights, Health and Medicine, Women). After selecting a category, the names and descriptions of organizations that fall within that category and that are within 20 miles of the user's home are presented. Users can then express their interest in particular organizations via the Internet, and Volunteermatch sends a separate e-mail to the organization informing it of the user's interest in becoming a volunteer. According to an internal study prepared for Volunteermatch, approximately 75% of those who give their names actually volunteer (T. Willets, personal communication, October 2, 2003). Penner et al. (2005) used data from the Volunteer match Web site to examine how 9/11 affected volunteering.

Figure 5.1 shows the weekly totals of people who offered to volunteer in 2000 and in 2001. The impact of the September 11 attacks on volunteering was quite dramatic. The critical weeks in this figure are the week of September 10 and the two weeks that followed. In 2000, the total number of people who offered to volunteer during the weeks of September 10, 17, and 24 were 4,039, 3,826, and 4,806, respectively. The totals for the same weeks in 2001 were 9,370, 13,227, and 8,459, a two- to threefold increase in volunteering. It should also be noted that the total for the week of September 10, 2001, substantially underestimates the effects of the attacks on volunteering. Because the attacks occurred on the morning of the third day of this "week," the total actually reflects only four days of postattack volunteering. Volunteering that benefited the Red Cross and other disaster-re-

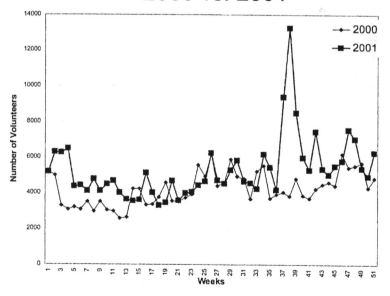

FIG. 5.1.   Rates of volunteering before and after September 11, 2002. From Penner et al. (2005), with permission.

lated agencies showed the greatest increase, but the increase in volunteering was not limited to the Red Cross or even to traditionally popular organizations (e.g, those that benefitted children or elderly people). Volunteering increased *for every single organization* listed on the Volunteermatch web site, including those that served groups that are often stigmatized (e.g., gays and lesbians) or that may be considered outgroups (e.g., immigrants). Penner et al. (2005) were not the only researchers who found increased volunteering after a disaster. St. John and Fuchs (2002) looked at the impact of the bombing of the Murrah Federal Building in Oklahoma City in 1995 on the residents of that city. In a survey conducted 10 months after the bombing, nearly 75% of the residents of the city reported that they had volunteered to help the victims of the bombing. Similar high levels of volunteering have been found after floods and other natural disasters (Dynes & Quarantelli, 1980).

We do not want to create the impression that people volunteer only in response to disasters and other highly dramatic events—what might be thought of as the organizational helping equivalent to emergency intervention. Indeed, such events probably account for only a small proportion of the volunteering that occurs on a daily basis. So let us look at some other factors that are associated with more "everyday" decisions to volunteer.

Who Volunteers?

Even though volunteering is a very common form of prosocial behavior, there are still significant individual differences involved in the decision to volunteer. These individual differences relate to demographic characteristics (related to a social group membership), socialization factors (related to social institutions), and personal characteristics.

Demographic Characteristics. There is considerable research (see Dovidio & Penner, 2001; Penner, 2002; U.S. Department of Labor, 2002; Wilson, 2000) that finds a consistent association between certain demographic characteristics and volunteering. The three demographic characteristics that are most commonly associated with volunteering in the United States (and other countries as well) are *education, income,* and *age* (Independent Sector, 2002; Penner, 2002; Putnam, 2002; Wilson, 2000). There is a relatively strong positive association between level of education and volunteering (Independent Sector, 2002; McPherson & Rotolo, 1996; Putnam, 2002). Penner et al. (2005) even found a strong positive association between education and the incidence of post September 11 volunteering. Income is also positively associated with volunteering up to a certain income level, but then begins to taper off. Still, the level of volunteering among the wealthiest segment of American society is much higher than that found among the poorest segment (Independent Sector, 2002; Putnam, 2002).

One possible explanation of these findings is that better educated, wealthier people have more free time to donate because they are less constrained by their jobs, because they are often salaried rather than paid by the hour. A problem with this "free time" explanation, however, is that volunteerism is substantially more common among employed than unemployed individuals (Hart, Atkins, & Donnelly, 2002; Independent Sector, 2002; National Centre for Volunteering Research, 2002; Reed & Selbee, 2000; Volunteering Australia, 2005). Nevertheless, among employed individuals, those with higher status jobs, more flexible work schedules, and greater job autonomy are the most likely to be volunteers (Freeman, 1997; Smith, 1994; Wilson & Musick, 1997a). Although flexibility in their work schedules among employed workers may be associated with greater volunteering, the broader relationship between economic status and volunteering cannot be explained simply by the amount of discretionary free time a person has. Thus, some researchers have posited more complex relationships; Wilson (2000), for example, suggested that "education boosts volunteering because it heightens awareness of problems, increases empathy, and builds self-confidence" (p. 219).

Another explanation of these findings is that people at upper socioeconomic levels, especially those who are also active members of some religious organization, are better integrated into and involved with their communities than are people at the lower socioeconomic levels. Active involvement and participation in the civic and social activities of one's community have been shown to be strongly associated with volunteering in both the United States and Canada (Bellah, Madsen, Sullivan, Swidler, & Tipton, 1985; Hart et al., 2002; Putnam, 2002; Reed & Selbee, 2000). People who are marginalized in their community are much less likely to become volunteers. In addition, people who are more engaged and involved in community activities are more likely to be asked to volunteer and then to agree when asked (Wilson & Musick, 1997b).

Finally, we consider gender and ethnicity as they relate to volunteering. In North America, women are somewhat more likely to be volunteers than men (Independent Sector, 2002; Reed & Selbee, 2000), but this gender difference is not found in Europe or Australia (Volunteering Australia 2005; Wilson, 2000). However, across all of these geographic locations, there are gender differences in the *kinds* of work volunteers do. According to Wilson (2000), women do "more of the caring, person-to-person tasks and fewer of the public, political activities, and they are less likely to be found in leadership positions" (p. 228).

In the United States, members of ethnic minorities (e.g., African Americans, Hispanics/Latinos) are less likely to volunteer than are European Americans, although the percentage of African Americans who reported volunteering showed a dramatic increase in the most recent Independent Sector survey (Independent Sector, 2002). Part of the reason for these ethnic differences is probably social exclusion. As we just mentioned, African Americans are less likely to be *asked* to volunteer than are whites (Ferree, Barry, & Manno, 1998; Hodgkinson & Weitzman, 1996), and we have already noted that being asked is often the critical first step to get someone to become a volunteer. Furthermore, when factors such as education, income, and other socioeconomic factors are statistically controlled, racial/ethnic differences largely disappear (Clary, Snyder, & Stukas, 1996; Latting, 1990; Wuthnow, 1998).

Of course, all these findings concerning demographic characteristics and volunteering are correlational. That is, they show that the two things are related, but they really do not allow us to conclude that one caused the other. We already noted some possible explanations for the links between education and income and volunteering. Other possible explanations for such relationships involve psychological processes. Bellah et al. (1985) suggested that well-educated and wealthy people have reached a point in their lives when they are more likely to concern themselves with the needs of others, as opposed to the needs of themselves and their immediate family. Thus, it should be kept in mind that the relationship between demographic characteristics and the decision to volunteer is almost always an indirect one.

Social Institutions. A substantial portion of the research literature on what causes a person to volunteer comes from the sociological literature. Indeed, the 2000 *Annual Review of Sociology* contained a contribution solely concerned with volunteering (Wilson, 2000). Not surprisingly, Wilson and other sociologists focus a good deal of attention on the social institutions that are associated with volunteering.

With regard to these social institutions, there is good agreement that the family and the church play vitally important roles in the initial decision to volunteer. For example, teenagers are more likely to volunteer if their parents are also volunteers (Janoski & Wilson, 1995; Rosenthal, Feiring, & Lewis, 1998; Sundeen & Raskoff, 1995), and long-term blood donors are more likely than short-term donors to have parents who were themselves donors (J. A. Piliavin & Callero, 1991). The specific processes responsible for these strong associations are not known. The parents serve as powerful prosocial models for their children, but they probably also use prosocial exhortations as well (Clary & Orenstein, 1991). We return to the issue of socialization and prosocial behavior and consider it more fully in chapter 6.

Other aspects of one's family also affect volunteering. For example, economic status of the parents is positively associated with volunteerism among their children (J. A. Piliavin, 2004; Sundeen & Raskoff, 1995). Mustillo, Wilson, and Lynch (2004) studied volunteering among mothers and their daughters in an attempt to understand how parents influence their children's decisions to be a volunteer. They compared two possible processes, both of which could be operating. Parents' influence might be due to the prosocial modeling they provide for their children; that is, children who see their parents doing volunteer work can be influenced by these prosocial models. Parents' influence could also be due to the socioeconomic status of the family; for example, wealthy families have the resources to allow the parents, and later their children, the freedom to spend some time working as a volunteer. Wilson (2000) suggested that the parents' economic resources may make it less necessary for their children to work and thus provide the young people with more time to volunteer.

Mustillo et al. found that both factors had effects on the initial levels of volunteering among the daughters: The highest level of initial volunteering was found among the better educated daughters of mothers who also volunteered. But when they looked at the daughters' subsequent volunteering over a 13-year period, they found that the increases in volunteering were almost completely due to a family's socioeconomic status. The authors proposed that mothers may have initially served as effective volunteer recruiters, because volunteer recruitment is more likely to succeed if there is a personal relationship between recruiter and target (Brady, Schlozman, & Verba, 1999). However, over time, it appears that the daughters' families provided them with the resources that allowed them the freedom to spend time as a volunteer.

Another social institution that is consistently associated with volunteerism is organized religion. Among youths and adults, there is a positive association between affiliation with some religion and being a volunteer (Lam, 2002; Lee, J. A. Piliavin, & Call, 1999; Musick, Wilson, & Bynum, 2000; Penner, 2002; Reed & Selbee, 2000; Uslaner, 2002). A recent study suggests that this relationship cuts across racial and ethnic groups; Mattis et al. (2004) studied volunteerism among Black men and found that religiosity was a significant predictor of volunteer activity. This consistent relationship could be due to the fact that volunteering for one's church, synagogue, or mosque is, at least in the United States, the most common form of volunteering (Independent Sector, 2002; U.S. Department of Labor, 2005). However, Penner (2002) and Piliavin (2004) excluded religious volunteering from their analyses, and both of these researchers still found a higher incidence of volunteering among people who identified with an organized religion. Further, within Penner's sample of volunteers, the most active volunteers were also more religious, even when religious volunteering was not included. Again, the causal processes responsible for this strong and consistent association have not been fully explored.

Personal Characteristics and Motivations.

Psychologists who study why people initially volunteer have focused much more than sociologists on how the personality, needs of potential volunteers, and the social situations they confront affect volunteering. For example, Davis et al. (1999) found an association between dispositional empathy and willingness to engage in certain kinds of volunteer activities. Both Penner and his associates (Penner, 2002; Penner, Fritzche, Craiger, & Freifeld, 1995; Penner, Midili, & Kegelmeyer, 1997) and Hart and his associates (Atkins, Hart, & Donnelly, 2005; Hart et al., 2004) demonstrated that a cluster of personality dispositions (which include empathy) plays a significant role in the decision to volunteer. Thus, personality differences may relate to spontaneous helping and volunteering in dynamically similar ways. We return to this research on the prosocial personality in chapter 7, where we discuss in more detail the personal characteristics of helpful individuals.

How do individual differences in background and personality actually translate into volunteering? Mark Snyder and his associates (e.g., Clary & Snyder, 1991; Omoto & Snyder 1995, 2002; Snyder, Clary, & Stukas, 2000) approached the question of how different people make the decision to volunteer from a somewhat different perspective. These researchers argued that people decide to volunteer because volunteering will serve some purpose or meet some need for them. Their *functional analysis of volunteering* is based on the principle that much of human behavior is motivated by goals and needs. Therefore, understanding why a person engages in a particular activity requires identifying the function the activity serves or the need that was satisfied for that person. The same behavior can serve different functions for different individuals or for the same individual at different times. Thus, Snyder and his colleagues extensively explored people's motives for volunteering and developed an instrument that assesses different volunteer motives (Clary et al., 1998). Clary et al. (1998) identified six motives for volunteering: *Values*, to express values related to altruistic and humanitarian concerns for others; *Understanding*, to acquire new learning experiences and/or use skills that otherwise are unused; *Social*, to strengthen social relationships or engage in behaviors favored by important others; *Career*, to gain career-related benefits; *Protective*, to reduce negative feelings about oneself or address personal problems; and *Enhancement*, to grow and develop psychologically. Initiation of volunteering depends on whether the person believes the act will meet one or more of these needs and serve the intended functions. According to the theory, whether volunteer activity is sustained depends on the extent to which the volunteering experience in fact satisfies the relevant motive(s) for the individual.

Many researchers find that volunteers say that they are most motivated by value-based, other-oriented, or prosocial motives (Independent Sector, 2002; National Centre for Volunteering Research, 2002; Reed & Selbee, 2000). For example, Penner and Finkelstein (1998) conducted a longitudinal study of motives of volunteers at an AIDS service organization. They measured male volunteers' motives for volunteering at the beginning of the study and found that the Values motive correlated most highly with the extent of volunteer activity and with time spent with HIV-positive clients 10 months later. Similarly, Clary and Orenstein (1991) also found that this altruistic or Value motivation was related to the amount of help given by crisis-counseling volunteers. However, Snyder and his colleagues have persuasively argued that sustained volunteering can also be motivated by other less selfless motives, such as advancing one's career or developing social relationships (Clary et al., 1998; Clary & Snyder, 1999; Omoto & Snyder, 1995).

Hart and his associates (2004) recently proposed an innovative model that attempts to integrate both the sociological and psychological approaches to volunteering. Using data from a national survey, they presented evidence that both personality factors and social structures (e.g., family, culture) play important roles in the incidence of volunteering, but the relationship is not a direct one. Rather, these factors affect things such as a person's attitudes, identity, commitment to ideals, and the richness of the person's social networks. It is these latter factors that directly lead to volunteering. Similarly, Wilson and Musick (1997b) presented a model in which both volunteering and informal helping are predicted from demographic variables, "human capital" (education, income, functional health), "social capital" (number of children, social interaction patterns), and "cultural capital" (religiosity and valuing helping). Omoto and Snyder (2002) also included "considerations of community" in their modeling of volunteering. They argued that being part of a community and identifying with it both can affect whether and for how long individuals choose to volunteer.

In summary, people's initial decision to volunteer are affected by multiple personal, social, and organizational factors. The forces that determine the initial decision to volunteer resemble those involved in spontaneous helping. Empathy, other-oriented and self-oriented motivations, and the recognized needs of others all contribute to the initial decision to volunteer. But, as we have mentioned, volunteering is a long-term activity. Longitudinal studies of volunteers find that once people decide to volunteer, a large percentage of them remain volunteers for several years (Finkelstein & Penner, 2004; Omoto & Snyder,

1995; J. A. Piliavin & Callero, 1991). In the next section, we consider what maintains this behavior.

Maintenance of Volunteering

There have been two major theoretical models that have sought to identify the factors that sustain volunteering over an extended period of time: Omoto and Snyder's (1995, 2002) Volunteer Process Model, and the Role Identity Model proposed by Piliavin and her associates (Grube & J. A. Piliavin, 2000; J. A. Piliavin & Callero, 1991; J. A. Piliavin, Callero, & Grube, 2002). These two models agree on many points (e. g., the inclusion of organizational variables) and are not "competitors" for the best explanation of sustained volunteer activities. However, they do diverge somewhat in terms of focus and emphasis. Omoto and Snyder's model gave most attention to intrapersonal variables (specifically, motives), while the Piliavin et al. model was more concerned with social roles and the social context in which volunteering occurs.

The Volunteer Process Model. The Volunteer Process Model views sustained volunteerism as being primarily determined by the extent to which there is a match between the motives or needs that led the person to first volunteer and that person's actual experiences as a volunteer. For example, someone who volunteered to learn more about the world and found that the volunteer experience met this need will continue in this role longer than someone whose needs were not met. The model posits that prosocial dispositions, social support for the volunteer's activities, satisfaction with the volunteer experience, and integration with the organization also play important roles in sustained volunteering.

Omoto and Snyder (1995) conducted a test of the Volunteer Process Model with AIDS volunteers and found that motives and social support did, in fact, predict duration of volunteering. Surprisingly (but in line with the egoistic motives found to mediate interpersonal helping), they found greater persistence among volunteers with relatively selfish values. They stated, "It was not the humanitarian desires to do good on behalf of others, nor concern for communities affected by HIV, that kept volunteers involved. Rather, it appears that the opportunity to have personal, self-oriented, and perhaps even selfish functions served by volunteering was what kept volunteers actively involved" (p. 684). A second factor that contributed to duration of volunteering was the level of support the volunteer's friends and relatives provided for this activity, although this effect was a negative one: The more support the volunteer reported receiving from friends and family, the shorter was the time period for which the person actually volunteered. Personality variables (specifically, empathy) were not related to duration of volunteering but were related to satisfaction with the volunteer experience and organizational integration. Similar results have been obtained by Penner and Finkelstein (1998) and Vecina (2001). Davis, Hall, and Meyer (2003) also found that satisfaction with volunteer work predicted the number of hours of volunteer work but not persistence over time. It appears that motives do play an important role in sustained volunteering, but how interactions between the volunteer's initial motives and other aspects of the volunteer experience (e.g., satisfaction with the organization) affect long-term volunteering is worthy of further study.

Role Identity Model. The other major model of volunteering, the Role Identity Model, was initially developed to explain the behavior of people who continued to donate blood over an extended period of time (J. A. Piliavin & Callero, 1991). The two key constructs in the theory are *perceived expectations*—beliefs about how significant others feel about the person's behavior—and *role identity*—the extent to which a particular role (e.g., being a volunteer) becomes part of the person's personal identity (Grube & J. A. Piliavin, 2000; J. A. Piliavin et al., 2002). The items that assess a person's role identity as a volunteer in this research are presented in Table 5.1. The model proposes that perceived expectations of others lead to becoming a volunteer, the experiences/behaviors associated with actually volunteering and organizational variables (e.g., prestige of the service organization) lead to the development of a volunteer role identity, and role identity is the immediate cause of sustained volunteering. The initial decision to participate is also influenced by past experience of need and the volunteer models provided by family members.

The Piliavin and Callero model was tested in a survey to see to whether it could be generalized to both volunteering and charitable do-

TABLE 5.1
Role Identity as a Volunteer (Grube & J. A. Piliavin, 2000)

1. Doing volunteer work is something I rarely think about. (reverse scored)

2. I would feel a loss if I were forced to give up volunteer work.

3. I really don't have any clear feelings about volunteer work. (reverse scored)

4. For me, being a volunteer means more than just volunteer work.

5. Volunteering is an important part of who I am.

nation (Lee et al., 1999). The analyses were based on the 1989 National Charity Survey, which consisted of telephone interviews with a national random sample of 1,002 respondents. The main dependent variable was the answer to a single question, "How likely do you think it is that you will donate [blood or time or money] sometime during the next twelve months?" People answered on a 4-point scale from "not at all likely " to "extremely likely." Using the Role Identity Model as their starting point (shown in Fig. 5.2), the researchers asked the following question: Do the factors of modeling by parents, being a past recipient of help, and expectations of others lead to both the habit of donating and the development of a volunteer role identity, and do habit and role identity predict intentions to donate in the future? Many of the other factors known to influence volunteering and giving (e.g., religiosity, income, education) were statistically controlled to allow a valid test of the model to be conducted. The model's predictions were largely supported for all three forms of helping, with the sole exception being that past receipt of help affected only blood donations. The authors explained the absence of a relationship between previously being helped and the other two kinds of donating by making the statistical argument that too few people had received or knew of people who had received charity or social services for the analyses to have the power to detect meaningful influence.

Grube and J. A. Piliavin (2000) conducted another test of aspects of the Role Identity Model using cancer volunteers and found that per-

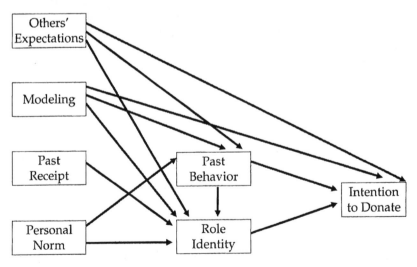

FIG. 5.2.   Factors leading to blood donation. From Lee et al. (1999), with permission.

ceived expectations and organizational attributes were again associated with the development of a volunteer role identity. This identity was strongly associated with intention to continue volunteering and number of hours devoted to the organization (see also Finkelstein & Penner, 2004; Penner & Finkelstein, 1998). Finkelstein, Penner, and Brannick (2005) used a sample of elderly volunteers in a hospice to study how a volunteer role identity might affect their behavior. They also found that the more strongly the participants identified themselves as a volunteer, the more time they spent volunteering each week and the longer their tenure as a volunteer. Finally, Marta, Manzi, and Vignoles (2005) did a 3-year longitudinal study of young adults volunteering with children in northern Italy, as a direct test of the role identity model. Using a questionnaire, they measured parents' and friends' expectations, years of past volunteering, attitude, and father's modeling as predictors of role identity, as well as behavioral intentions, hours of volunteering (habit), and perceived behavioral control at the beginning of the study. Three years later they called and asked the participants if they were still volunteering in the same capacity. Their results are shown in Fig. 5.3. The authors stated that "role identity as a volunteer did not just add to the variance predicted in behavioural intentions, it *fully mediated* the effects on behavioural intentions of both

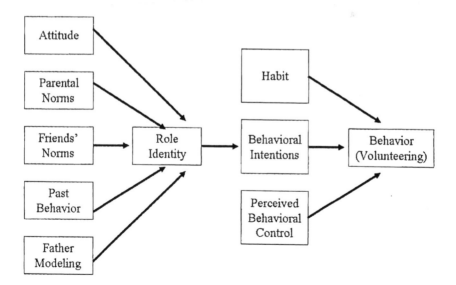

FIG. 5.3.   A 3-year longitudinal study of factors predicting volunteering. From Marta et al. (2005), with permission.

attitudes and subjective norms ... as well as effects of past behaviour and of parental modeling.... Thus it appears to be role identity ... which has the greatest impact on maintenance of volunteering activities in the long term" (p. 6).

Although all of these studies provide some support for the Role Identity Model of long-term volunteering, perhaps the strongest support comes from studies of blood donation. We now turn to this unique and interesting kind of organized volunteering.

Blood Donation

Giving blood is a unique kind of volunteering, referred to by one donor as "the most passive way of being a hero I can think of" (J. A. Piliavin & Callero, 1991). It is quite literally "giving of oneself." Because it is different from other forms of volunteering in many ways (e.g., involving some pain, discomfort, and anxiety; being a passive form of helping; being associated with the medical establishment), the factors related to individuals' initiating and continuing this activity are somewhat different from other forms of volunteering as well. For example, the role of emotion is stronger in blood donation than in other forms of volunteering; about one-quarter to one-third of blood donors report negative effects when they donate, including fainting or dizziness, fatigue, nausea, bruising, and pain (Newmann, 1997; Newmann, Pichette, & Dzaka, 2003; Nilsson Sojka & Sojka, 2003). In light of these negative experiences, how do blood donors come to their first donation, and what leads them to continue?

Initial Decision to Donate Blood. First, and consistent with the modeling effects described already, there is evidence that giving blood "runs in families." McCombie (1991) found that among undergraduates donating at a campus drive, those who had given most often reported more family and friends who gave blood; similarly, when asked how many times they could donate in the next year, those with family members who donated claimed they would give blood more times in the coming year than those who did not have a family member who donated blood. In a sample of students, there was a significant difference between donors and non-donors in the number of family members who were donors. J. A. Piliavin and Callero (1991) also found that both having parents who gave blood and knowing someone in the past who had needed blood are factors that help get someone "in the door" of a donation center the first time. Second, like other kinds of volunteering, potential blood donors respond to being asked. In fact, Drake, Finkelstein, and Sapolsky (1982) argued that the most important way to get people to give blood for the first time was to ask them. As noted earlier, this is also a critical factor in getting people to engage in volunteering of time and donation of money.

Maintenance of Blood Donation. What leads donors to return and donate blood repeatedly? The model presented by J. A. Piliavin and Callero (1991) proposes that what happens at the first several donation experiences can be critical. The donor who comes in without strong social pressure, is not temporarily deferred, has a "good stick" (i.e., the needle was easily inserted in the vein), does not faint, reports little pain, feels good afterward, and is treated in a warm and friendly way by staff has a much greater likelihood of returning. If the experience of blood donation comes off without a hitch, the donor is more likely to return. These factors are similar to "satisfaction" in the Omoto and Snyder (1995, 2002) Volunteer Process Model of volunteering.

Sauer and France (1999) actually carried out an experimental intervention to prevent fainting by giving either varying amounts of caffeine (which raises blood pressure and decreases the chances of fainting) or a placebo to female donors and then measured fainting as well as the number of subsequent donations. Those women given the highest amount of caffeine had fewer fainting episodes and were more likely to return than those who had been given placebos. Moreover, just observing others fainting significantly decreases return visits among occasional donors, suggesting that it is not the fainting per se but rather the fear of some negative event that affects decisions about making future donations (Ferguson & Bibby, 2002).

In addition, the more quickly the donor returns to give blood again, the more likely the person is to move to the next step of self-labeling oneself as a person who can give easily and intending to do so; this relationship was initially found by J. A. Piliavin and Callero (1991). In a more recent sample of over 179,000 first-time donors, those who gave more times in their first year of donation—meaning that they returned not only more often but also more quickly—were more likely to become regular donors (Schreiber et al., 2005). This is the beginning of the internalization of the role identity of "blood donor." In one longitudinal study, donors who described themselves as "a regular donor" early in their donation career were more likely to develop a habit of donation over a period of up to 3 years (J. A. Piliavin & Callero, 1991). In a later study of donors with varying past experience of donation, role identity was directly measured and demonstrated to be the strongest predictor of *intentions* to donate. Intentions combined with habit predicted actual donations over the following year (J. A. Piliavin & Callero, 1991). The quality of the social relations in the donation setting and perceived expectations have also been shown to be important for continued blood donations (J. A. Piliavin & Callero, 1991; Boccacin, 2000).

Role Identity Theory is not the only framework that attempts to explain blood donation. Giles and Cairns (1995) tested the applicability of the Theory of Planned Behavior (e.g., Ajzen, 1991) to blood donation. This theory says that intentions to engage in some behavior can be predicted from three things. These are attitudes toward the behavior, perceived social norms (i.e., beliefs about what other important people would want you to do), and perceived behavioral control (i.e., the extent to which the you believe the ability to perform the behavior in question is under your own control). Giles and Cairns measured these three variables and found that they could predict intentions to give blood, with perceived behavioral control being particularly important in this prediction. Consistent with the theory of planned behavior, the blood donation behavior itself was most accurately predicted from these intentions. Armitage and Connor (2001) also used a combination of the theory of planned behavior and concepts from identity theory to predict intention to donate blood. They found that perceived control was an important predictor of intention to donate; they also found that a sense of self-efficacy, self-identity, and moral norms predicted intentions to give blood as well.

As we have shown, there has been extensive research trying to understand why people volunteer and what makes them continue to serve in that prosocial role. In most cases, people offer their help to organizations that have already been established, and these organizations often have procedures in place that allow volunteers to easily make contributions of their time, effort, and, as we have seen, blood with some confidence that their donations will eventually be used to benefit others.

However, prosocial action does not necessarily have to occur *through* an organization; it can, and frequently does, happen *within* an organization. People spend a significant amount of their lives at the workplace. Although much of that time is spent performing the required responsibilities of their position, people often spend considerable time interacting with others informally on the job. Opportunities for helping others can thus come during people's "off times" (e.g., during lunch breaks) or occur in the course of job-related activities. These prosocial actions can be directed toward specific individuals or toward the organization as a whole. We discuss these kinds of planned helping in the next section.

LONG-TERM PLANNED BEHAVIORS
WITHIN ORGANIZATIONS

Within this section, we focus first on prosocial behaviors directly associated with people's roles in organizations, *organizational citizenship behavior* (OCB) and *principled organizational dissent* (POD). Perhaps the best way to introduce these two forms of prosocial actions is to differentiate them from the focus of the next section—informal interpersonal helping that occurs within the context of person's occupational role but involves efforts basically unrelated to that role or the organization that employs the helper. OCB and POD differ from interpersonal helping in four basic ways. First, because these behaviors occur within the context of an organization, the theories that explain these prosocial behaviors must consider not only the interpersonal processes that are operating, as with interpersonal helping, but also the characteristics of the organization in which the prosocial behaviors occur. Second, although interpersonal helping most often happens spontaneously, these types of prosocial action within organizations are much more frequently planned. Thus, feelings and emotions will often play much less of a role in the decision to engage in organizational prosocial actions than they do in interpersonal helping.

Third, OCB and POD are both long-term behaviors. People who engage in POD often spend months and even years trying to correct the wrongs they believe an organization or its representatives have done. In one prominent case, Coleen Rowley was an FBI agent in Minneapolis who uncovered evidence a few months before the September 11 attacks that terrorists might be planning to use planes to attack buildings in the United States. Her memos and requests for actions regarding this possibility were largely ignored by officials of the agency. After the attacks, Ms. Rowley spent 2 years trying to change the way the FBI operated; she made her concerns public in an open letter to the director of the FBI, an action that put her career with the FBI in jeopardy. She has now resigned from the agency, but she continues to question and challenge the ability of the FBI antiterrorism efforts on a number of fronts. Again, this kind of behavior can be contrasted with the emergency help given in bystander interventions that are usually transitory and severely time-limited.

It is also quite common that, in contrast to interpersonal helping, the goal of organizational helping is not to benefit a specific individual but rather to serve the goals of an organization or some even larger entity. OCB often involves behaviors that will help the organization perform its functions better, such as an employee working to keep up with the changing practices of the organization or doing community service to improve the organization's image in the community. To return to Ms. Rowley's whistle blowing about the FBI, the ultimate goal of her efforts was not the protection of any particular individual but rather to improve the safety of the citizens of the entire nation.

Having identified the new factors that will be operating within the organizational helping domain, let us now begin our investigation of the various types of long-term, planned prosocial behavior that we have briefly introduced.

Organizational Citizenship Behaviors

Most of us would agree that things such as organizing one's community to solve some crisis or shared problem, volunteering, and donating blood are selfless acts primarily meant to have the consequence of benefiting others, even if there are sometimes small secondary personal rewards for the helper. OCBs are also prosocial behaviors that serve to benefit other people and organizations, but these behaviors may also produce some direct and tangible rewards for the person who does them.

OCBs are typically defined as behaviors not formally part of an employee's job that are intended to either help others in the organization or to help the organization itself (Smith, Organ, & Near, 1983). OCB has two dimensions. OCB researchers refer to the help directed at individuals within the organization as the *altruism* dimension of OCB. This type of helping behavior can be *job-related*, such as assisting a coworker with a specific project or work task, or *non-job-related*, such as helping a co-worker or supervisor with a problem of a personal nature. The second dimension of OCB—helpful actions directed at the organization—is usually called the *conscientiousness* or *generalized compliance* dimension of OCB. This class of OCB might involve staying late to finish a project without being asked to do so, consistently following organizational rules and policies, and engaging in activities that would maintain or improve employee morale (e.g., by organizing social events).

Over 40 years ago, Daniel Katz (1964) suggested that OCB-like behaviors were "vital to organizational survival and effectiveness" (p. 132). Within the last 10 to 15 years, many large organizations and researchers who study organizations have rediscovered Katz's proposal, and the interest in OCB (and similar behaviors) has grown dramatically. These contemporary researchers (e.g., Borman, 2004; Borman & Motowidlo, 1993; Organ, 1988, 1990, 1997; Smith et al., 1983) believe that OCB can have a beneficial effect on the organization by "lubricating" certain aspects of its "social machinery," increasing efficiency, and reducing friction among employees.

A more cynical way of looking at OCB is that organizational leaders assume that when employees engage in citizenship behaviors, the organization gets more work from its workers at no additional cost to the company (Organ, 1988), and the research provides some support for this assumption (George & Bettenhausen, 1990; Podsakoff, Ahearne, & MacKenzie, 1997; Podsakoff & MacKenzie, 1994; Walz & Niehoff, 1996). For example, companies whose employees exhibit a high level of OCB generally produce more products that are of high quality, and, as a consequence, the companies experience greater financial success (Podsakoff & MacKenzie, 1997). The companies are not the only ones to benefit from OCB. OCB has also been shown to be a reliable predictor of employee success in the organization (Borman & Penner, 2001; Chen, Hui, & Sego, 1998). For example, Podsakoff, MacKenzie, Paine, and Bachrach (2000) found that supervisors frequently consider OCB when they evaluate their subordinates, even though the extra contributions are not part of the employees' formal job responsibilities. Employees who exhibit high levels of OCB are also more likely to remain with an organization, whereas those who exhibit low levels of OCB are more likely to leave a company (e.g., Orr, Sackett, & Mercer, 1989). Having said this, we must add that research does *not* suggest people engage in OCB simply because it may increase their salary or earn them a promotion. The causes of OCB are considerably more complex.

Causes of Organizational Citizenship Behavior. Because OCBs have been shown to be important for organizations and the employees who work for them, there has been extensive research directed at identifying the potential predictors of OCB. Perhaps the most comprehensive summary of the variables that might cause people to engage in OCB was provided by Organ and Ryan (1995). They examined the results of a large number of studies that investigated when people engage in OCB and then statistically combined the results of these studies (a technique known as *meta-analysis*) to identify some likely causes of this behavior. One of the best predictors was job attitudes, and one of the major job attitudes found to be related to OCB was satisfaction. Not surprisingly, employees who are more satisfied with their jobs are also more likely to engage in both kinds of OCB (that is, Altruism and Conscientiousness) than employees who are dissatisfied with their jobs (Organ & Ryan, 1995).

One possible explanation for this relationship is based on the notion of *reciprocity*, or the tendency to respond in kind when receiving some resource from another person or group (see chap. 2). This social norm was also discussed in chapter 4, when we addressed why someone might engage in interpersonal helping. In the context of a job, workers may receive some type of reward, such as a raise or complimentary "pat on the back" from their supervisors. However, because of the nature of their job, the workers may not always be able to reciprocate in terms of increased productivity or other forms of task-related performance, but they can engage in OCB as an alternative way of reciprocation. They are able to respond to the gesture made by their supervisor by responding with a gesture that benefits the organization.

Another variable that appears to be consistently related to OCB is *organizational commitment* (Moorman, Niehoff, & Organ, 1997; Organ & Ryan, 1995; Wagner & Rush, 2000; Williams & Anderson, 1991). For example, Vigoda (1999) reported a significant relationship between the commitment of Israeli public health employees to their jobs and their tendency to engage in OCB within the organization. Interestingly, organizational commitment is also associated with long-term volunteering (Grube & Piliavin, 2000; Penner & Finkelstein, 1998).

Organizational justice is another variable that appears to be related to OCB (e.g., Konovsky & Organ, 1996; Organ & Ryan, 1995; Skarlicki & Latham, 1996). The term *organizational justice* concerns the extent to which workers believe that they are being treated fairly by the organization. Organizational justice has two components: distributive justice, which refers to a person's perceptions of the fairness of outcomes he or she receives, and procedural justice, which refers to the fairness of the procedures used to determine those outcomes (e.g., Meyer, 1997; Thibaut & Walker, 1975). A number of studies have found that as employee perceptions of fairness increase, so does their tendency to engage in OCB. One suggested explanation for the positive association between employee perceptions of organizational justice and OCB is another theory discussed in earlier chapters, equity theory (e.g., Adams, 1965; Walster, Walster, & Bersheid, 1978). Recall that the basic premise of this theory is that people expect fairness in their dealings with others. In general, individuals see interactions as fair or equitable if the relationship between their contributions and their outcomes is roughly proportional to the contribution–outcome relationship of others. From the perspective of workers, if their outcomes exceed their contributions to the job, and equity cannot be restored by working harder or faster, then engaging in OCB is a reasonable way to restore equity in the relationship (Organ, 1990; Organ & Konovsky, 1989).

A field experiment by Skarlicki and Latham (1996) found support for this explanation of OCB. In their study, one group of union leaders received training in the effective implementation of organizational justice principles on the job, while another group of leaders did not receive this training. Skarlicki and Latham later collected self-reports of perceived leader fairness from workers of both groups, as well as peer ratings of the amount of OCB the workers displayed. The leaders who had received the organizational justice training were perceived by their subordinates as being fairer when compared to leaders who had not received the justice training. In addition, peer ratings of the workers' OCB were higher in the groups with justice-trained leaders.

In addition to the organizational variables already described, other research has found that the quality of the relationships between leaders and their subordinates can also have an effect on OCB. High-quality, positive interactions between supervisors and subordinates are associated with OCB (e.g., Deluga, 1998; Settoon, Bennet, & Liden, 1996; Wayne & Green, 1993). Equity theory has also been proposed as an explanation of this relationship. Specifically, workers who receive certain advantages from their supervisor (e.g., valued promotions, increased freedom regarding work tasks, career development support) will comply in return with the supervisor's expectations and may reciprocate by performing voluntary OCBs that benefit the supervisor and/or the organization (Deluga, 1998).

Finally, some researchers have also suggested that personality may play a role in OCB (Borman & Motowidlo, 1993; Borman, Penner, Allen, & Motowidlo, 2001; Organ, 1997). However, we defer a discussion of this possibility until chapter 7, when we discuss the personal attributes of people who consistently act prosocially.

Maintenance of Organizational Citizenship Behavior. Given that an organization (and its employees) typically gains from high levels of OCB, it seems reasonable to ask how this kind of behavior can be maintained over a long period of time. Penner and his associates (e.g., Connell & Penner, 2004; Finkelstein & Penner, 2004; Penner et al., 1997; Rioux & Penner, 2001) investigated whether the models of sustained volunteerism discussed earlier could be applied to organizational citizenship behavior (Borman & Penner, 2001).

For example, Rioux and Penner (2001) modeled Snyder's strategy of using a functional analysis to understand volunteering (e.g., Clary & Snyder, 1991; Omoto & Snyder, 1995, 2002; Snyder et al., 2000) in their attempt to understand the functions that OCB might play for employees. First, they identified the motives that might lead a person to engage in OCB. One of these was called Prosocial Values, which describes OCB motivated by a desire to help others and be accepted by them. A second motive was Organizational Concern, or engaging in OCB due to positive feelings held about the organization. The final motive was called Impression Management and describes OCB that is motivated by a desire to avoid negative evaluation by others or to gain material rewards. Rioux and Penner administered a scale that measured each of these three motives to a group of municipal employees. In addition, they obtained self, peer, and supervisor ratings of the extent to which the employees displayed behaviors that represented the Altruism and Conscientiousness dimensions of OCB. They found the Prosocial Values motive was shown to correlate most strongly with the Altruism dimension, whereas the Organizational Concern motive was shown to correlate most strongly with the Conscientiousness dimension. Thus, it is possible that motives specific to organizational settings may play an important role in the prediction of this type of prosocial behavior. More recent work by Connell and Penner (2004) found additional support for the notion that there are organizational motives that play an important role in OCB. In this study, they found that motives may explain why organizational commitment and procedural justice lead to OCB. For example, it appears that it is a person's commitment to an organization that activates the organizational concern motive, and it is this motive that directly leads to OCB.

Turning to role identity, Finkelstein and Penner (2004) and Krueger (2004) both measured an organizational citizen role identity and correlated this factor with independent ratings of employees' levels of OCB. In both studies, the researchers found significant correlations between self-reported role identity and the amount of OCB people displayed. More specifically, Krueger found that antecedents such as organizational justice motives correlated with employees' organizational citizen role identity, which in turn was correlated with how much OCB employees displayed. Thus, as was the case with volunteering, role identity appears to be a direct cause of OCB.

In some ways, the occurrence of OCBs depends on individuals feeling that they are being treated fairly and equitably by the organization in which they are employed and identifying themselves as part of that larger institution. In addition, as we have suggested, the tangible benefits realized by an individual by being a "team player" in an organization can be significant (e.g., pay raises, promotions), and, as we show in chapter 8, cooperative efforts in which people are willing to make some small personal sacrifices for the collective well-being of the group can benefit everyone. But it is also true that there are instances when individuals may be moved to action because their sense of institutional fairness or the validity of organizational citizen identity is threatened. To resolve discrepancies between the ideal and the reality of one's circumstances, the individual may be motivated to take some sort of personal corrective action, and principled organizational dissent may be the result.

Principled Organizational Dissent

Principled organizational dissent (POD) was defined by Graham (1986) as "the effort by individuals in the workplace to protest and/or to change the organizational status quo because of their conscientious objection to current policy or practice ... which violates [a] standard of justice, honesty, or economy" (p. 1). Behaviors that can be considered kinds of POD are resigning in protest, reporting incidents to interested parties inside or outside the organization (i.e., whistle blowing), engaging in collective actions that block the organization (e.g., "sickouts"), or attempting to change current organizational policies or practices. POD has, we have already noted, many attributes that make it similar to OCB. However, the attributes differ in one very important respect. Although OCB can be seen as part of an attempt to help an organization reach some goal, POD usually involves an individual's attempt to stop the company from reaching some inappropriate goal or at least to dramatically change the way the company tries to reach that goal.

Of course, not everyone would agree that POD is a prosocial action, but we have included it in this chapter because it can play an important role in identifying illegal, immoral, or unprincipled behavior and stimulating constructive organizational change. If these outcomes occur, the company's reputation will improve, and, perhaps more importantly, POD may cause people outside the organization to become aware of the company's inappropriate acts (VanDyne, Cummings, & Parks, 1995). Although painful, costly, and difficult in the short term, in the long run dealing with internal problems raised by POD may be in the organization's best interest. Principled actions may benefit the people who work for or deal directly with the organization or society in general.

These social benefits can easily be seen in the cases of three "whistle blowers" profiled by *Time* magazine in 2002 when they were named the magazine's "persons of the year." One of them, Cynthia Cooper, publicly pointed out the accounting irregularities at Worldcom, a large telecommunication company. This action by Cooper resulted in the indictments of the president of the company and several other high-level executives. Another woman, Sherron Watkins, tried to stop the elaborate accounting schemes that Enron was using to make itself appear more profitable than it actually was. Despite her efforts, the schemes continued until state and federal agencies stopped Enron from engaging in them and indicted several top-level Enron executives. Watkins's internal memos were discovered in the course of the investigations by the various agencies. And as we have already discussed, Coleen Rowley tried without apparent success to get the FBI to improve its antiterrorism efforts prior to the tragedy of 9/11. It is important to note that none of these women was simply an unhappy employee or looking to make a name for herself. Each claimed to love the organizations for which she worked, and each initially tried to achieve the changes through private communications within the organizations. It was only when these efforts were rebuffed or their attempts were disclosed to the media that these women became public figures.

Causes of Principled Organizational Dissent. What do we know about the determinants of POD? Organizational factors seem to carry more weight than personality factors. The climate of the organization, and particularly its openness to constructive self-criticism, is very important. Variables that have been identified as predictors of such challenging behaviors include value congruence with top managers, organizational climates that support speaking out, the existence of formal dissent procedures, reward structures for reporting problems, and the responsiveness of the organization to complaints. If workers believe their supervisor really wants to know when improprieties are occurring (value congruence) and if there are norms in the organization that support attempts to do things right, individuals may believe that such reporting will be valued, will not be punished, and may lead to beneficial changes. Similarly, if there are publicly available procedures to follow if an employee wants to report a problem, if there are rewards for suggestions and complaints, and if there is some past history that the organization has responded positively to workers' suggestions, a worker may feel more confident to file a complaint. However, for the most part, incidents are not reported, and if they are, the consequences can sometimes be negative for the complainant, occasionally including job loss or transfer (Bergman et al., 2002; Loy & Stewart, 1984; Schneider, Swan, & Fitzgerald, 1997).

VanDyne et al. (1995) suggested that whistle blowing and POD may result "when an employee feels as though he/she has allegiances to a higher cause or more important set of values" (p. 262). One mechanism for identifying with a higher cause may be emphasizing membership in one's professional group. That is, Breakwell (1986) suggested that a person's feeling about losing membership in one organization (i.e., one's employer) may be compensated for by finding other, more accepted memberships. The concept of role identity might be useful here. An employee is likely to have adopted a role identity as a member of his or her organization, or what is sometimes referred to as "organizational identification." We mentioned earlier that a specific role identity as a "volunteer for the American Cancer Society" predicted the number of hours worked for that organization and a lowered likelihood of quitting. Those with a stronger general role identity as a "volunteer," however, gave more hours to other organizations as well. For a potential organizational dissenter, there can be a conflict between an organizational identity, which argues against "blowing the whistle" that might harm one's employer, and some other identity as a professional (e.g., accountant, attorney, psychologist, physician) whose profession has standards that may override the specific organizational identity. We may be seeing evidence of this organization versus profession conflict in the fact that a large percentage of whistle blowers have been accountants, a field that has a strong code of ethics (and severe legal consequences for violating it).

Piliavin and her associates (J. A. Piliavin & Grube, 2001; J. A. Piliavin, Callero, & Grube, 2002) actually examined how conflicting role identities might influence POD. They discussed how the role identity construct might be used to understand when members of organizations will and will not confront the organization. J. A. Piliavin and Grube (2001) conducted a study of one specific type of POD—reporting by nurses of unsafe medical practices. Reporting errors so that better care can be provided is consistent with the very core of a professional nurse's identity. The profession's code of ethics states, "The nurse acts to safeguard the client and the public when health care and safety are affected by the incompetent, unethical, or illegal practice of any person" (American Nurses Association, 1985, p. 1). The nurse identity might serve the role of "a higher set of values." That is, nurses with a strong role identity as a "nurse" might be more likely to report any mistakes that are observed.

Piliavin and Grube found that role identity alone did not predict reporting of unsafe practices, but they did find that reporting was higher among nurses who had a strong role identity when the number of observed errors was high. Perceived congruence of values between the nurse and her supervisor was also a significant factor in reporting. Finally, nurses who felt valued by the organization *and* had a personality characteristic Piliavin and Grube labeled as "advocacy" were the most likely to report errors.

Volunteering, community activism, and OCB are almost always strongly encouraged and praised because they are intended to improve the well-being of individuals and organizations. POD and whistle blowing are different matters. Whistle blowers usually are shunned by their coworkers, lose their jobs more than half the time, and may be threatened with physical harm; it is rumored that some have even been killed (Greenberger, Miceli, & Cohen, 1987; Jos, Tompkins, & Hays, 1989).

The story of Jeffrey Wigand provides a dramatic example of what can happen to a whistle blower. Jeffrey Wigand was a biochemist who worked for a large tobacco company in the late 1980s, hoping to create a safer cigarette for smokers around the world. The project was dropped, but Wigand was forced to sign a confidentiality agreement not to disclose what he had learned and knew about the dangers of tobacco smoke. When Wigand saw tobacco executives testify to Congress in 1994 that nicotine was not addictive, it convinced him to start talking to the Food and Drug Administration (FDA). Wigand helped the FDA secure thousands of pages of evidence that nicotine was, in fact, addictive.

Wigand paid a great price, however, for blowing the whistle on his employers. He lost his $300,000-a-year job and any chance to be hired as a high-level researcher by any other tobacco company. He was publicly labeled a liar by representatives of the tobacco industry and received death threats. Three years after he went to the FDA, he was teaching high school science and living on $30,000 a year. Industry-paid detectives followed him constantly, and he was facing a lawsuit from his former employer, Brown & Williamson, for breaking the confidentiality agreement. It was only when magazine articles and a film (*The Insider*) about Wigand's ordeal appeared that he was publicly vindicated and labeled a hero (*Frontline*, 2001).

We have now described four types of long-term and planned prosocial behavior that typically occur through or within organizations. Community activists and volunteers contribute to the welfare of others by creating or contributing to organizations. OCB and POD are informal prosocial actions by employees of organizations to help others in the organization, to benefit the organization, or to prevent the organization from doing harm to others. In discussing these types of long-term, planned helping, we have shifted the focus of our consideration of prosocial behavior from the interpersonal helping discussed in the earlier chapters to organizational helping, in which the acts of individuals are coordinated by an organization to benefit large, often unseen groups of people in need. As we indicated in the introduction to this chapter, however, there is one other kind of helping that also deserves to be recognized. Although this final class of helping involves interpersonal helping, the fact that it often takes place over an extended period of time, is not necessarily given in response to an emergency, and may be seen as part of the helper's occupational role makes it more consistent with the class of organizational helping than with helping given as an emergency intervention. Therefore, we now turn our attention to informal helping.

INFORMAL HELPERS

There are many occupations that are organized around providing help to others: firefighters, police officers, social workers, clinical psychologists, and medical personnel. These individuals make their living helping others solve their problems, and they typically have formal training that allows them to handle problems effectively in their areas of expertise.

However, members of these formal helping professions provide only a small percentage of the help that is ultimately given to those in need. As we have seen in this and the two preceding chapters, most help is provided by untrained helpers. Between the untrained helpers who respond to emergencies and volunteer their assistance to charitable organizations and the professional helpers is an often overlooked class of helpers.

These people have occupations not normally defined as helping professions, but they are involved in one-on-one contact with clients on a regular basis. Because the people in these jobs are exposed to needs these clients have, they sometimes become *informal* helpers. There is research from both the United States and Germany concerning such "job-related helpers": taxi drivers, beauticians, masseurs, bartenders, even mail carriers, meter readers, and sales personnel. According to Nestmann (1991), many people in these jobs engage in helping behavior that is not formally part of their jobs, but that comes about in the performance of their occupational roles. It might even be considered a special type of OCB, except it is the clients and not other workers or the organization who are being helped. Listening and social support are most of what is being provided by these individuals, but the help may also involve just checking on the safety of a client, such as when a mail carrier notices that letters have not been taken from an elderly patron's mailbox and calls the authorities.

Emory Cowen (1982) and his colleagues used both face-to-face interviews and questionnaires to find out about informal helping by hairdressers, lawyers, industrial foremen, and bartenders. Hairdressers reported an average of 25 minutes of conversation with their customers and said that about a third of the customers discussed "moderate" to "serious" problems with them. Although Cowen's sample of lawyers worked on a very small number of family cases (i.e., divorce, custody), the lawyers reported that there were extensive discussions of the clients' personal problems in about 40% of their cases.

The topics discussed were broadest among bartenders and hairdressers; lawyers dealt primarily with problems and consequences of divorce, and foremen talked mainly about work and career difficulties (see Table 5.2). Nevertheless, in all four occupations, informal helpers consistently and repeatedly gave emotional support and provided active advice and help-giving as a consequence of the nature of their jobs.

Nestmann (1991) also reported an extensive study of informal helping among taxi drivers, hairdressers, bartenders, and masseurs. More than 95% of those interviewed reported either having clients mention problems or having provided help or support to them. In addition to surveys and interviews, Nestmann's data included direct observations of helping exchanges between these informal helpers and their clients and analyses of the conversations that took place. For example, one

TABLE 5.2
Most Frequently Heard Problems
for Four Job-Related Helping Professions

Rank	Bartenders	Lawyers	Supervisors	Hairdressers
1	Jobs	Anger with spouse	Problems with fellow workers	Difficulties with children
2	Marital Problems	Depression	Opportunities for advancement	Physical health
3	Finances	Managing contact with spouse	Dissatisfaction with job	Marital problems
4	Sex	Difficulties with children	Finances	Depression
5	Depression	Emotional/ psychological	Difficulties with children; and physical health	Anxiety

Note. Adapted from Cowen (1982, p. 369), with permission.

source of data was a month-long daily record of interactions in a "corner bar," and another was a set of 60 recorded conversations with taxi drivers and their fares. These covert, direct observations corroborated the self-report data, finding frequent mention of problems by customers and supportive responses from the workers. Some of the informal helpers interviewed even mentioned trying to elicit problems from regular customers whom they observed to be upset or "down." As Nestmann (1991) stated, "Everyday helpers are not restricted to reactive behavior, but also can stimulate and undertake help processes actively and on their own initiative" (p. 234).

These examples of informal helpers serve to underscore the point made several times in this section: It may be where people are in the social structure as much as who they are as individuals that affects their participation in both formal and informal helping activities.

THE ANSWER: SUMMARY AND IMPLICATIONS

We opened this chapter by explaining our intention to distinguish among different types of planned and long-term helping. Community activism relates to recognizing a need among groups within a community and mobilizing people to create structures and organizations to serve these groups. Volunteering involves giving freely of your time, efforts, resources, or, in the case of blood donation, yourself, to help others. People frequently volunteer through organizations specifically founded to help others or through broader organizations (e.g., churches) that encompass assisting others in need as part of their mission. Organizational citizenship behavior (OCB) and principled organizational dissent (POD) are prosocial actions by employees within an organization. Although OCBs are actions not specifically prescribed by one's position that directly benefit the welfare of others in the organization or help the organization as a whole, POD is an intervention to benefit others generally by preventing the organization from doing social harm or acting contrary to the best interests of others. Informal helping is actions taken by people whose occupations place them in a position to help others, but these actions extend beyond the specific responsibilities of the job.

We posed two basic questions at the beginning of this chapter. The first was: What factors initially lead people to engage in planned, long-term helping? The second question was: What sustains these behaviors? With respect to the first question, the decision to initiate long-term prosocial behavior is related to the same factors shaping short-term, spontaneous helping. This should not be too surprising. The first time the action takes place, it is not yet a long-term behavior. As we discussed in chapter 3, one of the most important elements both in spontaneous and long-term helping is recognition that an individual or a group of people is in need. Clarity and degree of the perceived need of others are important contextual factors for both classes of prosocial behavior.

An emotional reaction to others' situation is a second critical element. In chapter 4 we examined how empathy experienced as personal distress, upset, or empathic concern motivates spontaneous incidental and emergency helping. For planned helping, which often involves a more complex assessment of the situation, other emotions may be involved. For instance, people may experience anger in response to perceived injustice, which then stimulates action, such as community activism or principled organizational dissent. In addition, because planned prosocial behavior often takes more time to formulate and execute, emotional reactions play less of a role than in situations, such as emergencies, requiring immediate assistance.

Although individual differences are important for all types of helping, demographic factors and personal characteristics are particularly associated with variations in long-term, planned helping. Perhaps because of the investment involved, people weigh the costs and benefits heavily in their decisions. The balance is quite a bit different among people who have more free time or more money to give. In addition, in spontaneous nonemergency and emergency helping situations, bystanders are essentially amateurs and time to act is typically more important than skill in executing the actions. In contrast, in planned, long-term helping, which by definition is less time-sensitive, individual differences in skill and perseverance are much more important.

Because the activity associated with planned, long-term helping competes with a range of other responsibilities and interests over time, basic values, principles, motivations, and goals are critical for determining the priority of these helping activities in people's lives. Prosocial activities that are more functional in meeting one's needs, achieving one's goals, or meeting one's standards will be more likely to be engaged in and engaged in more frequently. Some behaviors, such as OCBs, may be strategic behaviors based on a desire for personal advancement. Other behaviors, such as volunteering time, may fulfill one's need for personal meaning or allow a person to express humanistic values.

One key aspect of planned, long-term helping that distinguishes it from spontaneous helping is its repetitive nature. The situation providing the opportunity happens over and over. This brings us to the second question we posed, about the factors that sustain these types of helping. In general, the consequences of these actions are the most important factor. These consequences can be quite immediate, such as feeling faint after giving blood or experiencing a sense of satisfaction. Positive experience increases the likelihood that people will engage in the behavior, whereas negative experiences reduce the likelihood.

The consequences of engaging in these behaviors, however, can be more gradual and long-term. As models of volunteering and blood donation indicate, behaving in these ways can become an integral part of an individual's identity. People see themselves not simply as helpful, but as a particular type of helper, such as a blood donor or as a volunteer for the homeless. They also develop valued social networks in these roles, and volunteering becomes embedded in their social life.

In conclusion, research on planned, long-term helping frames prosocial behavior in a quite different way than does the work on emergency intervention that stimulated so much research beginning in the 1960s. The Kitty Genovese incident, introduced in chapter 1 and described in more detail in chapters 3 and 4, led to the view that people were generally apathetic and unhelpful. The work on planned, long-term helping highlights the enormous generosity of others in everyday life. People give significantly to others whom they may never meet. And this type of helping becomes part of who we are. Despite these two seemingly contradictory perspectives, both lines of research produce similar conclusions about prosocial behavior. The decision to help is determined by contextual factors, emotional reactions, social motivations, and personal attributes and skills. The weight given to these factors may vary with different types of helping situations, but they are all important to understanding the dynamics of prosocial behavior—why people help initially and why they may choose to continue helping.

CHAPTER 6

The Development of Prosocial Behavior

I n chapter 2, we addressed the question of whether or not there is a genetic or biological basis for prosocial actions. As part of the discussion of this issue, we presented studies that examined the behavior of infants and toddlers. These studies provided impressive evidence that at least the antecedents of prosocial behaviors are present at a very early stage of life. For example, 1-day-old infants become upset when they hear other infants cry, and children who are 1 or 2 years old clearly display empathic reactions to others who are in distress.

As we discussed in chapter 4, empathy plays a very important role in helping. But do infants, children, and adults experience empathy in the same way? There may be very basic and substantial differences between what motivates infants and toddlers to help another person and what motivates adults. Among very young children, helping is usually under the control of external and tangible rewards, such as a smile or praise from a parent. This is not necessarily the case among adults; as we discussed in chapter 4, adults are much more likely to help because of internal and intangible influences, such as their feelings, standards about the importance of helping, or concern about the welfare of another person. In this chapter, we explore how helping and prosocial thoughts and feelings change as people develop, and some of the reasons why these changes occur.

THE QUESTION

The central questions in this chapter are: (a) How do helping and other aspects of prosocial behavior change as humans mature? (b) What processes are responsible for the developmental changes that influence helping and altruistic behaviors? (c) How do these processes affect the behaviors of adults? To answer the first question, psychologists conduct *cross-sectional* studies that look at the responses of *different* people of different ages and *longitudinal* studies that examine the responses of *the same* people over time as they age. These two strategies provide key information about age-related changes in the factors that motivate people to help, the way people think about helping, and how people engage in helpful and altruistic behaviors.

Turning to the second question, most researchers who study developmental trends in prosocial behavior believe that there are two interrelated processes responsible for the changes that occur. One of these processes involves natural maturational changes in certain cognitive skills and abilities. Researchers who study these changes focus on the ways that people think about themselves and the people around them. As children mature, there are substantial changes in the manner in which they think about helping, and these changes appear to be part of broader developmental transformations in cognitive skills and abilities. Just as people's physical characteristics (e.g., height, weight) change as they mature, changes also occur in the way they think about the causes of their own actions and of other people's behavior, in their feelings of responsibilities for others, and in their beliefs about what is "right" and what is "wrong." Thus cognitive maturation plays an important role in the development of helpful and altruistic behaviors.

The other explanation of the changes in prosocial thoughts and actions involves learning processes. Speaking very broadly, this approach to developmental changes argues that as people mature, their own experiences and the things they learn from others teach them to value being prosocial and to enjoy doing things that benefit others (Grusec, Davidov, & Lundell, 2002). These learning processes primarily involve what we learn from others and are usually referred to as the socialization process, or just *socialization*. As children grow up, they learn new behaviors, what other people expect of them, and that these expectations differ for men and women and change as they move from childhood to adolescence to adulthood and finally old age.

Of course, maturational changes in cognitive processes and learning experiences do not occur independently of one another. In fact, they typically combine and interact to produce the many changes in helping that are the focus of this chapter. Therefore, wherever possible, we discuss how the two processes jointly affect the development of helping and altruism.

This brings us to the third question in the chapter: How do biological factors and socialization interact to shape our prosocial behavior as adults? We address this question primarily by examining differences in the thoughts, feelings, and behavior of men and women. There are, as you know, substantial biological differences between men and women. But there are also substantial differences in how males and females are socialized—what they are taught and what others expect of them. These differences are manifested in male–female differences in helping and other prosocial actions.

In the first section of the chapter, we describe developmental changes in humans' prosocial thoughts and actions. We examine how people change with regard to what motivates them to help and how they make decisions about when and why they should help. In the next section, we examine the processes that are believed to be responsible for developmental changes in helping. Specifically, we discuss the kinds of cognitive development and learning experiences that appear to be responsible for these changes. Although most of the chapter focuses on developmental changes in children, humans change and develop throughout their entire lives. Thus, in the final sections we briefly consider prosocial actions among elderly people, and, as already noted, how developmental processes discussed in the chapter produce differences in the ways mature men and women provide help to others.

DEVELOPMENTAL CHANGES IN PROSOCIAL THOUGHTS AND ACTIONS

It is generally agreed that as children grow up different factors motivate them to help others. There are several models that describe these changes in children's motivations to help. Two of the more widely accepted ones are Robert Cialdini's socialization model (Cialdini & Kenrick, 1976; Cialdini, Kenrick, & Baumann, 1982) and Daniel Bar-Tal's (1982) cognitive learning model.

Cialdini's Socialization Model

According to Cialdini et al. (1982), as children mature, they go through three stages related to helping. In the *presocialization* stage, children are not aware that other people value and reinforce helping; they will help if asked or ordered to do so, but helping itself has no positive associations for children in this developmental stage. In the second stage, called *awareness*, children learn that the society in which they live desires and values helpfulness from its members. They become aware of and sensitive to social norms about prosocial behaviors. Children in this stage may initiate acts of helping, but such acts are motivated primarily by desires to please the adults who are present or by attempts to comply with norms about helping. Cialdini et al. (1982) estimated that the transition from the first stage to the second stage typically occurs when a child is 10 to 12 years old. By the time most children are 15 or 16 years old, they will have moved into the third and final stage of the socialization of helping, *internalization*. In this stage, helping is intrinsically satisfying and can actually make a person feel good. The external norms that motivated helping during the awareness stage have been internalized. Thus, as children get older, their motivations to help shift from entirely external to internal.

These developmental changes are illustrated in a study by Froming, Allen, and Jensen (1985). These researchers looked at how children who were in the presocialization or the awareness stage reacted to the presence of an adult who could evaluate them. They found that among children in the presocialization stage, the presence of the evaluative adult had no influence on how much they donated to a charity, but the adult's presence significantly increased donations among children in the awareness stage. Froming et al. explained these results by proposing that because the younger children had not yet learned that adults value helping and expect others to be helpful, there was no reason for the younger children to increase how much they helped in the presence of an adult. However, the older children had learned about the social norms for helping and how adults feel about compliance to those norms, and therefore the adult's presence motivated children in the awareness stage to be more helpful.

In another experiment concerned with motives for helping, Cialdini and Kenrick (1976) used the concept of negative state relief (see chap. 4) to test their socialization model. Recall that the negative state relief model proposes that adults who are sad are particularly motivated to help when they believe that the reward of helping will alleviate their negative mood. Relating this to developmental changes in motivations for helping, Cialdini and Kenrick investigated whether sadness would have this effect on helping among young children who had not yet learned that helping is rewarding.

There were three groups of participants in this study: 6- to 8-year-old children, preteens (10 to 12 years old), and adolescents (15 to 18 years old). Within each age group, half of the participants were asked to think about something sad from their past (e.g., the loss of a favorite pet), whereas the other half of the participants were told to think about a neutral past experience. This manipulation produced a negative or sad mood in the former group but not in the latter group. All participants were then presented with an opportunity to help other students anonymously by giving them some coupons (redeemable for prizes) the participants had previously won in a game. The number of coupons that each person donated was discreetly measured by the researchers.

Cialdini and Kenrick reasoned that most of the youngest children would be in the presocialization stage, and it was unlikely that they would intrinsically value helping or believe that helping would make them feel better. Thus, young children in the sad mood condition would not be more motivated to help than those in the neutral condition. In fact, giving away something they had won would probably make them feel even worse. As a result, children in the sad condition were expected to help less than those in the neutral condition. This difference would be much less among the 10- to 12-year-olds (preteens), because at least some of them had begun to learn that helping others could actually make them feel better. Finally, because most of the 15- to 18-year-olds would have presumably reached the internalization stage, they would value helping and recognize the reinforcing effects that could be realized by helping someone else. Adolescents in the sad mood condition could thus use helping to reduce their negative mood. Therefore, they were expected to help more than those in the neutral condition.

These predictions were confirmed. Among the youngest children, those in the sad mood condition donated less than half as many coupons as did those in the neutral mood condition. The preteens helped about equally in the two conditions. But among the late adolescents, those in the sad condition donated *more than four times* as many coupons as did those in the neutral condition. It is important to note that Cialdini and Kenrick believed that these developmental changes were due to learning and socialization experiences rather than some biologically based maturational process. In addition, they recognize that not all children will go through the stages at the same time; the rate at which children move through the stages depends on their learning experiences and their culture (Fiske, 1991). Indeed, some people may never reach the third stage.

Bar-Tal's Cognitive Learning Model

Social and developmental psychologists are sometimes criticized because they seem to use only one method—experiments—to study what they are interested in and because they often restrict their research subjects to people from the United States (or at least North America). Critics argue that one cannot be sure whether the same kind of results would be obtained if different methods of collecting data were employed or if different groups of people from different cultures were studied. Fortunately, this is not the case for developmental models of changes in helping. Other researchers, using different methods and studying children from other countries, have reached very similar conclusions about how children change as they mature.

We see this in the developmental model proposed by Daniel Bar-Tal, an Israeli psychologist. Bar-Tal based his model on observations of how children of different ages responded to different kinds of requests to help another child. The procedures used by Bar-Tal and his colleagues can be illustrated by one of the studies they conducted on helping among school children in Israel (Bar-Tal, Raviv, & Leiser, 1980).

In this study, pairs of children 4½ to 9½ years old played a game. One of the children was designated, on a random basis, as the "winner" and received several pieces of candy as a prize. The adult who gave out the prize then left the two children alone, with no instructions about sharing the candy. Unknown to the children, they were observed for the next few minutes. If, during this time, the winner had not shared some of the candy, the experimenter returned, read a story about sharing, and left the room again. Three minutes later, children who had still not shared the candy were told that their teacher would probably give an important part in a school play to a child who shared his or her candy. The child was given another chance to share, but if this again did not happen, the child with the candy was explicitly told to share it with the other child. If the child still did not comply, the experimenter repeated the request and offered the child a big additional prize for sharing. Note that the consequences for sharing became progressively more external and tangible.

The question Bar-Tal and his colleagues asked was, would children of different ages react differently to the requests? As you might expect, they did. In general, the older the children, the less external and tangible an inducement was needed to get them to share. For example, 38% of the oldest children had shared by the second phase of the study (hearing a story about helping), but only 7% of the youngest children had shared by then. Findings such as these led Bar-Tal (1982) to propose a stage model of helping much like that of Cialdini and his associates.

Bar-Tal's model proposes that as children mature, the things that motivate them to help others change. He argued that helping among very young children is usually motivated by the promise of a specific reward or the threat of a specific punishment. Without such rewards, there will be little or no helping. Like Cialdini, Bar-Tal (1982) believed that later in childhood, helping might also be motivated by a desire to receive the approval and praise of others. As children move into adolescence, these egocentric motivations for helping begin to be replaced by the final kind of motivation in Bar-Tal's model—altruism. In this stage, the person helps "out of a moral conviction in justice, ... [and may experience] self-satisfaction or raised self-esteem" (p. 110).

Table 6.1 presents the major stages in Cialdini's and Bar-Tal's models of the developmental changes in the motivation to help. We present these models side-by-side to provide a clear illustration that, despite the differences in their methods and the countries in which their studies were conducted, these researchers arrived at a very similar view of the developmental changes in prosocial behavior. They each propose that as children mature, helping changes from an action that occurs because it produces some external, concrete benefit for the helper to an action taken because it makes the helper feel better or because it benefits another person.

Although the models of Cialdini and Bar-Tal emphasize the role of feelings in developmental changes in helping, other approaches focus on changes in the way that children think about situations in which others need assistance. These approaches look at the process of moral reasoning.

Moral Reasoning

Developmental psychologists have long been interested in how children reason or think about themselves and the world around them. Although they may disagree in their theories of specific reasoning processes, developmental psychologists generally agree on this point: Children reason differently from adults and, as they grow up, the way they reason changes. One area of children's reasoning that has attracted considerable interest and attention from psychologists over the years is how they reach decisions about what is the "right" way to act and what is the "wrong" way. The study of *moral reasoning* concerns the principles people use when they make such a decision. Most developmental psychologists believe that children pass through several levels or stages of moral reasoning as they mature. At each level, the principles or criteria on which they base their moral judgments are qualitatively different. The best known model of the development of general moral reasoning is the one proposed by Lawrence Kohlberg (1985; Colby & Kohlberg, 1987).

TABLE 6.1
**The Cialdini et al. and Bar-Tal's Models
of the Development of Prosocial Behavior**

Cialdini et al.	*Bar-Tal*
Stage I. Presocialization: Individuals are unsocialized about helping and rarely act altruistically because it involves a loss of resources.	Phase I. Compliance—concrete: Individuals help because they have been ordered to do so, with explicit threat of punishment.
	Phase 2. Compliance: Individuals help if an authority requests them to do so. The threat of actual punishment is no longer needed.
Stage 2. Awareness of norms: Individuals help because they have learned that people expect them to help and may punish them if they do not. They are concerned about social approval.	Phase 3. Internal initiative—concrete: Individuals help because they expect a tangible award.
	Phase 4. Normative behavior: Individuals help because they know norms about helping and are concerned about social approval.
	Phase 5. Generalized reciprocity: Individuals help because they believe that the recipient would and should reciprocate.
Stage 3. Internalization: Individuals help because it makes them feel better.	Phase 6. Altruistic behavior: Individuals help because they want to benefit the other person, Helping increases their self-esteem and satisfaction.

Note. Adapted from Bar-Tal and Raviv (1982) and from Cialdini et al. (1982).

Kohlberg's Model. As part of the development of his model, Kohlberg presented people with what he called "moral dilemmas" and recorded the ways in which they resolved them. Here is one of the dilemmas people had to consider: A man's wife will die unless she receives an expensive drug. He has scraped together much of the money needed to buy the drug, but he does not have enough, and the pharmacist refuses to give him the drug. In desperation, the man later breaks into the pharmacy and steals the drug. Is the man's action right or wrong? Why?

People's responses to these dilemmas led Kohlberg to propose that there are three separate levels of moral development, and within each level there are two distinct, sequential stages. Each successive level and stage represents more mature and sophisticated kinds of moral reasoning. It is important to recognize that classifying people into the levels of moral development is not based on whether the person saw the protagonist's action in the moral dilemmas as being "right" or "wrong" but rather on the *reasoning* that the person offered to justify whatever moral judgment was made. The first level, which Kohlberg called *preconventional morality*, contains two stages or "orientations" toward whether an action is moral or immoral. In the first stage, people's judgments about the morality of their actions are based on fear of punishment. In the second stage of this level, people decide whether something is moral on the basis of whether it provides them with some kind of reward (particularly material rewards).

Kohlberg and his associates used cross-sectional and longitudinal studies to investigate developmental changes in moral reasoning. Until the age of 7 years, most children use this preconventional level of moral reasoning, making their moral decisions almost exclusively in terms of avoiding punishment and gaining rewards from others (i.e., Stages 1 and 2). As children mature, there are changes in the extent to which they reason in this way. After 7, the incidence of preconventional moral reasoning begins to decline, and by midadolescence, many people's judgments about what is "moral" and "immoral" have progressed to the next level of moral reasoning (Colby, Kohlberg, Gibbs & Lieberman, 1983; Kohlberg, 1963). Kohlberg called this level *conventional morality*, and in the first stage of this level (Stage 3), judgments of right and wrong are based on whether the person's actions would win the approval or disapproval of others. In the later stage (Stage 4), these judgments are based on whether an action conforms to society's formal and informal rules and laws (i.e., conventional standards). People have an obligation and duty to obey legitimate authority. The majority of people do not reach Stage 3 before their early teens (Colby et al., 1983); few people display Stage 4 moral reasoning before they are adults, but the majority of adults operate at this stage of moral development.

The highest level of moral reasoning, *postconventional morality*, involves internalized and personal moral standards. In the first stage at this level (Stage 5), moral decisions are based on concerns about the rights and well-being of others; an action that achieves these goals may be seen as being moral even if it challenges certain laws. Individuals at this stage may obey a law that they do not personally believe to be fair and just, but, unlike a person operating at Stage 4 who unquestionably accepts social standards, the Stage 5 individual will work within the social system to try to change that law. In Stage 6, moral decisions are made on the basis of the person's own ethical principles or conscience and reflect a concern for universal justice, even if this contradicts social norms and laws. A person at this stage may engage in nonviolent civil disobedience, believing that his or her personal actions should be governed more by personal conscience and universal ethical principles than by social conventions. Kohlberg considers this highest level to reflect the moral standards of leaders such as Mahatma Gandhi and Dr. Martin Luther King, Jr. The Colby et al. longitudinal study of moral development indicated that few people (less than 10% of the people studied) ever reach Stage 5, and almost no one reaches Stage 6. Similar (but not identical) patterns of moral development were found in Turkey and Israel (Colby & Kohlberg, 1987).

Although many people have used Kohlberg's general model of moral reasoning to explain developmental changes in altruism and helping, Nancy Eisenberg (1982, 1986) suggested that if one is interested in such changes, it may be more appropriate to examine developmental changes in reasoning specifically concerned with prosocial actions. She noted that Kohlberg's model was generated from people's responses to situations in which there was a conflict between some law or rule and the person's own sense of right and wrong; the person had to decide whether he or she should follow or break some rule. To understand developmental changes in helping, we may need to examine children's reasoning when there is a conflict between their own needs and wants and the needs and desires of others. Eisenberg and her associates developed a model that describes such changes. As we present this model, you may notice how closely related it is to the Cialdini and Bar-Tal models of changes in the factors that motivate children to help, incorporating developmental changes in the way children think and feel. This is not a coincidence; Eisenberg believes that a child's prosocial moral reasoning reflects, in part, the child's motives when his or her own needs are in conflict with the needs of others.

Prosocial Moral Reasoning. Eisenberg wanted her model of moral reasoning specifically to address developmental changes in what children think are good and bad reasons *to act prosocially*. To study this process, Eisenberg (previously Eisenberg-Berg) and her colleagues (e.g., Eisenberg-Berg, 1979; Eisenberg-Berg & Neal, 1981; Eisenberg-Berg & Roth, 1980) presented children with prosocial moral dilemmas and asked them what they would do. An example of one such dilemma is:

> A girl named Mary was going to a friend's birthday party. On her way, she saw a girl who had fallen down and hurt her leg. The girl asked Mary to go to her house and get her parents so the parents could take her to the doctor. But if Mary did run and get the child's parents, she would be late for the birthday party and miss the ice cream, cake, and all the games. What should Mary do? Why? (Eisenberg, 1982, p. 231)

In a more recent version of a test for prosocial moral reasoning, the Prosocial Reasoning Objective Measure (Carlo, Eisenberg, & Knight, 1992), children respond to additional dilemmas relating to (a) keeping food after a flood versus giving some to others who are without food, (b) helping children with physical disabilities strengthen their legs by teaching them to swim versus practicing for a swim meet to win prize money for themselves, (c) continuing to stay and play in one's own backyard versus trying to stop a bully who is picking on another child, (d) going to the beach with a friend versus helping a peer to study for a math test, (e) donating blood to a needy other leading to losing time and money at work and school, and (f) helping a peer who is being teased versus risking rejection from others.

The responses from children of different ages to these stories led Eisenberg to propose the developmental model of prosocial moral reasoning presented in Table 6.2. At the most basic developmental stages of her model, judgments about what is right and what is wrong are based on self-centered, pragmatic, and hedonistic concerns. For example, children say that if they help someone, it is because the recipient might help them later or because they are afraid that they would be punished by an adult if they do not help. But as children mature, their judgments become more pragmatic and less hedonistic. They begin to consider the feelings of those in need and the way other people react to helping. For instance, in dilemmas like the one just given describing the girl with the injured leg, children say that they would help because it would make the other child happy or because their parents would be proud of them. In the final stages of the model, prosocial moral reasoning is based largely on the person's sense of obligation to others and concern for their welfare. In these stages, individuals help because helping makes them feel good about themselves and they would think badly of themselves if they did not offer aid.

TABLE 6.2
Stages of Prosocial Moral Reasoning

Stage 1: Hedonistic, pragmatic orientation. The individual is concerned with selfish, pragmatic consequences rather than moral considerations. "Right" behavior is that which is instrumental in satisfying the actor's own needs and wants. Reasons for assisting or not assisting another include consideration of direct gain to self, future reciprocity, and concern for others whom the individual needs and/or likes.

Stage 2: Needs of others orientation. The individual expresses concern for the physical, material, and psychological needs of others even though the other's needs conflict with one's own needs. This concern is expressed in the simplest terms, without clear evidence of role taking, verbal expressions of sympathy, or reference to internalized affect such as guilt ("He's hungry" or "She needs it").

Stage 3: Approval and interpersonal orientation and/or stereotyped orientation. Stereotyped images of good and bad persons and behavior and/or considerations of others' approval and acceptance are used in justifying prosocial or nonhelping behaviors. For example, one helps because "It's nice to help" or "He'd like him more if he helped."

Stage 4a: Empathic orientation. The individual's judgments include evidence of sympathetic responding, role taking, concern for others' humanness and/or guilt or positive affect related to the consequences one's actions. Examples include, "He knows how he feels," "She cares about him," and "I'd feel bad if I didn't help because he'd be in pain."

Stage 4b: Transitional stage. Justifications for helping or not helping involve internalized values, norms, duties, or responsibilities, or refer to the necessity of protecting the rights and dignity of other persons; these ideas, however, are not clearly and strongly stated. References to internalized affect, self-respect, and living up to one's values are considered indicative of this stage if they are weakly stated. Examples include, "It's something I've learned and feel."

Stage 5: Strongly internalized stage. Justifications for helping or not helping are based on internalized values, norms, or responsibilities, the desire to maintain individual and societal contractual obligations, and the belief in the dignity, rights, and equality of all individuals. Positive or negative affects related to the maintenance of self-respect and living up to one's values and accepted norms also characterize this stage. Examples of Stage 5 reasoning include, "She'd feel a responsibility to help other people in need" or "I would feel bad if I didn't help because I'd know that I didn't live up to my values."

Note. Eisenberg (1982), with permission.

Eisenberg and her colleagues demonstrated support for their developmental model in longitudinal studies of prosocial moral reasoning (Eisenberg et al., 1987; Eisenberg, Miller, Shell, McNalley, & Shea, 1991). They found that preschool children engage in a good deal of hedonistic and self-centered moral reasoning, but by the late grade-school years, this kind of reasoning declines and more sophisticated and other-oriented kinds of reasoning increase. When boys reach early adolescence, they may regress to more hedonistic kinds of reasoning, but in late adolescence, both boys and girls began to display the higher level kinds of moral reasoning (i.e., Stages 4 and 5). Thus, the data show that moral reasoning seems to develop pretty much in the manner that Eisenberg originally proposed.

A second and equally important question is whether these changes in moral reasoning are, in fact, related to changes in helping. The relationship is not perfect, but Eisenberg and others have found that as children move toward more mature and sophisticated forms of reasoning about prosocial dilemmas, their propensity to display sympathy and empathy and to spontaneously help others also increases (Eisenberg et al., 1987, 1991; Raviv, Bar-Tal, & Lewis-Levin, 1980). For example, Janssens and Dekovic (1997) reported that prosocial moral reasoning correlates with actual prosocial behavior. Even among children as young as 4–5 years old, level of moral reasoning is positively related to expressions of emotional empathy and prosocial behavior (Miller, Eisenberg, Fabes, & Shell, 1996). Eisenberg and her colleagues (Eisenberg et al., 2002) measured prosocial moral reasoning, self-reported prosocial behavior, and a friend's report of the person's prosocial behavior for the same sample of people at ages 19–20, 21–22, 23–24, and 25–26 years. In general, participants were relatively stable on all three measures across the testing period, and at each age prosocial moral reasoning was positively correlated with self-reported prosocial behaviors (correlations between .39 to .54) and with a friend's report in 2 of the 3 years in which friends' assessments were available (correlations of .39 and .50). Measures of prosocial moral reasoning relate to prosocial behavior consistently across different points in people's lives.

With the exception of Bar-Tal's work, most of the studies that we have presented in this section were conducted in the United States. Would the same patterns of development be found elsewhere in the world? Studies of moral reasoning in different countries suggest that the *content* of prosocial moral reasoning (i.e., the specific kinds of actions that are judged as good or as bad) is probably affected by the culture in which one lives (Miller, 1994). However, the basic *patterns* of changes in what motivates helping and in moral reasoning that are described by the models can be found around the world.

Eisenberg (1992) reported that similar changes in moral reasoning occur in most western countries. For instance, although adolescents in the United States scored higher than adolescents in Brazil on prosocial moral reasoning overall, both groups showed the same age-related developmental trends (Carlo, Koller, Eisenberg, Da Silva, & Frohlich, 1996). In addition, as with previous work in the United States, prosocial moral reasoning was related to prosocial behavior among Brazilian children. Other research suggests that these developmental patterns do not appear to be confined to children raised in western cultures. Studies of Japanese children (Munekata & Ninomiya, 1985) and children of a tribe in New Guinea (Tietjan, 1986) find quite similar developmental patterns. After reviewing such research findings, Radke-Yarrow, Zahn-Waxler, and Chapman (1983) concluded that across all cultures that have been studied, as children mature, their thoughts and actions tend to become less egocentric and more other-oriented.

We must be careful, however, in how we interpret this relationship. We cannot say with certainty that changes in the things that motivate helping and in moral reasoning *cause* people to be more helpful. It is also possible that engaging in more prosocial action affects moral reasoning and causes changes in the way people think about their prosocial actions. For instance, in a 2-year longitudinal study, high school students' involvement in community activities at age 17 years predicted their level of moral reasoning at age 19 (Pratt, Hunsberger, Pancer, & Alisat, 2003). That is, prosocial activity preceded and appeared to influence the way high school students thought about moral issues. In addition, prosocial behavior (cooperativeness, helpfulness, and generosity) among third graders predicts how socially and academically responsible they are as adolescents (Caprara, Barbaranelli, Pastorelli, Bandura, & Zimbardo, 2000). In fact, prosocial behavior among third graders is a better predictor of academic achievement in adolescence than is their academic performance in the third grade. The relationship between prosocial behavior and moral reasoning goes in both directions. It does seem safe to conclude, however, that as children mature, the way they reason about what are good and bad prosocial actions changes, and that there are concomitant changes in the factors that motivate helping. Thus, it appears that as children get older, they also tend to become better—at least in terms of their prosocial orientation.

Summary

As children mature, there are substantial changes related to helping. One of the major changes is in what motivates a child to help. We saw

that young children do not seem to derive intrinsic pleasure from helping others, and, as a result, they are not often inclined to help spontaneously. Rather, they help either because they are directly asked to do so or
because they believe that helping will produce some tangible benefit for
them. However, as children get older, different considerations motivate
them to help. By the time they are adolescents, some are motivated to
help because it will earn them social approval, and by the time they
reach adulthood, many people help because it is intrinsically rewarding
and, as we discussed in chapter 4, makes them feel good.

Closely paralleling these motivational changes are developmental
changes in children's moral reasoning. As they get older, children's general moral reasoning becomes less egocentric and rule-bound and more
other-oriented and sophisticated. Moral reasoning about prosocial behaviors develops in a similar fashion. When asked to make decisions in
situations that pit their own needs against the needs of others, young children resolve these dilemmas in self-serving and egocentric ways. As they
mature, they become more sensitive to the rights and needs of others. By
the time they are adults, most (but not all) people believe they have a personal, moral obligation to further the welfare of others. Violating this personal norm has a negative effect on their self-image and self-esteem. As
we described in chapter 4, motivations to help others involve both cognitive and emotional elements, often operating in a coordinated fashion.

In general, then, psychological research offers a fairly clear answer to
the question about how helpful thoughts, feelings, and actions change
developmentally. We turn now to the second and more difficult question—what processes are responsible for these changes? In the pages
that follow, we turn our attention from *how* people change to *why* these
changes occur.

There are two basic processes that have been offered to account for
why developmental changes in prosocial behavior unfold as they do.
These are social/cognitive processes and learning processes. Social/
cognitive development involves changes in children's mental capacity
to understand their world; learning relates to the knowledge and skills
children acquire, which is shaped by what people around them say and
do. Consistent with the general theme of this chapter, maturational
changes in children's abilities and the effects of social learning typically work in combination to influence helpfulness.

SOCIAL/COGNITIVE DEVELOPMENT

In terms of maturational processes, as humans get older, their cognitive
skills, abilities, and capacities mature and change. These changes affect

the way people think about the physical world around them and about their social world as well. This results in changes in the things that motivate people to help, the reasons why they help, and the ways they think about helping. For example, Leahy (1979) presented first graders, fifth graders, and adults with descriptions of situations in which one child gave his lunch to another child; the rewards and punishments used to induce this behavior were systematically manipulated. After reading a scenario, the subjects indicated how kind they thought the helper in the story was. Among the young children, the act of giving the lunch to someone else was seen as kinder when it was rewarded than when it was not rewarded. Apparently, they focused on the *consequences* of the action. Fifth graders and adults responded in just the opposite way; they saw the unrewarded actions as kinder than those that were rewarded. They seemed to pay much more attention to the helper's *intentions*. Younger and older people see helping in very different terms.

Such differences are the result of natural maturational changes in human cognitive processes. When these changes involve cognitive processes related to social thoughts (or cognitions) and social behavior, the process is called *social/cognitive development*. To understand this kind of development, we must begin with a consideration of general cognitive development.

Cognitive Development

Jean Piaget (e.g., 1932/1965), whom many consider to be the "father" of research on cognitive development in children, believed that the differences between the thinking processes of children and adults reflected more than the simple fact that adults have accumulated more knowledge about the world around them. Piaget argued that children think about themselves and the world around them in ways that are qualitatively different from adults.

Developmental theorists (e.g., Flavell, 1985) propose that cognitive development proceeds in stages, with the thought processes in each successive stage becoming more sophisticated and complex than in the preceding one. Although people may differ with respect to how rapidly they move through these stages, all people within the normal range of intellectual abilities will pass through the stages in the same order. These changes are as natural a part of the maturational process as growing taller or heavier. The particular cognitive stage that individuals are in will largely determine how they think about helping others. More specifically, social/cognitive theorists believe that two cognitive abilities are critical to the development of spontaneous, internally motivated helping. The first of these is the ability to see things from the other person's perspective. This is called role taking, perspective taking, or *cognitive empathy*. The second is the tendency to make personal or *internal attributions* about the causes of one's own behavior and the behavior of others.

Cognitive Empathy. In the discussion of empathy in chapter 4, we distinguished between *affective empathy* (vicarious emotional responses to another person's circumstances) and *cognitive empathy* (the ability to understand the thoughts and perspectives of another person; Davis, 1994). As we saw in the previous chapter, the work of Carolyn Zahn-Waxler and her colleagues (e.g., Zahn-Waxler, Radke-Yarrow, Wagner, & Chapman, 1992) strongly suggests that by the time children are 2 years old, they are quite capable of experiencing affective empathy. The discussion of affective empathy in chapter 4 makes it clear that this kind of empathic response plays a critical role in helping and altruism among both children and adults.

Cognitive empathy is also quite important in the development and maintenance of prosocial behavior. However, the capacity for cognitive empathy, or perspective taking, appears to take somewhat longer to develop than does affective empathy. Piaget believed that when children are quite young (under 5 or 6 years of age), they have great difficulty taking the perspective of others, regardless of whether the task involves visual or social stimuli. For example, Piaget and Inhelder (1971) showed young children a papier-mâché model of some mountains and asked them how the mountains would look from the perspective of someone standing on the other side of the model. The children found this task extremely difficult. This led Piaget and Inhelder to conclude that before the age of 5 or 6 (during the *preoperational* stage), children were unable to adopt the perspective of others and have an extremely egocentric view of the physical world.

Similarly, children are *interpersonally* quite egocentric at this age. They are unable or unwilling to take another person's perspective and usually see interpersonal situations only from their own point of view. Thus, they often have difficulty understanding how other people feel or what they want. (However, more recent work on what is sometimes called the "theory of mind" suggests that young children may possess some perspective-taking skill in social situations [Gopnik & Meltzoff, 1997; Wellman, Cross, & Watson, 2001], although situational complexity and egoistic motivations inherent in many helping situations may distort or overwhelm the concern felt for another.) By the time children are 8 or 9 years old (Piaget's *concrete operations* stage), they are capable of true cognitive empathy; they are able to take the perspective of another person. However, they still have great difficulty simultaneously considering their own perspective and the perspective of another person (Selman, 1980). It is probably not until around the time of puberty that children are fully capable of the kinds of cognitive empathy that are displayed by adults.

According to Bar-Tal and Raviv (1982) and others (e.g., Eisenberg & Fabes, 1991), an understanding of the perspective of others is critical to helping and altruistic behaviors. Small children will help others in need or distress if the source of the distress also directly affects them or involves something they have also experienced (e.g., missing one's mother). Otherwise, children have great difficulty understanding what the other person is feeling. As a result, they will be unlikely to spontaneously come to a person's aid in an unfamiliar situation—not because of a lack of caring, but because of a lack of understanding. Note what is being suggested here: Very young children are *not* selfish—they are just egocentric. They fail to help others only because they lack the ability to understand the others' needs. As children mature, they develop the cognitive abilities to see physical events and social stimuli more from another persons' perspective, and as their ability to take the roles of others increases, so does their propensity to help others (Eisenberg & Fabes, 1991; Eisenberg & Miller, 1987). The ability to think about different aspects of a situation and inhibit an immediate response to salient stimuli is a critical cognitive ability that children need to develop to act prosocially toward others (Moore, Barresi, & Thompson, 1998).

Internal Attributions. The second cognitive process involved in the development of helpfulness concerns the manner in which children make attributions about the causes of their own actions as well as the actions of others. A behavior can be explained by internal, personal causes or by external, situational causes (Heider, 1958). According to Diane Ruble and her associates (e.g., Feldman & Ruble, 1981; Ruble & Rholes, 1983), children before the age of 7 or 8 react to information about other people quite differently than do adults. In general, younger children react only to a person's concrete, external characteristics (e.g., "She has red hair"), immediate actions (e.g., "He took my truck"), or the consequences of actions (e.g., "She received a prize"). They do not focus on unobservable aspects of other people (e.g., their personality traits or intentions). They are unable or unwilling to use traits to explain a person's behaviors or to make inferences about other people's underlying personality dispositions (e.g., "He did that because he is selfish; he is a selfish person"). The attributions offered by young children typically involve external rather than internal causes. By the time children are 9 or 10, they begin to make abstract inferences about other people and tend to make attributions much as adults do—recognizing that the contributions of both external and internal factors must be considered to understand fully the causes of any event.

The relationship between attributional tendencies and helping may not be as obvious as the relationship between cognitive empathy and helping, so perhaps a little more explanation is needed. As we discuss in more detail later, self-attributions play an important role in how children learn to be helpful. If children look at an instance in which they are helpful and infer that they helped because they are a "helpful" person (i.e., an internal attribution), it is likely that they will help more on subsequent occasions. However, before a certain age, children may be unable to fully comprehend internal attributions about their helpful actions. This is illustrated in the results of a study by Grusec and Redler (1980). When adults expressed an internal attribution about 8-year-old children's helpful behavior ("You are a helpful person"), this increased the child's subsequent prosocial behavior. However, the same statement had little effect on the actions of 5-year-olds. Therefore, for social labeling of helpfulness to be fully effective, the child must have reached a certain stage of social/cognitive development. The age-related shift in how children make attributions about behavior plays an important role in their likelihood of spontaneously offering help to others.

These developmental changes in cognitive processes are quite consistent across diverse groups of people. As we have already noted, there is an underlying similarity in how prosocial thoughts and actions change as children mature in many different cultures. These facts might lead you to conclude that there is a basic biological process at work here. That is, just as a genetic code directs humans' physical growth as they mature, a similar genetic code may directly and indirectly affect the development of helpful and altruistic tendencies. We do not dismiss this possibility, but we do not believe that genetically based maturational changes alone are able to adequately explain the kinds of changes in helping that we have been discussing. Socialization processes, which vary across cultures, also play a critical role.

Cultural Diversity. Although there are many cross-cultural similarities in prosocial development, there are also many differences. For example, Miller (1994) attempted to apply western models of moral development to moral development in India. She argues that Kohlberg's and other Western models (e.g., Carol Gilligan's gender-based model, 1982) are probably not applicable in India and other non-Western cultures in which individualism is not strongly stressed or valued. Other studies have found great differences in the absolute levels of helpfulness and cooperation in different cultures. For example, Whiting and Whiting (1975) compared the helpfulness of children from six countries (India, Kenya, Japan, Mexico, the Philippines, and the United States) on a scale of altruistic behaviors. Although all of the Kenyan children were rated above the median (i.e., the 50th percentile) "altruism" score for the entire sample of children, only 8% of the children in the United States were above this international norm. Thus, there are vast differences between cultures in how helpful their members are. The next section discusses the processes that are the most likely causes of these differences.

LEARNING EXPERIENCES: LEARNING TO BE A HELPER

We do not want to discount the possibility that biological factors are responsible for some of these cultural differences, but we think it is much more likely that cultural differences are due to differences in specific learning experiences across the cultures (Fiske, 1991; Moore & Eisenberg, 1984). In chapter 4 we introduced the concept of social learning and explained how it is relevant to helping. Social learning is also important for understanding developmental changes because different societies with somewhat different customs, values, and norms teach their children different things about prosocial behavior at different times in their lives.

Social Learning

Despite this variety and diversity in the characteristics and customs of different human cultures and societies, children in all cultures share one very basic experience in common: *socialization*. Socialization is a complex, multifaceted process that has two basic goals: (a) to teach children the norms and values of the society in which they live, and (b) to get children to accept and internalize these norms and values (Grusec et al., 2002). Joan Grusec (1982) noted that in the case of altruism and helping, the specific goal of the socialization process is to encourage children to "to show concern for others 'for its own sake'" (p. 142). The process that most people believe is responsible for this kind of socialization is *social learning* (see chap. 4). According to social learning theorists, the socialization of helpfulness and altruism involves three basic kinds of social learning: experiencing direct reinforcement for behavior, observing models in the environment, and being told things about helping (Rushton, 1982).

Direct Reinforcement. We previously discussed the role of classical conditioning in the acquisition of empathic reactions (Aronfreed,

1970), and in chapter 4, we considered *operant* or *instrumental* conditioning. The basic principle in operant conditioning is that behaviors that produce positive consequences are more likely to occur in the future, and behaviors that are associated with negative consequences are less likely to occur again. If rewards regularly follow some behavior, that behavior will be learned, and it will subsequently be performed more frequently when the conditions are appropriate. If punishments follow a behavior, the connection will also be learned, but the punished behavior will be performed less frequently. Some examples of research on the effects of rewards and punishments on helping are presented below.

Interest in the effects of *rewards* or *reinforcement* on helping is based on the simple premise that if you reward a child for being helpful, the child will learn and subsequently perform this behavior. In some cases, rewards can be very tangible. For example, giving children even a few pennies every time they help increases their helpfulness in the future (Smith, Gelfand, Hartmann, & Partlow, 1979). But how long-lasting and generalizable are the effects of rewards? The effects of *social* rewards appear to be quite resistant to extinction. In study by Rushton and Teachman (1978), for instance, an adult subtly induced children to donate tokens they had won to a charity. Some of the children were praised (rewarded) for their actions, others were criticized (punished), and still others experienced no consequences for their generosity. Two weeks later, the children's generosity was measured again. The effects of the praise on the children's generosity were still evident. Children in the praise group were the most generous, and the children in the criticism group were the least generous.

In fact, social rewards, such as praise, seem to be even more effective reinforcers for helping than material rewards, such as money (Gelfand & Hartmann, 1982; Grusec, 1991a; Rushton, 1982). For example, in the previous paragraph, we described a study in which some children received pennies as reinforcers for helping (Smith et al., 1979). Other children in that study received praise instead of money when they helped. Later, both groups of children were asked *why* they had helped. The children who received the pennies said they helped to get the money, but the children who received the social reward said they helped because they were concerned about the welfare of the child whom they had helped.

Not only are material reinforcers less effective in eliciting prosocial behavior from children, but in some instances they may actually reduce the probability that a child will spontaneously act prosocially. A study by Richard Fabes and his associates illustrates this (Fabes, Fultz, Eisenberg, May-Plumlee, & Christopher, 1989). Fabes et al. examined the behavior of grade-school children whose mothers had said they often used rewards to get their children to act prosocially. These children were placed in a situation where they had two opportunities to help "sick and poor children in the hospital" (by making games for them). Some of the children received a material reward (a toy) the first time they helped; others did not. Then all the children were given a second chance to help.

Fabes et al. (1989) found that although less than half (44%) of those who received the toy for helping were willing to help the second time, all of the children in the no-toy condition spontaneously helped the second time. How can this be explained? The researchers speculated that the reward may have decreased spontaneous helping because it undermined intrinsic motivations for helping (e.g., Lepper, 1981). That is, giving the children the toy may have caused them to believe that they were helping *because of this toy* rather than because they wanted to help the people in the hospital. When there was no longer any extrinsic motivation for helping (i.e., no toy being offered), the children saw no reason to be helpful. Thus, material reinforcers may be relatively ineffective in motivating future helping because they provide children with an extrinsic explanation of why they have helped. Children who continuously receive material reinforcers for helping may come to believe that they help not because they are helpful people but because of the external rewards for doing so. As is discussed shortly, such self-perceptions can have a strong influence on how people react to requests for help.

Parents appear to understand intuitively the short- and long-term effectiveness of social reinforcers on helping. Grusec (1982, 1991b) trained the mothers of 4- to 7-year-olds to record how they reacted to their children when the children were prosocial or helpful. Parents almost always responded to such actions in some manner, usually with social reinforcements, such as thanking the children, smiling at them, or praising them. They almost never rewarded their children's prosocial behaviors with a material reward. This finding suggests that parents just seem to know that giving material rewards is not the most effective way to teach their children to be helpful.

There is, of course, another side of the consequences coin. It is the use of *punishment* or *discipline* to teach a child to be helpful by using sanctions when some prosocial behavior is not performed. This is not the first time we have discussed the costs of not helping. Recall from chapter 3 that Piliavin et al. (1981) included such costs in the arousal: cost–reward model, which helped explain when bystanders will or will not intervene in an emergency. However, that model has focused mainly on helping by adults, and most of the costs considered are internal and self-generated. Here we focus more on externally administered costs for failing to help. To train prosocial behavior, punishment could be administered by an adult if a child either failed to be helpful or acted selfishly.

There is wide consensus about the effects of rewards on helping, but the picture with regard to punishment is more complex. Martin Hoffman (1970, 1994) argued that there are different techniques of discipline, and some may be more effective than others in promoting prosocial actions.

One kind of discipline involves the use of power and threats and is based on the fact that adults are larger and stronger than children and can, if they desire, physically punish or withhold rewards from a child; Hoffman called this kind of discipline *power assertion*. Another kind of discipline is *love withdrawal*, in which parents attempt to control or modify children's actions by ignoring them or withholding their approval or attention. In each case, the expectation is that children will change their behavior (hopefully by becoming more prosocial) to avoid these punishments.

The final kind of discipline identified by Hoffman does not involve punishing children, but rather reasoning with them. He called this *induction* (or other-oriented induction) discipline. Using this approach, parents explain to the child why a behavior was wrong, point out the effects of the child's behavior on another person, and suggest ways in which the child might right the wrong that he or she has committed. Hoffman (1994) argued that children disciplined with induction are more likely to display mature moral reasoning, compassion, and sympathy than are children who are disciplined with either power assertion or love withdrawal. There have been several studies that have attempted to test Hoffman's ideas about discipline. The results of these studies are complex. One reason for this is that parents in the real world rarely use a single kind of discipline. Rather, when parents discipline a child, they often say things that contain elements of all three discipline techniques (Grusec & Lytton, 1988). However, the results of these studies generally suggest that induction-based discipline is more likely to result in prosocial thoughts and actions than discipline that primarily involves either power assertion or love withdrawal (e.g., Brody & Shaffer, 1982; Crockenberg & Litman, 1990).

Why is discipline based on power assertion and love withdrawal less effective than induction in promoting prosocial thoughts and behaviors? One reason is that power assertion and love withdrawal often involve threat and perhaps actual punishment, and this may produce considerable negative affect and arousal in a child. High levels of arousal will probably cause children to focus on themselves and react in a self-centered or egoistical way (Fabes, Eisenberg, & Eisenbud, 1993). Discipline that causes heightened arousal may also interfere with children's ability to remember *why* they are being disciplined or the content of what their parents are saying to them (Hoffman, 1990). Finally, Grusec and Goodnow (1994) proposed that if discipline threatens a child's independence and autonomy (as would almost certainly be the case in power assertion), the punishment may actually arouse reactance (Brehm, 1966; Brehm & Brehm, 1981) and increase the child's motivation *not* to comply with these wishes.

In contrast, there are several reasons why inductive discipline should be effective. It provides children with standards against which they can evaluate their actions in the future (Hoffman, 1977). Induction also enables parents to discuss emotions that would lead to concern for others (e.g., guilt, shame), teach children how to empathize with people in distress, and provide them with information about how they *should* behave toward others (e.g., Eisenberg, 1992; Grusec & Goodnow, 1994; Hoffman, 1994). Thus, induction does more than control children's behavior; it also serves to teach them how to act prosocially. As a result, it may increase a child's tendencies to spontaneously act in a prosocial manner.

Observing Helpful and Altruistic Models. The second process that is involved in learning to be helpful is called *observational learning* or *modeling*. This concept was introduced briefly in chapter 4. According to social learning theorists, such as Albert Bandura (e.g., 1977, 1986), much of what children learn about helping (and other social behaviors) is the result of observing the actions of models in their environment.

Modeling can affect the development of helping in at least two ways. First, it can teach children helpful behaviors that they did not previously know. Second, it can show children what will happen when they engage in certain helpful (or selfish) behaviors that they already know. For both of these reasons, it is important that models behave consistently (Lipscomb, McAllister, & Bregman, 1985). Thus, what models *say* and what models *do* are both important. But which is *more* important?

In one study (Rushton, 1975), half of the children saw an adult model act generously; the other half saw a model behave selfishly. Within each of these two groups, half of the children heard the model preach generosity, and half heard him preach selfishness. The children in each of these four conditions were then given a chance to donate money to "Bobby," a poster boy in a charity campaign. The immediate effects of the models' actions and words on the children's behavior are presented in Fig. 6.1. Children were only minimally influenced by what the model said—children exposed to the model who preached selfishness donated slightly less than did children who heard the model preach generosity. The immediate effects of the model's *actions* were much more powerful. Regardless of what the model said, the children donated more when the model acted generously than when he acted selfishly. When the children were tested again, 2 months later, the impact of the model's actions were still present, but now the models' words affected the children as well. Those exposed to a model

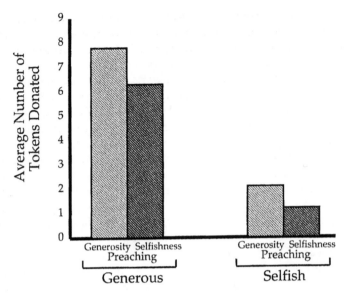

FIG. 6.1. A model's actions are more influential than words for promoting prosocial behavior. Adapted from Rushton (1975), with permission.

who preached generosity donated more than did those exposed to a model who preached selfishness. So although in the short run "actions speak louder than words," in the long run what a model does and what a model says both affect children's prosocial actions.

Models do not have to be "live" and physically present to make an impression on children. For example, the models that children see on television are important (Liebert & Sprafkin, 1988). Children between the ages of 4 and 16 years typically spend between 2.5 and 4 hours per day watching television, and in many homes, they may spend more time watching television than interacting with their parents (Liebert & Sprafkin, 1988). Most people are aware of the impact that watching violent models on television can have on aggression in children (Anderson et al., 2003). Can televised models also have an impact on how helpful children are?

Several field studies have examined whether television shows with prosocial characters or themes have a long-term influence on the behavior of children who watch them. In a study conducted in Australia, Ahammer and Murray (1979) found that exposing children to prosocial television shows for half an hour a day for 5 days produced increases in the children's cooperativeness and willingness to help others. Furthermore, exposure to prosocial television programs combined with training in prosocial behavior has a consistent and powerful effect on children's cooperativeness, helpfulness, and generosity (Friedrich & Stein, 1975; Friedrich-Cofer, Huston-Stein, Kipnis, Susman, & Clewett, 1979). Hearold (1986) conducted a comprehensive review of the research on how television programs with prosocial themes or messages affected the children who watched them. She concluded that these programs had a strong positive impact on children—much stronger, in fact, than the negative impact of programs with aggressive or antisocial themes.

Studies of the effects of real-life models have identified some of the factors that make one model more effective than another. In general, models who are seen by a child as powerful and those who have a warm, nurturant relationship with the child produce the strongest modeling effects (Grusec, 1982; Moore & Eisenberg, 1984). Perhaps because of these qualities, parents are often the most important models for young children.

Some parents, however, are more effective prosocial models for their children than are others. Why? One explanation is based on *attachment theory* (Ainsworth, 1973; Bowlby, 1969). Attachment theory deals with the quality of the relationship between parents and their children, and there is a powerful relationship between attachment and helping. First, helping can increase attachment between parents and children. Helpful parents tend to have closer relationships with their children. Then, because of these close relationships, these parents become increasingly effective models. As a result, these children are more likely to internalize the behavior and values of their parents than are children without strong attachments. One of the consequences of this internalization is that the children come to see themselves as people who are concerned about other people and also to see other people as worthy of such concern. This, in turn, makes them more likely to help others. (We discuss other aspects of attachment theory and prosocial behavior in chap. 7.)

This process begins quite early and appears to have fairly long-term effects. For example, several researchers have recorded the quality of parental attachments of infants and correlated this with prosocial reactions a few years later when the children are in preschool. The general finding is that the stronger and more secure the early relation with the parent, the more empathic and prosocial these children are when they interact with their preschool classmates a few years later (Grusec, 1991a; Kestenbaum, Farber, & Sroufe, 1989; Main & Weston, 1981).

The impact of prosocial parents can been seen throughout a child's lifetime. For example, Fabes, Eisenberg, and Miller (1990) found that primary school girls who were sympathetic to children in distress had mothers who also were sympathetic in such situations, suggesting that the children were in part modeling their mothers' reactions. There is also evidence that prosocial parental models may exert a strong influence on the behavior of their children even after they have reached adulthood. For instance, Whites who actively participated in the Black civil rights movement in the early 1960s had parents who regularly displayed prosocial behaviors (Rosenhan, 1969). Many of the people who risked their lives to rescue Jews in Europe during World War II had parents who displayed strong commitments to prosocial moral actions (London, 1970; Oliner & Oliner, 1988); we address this relationship in more detail in chapter 7. The effect is also evident in more day-to-day types of helping. Piliavin and Callero (1991) reported that almost 60% of a sample of first-time blood donors said that someone in their family gave blood. Given the fact that no more than 10% of those eligible to give blood in the United States actually donate blood, it would appear that modeling the actions of family members may be a strong factor in a person's initial decision to donate blood. Parental modeling of giving time and money also relates to willingness to help in these ways (Lee, J. A. Piliavin, & Call, 1999). Thus, the prosocial behavior of parents has a profound impact on children throughout their lifetimes.

Parental influences can also help explain cross-cultural differences in helping. As noted earlier, there are considerable differences in the levels of prosocial behavior and helping in different countries. For example, children from Kenya, Mexico, and the Philippines were much more helpful than children from the United States (Whiting & Edwards, 1988; Whiting & Whiting, 1975), and some of these differences may be explained by different kinds of family socialization. Helping was more frequent in those areas where children were expected to cooperate with other family members when performing chores and to share in the care and raising of other children. Helping was less frequent in cultures in which children were not expected to assume family and household responsibilities and were encouraged to compete with others.

The adults in a child's environment do more than serve as models; they are also teachers who directly and indirectly instruct children about what is good and what is bad—what they should and should not do. This kind of social learning is considered next.

Talking About Helping and Altruism.   Although actions often speak louder than words in modeling prosocial behavior, words are still important. Most of us can recall more than one instance when we acted selfishly and our parents gave us a lecture about being helpful, cooperative, considerate of others, or concerned about the welfare of someone else. Two of the male coauthors of this book can vividly recall the lectures on the rights of others they received when they refused to share toys with their quite deserving, but younger (and not coincidentally, smaller) sisters. What kinds of words and approaches are most effective with children? Three kinds of verbal communications will be considered here: direct instruction, preaching, and how parents explain why their child has acted prosocially.

Direct instruction is the most specific type of verbal communication. It involves telling the child explicitly what to do. For example, Grusec, Saas-Kortsaak, and Simutis (1978) simply told children that they were to share half of the prizes they won in a game with poor children. Not surprisingly, this induced a high level of donating immediately after the children received the instruction. But can specific instructions produce long-term and generalized increases in helping? In fact, direct instructions have been found to affect helping as long as 4 weeks after the children receive explicit commands to share (Israel, 1978; Israel & Brown, 1979), and these instructions can cause an increase in subsequent prosocial behaviors that were not specifically mentioned in the instructions (Barton & Osborne, 1978; Staub, 1993). Apparently, once children understand what should be done, they are willing and able to generalize these ideas about prosocial behavior to new situations.

Preaching (also called "moral exhortation") is a rather common way by which parents try to induce prosocial behavior in their children; it involves teaching children the *value* of helping. For example, Grusec (1982) trained mothers to record their own responses to altruistic and selfish behaviors by their children. Preaching to the child about the virtues of helping others was the most common response when a child failed to act spontaneously in a prosocial manner and the second most common response when a child failed to comply with a specific request to be helpful.

Moral exhortations can, in fact, be quite effective in producing prosocial behaviors in children (Grusec, 1982; Moore & Eisenberg, 1984), and, as with direct instructions, the effects appear to persist for some time and to generalize beyond the specific situation in which the "sermon" was delivered. However, it also appears that some forms of preaching about behaving prosocially are more effective than others. For instance, Grusec, Kuczynski, Rushton, and Simutis (1978) presented children with two kinds of exhortations. One was relatively specific in its message, discussing one particular kind of helping and the reason for it; the other message discussed the importance of being helpful to others in more general terms. Initially, the two kinds of messages were equally effective in promoting prosocial behavior, but a month later, when the children were asked to help an adult they had never seen before, the children who heard the general message were much more generous than those that heard the specific message. Thus, although children respond to both methods, teaching children that it is good to be helpful as a general rule is more effective than teaching children that helping is appropriate in specific situations.

The final, and most indirect, kind of verbal communication that appears to affect helping relates to the *explanations* that are made about the child's helpful actions. In social psychology, these are called *attributions*. Attributions were discussed briefly earlier, but now we consider their effects on helping in a bit more detail. Attribution theory (e.g., Heider, 1958; Kelley, 1967, 1973) suggests that if we believe that we have taken an action on our own, without external coercion or expectation of a large reward, we are likely to make a personal or internal explanation of our behavior. We will *attribute* our behavior to an enduring characteristic or disposition that we possess (e.g., "I am the kind of person who helps others in need"). Once we believe that we are the kind of person who does helpful things, we will be more likely to act in ways consistent with that self-perception in the future.

Attributions offered by others may also be accepted, internalized, and serve as guides for future behavior. Imagine, for example, that one of us had actually shared a toy with his younger sister. Our father could have said, "What a generous boy you are!" and made an internal attribution about his son's behavior. Alternatively, he could have remarked, "You knew it would make me happy that you shared with your sister" and made an external attribution about his son's behavior. Which would be more effective? Among children 8 years old or older, internal attributions typically produce more generalized helping than do external attributions (Grusec et al., 1978).

Grusec and Redler (1980) directly compared the short-term and long-term effects of social reinforcers and internal attributions. Children were induced to share some tokens they had won in a game with poor children. The experimenter then either verbally praised the child ("It was good that you gave your tokens to those poor children ... that was a nice and helpful thing to do"), or they made an internal attribution about the child's behavior ("I guess you're the kind of person who likes to help others whenever you can.... You are a ... helpful person"). The researchers recorded how helpful the two groups were immediately after the attribution or praise. They also assessed helpfulness 1 week and 3 weeks later. The results of this study are presented in Fig. 6.2. Initially there were no differences in how helpful the children were, but when they were observed on the two later occasions, the children who received the internal attributions were much more helpful than those who received the social reinforcers.

In summary, it is clear that social learning and the socialization process play important roles in developmental changes in helping, sharing, and prosocial behavior in general. However, to understand this process

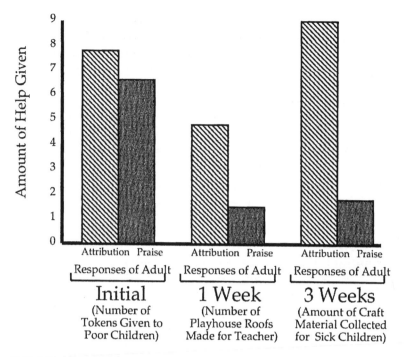

FIG. 6.2. Attributions of helpfulness can have more enduring effects on prosocial behavior than social reinforcers such as praise. Adapted from Grusec and Redler (1980), with permission.

fully and to answer the question about how developmental changes in prosocial behavior occur, we must also ask *why* these learning processes are so effective. The social learning theorists would argue that children learn to self-regulate prosocial behaviors as the product of these learning experiences. Repeated learning experiences teach children the benefits of helping and altruistic actions. Having once learned this lesson, children act prosocially without the aid of external reinforcers, models, or instructions from their parents.

A second possibility, proposed by Grusec (1991a) and others (e.g., Moore & Eisenberg, 1984), is based on some of the cognitive processes discussed in the previous section. These authors give special attention to self-attributional processes. They propose that if children repeatedly act prosocially, they will come to believe that they are doing so because they are "prosocial people." They make internal, personal attributions about their behavior, and, as a consequence, they are more likely to help even when there are no external reinforcers, models, or exhortations to be helpful. Of course, these theorists add a very important qualifier to this explanation. Before a certain age, children are not capable of engaging in such complex cognitive processes. Thus the effectiveness of learning processes depends on a child having attained a certain level of cognitive and social development. As we noted at the beginning of this chapter, one needs both the cognitive and learning approaches to understand developmental changes in helping. In the next sections of this chapter, we extend our consideration of developmental trends in prosocial behavior across the life span, examining general changes that occur throughout adulthood, and then we explore male–female differences in helping.

ADULT SOCIALIZATION OF HELPING: IT AIN'T OVER 'TIL IT'S OVER

Development is not a process that ends after people mature from childhood to adolescence to adulthood. Obviously, physical, mental, and emotional changes occur across the entire life span. As with children, both physical maturational and learning processes continue to influence developmental changes in adults as they age. Physical problems relate to less helpfulness among older adults; older adults help others less when they are less physically able or feel less able to function effectively with others (Caprara & Steca, 2005; Kim, Hisata, Kai, & Lee, 2000). Nevertheless, even among adults, there are events and experiences that can exert long-term influences on how much people help and the reasons why they do so. Regardless of their physical condition, helping remains an important social activity for the elderly; helping others is positively related to life satisfaction and, in fact, is more strongly related to the experience of quality of life for older adults than is being helped (Caprara & Steca, 2005; Kim et al., 2000). In addition, as with children, prosocial moral reasoning, particularly in the form of individuals' personal and internalized principles, is strongly related to prosocial behavior in older adults (Midlarsky, Kahana, Corley, Nemeroff, & Schonbar, 1999). Thus, the processes underlying prosocial behavior appear to be similar across the life span. We now consider some of these adult socialization experiences.

Modeling

Just as observing prosocial models influence the helping behavior of children, social models for helping influence adults as well. As we noted in chapter 4, many studies have shown that there are increases in donations and other forms of helping with the presence of models who display prosocial actions (e.g., Hornstein, 1970; MacCaulay, 1970). For example, Rushton and Campbell (1977) demonstrated the impact of modeling on blood donation decisions among adults. Students walking with a confederate either were asked to give blood or observed the confederate's positive response to a request to donate blood. When the student was asked first, only 25% agreed, and none actually showed up for their appointment. Among those exposed to the complying model, however, 67% also agreed to give blood, and 33% actually donated. Thus, the principles of observational learning and modeling apply as much to adults as to children.

Self-Attributions and Roles

Earlier in this chapter, we told you that if children make internal attributions about why they help, this will often lead to long-term increases in helpfulness. The same process appears to operate with adults as they consider the consequences of their helping to determine *why* they helped. If adults are offered money to help, are subjected to external social pressure to offer help, or help a person who has previously helped them (arousing the reciprocity norm), they perceive themselves to have acted less altruistically than if they helped without such external inducements (Batson, Fultz, Schoenrade, & Paduano, 1987; Thomas & Batson, 1981; Thomas, Batson, & Coke, 1980). Thus, inducing helping with obvious external and tangible incentives may make adults *less* helpful in the future.

When adults identify themselves as "helpful people," they may become even more helpful. How can adults be induced to label themselves this way? The most direct way is by telling them that they are! Because helping is valued in our society, most people will quite willingly adopt the label of a "helpful person." For example, in one study by Swinyard and Ray (1979), experimenters conducted door-to-door interviews. At the conclusion of the interview, the interviewer told half of the respondents that they were the type of person who was "interested in their fellow man." Some time later, all of the people who were interviewed received mailings asking them to volunteer for Red Cross activities. Although the assignment to conditions was done randomly, those people who had been told that they were concerned about others were significantly more likely to volunteer than those who had not received such an attribution.

There are also more subtle techniques for influencing people's self-images and then finding them to be more receptive to requests for help. One of these is called the *foot-in-the-door* technique (Freedman &

Fraser, 1966). The foot-in-the-door technique involves getting a person to comply with an initial request for a small favor and then following the small request with a request for a much larger favor. The technique gets its name from the actions of door-to-door salespeople; to keep customers engaged and to make sure they could make their "pitch," they would literally put their foot between the door and the door jamb, so that the customer could not slam the door in their face. These salespeople correctly believed that getting potential customers to agree to watch a brief demonstration would greatly increase their likelihood of making a sale. Freedman and Fraser demonstrated the effectiveness of this technique. In one study, they were able to get a large number of people to agree to place a very large and ugly sign in the middle of their front yard (a large commitment) by first getting them to agree to place a small, inconspicuous sign in a window of their house or in their car (a small commitment—the foot in the door). One explanation of this effect is that after individuals comply with the initial request, they come to define or see themselves as "helping people" and will continue to comply in order to maintain that self-perception. In general, the foot-in-the-door technique produces small, but consistent increases in compliance with requests for favors (Beaman, Cole, Preston, Klentz, & Steblay, 1983).

Of course the "foot" in the foot-in-the-door technique may also be one's own. If a person repeatedly engages in a behavior, this can change the person's self-image and perceptions about why she or he is engaging in the activity. Think about an activity that you regularly engage in. Why, for example, do you jog every day, even when the weather is rainy or cold? Perhaps it is because running has become an integral part of your identity: Runners run, and to not run would be inconsistent with your self-image and thus would be distressing. This process also applies to helping. For instance, college students who donate blood more regularly develop strong personal feelings of moral obligation to donate in the future. They become more intrinsically motivated to give blood, and, as attribution theory suggests, these effects are even stronger among donors who have no external justifications (e.g., a blood drive) for their most recent donation (Piliavin & Callero, 1991). The donors' own behaviors change their self-image and perceptions of the causes of their behavior. One might say they are able to socialize themselves to be blood donors.

Regular and public commitments to helping can lead to the development of social roles for helping. A *role* is defined as the set of expectations for the behavior or performance of a person who occupies some position. Although self-attributions may lead to a person's *own* identity as a helper, roles involve expectations that others have for the person as well. For example, we have expectations about how a police officer, a school teacher, or even a drug dealer should behave. We also acknowledge and share others' expectations about our own roles (e.g., student, parent, faculty member). Although roles have not received much attention in studies of children, researchers interested in changes in adult social behavior place great importance on the concept of roles. They believe that part of the socialization process of adults involves people identifying themselves with certain long-term roles—establishing a "role identity." Such an identity becomes an important aspect of the person's self-schema or self-image and may subsequently influence the individual's behavior.

Some theorists have suggested that simply committing to some behaviors can lead to the development of a role identity consistent with those behaviors (McCall & Simmons, 1978; Stryker, 1980; Turner, 1978). For example, not only are one's own feelings of moral obligation and personal identity important in deciding whether to donate blood, but the perceived expectations of significant others (e.g., friends, family) are also critical. Students who believe that others expect them to continue giving blood express stronger intentions to give blood in the future, and as a consequence, they *are* more likely to donate blood (Callero, 1985/1986; Charng, J. A. Piliavin, & Callero, 1988; J. A. Piliavin & Callero, 1991). Thus, one's self-identity, which can itself motivate people to donate blood, can become more publicly formalized in terms of social roles and others' expectations. Similarly, people may perform volunteer work in hospitals or for charity because it has become a part of their own identity and what others expect of them. These influences continue to develop across an entire lifetime. Older volunteers who help others, for example, report that they are motivated to fulfill a "meaningful role" (Bengtson, 1985; Midlarsky & Hannah, 1989).

In summary, developmental changes in helping do not stop at a certain age. People grow and change in this respect throughout their entire lives. Although there are certainly many differences between the processes affecting changes in children and those influencing changes in adults (e.g., biological maturation), there are many similar influences (e.g., modeling, self-perceptions). Through social learning and direct reinforcement, people can learn new ways to benefit others. Through self-attributions and regular activities, they can also develop new roles and identities. Among the elderly, for instance, these helping identities and roles contribute to the maintenance of high self-esteem and a positive outlook on life (Midlarsky, 1991). Thus, the development of prosocial behavior is a lifelong process.

MALE–FEMALE DIFFERENCES IN HELPING

One major source of differences in how humans are socialized is their biological sex. Children who are female are raised differently from those who are male. These socialization differences, in combination with differences in behavior that are directly due to the biological differences between males and females (e.g., hormone production, size, physique), can result in some substantial differences in the behavior of males and females. In this section, we consider male–female differences in prosocial behavior. But first we begin with a brief history of research on sex differences in helping and other prosocial behaviors.

Research on Sex Differences in Prosocial Behaviors

Today, there is substantial interest in whether men and women differ with regard to most social behaviors, including prosocial ones, and perhaps even more interest in why. But until the 1970s, male–female differences in helping and other prosocial behaviors were largely ignored. This was partially because helping researchers focused so intently on how the situation affected people's decisions to intervene in emergencies that individual differences of any kind did not receive much attention. Unfortunately, it is also true that at that time many social psychologists did not believe that differences in the social behaviors of men and women were of particular theoretical or practical importance. The emergence of the women's movement in the 1970s played a major role in making social psychologists aware that if they were to fully understand human social behavior, their research had to consider the similarities and differences between the sexes. By the 1980s, researchers were asking many more questions about how a person's sex might affect his or her willingness to offer help.

Reviews of the literature conducted at that time (Eagly & Crowley, 1986; Piliavin & Unger, 1985) found that in the majority of the studies men were more likely to help than women. A few years later, Johnson et al. (1989) obtained people's self-reports of helping in a cross-cultural comparison of helping in five countries (Australia, Egypt, Korea, China, the United States, and Serbia). Across these five countries, men reported that they were more likely to give help than were women. These kinds of findings led some researchers to conclude that men were, as a group, more helpful than women, but there are several reasons to be skeptical about the validity of this conclusion.

First, it is very difficult to conclude that these differences were due solely to differences in people's sex. Researchers who study sex differences cannot manipulate a person's biological sex in the same way they manipulate independent variables in a "true" experiment; that is, they cannot randomly assign a participant to one or the other sex when they come to the lab for a study. Random assignment is done in experiments to make the experimental groups that will be compared as equivalent as possible before conducting their studies; randomization is done to eliminate any systematic biases among the groups. In the absence of random assignment, a researcher cannot ensure that the different groups are equivalent on all the characteristics that might affect their responses to the experimental manipulation or treatment. When the variable of interest is a person's biological sex, you can in fact be quite sure that male and female subjects *will* differ in many ways other than their biology. As a result, even if a study finds sex-related differences in helping, the researcher is not able to specify the exact cause of "sex-different behaviors" (Piliavin & Unger, 1985); the observed differences may be due to (a) biological differences between men and women, or (b) differences associated with the way men and women are raised and socialized in our society, or (c) differences in what is viewed as socially appropriate or acceptable behavior for men and for women in a particular situation. Thus, like other demographic and organismic variables, sex is a "carrier variable," reflecting a range of other physical, social, and personal differences.

Second, as we have already discussed in several places in this book, when research interest in prosocial actions began in the 1960s and then grew in the 1970s and the 1980s, the vast majority of this research focused on one very specific form of prosocial behavior—bystander intervention in emergencies—and thus most of the studies on male–female differences in helping were conducted in such situations. As we discuss later in somewhat greater detail, there are several reasons why the need for help in emergencies is more likely to elicit helping from males than females. Thus, as Alice Eagly and others pointed out (Becker & Eagly, 2004; Eagly & Crowley, 1986; Piliavin & Unger, 1985), it was highly questionable to generalize from laboratory studies of bystander interventions to all forms of prosocial behavior.

These problems do not mean, however, that one cannot conduct valid research about *whether* men and women differ in their willingness to help others; nor does it mean that one cannot study *why* such differences occur. We address both of these issues in the next section.

Sex Differences in Helping: Myth or Reality?

Do men and women differ in their propensity to engage in prosocial actions? As we have just suggested, to provide a meaningful answer to this question, we need to consider the *kind* of prosocial behavior we are talking about. For example, one rare but very interesting kind of prosocial action is heroism. According to Becker and Eagly (2004), heroism involves *both* risk taking and "service to a socially valued goal" (p. 164). Examples of heroic acts include running into a burning building to save a child, attempting to stop an armed robbery, or the kinds of rescues that occurred in the Twin Towers immediately after the September 11 attacks (see chap. 1). Some researchers interested in male–female differences in prosocial actions have looked at the relative frequency of heroic actions by men and by women. One source of information about this issue comes from the Carnegie Hero Fund Commission, which has been making awards for the last hundred years to people who voluntarily and knowingly risk their own lives "while saving or attempting to save the life of another person" (Carnegie Hero Fund Commission Requirements Section, paragraph 1). The commission excludes from consideration people such as firefighters and police officers (because their jobs might require such actions) and instead only considers "ordinary" people who engage in these heroic acts. From 1904 through 2003, there were 8,706 Carnegie Medalists, and less than 10% have been women (Becker & Eagly, 2004). Studies of other heroes yield similar findings (e.g., Huston, Ruggiero, Conner, & Geis, 1981). But can we infer from these studies that men are more helpful than women?

Becker and Eagly (2004) suggested that this is not the case. For example, they looked at Christians who risked their lives to save Jews during the Holocaust in Europe in the 1940s (for more on this, see chap. 7) and found that women were significantly more likely to have offered that kind of help than men. Women are also more likely than men to work in "caring" professions (e.g., nursing), to become volunteers, and to be organ donors (Becker & Eagly, 2004; Biller-Andorno, 2002; Cancain & Oliker, 2000; Fletcher & Major, 2004; Independent Sector, 2002; Zimmerman, Donnelly, Miller, Stewart, & Albert, 2000).

Studies of interpersonal helping when there is not an emergency also seem to show that women are more helpful than men (Otten, Penner, & Waugh, 1988; Pomazal & Clore, 1973). Further, studies of both young children and adolescents find that girls are more likely to act prosocially, place importance on prosocial values, and experience empathy and concern for people in distress than are boys (Beutel & Johnson, 2004; Pakaslahti, Karjalainen, Keltikangas-Järvinen, 2002; Persson, 2005). These sex differences in helping also vary somewhat by culture. In one study comparing children in Brazil and the United States, girls generally shared resources more than boys, but this difference was greater in Brazil than in the United States (Carlo, Roesch, Knight, & Koller, 2001). If all this is true, why are women less likely to engage in risky emergency interventions than men?

The Costs of Helping

Is there something about helping in emergencies that might lead men to intervene more than women? One possible explanation of sex differences in such situations is based on the concept of costs of helping (discussed in chaps. 3 and 4). As you may remember, the arousal: cost–reward model proposes that once potential helpers are aroused, they consider the costs of helping (and not helping) before they make a final decision about intervening. As the costs for helping increase, the likelihood that a bystander will help usually decreases.

Piliavin and Unger (1986) suggested that women may help less in these emergency situations not because they are less helpful people than men, but because it would cost them more to be heroic than men. For example, the fact that men, on average, are larger, have greater upper body strength, respond more quickly, and are better at tasks that require intensive bursts of strength and energy (Wood & Eagly, 2002) might make the cost of emergency interventions less for men than for women. If costs are playing a role in sex-related differences in this kind of helping, then researchers should find that they affect helping even among members of the same sex. Data that speak to this come from the Huston et al. (1981) study of people who had intervened to prevent dangerous crimes (e.g., muggings, bank robberies). Huston et al. compared these heroes (all male) to a comparison group of other men who had not intervened to save or rescue someone. Huston et al. found that their heroes were taller, heavier, and had more police and medical training than did the members of the comparison group. The researchers argued that the heroes were more likely to intervene at least in part because they believed it would cost them less to do so: Because of their size and previous experience, they were less likely to be injured and more likely to be successful when they intervened.

Physical differences between men and women cannot, however, completely account for the sex-related differences in helping. Another important part of understanding when and why such differences might occur lies in the concepts of gender and gender role.

Sex and Gender

Although many people use the terms *sex* and *gender* interchangeably, most social psychologists make a distinction between them. Eccles (1991) proposed that the term *sex* be used to refer to a person's "personal and reproductive status (solely) on the basis of genitalia." In contrast, *gender* should refer to "one's personal, social, and legal status as male and female, or mixed, on the basis of somatic and behavioral criteria" (p. 164). To social psychologists, a person's gender is usually considered to be a more important determinant of social behavior than the person's biological sex. The gender that a person assumes is partially determined by biological sex but probably more strongly influenced by the manner in which the person has been socialized. In essence, the processes and mechanisms discussed earlier in this chapter (e.g., conditioning, observational learning) "teach" children how to be a boy and how to be a girl. A person's gender affects the way he or she sees and reacts to the world and how other people see and react to the person.

A very important aspect of a person's gender status is his or her gender role. As we have already discussed, a role is a pattern of behavior expected of a person who occupies a certain position or status. Associated with any given role is a set of social norms or standards, and the expectations about these social norms are usually shared by the person who occupies the position and those who come into contact with the person. Compliance with these norms may bring positive social consequences; failure to comply with them may bring social disapproval. Most people simultaneously occupy many roles. For example, consider some of the many positions that you might presently occupy: sister or brother, student, employee, and, of course, being a woman or a man. The last role is associated with your sex status and is called your *gender role*, which Eagly and Crowley (1986) defined as a set of norms about how people should behave based on their presumed biological sex.

Although gender role differences would not automatically lead to differences in how much people help, gender role could lead to differences in *when* people help and in the kinds of help they offer (Eagly & Crowley, 1986). For example, the female gender role encourages women to be compassionate, caring, kind, and nurturant, especially to their friends and family. In addition, even though men and women may not differ physiologically in how much physiological arousal other people's distress causes them (Eisenberg & Lennon, 1983), traditional gender roles may lead women be more likely to *interpret* this arousal as empathic emotion (see chap. 4) or to express these feelings as empathy on self-report measures (Becker & Eagly, 2004). In a similar vein, women are much more likely than men to provide their friends with personal favors, emotional support, and informal counseling about personal or psychological problems (Cross & Madson, 1997; Eisenberg & Fabes, 1991).

Now let us consider the male gender role. Relative to the female role, it is much more likely to be associated with traits such as being daring, risky, adventurous, and courageous than the female gender role (Diekman & Eagly, 2000; Williams & Best, 1990). These differences should result in somewhat different kinds of prosocial actions. Specifically, because of the norms associated with the male gender role, men are more likely than women to take physical risks and to engage in "chivalrous," behaviors, in which they protect individuals who are less able and powerful than they are. This would include such things as acts of heroism and bystander interventions in emergencies, as we described previously.

Reviews of the literature (e.g., Eagly & Crowley, 1986; Piliavin & Unger, 1985) have found that gender roles do, in fact, explain a substantial amount of the differences between men and women in prosocial actions. One consistent finding from the studies reviewed by these authors was that people tend to offer the kinds of help that are most consistent with and appropriate for their gender roles. For example, men are more likely than women to help someone whose automobile has broken down but are less likely than women to help someone who has a personal or emotional problem (Johnson & Aries, 1983; Penner, Dertke, & Achenbach, 1973).

More recently, Kidder (2002) studied how gender roles can affect organizational citizenship behavior (OCB). As we discussed in chapter 5, OCB consists of prosocial actions performed by paid employees of large organizations. These actions can be directed at coworkers (usually called *altruism*) or at the organization itself (usually called *generalized compliance* or *conscientiousness*). As she hypothesized, men and women engaged in the kinds of OCB that were most consistent with their gender roles. Specifically, women were more likely than men to help their coworkers, and men were more likely than women to help the organization itself. Further, the gender orientations of the jobs people held affected the kinds of OCB in which they engaged. For example, people who worked as nurses—a female-dominated profession—were more likely to engage in altruism than in generalized compliance, whereas people who worked as engineers—a male-dominated profession—were more likely to engage in generalized compliance than in altruism.

Even among people of the same sex, gender role can influence helping. Some individuals are *sex typed*; that is, they almost always engage in behaviors that are expected of people of their biological sex. There are, however, people who engage in behaviors that are appropriate for people of both sexes (e.g., men and women who are both assertive and sensitive to the feelings of others; men and women who enjoy playing basketball and doing needlepoint); such people are called *androgynous* (Bem, 1981). Mikolay, Dovidio, Ellyson, Maggiano, and Keating (1989) found that on traditionally feminine helping tasks, sex-typed women were more likely to help than were androgynous women; the pattern was reversed on less traditionally feminine tasks.

Before closing this section of male–female differences in helping, it should be noted that there are those who dissent from this gender roles explanation of these differences. Specifically, evolutionary psychologists would argue that male–female differences in the kinds of prosocial actions each gender is most likely to perform are the result of different strategies that males and females have used in the past to maximize the likelihood that they would be evolutionarily successful (see chap. 2). For men, being more risky and courageous than other men would give them greater access to fertile women and higher status in the group, both of which would increase their inclusive fitness. For women, however, the best strategy to increase their inclusive fitness was to care for others, in particular their own children (Campbell, 1999). According to this argument, sex differences seen among contemporary men and women reflect these different evolutionary strategies. Here we find another instance of the disagreements between the advocates of nature (i.e., genetic determinants) and the advocates of nurture (i.e., socialization) as explanations of human behavior. In this case, we believe that role theory provides a better explanation of how and why men and women differ with regard to their prosocial actions. However, we also suspect that, as is true for most social behaviors, the best explanations to be offered to account for female–male differences in prosocial behavior draw on both environmental and biological causes and emphasize the interactions between them.

Summary

Men and women differ in *how* and *when* they help. Men are more likely than women to engage in heroic actions that involve some danger. Women are more likely to engage in acts of caring and support for other people who are in distress. Although part of the reason for these differences lies in the physical differences between men and women (e.g., size, strength), gender norms and gender roles probably provide better explanations for the differences than does biological sex. Specifically, gender roles, which are largely the result of how people have been socialized, influence the kinds of prosocial actions in which men and women are most likely to engage. In general, people are more likely to act if the prosocial action is consistent with their gender role than if it is inconsistent.

THE ANSWER: SUMMARY AND IMPLICATIONS

This chapter sought to answer three important questions about helping and prosocial behavior: First, as people mature, how do they change with regard to the things that motivate them to help and the way they think about helping and altruism? In general, as we go through infancy to childhood to adolescence to adulthood, there is an increase in the extent to which helping is motivated by internal and intangible things. Accompanying this change is an increase in the extent to which people consider the rights and well-being of others when they have to make decisions about helping. As a result, adults are more likely to help spontaneously than are small children. However, developmental changes do not simply occur with the transition from childhood to adulthood; they occur throughout people's lifetimes.

This led us to the second question: What processes or mechanism are responsible for these developmental changes? The research suggests that two general processes are primarily responsible. The first involves more or less natural developmental changes in how children think about helpful and altruistic behaviors. It appears that as children mature, there are quantitative and qualitative changes in the ways they think and reason about the physical and social world around them. These affect children's thoughts and actions related to helping. For example, although the very young child (3 to 5 years of age) sees the world primarily from an egocentric perspective, the young adult is able to also see the world through the eyes of other people. As a result, young adults are more likely to understand that other people have needs and are more likely to help them satisfy these needs.

The second process involves social learning and socialization. As the result of social learning mechanisms such as direct reinforcement, modeling, and verbal communications, long-term and generalized changes in children's prosocial behavior take place. These changes occur initially because children learn that society values prosocial actions and they then internalize these values. At the same time, engaging in helpful actions produces changes in children's perceptions of themselves and the explanations they offer for their own behavior. Among older children and adults of all ages, repeatedly engaging in prosocial actions may shape their personal identities and social roles, and these roles and identities, in turn, can motivate future helpful behaviors.

Although the two processes were presented separately, they are actually highly interdependent. Children cannot learn from certain experiences until they are cognitively ready. Similarly, many of the changes in the way children reason and make moral decisions are the product of learning experiences they have had.

Finally we asked how these development processes affect the behaviors of adults. We saw that changes in the physical abilities and cognitive capacities of adults can influence their motivations to help, which in turn can produce experiences that reinforce their helpfulness and influence how they perceive of themselves in relation to others. In the last section of the chapter, we saw how physical and strong socialization differences between women and men combine in intricate ways to determine when, how, and why differences in helping between men and women occur.

This chapter (along with the preceding chapters) illustrates the profound, joint influence of nature and nurture on prosocial behavior. There is surely a genetic basis for helping and altruism among humans (see chap. 2), and maturational processes play an important role as well. However, we cannot explain and understand many of the helpful actions that we observe in humans unless we also consider the social circumstances and culture in which they live and the learning experiences they have had.

Thus far, in considering the different processes that contribute to prosocial behavior, we have focused on the *similarities* in how people react to certain situations, the *common* genetic heritage of humans, and the *shared* experiences that socialize human beings. However, within a culture, a group, or a social setting, there are also palpable differences in how various people respond to the same event. Developmental influences are certainly involved, but the unique qualities of the individuals are also important. Therefore, in the next chapter, we turn our attention to individual differences in helping.

CHAPTER 7

Being the Helper and Being Helped: Causes and Consequences

T he material presented in the previous chapters might lead you to conclude that helping is a behavior that is pretty much a part of human nature and to believe that everyone is equally helpful. For example, in chapter 2, which considered the biological bases of prosocial actions, we argued that there may be an evolutionary advantage for those who are helpful to both relatives and strangers, and we even suggested that humans might be genetically "hard-wired" to be helpful. In the subsequent chapters, we discussed how situational factors can cause most people to act prosocially (or not to do so). When we discussed collective forms of helping in chapter 5, we more or less skirted the issue of individual differences in the likelihood that people would engage in such actions, focusing instead primarily on demographic, situational, and organizational variables. Only in the previous chapter, which examined the development of prosocial tendencies and sex differences in prosocial actions, did we really discuss the possibility that people could have different socialization experiences that could result in differences in how prosocial they were. But now it is time to directly consider individual differences in the willingness to help. In addition, we expand our view of the helping *relationship*, considering the perspective of the person being helped.

THE QUESTION

In this chapter our focus turns from prosocial actions to the people who perform them and the people who are the recipients of these actions. In terms of helpers, we begin by considering whether there are reliable individual differences among people in their propensity to offer aid to others. This leads to an examination of when and how certain personality traits and other personal attributes are related to various kinds of prosocial actions. Therefore, one major goal of the first section of this chapter is to identify the personal characteristics that are most clearly related to different kinds of helping and to understand why these relationships exist. From there we turn to the consequences of helping for the person who helps. We examine the ways in which helping might benefit the helper.

In this chapter, we also look at the other side of the coin and consider helping from the perspective of the person who may need assistance. In this part of the chapter, we explore the circumstances that lead people to seek help or inhibit them from asking for assistance. People with problems do not invariably seek help or accept it when it is offered. In addition, we examine the impact of receiving assistance on the recipient of help. Although each section of this chapter addresses a somewhat different aspect of prosocial behavior, they all share a common focus on individuals and the causes and consequences of their actions. The core questions that are asked in this chapter are: (a) What personal characteristics are associated with individual differences in helpfulness? (b) What are the consequences of helping for people who engage in prosocial action? (c) What factors influence people's decision to accept or seek assistance?

THE HELPER: INDIVIDUAL DIFFERENCES IN PROSOCIAL BEHAVIOR

There is little question that people differ in their reactions to others in distress and their willingness to act. Consider bystander intervention in emergencies. Among the researchers who study this kind of short-term interpersonal helping, there is a very strong emphasis on how the situation can influence a person's willingness to help (see chaps. 3 and 4). But these researchers will acknowledge that even when people are in the same situation, there will be differences in their reactions when they see someone who needs their help (e.g., Dovidio et al., 1991). For example, some potential helpers will become quite aroused by the emergency, whereas others will not. Some people may empathize a great deal with the victim, whereas others may not. Confronted with the same emergencies, some people will help; others will not.

Evidence of individual differences can be found in collective long-term helping as well. Consider volunteering, for example. The most common reason why people say they volunteer is simply because someone asked them to do so (Independent Sector, 2002). But people differ greatly in how they respond to such questions, and even among those who become volunteers, there are substantial differences in their commitment to the volunteer organization (Omoto & Snyder, 1995). We now consider some of the reasons for these differences.

In this section we discuss three different but related areas of research on individual differences in prosocial behavior: personality traits, attachment styles, and motives, values and culture.

Personality Traits and Prosocial Tendencies

Do people differ in their prosocial tendencies because of their personalities? Although many people outside of psychology would quickly answer "yes" to this question, over the years there has been considerable disagreement among psychologists about the actual importance of personality characteristics as *causes* of social behaviors. Before we can discuss personality traits and prosocial tendencies, we must briefly discuss this debate.

In the 1930s, Kurt Lewin, one of the most influential figures in the history of social psychology, laid out his general theory of the causes of human social behavior. Behavior, said Lewin, is a function of both the person and the environment or, in Lewin's (1936) shorthand formula, $B = f(P,E)$. Lewin believed that in order to understand completely a person's social behavior, one must know about the characteristics of the person (P) and the characteristics of the situation in which the behavior occurs (E). In addition, he noted that the characteristics of the situation and the personality might interact with each other in complex ways. However, Lewin's students, who dominated social psychology for many years, mostly focused on the "E" in his formula. They believed that situational characteristics were the key to understanding social behavior and ignored to a large extent the role of individual difference variables in their theories and experiments.

A much smaller number of psychologists focused on the "P" in Lewin's equation. These were the personality theorists, most of whom took a trait approach to personality. Specifically, they argued that our personalities are comprised of traits. What exactly is a trait? Traits are characteristics of individuals. Some traits are physical, observable characteristics, such as a person's height, eye color, and the like; other traits are not directly observable but must be inferred from observable behaviors. Among these are intelligence and, of primary interest here, personality traits. Like other traits (e.g., height, intelligence), personality traits are usually assumed to be normally distributed throughout the entire population, and people differ widely with respect to where they fall on these distributions. That is, just as some people you know are much taller than others, some people you know possess more of a given personality trait (e.g., extraversion) than others.

Thus, a *personality trait* is an enduring aspect of a person's character that manifests itself in that person's thoughts, feelings, and actions. Personality theorists acknowledge that these responses are also influenced by the situations people confront, but they believe that much of the consistency in people's thoughts, feelings, and actions across time and across situations is due to personality traits. With regard to helping, personality theorists believe that some people do consistently exhibit prosocial tendencies across time and across situations, and some of the differences between people in their willingness to help are due to differences among them in their personality traits (e.g., Rushton, 1984).

The trait theory perspective has been sharply challenged by many social psychologists who believe that the primary determinants of most social behavior can be found in the characteristics of the situation in which the behavior occurs. They argue that if the situation a person is in changes, the person's behavior will also change. Furthermore, they claim there has been little evidence of consistency in people's behavior across different situations. To quote Richard Nisbett (1980), a foremost proponent of situational explanations of social behavior, "The trait approach to the determination of social behavior … is largely wrong" (p. 110). The status of personality variables as explanations of why people help was succinctly summarized by J. A. Piliavin et al. (1981): "The search for the 'generalized helping personality' has been futile" (p. 184).

The debate about the roles of the environment and the person as causes of behavior continues. However, in the 25 or so years since these two judgments about personality as an explanation of differences in prosocial and other actions were offered, most researchers have tempered their views about the value of studying personality traits as causes of prosocial behavior. Although most contemporary social psychologists still believe that situational variables are very important causes of social behavior, they have also come to believe that traits and other personality variables play important roles as well. For example, in 1991, the same authors who had described the search for the altruistic personality as "futile" in 1981

— consistency based on strength of sit
• strong /unambiguous → P no matter
• weak / ambiguous cues → P important

PxF

BEING THE HELPER AND BEING HELPED • **227**

wrote that "despite the pessimism of earlier reviews of this area ... , a growing body of literature suggests the importance of individual differences in helping" (Dovidio et al., 1991, p. 101).

These theorists do not believe that personality traits operate independently of the situation. Rather, they have concluded that Kurt Lewin was right almost 60 years ago when he said that _both_ the person and the environment affect social behavior, that is, B = f(P,E). In contemporary psychology this position is called _interactionism_, or the person × situation framework. As the symbol × between the person and situation suggests, behavior is the _product_ of both the person and the situation. Behavior will change as a function of changes in situations, but within the new situations, people will differ in the behaviors they display. The extent to which people's behavior will vary will depend on the strength of the situational demands. In circumstances in which there are strong and unambiguous cues about how a person should behave, personality traits will not be important causes of behavior. But in circumstances in which these cues are weak and the norms about how a person should be expected to act are ambiguous, personality traits will be important causes of behavior (Penner, 2004; Snyder, 1992; Snyder & Ickes, 1985). For example, if an elderly woman carrying a cane falls down, cries out in pain, and directly asks for help, there will be few differences in how people respond. Most will probably offer assistance. In contrast, if an apparently able young man falls, makes no sound, and says nothing about needing help, there may be large differences in how people respond to his problem. Some will help, others will walk by, and some may even snicker about the victim's clumsiness.

Similarly, when a service organization puts out a call for volunteers, some people will respond, and some will not. And, as we have mentioned throughout the book, there are heroic altruists such as Paul Rusesabagina, who risked his own life to save the lives of hundreds of his Rwandan countrymen during the genocidal civil war in that country; Oskar Schindler, a German citizen, who defied the Nazis and helped hundreds of Jews escape death in Hitler's gas chambers; and the men and women in the Twin Towers on 9/11 who did not leave the buildings until they had helped others escape from the structures. What are the sources of personal variation in these kinds of behaviors?

The Prosocial Personality.   Researchers interested in understanding the sources of differences in prosocial tendencies have tried to identify the personality traits that are consistently associated with prosocial actions. Some researchers (Ashton, Paunonen, Helmes, & Douglas, 1998; Graziano & Eisenberg, 1997) proposed that some of the "big five" core dimensions of personality (i.e., Neuroticism,

Extraversion, Openness, Agreeableness, Conscientiousness; see Mc-
Crae & Costa, 1999) are responsible for individual differences in
prosocial actions. The two dimensions that are most frequently implicated in prosocial behavior are Agreeableness and Conscientiousness. Agreeableness is associated with trust and tender-mindedness
(Graziano & Tobin, 2002). In general, people higher on Agreeableness
are more cooperative with others (Ross, Rausch, & Canada, 2003) and
volunteer more to help others (Carlo, Okun, Knight, & de Guzman,
2005). People higher on conscientiousness, which relates to competence and reliability, are more active blood donors (Ferguson, 2004).
In addition, there are people with particular combinations of these
traits who may be particularly likely to help in certain situations.
Supportive of this possibility, King, George, and Hebl (2005) found
that although people higher in Agreeableness were generally more
helpful to others at work (organizational citizenship behaviors; see
chap. 5), this was primarily the case for those who also tended to be
high in Conscientiousness. These people both were oriented toward
the needs of others and felt competent to assist them.

Still other researchers have focused on sets or groups of personality
characteristics that are highly correlated with one another, and all related to prosocial thoughts, feelings and actions. This cluster of traits is
what Penner, Fritzsche, Craiger, and Freifeld (1995) called the prosocial
personality. There is reason to believe that some of the characteristics
that make up the prosocial personality develop fairly early in people's
lives and remain fairly stable over time. For example, Eisenberg et al.
(2002) found that ratings of empathy and prosocial responding among
a group of children were correlated with self-reports of prosocial personality characteristics when these children had grown into young
adults. Further, these prosocial dispositions remained stable among
the young adults for a substantial period of time.

More generally, there is consistency in prosocial behavior across extended periods of time. For example, 40 years after World War II ended,
people who had risked their lives to save Jews from the Nazis were still
more helpful than people who had not rescued Jews (Oliner & Oliner,
1988). Marwell and his associates (e.g., Marwell, Aiken, & Demerath,
1993) conducted a long-term study of some of the White college students who had actively worked for civil rights for African Americans
in the 1960s. Twenty years later, these people were compared to people
of the same age who had not engaged in these prosocial actions as college students in the 1960s. The former civil rights activists were much
more likely than members of the comparison group to be involved in
prosocial activities, such as fund-raising, donating money, organizing
for social causes, and volunteering for charities.

- get small group of 1 pro beh → indepthexam of background & personality
↳ what makes them diff?

BEING THE HELPER AND BEING HELPED • **229**

Such findings have led some researchers to try to identify the set of personality characteristics responsible for this consistency in prosocial actions. One strategy to do this is to find small groups of people who have already been identified as prosocial individuals—individuals who have engaged in exceptional acts of helping others. After locating these people, the researcher conducts in-depth examinations of these helpers, focusing on their personal backgrounds and their personalities. The goal is to find out what makes these individuals different from ordinary people. Another approach is to study large groups of people drawn more or less at random from the population and to identify the personality characteristics that make some of them consistently more helpful than others. The results from studies that have used each approach are presented in the following sections.

→ large randomly chosen group → what makes them consistently better?

Uncommon People: The Traits of Heroes. Adolf Hitler's campaign to exterminate all Jews formally began on November 9, 1938, in Germany, on a night that has come to be called *Kristallnacht*—literally, the night of broken glass. Jewish synagogues were destroyed, Jewish-owned businesses were set afire, and mobs of Hitler's followers drove Jews from their homes, took their property, and beat them. Shortly thereafter, the Nazi leadership decided that the "final solution" to the so-called "Jewish problem" was to kill them all. As Germany conquered other countries in Europe, the scope of the genocide against the Jews increased. In some countries, large numbers of people actively resisted the Germans' attempt to slaughter the Jews who lived there. For example, when all the Jews in Denmark were ordered to wear an arm band with the Star of David on it, the King of Denmark, a Christian, appeared wearing such an arm band. In one night, Danish citizens helped over 7,000 Jews escape from the Nazis to neutral Sweden (Arnold, 1967). But in other countries, the citizens aided the Nazis in the mass extermination of the Jews, other ethnic minorities (e.g., Roma or Gypsies), homosexuals, and people with physical and mental disabilities.

There were, however, individuals in countries that were sympathetic to Germany's Third Reich who refused to go along with the extermination of the Jews. There have been several studies of the people who helped those targeted for extermination; one of the more notable studies was conducted by Samuel and Pearl Oliner (1988). Samuel Oliner was, himself, a survivor of the Holocaust. Although the rest of his family died in a concentration camp, he was rescued by a Christian family who were friends of his parents (Hunt, 1990). Many years later, he and his wife, Pearl, began a systematic study of the characteristics of people who, like the family who had rescued him, had attempted to save Jews from the Nazis. The Oliners were able to locate 231 such individuals. These *rescuers* were com-

Holocaust survivor → study of characteristics of ppl who attempted to save Jews.

[handwritten note: compared rescuers to same demographic ppl who didn't rescue Jews.]

pared to a sample of 126 individuals with essentially the same demographic characteristics as the rescuers (i.e., their age, sex, education, the place where they had lived during the war) but who had not helped any Jews escape from the Nazis. The specific question that the Oliners asked was: What characteristics differentiated the two groups of people?

Some of the differences between the rescuers and nonrescuers did not seem to have much to do with a prosocial personality. For example, compared to nonrescuers, the rescuers reported greater actual and perceived similarity between themselves and people of Jewish ancestry. This finding has also been obtained in other studies of different rescuers (e.g., London, 1970; Midlarsky, 1985/1986), and it is consistent with the general finding that perceived similarity leads to helping (see chap. 3). The rescuers were also more likely than the nonrescuers to have been directly asked to help a Jew escape the Nazis. Again, as you have already read, a direct request for help usually produces results. These findings indicate that situational differences may have produced at least some of the differences among the people the Oliners studied.

But there were other differences between the rescuers and the nonrescuers that do appear to be related to socialization and to personality differences. One of the socialization differences involved how they had been disciplined by their parents. The parents of the rescuers were more caring individuals who were much less likely to use physical punishment to control the behavior of their children. Instead, the rescuers' parents reasoned with their children and explained what the children had done wrong and what kinds of behaviors were expected of them. As you may recall from chapter 6, Martin Hoffman (1970) called this induction or other-oriented discipline and proposed that it is more likely to produce helpful, prosocial children.

[handwritten margin note: less phys punish by parents]

Another difference involving the parents was that rescuers were much more likely to identify strongly with a parent who was very moral and provided a model of moral conduct. This relationship was also found by London (1970) in his study of other rescuers and is consistent with the results of studies of other groups of heroic altruists. For example, David Rosenhan (1970) reported that White Americans who made great sacrifices to help African Americans in their struggle for civil rights in the 1960s also had parents who served as strong role models of moral conduct.

The remaining differences between the rescuers and nonrescuers more directly involved personality traits. Two of these would be predicted from knowledge of how a situation can change the emotions and thoughts of potential helpers and how these changes can affect the likelihood that bystanders will intervene (see chaps. 3 and 4). For example, as we noted earlier in this chapter (and in chap. 4), Daniel Batson (1991) found that if people are made to empathize with someone in distress, the likelihood that they will help increases, even when the costs of helping are relatively high. Thus, it is not surprising to learn that the tendency to empathize with other people's feelings was greater among the rescuers than the nonrescuers. However, this was not simply the transitory kind of empathic responses discussed in chapter 4; rather, the rescuers were higher in *dispositional empathy*—a consistent tendency to respond emotionally to other people's emotional experiences and to understand their point of view. A second personality characteristic that distinguished the two groups was the *willingness to accept responsibility* for one's own actions and, more importantly, for the well-being of other people. This is also consistent with the finding from experiments on bystander interventions (also discussed in chap. 4) that if something causes an increased sense of personal responsibility among bystanders they are more likely to help (Berkowitz & Daniels, 1963).

Other personality traits that differentiated rescuers and nonrescuers were more complex. One of these was labeled *extensivity*. Extensivity involves the combination of empathy, a sense of responsibility, and the capacity to feel concern for and attachment to other people. In particular, people high on extensivity are distinguished by unusually high levels of empathy and feelings of social responsibility toward members of groups other than their own. Although most people would reserve these feelings primarily for someone who is similar to them and part of their own group, the rescuers felt this same concern for dissimilar people who were members of other groups. Thus, although most of the nonrescuers were biased in favor of members of their group (i.e., other Christians), most of the rescuers had the same feelings for members of other groups (e.g., Jews) as they had for members of their own group. They felt that "justice is not just for yourself and your own kind, but for others beyond your group" (Oliner, quoted in Hunt, 1990, p. 204). It is unusual for people to feel this way (e.g., Dovidio & Gaertner, 1993) and makes the rescuers different from most people.

Finally, the rescuers were people who "felt that they could control events and shape their own destinies and ... perceived themselves as actors capable of making and implementing plans and willing to accept the consequences" (Oliner & Oliner, 1988, p. 177). Such people are often described as having a sense of personal control (Paulhus & Van Selst, 1990) or having feelings of *self-efficacy* (e.g., Bandura, 1997); they believe they will succeed in the things they attempt to do. This characteristic has also been found in other studies of "altruists." For example, Colby and Damon (1992) conducted in-depth interviews with 23 exceptional individuals who had made significant, long-term contributions to the betterment of other people. According to Colby and Damon, one of these people's most salient traits was that they almost welcomed the challenges to achieving their goals and were unlikely to be discouraged by the obstacles that stood in the way of helping others.

More recently, Midlarsky, Jones, and Corley (2005) conducted another comparison of rescuers with people from their countries who did not offer help to victims of the holocaust. Their results were quite similar to those of the Oliners. That is, the rescuers scored higher on measures of empathy, social responsibility, and sense of control over their lives.

Although the findings from these studies are very impressive, the research is not without its weaknesses. There is a subtle but potentially serious problem with studies that use this approach to learn about the personality characteristics of altruistic individuals. Long before they were interviewed, the rescuers had already been publicly identified (and honored) as heroes or "true altruists." Being labeled as such by others may have affected how these people viewed themselves and formed their own self-image. This may have resulted in their answering questions from the Oliners and others about their personality in the way they thought an altruist should. Thus, their earlier actions and the reactions of others to them as a consequence of their prosocial actions may have been a cause of subsequent personality differences, rather than their personalities having caused their earlier prosocial behavior. This potential problem with this approach to defining the prosocial personality means that we must continue a little further before we can draw any firm conclusions about the personality traits that are part of it.

Common People: Prosocial Traits. In a second approach to understanding the prosocial personality, researchers have had people fill out questionnaires that measure personality traits and then examine the association between scores on the questionnaires and prosocial thoughts, feeling, and actions. Of special interest is whether the traits identified by this approach are the same as those identified by the other one—is there a convergence of the findings from these two different research strategies? To anticipate the results of this comparison, it would appear that there is such a convergence.

One key component of the prosocial personality is empathy. There have been several studies that have examined the relationship between dispositional empathy—a consistent tendency to respond emotionally to other people's emotional experiences and to understand their point of view—and helping. Most commonly dispositional empathy has been measured with Mark Davis's (1980) Interpersonal Reactivity Index (IRI). Some of the items from Davis's index are presented in Table 7.1.

TABLE 7.1
Sample Items from Davis's IRI
Reflecting Individual Differences in Empathic Concern

1. I often have tender, concerned feelings for people less fortunate than me.
2. When I see someone being taken advantage of, I feel kind of protective toward them.
3. I would describe myself as a pretty soft-hearted person.
4. I am often quite touched by things that I see happen.

Several studies have found that empathy is related to prosocial actions, particularly actions that require some planning and thought (e.g., Eisenberg & Miller, 1987). For example, Davis (1983) administered the IRI to students who had watched the annual Jerry Lewis Muscular Dystrophy telethon and obtained self-reports of how much money they had donated to this charity. Davis found a significant correlation between empathy and how much students donated to the telethon. Otten, Penner, and Altabe (1991) found that even among professional helpers (psychotherapists), those who scored high on Davis's measure of empathy were more likely to help a person with a work assignment (writing an article about psychotherapy) than were therapists who had scored low. The trait of empathy is also related to long-term commitment to help by working as a volunteer (Davis et al., 1999). Thus, studies of both heroes and everyday helpers suggest that people who are dispositionally more empathic are generally more helpful.

A second element of the prosocial personality is *a sense of responsibility.* As was the case with the rescuers, a number of studies have found that a sense of responsibility for the welfare of others is associated with prosocial behavior. For example, Staub (1974) found that participants who accepted social responsibility and engaged in other-oriented moral reasoning were likely to come to the aid of a person who was feeling ill (see also Staub, 1996). Berkowitz and Daniels (1964) found that people who scored high on their measure of social responsibility were, relative to people who scored low, more likely to help someone who was dependent on them for help.

The final attribute that appears to characterize both the rescuers and the life-long altruists studied by Colby and Damon was a sense of *self- or personal efficacy.* They were self-confident individuals who believed they could successfully meet the challenges that confronted them. Is there any evidence that this personality characteristic causes people to act prosocially? In younger age groups, children who are assertive are more likely to initiate prosocial acts than those who are not assertive

(Graziano & Eisenberg, 1997). Rushton (1984) found that people who were volunteers at a community mental health center were independent individuals who were particularly likely to believe that they controlled what happened to them. And finally, Penner and Fritzsche (1993) found that helpful people are also self-assured and confident of their abilities.

Measuring the Prosocial Personality. Penner and his associates attempted to combine these traits into a single measure of the prosocial personality. The resulting questionnaire was called the Prosocial Personality Battery (Penner et al., 1995). A factor analysis of responses to the items in this battery indicates that it measures two separate dimensions of the prosocial personality. The first, called *other-oriented empathy,* concerns prosocial thoughts and feelings. People who score high on this dimension are able to empathize with others' feelings and thoughts, have a sense of responsibility for the welfare of others, and consider the feelings of others when they are making decisions. This dimension of the prosocial personality is very highly correlated with measures of Agreeableness (Penner et al., 1995), and it also appears to be very similar to what the Oliners called *extensivity.* Even among "ordinary" people, the traits that comprise other-oriented empathy appears to be related to a number of prosocial feelings and behaviors. For example, people who score high on this scale estimate the cost of helping others as lower, report more sympathy and concern for someone who is in trouble, and are more likely to help a friend with a personal problem (Carlo, Eisenberg, Troyer, Switzer, & Speer, 1991; Penner et al., 1995). Bierhoff, Klein, and Kramp (1991) found that witnesses who intervened to help victims of traffic accidents were more empathic and had a stronger sense of social responsibility than bystanders who did not intervene. Finally, Helen Harton (personal communication, May, 1997) found that the higher someone scored on other-oriented empathy, the faster they responded in an emergency.

This dimension of the prosocial personality is also related to more planful helping. People who are high on the traits that comprise other-oriented empathy are more likely than people who score low to be volunteers (Penner, 2002; Penner et al., 1995; Penner & Fritzsche, 1993; Unger & Thumuluri, 1997). In a study of volunteers at an AIDS service organization, Penner and Finkelstein (1998) found that scores on the other-oriented empathy dimension taken at the beginning of the study predicted how much time male volunteers spent with people with HIV/AIDS 11 months later. Finally, other-oriented empathy has also been found to be related to how willing people were to engage in organizational citizenship behavior (OCB; see chap. 5), especially OCB that is directed at other people rather than the organization (Borman, Penner, Allen, & Motowidlo, 2002; Tillman, 1998).

The other dimension of the prosocial personality identified by Penner et al. (1995) was called *helpfulness* and concerned a propensity to *act* prosocially. Interestingly, this helpfulness is not that strongly related to other-oriented empathy or to other personality attributes of prosocial people, such as agreeableness. In other words, people who are high on this dimension are inclined to perform prosocial actions, but they do not necessarily experience prosocial thoughts or feelings. Scores on the helpfulness dimension of the Prosocial Personality Battery have been found to correlate with willingness to be an organ donor (Cicognani, 1999), the number of charities for which a person volunteers (Penner, 2002), organizational citizenship behavior (Connell & Penner, 2004), and willingness to serve as a mentor in a large organization (Allen, 1999).

Other research has shown that scores on the helpfulness dimension are positively associated with a sense of self-efficacy, personal competence, and a need to master and control one's environment (Penner et al., 1995). This finding is consistent with Graziano and Eisenberg's (1997) ideas about what constitutes "altruism" (or prosocial behavior): "[It] involves not only an other-orientation but also the ability to enact helping actions, [therefore] it is reasonable to expect [positive] correlations between altruism indices and [measures of] individual competence and control" (p. 59). Similarly the ability to control one's emotions is associated with prosocial tendencies (Lopes, Salovey, Côté, Beers, & Petty, 2005). Thus, people not only need to possess the inclination to act prosocially but also to believe that they are capable of helping others.

This brief review suggests that there may well be such a thing as the prosocial personality, and it is comprised of the following relatively enduring personal attributes: empathy, a sense of responsibility, concern for the welfare of others, a willingness to actually act prosocially, and a sense of confidence about the outcomes of those actions.

Personality and Situations.   Before leaving the prosocial personality, we need to put it in context. Personality characteristics do appear to play important roles in individual differences in prosocial thoughts, feelings, and actions. The conventional wisdom of 25 years ago appears to be incorrect. But it would be just as incorrect to ignore the role of social circumstances or situations as causes of difference, in prosocial responses. Most importantly, as noted earlier, personality characteristics and situational factors can *interact* to affect people's thoughts, feelings, and actions—prosocial and otherwise. For example, personality attributes influence the decisions individuals make about places they should go and/or the people with whom they will interact (Carver & Scheier, 2004). But as we saw in chapters 3 and 4, once a person is in a particular situation or with certain people, his or her actions will be greatly influenced by the characteristics of the situation and the behavior of the other people in it.

Attachment Styles   *result of experience w/ caretaker @ infancy.*

In the last few years, Mario Mikulincer and Philip Shaver (2001, 2003, 2005) began an interesting line of research about another source of individual differences in prosocial responses. Specifically, they explored how differences in *attachment styles* might affect people's willingness to respond prosocially. Briefly, attachment style refers to how a person relates to other people, especially people with whom the person has a close personal relationship.

According to attachment theorists (e.g., Bowlby, 1988), people's attachment styles are the result of their experiences as infants with their parents or other caretakers. To be more precise, the crucial experiences involve how the caretaker responded when the infant was in distress and needed either physical (e.g., food, water) or emotional (e.g., comfort, safety) help. For most children, parents or other adult caretakers consistently respond to the child's distress by offering support and comfort. But other parents may respond inconsistently, sometimes being comforting and sometimes not, and still others may not respond very positively to their children's distress (Mikulincer & Shaver, 2003). According to attachment theory, these experiences lead to the formation of "working models" or general ideas of how other people with whom they are close will treat them. These different working models produce different styles of relating to or attaching to others. The most commonly identified styles are *secure,* in which people desire close relations with others and find them calming; *fearful–avoidant,* in which the person desires intimate contact with others but it makes him or her anxious; and *dismissing–avoidant,* in which the person does not desire a lot of contact with intimate others (Bartholomew & Horowitz, 1991).

Mikulincer and Shaver (2005) reasoned that people who have a secure attachment style are able to concern themselves with other people's need and welfare because they are not as worried about what will happen to themselves, and because "[this] sense of security is closely related to optimistic beliefs and feelings of self-efficacy when coping with one's own or [another's] distress." (p. 35). Such feelings would not be as strong among people with fearful or dismissive attachment styles. In some recent studies, researchers have examined how the feelings associated with different attachment styles were related to willingness to offer help. Consistent with the theoretical expectations, Gillath, Shaver, and

• secure → can concern self to others welfare → b/c secure in self
↳ optimism, SE, cope w/ own distress

Mikulincer (2005) found that the avoidant attachment style was negatively associated with willingness to volunteer or donate blood, and that people who had an anxious style said they would volunteer primarily for selfish or egoistic reasons (e.g., to make themselves feel better).

These findings are, of course, correlational, and therefore we cannot say whether the attachment styles were the causes or the effects of willingness to volunteer. In another study, Mikulincer, Shaver, Gillath, and Nitzberg (2004; cited in Mikulincer & Shaver, 2005) experimentally investigated the effects of attachment style on willingness to offer help to a distressed person. This experiment (conducted in both the United States and Israel) used a procedure somewhat similar to that used by Batson and other bystander intervention researchers. The participants were randomly divided into three groups, with members of each group receiving a different subliminal prime to activate the thoughts and feelings associated with a secure attachment style. Members of the "security prime" group were very briefly shown the name of someone with whom they associated strong feelings of safety and security; people in a second group were shown the name of a good friend, and those in the final group were shown the name of a more casual acquaintance. The participants then watched as another person (really a confederate of the experimenters) was asked to perform some extremely unpleasant tasks (e.g., pet a snake, let cockroaches crawl on her arm). As the tasks proceeded, the confederate became more and more uncomfortable and finally asked to take a rest. (This was, of course, all staged.) At this point the experimenter approached the participants and asked how willing they would be to take the woman's place and engage in several more unpleasant tasks. The results of this study are presented in Fig. 7.1.

About 30% of the participants who had previously received the close friend and casual acquaintance primes were willing to help, but almost 70% of those who received the secure prime were willing to help. This suggests that feelings of safety and security are associated with greater willingness to help, even when the helping involves some element of difficulty and danger. In the same study it was also found that people who scored high on a measure of an avoidant attachment style reported less compassion for the woman and were less likely to help her. The same results were found in both the United States and Israel.

This line of research is new, and it would be premature to definitively conclude that differences in attachment styles are an important source of differences in prosocial thoughts, feelings, and actions. However, this line of research certainly merits further examination, as it suggests another source of individual differences in prosocial tendencies.

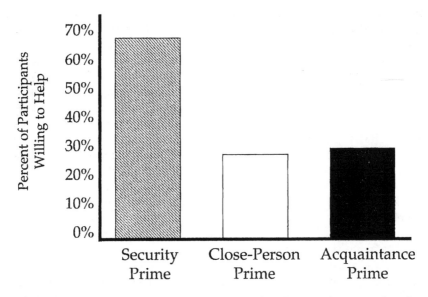

FIG. 7.1. Participants were more willing to help a distressed person when they were primed subliminally with the name of an attachment figure (Security Prime) than when they were primed with the name of a close person who was not an attachment figure or with the name of an acquaintance. From Mikulincer, Shaver, Gillath, and Nitzberg (2004, Study 1), with permission.

Motives, Needs, and Values

Before leaving the discussion of individual differences in prosocial tendencies, we briefly discuss some other possible sources of these differences. One of these is people' needs or motives. As has already been discussed in chapter 5, Mark Snyder and his associates proposed a *functional analysis* of volunteering, in which they suggest that people often act prosocially because it serves some personal or social need (e.g., Omoto & Snyder, 2002). As part of this research program, Clary et al. (1998) identified six motives that they believed represent most people's reasons for volunteering. Other researchers (e.g., Clary & Orenstein, 1991; Davis, Hall, & Meyer, 2003; Penner & Finkelstein, 1998; Snyder & Omoto, 2001) all found significant relationships between one or more motives and some aspect of volunteering. Further, Connell and Penner (2004) and Rioux and Penner (2001) both found that differences in the strength of certain motives are associated with differences in the amount of organizational citizenship people display. For instance, in an organizational setting, prosocial value motives relate to helping individuals on the job, whereas organizational concern motives are associated with behaviors directed at helping the organization (Rioux & Penner, 2001). Also, Piliavin (2005a) found that individuals with a long history of volunteering score higher on the Clary et al. "values" motive than those who have volunteered less or not at all.

Differences in values are another very likely source of differences in prosocial tendencies. According to Shalom Schwartz (1994), *values* are ideas of what is desirable that guide the way people choose among various actions, evaluate people and events, and explain their own actions and evaluations. People's decisions as to what action they should take reflect the relative importance they place on certain values. One set of values proposed by Schwartz is concerned with universalism and benevolence. These values would seem especially relevant for prosocial behaviors, that is, we would expect a person who places great importance on such values would be more prosocial than one who consider these values of lesser importance.

However, despite the apparent relevance of values to an understanding of individual differences in prosocial tendencies, there has been almost no empirical work on this relationship (S. Schwartz, personal communication, April 2005). The one exception is a study by Hitlin (2003), who examined the correlation between the importance placed on certain values and the strength of college students' volunteer role identity. Hitlin found a significant positive relationship between the value of "benevolence" (as measured by the importance assigned to things such as true friendship, honesty, forgiveness, helpfulness) and volunteer identity. He also found significant negative relationships between values associated with a desire for power and personal achievement and a volunteer identity. It must again be noted, however, that these findings only showed that certain values and a volunteer identity were related; they did not demonstrate that differences in values *caused* differences in volunteer identity. Despite this, we would argue that one potentially very valuable line of future research would be to study the role of values in individual differences in prosocial tendencies.

CONSEQUENCES FOR THE HELPER

Most people assume that both the primary motive for and consequence of helping is to improve the well-being of some person, group, organization, or country that is in need of help. But there can be unintended consequences as well, both positive and negative. Woody Hayes, the legendary Ohio State football coach, once said, "When you throw a forward pass, there are three things that can happen, and two of them are bad." There is also a variety of things that can happen when a person attempts to help another, and some of them can be bad—for the recipient, the helper, or both. Therefore, we now turn our attention to the effects of helping on the person who helps. First we consider the emotional consequences of offering help, and we begin with situations where the offer of help is refused.

potential helpers expect acceptance → when rejected → tension.

Reactions to Spurned Offers of Help

Sidney Rosen and his colleagues were among the first researchers to study how people reacted when their offers of help were rejected by others. Rosen, Mickler, and Collins (1987) proposed that most would-be helpers expect that a person who needs help will accept it from them, and if their offer of help is then rejected, the violation of an expectancy creates tension in the spurned helpers. To test this notion, Rosen et al. conducted a laboratory experiment in which a confederate either accepted or rejected subjects' offers of help. The helpers' reactions were then measured. Rejection created negative feelings in the potential helpers and decreased their liking for the person who rejected them. The spurned helpers also provided explanations for the rejection, some of which were unflattering to the recipient of their offer (including stubbornness, pride, and lack of trust). These results are consistent with the well-known theory of cognitive dissonance (Festinger, 1957). Specifically, as dissonance theory would predict, the rejected helpers were trying to rationalize or explain away this unpleasant and unexpected outcome. Rosen and his colleagues subsequently applied their ideas about the effects of rejected attempts to help to burnout among people who earn their living as "professional" helpers, such as medical personnel and teachers. Rosen et al. linked consistent spurning to burnout in such occupations. They proposed that these effects might be reduced, however, by teaching members of these professions to expect that some people would reject their attempts to help them and by the development of emotional coping skills to buffer the effects (Cheuk & Rosen, 1993; Cheuk, Wong, Swearse, & Rosen, 1997; Mickler & Rosen, 1994).

Reactions When Help Is Accepted

The fact that people react negatively when their offers of help are rejected might lead to the conclusion that they must react positively when help is accepted, but, surprisingly, there is little *direct* evidence that helping others actually makes the helper feel good (cf. Williamson &

Clark, 1989; Yinon & Landau, 1987). There is, however, a fair amount of evidence that most people believe they will feel better if they have helped others (Wuthnow, 1991). For example, Harris (1977) reported that college students she surveyed *believed* that altruistic actions have a mood-enhancing component. Another study of older adults (55 to 85 years) who volunteered to work in schools found that 65% of the volunteers reported improved life satisfaction; 76% reported feeling better about themselves; and 32% said that volunteering had improved their mental health (Newman, Vasudev, & Onawola, 1985). We would point out, however, that in this and many other studies (e.g., Hodgkinson & Weitzman, 1990, 1992) the major outcome variable has been *perceptions* of benefits from volunteering rather than *actual* benefits.

The most direct evidence that helping leads to positive feelings comes from a series of laboratory experiments by Weiss and colleagues (Weis, Boyer, Lombardo, & Stich, 1973; Weiss, Buchanan, Alstatt, & Lombardo, 1971). These studies demonstrated that being able to terminate shock to another student (clearly helping that person) served as a reinforcer in a classic operant conditioning setting. The faster subjects pressed a button, the sooner the shock was stopped, and the subjects learned to press it faster and faster. The reasoning is that helping in this way must have felt good, or the participants would not have learned the response. They concluded that "altruism is rewarding" (Weiss et al., 1971, p. 1262).

In terms of "real world" helping, the only direct evidence on the emotions that follow helping comes from studies of blood donation. J. A. Piliavin and Callero (1991) measured people's moods before and after they had donated blood. These blood donors included high school and college students and adults from the general public. Piliavin and Callero consistently found significant decreases in anxiety in all samples, and they also found significant changes in positive mood for the adult samples but not for the students. The authors explained this difference by suggesting that the students were generally in better moods than the adults *before* they gave blood, and thus it was harder to find an improvement in their moods after donating. In two separate samples of high school students who gave blood at least twice, there was a highly significant decrease in nervousness before donation and a borderline increase in warm feelings. More importantly, there were highly significant decreases in pulse rate and systolic blood pressure, physiological measures associated with anxiety (J. A. Piliavin & Callero, 1991). As might be expected, people's feelings when they donated blood predicted the amount they donated in the future.

More recently, Nilsson Sojka and Sojka (2003) asked 600 blood donors to answer an open-ended question asking "whether the blood donation had any impact" on them. Twenty-nine percent spontaneously reported only positive effects, including feelings of satisfaction and of feeling better than before the blood donation; exclusively negative effects were reported by only 19%. The positive effects of blood donations often lasted for weeks and persisted much longer than the negative effects.

Another way to examine the effects of helping on helpers is to examine how their behavior changes as the result of some prosocial action. In this vein, there is a fairly large amount of research on the long-term effects of volunteering and other forms of community services.

The Consequences of Volunteering

In this section we address how being a volunteer affects the volunteer's subsequent behavior, involvement in the community, career choices, and mental and physical health (Wilson & Musick, 2000). Research concerning psychological well-being, self-esteem, life satisfaction, and happiness has looked at volunteers all ages, but research on how volunteering affects people's life paths has focused almost exclusively on adolescents and young adults, and the research on physical well-being (including mortality) has focused mainly on older adults and the elderly. This separation by age seems to make sense. Adolescents have not yet developed all of their cognitive and social skills or been socialized completely to their social roles, and their sense of what kind of person they are (their "sense of self") is still developing. Thus, community service activities may have the potential of helping them to develop desirable personality traits, skills, and habits and to internalize helping roles as part of their self-concept. In contrast, the elderly are generally thought of as fully socialized but potentially alienated from society by virtue of retirement, loss of family roles, and decreasing physical abilities. Thus the focus of research on the elderly has been not on developmental issues but on things such as feelings of being part of society, avoiding depression, preserving physical health, and forestalling mortality.

Effects of Volunteering Among Adolescents and Young Adults. Adolescence and early adulthood is often a time of experimentation and rebellion. People in these age groups are more likely to engage in antisocial and deviant acts than are older people (I. M. Piliavin, Gartner, Thornton, & Matsueda, 1986; Sampson & Laub, 2002). Thus, one question asked by both researchers and people at large concerns what kinds of activities might reduce these tendencies. One suggestion is getting younger people involved in community service (Box 7.1).

Box 7.1

PERSONAL IMPACT OF SERVICE LEARNING ON OUTCOMES RELATED TO VOLUNTEER MOTIVES

Service learning is a specific kind of community participation that combines service in the community with a "reflective" component. For example, students in a course on the psychology of aging may, as part of the class, volunteer at a local nursing home. They may keep a diary of their activities there, reflect on its significance and relation to the material they are studying, and discuss aspects of what they observed in the class. Many students have had experience with this kind of volunteering. Stukas, Clary, and Snyder (1999b) concluded that "it is the reflection component and the surrounding educational context that serves to highlight the reciprocal nature of the community service activities at the center of service-learning programs. In other forms of service and helping, it may not be nearly as clear that both the recipient of help ... and the helper receive benefits from their partnership" (pp. 2–3).

Stukas et al. framed their review of the literature in terms of their functional approach to volunteering, which assumes that volunteers receive a variety of benefits related to six possible goals for volunteering: self-enhancement, understanding of self and the world, value expression, career development, ego protection, and social experiences. They claim that there is evidence for some effect related to each of the motives.

1. Self-enhancement. Service learning can enhance feelings of personal efficacy, self-esteem, and confidence (Giles & Eyler, 1994, 1998; Williams, 1991; Yates & Youniss, 1996b).

2. Understanding. Service learning increases:

a. Students' appreciation for and attitudes toward diverse groups in society, including the elderly and people from other cultures or races (Blyth, Saito, & Berkas, 1997; Bringle & Kremer, 1993; Myers-Lipton, 1996a, 1996b; Yates & Youniss, 1996a). There can be a backlash, however, if the exposure is too short or if participation is compulsory (Vadeboncoeur, Rahm, Aguilera, & LeCompte, 1996).

b. Specific learning of course content (Hamilton & Zeldin, 1987).

c. The ability to connect academic concepts to real situations (Kendrick, 1996; Miller, 1994a).

3. Value expression. Service learning can increase altruistic motivation and social and personal responsibility (Markus, Howard, & King, 1993; Sax & Astin, 1997; Yogev & Ronen, 1982).

Box 7.1 *(continued on next page)*

BOX 7.1 (CONTINUED)

4. *Career.* Service learning predicts students' academic commitment, importance of career plans, and desire for future community involvement, even when factors related to self-selection ... were taken into account (Johnson, Beebe, Mortimer, & Snyder, 1998).

Stukas et al. emphasized four features of the programs that appear to be related to positive effects: (a) being autonomy-supportive—that is, allowing participants a voice in determining the details of service activities; (b) matching goals and activities—that is, allowing students' needs and interests to help shape the activities so as to contribute to the attainment of goals; (c) paying attention to the relationship among all participants, involving mutual respect among instructors, students, and community participants; and (d) including opportunity for reflection, which "cement[s] the link between experience and theory" (p. 14).

Programs such as the Valued Youth Program (reviewed by Moore & Allen, 1996) directly investigated how volunteering can affect antisocial and deviant behavior among adolescents. This program focused on children in middle school in San Antonio, TX, all of whom had scored below grade level on reading tests. They were randomly assigned to a control group or to do tutoring of other children. These students were compared at the beginning and end of a two-year evaluation period on grades, disciplinary action, school absences, and school dropout, as well as self-concept and perception of quality of school life. Moore and Allen found lower dropout rates and better reading grades, self-concept, and attitudes towards school among the students who had been assigned to be volunteers. This is an important study because by using random assignment to the two groups, the researchers eliminated an alternative explanation of the finding, namely, that adolescents who volunteer are less deviant than nonvolunteers to begin with. This is called a *selection bias*, and it is a problem in many field studies of the effects of volunteering, including the next one we discuss.

Another program, the Teen Outreach Program, involved volunteer work that was meaningful to students for an average of 31 hours over an academic year (slightly less than an hour a week). The participants were from 11 to 21 years old, an ethnically diverse group, and identified as "at risk" for problem behaviors (e.g., teenage pregnancy or being suspended from school; Allen, Philliber, & Hoggsen, 1990; Allen, Philliber, Herrling, & Kuperminc, 1997). The students who chose to work as volunteers and a group of their classmates who did not volunteer were followed for 8 years. Over this time, Teen Outreach volunteers were somewhat less likely to fail a course or to be suspended from school, and the volunteers had a 33% lower rate of pregnancy and a 50% lower rate of school dropout (Moore & Allen, 1996). Furthermore, the more time the students spent volunteering, the fewer problem behaviors they displayed. This latter finding makes it less likely that the volunteer–nonvolunteer differences were an effect of selection. Similar results were obtained in a study by Uggen and Janikula (1999).

In addition to looking at how volunteering reduces anitisocial behavior among adolescents, additional research has explored how it influences other prosocial behavior later in life (e.g., people's willingness to volunteer and engage in other kinds of community activities at a later age). Overall, greater community activism when you are young appears to increase the likelihood of community involvement when you are older. For example, students who volunteered to do civil rights work in the American South in the 1960s were more involved in their community in later life than those who applied but did not go (Marwell, Aiken, & Demerath, 1987; McAdam, 1988). Also, Fendrich (1993) found that alumni of two universities in Florida who had been active in volunteer organizations and social movements as students were more politically and socially engaged 10 years later. However, these differences were no longer significant 25 years later.

Today, many schools require compulsory involvement in some sort community service program. The effects of such programs on the students who participate in them are mixed. Warburton and Smith (2003) interviewed students who had been required to do community service and found that, first, the students were bothered by the lack of choice involved in these programs and that this weakened their sense of control over their own behavior. Second, students in the programs did not develop positive community attitudes or active social behaviors. In fact, such programs may actually weaken the students' "citizenship identities," perhaps due to a process akin to the "overjustification" effect (e.g., Deci, Koestner, & Ryan, 1999).

Stukas, Clary, and Snyder (1999a) also found mixed effects in an experiment on what they call "mandatory volunteerism." Individuals who had volunteered before were not negatively affected by being required to volunteer; however, those who had not previously volunteered were *less* likely to volunteer in the future. This appears to be an example of "psychological reactance" (Brehm, 1966; Brehm & Brehm, 1981), in which people rebel to reassert their behavioral freedom when they believe their freedom of choice has been constrained.

Volunteering also relates to later personal accomplishment, such as academic achievement. Adolescents engage in a number of different kinds of volunteering. One of the more common kinds is students tutoring other students with their school work. The goal is to help both the tutor and the learner in various ways, both academic and social. When the tutoring involves reading, both the tutors and the tutees' reading skills appear to improve (Elbaum, Vaughn, Hughes, & Moody, 1999; see also Osguthorpe & Scruggs, 1986; Scruggs, Mastropieri, & Richter, 1985).

Nonacademic volunteering appears to contribute to academic and professional achievement. There is, for instance, a positive relationship between volunteering during college and the highest academic degree that people earn (Astin, Sax, & Avalos, 1999). In addition, Wilson and Musick (2003) studied a group of women for more than 20 years and assessed the relationship between earlier volunteering and the subsequent prestige of their occupations. The results of their study are shown in Fig. 7.2. As you can see from the figure, in 1973 volunteers and nonvolunteers did not differ in the status of their occupation, but by 1991 a strong difference had emerged. The women who volunteered occupied much higher prestige occupations than did the women who did not volunteer. Again, this difference was found even when the effects of factors such as the women's education, IQ, marital status, and number of children were controlled.

Adolescents who engage in volunteer activities also appear generally (but not universally) to benefit in self-esteem and psychological well-being. In terms of self-esteem, research conducted in places as diverse as in-

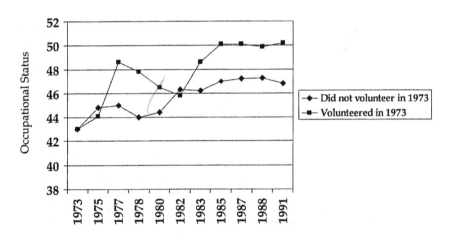

FIG. 7.2. Wilson and Musick (2003) studied a group of women for more than 20 years and assessed the relationship between earlier volunteering and the subsequent prestige of their occupations. In 1973 volunteers and nonvolunteers did not differ in the status of their occupation, but by 1991 women who volunteered occupied much higher prestige occupations than did the women who did not volunteer. From Wilson and Musick (2003), with permission.

ner-city Detroit and Israel has found that students who volunteer to tutor show significant increases in their self-esteem (Gardner, 1978; Yogev & Ronen, 1982). Winter (1996) also found increases in self-esteem and feelings of general self-worth among girls who volunteered and gains in intrinsic motivation to learn among all students. However, these effects do not appear to generalize to students who are handicapped or emotionally disturbed (Osguthorpe & Scruggs, 1986; Scruggs et al., 1985). In addition, Lee (1997) found no impact of volunteering during the first year of college on self-esteem or academic self-efficacy. In fact, the students' self-esteem generally went down over the year, and the most powerful variable contributing to this decline was grade point average.

With respect to measures of general well-being, however, the findings for the psychological effects of volunteering on teenagers are inconsistent. On the one hand, a number of studies that investigated psychological effects of volunteer work on adolescents (e.g., Calabrese & Schumer 1986; Conrad & Hedin, 1982, 1989; Newmann & Rutter, 1983) have found significant positive effects not only on variables such as those discussed earlier (e.g., discipline problems, level of alienation, moral development, positive attitudes towards adults) but also on self-acceptance (Moore & Allen, 1996). However, other studies have revealed no effects of volunteering on subsequent levels of depression, academic achievement, or self-esteem and other well-being factors (Johnson, Beebe, Mortimer, & Snyder, 1998).

Overall, then, there is evidence for social and psychological benefits of volunteering among adolescents, but the findings are also somewhat mixed in this age group. The situation is quite different, however, for studies of how volunteering affects adults and the elderly.

Effects of Volunteering and Helping on Adults and the Elderly. Being a volunteer requires that a person take on new responsibilities and assume roles in addition to those he or she occupies at work and at home. Sociologists such as Sieber (1974) and Thoits (1986) suggested that adding social roles will enhance psychological and physical well-being, and empirical research on this question quite strongly supports this position (Miller, Moen, & Dempster-McClain, 1991; Thoits, 1986). This is known as the *role accumulation approach.* Thoits (1992, 1995) suggested that the social roles a person assumes voluntarily (e.g., friend, volunteer) may be more responsible for the positive effects of multiple roles than are obligatory roles (e.g., being a parent). This again would be consistent with reactance theory. Does volunteering lead to psychological and physical well-being? We consider adults from early adulthood through later adulthood and the elderly separately.

With respect to adults, most of the research on this question has looked at membership in voluntary associations rather than the number of hours volunteered, but the results are quite clear. There is a positive relationship between the number of voluntary memberships and indicators of psychological health, such as increased self-esteem, decreased depression, and greater life satisfaction (Brown, Gary, Green, & Milburn, 1992; Ellison, 1991; Gecas, 2000; Gecas & Burke, 1995; Reitschlin, 1998). Most of this research is correlational, but, as we noted earlier, the researchers looked at people over an extended period of time in some of these studies and therefore have been able to statistically control other variables that could be the true causes of effects observed (e.g., Reitschlin, 1998). These methodological features can increase our confidence in the conclusions the researchers have drawn.

These studies do not tell us about the effects of volunteering per se, but others studies do. For example, Van Willigen (1998) found positive effects of both attending voluntary association meetings and the number of hours of volunteer work on life satisfaction and depression. Thoits and Hewitt (2001) studied the long-term impact of the number of volunteer hours on six measures of well-being: happiness, life satisfaction, self-esteem, mastery, depression, and physical health. The most significant positive effects were on life satisfaction and feelings of mastery. These effects remained even after other possible causes of well-being were statistically controlled.

Other studies have examined whether people's well-being increases as the amount of volunteering they do increases (a so-called *dose-response* effect—a term from medical research meaning that the greater the amount of a drug, the greater the effects), or whether increased volunteering is beneficial only up to a certain point. In other words, if some volunteering is good, is more better?

In general, among adults, higher levels of volunteering are directly associated with better personal outcomes (i.e., a dose–response effect). People who volunteer more subsequently show lower levels of depression (particularly after age 65; Musick & Wilson, 2002), greater psychological well-being (J. A. Piliavin, 2005b), and a lower likelihood of Alzheimer's disease at age 70 (Friedland et al., 2001). Luoh and Herzog (2002) also found that volunteering leads to better health and lower mortality, but beyond a certain point (100 hours a year), an increase in volunteering was unrelated to health outcomes.

Research conducted among older people, the elderly, produces even stronger findings. There is a positive relationship between the amount of volunteering an elderly person does and his or her psychological well-being (Morrow-Howell, Hinterlong, Rozario, & Tang, 2003; Wheeler, Gorey, & Greenblatt, 1998). There also appears to be a relationship between volunteering and physical health (and mortality rates) among the elderly. For example, Moen, Dempster-McClain, and Williams (1989) found that higher levels of participation in clubs and volunteer activities were associated with lower levels of mortality among elderly women. In another study with the same women, Moen et al. found the same effects on three other measures of health: self-appraised health, time to serious illness, and functional ability (Moen, Dempster- McClain, & Williams, 1992). Moreover, the impact of volunteering on lowering mortality rates increases as those volunteering get older (Oman, Thoresen, & McMahon, 1999). Finally, Midlarsky and Kahana (1994) did an experiment in which some elderly volunteers received specific individualized information that would aid them in their volunteering, whereas other elderly volunteers did not; those given the information did indeed volunteer more often. This intervention resulted in increases in self-esteem as well as subjective social integration (i.e., a positive sense of being more a part of their community).

Findings such as these led Midlarsky and Kahana (1994) to propose a model of how volunteering and other kinds of helping may contribute to healthy aging. It is shown in Fig. 7.3.

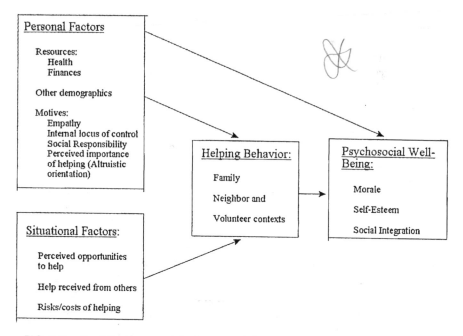

FIG. 7.3. Contributory model of successful aging. From Midlarsky and Kahana (1994), with permission.

The model first proposes that, consistent with the position taken throughout this book, helping is the product of both situational and personal variables. Note that some of the specific personal factors identified in the model are the ones we discussed earlier (e.g., empathy, personal responsibility). Similarly, the situational variables included in the model have been discussed in this and other chapters in the book (e.g., risks/costs of helping). These two kinds of variables combine to affect the amount of helping in which people engage ("helping behavior"). Helping behavior, in turn, is directly related to "psychosocial well-being": The more people help, the better they feel. Although Midlarsky and Kahana were not able to directly test the validity of their model, it is consistent with the results of their experiment as well as the other studies we have presented.

Although the studies with adults show a consistent relationship between volunteering and a range of personal outcomes, the meaning of this relationship (along with the findings for adolescents) needs to be interpreted with caution. Most of these studies are nonexperimental; participants were not randomly assigned to conditions and there was no direct manipulation of volunteering involved. There is always the problem with nonexperimental data of whether the presumed effect—here, well-being and health—is a real causal effect, merely a correlate of the effect of interest, or perhaps one of a larger set of factors that *causes* the volunteering. However, the causal impact of volunteering is supported by the experimental studies that have been conducted (e.g., Midlarsky & Kahana, 1994) and by longitudinal studies that not only show that volunteering precedes changes in well-being but also that statistically controlling for reciprocal effects (e.g., that healthier people are more likely to volunteer; Thoits & Hewitt, 2001) does not eliminate the consistent finding that volunteering is, indeed, good for you.

Explanatory Mechanisms

All of these findings beg the question of *why* volunteering has these positive effects. We first consider the psychological consequences of being a volunteer. Thoits and Hewitt (2001) suggested two potential mechanisms by which these effects might be produced: First, it gives people a sense that they "matter" (Rosenberg & McCullough, 1981); second, volunteering is a role identity that gives meaning and purpose to life (Thoits, 1992). Midlarsky (1991) proposed five reasons why helping others may benefit the helper: (a) by providing a distraction from one's own troubles, (b) by enhancing the sense of meaningfulness and value in one's life, (c) by having a positive impact on self-evaluations, (d) by increasing positive moods, and (e) by enhancing social integration based on social skills and interpersonal connections. Related work by others (e.g., Haidt & Rodin, 1999; Rodin & Langer, 1977) has added to this list the possibility of enhanced feelings of efficacy and control.

There has been relatively little research that has directly examined the validity of these reasons and explanations. But Musick, Herzog, and House (1999) did find that volunteering was most likely to lead to better physical and mental health among people who were relatively socially isolated. Li and Ferraro (2005b), using the same data set, found that widows increased their volunteering after widowhood and that these new roles protected against depressive symptoms. Further, the number of volunteer hours enhanced self-efficacy. Thus volunteer participation can help to offset the negative impact of widowhood on well-being. J. A. Piliavin (2005b), using the Wisconsin Longitudinal Study, also found that people in their fifties who were less well integrated into society (e.g., unmarried, not working, with low levels of perceived social support) benefitted more psychologically from doing volunteer work. Thus, volunteering could have served to prevent or ameliorate alienation and anomie. She also found that psychological well-being—a measure that includes a sense of purpose in life—mediated the impact of volunteering on self-reported health.

In more recent analyses, Piliavin, studying the same people when they were 64–65 years old, attempted to investigate whether other mechanisms (e.g., volunteer identity, volunteer motives, and the feeling of "mattering") mediate these relationships. Figure 7.4 shows the findings of both analyses. Volunteering earlier in life leads to stronger volunteer motives (Clary et al., 1998), volunteer identity (Grube & J. A. Piliavin, 2000), and the sense of mattering (Rosenberg & McCullough, 1981) for individuals in their 60s. Another contribution of this study is to suggest that, over and above the direct impact of both their volunteering activities and how psychologically healthy these individuals felt in their 50s, mattering may further contribute to their well-being in their 60s. That is, it is possible that early volunteers have better psychological well-being in their 60s *because* their earlier volunteering made them feel that they mattered in the world. (However, caution must be exercised in drawing this conclusion because mattering and well-being are being measured at the same point in time.)

With regard to the effects of volunteering on physical health and mortality, Oman et al. (1999) suggested that several of Midlarsky's proposed mechanisms (e.g., improved morale, self-esteem, positive affect) could influence the body through psycho-neuro-immunologic pathways, thus reducing mortality rates in aging populations. However, no one has yet attempted to measure immune function in relationship to volunteering.

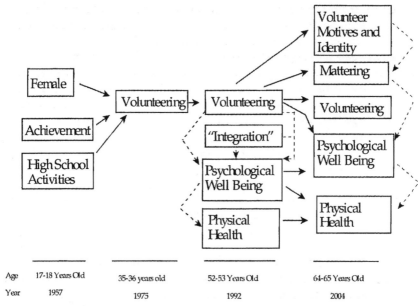

Age	17-18 Years Old	35-36 years old	52-53 Years Old	64-65 Years Old
Year	1957	1975	1992	2004

FIG. 7.4. Effects of volunteering on well-being are strongest for those who are at least socially integrated in their 50s. Volunteering earlier in life leads to stronger volunteer motives, volunteer identity, and the sense of mattering for individuals in their 60s. Mattering may mediate the path from volunteering to psychological well-being (J. A. Piliavin, 2005b). Dashed lines indicate relationships of variables at the same point in time.

Finally, it needs to be mentioned that different kinds of volunteering and helping will have different effects, and that not all forms of helping may be beneficial for the helper. For example, most of the AIDS volunteers in Snyder and Omoto's research dropped out because their work was emotionally debilitating. The generally positive impact of volunteer helping on mental and physical health also may not extend to long-term family caretaking (Schultz, Williamson, Morycz, & Biegel, 1991).

THE RECIPIENT OF HELP: REACTIONS TO HELP AND HELP SEEKING

Through the previous chapters, we have approached our study of prosocial behavior by examining the multiple factors that affect a helper's decision of whether or not to provide aid and assistance to a person in need. Understanding why a person does or does not help another has been the primary goal to this point. But now our focus of attention shifts from the helper to the recipients of help, and a very specific question is asked: What factors affect a person's decision to seek and accept help from others? As we briefly discussed in the previous section, people in need will sometimes reject offers of help. It is even more common for a person to have a problem and to be unwilling to seek help from others. Why would people *not* seek or accept help from others? One basic reason is that receiving help has implications for how one feels about himself or herself and how a person is perceived by others.

[handwritten: affects how they feel bout self/are perceived.]

Impact of Being Offered Help

Offers to help a person meet a need, no matter how well intended, can at times also have negative consequences. On the one hand, it seems that the recipient should be pleased that the problem has been confronted and dealt with successfully. One would expect the recipient to be thankful for the helper's contributions and appreciative of the assistance. This is certainly the expectation of many egoistically motivated helpers who may have offered the assistance primarily to make themselves feel good and who are looking for a word of thanks to bolster their own self-image (see chap. 4). On the other hand, the recipient may experience self-doubts about his or her competence and feel that the relationship with the helper has been changed as a result of the help received. These consequences are the costs that were considered when deciding whether or not to ask for assistance, and these reactions represent the "bill" that comes due after the help has been received.

[handwritten: expect thanks]

Arie Nadler and Jeffrey Fisher proposed a comprehensive model that attempts to predict and explain people's positive and negative reactions in situations such as these. It is called the Threat to Self-Esteem Model of reactions to help (Fisher, Nadler, & Whitcher-Alagna, 1982; Nadler & Fisher, 1986) and is presented in Fig. 7.5.

The Threat to Self-Esteem Model provides a comprehensive description of how people react to help they receive from others. A very important premise of the model is its assumption that receiving help is neither all good nor all bad; it is the relative amounts of self-threat and self-support that ultimately determine a particular recipient's reaction to being helped.

The model begins with the kind of help that is given, the person who gives it, and the person who receives it (see the box on the far left of Fig. 7.5). As we have seen, these variables individually and in combination affect how the recipient perceives being helped. Helping can either be seen as threatening or supportive by the recipient (the next boxes in the model). Let us consider each of these reactions.

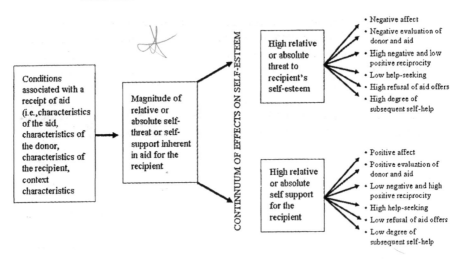

FIG. 7.5. Threat-to-Self-Esteem Model for recipient reactions to aid. Adapted from Fisher, Nadler, and Whitcher-Alagna (1982), with permission.

People who are offered or who receive assistance are most likely to see help as threatening when it challenges the recipient's freedom and autonomy; implies an obligation to repay the favor, but provides no opportunity to do so; suggests that the recipient is inferior to and dependent on the helper, particularly someone originally perceived as socially comparable to the recipient; is received for an ego-central task; and is inconsistent with the positive aspects of the recipient's self-concept. Such help produces defensiveness and negative feelings in the recipient because of three basic processes. First, helping that makes someone feel dependent and obligated in the future arouses *psychological reactance,* which is a negative state related to feeling that one's freedom is compromised (Brehm, 1966; Brehm & Brehm, 1981). Second, helping that a person cannot reciprocate violates a sense of *equity,* a feeling of balance, which is violated when they receive more than they can give back (Hatfield & Sprecher, 1983). And third, receiving assistance can produce negative *attributions* about oneself (e.g., the lack of competence to deal with one's own problems) or the intentions of others (e.g., concerns about being taken advantage of). Receiving assistance from someone formerly seen as comparable to you can imply that you are now inferior to them; as a consequence, receiving unsolicited help from them may be experienced as particularly threatening (Tesser, 1999). Claude Steele (1992) discussed one implication of these attributional processes for people of color. In particular, he proposed that programs that are designed to be helpful but that primarily emphasize the deficiencies of a particular

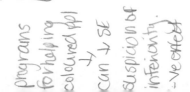

group create a "suspicion of inferiority" for recipients. This suspicion, if it is compounded by traditional stereotypes, is especially detrimental to participants' self-esteem. As a consequence, affirmative action programs may have many benefits for targeted groups, but they also can, under some circumstances, have damaging negative effects on the self-esteem of the beneficiaries (Turner & Pratkanis, 1994).

Of course, it is also possible that the help will be seen as supportive. Supportive help is pretty much the polar opposite of threatening help: It usually comes from a noncomparable donor, it does not threaten the recipient's freedom and autonomy, it does not communicate inferiority or dependence, and it is much more consistent with the recipient's positive self-concept. Supportive help produces a nondefensive reaction and positive feelings in the recipient (Fisher, Nadler, & Whitcher-Alagna, 1983; Nadler & Fisher, 1986).

The Threat to Self-Esteem Model also considers how people react to help that is perceived as threatening or as supportive. As you can see in Fig. 7.5, if the help is seen as supportive (the arrow in the figure that points down), this has the "self-consequences" of providing support for the recipient's self-esteem. This, in turn, produces certain "immediate reactions," such as a good mood in the recipient, good feelings about the helper, more help seeking, and a decrease in the tendency to engage in self-help and self-improvement.

However, if the help is seen as threatening (the arrow pointing up), this challenges the recipient's self-esteem and produces quite different "immediate reactions." The specific character of these reactions depends on how threatening help affects the recipient's sense of control over the problem. If it *increases* the sense of control, the recipient will react negatively to the help and the helper and will be less likely to seek help from others; instead, the recipient will engage in more self-help and self-improvement and become more independent. Threatening help that *decreases* the sense of control produces negative reactions toward the help and the helper as well, but it also produces an increase in help-seeking and decrease in self-help. Recipients become more dependent and continue to seek help because they believe that they cannot solve their problems on their own.

The final part of the Threat to Self-Esteem Model concerns the long-term consequences of receiving help. If the help is supportive of recipient's self esteem, these consequences are the same as the immediate reactions—positive feelings about being helped and little inclination toward self-help. The long-term effects of help that threatens a person's self-esteem depend on how this action also affects the person's sense of control. If the aid is seen as threatening but *increases* the recipient's sense of control, there are immediate negative immediate reactions, but later these feelings become positive. Why? It is because the help has enabled the person to feel that he or she can solve his or her own problems and it has improved the person's self-image. The person is a more competent, independent individual. For example, earlier we asked you to place yourself in a hypothetical situation where you could not solve a math problem but a classmate could. Now imagine that the classmate who had no trouble with the problem tells you that she wants to show you how to solve it. This may be very threatening to you, but if, in the course of helping you, she gives you information that makes you "see the light" and realize how to solve this particular problem and other similar ones, this may increase your sense of control and self-confidence in dealing with mathematics. As a result, your long-term reactions to this help will be positive.

Assistance that is threatening and *decreases* the sense of control produces negative immediate reactions and long-term feelings of helplessness and dependency. It convinces the person that he or she needs help to solve problems because he or she is not very competent. The person continues to seek help, but this causes him or her considerable distress.

In general, Nadler and Fisher's model has provided a comprehensive framework that describes how adults react to help. It explains and integrates diverse findings on this topic, and it has stimulated productive new research. Shell and Eisenberg (1992), for instance, adapted the Threat to Self-Esteem Model to explain how children react to being helped. One of the major new factors considered in Shell and Eisenberg's model involves the effects of social/cognitive development on reactions to being helped. Specifically, their model proposes that a recipient's initial reaction to being helped (i.e., whether the help is seen as threatening or supportive) partially depends on where the recipient is in his or her social and cognitive development. As discussed earlier in chapter 6, the cognitive development of young children (under 8 or 9 years) is still in its early stages, and they do not explain their own behavior and the behavior of others in the same way as do adults. As a result, they do not react to being helped in the same ways as do adults. For example, they respond very favorably to a helper even when they know the helper was told to offer then assistance, and they do not necessarily evaluate themselves negatively when they require help with some task (Shell & Eisenberg, 1992).

Nadler (2002) also extended some of the ideas of the Threat to Self-Esteem Model into the domain of intergroup behavior. In an intergroup context, Nadler (2002) proposed that intergroup helping can be a way of groups to gain or maintain status over members of other groups. As a consequence, groups striving for or possessing high status will tend to give dependency-oriented help, in which the assistance fully addresses the other's need, rather than autonomy-oriented help, which allows recipients to maintain some independence. Arie Nadler and Samer Halabi (2005) further proposed that the reactions of recipients of intergroup helping will depend on the relative status of the groups, degree of group identification, the perceived stability of intergroup status relations, and the type of help (dependency oriented or autonomy oriented) offered. Specifically, they hypothesized that low-status group members' reactions to assistance will be more negative, arousing negative affect and bias toward the other group, when status relations are unstable and the type of assistance offered is dependency oriented. Receiving help under these circumstances is threatening because dependency on the other group is unwanted as well as an impediment to social change.

Nadler and Halabi (2005) found support for this model across a series of studies involving "minimal groups," students randomly told that they were either "global perceivers" or "specific perceivers" on the basis of their performance on a dot estimation task, and real groups, Israeli Jews and Israeli Arabs. In Israel, Israeli Arabs have lower status than Israeli Jews. In one of their studies (Nadler & Halabi, 2005, Study 2), for example, Israeli Arab students were assigned the task of solving 12 anagram "psychometric problems," which they were told most people can solve in 10 minutes. To reinforce status differences, students read an information sheet indicating that Israeli Jews perform better on the task than do Israeli Arabs. The stability of this status difference was manipulated by additional information stating that these differences have remained constant over the years (Stable Status) or has been consistently narrowing (Unstable Status). Six of the problems that participants received were very difficult to solve. Partway through the session, the experimenter, who was identifiable as an Israeli Jew or Israeli Arab by the name he introduced himself with, discreetly pointed to the answers to four of the six difficult items. Thus, Israeli Arab students received unsolicited help from a member of the ingroup (Israeli Arab experimenter) or a member of the outgroup (Israeli Jew experimenter) while believing that status differences were stable or unstable. As Nadler and Halabi (2005) predicted, the Israeli Arab students tended to respond more negatively, in terms of affective reactions (e.g., more sad, insecure, and dissatisfied) and attitudes toward the outgroup, when they received help from an outgroup than from an ingroup member. Moreover, as expected, this difference was particularly pronounced when status relations between the groups were unstable.

Taken together, the findings and theories we have reviewed in this section reveal that people's reactions to receiving unsolicited help can vary greatly, depending on the type of help, the source of assistance, the developmental maturity of the recipient, and the personal and social relationship between the helper and recipient. The same action by the helper can be interpreted as threatening or supportive, depending on the perspective of the recipient. These same principles extend to the processes that determine whether people will actively seek help. According to Arie Nadler (1991), such decisions are influenced by (a) the characteristics of the person in need—some people are more inclined to seek help than are others; (b) the specific kind of assistance needed—there are some problems for which people readily seek help, there are other types that they prefer to deal with alone; and (c) their relationship with the potential helper. We briefly consider the dynamics of help seeking in the next section.

Help Seeking

Just as we found in our investigations of potential helpers and the factors that contribute to their decisions to help, both demographic variables (i.e., gender, race, age, socioeconomic status) and personal characteristics (e.g., self-esteem) have been found to play important roles in determining whether a person will request aid. We examine the demographic variables first.

Demographic Characteristics and Help Seeking. Demographic characteristics are qualities associated with a person's group membership. Three demographic characteristics that are most strongly related to help seeking are gender, race/ethnicity, and age.

Gender plays a substantial role in the decision to seek assistance. The research literature demonstrates that women are significantly more likely to seek help than are men, even when the need for assistance is the same (e.g., Berger, Levant, McMillan, Kelleher, & Sellers, 2005; Sen, 2004; Sheu & Sedlacek, 2004). Anita Barbee and her associates (Barbee et al., 1993; Derlega, Barbee, & Winstead, 1994) argued that it is gender and gender roles, rather than a person's biological sex, that are responsible for these differences in help seeking. That is, it is people's beliefs about how males and females should act, rather than some biological process (e.g., hormonal levels), that best explain this difference. Barbee et al. focused their interest on a particular kind of help, social support. Barbee et al. believed that social support involves a dynamic, interactive process between the person who seeks this kind of help and those who provide it. The actions of the person who needs social support play a major role in the quantity and the quality of the support the individual receives, and gender roles affect both the quantity and the quality. Men are more likely than women to worry about people's reactions if they ask for help with a problem (Bruder-Mattson & Hovanitz, 1990). Because strength, competence, and autonomy have traditionally been associated with the male gender role and dependence and naivete have been associated with the feminine gender role, a man who subscribes to the traditional male gender role may estimate that the social costs of asking for social support (even from close associates) are too high. Rather than suffer the potential embarrassment of asking for assistance, men are more likely to forego the help that they may truly need. A woman seeking social support, however, may be perceived as satisfying her gender-role requirements, while also securing the help that she may need (Barbee et al., 1993; Derlega et al., 1994). Recent research provides strong support for Barbee's position. For example, Berger et al. (2005) found that the more strongly men endorse traditional male ideologies, the less likely they are to seek professional help.

People from different *racial and ethnic* groups may also show systematic differences in their willingness to seek help (e.g., Takeuchi, Leaf, & Kuo, 1988). For example, Black college students and adults are usually more likely than Whites to seek formal help (i.e., mental health professionals, teachers, lawyers, social workers, and emergency medical personnel (e.g., Broman 1987; Broman, Neighbors, & Taylor, 1989; Sheu & Sedlacek, 2004). As members of an ethnic minority that is often the object of prejudice and discrimination, Blacks may simply experience more stress in their day-to-day lives than do Whites. This appears to be true; studies that have compared stress levels in various ethnic groups have found that non-Hispanic Whites report less stress than do Blacks, Puerto Ricans, or Mexican-Americans (Golding & Burnam, 1990; Sen, 2004; Sheu & Sedlacek, 2004).

Help seeking also varies with *age*. Young children are less likely than adults to shy away from seeking help when they are faced with new challenges (e.g., Shell & Eisenberg, 1992). One reason for this is that young children understand and accept their dependence on adults and assume that they are entitled to help and protection. In addition, because children younger than 8 years of age are not likely to make global judgments about their self-worth (Harter, 1986), concerns about self-esteem do not inhibit their help seeking. But as children get older, they become more reluctant to request help. Even by the second grade, some children begin to express concern about how others will view them if they seek help for schoolwork. They are also aware of specific social expectations: Girls, for example, say that they fear that their parents and teachers will think they are "dumb" if they ask for assistance in math (Newman & Goldin, 1990).

This trend continues through adulthood. Older adults (particularly those over 60 years of age) are less likely to seek help than are younger

older adults < young adults.
b/c wanna maintain indept SEfficacy.

adults (Veroff, 1981). Elderly people may be particularly concerned about maintaining (and perhaps projecting to others) a sense of personal independence and self-efficacy in their lives (Lieberman & Tobin, 1983). These feelings of control are important to their psychological and physical well-being (e.g., Langer, 1989; Langer & Rodin, 1976). Thus, just as men may not seek help for their problems in order to behave in a manner consistent with their traditional gender role, older people may be particularly reluctant to seek help in those areas of their lives in which they feel most vulnerable (Fox, 1984). Not coincidentally, these may be the areas in which their need is greatest.

Personal Attributes and Help Seeking. Turning to personal traits, self-esteem is particularly relevant to help seeking behavior. However, the relationship between self-esteem and help seeking appears to be moderated by the relationship between the help seeker and the potential helper. If that person is a stranger, people with high self-esteem are often less willing than people with low self-esteem to ask for help (e.g., Miller, 1985; Nadler & Fisher, 1986; Weiss & Knight, 1980; Wills & DePaulo, 1991). For instance, abused women with high self-esteem are less likely to seek treatment or counseling than abused women with low self-esteem (Frieze, 1979). Maintaining self-esteem seems particularly important to people who have a very positive self-image. Because of the potential damage of help seeking to their image of competence and control, these people are hesitant to seek assistance from others.

When there is a close relationship with the potential provider of support, the relationship between help seeking and self-esteem reverses. For example, Caldwell and Reinhart (1988) found that students with high self-esteem were somewhat more likely to receive social support from their families than were students with low self-esteem. It is reasonable to surmise that the students with high self-esteem had good relations with their families and did not feel that their self-esteem would be threatened by asking their parents or siblings for help.

Another personality trait that appears to be related to help seeking is shyness. Indeed, in his book on shyness, Philip Zimbardo (1977) argued that one of the most serious consequences of being shy is an unwillingness to ask for help. People who are shy usually have low self-esteem (Cheek, Melchior, & Carpentieri, 1986), but there is more to shyness than just low self-esteem. Shy individuals are also anxious and unsure of themselves in social situations and often try to avoid interacting with others (Wills & DePaulo, 1991), and this social anxiety affects people's ability to obtain aid from their social support network. Caldwell and Reinhart (1988) found a negative relationship between social anxiety and the amount of social support college students received from

• stranger → ↑SE < ↓SE
• close → ↑SE > ↓SE

SE ——→ seek
    ↑
relationship.

friends, especially friends of the other sex (see also DePaulo, Dull, Greenberg, & Swaim, 1989).

An additional reason why shy individuals may be reluctant to seek help is because they fear either that they will do poorly in the interaction with the helper or that the helper may simply reject their request. This latter fear has some basis in fact. DePaulo et al. (1989) found that shy people were less likely to get help from a member of the opposite sex. This may have been a case of a self-fulfilling prophecy; that is, because the shy people expect their requests to be rejected, they act in a manner that makes this more likely.

Situational Influences on Help Seeking. Although the demographic and personal attributes of the help seeker play an important role in help seeking, the situation a person is in when the decision about seeking help arises probably has an even stronger influence on help seeking. One of the major situational determinants is the nature of the problem that confronts the person.

Some problems make it less likely that people will ask for help. For example, the controllability of the problem is critical: People are particularly motivated to seek help when they believe that they are losing control of an important aspect of their life that is ultimately controllable. However, if problems persist and become so serious that people come to believe that the problems are uncontrollable, they will no longer be motivated to seek help; people may simply decide to give up. For example, Wolcott (1986) surveyed nearly 300 recently divorced people about their help-seeking actions prior to divorce. The primary factor that differentiated those couples who did seek help from those who did not was their beliefs about whether there was anything they could do to avoid a divorce. The people who did not seek help believed that the relationship could not be saved, "things" could not be changed, and therefore there was no need to seek help.

A second important issue is how the problem relates to a person's self-concept or self-identity. When people are confronted with problems that might be seen as reflecting their self-worth or self-image (e.g., being abandoned by a spouse or lover), they might be more reluctant to seek help than those whose problems are unrelated to such considerations (e.g., the unexpected death of a spouse/lover). Nadler (1987) found almost exactly this pattern among students seeking help for academic problems; they were more reluctant to ask for help with "ego-central" problems. This tendency was greatest among the students who were high in self-esteem.

This suggests one reason why people with problems may refuse to ask for help—they may fear the psychological costs of requesting aid (e.g.,

[handwritten: study → male, male oriented job, core competence of org → ↓ seek.]

embarrassment, threat to self-esteem). A study by Lee (2002) generally supports this conclusion. Lee examined help seeking by physicians and nurses with a new computer system within a large hospital. Individuals were less likely to seek help when they were male, in male-oriented occupations, and when the task was central to the organization's core competence. Lee found that the direct cause of this behavior was the men's perceptions of the social costs that would accompany asking for help.

There are instances, however, in which people with problems related to their self-image or self-concept do turn to other people for help. The relationship with the potential helper is a key factor in the decision to initiate this action.

Relationship With the Helper. How people view their relationship with others has a profound impact on whether help seeking will be seen as supportive or threatening. Feelings of closeness with the potential helper, the nature of the preexisting relationship with the person, and how people see themselves in relation to others critically shape these perceptions, and ultimately determine whether people will ask others for assistance.

[handwritten: Seek more help if closer + more similar]

Closeness. In general, people anticipate that others with whom they are *close* will be supportive. Therefore, when people do seek help, most commonly they approach someone who is similar to them and with whom they have a close relationship. Experiments consistently show that people are more likely to ask friends for help than strangers (e.g., Barbee, 1990; Barbee et al., 1993; Derlega et al., 1994).

This effect also occurs when the strangers are professionals who are trained to give assistance. According to Wills (1992), people who seek help for psychological problems are about two to five times as likely to seek it from their friends, other family members, or other acquaintances as they are to seek it from professionals, even though the professionals may be better trained and more capable of effectively dealing with the problem. For example, Wills reported that people with personal or emotional problems were more than twice as likely to ask for informal help from people in their social support network than to ask for help from a professional. Even when people do seek organized formal support for a specific problem, they are as likely to join a "self-help" group comprised of people with the same problem (e.g., an alcoholic joining Alcoholics Anonymous) as they are to go to a professional who treats such problems.

The reason for this effect of closeness on help seeking probably lies in the differences between the dynamics that exist in different kinds of relationships. Relationships can be classified as one of two types, exchange or communal. Clark and Mills (1993) characterized exchange

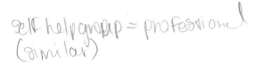

[handwritten: self help group = professional (similar)]

relationships as interactions in which the participant's behavior is largely controlled by "economic" considerations. People in such a relationship carefully consider the effort (i.e., costs) they will have to expend when they do something for another person, and they also fully expect that such actions will be reciprocated. Conversely, those in exchange relationships are aware that if the other person helps them, they will owe that person something in return. Think about your relationships with your boss, a classmate with whom you are working on a class project, or a person who lives down the hall from you in the dormitory. These may be examples of exchange relationships.

In contrast, people in *communal relationships* are less interested in the costs and benefits associated with their actions and are more interested in the quality of the relationship and the well-being of the other person. Because the parties involved in the relationship care more about one another, they assume that kindnesses and favors will eventually be repaid (Webley & Lea, 1993), but they do not keep close track of who owes what to whom. Additionally, because the people in a communal relationship know one another fairly well, they are more willing to "let their guard down" and are (somewhat) less concerned about someone ridiculing or rejecting them if they disclose something negative about themselves.

In Nadler's (1987) experiment discussed earlier, the participants who needed help with academic problems probably (correctly) saw themselves as in an exchange relationship; thus, they were reluctant to ask a stranger for help. To do so would have made them feel indebted to that person and, more importantly, concerned that the person would think less of them for asking for help. But in communal relationships, help seekers may feel that they can expose their weaknesses and problems to people like them without a great deal of fear that they will suffer any negative consequences. Studies of homosexual men coping with their concerns about HIV and AIDS are supportive of this interpretation (e.g., Hayes, Catania, McKusick, & Coates, 1990; Pryor, Reeder, & McManus, 1991).

Another characteristic of the potential helper that may influence help seekers' choices is their own status and abilities relative to those of another person. If help seekers are making the request primarily because they want the person to help them solve a problem and improve themselves, they will probably choose a helper with more competence, expertise, or information about the matter at hand than they possess (Medvene, 1992). In contrast, if people's self-esteem is seriously threatened by the problem and they want to bolster their self-image, they will probably select someone who has less experience or expertise than they, who is not doing as well as they are with the problem (Taylor & Lobel, 1989; Wills, 1983).

If a person is threatened by a problem and chooses a helper of higher status or ability, this may produce what Wills (1983) called the *paradox of help seeking*—the person seeks help from someone who could threaten his or her self-image and cause further self-devaluation. What do people actually do when seeking help? Although laboratory experiments suggest a preference for lower status helpers, there is evidence from field studies that help seekers are also interested in finding someone who can actually help them solve their problem and thus may strike a balance between the two options—successful problem solving and maintenance of a positive self-image.

For example, Medvene (1992) examined college students' preferences for selecting someone to help them with their academic and social problems. They were asked to choose between several different potential helpers. Among their choices were other students with the same problems as theirs, who were either better, worse or equal to them in their ability to solve them (so-called *similar peers*); other students who did not have the same problems, but who did have formal training and expertise in solving these problems (*trained paraprofessionals*); and professional experts in the problem area.

The students' choices reflected concern for both self-improvement and for their self-image. Specifically, the most frequent choice by far for a helper (50% for academic problems; 58% for social problems) was a similar peer who was *better* at solving their problem than the help seekers. The most common reason the students gave for doing this was that it would lead to self-improvement. The fact that they chose the best peer supports this claim. But notice that they did not select the *most* qualified individuals—the paraprofessionals or the professionals. Medvene suggested that this preference represents a compromise between self-improvement and self-enhancement concerns. He further noted that this is the kind of choice usually found in field studies of help seeking. For example, when people join support groups such as Alcoholics Anonymous, they are given a "sponsor" (someone farther along in their treatment program) who is able to help them, but very soon the new members agree to serve as a sponsor themselves, helping someone not as far along in the recovery process as they are (Medvene, 1992).

THE ANSWER: SUMMARY AND IMPLICATIONS

In this chapter we moved our focus from prosocial tendencies to the people who engage in prosocial actions and the people who receive them. We addressed three broad questions: What personal characteristics might be associated with differences between people in their prosocial tendencies? What benefits if any accrue to people who engage in prosocial actions? What factors influence people's decisions to ask for help? With regard to the first of these issues, it does appear that a set of interrelated personality characteristics play an important role in individual differences in prosocial thoughts, feelings and actions. That is, there is a convergence of findings across a fair number of different studies that leads us to conclude that: (a) there is such a thing as a "prosocial personality," and (b) differences in this personality attribute are associated with differences in prosocial actions that range from willingness to help a distressed individual, to heroic rescues of people whose lives were in danger, to willingness to serve as a volunteer.

Some important qualifications must be placed on these findings, however. First, as we have pointed out several times, prosocial behaviors do not occur in a vacuum. Situational factors play a critical role in people's decisions to act or not act prosocially, and, more importantly, personal attributes and the characteristics of the situation interact to affect what a person thinks, feels, and does. In sum, one cannot focus just on personality (or just on situational) variables if one wants to understand fully prosocial responses. Second, almost all of the findings regarding the personality correlates of prosocial actions are correlational. Thus, one must be very cautious about inferring cause-and-effect relations from these correlations. For example, the relatively consistent findings of relationships between certain personality traits and volunteering could be due to the impact of volunteering on people's self-reports of their personality characteristics. That is, they could describe themselves as prosocial because they are volunteers, rather than vice versa. Thus, until there is a body of research that consistently shows that differences in personality traits *precede* and *predict* differences in volunteering, we cannot be sure what is cause and what is effect: Does personality make one volunteer, or does volunteering make one have a more prosocial personality? Finally, even if causality is established, research is still needed on the specific mechanisms that link prosocial attributes with prosocial actions. It is not enough to show that personality predicts prosocial responses; it is also necessary to understand why this relationship exists. What are the processes that turn prosocial personal traits into prosocial actions?

Some of the same problems in making causal inferences are present in the research on the consequences of prosocial actions for the people who perform them. There seems to be little question that there is a positive relationship across a wide variety of kinds of helping and kinds of helpers between people's willingness to volunteer (and similar behaviors) and outcomes ranging from academic achievement and occupational success to psychological health and feelings of well-being to physical health. The critical question again is whether volunteering is the cause or the effect in these relationships. However, in this instance, it is a little easier to answer this question. This is because many of the studies of the consequences of volunteering have used longitudinal designs that measure volunteering early in the research and then use differences in this behavior to predict subsequent feelings and behaviors. Furthermore, these studies employ sophisticated statistical techniques to control for other possible causes and explanations of the positive relationships found. Thus, we feel fairly confident in stating that volunteering seems to produce a host of benefits for the volunteer.

At the same time we must note that no one has yet explained *why* engaging in volunteering would necessarily make a person physically and psychologically healthier. What, for example, are the biological pathways from being a volunteer to better health? Until these pathways can be identified, we must entertain the possibility that both volunteering and the positive effects that follow could simply have some common cause. Investigating the consequences of volunteering seems to be an area in which collaborative efforts between social psychologists and sociologists interested in volunteering and more biologically inclined researchers could prove very productive.

Turning to the final topic covered in this chapter, help seeking, the major question of interest was what variables affect people's reactions to assistance and willingness to ask for help. The general answer to this question is fairly straightforward: the characteristics of the person in need, the specific kind of assistance needed, and the relationship between one in need and the potential helper. Perhaps the most intriguing aspect of help seeking is that it does not always occur when a person is in trouble. That is, despite the material benefits that would almost certainly result from asking for help (e.g., relief from distress and pain, help with personal and professional problems, improved physical or psychological well-being), people often refrain from asking for help. A substantial number of different personal, social, and situational variables have been found to affect help seeking, but most of these variables appear to be related to help seeking in one common way: They affect the *psychological costs* of receiving unsolicited assistance or asking for help.

Consider the relationship between the potential helper and the recipient. People in need do not request help from just anyone; instead, they select individuals who can offer help to them at the minimum cost to their self-image and self-esteem. They may not select the person who could offer the most help most efficiently, but they may ask the person who can provide the help with the fewest psychological costs to themselves. If such a "low-cost" helper is not available, then people may refrain from asking for any help and simply "go it alone." Alternatively, they may seek and accept help from another person but then harbor negative feelings toward their benefactor because of the costs that they have to bear.

One area in which these help-seeking findings would seem especially relevant is in interactions between people from different social groups or between the groups themselves. Prosocial exchanges between groups that differ racially or ethnically would seem to be a fairly obvious way to promote increased intergroup harmony. But, of course, things are much more complicated than this. There are a multitude of factors that impede one group's willingness to ask another for aid, and still other factors that will affect reactions to the aid if it is given. We explore prosocial behaviors in a group and intergroup context in the next chapter and discuss the consequences that prosocial behavior might then have on intergroup relations.

CHAPTER 8

Prosocial Behavior in Collectives: Cooperation Within and Between Groups

*I*n chapter 1, we described distinctions among three types of prosocial behavior: helping, altruism, and cooperation. In most of the subsequent chapters, we have focused on helping of various types primarily (although not exclusively) in situations that involve two individuals—one in need and one who provides assistance. This emphasis on dyads is largely due to the early bystander intervention studies that stimulated so much interest in helping in the 1960s (for examples, see chaps. 3 and 4), and by the traditional individualistic orientation of U.S. social psychology. In chapter 5, we expanded our consideration of situations in which one person helps another by looking at collective kinds of helping such as community activism and volunteerism, in which one person's assistance is directed to a *class* of individuals who share a common need but who may not be even known by the activists or volunteers. In this chapter, we consider the final category of prosocial behavior, cooperation.

Cooperation shares many common features with the prosocial behaviors we have previously examined, but it differs from interpersonal and collective helping in at least two important ways. First, in helping, the parties involved typically are not equal partners. With one-on-one helping, there is one person who needs help and another who has the resources (e.g., time, effort, money) necessary to provide it. With volunteerism, there is a class of people in need, and there are many individuals who are willing to give or do something to benefit them. In contrast, cooperation involves two or more people coming together as more-or-less equal partners, who work interdependently toward a common goal that will benefit all of the parties involved.

Second, research on interpersonal and even collective helping usually focuses on psychological and decision-making processes affecting a single person (the helper or the recipient of assistance) and typically takes an individual level of analysis, whereas cooperation is best understood using the group as the level of analysis (Penner et al., 2005). By pooling their resources (e.g., expertise, strength, money, time), members of groups may be able to accomplish what a single individual cannot. The early Gestalt psychologists who studied perceptual processes claimed that "the whole is greater than the sum of its parts." Similarly, the collective actions of individuals cooperating with one another can often lead to a greater payoff than the individuals working alone could have earned. Although some individuals might have been personally better off if they had "each done their own things," the group as a whole benefits when everyone pulls together for the "common good" through cooperation.

THE QUESTION

In this chapter, we explore the various factors that promote cooperation among the members of groups and compare these to the factors previously identified as promoting helping and altruism. The first major question is how processes associated with helping translate into processes associated with cooperation. The second is whether there are different psychological processes that operate within the group setting to produce cooperation. Third, we ask whether the processes that determine cooperation *within* groups are the same as those that determine cooperation *between* groups. Finally, as with our review of helping, we examine the consequences of cooperation between groups. Before we begin this exploration, we first discuss what is meant by cooperation.

DEFINING COOPERATION

One of the best definitions of the benefits of cooperative behavior is offered by Alfie Kohn (1986) in his book *No Contest: The Case Against Competition*. As you read in chapter 1, Kohn (1986) defined *cooperation* as "an arrangement that is not merely noncompetitive but requires us to work together in order to achieve our goals" (p. 6). In cooperative exchanges, because of the absence of a power hierarchy and the realization of common rewards, greater group cohesiveness and more positive interpersonal relations usually occur.

Although there are other definitions of cooperation (see also Argyle, 1991; Raven & Rubin, 1983), in all of them the key elements of cooperation are that the parties involved all participate in an *interdependent relationship* and are expected to *coordinate* their actions, to pursue *common goals*, and to promote *mutually beneficial* (i.e., prosocial) outcomes that may include social as well as material rewards. Although helping may be thought of as being *unidirectional*—the helper (or helpers) provide assistance to someone in need (see chap. 1)—cooperation represents a *bidirectional* social interaction of supposed "equals," who understand the benefits of pursuing the best *joint outcomes* for all, and thus coordinate their efforts and actions. Cooperation is commonly found in groups where members "interact on a regular basis, have affective ties with one another, share a common frame of reference, and are behaviorally interdependent" (Levine & Moreland, 1994, p. 306). However, basic kinds of cooperative behavior (e.g., turn-taking) can occur in informal collectives of people who just happen to find themselves in the same place at the same time and recognize that they have a common goal. A good example of this is what happens when a set of traffic lights goes out at an intersection, and, without any help from the police, cars take turns going through the intersection.

In the remainder of this chapter we explore cooperation within and between groups. We consider both the causes and consequences of cooperation.

COOPERATION WITHIN GROUPS

Cooperation within groups requires individuals to coordinate their efforts, often foregoing some individual gain to maintain or achieve some collective good. It is important to understand these processes because the consequences of individuals achieving (or not achieving) cooperation can directly affect your life. For example, the ways politicians, heads of industry, voters, and consumers reach decisions about problems such as air pollution, health care, restricting over-development, and supporting public education have a significant impact on your future. In this section of the chapter, we consider whether and why people come together to work cooperatively to maintain or achieve a common good. We first review how psychologists study what are called "social dilemmas," and then we discuss the processes that facilitate or inhibit cooperative action.

Studying Cooperation With Social Dilemmas

One of the recurring themes in the previous chapters on helping and altruism concerned the helper's motivation to provide assistance for another. In particular, we examined the internal struggle between selfish, egoistic desires and selfless, altruistic motives within a potential helper (see chap. 4). Very similar conflicts exist within individual members of groups as they try to decide whether to pursue a course of action in their own best interest or to act cooperatively to promote the collective well-being of their group. It is exactly this "mixed-motive" conflict between individual versus collective payoffs that defines *social dilemmas*. Therefore, it should not be a surprise that much of the current research on cooperation has been conducted in the context of social dilemmas (Dawes, 1980; Hardin, 1968; Komorita & Parks, 1994; Weber, Kopelmann, & Messick, 2004).

Social dilemmas are perhaps best illustrated by "the tragedy of the commons," which we mentioned in chapter 1. Garrett Hardin (1968) first brought the commons tragedy to the attention of contemporary researchers. This tragedy occurred among the citizens of a small community who were permitted to graze their cattle on the town's shared grassland (the commons). The cost incurred for grazing these cattle—the grass eaten on the common pasture land—was effectively *shared by the community* as a whole. However, each citizen who chose to take advantage of this opportunity *profited individually* by grazing the cattle that he or she privately owned on the public land. In this situation, each individual's most rational course of action (i.e., the way to maximize his or her personal profits) is to graze as many cattle as possible on the commons.

When too many citizens of the community decided to pursue this individually rational course of action, however, the cumulative consequences of their collective actions were tragic. So many cattle were brought to the commons that it was overgrazed, the grass was destroyed, the commons was lost as a resource, and all members of the community suffered. Hardin (1968) viewed this final outcome of the commons dilemma as being inevitable: "Ruin is the destination toward which all men rush, each pursuing his own best interest in a society that believes in the freedom of the commons. Freedom in a commons brings ruin to all" (p. 1244).

Hardin believed that there were no technological solutions to the tragedy of the commons because we live on a planet where many valuable resources are limited, and some of them (e.g., fossil fuels) cannot be replaced—our world has a limited *carrying capacity*. Because the earth's resources are limited, Hardin argued that the only solution to the commons tragedy was in the sociopolitical arena, in which restrictions (e.g., conventions, contracts, regulations, laws; see Schroeder et al., 2003) must be placed on individual freedoms for the well-being of the group. For our purposes, we can think of these restrictions as ways to promote cooperation.

Social dilemmas have two fundamental characteristics: (a) Each individual receives a higher payoff for defecting from what is in the group's best interest (e.g., using all the available resources for one's own advantage) than for cooperating, no matter what the other individuals in the group might do, but (b) all individuals are better off if they *all* cooperate than if they *all* defect (Dawes, 1980). In these characteristics we see that the mixed motives—the egoistic–altruistic conflict—that operate for individuals also operate at the group level. Social dilemmas are pervasive, and a wide variety of social problems can be classified as social dilemmas (e.g., the energy crisis, preservation of the rain forests, global warming, recycling efforts, support of charitable organizations). Because the typical solution for social dilemmas is for individuals to hold their selfish tendencies in check for the common good, using social dilemmas to study ways to promote cooperation can provide important insights into the psychological processes that underlie the decision to cooperate. Although the specific characteristics of particular social dilemmas may vary greatly, there are only three major types of social dilemmas: Prisoner's Dilemmas, common pool dilemmas, and public goods dilemmas. We discuss each of these types in turn.

Prisoner's Dilemmas. Although our focus in this chapter is on larger groups, the two-person Prisoner's Dilemma has played an important role in the investigation of cooperation. The origins of this game can be found in attempts by von Neumann and Morgenstern (1944) to better understand conflicts, including international conflicts, by reducing them to the most basic level—the potential costs versus payoffs that would be produced by the joint actions of two parties, when neither of them had full information about the goals or intentions of the other party (see Poundstone, 1993). This *rational choice theory* approach assumes that the decision-making processes used by most people are based largely on economic considerations, with individuals trying to maximize their own payoffs.

The original Prisoner's Dilemma involved this hypothetical situation: Two suspects have been arrested and charged with burglary. They are taken to the police station and immediately separated for further interrogation. The police tell each that they already have sufficient evidence to convict them and that each will receive a sentence of 5 years for the current crime. They are also told that they are strongly suspected of having been involved in a major crime spree and that they will probably be charged with more serious offenses after further investigation has been completed. Both suspects know that they committed these other crimes. The police tell them that if they both confess now, they will be prosecuted but that a reduced sentence will be recommended—15 years. But the interrogator gives each of them the opportunity to "turn state's evidence": If he (in the original dilemma the prisoners were men) confesses now and testifies against his partner and his partner refuses to confess, he alone will receive a substantially reduced sentence—only 2 years—for his assistance. His partner will have the book thrown at him, receiving a sentence of 25 years in prison. Both are told that their partner has been offered the same deal.

The dilemma concerns the decision to be made by each suspect of whether he should cooperate with or defect from his partner. As indicated in Fig. 8.1, there are four possible outcomes in this situation. If

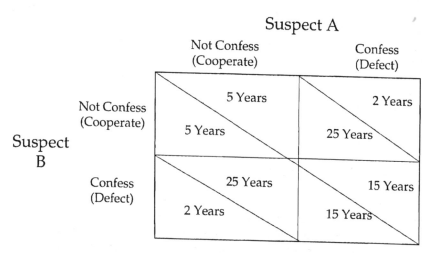

FIG. 8.1. The Prisoner's Dilemma matrix.

both refuse to confess—essentially to *cooperate* with one another—they will each go to jail for 5 years. If one of the suspects confesses—the *defecting* choice—but the other refuses to confess, the one who confesses gets only 2 years in jail, but the one who does not gets 25 years. If both suspects decide to turn state's evidence—that is, if both defect—each will be in jail for 15 years—far more than they would have gotten if they had cooperated with one another by refusing to turn state's evidence! Remember that these "partners in crime" cannot talk to one another. Do they trust one another not to squeal? Of course, if one of the suspects turns state's evidence and the partner does not confess, the "squealing" suspect could get off with only 2 years in jail, while his unhappy partner stays in jail for 25. What would you do?

The Prisoner's Dilemma can be considered a special case of a social dilemma (e.g., Komorita & Parks, 1994). It meets the criteria for a social dilemma because the players are better off if both cooperate than they would be if both defected, but if only one of the players defects, the defector is better off than the cooperator. The biggest difference between the Prisoner's Dilemma and the two types of social dilemmas we discuss next is that the Prisoner's Dilemma involves only two individuals instead of a group of people. Thus, each player in the prisoner's dilemma knows exactly what choices the other player made and can therefore modify his or her subsequent choices to try to affect what the other player does (Orbell & Dawes, 1981). But in the group social dilemmas, it is often impossible for a player to know the decision made by any particular member of the group.

Common Pool Dilemmas. Common pool dilemmas (Dawes, 1980; Messick & Brewer, 1980; Ostrom, Gardner, & Walker, 1994; Weber et al., 2004) represent situations in which the members of a group "harvest" or withdraw some valued resource or commodity from a common resource pool. Real-world examples of this dilemma include commercial fishing, removing oil from petroleum reserves, or, to use Hardin's example, grazing cattle on shared commons areas. Common pool dilemmas are sometimes called "take-some" situations. In some common pool dilemmas the resource may be able to replenish itself (e.g., pastures, fishing banks, forests and timberlands); in other cases, the resource cannot be replenished (e.g., fossil fuels, such as oil and coal). In common pool dilemmas, if the resource is depleted to such an extent that it can no longer replenish itself (e.g., overfishing in some part of the ocean), or if the limited supply of a finite resource has been fully exhausted, people will no longer be able to obtain the resource and everyone will be worse off. So what is the dilemma? It is this: Those people who make individualistic selfish choices (e.g., exploiting the common resource pool) are always at a competitive advantage relative to those who choose to cooperate (e.g., limiting how much they take from the pool). That is, at least in the short run, people who overuse a common resource pool (sometimes called *defectors* or *competitors*) will have more of the valued resource than will those who have restricted their use. In these social dilemmas, the individual who cooperates for the well-being of the group will always be in a disadvantageous position. Thus, if everyone overuses the resource, it will quickly be depleted and everyone will suffer. However, if those who have access to the resource can coordinate their actions, recognize the long-term benefits of restricting how much each one takes from the resource, and consider the well-being of the group—that is, learn to cooperate—the resource will continue to be available and everyone will benefit. This, of course, requires cooperation among the group members.

Public Goods Dilemmas.   The third class of social dilemmas is the *public goods dilemma*, sometimes called the "give-some" situations (Baden, 1998b; Komorita & Parks, 1994; van de Kragt, Orbell, & Dawes, 1983). In public goods dilemmas, members of a group must decide whether to make a contribution to a cause or project that will be shared by *all* members of the group—contributors and noncontributors alike. (One defining characteristic of public goods dilemmas is that no one can be excluded from the benefits of the good.) Contributions to keep National Public Radio (NPR) on the air or donations to organizations such as the Red Cross or the American Cancer Society are illustrations of public-good dilemmas. If a sufficient number of group members choose to make enough contributions to the public good—that is, cooperate to meet the *provision point* for the good—the good will be available to all members of the group. The problem for contributors is that although they benefit from the public good (e.g., get to listen to the NPR programs), their neighbors who did not make a contribution (sometime referred to as *free riders*) will be able to enjoy the broadcasts too, and still have the money that they did not contribute to the public good of keeping NPR on the air.

If the provision point is met, the free rider who did not contribute to a public good still gets to enjoy the public good that was provided by those who did contribute. Those who made the contributions can be labeled as cooperators, because their prosocial actions benefit both themselves and others. (Of course, free riders often think of the cooperators as being *suckers!*) If the group as a whole fails to contribute enough for the public good to be provided, however, everyone is a loser because the potential benefit is lost, but those who had contributed and lost their stake are doubly disadvantaged. So again, cooperation would yield the most desirable outcome.

Dynamics of Cooperation in Social Dilemmas

Prisoner's Dilemmas, common pool dilemmas, and public goods dilemmas are important tools that psychologists use to understand when those caught in social dilemmas will or will not cooperate to achieve the best *collective* payoff possible. Researchers create experimental games that capture the defining characteristics of social dilemmas (see Komorita & Parks, 1994). Players in these games then make either a single decision or a series of sequential decisions, with each player trying to maximize his or her own payoff. As the players make their choices, the researcher usually manipulates some aspect of the situation to determine the effect of that variable on the players' behavior, particularly prosocial, cooperative behaviors.

Many of the factors that influence cooperation in social dilemmas have direct ties to the factors that were discussed previously in the chapters on helping behaviors. These factors include evolutionary-based predispositions to benefit others (chap. 2), cost–reward considerations (chap. 3), social influence and social identity (chap. 3), social motivations (chap. 4), and individual difference variables (chap. 7). In addition, the unique dynamics of cooperation in many social dilemmas, which require interdependence over time and changing circumstances if the benefits of group processes are to be realized, mean that additional motivational factors (greed and fear), other aspects of social relationships (trust), and structural solutions to complex situations become important as well.

Evolutionary-Based Influence Factors. Genetic and evolutionary factors that have been shown to be important for helping and altruism (as defined by sociobiologists) play important roles in cooperation as well. As we discussed in chapter 2, kin selection operates to promote the collective well-being of the family unit, and the benefits of this prosocial strategy accrue to all members of the family over time. For example, parents normally care for their dependent children when they are young; however, the parents may also see this care as an investment in their own future, expecting that their offspring will provide support when they are unable to care for themselves later in life. Kinship relations may also promote cooperation in more subtle ways. Because the benefits of kin selection are not necessarily restricted to members of one's immediate family (who are presumably quite well known), people may also use perceptual cues such as appearance similarity as a "trigger" for prosocial actions. For example, van Vugt and van Lange (in press) reported that both physical and psychological similarities (such as social identities, shared values and attitudes) may serve as "kin-recognition heuristics." That is, in the large and diverse populations that now exist, people may interpret similarities in appearance and in social group memberships as signs of genetic relatedness. Presumably as a consequence, these signs lead to increases in group loyalty and cooperation within groups. These observable characteristics may also give rise to the arousal of empathy and other psychological states that are associated with helping in dyadic situations (see chap. 4), and this sense of "we-ness" with similar others can heighten prosocial concerns in groups as well.

The research in evolutionary psychology also points to the importance of reciprocity (e.g., Trivers, 1971) for cooperation within a group. There are two categories of reciprocity that may have evolutionary bases and contribute to actions in the best interest of the group. The first of these is *direct* (or *strong*) *reciprocity* (e.g., Fehr & Henrich, 2003), which like reciprocal altruism involves the "return of a favor" to someone who has given assistance to another person, but strong reciprocators are also willing to punish—even at some cost to themselves—those who violate the norm of reciprocity (i.e., free riders, overharvesters). The other, *indirect reciprocity*, does not lead to immediate repayments, but rather it is behavior that increases the likelihood that the benefactor will receive some prosocial responses *in the future* from either the original recipient or others who might have been aware of the prior help.

Direct reciprocity is a critical component of the most effective strategy for achieving mutual cooperation in a Prisoner's Dilemma game. Several years ago, Robert Axelrod (1984) conducted an international computer simulation contest to determine the strategy that would be most successful against all other strategies in a multitrial Prisoner's Dilemma (i.e., two players play several trials or rounds of this game). Many different approaches were submitted, but the best strategy (i.e., the one that beat all others in the computer simulation) was also one of the simplest—the "tit-for-tat" strategy: The computer started the game by making the cooperative choice, and thereafter simply matched what the other player did on the immediately preceding round. That is, if the other player cooperated on one trial (the nth trial), the rule was to cooperate on the next (nth + 1 trial); if the other player defected on the nth trial, then the rule was to defect on the nth + 1 trial. Because players can exert direct reinforcement control over their partners in Prisoner's Dilemmas, this tit-for-tat strategy can work well by managing the consequences for the other player's actions.

Another instance in which strong reciprocity may occur is when there are defectors or "free riders" in the group (e.g., Gintis, Bowles, Boyd, & Fehr, 2003). Other members of the group with a strong commitment to the norm of reciprocity punish those who violate the norms of reciprocity and cooperation, even if such punishment requires some personal cost and there is no expectation that the costs will ever be recouped. Fehr and Gachter (2002) called this willingness to bear costs to punish defectors *altruistic punishment*. Recall that in chapter 2, we suggested that there may be an evolutionary or biological basis for reciprocity and noted that consistent with this, when altruistic punishment occurs, there is neural activity in the dorsal striatum part of the brain, a region that is activated when people are rewarded for their behaviors (de Quervain et al., 2004).

Indirect reciprocity (e.g., Nowak & Sigmund, 1998) involves taking some prosocial or cooperative action that will be witnessed by others, even if you know that you may never interact with the person who benefited from your action again. This idea is related to generalized reciprocity in the helping literature, which was discussed in chapter 4. Such cooperation sends two messages to others who have observed the action. First, it shows that the helper is a person of means who is in a position to offer aid to others with no expectation of repayment. Second, it suggests to others that this person can be counted on to provide aid when necessary. By being helpful in situations in which others know that the person will not benefit but in which others will be aware of his or her helpfulness, the person is building a *reputation* of being someone who can be trusted to reciprocate and who will not cheat or violate the norms of reciprocity. As a result of what might be seen as a social investment, the helper increases the chances that others, even those that have not directly benefited, will be willing to step forward to offer assistance to the helper in the future.

Costs and Rewards: Payoffs for Cooperation and Competition. Another example of this correspondence between the interpersonal level of helping and the group level of cooperation is seen in the impact of costs and rewards on prosocial behavior. The net payoffs (benefits minus costs) anticipated by the players in social dilemma situations are primary determinants of the choices they make. If a player looks at a payoff matrix such as that shown in Fig. 8.1 and realizes that he or she can get more points by making the defecting choice regardless of the decision made by other players (what is sometimes called the *dominating choice*), that player is likely to make the defecting choice. The self-interested economics of the games is seen as being the prime motivation that underlies each player's decisions (van Dijk & Wilke, 2000).

When the payoff matrix is changed, the decisions made by the players in a dilemma situation will change as well. For the sake of simplicity, we will illustrate this with the two-person Prisoner's Dilemma game, although the basic processes extend to multiperson social dilemmas as well. Imagine that the sentence that would be given if both players cooperate and refuse to confess was only 1 month for a misdemeanor charge, but the sentence if both players confess would be life in prison. In such a case the *incentive to cooperate* is extremely high: Why run the risk of receiving a harsh sentence when not confessing is such an attractive option to both of you? The principle here is that the larger the difference between the payoffs for both cooperating (the "reward payoff") and both defecting (the "punishment payoff"), the less likely either player is to defect. An illustration of this was the relationship between the United States and the former Soviet Union during the Cold War era of the mid-20th century. Although the two governments disliked and distrusted one another, the punishment payoff for defecting—of engaging in a nuclear attack—was massive retaliation by the other side (what was sometimes called "mutually assured destruction"). This was seen as the major reason peaceful relations were maintained.

Social Influence. Another similarity between the spontaneous helping discussed in earlier chapters and cooperation in social dilemmas is the role of social influence (see chap. 3). There is a degree of ambiguity, "noise," and complexity in social dilemmas that makes it difficult for those involved to feel that they fully understand what is the best course of action for them to take. Under these conditions, people tend to engage in *comparative appraisal*—observing what others are doing and then simply mimicking that behavior. Unfortunately, these appraisals often occur without the observer having the ability (or perhaps even the inclination) to critically think about the wisdom or appropriateness of those action (e.g., Schroeder, Jensen, Reed, Sullivan, & Schwab, 1983). As a result, these relatively mindless actions are often counterproductive and contrary to the best interests of the group, in much the same way that unresponsive bystanders to emergencies inappropriately use the *in*actions of others to convince themselves that there is no reason to get involved.

Consistent with a large body of research on how such "pluralistic ignorance" inhibits bystander intervention in emergencies (e.g., Latané & Nida, 1981), cooperation becomes less likely as the number of people involved in the dilemma increases (Martichuski & Bell, 1991). As the group gets larger, each person believes that his or her contribution has less impact on what happens to the group (e.g., Messick, 1973; Olson, 1965; Williams, Jackson, & Karau, 1995). In addition, the more anonymous a person feels, the more likely an individual will be to free ride, attempting to benefit from the group's actions without personally contributing (Kerr & MacCoun, 1985).

Direct communication is one of the most effective ways of combating the effects of pluralistic ignorance: Allowing group members to communicate with one another has consistently been shown to increase cooperation (e.g., Dawes, McTavish, & Shaklee, 1977; Ostrom, Gardner, & Walker, 1994). Just as the prosocial action of even one individual makes the situation clearer and increases helping (see chap. 3), the beneficial effects of direct communication in a group are largely due to the opportunity for the members to clarify the dilemma that they face.

A study by Dawes et al. (1977) illustrates this point quite well. These researchers had participants play an eight-person commons dilemma game (in which participants draw from some common resource) in which they had one chance to make a cooperative or competitive choice. Prior to making that choice, however, some groups were given the chance to talk among themselves. Some groups were allowed to tell other members something about themselves, but they were not permitted to discuss the game that they were about to play. Other groups were allowed to talk about the game and to share their ideas about its nature; they were not, however, allowed to discuss possible strategies or indicate anything about what they intended to do with their choices. Still other groups were not only allowed to talk about the game but were also asked to express a nonbinding statement about the choice they intended to make. Groups in a control condition were not allowed to communicate with each other at all.

The results of this study help to show what it is about communication that promotes cooperation. Players in the groups that were only allowed to talk about things irrelevant to the game showed as low a rate of cooperation as did the control groups; simply getting to know others in the group did nothing to increase cooperation. If the members of the group were able to discuss the task, however, the rate of cooperation significantly increased. Sharing information relevant to the problem to be faced clarified the pros and cons of the consequences of the alternative choices, and the individuals were able to recognize the wisdom of the cooperative response. Interestingly, taking a nonbinding straw vote after having discussed the nature of the task but before the members made their private choices did nothing to further increase the cooperation rate. At least in this game, the value of the communication seems to have been in increasing the players' understanding of the situation rather than in better social coordination.

In more complex social dilemma situations that involve dynamic interactions over time, being able to discuss and commit publicly to a common strategy increases cooperation beyond simply exchanging information relevant to the situation. One reason why such communication may be effective for promoting cooperation is that it provides the opportunity to coordinate actions and thereby minimizes the risk of unexpected responses by other group members that might threaten the viability of a resource pool or lead to misinterpretations of their intentions. In a study by van de Kragt, Orbell, and Dawes (1983), players allowed to communicate while playing a public goods (or give-some) game reached an agreement that assigned just enough group members to contribute to the pool to achieve an outcome that guaranteed a bonus for all players. Although there was no way that free riders in this group could have been punished, virtually everyone (96%) designated as contributors actually contributed to the public good as agreed upon.

A second reason why communicating specific intentions about how one will behave may increase cooperation in commons dilemma involves the impact of making a commitment and the social pressure felt by individuals to do what they say they are going to do. Kerr, Garst, Lewandowski, and Harris (1997) found that the act of making a *public commitment* to cooperate leads to greater subsequent cooperation, even if the person to whom the original commitment was made would never be able to find out if the promise had been kept. These researchers suggest that internalized *personal* norms ("a still, small voice" of conscience) were responsible for promoting the prosocial action in this study. Similar findings have been reported by Kerr (1995, 1999) and by Orbell, van de Kragt, and Dawes (1991).

A related issue is whether knowing that someone has made a commitment to act in a particular way has any real impact on the actions of the others. Does knowing that *you* say you are going to cooperate make *me* more likely to cooperate, and if so, why? One critical influence for cooperation, which has received little attention in the helping literature, is *trust*. Trust is the expectation that others will behave with goodwill and in a socially responsible manner (see Insko, Kirchner, Pinter, Efaw, & Wildschut, 2005). In an early analysis of social dilemmas, Robyn Dawes (1980) saw trust, together with morality and communication, as being the foundation of cooperation. According to Kramer (1999), trust promotes greater cooperation by minimizing the costs of interacting with others, particularly the cognitive costs of the choice. That is, people do not have to worry as much when they trust others in the group, and they do not have to think about all the different possibilities if another person does not cooperate.

Russell Hardin (2002) posited that what he called "encapsulated trust" operates to promote cooperation in group settings. According to this view, people not only recognize the benefits of trusting others to cooperate but also recognize that the ones being trusted understand that it is in their best interest to cooperate as well. When all parties realize that cooperation will maximize the joint payoff and, perhaps equally important, that there may be serious consequences if they defect from the common good (Axelrod, 1984, 1997; Fehr & Gachter, 2002), the mutual benefits of cooperation will be realized.

There is considerable research that shows the important role of trust in promoting cooperation in social dilemmas. Brann and Foddy (1987) defined trust as an expectation that a risky choice will be reciprocated and suggested that low trust induces defensive behavior. In social dilemmas, defensive behavior means a competitive, noncooperative choice will be made to avoid being a sucker. Brann and Foddy used Rotter's Interpersonal Trust Scale (Rotter, 1967) to classify people as high or low in trust and then had them play a common pool game, in which they believed they were in five-person groups. False feedback was given indicating that the size of the common resource pool either remained the same across several trials of the game or was being depleted by the players at a slow, moderate, or rapid rate. Brann and Foddy found that low-trust participants took the same (moderate) amount of the resource regardless of the rate at which the resource pool was depleting. High-trust participants took the status of the resource pool into account as they made their choices. When the pool was in no danger of being depleted, high-trust participants actually took more of the resource than low-trust participants. But when the resource pool was at risk of being depleted because of the behavior of the other group members, the high-trust participants significantly reduced their consumption, apparently to help preserve the pool for the group as a whole.

De Cremer, Snyder, and Dewitte (2001) reported similar results, using a modified two-person public goods dilemma. Overall, high-trust participants showed greater cooperation than low-trust participants. Low-trust participants contributed less than high-trust participants when they believed their cooperation choices would be anonymous. However, when low-trust participants thought that others would know their choices, they were as cooperative as the high-trust participants. This was particularly true among those participants who were most concerned with how they might appear to others. The reactions of the low-trust participants in the De Cremer et al. (2001) study suggest that they may be particularly sensitive to external forces that might affect their actions. Toshio Yamagishi (1986) showed that the low trusters demonstrate their lack of confidence in the prosocial motives of others by wanting to establish external procedures that will encourage greater cooperation. Specifically, low-trust individuals are more interested than high-trust individuals in establishing sanctioning systems to punish defectors in social dilemmas, and, in line with the altruistic punishment notions discussed earlier (e.g., Fehr & Gachter, 2002), they are also willing to contribute their resources to support such a system. They desire solutions to the dilemma that promote cooperation by instituting reward–punishment contingencies that will prevent individuals from gaining an unfair advantage. The low-trust individuals seem to be particularly concerned with not being a sucker, and they would like a system that gives them a basis to trust that others will cooperate, if only to avoid some punitive sanctions. However, low-trust individuals do not respond well to appeals to cooperate simply for the well-being of the group, which explains why they are not very cooperative when left to their own devices.

Social Identity. In chapter 3, we discussed social identity theory (Tajfel & Turner, 1979) and the changes in perspective and motivations that accompany a shift from personal to social identity. For example, when social identity is salient, people see themselves as more similar and connected to others in the group. They become concerned for the well-being of others in their group because their outcomes all become linked. Furthermore, once people develop a common social identity, this shared identity leads to more trust and therefore more cooperation (e.g., De Cremer & Stouten, 2003).

The impact of a shared social identity on cooperative behavior has been shown in numerous studies. For example, Kramer and Brewer (1984) led participants to focus either on a subordinate group identity (e.g., they were college students, and other participants were not) or on a superordinate identity (e.g., all the participants were residents of the same city). Then they played a common pool dilemma game. When the resource pool began to deteriorate, participants taking the superordinate perspective did more to conserve the pool than those who saw themselves as part of a smaller subgroup. Similar results have been reported for participants in a public goods game (De Cremer & van Vugt, 1998). If individuals feel a strong attachment to and respect from the other members of the group, they make greater contributions in a public goods dilemma (De Cremer, 2002) and show a greater willingness to remain in the group, even if greater rewards could be realized by moving to another group (van Vugt & Hart, 2004).

Social Motivations. As we have seen, helping (chap. 4) and volunteering (chap. 5) may be motivated by a range of personal motivations. Some of the work on social motivations and helping extends to processes involved in cooperation. For instance, Batson and his colleagues (see Batson, 1991) demonstrated that empathic concern promotes altruistically motivated spontaneous helping. Similarly, Batson and Moran (1999) found that participants induced to experience empathic concern for their partner in a one-trial Prisoner's Dilemma game were more likely to cooperate than were those in a control condition. In addition, people who experienced empathic concern tended to show high levels of cooperative responses even when they knew that their partner had already made a competitive choice (Batson & Ahmad, 2001). This is consistent with the assumption that the motivation aroused by empathic concern is to improve the welfare of the other person.

In social dilemmas involving more than two people, empathic concern can have some paradoxical effects. For example, Batson et al. (1995) gave participants in a modified public goods dilemma a chance either to (a) allocate lottery tickets to specific individuals in their four-person group (with an option to keep tickets for themselves) or (b) contribute their tickets to the group as a whole. If participants gave tickets to the group, the number of tickets would be increased by 50% (the public good bonus) before being distributed. Prior to making their choices, however, some participants were told that two members of their group would be allowed to send a brief note "about some recent event in his or her life" to others in the group. Batson et al. manipulated and measured the amount of empathy these messages generated in the people who received them. The most interesting finding was that participants who experienced high levels of empathy allocated more tickets to the individual whose message they had read than did low-empathy or control (no communication) participants, but did not allocate more tickets to the group as a whole. The arousal of an altruistic motivation directed toward one person thus increased the prosocial behavior at the individual level while undermining it at the group level.

Other motivations are also important in social dilemmas. One that has been shown to have a substantial impact on people's choices in a social dilemma is personal *greed*. Trying to maximize one's own situation in a social dilemma is wholly consistent with the dominance of egoistic motives in helping and emergency intervention situations. Thus, it should come as no surprise that egoism's best friend, greed, should be an important motivation for group members as well (Eek & Biel, 2003). A second motive that may drive social dilemma choices is the desire to avoid exploitation. As we have noted, players who cooperate will be at a relative disadvantage, and competitors may be seen as taking advantage of those who are more prosocial. To avoid the *fear* of exploitation—of being a "sucker"—a player whose natural inclination is to be cooperative and prosocial may choose not to cooperate.

One way to study the effects of these two motives is to create situations in which greed and fear of exploitation are systematically eliminated as possible motives and then to see if there are changes in group members' choices. Two studies did just this (Dawes, Orbell, Simmons, & van de Kragt, 1986, done in the United States; Rapoport & Eshed-Levy, 1989, conducted in Israel). To eliminate fear of exploitation, participants were told that if they contributed to the public good but the provision point was not met because others had not given enough, they would have their contributions returned to them: No one could be "played for a sucker." To eliminate greed, participant were told that if a specified level of contribution was achieved, those members who had not initially contributed to the public good would be forced to give up their endowment: Free riding would not pay off.

The results of both of these studies showed that eliminating greed for the participants' decision-making equation led to greater cooperation than that seen in their control conditions (an average of a 30% difference). Eliminating fear also increased the amount of cooperation in the study done in Israel (by 26%). However, Dawes et al. did not find a significant difference in the United States. Cultural differences have been suggested as a plausible explanation for this discrepancy (Komorita & Parks, 1994). The important point in these studies is that players are quite sensitive to the nature of the possible payoffs, changing their motivation and behavior in accord with the options that will provide the best outcome.

Individual Differences: Social Value Orientation. Research on individual differences in volunteering (chap. 5) and helping (chap. 7) has examined a rather large number of personality variables, but research on individual differences in reactions to social dilemmas has primarily focused on one set of characteristics: an individual's *social value orientation*. Social value orientations can be thought of as general preferences for different outcome distributions between oneself and another person (McClintock, 1978; van Lange, 1999). Unlike many personality constructs, social value orientations are primarily rooted in social relations rather than in specific characteristics of an individual. Nevertheless, like personality variables, van Lange, van Vught, and Bekkers (2005) found that social value orientations are related to a range of different prosocial behaviors, beyond cooperation in social dilemmas. In addition, van Lange et al. suggested that there may even be a genetic basis that predisposes people to characteristically adopt different value orientations.

The three most consistently identified social value orientations are *Cooperators* (sometimes called *Prosocials*), *Individualists*, and *Competitors* (Kuhlman & Marshello, 1975). People who hold one of these three social value orientations differ fundamentally in their preferences for allocating resources to themselves and others. The "triple dominance" classification scheme developed by Kuhlman and Marshello (1975; see also van Lange, Otten, DeBruin, & Joireman, 1997) is used to show how the different personality types differ in terms of their preferences for distributing resources (see Table 8.1).

People are typically given a set of nine resource distribution situations similar to those displayed in Table 8.1. Classification into one of the three main categories is made only if the person's preferences for a

TABLE 8.1
Measuring Social Value Orientation

To measure social value orientation (SVO), individuals are asked to make a series of decisions about how to distribute a valued resource (represented by "points") between themselves and a randomly paired partner (typically referred to as the "Other") whom they did not know and whom they would never meet. The individuals are also told that the Other is making a similar set of choices; to convey a sense of interdependence, players are told that the number of points that they will receive at the end of the task will be based on the results of the distribution decisions that they have made and the decisions that have been made by the Other. Everyone is told that the more points they accumulate, "the better for you." If these were the instructions that you received, what kind of decisions do you think you would make? Here is an example.

	Options				*Options*		
	A	*B*	*C*		*A*	*B*	*C*
Decision 1:				Decision 2:			
You get	480	540	480	You get	560	500	500
Other gets	80	280	480	Other gets	300	500	100
Decision 3:				Decision 4:			
You get	520	520	580	You get	500	560	490
Other gets	520	120	320	Other gets	100	300	490
Decision 5:				Decision 6:			
You get	560	500	490	You get	500	500	570
Other gets	300	500	90	Other gets	500	100	300
Decision 7:				Decision 8:			
You get	510	560	510	You get	550	500	500
Other gets	510	300	110	Other gets	300	100	500
Decision 9:							
You get	480	490	540				
Other gets	100	490	300				

For this version of the SVO test, the choices indicating a Cooperative orientation are 1C, 2B, 3A, 4C, 5B, 6A, 7A, 8C, and 9B; the Individualistic choices are 1B, 2A, 3C, 4B, 5A, 6C, 7B, 8A, and 9C; and the Competitive choices are 1A, 2C, 3B, 4A, 5C, 6B, 7C, 8B, and 9A. How did you do? To be classified into one of these categories, you have to have made six or more consistent choices across the nine decisions that are usually used to make the SVO assessment. The SVO measure has been shown to have good test–retest reliability, and its validity has been shown in the many studies described in the text in which Cooperators, Individualists, and Competitors behave in different and predictable ways in a wide range of experimental situations. (Adapted from van Lange et al., 1997, with permission.)

particular distribution pattern are consistent for at least six of the nine choices. About 80% of people studied show a consistent choice preference. Among them, about 55% have a Cooperative orientation and show greater concern for the common good than do Individualists (approximately 30–35%) and Competitors (approximately 10–15%; van Lange et al., 1997).

Cooperators weigh most heavily the *joint outcomes* of themselves and others. If you look at the options that count toward the Cooperative category in Table 8.1 (e.g., Option A for Decision 1), the combined payoffs for the individual and the other person are higher than the combined payoffs possible in either of the other two options. Prosocial cooperators are also interested in trying to minimize differences between the individual outcomes for themselves and others; they favor an equal distribution of resources (van Lange, 1999). Individualists, by contrast, are most inclined to consider only their own outcome, largely ignoring the consequences for the other person; they primarily look for the option that provides them with the largest *personal* payoff. This preference pattern is seen in options that count toward the Individualist category (see Table 8-1). Finally, Competitors try to maximize their *relative outcomes*, that is, how much better they fare compared to the other person, even if that choice means accepting a lower personal payoff. In the options that count toward this category, the player could get a bigger personal payoff by taking either of the other two options, but there is no other option that gives the player such a large difference between his or her payoff and that of the other person.

Numerous studies show that individuals differing in social value orientation behave differently in social situations. The research also helps to provide a better understanding of when these difference occur. For example, Paul van Lange (1999, Study 2) had participants play a standard Prisoner's Dilemma game and, as expected, found that Prosocial individuals showed greater cooperation than either Individualists or Competitors. Of greater interest, however, was the finding that the Prosocials were strongly affected by the level of their partner's cooperation and showed levels of cooperation that closely matched the rate of cooperation of their partners. Individualists and Competitors, however, were only mildly affected by the actions of their partners, and invariably showed higher levels of defection than did their partners. In a subsequent study, van Lange found that Prosocials also showed levels of cooperation that mirrored their *expectations* about what their partner would do, but Individualists and Competitors acted solely with self-benefit in mind. These results were in line with van Lange's value-reciprocity hypothesis, which suggests that Prosocials are interested not only in maximizing the joint outcome of an exchange but also in maintaining the equality of the outcomes among the players.

Characteristics of the partner also seem to differentially influence the actions of people with different social value orientation types. van Lange and Kuhlman (1994) had participants play social dilemma games after being given information about their partner's honesty and intelligence. As before, Prosocial individuals were more cooperative overall than Individualists or Competitors. In addition, although all participants were generally more cooperative toward honest partners than toward dishonest partners, Prosocials appeared to give greater weight to the moral characteristics of their partners, a response consistent with their interest in fair exchanges between parties. Individualists and Competitors were again more interested in their personal outcomes—which may be independent of their partner's honesty—rather than in fairness for all. Finally, participants cooperated less overall with partners of supposed low intelligence. The authors suggested that this may be due to a lack of predictability about what an unintelligent partner might do, and no one (not even Prosocials) wants to be exploited.

That Individualists and Competitors are often similar in their behaviors might not be a surprise, but there are instances in which Individualists may look quite similar to Prosocials. van Lange and Visser (1999) found that Prosocials and Individualists were satisfied to play a game with a partner who consistently followed a tit-for-tat strategy in a game with highly interdependent payoffs, although for somewhat different reasons. For Prosocials, their cooperating within a tit-for-tat exchange maximizes the joint payoff for both parties; for Individualists, cooperating with a partner employing a tit-for-tat strategy maximizes their personal payoffs. In contrast, when given the opportunity, Competitors desired to switch to a game involving less interdependence because the tit-for-tat strategy punishes defections. Competitors need to defect if their goal to maximize payoff differences is to be realized.

Although it may be interesting to find that individuals within the three major social value orientation categories behave differently in social situations, the question remains of why these differences in prosocial behavior exist. van Lange and De Dreu (2001) suggest that these differences can be understood within the framework of interdependence theory (Kelley et al., 2003; Kelley & Thibaut, 1978; Rusbult & van Lange, 1996; Thibaut & Kelley, 1959). *Interdependence theory* is based on the notion that two people engaged in a relationship give consideration to the joint payoffs received as they act together. In many ways, the framework of interdependence theory is very much like that of a Prisoner's Dilemma game, but interdependence theory is most applicable when people can communicate, which is not usually the case in the Prisoner's Dilemma.

For a very simple example, imagine two friends, Terry and Chris, who are trying to decide what to do one day. Terry sees the alternatives as either going hiking or staying home and listening to some music. Chris sees the alternatives as either going shopping at the mall or going hiking. There are four possible combinations of behaviors for these two friends: (a) Terry could listen to music, and Chris could go to the mall; (b) Terry could go hiking alone, while Chris goes shopping; (c) Terry could listen to music, while Chris is hiking; or (d) finally, Chris and Terry could go hiking together. The degree of satisfaction (i.e., the payoff) for each person associated with each of these four possibilities can be represented in what Thibaut and Kelley called an *outcome matrix*, with the values in the matrix representing how happy each person would be with each particular combination of behaviors (see Fig. 8.2).

van Lange and De Dreu (2001) put the social value orientation classification scheme together with interdependence theory and suggested

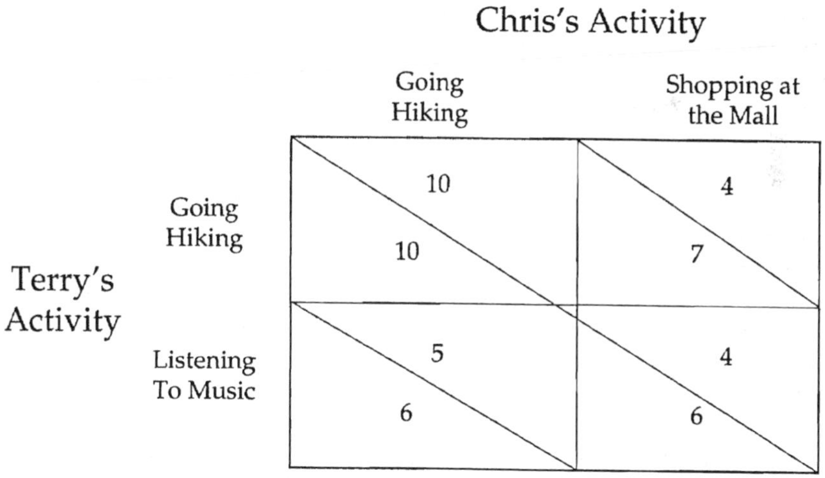

FIG. 8.2. A simplified outcome matrix of how satisfied Terry and Chris would be as a function of their decision of how to spend their day. The numbers in each cell represent the degree of satisfaction the two individuals would experience for different outcomes. Higher numbers signify greater satisfaction. The number above the diagonal in each cell shows Chris's satisfaction; the number below the diagonal shows Terry's satisfaction. As shown in the interdependence matrix, the higher payoffs in the cells in which Terry and Chris are doing things together may be taken as an indication of their friendship.

that different individuals may cognitively combine the objective payoffs in different ways as a function of their different social values. Because of their social value orientation, people may psychologically redefine the payoff matrix to take into account things such as the collective outcomes for all parties and the long-term social consequences of one's actions for the relationship. For example, although Chris might want to go to the mall, the combined satisfaction payoff for going hiking with Terry (the cooperative outcome), together with the confirming evidence that such a choice sends to Terry about Chris's commitment to a long-term friendship, may be appealing if Chris is a Cooperator. However, if Chris is an Individualist, the greater personal payoff for going to the mall will determine the behavior. Thus, van Lange and De Dreu believed that these transformed cost-benefit analyses will guide people's future actions.

Simpson (2004) tested this transformation notion. He argued that the unexpectedly high rates of cooperation found in most Prisoner's Dilemma studies may be due to certain types of people psychologically transforming the Prisoner's Dilemma game into what he called an "assurance" game, in which competition is no longer the dominant response. According to Simpson, Prosocials are more likely than Individualists to make this transformation and therefore are more likely to respond cooperatively as they react to the transformed effective matrix. If Simpson's argument is correct, the effect should be seen in a *sequential* Prisoner's Dilemma game in which the players make their response in sequence, and the second player to respond already knows what option the first player has chosen before making his or her own response. If Prosocials have made the transformation to an assurance game and are primarily concerned with maximizing the joint outcomes, they should cooperate even after finding that the other player has already selected the cooperative choice and could be exploited by simply making the defecting choice. Alternatively, Individualists should be most concerned with their own personal outcomes and therefore defect. Consistent with this reasoning, Simpson found that Prosocials were nearly twice as likely as Individualists to choose the cooperation option, even though the defecting choice would have guaranteed a higher personal payoff.

Structural Solutions. As we noted earlier, one of the aspects of most social dilemma situations that distinguishes them from many helping situations is that social dilemmas involve some sequence of decisions across time and across changing circumstances. As the members of a group receive feedback about how well they are doing collectively and individually, they can discuss what they have done and change their behavior from trial to trial to improve their outcomes. Alternatively, those caught in a social dilemma may decide to take a direct approach by imposing *structural solutions* on the situation; they may realize that they need to change the very nature of the dilemma situation if they are to have any hope of escaping the trap in which they are caught.

What structural solutions often do is to eliminate individual versus group conflict—essentially eliminating the root of the dilemma. As a consequence, the group might decide to impose a *sanctioning system* similar to that suggested by Yamagishi (1986) and change the nature of the objective payoff matrix. By changing the reinforcement/ punishment contingencies to make selfish defections more costly for all group members, the system increases group cooperation by reducing fears that others will defect. Groups may also pursue the structural solution of selecting a "superordinate authority" (or leader) to help them help themselves (e.g., Platt, 1973). What leads groups to be willing to impose this structural solution upon themselves? David Messick, Charles Samuelson, and their colleagues (Messick et al., 1983; Samuelson & Messick, 1986a, 1986b; Samuelson, Messick, Rutte, & Wilke, 1984) found that groups were more willing to elect a leader to manage resource allocations if the common resource pool was being depleted than if it was being satisfactorily managed by the group. That is, if the group's outcome was acceptable, there was no need or interest in changing the status quo; it was only when things started to get bad that group members were willing to hand over control to a leader.

When groups do decide they need a leader, their members' social value orientations may influence the kind of person they choose. For example, De Cremer (2003) found that Prosocials were particularly interested in leaders who would emphasize group goals, let others know what was expected of them, and plan carefully what was needed to do well in the future (see also van Dijk, Wilke, & Wit, 2003).

Cooperation Within Groups: Pulling Things Together

The various factors that have been discussed as promoting cooperation can be seen as being part of an extensive decision-making process engaged in by group members. Although we used social dilemma situations as our prototype for the study of cooperation, the processes that we have identified will operate in most other group settings as well. Moreover, although we discussed a range of factors that can independently influence cooperation, it is also important to consider how these elements operate in concert.

An Integrated Model of Cooperation. Schroeder, Sibicky, and Irwin (1995) attempted to integrate these disparate factors into a coherent system that captured the dynamic aspects of group decision making and cooperation. Their model is illustrated in Fig. 8.3.

The first set of factors can be seen as representing the *objective* features of the situation. These factors include not only the nature of the dilemma situation itself (i.e., what kind of dilemma the participants face; the given payoff matrix; constraints on communication) but also individual differences in the personality characteristics of the players (i.e., social value orientations). These are the raw materials that go into the social processes that may eventually lead to cooperation and prosocial behavior.

As we move through the decision-making sequence, the perceptions of those involved move to the forefront—"what is" becomes less important than "what I think it is" in the minds of the players. These *subjective* interpretations operate in at least three ways. First, players begin to impose their personal motives and goals, represented by the personality factors, on their understanding of the dilemma to be solved. For example, people with different social value orientations transform the given payoff matrix into one that is consistent with the way they see the world (Simpson, 2004). These transformations result in the players responding to the *effective payoff matrix*, an idiosyncratic interpretation of the social situation they face.

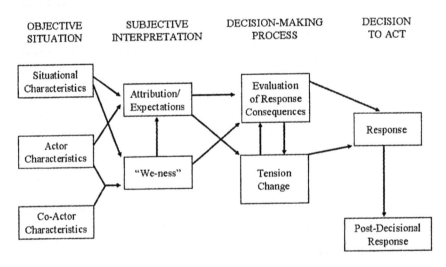

FIG. 8.3. An integrated model of the decision-making process in social dilemmas. From Schroeder, Sibicky, and Irwin (1995), with permission.

Second, social attributions made about others in the group lead to different expectations and levels of trust about their likely actions, and players and these expectations influence their decisions about how they should act. If one expects all of the other members of a group to take as much of a common resource as they possibly can, it makes little sense for any one individual to be cooperative. In contrast, if a player believes that others will conserve the common pool or will make sufficient contributions so that the public goods will be provided, that player might be less inclined to try to defect or free ride. The interpretation of the social situation and the expectations about what others will do become critical elements in decision making about whether to cooperate.

Third, in addition to making attributions about individuals involved in the situation, people will make attributions about the group as a whole. Working to solve a common problem ("How will we preserve the commons?") and sharing a common fate ("If we don't solve this problem, the commons will be lost to all") may pull the individuals closer together psychologically, leading to a shared social identity and heightened concern for the group. This concern then results in a sort of self–other merging, in which the boundaries between "you" and "me" blur into "we" and cooperation that mutually benefits "us" is seen.

These perceptions then shape the decisions that individuals make about whether to cooperate. Rational choice theory might suggest that the players will use the given payoff matrix when weighing their options, but the factors included in the subjective components phase suggest that extrarational considerations may come to play an even larger role (see Colman, 2003; Weber et al., 2004).

Once everyone has made their decisions about how to respond to the dilemma and results are known, the group can turn its attention to assessing how satisfactory the outcome has been. There will be winners (some of whom won by defecting) and losers (some of whom lost by cooperating), but in many cases these same individuals will have to continue to work together as they face the dilemma again and again. Moreover, if the group has been drawing from some common pool, the impact of their collective actions may have taken some toll on the resource, and the status of the resource pool may need attention. This is a time of reflection and reevaluation, and if the outlook for the future is not good either for a significant number of members of the group or for the resource pool, some action may be required to keep the group together and to keep the situation viable. The action required may be some type of structural solution changing the very nature of the situation in ways that are intended to promote greater cooperation, to preserve the common resource pool, and to increase contributions for public goods.

Even if the postdecisional evaluation is not dire enough to stimulate the group to take drastic action such as imposing structural solutions, there will still be consequences in terms of new information that will feed back through the system to change its objective nature (e.g., the resource pool status), modify the expectations that players have about the likely actions of others in the future, and/or help to bring the members of the group closer together psychologically to promote greater ingroup solidarity. Thus, it is important to view cooperation as a process, not simply as a discrete action at a particular time (Ostrom, 2003).

Summary. Not surprisingly, the factors that promote cooperation in social dilemmas are not that dissimilar from the factors that promote dyadic forms of prosocial behavior. Reciprocity (chap. 2), cost–reward (payoff) considerations (chap. 3), social influence factors (chap. 3), and individual differences in social value orientation (chap. 7) are critical determinants of cooperation in social dilemmas. Thus, the underlying mechanisms that operate to promote spontaneous helping and facilitate volunteering are quite similar to the forces that influence cooperation within groups; it is only the overt manifestations of these processes that differ as the demands of the situations and circumstances change.

COOPERATION BETWEEN GROUPS

Research on cooperation within groups has focused primarily on identifying the factors and processes that underlie people's decisions and their consequences on tangible group outcomes. In contrast, work on cooperation between groups has largely focused on the consequences of cooperation on subsequent relations between groups and places less emphasis on the processes that produce cooperation. One reason why researchers have placed so much emphasis on the consequences of cooperation between groups is the special nature of intergroup relations. Relations between groups tend to be much more contentious than between individuals, and there are some basic psychological explanations for why this is so.

Perhaps because of the evolutionary survival value and social importance of identifying who is a member of your group and who is not (Olsson, Ebert, Banaji, & Phelps, 2005), humans are able and likely to sort people, immediately and with minimal effort or awareness, into a smaller, cognitively manageable number of meaningful groups or categories (Brewer, 1988; see also Fiske, Lin, & Neuberg, 1999). Given the centrality of the self in social perception, this *social categorization* process further involves a basic distinction between the group containing the self—one's ingroup (us)—and other groups—the outgroups (them). A great deal of research has been done on these issues using social identity theory and self-categorization theory (Tajfel & Turner, 1979; Turner, Hogg, Oakes, Reicher & Wetherell, 1987).

Let us describe a typical experiment on social categorization. Imagine that you are in a study with several other students. The experimenter shows you a series of slides with a large number of dots and asks you to estimate the number of dots on each slide. At the end of the task, the experimenter scores the responses and tells about half of the students that they are "overestimators," whereas the others are "underestimators," and says this difference reflects how different types of people view the world. You are informed that you are an overestimator (although unbeknownst to you, this label was randomly assigned). Would this change your view of the other people in the room? Would you think about and feel differently about your fellow overestimators than about underestimators? Considerable research suggests that you would.

The recognition of different group memberships, even on the basis of something as apparently trivial as how many dots you saw, has a profound influence on social perception, emotions, cognition, and behavior. With regard to perceptions, when people or objects are categorized into groups, actual differences among members within the same category tend to be minimized and often ignored in making decisions or forming impressions, while between-group differences tend to become exaggerated (Tajfel, 1969). Emotionally, people are more attracted to members of their own group than to other groups and spontaneously experience more positive feelings toward them (Otten & Moskowitz, 2000). Cognitively, people remember more positive information and recall information in greater detail for ingroup members than for outgroup members (Park & Rothbart, 1982). These biases in the way people think and feel about members of different groups occur spontaneously when people are categorized into groups, and these biases form the foundation for intergroup prejudice and conflict.

The biases associated with the mere classification of people into different groups develops into more intense conflict when groups come in contact with one another in more naturalistic settings. Distinguishing people as ingroup and outgroup members arouses perceptions of competition between the groups, particularly when resources are scarce. According to social identity theory (Tajfel & Turner, 1979), people automatically become motivated to see their group as better than other groups and will look for ways to achieve this "positive distinctiveness." Competition and discrimination are two ways to establish the superiority of one's own group over others. Perhaps because of these fundamental psychological processes, groups of people universally organize themselves within a society in a hierarchical way (a "pecking order") and as a result, some groups have more status and power than others (Sidanius & Pratto, 1999).

Many theorists see the psychological processes that produce competition between groups and the perceived threat that follows as a fundamental cause of intergroup prejudice and conflict.

It does not stop there, though. Not only do psychological biases produce perceptions of competition and motivate actual competition between groups, but the competition between groups itself further increases bias (see, e.g., realistic group conflict theory; Campbell, 1965; Sherif, 1966). This process was illustrated in the classic work of Muzafer Sherif and his colleagues (Sherif, Harvey, White, Hood, & Sherif, 1961). In 1954, Sherif and his research team conducted a field study on intergroup conflict in a camp adjacent to Robbers Cave State Park in Oklahoma. In this study, twenty-two 12-year-old boys attending the summer camp were randomly assigned to one of two groups (who subsequently named themselves Eagles and Rattlers). Over a period of weeks, they became aware of the other group's existence, engaged in a series of competitive activities that generated overt intergroup conflict, and ultimately participated in a series of cooperative activities designed to reduce conflict and bias. But let us begin with the effects of competition and hold off on the last phase of this study for a little while.

The two groups were initially kept completely apart for 1 week to permit time for group formation (e.g., development of norms and a leadership structure). Then during the second week of camp, the researchers had the two groups engage in a number of competitive athletic activities such as tug-of-war, baseball, and touch football, with the winning group receiving prizes. As expected, the introduction of competitive activities generated conflict and derogatory stereotypes between the groups. These boys did not simply show the ingroup favoritism frequently seen in laboratory studies. Rather, in this naturalistic situation, there was genuine hostility between these groups. They conducted raids on one other's cabins that resulted in the destruction and theft of property. The boys carried sticks, baseball bats, and socks filled with rocks as potential weapons. Fistfights broke out between members of the groups, and food and garbage fights erupted in the dining hall. In addition, group members regularly exchanged verbal insults (e.g., "ladies first") and name calling appropriate to the 1950s (e.g., "sissies," "stinkers," "pigs," "bums," "cheaters," and "communists"). During the third week, Sherif and his colleagues changed things a little bit and arranged for the groups to have contact under neutral, noncompetitive conditions (e.g., watching a movie together). These interventions did not reduce the ferocity of the exchanges, however. Mere intergroup contact was not sufficient to change the nature of the relations between the groups. As we discuss in more detail shortly, contact between groups must be structured in particular ways to reduce intergroup conflict successfully (Allport, 1954; Dovidio, Gaertner, & Kawakami, 2003; Pettigrew, 1998).

All of this suggests that it might be more difficult to get groups to co-operate than individuals. Is that actually the case? Chester Insko and John Schopler and their colleagues investigated this question in an extensive program of research (see Schopler & Insko, 1992; Wildschut, Pinter, Vevea, Insko, & Schopler, 2003). In their studies, participants first learn about a social dilemma, typically a Prisoner's Dilemma (see Fig. 8.1), and they then are randomly assigned to the individual or group condition. In the individual condition, two participants play the Prisoner's Dilemma game in the usual way. They each simultaneously select a response. In the group condition, two three-person groups are formed, and each group discusses the matrix and selects a representative to play the game. Groups are much more likely to compete (and thus much less likely to cooperate) than are individuals. In one study (Schopler et al., 2001), for example, although individuals chose competitive options only 1% of the time in a prisoner's dilemma game, groups chose the competitive action 30% of the time! These effects generalize to other types of social dilemma games (Insko et al., 1994) and to competition and cooperation in other situations (e. g., involving profits for producing paper origami figures; Schopler et al., 2001). These findings illustrate the *interindividual-intergroup discontinuity effect*, in which, under the same conditions, groups cooperate less often than do individuals.

How might this strong tendency for groups to compete be changed? In the next section, we explore whether the processes that influence prosocial behavior and cooperation within groups also apply to cooperation between groups.

Dynamics of Cooperation Between Groups

In the preceding section and earlier chapters we discussed several factors that relate consistently to helping, volunteering, and cooperation within groups: reciprocity, cost–reward (payoff) considerations, social influence factors, and individual differences in values and personality. Although these same factors generally influence cooperation between groups, they are less consistently related to intergroup cooperation, in part because they are more difficult to vary in these situations.

Reciprocity. We saw in chapter 2 that reciprocity, especially among relatives ("kin selection"), promotes inclusive fitness, because it provides benefits to relatives whose survival increases the likelihood that their shared genes will be transmitted to future generations. This suggests that reciprocity would likely be a more potent factor within groups than between groups, where differences are exaggerated and often attributed to biological factors (Campbell, 1958; Yzerbyt, Rocher, & Schadron, 1997). As we noted in chapter 2, genes for reciprocal altruism are most likely to develop when groups of related people remain isolated from other groups (Morgan, 1985).

In addition, as we discussed in chapter 7, experimental studies indicate that people may actually resent assistance from members of other groups because it signals the other group's superiority over their group (Nadler, 2002, 2005; Nadler & Halabi, in press). This kind of reaction is especially likely to occur for groups that do not have the resources or opportunity to reciprocate (Gergen, Morse, & Gergen, 1980). However, because cooperation involves reciprocity, it can help reestablish a group's status relative to the other group. Consistent with this idea, Worchel, Wong, and Scheltema (1989) found that when groups had a competitive history, an offer of unilateral help intensified negative intergroup attitudes, but an offer of cooperation by a member of the other group improved attitudes toward the group.

Costs and Rewards. In general, changing the payoff matrices in Prisoner's Dilemma games affects intergroup cooperation in much the same way as it influences intragroup cooperation. However, an additional element that is more important for intergroup than intragroup cooperation is the correspondence of outcomes—the degree of symmetry—between the players (either individuals or groups). Correspondence occurs when the payoffs produce similar consequences for the participants; noncorrespondence refers to the degree to which the payoffs are different for the two groups. Consistent with the idea that groups are more competitive than individuals, increasing the asymmetry of outcomes promotes competitive responses in a Prisoner's Dilemma game much more sharply for groups than individuals (Schopler et al., 2001). Groups become much more competitive when they can gain more advantage over other groups.

Social Influence. As we discussed in chapter 3, other people play an important role in defining the nature of social situations and of the responses people should make in these situations. This social influence is also integral to cooperation and competition between groups. One of the reasons why groups are more competitive than individuals, according to Insko, Schopler, and their colleagues (e.g., Wildschut,

Insko, & Gaertner, 2002), is that within groups a norm of self-interest is established. This norm encourages exploitation of other groups. As a consequence, in a Prisoner's Dilemma game, groups are more likely than individuals to take advantage of cooperation and choose a competitive response. Moreover, consistent with the processes of social influence, the behavior of group members can influence these types of decisions in significant ways.

Imagine you are in a group about to play a Prisoner's Dilemma game with another group. One of your group members argues that your group should make a cooperative choice. Can this weaken the norm of self-interest? The answer is yes, at least to some degree. Schopler et al. (1993) found that when groups contained someone who advocated for cooperation in their preparation for the game, they were more cooperative in their initial choices than were groups with a member who argued for competitive action, particularly when cooperation from the other group was anticipated. In addition, someone arguing for competitive action increased competition between groups even more than what normally occurs for groups (Wildschut et al., 2002). However, the impact of social influence is much more limited when the situational demands are strong, such as when competition offers substantial advantage to one's group (Wildschut et al., 2002) or the groups already have a competitive relationship (Schopler et al., 1993).

Social Identity. The research on the effects of categorizing other people in terms of ingroup and outgroup membership also demonstrates the importance of social identity. In general, intergroup bias is greater among people who strongly identify with and are invested in their group (Mullen, Brown, & Smith, 1992), and greater identification with one's group produces more negative orientations toward other groups when the groups are seen as being in competition with each other in some way (Brown & Zagefka, 2005). Similarly, the more interdependent members of a group are, the more competitive toward other groups they are in social dilemmas (Wilschut et al., 2003). Conversely, the more personally identifiable people in groups feel, the less competitively they behave toward other groups (Schopler et al., 1995).

Gaertner, Dovidio, and their colleagues (Gaertner & Dovidio, 2000; Gaertner, Dovidio, Anastasio, Bachman, & Rust, 1993) proposed that the salience or importance of social identities can change over time and in different contexts, and as a result, the way people feel toward others can vary depending on which social identity is most salient at the time. Have you ever bumped into someone from your school in a distant city or country?

Even if you had previously felt little connection to that person and rarely interacted, your common social identity becomes especially salient in this situation, and you react to each other like long-lost friends.

This idea provided the basis for Gaertner and Dovidio's (2000) Common Ingroup Identity Model. They proposed that it might be possible to harness the psychological forces that normally produce negative orientations when people are seen as members of a different group and use them instead to promote positive orientations when people come to see others as members of their own group. That is, intergroup bias and conflict can be reduced by factors that transform people's representations of memberships from two groups to one, more inclusive group. With this common ingroup identity, the cognitive and motivational processes that initially produced ingroup favoritism are redirected to benefit the larger common ingroup that now includes former outgroup members. As we described in chapter 3, emphasizing a common group identity increases spontaneous helping toward others who would otherwise be seen only in terms of their membership in a different group (Dovidio et al., 1997; Levine et al., 2005; Nier et al., 2001).

Wit and Kerr (2002) examined the kinds of choices people make when there are conflicts among individual, subgroup, and collective interests (this is called a *nested social dilemma*). The experimenters manipulated the salience of participants' social identity by emphasizing that the person would be participating as one of six individuals in the session, as a member of one of two different three-person groups in the same session, or as a group of six people in the same session. Later in the study, participants had the opportunity to allocate points, which could be redeemed for money, to their personal (individual) account, to an account for three people in their session (coinciding with their three-person group in the two subgroups condition), or to the collective account for all six people in the session. The results are presented in Fig. 8.4. As illustrated in the figure, participants allocated the fewest resources to the six-person account (a cooperative action) when the subgroup social identity was salient and intergroup conflict was emphasized, and they allocated the most resources cooperatively when the situation was framed so the players believed things such as "we are all in this together." In other words, cooperation increased when there was a recategorization or change to one collective social identity. One explanation for why people may be more cooperative when common group membership is emphasized is that when people perceive themselves to be members of the ingroup, concerns about fairness and justice increase in importance relative to personal outcomes (De Cremer & Tyler, 2005; Tyler & Blader, 2000, 2003).

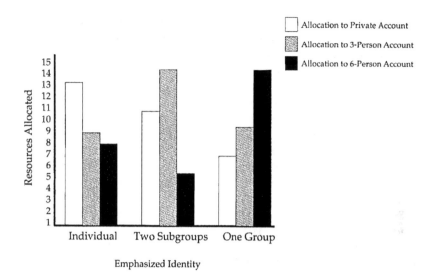

FIG. 8.4. Participants allocate the most resources to the six-person group when their common identity is emphasized and the least when the identities of two different three-person subgroups are emphasized. Adapted from Wit and Kerr (2002), with permission.

Social Motivations. The role of empathy is more limited in intergroup relations than in interpersonal relations because it is more difficult to empathize with groups than with individuals. In the case of the tsunami disaster described in chapter 1, appeals for donations generally portrayed the tragic plight of particular individuals, typically ones who were connected to the identities of the audience in some way. Why? Recall the effects of social categorization. When we think of someone as a member of a different group, differences between "us" and "them" become exaggerated, and we no longer think of them in personal ways. In fact, people tend to see members of other groups as less "human" in many ways than members of their own groups (Leyens et al., 2003). These processes make it difficult to empathize with members of other groups, and particularly with the other group as a whole.

Without the positive influence of empathy, intergroup relations tend to be largely determined by different motivations. Schopler and Insko (1992) identified greed and fear as two of the most important. Fear and greed foster a climate of distrust, in which groups are neither trusting nor particularly trustworthy (Insko & Schopler, 1998). Evidence for the importance of greed as a motivation fostering competition between groups comes from two findings: (a) discussion of exploitation within a group preparing to play a Prisoner's Dilemma game results in subsequent competitiveness (Schopler & Insko, 1992), and (b) as described in the section on social influence, having someone initiate conversation about exploiting the other group increases intergroup competition.

Similarly, the more a group discusses concerns about *being* exploited, which is related to fear and distrust of the other group, the more competitive the group members are in their intergroup orientation (Insko & Schopler, 1998). One consequence of this fear and distrust is that whereas greater communication substantially increases cooperation between individuals, it has a much weaker effect on cooperation between groups (Insko et al., 1993). If you do not trust what someone says, simply giving the person an opportunity to say something will have little effect on your behavior. Also consistent with the explanation of the role of fear in intergroup relations, increasing feelings of safety and security by limiting one's vulnerability to another person's or group's actions reduces the difference in competitiveness between both groups and individuals (Schopler et al., 1993).

Individual Differences. Research on cooperation and competition at the group level places less emphasis on individual differences than does research that studies these phenomena at the individual level. When social or group identity is salient, personality characteristics have a weaker effect on behavior toward members of other groups (Verkuyten & Hagendoorn, 1998). Rather, differences in the groups with which people identify represent the most relevant individual difference.

However, individual differences can operate indirectly in intergroup situations by affecting people's willingness to adopt a common identity instead of maintaining separate group identities. In particular, recategorization processes, such as shifting one's perspective from an individual and subgroup identity to a common group identity, may also be affected by the social value orientations we discussed earlier. For instance, van Lange, van Vugt, and De Cremer (2000) reported that people with a Prosocial value orientation (i.e., Cooperators) are more likely to view real-world transportation dilemmas (e.g., overcrowded highways) as society-level environmental problems and are more willing to use mass transit systems than people classified as Individualists or Competitors. People with Prosocial value orientations seem to have a broader conception of their ingroup, perhaps due to their willingness to recategorize many subgroups (e.g., my neighborhood, wealthy people, poor people) into a superordinate group (e.g., my town or state).

As we noted in our discussion of cooperation within groups, cooperation is a process, not a static outcome. And, as illustrated by the Schroeder, Sibicky, and Irwin (1995, p. 184) integrative model, the process is self-reinforcing. For example, having an inclusive common identity can promote cooperation among individuals or between groups, and cooperation then can create or strengthen a common group identity. And this leads us to the final topic of this chapter—the consequences of intergroup cooperation.

Consequences of Intergroup Cooperation

Perhaps because intergroup relations so often involve competitive intergroup relations, there is a considerable body of research that examines the impact of inducing cooperation between groups on subsequent intergroup attitudes. Cooperative interdependence is a cornerstone of the "contact hypothesis" (Allport, 1954; Dovidio et al., 2003; Pettigrew, 1998; Pettigrew & Tropp, 2000), which has been the most important approach for reducing intergroup bias and conflict over the past 50 years (see Dovidio, Glick, & Rudman, 2005). This hypothesis proposes that simple contact between groups is not automatically sufficient to improve intergroup relations. Rather, for contact between groups to reduce bias successfully, certain features must be present. These include equal status between the groups; cooperative (rather than competitive) intergroup interaction; opportunities for personal acquaintance between the members of the different groups, especially with those whose personal characteristics do not support stereotypic expectations; and supportive norms by authorities within and outside of the contact situation (Pettigrew, 1998). Research in laboratory and field settings generally supports the efficacy of this list of conditions for achieving improved intergroup relations (see Pettigrew & Tropp, 2000). Pettigrew and Tropp (in press) meta-analyzed 713 findings from 515 different studies involving participants from 38 countries and found that intergroup contact generally reduced intergroup bias, but particularly so when the contact situation more closely represented the optimal conditions specified by the contact hypothesis.

In a similar vein, Sherif et al. (1961) used superordinate goals to induce cooperation and thus reduce conflict and bias between the Rattlers and the Eagles in their Robbers Cave study. Recall that Sherif and his colleagues stimulated intergroup conflict by placing the two groups of boys in competition. After all other attempts at reconciliation failed, they introduced a series of superordinate goals intended to elicit intergroup cooperative activity among the conflicting groups. The researchers had total control over the environmental features of the camp; thus they were able to place these groups in a series of predicaments that required their mutual cooperation to resolve. For example, the groups had to work together to find a clog in the camp's water system that interfered with their water supply, to contribute money to rent a film both groups of boys wanted to see, and to push a truck up a hill to get food supplies. As a consequence of these activities, the boys' attitudes toward the other group improved. They began to think of themselves more as members of one common group (frequently using the inclusive term "we" to refer to members of the other group) and became more spontaneously cooperative. Sherif et al. (1961) observed, "While waiting in line for breakfast ... the two groups discussed and reached an agreement that the Rattlers would go into breakfast first, and at lunch the Eagles would be first.... Thus the notion of 'taking turns' was introduced ... on the intergroup level to regulate matters of mutual concern" (Sherif et al., 1961, p. 168). After the third task, Sherif et al. further noted that "the successful, interdependent efforts of both groups in pulling the truck, which was to get their food, had an immediate effect similar to that of superordinate goals introduced on previous days at the camp—intermingling of members of the two groups and friendly interaction between them" (Sherif et al., 1961, p. 171).

Several additional explanations have been proposed for why cooperation between groups improves intergroup relations. For example, cooperation may induce greater intergroup acceptance as a way of rationalizing the positive interactions with the other group, which was originally disliked (Miller & Brewer, 1986). As Leon Festinger (1957) observed in his classic theory of cognitive dissonance over 50 years ago, humans desire that their social relations be balanced or make sense. When intergroup contact is favorable and has successful consequences, the psychological processes that serve to restore cognitive balance or reduce dissonance produce more favorable attitudes toward members of the other group and toward the group as a whole. That is, now the attitudes are consistent with the positive nature of the interaction and things are logical or "make sense."

It is also possible that cooperation can have positive, reinforcing outcomes. The rewarding properties of achieving success may become associated with members of other groups (Lott & Lott, 1965), thereby increasing attraction (Gaertner et al., 1999). Also, as supported by experimental evidence related to the Common Ingroup Identity Model (Gaertner, Mann, Dovidio, Murrell, & Pomare, 1990), cooperation changes the way people think about one another from being in "different groups" to being in one "common group." This shift in social identity improves people's feelings toward those formerly seen as members of another group. This leads to more cooperation, which in turn reinforces positive and constructive relations.

THE ANSWER: SUMMARY AND IMPLICATIONS

We began this chapter with four questions. First, we asked if the processes that influence helping and volunteerism translate to cooperative behavior. Second, we questioned whether there were new or different processes that operate uniquely for cooperative behavior. Third, we posed a question about whether the processes that determine cooperation within groups are the same ones that influence cooperation between groups. And fourth, we inquired about the potential social consequences of cooperation.

The answer to the first question was "yes"—essentially the same processes that promote prosocial behavior in the forms of spontaneous and long-term, planned helping also apply to the promotion of cooperation. In particular, reciprocity, costs and rewards (in terms of the payoffs associated with different outcomes), clarity of need for prosocial action, social influence (e.g., pluralistic ignorance), and relationship to others involved in the situation are as important for cooperation as they are for helping.

The answer to the second question is also affirmative: Some factors operate a bit differently for cooperation than for helping, and there are some new elements that are important in the group setting. Although various different personality and demographic variables relate to helping and volunteering and exert their influences through a variety of different mechanisms (e.g., level and type of emotion experienced, assessment of costs and rewards), research on individual differences in cooperation in social dilemmas has focused primarily on one type—social value orientations (i.e., Prosocial, Individualist, Competitive). Unlike many personality constructs, social value orientations are based on social relations, as reflected by different preferences for the distribution of resources between oneself and others, rather than qualities solely within the individual. However, like personality variables, social value orientations consistently relate to cooperation in specific social contexts, as well as to a range of prosocial actions beyond cooperation in social dilemmas.

In addition, because cooperation involves mutual interdependence, the role of trust is much more important in cooperation than it is for the unilateral prosocial actions of helping and volunteering. Also, because cooperation relies on coordinated actions over some period of time, there is more emphasis on the iterative effects of cooperation on subsequent evaluations and cooperative actions than there is for spontaneous interpersonal helping, which is episodic, and for volunteering, which often involves helping others whom you will never meet. Because of the continuing nature of many cooperative relations and the opportunities these continuing relations afford for finding ways to deal with social dilemmas, people will often turn to structural solutions that eliminate the fear of exploitation and thereby instill the trust necessary to achieve mutual cooperation over time.

In terms of the third question posed at the beginning of the chapter, we concluded that there are both differences and similarities for cooperation within and between groups. In general, one fundamental difference between intergroup and intragroup cooperation is that relations between groups initially tend to be more negative and contentious than relationships between individuals within groups. Even the random and arbitrary assignment of people to groups is sufficient to initiate biases that lead people to value their own group more than others. Competition between groups produces higher levels of intergroup bias, and under these conditions, groups display higher levels of fear and greed than do individuals in comparable circumstances—what has been called the interindividual–intergroup discontinuity. In addition, collective identity is more important than individual identity in intergroup contexts.

Nevertheless, despite the fact that there are obviously more obstacles to overcome to achieve cooperation in intergroup contexts than in intragroup situations, many of the dynamics are actually quite similar; reciprocity, perceived costs and rewards, social motives, and social influence all remain critically important for the promotion of cooperation between groups.

The final question we asked was about the consequences of cooperation. The impacts of helping and being helped are often quite variable, depending on people's personality and circumstances, but the effects of cooperation are more consistently positive. One reason is that helping is a status-differentiating behavior; that is, the helper assumes superior status relative to the recipient of assistance. In contrast, cooperation is bilateral, reciprocal, and coordinated; as a consequence, cooperation tends to reduce status differences between groups and to create a stronger sense of common identity relative to separate personal or ingroup/outgroup identities. The shift in collective identity is an important element contributing to how practical interventions, such as cooperative learning in schools (Cooper & Slavin, 2004; Johnson & Johnson,

2000) and jigsaw classrooms (Aronson & Patnoe, 1997), reduce intergroup bias and conflict.

In conclusion, cooperation is an important kind of prosocial behavior, both conceptually and practically, that is similar in many ways to other forms of prosocial behavior but that also reflects its own distinctive qualities. Understanding cooperation requires the understanding of the psychology and behavior of groups, highlights the critical distinction between individual and collective identity, and offers a more complete picture of the role of prosocial behavior in social life.

CHAPTER 9

Prosocial Behavior: The Past, Present, and Future

O ver the past eight chapters, we have examined some fundamental questions about prosocial behavior. Are people altruistic by nature? Why do people engage in both spontaneous and planned kinds of helping? What leads to sustained donations of things such as time, money, and even blood? How do
prosocial behaviors develop and change across people's lives? What
are the attributes of people who help others with minor or serious
problems? What are the short- and long-term consequences of being
a prosocial person? What leads to cooperation within and between
groups? In addition, we asked how people seek help and respond to
being helped by others. This chapter attempts to summarize the development and growth of prosocial research, what is currently
known about prosocial behavior, and where research on this topic is
likely to go: the past, the present, and the future of the social psychology of prosocial behavior.

THE PAST: THE GROWTH
AND DEVELOPMENT OF PROSOCIAL RESEARCH

Over the history of social psychology, the study of helping and altruism has reflected a range of different interests and perspectives. As we discussed in chapter 1, William McDougall appears to have been the first social psychologist interested in prosocial behavior. In his 1908 social psychology textbook, McDougall argued that prosocial behavior is the result of "tender emotions" created by the parental instinct, a biologically based explanation of prosocial tendencies among humans that is not entirely inconsistent with some contemporary explanations of the origins of these tendencies. However, McDougall's ideas were largely untestable and flew in the face of behaviorism's environmental explanations of social behavior, which dominated American psychology in the first half of the 20th century. It is perhaps because of this that there were virtually no references to prosocial actions among adult humans in either Murchison's (1935) or Lindzey's (1954) initial versions of handbooks in social psychology. There were only 16 entries on any aspect of prosocial behavior in the over 3,500 pages of the second edition of Lindzey's *Handbook of Social Psychology* (Lindzey & Aronson, 1969).

By 1985, however, the *Handbook of Social Psychology* (Lindzey & Aronson, 1985) devoted one-half of a chapter to helping and altruism (Krebs & Miller, 1985), and numerous other entries throughout this edition also concerned issues related to prosocial behavior. The most recent edition of this handbook (Gilbert, Fiske, & Lindzey, 1998) contains an entire chapter on helping, altruism, and prosocial behavior (Batson, 1998), as does Hewstone and Brewer's more recent *Blackwell Handbook of Social Psychology* (chapter by Dovidio & Penner, 2001). Between 1970 and today, there have been at least 20 monographs or edited volumes devoted to the social psychology of prosocial behavior, and the most popular contemporary social psychology textbooks all dedicate at least one half of a chapter to some aspect of prosocial behavior.

What forces were responsible for these changes? Although research on prosocial behavior, particularly work on how norms of reciprocity and social responsibility govern help-giving, began to appear in the early 1960s, the remarkable growth of interest in prosocial behavior in general and helping behavior in particular can primarily be traced to the brutal murder of Kitty Genovese in 1964, in which 38 of her neighbors either watched or listened as she was attacked, escaped, and then hunted down, raped, and murdered by a lone assailant (see chaps. 1 and 3). The news media fueled the public's outrage over Kitty Genovese's neighbors' alleged callous indifference to her plight, and the incident led to Bibb Latané and John Darley's (Darley & Latané, 1968; Latané & Darley, 1970) seminal work on bystander responses to emergencies. Latané and Darley were able to identify situational factors that could facilitate or inhibit helping in this context. The publicity given Ms. Genovese's murder and Latané and Darley's research program opened the floodgates for empirical investigations on when and why people do and do not offer help. The focus of much of the research through the 1970s was on factors that influence the likelihood of helping others in episodic emergency and nonemergency situations.

As the field matured, from the mid-1970s into the 1980s, emphasis shifted from the question of *when* people help to the issue of *why* people engage in prosocial behavior. During this period, scholars such as Batson, Cialdini, and Piliavin and their associates further fueled the field's interest in prosocial actions with their long-running debates about the motivational mechanisms that underlie helping (see Batson, 1991; Cialdini & Fultz, 1990; Dovidio, 1984; Dovidio et al., 1991; J. A. Piliavin, Dovidio, Gaertner, & Clark, 1981). These debates considered fundamental questions about whether prosocial behaviors were always driven by some form of self-interest (egoism) or could involve other-oriented (altruistic) motivations (see chap. 4). The roles of empathy and affect, as well as cognitive deliberations on the costs and rewards of helping, became incorporated into more comprehensive models of prosocial action. This research was widely viewed as addressing prosocial behavior in general. However, in retrospect it can be reasonably argued that, in fact, it addressed only a fairly specific form of prosocial action—the behavior of helper–victim dyads within the context of a specific situation, or what we have called a *meso level* of analysis (Penner, Dovidio, J. A. Piliavin, & Schroeder, 2005).

Over time, as the topic area matured and the issues became very focused, the debates began to center on specific methodological issues and fine conceptual distinctions. But outside of the people directly involved in these debates, scholarly interest in helping and altruism began to decline in social psychology. Although approximately 6% of the articles published in the major social psychology journals during the 1970s investigated this topic, the percentage steadily declined throughout the next decade: 4.3% from 1982 to 1984, 3.1% from 1985 to 1987, 3.0% from 1988 to 1990, and 1.8% from 1991 to 1993 (Batson, 1998). Since the mid 1990s, however, the downward trend has been reversed. But rather than continuing to focus narrowly on a few traditional topics involving helping between individuals (chaps. 3 and 4), researchers began to think more broadly. Some of them addressed the genetic and neural underpinnings of prosocial motivation (what we call the *micro level* of analysis), whereas others studied helping, cooperation, and prosocial behavior involving groups and organizations (the *macro level* of analysis).

Certainly there continues to be theoretical and empirical interest in work on interpersonal helping, but research over the past decade has branched out to these other levels of analysis. Some of this work builds on principles established in earlier studies of helping. For example, some studies at the micro level have pursued whether the distinction between altruistic and egoistic motivation might have implications for the understanding of hemispheric brain function (Buck, 1999, 2002; Gray, 2002; see chap. 2). Similarly, research at the macro level has explored the influence of egoistic and altruistic motivation on community involvement (Batson, 2002; see chap. 5) and cooperative behavior (Batson & Ahmad, 2001; see chap. 8). However, much of the work at these new levels of analysis relies less on the prior social psychological research on interpersonal helping and draws much more on research from other disciplines (e.g., biology and sociology) and the unique qualities of the phenomena that occur at these levels. This brings us up to the present, and the theory and research presented in this book. The next section uses this theory and research to summarize what we presently know about prosocial behavior.

THE PRESENT: WHAT DO WE KNOW ABOUT PROSOCIAL BEHAVIOR?

Throughout the book we identified a number of important and enduring questions in the study of prosocial behavior. In this section, we restate the questions that have guided our investigation of helping in the previous chapters and provide brief answers to them. The answers represent highlights of the major conclusions that were reached in response to each question. The questions and their answers are not intended to substitute for the chapter summaries or to suggest that the questions that have been asked can be answered in a few simple sentences. The full answers are rarely so simple or straightforward. Also, rather than simply leaving these "facts" in isolation, in the second part of this section we attempt to organize what we know within a general framework for prosocial behavior.

Are Humans Prosocial and Altruistic by Nature?

The central question of chapter 2, "The Origins of Prosocial Behavior," is, "Are people naturally inclined to be selfless and altruistic?" That is, is there a biological basis for prosocial actions among humans? The evidence from studies of cross-cultural and cross-species behaviors, research in behavioral genetics, and observations of newborn infants leads to the following conclusions about the biological bases of human prosocial actions.

- Humans are biologically predisposed to act prosocially.
- There are at least two evolutionary processes that could produce such tendencies in humans: kin selection and reciprocal altruism. Kin selection produces prosocial tendencies because helping one's kin can increase the likelihood that the helper's relatives will survive and reproduce some of his or her genes, even if the helper dies without reproducing. Reciprocal altruism may have this same effect because helping an unrelated person can increase the likelihood that the altruist will receive aid from people he or she has helped, which in turn increases the altruist's chances of surviving and reproducing. Thus in our evolutionary past, altruistic actions increased the *inclusive fitness* of our ancestors; that is, there were more of their genes in subsequent generations.
- Among humans, genes do not directly cause prosocial actions. Instead, genes provide humans with the capacity and inclination to engage in such behaviors. The innate abilities to empathize with other humans and to effectively communicate one's emotions and feelings serve this function for prosocial behaviors. Although these abilities are substantially influenced by heredity, learning experiences influence them as well. This appears to be especially true of empathy, which is often fostered by parents. This is one of many examples of why it is wrong to attribute complex social behaviors to "nature" or to "nurture." Prosocial (and most other human) behaviors are influenced by a complex, interdependent relationship between our genetic heritage and environmental influences.
- Although humans are predisposed to act prosocially, their actual behavior is shaped jointly by interactions between such tendencies and the environment. That is, whatever the predisposition is, an individual's immediate social and situational contexts play a critical role in whether or not helping occurs.

When Will People Help?

In chapter 3, "The Context: When Will People Help?," the central question posed was: "When *will* people help and when will they *not*?" The conclusions were:

- Before bystanders offer help, they must decide that something is wrong, that another person's help is required to solve the problem, and that they have personal responsibility to provide this help. Then they have to decide whether they can provide the kind of assistance that is needed. If the answer to each of these questions is "yes," bystanders will help.
- When presented with a potential helping opportunity, people weigh the costs and rewards associated with various courses of action. Besides helping directly, people can help indirectly (e.g., call someone else for help), reinterpret the situation as one that does not require their personal assistance, or simply leave the scene. People will help directly when they believe that helping represents the most cost-effective action, considering all of the interests involved.

What Motivates People to Offer Help?

The basic question posed in chapter 4 is represented by its title, "Why Do People Help?" The answers to this question relate to both thoughts and feelings (i.e., cognitions and emotions).

- People are sometimes motivated to help because they have learned through direct experiences and by observing others that helping will produce both tangible and intangible benefits for them. People will seek these rewards particularly when they are feeling sadness or other negative states.
- Social and personal norms about what is appropriate or acceptable behavior may also motivate people to help. People may be motivated to help because they feel external or internal pressure to comply with these norms.
- People's emotions and feelings also motivate helping. People typically experience empathic arousal when they see someone in distress. Usually (but not invariably), this arousal increases the motivation to help. This motivation may be

egoistic and self-serving. By eliminating the other person's problem, helping can reduce the negative feelings that people experience as a result of the other's distress.

- In circumstances in which there are feelings of connectedness between the bystander and the person in need, the motivation to help can originate from a feeling of empathic concern about the other person. Empathic concern motivates altruistic helping, in which the primary goal is to improve the other person's welfare.

Why Do People Engage in Long-Term Efforts to Help Other People?

In chapter 5, "Planned and Long-Term Helping," we described five different types of planned, long-term helping: community activism, volunteering, organizational citizenship behaviors, principled organizational dissent, and informal helping. We posed two main questions. First, what factors initially lead people to engage in long-term planned helping? Second, why do people continue to perform these behaviors over long periods of time? That is, what sustains these behaviors, sometimes in the face of considerable costs and effort? We found:

- The decision to initiate long-term prosocial behavior is related to some of the same factors shaping short-term, spontaneous helping. Clarity and the degree of the perceived need of others are important contextual factors for both classes of prosocial behavior. An emotional reaction to others' situation is a second, critical element.
- Although individual differences are important for all types of helping, demographic factors and personal characteristics are particularly associated with variations in long-term, planned helping. Perhaps because of the investment involved, people weigh the costs and benefits heavily in their decisions of whether to help. Because the activity associated with planned, long-term helping competes with a range of other responsibilities and interests over time, basic values, principles, motivations, and goals are critical for determining the priority of these helping activities in people's lives.
- The consequences of prosocial actions are the most important factor determining whether they will be sustained. The consequences may be immediate (such as physical reactions to

giving blood), somewhat delayed (the prosocial action meeting the needs and desires of the person), or develop gradually over time (performing the prosocial actions becoming part of the person's personal identity or self-concept).

Does Prosocial Behavior Change as People Mature?

The central questions in chapter 6, "The Development of Prosocial Behavior," were (a) How do helping and other aspects of prosocial behavior change as humans mature? (b) What processes are responsible for the developmental changes that influence helping and altruistic behaviors? and (c) How do these processes affect the behaviors of adults? The answers to these questions are:

- As humans mature, there is an increase in the extent to which helping is motivated by internal processes and intangible factors. Accompanying this change is an increase in the extent to which people consider the rights and well-being of others when they have to make decisions about helping.
- Two interrelated developmental processes are responsible for these changes: social learning and social/cognitive development. Social learning involves direct reinforcement, observing other people, and direct instruction. Through these processes, children learn that helping is socially valued. Social/cognitive development involves maturational changes in the way children think about the causes of their own behaviors and of the actions of others. As children mature in the way they think about helping and being helped, the reasons why they help also change.
- Both social learning and social/cognitive development produce changes in moral reasoning—judgments about "right" and "wrong." As children mature, moral reasoning usually becomes more prosocial and other-oriented; others' needs and welfare become more important at more advanced levels of moral reasoning.
- Developmental changes do not only occur with the transition from childhood to adulthood; they occur throughout people's lifetimes.
- In many instances, men and women react differently to someone in need of help. These differences not only involve whether assistance is offered but also include the ways in

which help is given. These male–female differences are due, for the most part, to socialization and norms about how members of each gender should behave. People are most likely to help in ways that are consistent with these gender role norms.

Are Some People More Helpful Than Others?

This was one of the main questions posed in chapter 7. The conclusion was that differences in personal attributes are important, but often in combination with other factors.

- There are stable individual differences in the willingness to help others. In particular, there appears to be a set of interrelated personality characteristics that play an important role in individual differences in prosocial thoughts, feelings, and actions. Our conclusions were (a) that there is such a thing as a "prosocial personality," and (b) that differences in this personality attribute are associated with differences in prosocial actions that range from willingness to help a distressed individual to heroic rescues of people whose lives were in danger to willingness to serve as a volunteer.
- Characteristically helpful and nonhelpful people differ with respect to personality traits. Helpful people are inclined to be empathic individuals who are concerned about and willing to accept responsibility for the well-being of others. Helpful people are individuals who also have a sense of self-efficacy—they believe that if they attempt to do something they will succeed.
- As is true of all complex social behaviors, prosocial behavior is the *joint product* of the person and the situation in which the behavior occurs.

What Are the Consequences of Helping Others and Being Helped?

Chapter 7 also focused on the consequences of helping for the benefactor and recipient. Although the effects for helpers are generally consistent and straightforward, the issues related to recipients of help and potential help seekers are more complex. But here are some answers to questions about the consequences of giving and receiving help.

- There is a relationship across a wide range of types of helping and kinds of helpers between the people's willingness to volunteer (and similar behaviors) and positive outcomes ranging from better academic achievement and occupational success to better psychological health and feelings of well-being to improved physical health.
- Before asking for help, people make decisions similar to those made by potential helpers. They must decide if a problem really exists and whether it could be solved with help from another person. If the answers to these questions are "yes," then they decide which person is most capable of providing the needed help.
- Decisions about when to ask for help and whom to ask are greatly influenced by concerns about self-esteem. People will ask for help if making the request does not threaten their self-esteem. As a result, people are usually reluctant to ask for help with a problem that involves a central aspect of their personality or character. This reluctance to ask for help may be reduced if the help seeker has a long-term, close relationship with the potential help provider or the help seeker believes that the favor can be reciprocated.
- Self-esteem considerations also strongly influence people's reactions to receiving help. Help that increases a person's sense of control over the problem will produce long-term positive reactions and increase independence in solving subsequent problems. Help that threatens self-esteem, however, will produce immediate negative reactions.

When and Why Do People Cooperate With Others?

There were four questions that we asked in chapter 8, "Prosocial Behavior in Collectives: Cooperation Within and Between Groups." First, we asked if the processes that influence helping and volunteerism translate to cooperative behavior. Second, we questioned whether there were new or different processes that operate uniquely for cooperative behavior. Third, we posed a question about whether the processes that determine cooperation *within* groups are the same ones that influence cooperation *between* groups. And fourth, we inquired about the potential social consequences of cooperation. Although cooperation is distinctly different from helping in that it involves the reciprocal and coordinated responses of two or more parties, the conclusions about cooperation are generally quite compatible with those for other types of prosocial behavior. The answers to these questions follow:

- In general, people will act cooperatively and contribute to the betterment of society when they believe it is in their self-interest to do so. People are unlikely to cooperate in situations in which they will immediately benefit from being selfish—even if selfishness may cause negative consequences for them and others in the long run. Communicating with other people or identifying with them can increase voluntary cooperation, but sometimes it is necessary to create stronger situational incentives to promote cooperation within the group.

- The same processes that promote spontaneous helping and long-term, planned helping also apply to the promotion of cooperation. In particular, reciprocity, costs and rewards (in terms of the payoffs associated with different outcomes), clarity of need for prosocial action, social influence (e.g., pluralistic ignorance), and relationship to others involved in the situation are as important for cooperation as they are for helping.

- However, some factors operate a bit differently for cooperation than for helping, and there are some new elements that are important in the group setting. Although a variety of different personality and demographic variables are related to helping and volunteering and exert their influences through a variety of different mechanisms (e.g., level and type of emotion experienced, assessment of costs and rewards), research on individual differences in cooperation in social dilemmas has focused primarily on one type—social value orientations (i.e., Prosocial, Individualist, Competitive).

- There are both differences and similarities for cooperation within and between groups. In general, one fundamental difference between intergroup and intragroup cooperation is that relations *between* groups initially tend to be more negative and contentious than relationships between individuals *within* groups.

- Because cooperation is bilateral, reciprocal, and coordinated, it tends to reduce status differences between groups and to create a stronger sense of common identity relative to separate personal or ingroup/outgroup identities and to reduce intergroup bias and conflict.

These short and very simple answers represent summaries of the field's answers to the focused and discrete questions asked in each of the chapters of the book. However, throughout this book we have attempted not only to identify the important elements for understanding prosocial behavior but also to illustrate their dynamic integration. Therefore, in the next section we attempt to organize the different elements of prosocial behavior that we have discussed into a "big picture" of the causes of prosocial behavior.

Organization of the Elements

Our depiction of the processes and mechanisms that form the foundation of prosocial behavior and how they affect helping and altruism is presented in Fig. 9.1. At the base of the diagram are the most distal causes of a prosocial action; the causes become progressively more proximal as we move toward the top. Thus, the diagram begins with the evolutionary processes associated with natural selection and inclusive fitness. Among humans' ancestors, helping was a behavior that, under many circumstances, served to increase inclusiveness fitness, and thus it is a characteristic that is likely to be reflected in prosocial genetic predispositions among contemporary humans. This should be especially

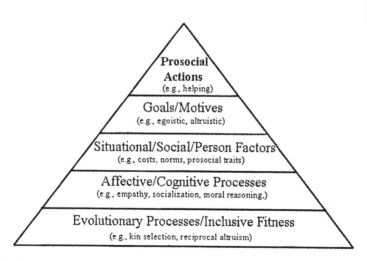

FIG. 9.1. Processes in prosocial behavior.

likely for helping biological relatives, because this action most directly and efficiently increases the likelihood that one's own genes will be transmitted to future generations. In addition, helping unrelated others may ultimately be beneficial to one's own survival or the survival of relatives through the process of reciprocity.

Humans are both feeling and thinking organisms. Thus, our organization suggests that affective and cognitive processes provide mechanisms for translating predispositions with genetic origins into prosocial actions. With respect to affect, Zajonc (1980) proposed, "Affect is the first link in the evolution of complex adaptive functions" (p. 156). As we noted earlier in this chapter, the capacity to experience empathy and empathic arousal is universal. The neurological structures that are responsible for feelings and emotions (i.e., the limbic system) are among the oldest in the human brain. Moreover, consistent with an evolutionary perspective, empathy is a highly heritable characteristic, and empathic arousal increases with closeness to the person in need.

From a cognitive perspective, people have the capacity to learn about helping and how to be helpful in the same ways that they learn other social behaviors, through direct or vicarious rewards and punishments. Socialization experiences and culture also affect the way they think about helping (Miller & Bersoff, 1994). Affective and cognitive processes are, of course, reciprocally intertwined. For example, recognition of a discrepancy between one's self-concept and actions may generate unpleasant emotional arousal. Arousal may in turn influence how different costs and rewards for helping are attended to and ultimately how they are weighed in decisions to help.

The characteristics of the situation, the victim, and the potential helper may cause particular affective and cognitive mechanisms to be activated selectively and to varying degrees. For example, situations of greater clarity and severity produce higher levels of empathic arousal and are associated with stronger norms supporting intervention and greater guilt for not helping. People have higher levels of cognitive and affective empathy with others who are similar to them, with whom they share group membership, and with whom they are psychologically closer. Personal dispositions may also affect affective and cognitive factors and thus produce individual differences in helpfulness. For example, people who are higher in traits such as Other-Oriented Empathy and who are more self-confident and higher in self-efficacy display affective and cognitive responses that typically produce helpful actions.

At the next level are the goals and motives that are relevant to the prosocial action. The nature of the motivation for helping and the ultimate objectives of the action are shaped by how affective and cognitive processes operate, which are influenced by the situational, personal, and interpersonal context in which the behavior occurs. And finally, we come to the behavioral outcome of all these causes—the prosocial action. It may involve interpersonal helping, volunteering for a large organization, or working with other members of a group to achieve some goal. It may be short-term or involve long-term commitments. It may even be reflected in inaction (Sibicky et al., 1995) or the refusal to acquiesce to a request for assistance that might ultimately cause another harm (e.g., an alcoholic's request for a drink).

A core assumption of this view of the causes of prosocial actions is that such actions are all immediately preceded by a moment (or maybe sometimes a fraction of a second) when the decision to act is made. This "decision" may reflect careful thought and reflection, or it may represent implicit processes, occurring outside the person's awareness and sometimes appearing "reflexive." Both affective and cognitive processes play critical roles in shaping this decision and thus people's prosocial behavior. In the next two sections we look at how prosocial actions are affected by affective and by cognitive processes. The goal of these sections is to further explore what we know about the causes of prosocial actions by taking information from each of the chapters and integrating it in comprehensive models of the causes of prosocial actions .

Affective Bases of Prosocial Actions

Figure 9.2 presents our model of the affective bases of prosocial actions. On the left-hand side of the model are innate, genetically-based human characteristics that we believe represent the origins of affective reactions in humans. On the right-hand side are the prosocial actions people may exhibit. The goal of the model is to link these two sides. As we outlined in chapter 1, prosocial behavior encompasses a wide range of action, from immediate, spontaneous responses to behaviors sustained over years. We propose that affective reactions may relate to this full range of behavior, including both individual and collective action, although their role is more likely to be primary in spontaneous helping situations or in the very initial stages of what may eventually develop into long-term helping, volunteering, or donating.

A basic premise of this model is that affective kinds of helping are, in part, caused by tendencies that we have inherited from our ancestors. That is, as we have discussed, there is sufficient evidence that humans are genetically predisposed to react to distress in another person in ways that may cause them to help that person. The first part of the model presents the mechanisms responsible for this reaction.

322

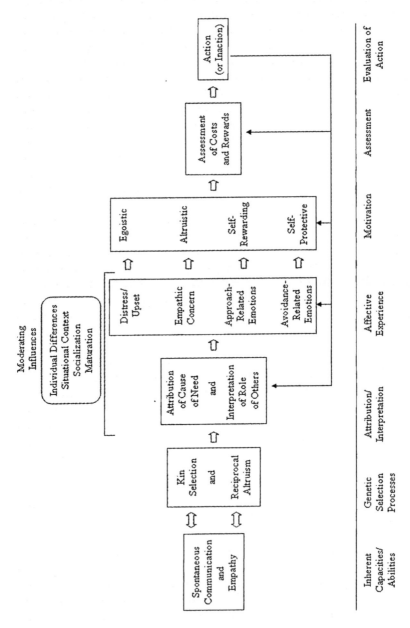

FIG. 9.2.   Affective bases of prosocial action.

Moderating
Influences

Individual Differences
Situational Context
Socialization
Maturation

| Spontaneous Communication and Empathy | Kin Selection and Reciprocal Altruism | Attribution of Cause of Need and Interpretation of Role of Others | Distress/ Upset, Empathic Concern, Approach-Related Emotions, Avoidance-Related Emotions | Egoistic, Altruistic, Self-Rewarding, Self-Protective | Assessment of Costs and Rewards | Action (or Inaction) |

| Inherent Capacities/ Abilities | Genetic Selection Processes | Attribution/ Interpretation | Affective Experience | Motivation | Assessment | Evaluation of Action |

The neurological structures that are responsible for feelings and emotions (i.e., the limbic system) were among the first to appear in the human brain (see chap. 2). If there is an evolutionary basis for helping and altruism, the mechanisms for translating these *inherent capacities and abilities* into behavior are likely to involve emotions. The innate tendency of humans to communicate their emotions may have given rise to other more specific kinds of communication between humans, such as empathy. As we also discussed in chapter 2, evolutionary processes and genetic influences shape the social relations among humans and produce fundamental orientations to others who are genetically related (kin selection) and to others in general (reciprocal altruism). Our model proposes that spontaneous communication and empathy probably provided the capacities and abilities needed for these two *genetic selection processes* that could lead to the evolution of helpful and altruistic tendencies in humans.

With respect to *kin selection*, the key to the survival of some trait or characteristic in a species is whether it contributes to the reproductive success of individuals who possess that characteristic (i.e., inclusive fitness). Thus, even altruists who died before they had offspring could have contributed to the reproductive success of their genetic characteristics by helping relatives with whom they shared these genetic characteristics survive and reproduce. If helpers' actions greatly increased the chances of their genetic relatives' survival and reproduction, then now-dead altruists would still have succeeded in transmitting a portion of their genes to future generations. Some of these genes would predispose people to be particularly responsive to the distress of those close to them. Spontaneous communication, which involves interpreting the situation of need and experiencing consequent emotional reactions, greatly facilitates the process of kin selection. The spontaneous communication approach suggests that people will communicate most often and most effectively with those with whom they share positive relations. These people are typically family members or others who live in close proximity.

Reciprocal altruism is mutual helping that increases the likelihood that unrelated but cooperating individuals will survive. Successful reciprocal altruism also depends on effective communication. For reciprocal altruism to benefit helpers and their descendants, a potential helper must not only be able to effectively and efficiently recognize that another person needs help but also be able to correctly distinguish between (a) those people who will reciprocate the aid, and (b) potential cheaters who will accept the assistance but not reciprocate by helping. Thus reciprocal altruism involves a careful interpretation of the situation and evaluation of the person or group of people in need.

This brings us to the next critical step in the model, the *attributions and interpretations* that people make about the causes of the other person's need (or, in the case of interdependence, the group's needs and their interpretations of the potential actions of others; see chap. 8). In spontaneous helping situations, one of the most basic attributions that people make is whether the person is responsible for his or her problem and deserving of assistance. In social dilemma situations (see Fig. 8.3 in chap. 8), people assess the nature of the dilemma itself (e.g., the payoff matrix) and their impressions of others involved (e.g., their personality and traits, such as trustworthiness) initially and in ongoing interactions. These attributional and interpretational processes relate to the evaluation of others along dimensions central to the concept of reciprocal altruism.

The next step in the model involves the *affective experiences* of the potential helper. In the model, affect is directly determined by the attributions and interpretations a person makes. The *situational context* (chap. 3), *maturation, socialization* (chap. 6), and *individual differences* (chap. 7)—what we have labeled as *moderating influences*—can all also influence affect directly (e. g., through differences in temperament) or indirectly by shaping attributions and interpretations. For example, as indicated in Fig. 9.2, the *situational context* can determine how much information a person has about another person, which determines what attributions and interpretations are made. If the situation limits information about why a person developed a drug addiction, people are likely to assume that the person is responsible for her problem because of a reckless lifestyle or a lack of personal control and, therefore, experience disgust or contempt. However, if the situation allows you to learn that the person developed the addiction as the result of medical treatment for chronic pain, your view of the person and the appropriateness of help would be quite different (see Weiner, Perry, & Magnusson, 1988), and you are more likely to experience compassion and sympathy. Aspects of the situation (e.g., relating to what and how much is communicated) can be a critical factor shaping attributions and interpretations of whether the prosocial actions under consideration involve assisting a stranger in need (chap. 3), helping an entire class of people in need (chap. 5), or resolving an interdependence problem (e.g., in a social dilemma situation; chap. 8).

The attributions that are made of others, as individuals or as groups, largely determine emotional reactions to the situation. When the cause of the other person's problem is perceived as uncontrollable (Weiner, 1986), people are likely to experience empathic emotions. As we discussed in chapter 4 and illustrated in Fig. 9.2, empathic affective reactions to potential helping situations can take a variety of different forms. Through the process of empathy, people may experience negative emotional states such as personal distress and upset. But under some circumstances, people may feel *empathic concern* (e.g., feelings of compassion and concern for a victim; Batson, 1991). Empathy is most likely to generate empathic concern when there is a special bond between a potential helper and the person in need. This bond may result from characteristics of the immediate situation (e.g., perceptions of shared fates or focusing on the other person's feelings), a long-term personal relationship between the people involved, or even genetic relatedness, as suggested by evolutionary theories.

The other affective reaction identified by the model is the consequence of violating the potential helper's standards of fairness and reciprocity (see chap. 4). Social standards of fairness, such as the norm of reciprocity, are universal across cultures, and people are generally motivated to act in ways that maintain these standards of fairness and to act in ways that benefit others perceived to be deserving of assistance. Thus, emotions such as guilt, which potential helpers may experience if they violate these standards (see chap. 4), or pity ("approach-related emotions") may also lead people to help both individuals (Cottrell & Neuberg, 2005) and groups (Fiske, Cuddy, Glick, & Xu, 2002). However, when the need is perceived to be caused by the person or group requiring help, people may experience emotions, such as anger, disgust, or contempt ("avoidance-related" emotions), that inhibit prosocial actions (Cottrell & Neuberg, 2005). In the same vein, when the situation involves groups rather than individuals, people may experience fear, which promotes competition rather than prosocial action.

Affective reactions directly influence the next component of the model—*motivation*. The motivation to help that is produced by feelings of distress, upset, guilt, and sadness is primarily *egoistic*: People help in order to relieve their own discomfort aroused by observing the distress of another. Nevertheless, as the arousal: cost–reward model (see chaps. 3 and 4) suggests, one's own needs and the needs of others frequently become intertwined through the mechanism of affective empathy. These affective reactions lead to helping primarily because the person believes that helping will make him or her feel better by eliminating the negative mood or will produce some rewarding outcome. This portion of our affective model of helping is primarily based on the negative state relief model and other similar models (see chap. 4) that propose people have learned that helping is often an effective way of making themselves feel better.

But helping is not always due to egoistic motivations. According to the empathy–altruism hypothesis (Batson, 1991), the affective reaction of empathic concern may elicit a truly *altruistic* motivation, in which the primary goal of the help given is to improve the other person's welfare. Thus, our model proposes that there are some prosocial actions that are truly other-oriented and solely motivated by an altruistic concern for another person's well-being. However, as we noted in chapter 4, because of the special conditions and social relations that must be present for empathic concern to be the predominant affective reaction, altruistically motivated helping is probably much less common than egoistically motivated helping. Finally, there are instances in which the motivation may not be either purely egoistic or altruistic. For example, people's motives may be rooted in their collective identities and involve promoting and/or protecting the interests of one's group rather than their own personal benefit (chap. 8).

Affect does not operate in isolation from cognitive processes, however. People *assess the costs and rewards* for various actions, specifically, the costs for helping, costs for not helping, and rewards for helping in spontaneous helping situations (chap. 3), in long-term helping (chap. 5), and in cooperation and competition (chap. 8). Even people who experience altruistic concern and are altruistically motivated to help in spontaneous helping situations may be inhibited if the costs for helping are too high (Batson et al., 1983). With respect to volunteering, this assessment is intimately related to the functions that volunteering serves for the self. Finally, "rational choice" models also propose that the decision to cooperate or compete in social dilemmas is the result of how people weigh these perceived costs and rewards.

The next step in the model presented in Fig. 9.2 involves the *action* that people take as a result of the preceding steps. But this is not the end of the process in our model. On the contrary, how people evaluate their own action, including their *affective experience* after acting, "feeds back" to shape interpretations of subsequent experiences, affective reactions, motivations, assessments, and actions. The impact of the behavior on the other parts of this model is particularly important for understanding sustained prosocial activities, such as volunteering or blood donation (chap. 5). Emotional reactions to others' competitive or untrustworthy behavior are critical factors in how people respond in social dilemma situations over time (chap. 8). The affect that people experience for their action may also apply at times to spontaneous helping. For example, the good feelings associated with being rewarded for helping in one instance may predispose people to be more responsive to others' needs in subsequent situations (chap. 3).

In summary, the affective bases of helping depicted in Fig. 9.2 are likely to have their origins in genetic predispositions that have been shaped by long-term evolutionary forces. These genetic tendencies are related to how people orient themselves in situations of need and are expressed in affective mechanisms related to empathy and emotional reactions associated with adherence to or violations of standards of fairness and reciprocity. As current theories of behavioral genetics suggest, however, these genetic predispositions do not automatically or completely determine our actions. Social, environmental, cultural, and personal factors influence the extent to which people exhibit these emotional reactions, as well as the specific nature of the emotion (e.g., empathic concern vs. personal distress) that they experience. These emotions then determine whether people engage in *altruistically motivated* helping (the result of empathic concern) or *egoistically motivated* helping (the result of distress, guilt, or sadness), or perhaps do not help at all (as a consequence of anger). Whether people's motivations result in actual prosocial action also depends on assessments of costs and rewards (the weights of which may be influenced by different motivations) for various courses of action. Moreover, once people take action, subsequent interpretations of and emotional reactions to what they have done and to other situations that may involve prosocial action are affected. Thus, the model is dynamic in suggesting that the process does not end with the prosocial action. To the contrary, acting prosocially involves iterative processes and reciprocal influences over time.

What kinds of prosocial behavior are best explained by a model of the affective bases of helping? As we noted at the outset of the section, we believe that this model is most applicable to informal, unplanned, and short-term acts of helping. Furthermore, affect exerts its strongest influence when another person is in extreme distress or great danger, and it is also most likely to explain helping among friends and family members—people who are likely to evoke strong emotions in the helper—as well as some forms of cooperative action (chap. 8). In these situations, it is probably the helpers' hearts rather than their heads that determine their actions.

Cognitive Bases of Helping

As we said earlier, humans are both feeling and thinking beings, and thus affect is not the whole story of helping. The capacity for higher level thought and reasoning distinguishes humans from other animals. Although there may be a strong affective basis of helping rooted in our evolutionary history, cognitive processes can also have a significant and perhaps an even more important influence on prosocial behavior. Figure 9.3 summarizes and integrates the major cognitive mechanisms discussed in the previous chapters. This aspect of prosocial action involves primarily the potential helper's assessments of the costs and benefits associated with offering help. Our task is to explain how the other parts of the model affect this critical decision.

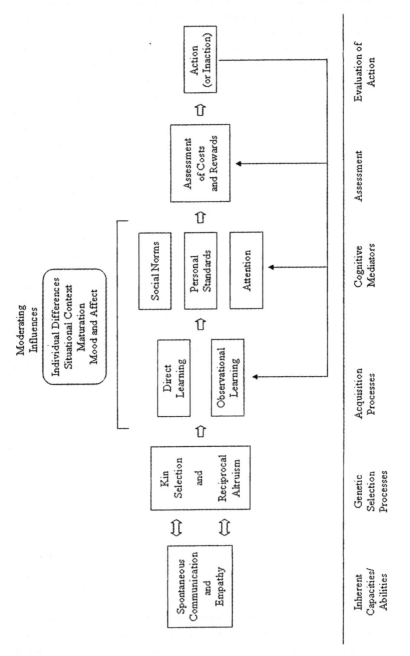

FIG. 9.3.   Cognitive bases of prosocial action.

We begin our discussion at the left portion of the diagram. The most distal causes of cognitive routes to prosocial actions are actually the same as those discussed in the affective model—*inherent capacities/abilities* and *genetic selection processes*. Predispositions to spontaneous communication and to empathize with others and genetic selection processes, such as kin selection and reciprocal altruism, influence people's orientation to the people and objects in their environment. In chapter 3, for example, we illustrated how people are more influenced by others whom they perceive to be more similar to themselves when deciding whether to intervene in an emergency. These processes also affect *acquisition processes*—how people learn about helping. From a cognitive perspective, people learn about helping and how to be helpful in the same ways that they learn other social behaviors. As we saw in chapters 4 and 6, both children (and adults) are strongly influenced by *direct learning* (by classical conditioning and operant learning) and by *observational (social) learning*. People learn more directly from others close to them, and they learn more by observing others whom they see as being similar to themselves. By watching prosocial models, children not only can learn that helping is valued but also can learn *how* to help and what happens to them when they help. As we saw in chapter 5, family influences are significantly related to planned, long-term forms of helping, such as volunteering and donating blood. People in social dilemmas are strongly influenced by what others in their group say and do (chap. 8).

This brings us to the *moderating influences* (similar to those identified within the affective model shown in Fig. 9.2) that are represented at the top of the model. Of course, people's *socialization* experiences affect the way they think about helping. Differences in families, social environments, and cultures can produce dramatic differences among people with respect to direct learning experiences, the social models to which they have been exposed, and the cultural and social values that they have learned. Individual families and entire cultures can differ significantly in what they teach a child about helping. For example, American and Hindu Indian cultures differ in what they teach children about repaying favors; Indians are more likely than Americans to believe that one has a moral (as opposed to a legal) responsibility to reciprocate favors (Miller & Bersoff, 1994). These variations in personal and cultural histories can obviously lead to individual differences in thoughts about helping.

Cognitive processes, like affective processes, may be influenced by *individual differences* in the personality characteristics and social roles of the potential helper (chap. 7), which have been shaped by learning and socialization processes. *Maturational changes* in cognitive processes, which were considered in chapter 6, are also critical moderating influences. Young children are cognitively egocentric: They find it difficult to learn to be helpful because they lack the cognitive ability to imagine themselves in another person's situation and to truly appreciate another person's problem or needs. As children mature, they develop the necessary cognitive skills to perceive events from another person's perspective. As a result, they are better able to understand when and how to help. Similar changes occur in actual helping; external and tangible rewards for helping become less important as children mature.

When a helping situation arises, the *transitory moods and affect* of a potential helper and the immediate *situational context* come into play. As we discussed in chapters 3 and 4, positive and negative moods can directly influence assessments of the costs and rewards of offering help. For example, people in good moods may help more because their positive mood makes them think more about the positive consequences of helping others. chapters 2 and 3 also provided considerable evidence about the effects of the social situation on helping. Such situational factors have a very important and direct influence on a potential helper's assessment of the rewards and costs of certain actions. Recall, for example, the concept of diffusion of responsibility (chap. 3); when there are other people who also see the person in distress and could offer help, their presence substantially lowers a person's estimates of the costs of not offering help. As a consequence, helping is reduced.

In Fig. 9.3, we propose that personal characteristics and immediate social circumstances indirectly affect helping through their effects on a limited number of *cognitive mediators*. These *cognitive mediators* include social norms, personal standards, and focus of attention, which we discussed in chapter 4. *Social norms* are widely held expectations about what is and what is not acceptable behavior. These expectations have their roots in individual differences in social and cultural experiences. Through personal experiences and observational learning, people learn about the social norms their society or group values (e.g., norm of social responsibility—helping those dependent on you; norm of reciprocity—helping others who have helped you). But there is also explicit and implicit communication with other people in the same circumstances through which individuals learn what norms are operative in a specific situation and what response is expected of them. Thus, observers' learning experiences and the immediate situation contribute to their understanding of which social norms are most relevant in a particular situation.

Although social norms provide general guidelines about what people should do across a range of situations, *personal standards* relate to an individual's own ideals and feelings of moral obligation (see chaps. 4 and 7). Personal standards are intimately related to a person's self-concept, and there may be considerable variation in personal standards within the same culture. Moreover, maturational processes affect the extent to which personal norms affect judgments about helping. For example, among young children who have not yet developed a stable sense of self, personal standards are not important determinants of helping. However, by the age of 8 or 9 years, children begin to make internal attributions about their own helpfulness and the helpfulness of others, and personal norms begin to play a greater role in helping decisions.

Another mediating process in the model concerns where potential helpers focus their *attention* when another person is in need. All the personal and situational variables we have been discussing influence the extent to which people pay attention to the needs of others as well as to their own needs. For example, because of different socialization experiences, men and women may attend differently to the needs of others (see chap. 6), with women traditionally being more socially sensitive. With regard to temporary moods, positive affect leads people to attend more to others, while some negative states (e.g., depression) make them less attentive and more self-absorbed. In terms of the effects of the immediate circumstance, we saw in chapter 3 that in overly stimulating environments, people are usually less attentive to the needs of others.

According to this model, social norms, personal standards, and attention directly affect the final and most critical part of the cognitive model, an observer's *assessment of the costs and rewards* associated with the decision about whether or not to help. A cost–reward analysis of prosocial actions assumes an economic view of human behavior—people are motivated to maximize their rewards and to minimize their costs. This represents a decidedly egoistic perspective toward the motivation of helping, one in which people are assumed to be mainly concerned about their own self-interest. The arousal: cost–reward model of emergency intervention (see chaps. 3 and 4) is perhaps the most explicit in incorporating these considerations into the decision to help, and the rational choice theory approach to cooperation (see chap. 8) is also predicated on the assumption that individuals engage in such analyses when weighing their behavioral options.

Finally, there is prosocial *action* (or inaction)—the end product of all the preceding steps in the model. Depending on the net effect of the various personal and situational factors that we have identified, an individual will either help or not help or, in group situations, will either cooperate or compete. Of course, the process does not end here. Performing (or not performing) a prosocial action has important consequences for the helper as well as the recipient (chap. 7) or for cooperators and their groups (chap. 8). This is especially true in the case of planned, long-term prosocial behaviors (see chap. 5), but it is applicable in some instances of unplanned, short-term helping as well. Sustained prosocial actions and how people *evaluate their own actions* can have a profound influence on how people see themselves, view others, and conceive of their relationship to other people and to their groups and organizations over time. That is, as we noted with the affective model, helping is not simply an outcome of the processes portrayed in Fig. 9.3 (e.g., personal standards and social norms); it feeds back and shapes these processes and, over time, can produce individual differences that maintain prosocial action and other interpersonal orientations in profound ways. As illustrated in Fig. 5.2 of chapter 5, for instance, giving blood repeatedly over time influences people's role identity as a blood donor, which further promotes giving blood in the future.

We believe that this cognitive model, like the affective model of helping presented earlier, can explain many acts of spontaneous, unplanned, and informal helping that occur among friends and even relatives. But we believe the cognitive model is much more useful than the affective model in explaining the kinds of collective prosocial behavior that were discussed in chapter 5 and the cooperative actions examined in chapter 8. As noted in the questions and answers section of those chapters, the research strongly suggests that decisions to contribute time or money to public goods or charities are most often determined by cost-reward calculations. Volunteers, contributors, and cooperators in general are usually individuals who have decided that it is in their own long-term best interests, as well as the long-term best interests of others in the community, to engage in work for the public good. Thus, we believe that most (although perhaps not all) action of this type represents cognitively-based forms of helping.

Affect and Cognition

Before we conclude our discussion of the two models, it is important to reiterate a point we made earlier: Although we can talk about the affective and cognitive bases of helping separately, in reality these two processes are inextricably intertwined in the decisions that people make about prosocial actions. Note that the models depicted in Figs. 9.2 and 9.3 in fact share several common components (e.g., inherent capacities/abilities, genetic selection processes, assessment of costs and rewards). For example, the degree to which we experience affective empathy strongly influences the cognitive assessment of costs for not helping when we are deciding what action we should take. The more unpleasant the arousal we experience by empathizing with a person in distress, the greater will be the anticipated costs for not helping, and, as a consequence, the more likely we will be to help.

Similarly, assessments of costs can influence the level of arousal that a person experiences. Suppose you see someone fall into a fast-flowing river—you immediately become aroused and distressed. Then you realize that the victim is your brother! The guilt, shame, and sorrow that you anticipate if you were to do nothing make you even more aroused and more upset. This higher level of unpleasant arousal may now impel you to immediate action. You may not know exactly what to do, but you know you must do *something*.

Alternatively, alterations of the perception of costs for helping may eventually reduce the amount of arousal you experience. Recall, yet again, the Kitty Genovese incident. The potential costs for direct help for the bystanders were high (e.g., the possibility of being stabbed if they intervened), but the costs for not helping were also high (e.g., her death). One way such "high cost for helping–high cost for not helping" dilemmas can be relieved is by reinterpreting or redefining the situation, as described by the arousal: cost-reward model. The observers of Kitty Genovese's murder did just this by diffusing responsibility. By convincing themselves that someone else would help, bystanders could come to believe that the emergency was over; by construing the situation in this way, their level of arousal could be decreased, further reducing the likelihood of helping.

The mutual influence of affect and cognition can also occur at a more fundamental level. As we observed in chapter 4, high levels of arousal can influence how we perceive situations and our assessment of costs and rewards. Specifically, high levels of arousal focus our attention very narrowly on the most salient central stimuli at the expense of less salient, peripheral stimuli. We process the most important information thoroughly and exhaustively, but we may largely ignore the peripheral information that is available. People who have been in a car accident sometimes report that they can provide vivid details about the hood ornament or shape of the bumper on the oncoming car—the salient stimuli in the situation. But they recall almost nothing about what was happening on either side of them—the peripheral information. As we saw in chapters 3 and 4, the impact of this focusing process on helping can be profound. People who are unable to "rationally" assess the full range of costs in the situation because of their extreme levels of arousal may help impulsively—jumping into the raging river to save your brother. Because this type of impulsive helping is nonrational, in some cases it can seriously jeopardize the lives of both the bystander and the person in need. Ironically, the problem here is not too much apathy but instead is too much empathy.

Alternatively, affective and cognitive processes can combine to influence prosocial action much later in the process. For instance, once egoistic motivations for action are aroused, there is a range of responses in which people can engage, besides immediate helping, to improve one's mood or relieve one's own empathic distress. With regard to cognition, egoistically motivated helping may reaffirm one's positive self-image or satisfy a wide range of personal goals (e.g., job advancement, distraction from personal problems). Helping may even be used strategically to gain advantage over another person by making the person dependent on assistance, by undermining his or her self-confidence, or by shaping more negative impressions of the person by others (Gilbert & Silvera, 1996).

In summary, although many manifestations of helping (particularly those commonly studied in the laboratory) appear simple and straightforward, prosocial behavior is a complex, multidetermined behavior. Whether it is spontaneous and short-term or planned and sustained, helping is an evolutionarily important behavior that is shaped by fundamental cognitive and affective processes, involves self- and other-directed motives, and has consequences central to one's self-image and social relationships. Thus, an understanding of the processes underlying helping can illuminate a wide range of other behaviors while offering genuinely unique insights to human motivation.

Despite the maturity of the field at the meso level of theory and research, the recent resurgence of interest in prosocial behavior stimulated by research at the micro and macro levels clearly demonstrates that we still have much to learn. It is obviously easier to describe what is known than what is not known; we cannot fully know what is yet to be discovered. Nevertheless, in the next, concluding section of this chapter and book, we identify what we see as promising new directions.

THE FUTURE: WHAT WE NEED TO LEARN

The study of prosocial behavior still has much to contribute to psychology and other disciplines. We asked a number of leading scholars, whose work we have described in this book, to also think about the future of the study of prosocial behavior. They agree that this is still a rich area of study, with much to offer. As we present our own ideas in this section about what we still need to learn about prosocial behavior, we will also intersperse related observations and projections by these distinguished scholars.

Although it may still be valuable to refine some of the current more focused meso-level theories about when and why people offer help, we believe that the best way to maximize new contributions at this time is to adopt a more comprehensive perspective on the topic. In the next section, we elaborate on one such perspective, the multilevel approach that we introduced briefly at the beginning of this chapter. (For a more complete description, see Penner et al., 2005.)

A Multilevel Approach to Prosocial Behavior

As we have suggested at various places throughout the book, prosocial behavior can perhaps best be viewed from three distinct but related levels of analysis: meso, micro, and macro. We call studying the behaviors of helper–recipient dyads within the context of a specific situation the *meso level of analysis*. This perspective is best illustrated by Darley and Latané's (1968) classic bystander intervention paradigm, in which participants' responses to others' accidents and medical emergencies (e.g., an apparent epileptic seizure) are studied. Meso-level research, which we examined most directly in chapters 3 and 4, has primarily focused on *when* people help and the motivational mechanisms responsible for bystander interventions and other forms of interpersonal helping. This type of research has been the traditional focus of psychological work on prosocial behavior (see Batson, 1998; Dovidio & Penner, 2001), and it is difficult to overstate its importance to the topic. However, researchers now recognize that this focus offers a limited view of the topic of prosocial behavior and that a broader perspective is needed (see Table 9.1). Moreover, as the com-

TABLE 9.1

Expanding the Perspective

Mark Davis (Eckerd College): My hope is that the next few years will see an increased interest in the way that empathy influences prosocial behavior outside the confines of the laboratory. For instance, considerable research has demonstrated that explicit instructions to imagine another's perspective (or to *not* do so) lead to predictable changes in thoughts, feelings, and behavior. But how do we typically act in everyday life, *without* such explicit prompts? Do we tend to empathize with other people more or less automatically, or is our usual tendency to remain emotionally and psychologically "separate" from others?

Alice Eagly (Northwestern University): The scope of research helping behavior should be broadened beyond its traditional focus on bystander intervention, polite and chivalrous behavior, and volunteering. Caring and nurturing behaviors have received some emphasis, but perhaps more among sociologists than psychologists. The shaping of caring by gender roles and other influences demands our attention.

ments in Table 9.2 reveal, there is still much to learn about the implications of prosocial motivation, as well as about what sustains these motivations and fulfills related needs.

Perspectives from other levels of analysis are now needed to more fully understand the entire spectrum of prosocial behaviors. One such perspective explores the characteristics of the individual who performs the prosocial action; we call this the *micro level of analysis*. Research at this level is primarily concerned with the origins of prosocial tendencies in humans and the etiology of individual differences in these tendencies. Thus, in chapter 2, which focused on the micro level of analysis, we considered how evolutionary theorists, neuroscientists, and behavioral geneticists explain general prosocial tendencies among humans. We returned to the micro level when we examined the work of developmental and personality psychologists (chaps. 6 and 7) on the causes and consequences of variations in prosocial behavior. We believe that much more work is needed at this level of analysis.

Finally, research conducted at the *macro level of analysis* considers prosocial actions that occur within the context of groups and large organizations. We explored the research literature on forms of prosocial action that usually occur among people who are members of an organization in chapter 5. This review focused primarily on volunteering and community service, but it also included related phenomena such as organizational citizenship behavior and whistle blowing. We need to know much more about both the antecedents and consequences of these behaviors. We also considered intragroup and intergroup helping and cooperation in chapter 8 and examined how feelings and beliefs about the intentions of others can shape one's own inclinations to act in a cooperative, prosocial manner.

Two promising ways to use this three-level framework in future research might involve (a) developing an integrative understanding of how certain cognitive, neurological, and genetic processes and mechanisms affect prosocial behavior at all three levels of analysis, and (b) conceptualizing prosocial behavior as an element of ongoing interpersonal and intergroup relations.

Integrative Understanding

One way to develop a broader and more integrative understanding of prosocial behavior might be to focus more attention on the proximal causes of prosocial actions. For example, recent research has begun to investigate how priming affects helping, often without conscious awareness (e.g., Garcia, Weaver, Moskowitz, & Darley, 2002). However, the

TABLE 9.2
Understanding the Motivational Implications

C. Daniel Batson (University of Kansas): The available evidence now strongly suggests that empathic emotion produces altruistic motivation. If this is true, then there are implications for philosophy, theology, economics, business, and law. These implications are being and will continue to be explored. There are also additional research questions: Are there sources of altruistic motivation other than empathy? Are there forms of prosocial motivation other than egoism and altruism? What produces empathy? What are the psychological implications of empathy-induced altruism?

Dan Hart (Rutgers University): The deep, life-transforming commitment to advancing the welfare of others that has as its cost the rejection of conventional social and material goals is deeply admired in our society but little understood. Individuals dedicated to altruism—for example, Paul Farmer, the subject of the recent biography *Mountains Beyond Mountains: The Quest of Dr. Paul Farmer, a Man Who Would Cure the World*—do not seem characterized by exaggerated personality traits, unique childhoods, or unusual social and cultural experiences, the factors that provide such powerful explanations of ordinary prosocial behavior. If we are to understand extraordinary lives of altruism, we will need to focus on the processes that result in identities, or integrated composites of values and commitments, that allow individuals to sustain enduring plans of action that are contrary to hedonic impulses and to societal norms.

Melvin Lerner (University of Waterloo): There is considerable evidence from the laboratory and everyday observation that the impulse to help someone and intervene on their behalf can be an automatic, virtually thoughtless response to familiar cues of distress/or harm. If accompanied by sufficient emotional arousal, people may act on the moral imperative seemingly without any thoughtful or rational considerations of the consequences for themselves or others. On the other hand, people may modify or override the initial impulse to help in the service of other motives. But from what I can tell, we have no systematic understanding of when either will occur and what form the subsequent response will take. When will the impulse to act on the moral imperative be manifested in the subsequent behavior, rather than be modified by more thoughtful, "intelligent" considerations?

Ervin Staub (University of Massachusetts): I have been concerned for many years now about how core orientations to the self and to other people develop, which I see as the underpinnings for empathy and sympathy and for a feeling of responsibility for other people's welfare (an aspect of what I have called a "prosocial value orientation"). In my view, these core orientations, the substrates for empathy, sympathy and feelings of responsibility, are the result of the fulfillment of basic human needs, such as a positive identity, feelings of effectiveness, positive connections to other people, and a constructive understanding of reality. It seems of great importance to me to explore to what extent the fulfillment of these needs is required for or makes more likely the development of empathy and sympathy, of feelings of responsibility for others, and in turn of helping and altruism, while their frustration makes it less likely.

emphasis of these studies has been more on the cognitive processes involved than on the prosocial behavior. Nevertheless, it is likely that many of the personal tendencies, motives, cost–reward calculations, and responsiveness to situational demands that are hypothesized to guide prosocial actions are not consciously accessible to potential helpers. Thus, we suggest that the large body of work on implicit cognitive processes that immediately precede social behaviors (e.g., Greenwald et al., 2002) might be useful to developing a more comprehensive understanding of why people act prosocially in interpersonal as well as in interdependent and group contexts, as well as why they do not.

The model for this inquiry might be the one that has been used for the study of racial and ethnic prejudice. This work has demonstrated that the direct or symbolic exposure of Whites to Blacks automatically activates racial associations (stereotypes and attitudes) that may not be consciously accessible and may even be inconsistent with their conscious expressions (Dovidio, Kawakami, & Beach, 2001). Moreover, implicit (unconscious) and explicit (conscious) attitudes predict different kinds of responses: Implicit attitudes best predict spontaneous responses, whereas explicit attitudes best predict deliberative behaviors (Dovidio, Gaertner, Kawakami, & Hodson, 2002). Information about these nonconscious processes has more fully informed prejudice researchers about the proximal mechanisms that underlie discriminatory behaviors, and similar research strategies might provide valuable insight and information about the proximal causes of prosocial actions and further illuminate when and how prosocial behavior occurs. This research might also add to an understanding of how the prosocial tendencies posited by evolutionary theorists are translated into actual prosocial behaviors. That is, they may link these distal evolutionary causes with the proximal causes of prosocial actions.

Yet another promising integration would be between prosocial research and social neuroscience. In recent years psychologists not trained as neuroscientists have become intrigued by the rapid advances in neural imaging and other aspects of neuroscience. Indeed, many social psychologists now describe themselves as social neuroscientists (see Cacioppo & Berntson, 2002). Their usage of functional magnetic resonance imaging (fMRI) and other imaging techniques has yielded some potentially interesting findings about the proximal causes of racial prejudice and other important social behaviors (Phelps et al., 2000). It would seem that these same research strategies might be applied to prosocial action. For example, it is well established that empathic responses are integral to many prosocial behaviors. Thus, it might be quite useful to researchers interested in prosocial behavior at all three levels of analysis to learn about those brain structures and functions that are activated when empathy is elicited. Neural imaging seems to afford this possibility (see also Table 9.3).

A more complex but worthwhile investigation would be to study how stable and observable individual differences in prosocial tendencies are manifested at the neurological level. Future research might thus compare the brain structure and functions of people who are well identified as consistently prosocial with those who do not characteristically display such behaviors. The research could focus on people who possess enduring personality traits that are associated with prosocial tendencies (e. g., the prosocial personality; Penner et al., 1995) or on people who have incorporated a prosocial identity into their self-concept because of their social role and others' expectations (e.g., a volunteer role identity, Grube & J. A. Piliavin, 2000). This research would inform the prosocial researcher, but it could have value to other researchers as well. Most obviously, it could help social neuroscientists better understand the neurological processes that underlie complex social behaviors. It might also be quite valuable for personality researchers. Most personality research simply demonstrates that some (often self-reported) personal characteristic is related to some behavior, but it does not really explain *why* this relationship exists. Identifying factors at the neurological micro level that differentiate "helpful" from "nonhelpful" people would begin to answer that question.

TABLE 9.3
Exploring Biological and Genetic Influences

C. Daniel Batson (University of Kansas): Affective neuroscience is an area where skies look brighter. If we can move beyond the level of putting people in scanners to "see what lights up" and instead—guided by what we already know about prosocial emotion and motivation—integrate neurophysiological measures with (a) experimental manipulations and (b) behavioral as well as self-report measures, we could learn lots.

David de Cremer (Tilburg University, The Netherlands): I think one development is the integration between biology and social sciences in studying prosocial behavior. Some hormones do have effect on how empathic and belonging people feel and that in turn affects prosocial acts. For example, an article in *Nature* in 2005 showed that the hormone "oxytocin" increased levels of trust among people.

Mark van Vugt (University of Kent, England): I foresee a convergence between social psychological and evolutionary models of altruism and prosocial behavior. When studying a particular aspect of prosocial behavior, researchers will have to ask themselves: "What are the functions of this behavior in both a psychological and a genetic sense?"

Future research also needs to pursue the behavioral genetics of prosocial actions. Psychology has moved well beyond the simplistic "nature versus nurture" question and now recognizes that, as we have repeatedly noted, both genes and the environment influence social behavior in a complex and interdependent manner. It would be useful to gain a better understanding of how this occurs. One way would be to conduct more studies in which the variance in prosocial dispositions is partitioned among the genetic and environmental components of a model that attempts to explain the differences in these tendencies (e.g., Krueger, Hicks, & McGue, 2001). These studies must ensure, however, that their phenotypic measures of the characteristics of interest are construct valid. Another way would be the approach used by Caspi and his colleagues (2002) in their longitudinal studies of how genetic characteristics interact with people's life experiences to affect adult behavior. This research has been primarily limited to how genetic anomalies interact with negative life events (e.g., child abuse) to affect antisocial tendencies in adults. However, we believe that this same methodology could be applied to understand better the etiology of prosocial tendencies in adults. Combined with the work of researchers such as Eisenberg and her associates (e.g., Eisenberg, Fabes, Guthrie, & Reiser, 2000), it would greatly advance knowledge of why some people are more prosocial than others. Several scholars in the field share this view and predict more emphasis on the topic of the development of prosocial tendencies in the future (see Table 9.4).

Before we leave this section, it should also be mentioned that the potential of merging the study of prosocial behavior with more biological approaches is not limited to neuroscience or behavioral genetics. For example, as we discussed earlier, certain prosocial behaviors (e.g., volunteering and the provision of interpersonal help) have positive health benefits for those who engage in these activities (Brown, Nesse, Vinokur, & Smith, 2003; Thoits & Hewitt, 2001). Are there biochemical processes responsible for these benefits? Is it possible, as some have suggested, that acting prosocially benefits the immune system? Using the prospective, longitudinal methodology employed by many volunteerism researchers, this may be an answerable question.

Prosocial Behavior and Ongoing Relations

The second strategy may be to widen the "lens" through which prosocial behavior is viewed. Specifically, rather than consider helping, cooperation, and volunteering as endpoints, these behaviors may be conceived of as parts of ongoing processes. Several of our colleagues saw this as an

TABLE 9.4
Investigating the Development of Prosocial Orientations

Gustavo Carlo (University of Nebraska): We know little about the socialization of sociocognitive and socioemotive traits associated with prosocial behaviors. How do socialization agents (e.g., parents, siblings, peers, media) foster traits and skills such as prosocial values, perspective taking, empathy, moral reasoning, and guilt? How do these traits and skills, in turn, promote prosocial behaviors? Our ability to explain how some individuals develop a deep commitment to prosocial activities is still limited. Work on care and moral exemplars is needed to understand the mechanisms that account for such behaviors over a long period of time.

Elizabeth Midlarsky (Columbia University): There are questions about people whose motives and values are altruistic, who are measurably empathic and socially responsible, but who cannot be helpful in the usual ways due to extreme old age and/or disability. What are the relative, separate impacts of the altruism and helping (to the extent that it does occur) by these people with disabilities on others and on their own well-being?

Ervin Staub (University of Massachusetts): A seeming paradox is that some people who have been victims of violence or abuse become caring, helpful, altruistic people, a phenomenon I have called "altruism born of suffering." What are the experiences that move people who have suffered to become caring and helpful, rather than aggressive, which is what research has primarily focused on? Are the characteristics they develop and the processes that lead them to help the same as among people who have become helpful through positive socializing experiences?

important future direction for the study of prosocial behavior, as indicated by the comments in Table 9.5. The research on volunteering has already provided a glimpse at the value of this approach, as it has examined the social, mental, and medical sequelae of being a volunteer. Future research could also consider the ongoing contribution of prosocial actions to interpersonal and intergroup relations.

Interpersonal Relations. In terms of interpersonal behavior, research with nonhuman primates has suggested that rather than viewing aggression as an antisocial orientation that interferes with relationships, it should be considered as a tool for negotiation that, when coupled with appropriate reconciliation responses, produces stronger and better relationships. For example, chimpanzees kiss and embrace after fights, and other nonhuman primates engage in similar "reconciliations" (de Waal, 2000, p. 586).

Among humans, forgiveness is an important contributor to stable relationships, including marriages (Ripley & Worthington, 2002). Al

TABLE 9.5
Understanding Prosocial Behavior and Social Relations

Wally Borman (University of South Florida): I believe an important next area of research in citizenship performance and OCB (organizational citizenship behavior) is in training organization members to be more effective in this performance domain. We and several others have demonstrated a link between supervisory (and peer) judgments of OCB effectiveness and overall job performance. So, with that contribution to overall effectiveness judgments of OCB effectiveness and the link Podsakoff and others have shown between organizational level OCB and indices of organizational effectiveness, encouraging and even actively training for enhanced OCB seems warranted.

Ross Buck (University of Connecticut): In anarchy such as that following hurricane devastation in New Orleans, violence is typically caused by gangs—social structures born out of chaos—not lone individuals. This spontaneous emergence of gangs actually reflects prosociality: When the social order is challenged, new forms of social organization arise, sometimes violently. In my current research, I approach social and moral emotions as aspects of self-organizing dynamical systems that emerge effortlessly from social interaction and communication, based biologically on attachment. Morality is a natural outcome of normal human socioemotional development, trustworthiness is signaled by expressive nonverbal displays, and authentic altruism evolves via communicative genes.

Arie Nadler (Tel-Aviv University, Israel): Although helping is often motivated by motivations of caring and empathy for those in need, helping relations also have implications for power and status relations between helper and recipient. Giving assistance may be motivated by the helpers' wish to make recipients dependent on them and relatively inferior to them. Habitual and ready acceptance of such help may signal recipients' acknowledgment of dependency and relatively lower status, whereas reluctance to seek or receive such help may indicate their wish for a change in status relations towards greater equality with the helper. From this perspective, helping relations may *create, maintain,* or *challenge* status and power relations between individuals and groups.

Alice Eagly (Northwestern University): Currently exciting to me is the study of heroism, a type of prosocial behavior in which people place themselves at considerable risk, often risk of serious physical harm or death. Although heroism is culturally associated with militarism and masculinity, it can occur in many other contexts, such as donating a kidney to a family member and even to a stranger in some cases. The social construction of heroism also warrants study. In daily life, people do not necessarily believe that heroism requires physical risk. Instead, sometimes individuals who have shown long-term commitment to others in difficult circumstances are re-

(continued on next page)

TABLE 9.5 (*continued*)

garded as heroic. For example, a person might label a family member as heroic because that individual has loyally served his or her family, despite considerable challenge and hardship.

Craig Parks (Washington State University): Cooperation researchers will increasingly look for variables and factors that can repair damaged cooperative relationships. For example, we are just starting to see systematic research on the importance of forgiveness: its ability to reinstate mutual cooperation; under what conditions people are and are not willing to forgive others who attempt to exploit goodwill; and the behavioral and psychological impact of not being forgiven a transgression.

though the role of prosocial orientation, in terms of empathy, is recognized as an important antecedent of forgiveness (McCullough, Worthington, & Rachal, 1997), the role that overt prosocial behaviors (e.g., reciprocated prosocial or cooperative actions) have in solidifying interpersonal relationships has not received direct empirical attention. Nevertheless, the research on reconciliation in primates suggests that this would be a promising direction for future inquiry. Similarly, McCullough (2001) proposed that forgiveness functions not only to reduce motivations to seek revenge but also to allow prosocial motivations to emerge or reemerge. This is just one example of how prosocial behavior can be seen as an integral part of an ongoing interpersonal relationship. Future research on this topic might explore, for example, whether a former transgressor's prosocial actions can facilitate forgiveness by eliciting a reciprocal empathic response. Relatedly, laboratory and field work at both the meso and macro level might reveal whether the occurrence of reciprocal prosocial behaviors during periods of reconciliation promotes the subsequent stability of relationships better than reconciliation when no prosocial action or unilateral prosocial behavior is involved. Countries such as South Africa and Northern Ireland, where the formal attempts at reconciliation between different groups (Blacks and Whites, Protestants and Catholics) still continue, might provide fertile sites for such research.

Intergroup Relations and Emerging Intragroup Processes. Prosocial behavior is also a potentially important factor in intra- and intergroup processes (see chap. 8). In terms of intergroup behavior, cooperation has long been recognized as a critical element of the Contact Hypothesis (Allport, 1954), which outlines how intergroup contact can improve intergroup relations. Similarly, in his general perspective on how to improve intergroup relations, Sherif (1966) proposed that the functional relations between groups are critical in determining intergroup attitudes. According to this position, competition between groups produces prejudice and discrimination, whereas intergroup interdependence and cooperative interactions that result in successful outcomes reduce intergroup bias (see also Bobo & Hutchings, 1996). More recent work on the Contact Hypothesis (e.g., Dovidio, Gaertner, & Kawakami, 2003; Pettigrew & Tropp, 2000) and on realistic group conflict (e.g., Esses, Dovidio, Jackson, & Armstrong, 2001) has confirmed the central function of cooperation in achieving and maintaining positive ongoing intergroup relations. Similarly, work on achieving stable peaceful relationships between groups that have a history of intense conflict (e. g., Bar-Tal, 2000; Kenworthy, Turner, Hewstone, & Voci, 2005) identifies mutual trust, cooperation, forgiveness, and empathy as key elements in the reduction of conflict.

Although it is well established that cooperation is an essential element for intergroup contact to reduce prejudice, future research might explore at what point in the process of intergroup contact cooperation is most important, and whether the optimal timing differs as a function of the historical relations between the groups. For example, among groups without a history of conflict, it might be relatively easy to facilitate empathy and perspective taking and to build trust by introducing activities in which members of the different groups simultaneously cooperate. In contrast, when groups have been in intense conflict, interventions that involve a series of sequential and reciprocal prosocial responses may be needed first to reduce tensions and build enough trust to engage in simultaneous cooperative activities. Thus, the role and functions of prosocial behavior might be studied within the context of different types of intergroup relations.

Another area in which the exploration of the instrumental role of cooperation and other prosocial action might be of considerable value is in interdependent *intra*group contexts, or social dilemmas. *Sustaining* cooperation in such settings is critical, but often difficult to achieve because defecting individuals will always have an advantage if they "free ride" or selfishly exploit a common pool resource. Informal coordination rules (van Dijk & Wilke, 1995; van Dijk, Wilke, Wilke, & Metman, 1999) and general interaction norms (Kerr, Garst, Lewandowski, &, Harris, 1997)—social standards that influence prosocial actions—may be sufficient to maintain group cooperation initially, and the fear of social sanctions if one deviates from implicit group standards may exert sufficient social pressure to temporarily suppress an individual's more egoistic, selfish desires.

Eventually, however, the suppressed egoistic desires are likely to resurface, competition will reemerge, and the trust that one once might have had in one's fellow group members will be eroded. To combat these urges, new social arrangements may need to be implemented in social dilemmas to preserve cooperation. Recent works by De Cremer and Tyler (2005), Schroeder, Steel, Woodell, and Bembenek (2003), and Tyler and Blader (2000, 2003) suggested ways in which more formal, justice-based procedural systems can serve to maintain intragroup harmony by reducing defections. The most effective procedural justice systems are likely to specify the *structural* justice rules for the allocation of both the goods (e.g., profit distribution) and the "bads" (e.g., taxes) of the situation and to prescribe the means to make amends for those who have violated the group standards. Relational procedures could also be incorporated into such justice systems, instilling within group members a sense of being valued, respected, and belonging, as well as a sense of collective, interdependent identity. But it is important to recognize that the formulation and implementation of *intra*group justice arrangements—in merged groups—may not be possible if the recategorization resulting from *inter*group conflict reduction has not provided the environment for reciprocity, trust, and cooperation to be fostered. That is, cooperation leads to procedural justice systems that in turn lead to stable, systemic cooperation.

This analysis and the linkage of prosocial behavior and justice suggest research that would address at least two questions. First, what factors in recategorized groups make them vulnerable to exploitation by individual group members? Understanding the limits of trust and reciprocity in newly formed groups would provide a starting point for identifying the variables that cause groups to consider the implementation of justice systems intended to produce fair outcomes for all members. Second, if sustained cooperation is one of the ultimate goals of justice systems, what are the necessary characteristics of such systems so that they will successfully suppress the egoistic desires of individual group members without imposing excessive restrictions of their freedom? Although the research that we envision would often address how prosocial behavior can best be elicited at the intra- and intergroup macro level, we also believe that it could have important implications for public and organizational policy development.

Intergroup Processes and Social Relations.   Different forms of prosocial behavior may function quite differently in intergroup contexts. Although successful cooperation, which involves mutual coordination and trust, may be a critical element in reconciliation and social integration between groups, helping behavior can have the opposite effects. The act of helping can be used to establish or reinforce perceptions that the helper (or the helper's group) has greater power, status, and re-

346 • CHAPTER 9

sources than the recipient (or the recipient's group), and helping over time can create a sense of dependency and powerlessness among recipients (Dovidio & Gaertner, 1983; Nadler & Fisher, 1986). With respect to intergroup processes, Nadler (2002) presented a model that suggests that high-status groups often offer low-status groups dependency-oriented help to establish and maintain dominance. The receptivity of low-status groups to this assistance may indicate their acceptance of inequality, and rejection may indicate an individual effort toward social mobility or a collective action to achieve social equality. Future research might build on earlier research on helping, using new integrative frameworks such as that proposed by Nadler to consider how the conditions under which help is given (e.g., to a member of another group in a superior or subordinate position; Dovidio & Gaertner, 1981), the type of help that is offered (Gergen, Ellsworth, Maslach, & Seipel, 1975), and the characteristics of the group identities involved (Taormina, Messick, Iwaki, & Wilke, 1988) influence intergroup relations over time.

Although studying prosocial behavior at the micro, meso, and macro levels of analysis separately will provide a more comprehensive view of prosocial behavior, as the comments of scholars in Table 9.6 articulate, the most significant advances will come from an *integrated* understanding—an appreciation of how these levels function interdependently. Humans are complex beings; our behavior is shaped by the intimate interaction of biological forces and predispositions, immediate perceptions and motivations, and social constraints and goals. Each factor is important, but a true understanding of prosocial behavior relies on appreciating how these forces combine to determine who helps, when they help, and why they respond prosocially.

CONCLUSION

The research presented in this chapter strongly suggests that far from being a moribund field, the study of prosocial behavior is growing and expanding. We began our review by discussing the origins of modern psychological research on prosocial behavior, with its meso-level analysis of the situational determinants of interpersonal helping. Then we examined how this research expanded both *inward* to the micro level and *outward* to the macro level. In doing this, we identified a host of interesting questions yet to be answered about the causes and consequences of the enormous variety of behaviors that are included under the prosocial rubric. These questions range from ones that are relevant to evolutionary psychology, behavioral genetics, and neuroscience to those that are relevant to social psychology, developmental psychology, personality

TABLE 9.6
Recognizing the Importance of Integration

Joan Grusec (University of Toronto, Canada): We need to differentiate among different kinds of actions that are lumped into the category of "prosocial" and treated as equivalent or interchangeable. Are comforting and helping and making restitution for some deviation governed by the same mechanisms? Or are they qualitatively different actions that need separate treatment? In a parallel fashion, the same act may have different underlying motivations and it makes little sense to lump these same acts together. Failing to make these kinds of differentiations makes the task of studying prosocial behavior all the more difficult.

Mark Snyder (University of Minnesota): As much as we know about when and why people help others in so many ways, what is less clear is whether there is a common core that transcends these diverse phenomena, a core set of psychological processes (whether motives, dispositions, instigators) that underlie and generate them, or whether these phenomena share a common name, prosocial behavior, but are reflections of quite different causal mechanisms beneath any surface similarities that they share. Thus, a clear challenge for the next generations of theory and research on prosocial behavior is to step back from the study of individual phenomena to gain a wide-angle perspective and construct the "big picture" of what diverse instances of prosocial behavior share in common and what marks each instance as a distinct phenomenon.

Paul van Lange (Free University, Amsterdam, The Netherlands): Prosocial behavior is one of the basic research areas to which almost any other area of social psychology can (and needs to) contribute, as well as several areas studied by biologists, sociologists, economists, political scientists, or anthropologists. Apart from interpersonal and group processes, insights derived from the literatures of social neuroscience (e.g., a neurological analysis of empathy and other emotions), social cognition (e.g., priming, implicit and explicit attitudes), social institutions (e.g., child care and education, family structure), and social change (e.g., urbanization, unemployment) are exceptionally important. I predict that a functional and comprehensive analysis of social value orientation, empathy, trust, and justice will appear to be essential for understanding prosocial behavior at various levels of analysis.

theory, industrial/organizational psychology, and the study of intra- and intergroup behavior.

Research on prosocial behavior also creates possible connections between psychology and other disciplines such as sociology, political science, and economics. There is a great need for interdisciplinary and multidisciplinary collaborations on prosocial behavior that use the multiple levels of analysis we have proposed. For example, social psychologists, sociologists, and political scientists might collaborate on issues such as how organizational factors impinge on the forms prosocial behavior takes, who it is that acts prosocially, and even what behaviors we define as prosocial. Psychologists might also join with sociologists, economists, and political scientists to jointly study the public policy implications of promoting large-scale, collective prosocial activities. And researchers interested in public health issues might join with psychologists, sociologists, and medical researchers to study the physiological costs and benefits of prosocial behavior.

We eagerly await the outcomes of these and other similar efforts.

References

Abrahams, R. D. (Ed.) (1985). *Afro-American folktales: Stories from Black traditions in the New World*. New York: Pantheon.

Adams, J. S. (1963). Towards an understanding of inequity. *Journal of Abnormal & Social Psychology, 67*, 422–436.

Adams, J. S. (1965). Inequity in social exchange. In L. Berkowitz (Ed.), *Advances in experimental social psychology* (Vol. 2, pp. 267–299). New York: Academic Press.

Adelmann, P. K. (1994). Multiple roles and physical health among older adults. *Research on Aging, 16*, 142–166.

Ahammer, I. M., & Murray, J. P. (1979). Kindness in the kindergarten: The relative influence of role playing and prosocial television in facilitating altruism. *International Journal of Behavioral Development, 2*, 133–157.

Ainsworth, M. D. S. (1973). The development of infant-mother attachment. In B. M. Caldwell & H. N. Ricciuti (Eds.), *Review of child development research* (Vol. 3, pp. 1–91). Chicago: University of Chicago Press.

Ajzen, I. (1991). The theory of planned behavior. *Organizational Behavior and Human Decision Processes, 50*, 179–211.

Albrecht, T. L., & Adelman, M. B. (Eds.). (1987). *Communicating social support*. Newbury Park, CA: Sage.

Alcock, J. (1989). *Animal behavior* (4th ed.). Sunderland, MA: Sinauer Associates, Inc.

Alcock, J. (2001). *Animal behavior* (7th ed.). Sunderland, MA: Sinauer Associates, Inc.

Allen, B. C., Sargeant, L. D., & Bradley, L. M. (2003). Differential effects of task and reward interdependence on perceived helping behavior, effort, and group performance. *Small Group Research, 34*, 716–740.

Allen, J. P., Philliber, S., & Hoggson, N. (1990). School-based prevention of teenage pregnancy and school dropout: Process evaluation of the national replication of the Teen Outreach Program. *American Journal of Community Psychology, 18*, 505–524.

Allen, J. P., Philliber, S., Herrling, S., & Kuperminc, G. P. (1997). Preventing teen pregnancy and academic failure: Experimental evaluation of a developmentally based approach. *Child Development, 64*, 729–742.

Allen, T. D. (1999, April). *Mentoring others: Mentor dispositions and desired protégée characteristics.* Paper presented at the fourteenth annual meeting of the Society of Industrial and Organizational Psychology, Atlanta, GA.

Allport, G. W. (1954). *The nature of prejudice.* Cambridge, MA: Addison-Wesley.

American Nurses Association. (1985). *Code for nurses and interpretive statements.* Washington, DC: Author.

Anderson, C. A., Berkowitz, L., Donnerstein, E., Huesmann, L. R., Johnson, J. D., Linz, D., Malamuth, N., & Wartella, E. (2003). The influence of media violence on youth. *Psychological Science in the Public Interest, 4,* 81–110.

Anderson, S. E., & Williams, L. J. (1996). Interpersonal, job, and individual factors related to helping processes at work. *Journal of Applied Psychology, 81,* 282–296.

Applebaum, L. D. (2002). Who deserves help? Students' opinions about the deservingness of different groups living in Germany to receive aid. *Social Justice Research, 15,* 201–225.

Archer, R. L. (1984). The farmer and the cowman should be friends: An attempt at reconciliation with Batson, Coke, and Pych. *Journal of Personality and Social Psychology, 46,* 709–711.

Archer, R. L., Diaz-Loving, R., Gollwitzer, P. M., Davis, M. H., & Foushee, H. C. (1981). The role of dispositional empathy and social evaluation in the empathic mediation of helping. *Journal of Personality and Social Psychology, 46,* 786–796.

Argyle, M. (1991). *Cooperation: The basis of sociability.* London: Routledge.

Arlitt, A. H. (1930). *Psychology of infancy and early childhood.* New York: McGraw-Hill.

Armitage, C. J., & Connor, M. (2001). Social cognitive determinants of blood donation. *Journal of Applied Social Psychology, 31,* 431–458.

Arnold, E. (1967). *A night of watching.* New York: Fawcett.

Aronfreed, J. (1970). Socialization of altruistic and sympathetic behavior: Some theoretical and experimental analyses. In J. Macaulay & L. Berkowitz (Eds.), *Altruism and helping behavior* (pp. 103–123). New York: Academic Press.

Aronfreed, J., & Pascal, V. (1965). *Empathy, altruism, and the conditioning of positive affect.* Unpublished manuscript, University of Pennsylvania, Philadelphia, PA.

Aronson, E., & Patnoe, S. (1997). *The jigsaw classroom.* New York: Longman.

Aronson, E., Wilson, T. D., & Akert, R. M. (2004). *Social psychology.* Upper Saddle River, NJ: Pearson Prentice Hall.

Ashton M., Paunonen, S. V., Helmes, E, & Douglas, N. (1998). Kin altruism, reciprocal altruism, and the Big Five personality factors. *Evolution and Human Behavior, 1,* 243–255.

Astin, A. W., Sax, L. J., & Avalos, J. (1999). Long-term effects of volunteerism during the undergraduate years. *Review of Higher Education, 22,* 187–202.

Atkins, R., Hart, D., & Donnelly, T. (2005). The influence of childhood personality on volunteering during adolescence. *Merrill Palmer Quarterly, 51,* 145–162.

Ausubel, N. (Ed.). (1948). *A treasury of Jewish folklore.* New York: Crown.

Axelrod, R. (1984). *The evolution of cooperation.* New York: Basic Books.

Axelrod, R. (1997). *The complexity of cooperation: Agent-based models of competition and collaboration.* Princeton, NJ: Princeton University Press.

Baden, J. A. (1998a). Communitarianism and the logic of the commons. In J. A. Baden & D. S. Noonan (Eds.), *Managing the commons* (2nd ed., pp. 135–153). Bloomington: Indiana University Press.

Baden, J. A. (1998b). A new primer for the management of common-pool resources and public goods. In J. A. Baden & D. S. Noonan (Eds.), *Managing the commons* (2nd ed., pp. 51–62) Bloomington: Indiana University Press.

Bandura, A. (1977). *Social learning theory.* Englewood Cliffs, NJ: Prentice Hall.

Bandura, A. (1986). *Social foundations of thought and action.* Englewood Cliffs, NJ: Prentice Hall.

Bandura, A. (1997). *Self-efficacy: The exercise of control.* New York: W. H. Freeman.

Barbee, A. P. (1990). Interactive coping: The cheering up process in close relationships. In S. Duck (Ed.), *Personal relationships and social support* (pp. 45–65). London: Sage.

Barbee, A. P., Cunningham, M. R., Winstead, B. A., Derlega, V. J., Gulley, M. R., Yankeelov, P. A., & Druen, P. B. (1993). Effects of gender role expectations on the social support process. *Journal of Social Issues, 49,* 175–190.

Baron, R. A. (1997). The sweet smell of … helping: Effects of pleasant and ambient fragrances on prosocial behavior in shopping malls. *Personality and Social Psychology Bulletin, 23,* 498–503.

Barrett, D. W., Wosinska, W., Butner, J., Petrova, P., Gornik-Durose, M., & Cialdini, R. B. (2004). Individual differences in the motivation to comply across cultures: The impact of social obligation. *Personality and Individual Differences, 37,* 19–31.

Barrett, L., Dunbar, R. I., & Lycett, J. (2002). *Human evolutionary psychology.* Princeton, NJ: Princeton University Press.

Bar-Tal, D. (1982). Sequential development of helping behavior: A cognitive-learning approach. *Developmental Review, 2,* 101–124.

Bar-Tal, D. (2000). From intractable conflict through conflict resolution to reconciliation: Psychological analysis. *Political Psychology, 21,* 351–365.

Bar-Tal, D., & Raviv, A. (1982). A cognitive-learning model of helping behavior development: Possible implications and applications. In N. Eisenberg (Ed.), *The development of prosocial behavior* (pp. 199–218). New York: Academic Press.

Bar-Tal, D., Raviv, A., & Leiser, T. (1980). The development of altruistic behavior: Empirical evidence. *Developmental Psychology, 16,* 516–524.

Bartholomew, K., & Horowitz, L. M. (1991). Attachment among young adults: A test of a four category model. *Journal of Personality and Social Psychology, 61,* 226–244.

Barton, E. J., & Osborne, J. G. (1978). The development of classroom sharing by a teacher using positive practice. *Behavior Modification, 2,* 231–251.

Batson, C. D. (1987). Prosocial motivation: Is it ever truly altruistic? In L. Berkowitz (Ed.), *Advances in experimental social psychology* (Vol. 20, pp. 65–122). New York: Academic Press.

Batson, C. D. (1991). *The altruism question: Toward a social-psychological answer.* Hillsdale, NJ: Lawrence Erlbaum Associates.

Batson, C. D. (1998). Altruism and prosocial behavior. In D. T. Gilbert, S. T. Fiske, & G. Lindzey (Eds.), *The handbook of social psychology* (4th ed., Vol. 2, pp. 282–315). New York: McGraw-Hill.

Batson, C. D. (2002). Four motives for community involvement. *Journal of Social Issues, 58,* 429–445.

Batson, C. D., & Ahmad, N. (2001). Empathy-induced altruism in a prisoner's dilemma II: What if the target of empathy has defected? *European Journal of Social Psychology, 31,* 25–36.

Batson, C. D., Batson, J. G., Griffitt, C. A., Barrientos, S., Brandt, J. R., Sprengelmeyer, P., & Bayly, M. J. (1989). Negative-state relief and the empathy-altruism hypothesis. *Journal of Personality and Social Psychology, 56,* 922–933.

Batson, C. D., Batson, J. G., Slingsby, J. K., Harrell, K. L., Peekna, H. M., & Todd, R. M. (1991). Empathic joy and the empathy-altruism hypothesis. *Journal of Personality and Social Psychology, 61,* 413–426.

Batson, C. D., Batson, J., Todd, R., Brummett, B., Shaw, L., & Aldeguer, C. (1995). Empathy and the collective good: Caring for one of the others in a social dilemma. *Journal of Personality and Social Psychology, 84,* 619–631.

Batson, C. D., Dyck, J, L., Brandt, J. R., Batson, J. G., Powell, A. L., McMaster, M. R., & Griffitt, C. (1988). Five studies testing two new egoistic alternatives to the empathy-altruism hypothesis. *Journal of Personality and Social Psychology, 55,* 52–77.

Batson, C. D., Fultz, J., Schoenrade, P .A., Paduano, A. (1987). Critical self-reflection and self-perceived altruism: when self-reward fails. *Journal of Personality and Social Psychology, 53,* 594–602.

Batson, C. D., & Moran, T. (1999). Empathy-induced altruism in a prisoner's dilemma. *European Journal of Social Psychology, 29,* 909–924.

Batson, C. D., & Oleson, K. C. (1991). Current status of the empathy-altruism hypothesis. In M. S. Clark (Ed.), *Review of personality and social psychology: Vol. 12. Prosocial behavior* (pp. 62–85). Newbury Park, CA: Sage.

Batson, C. D., O'Quin, K., Fultz, J., Vanderplas, M., & Isen, A. M. (1983). Influence of self-reported distress and empathy on egoistic versus altruistic motivation to help. *Journal of Personality and Social Psychology, 45*, 706–718.

Batson, C. D., Sager, K., Garst, E., Kang, M., Rubchinsky, K., & Dawson, K. (1997). Is empathy-induced helping due to self-other merging? *Journal of Personality and Social Psychology, 73*, 495–509.

Beaman, A. L., Cole, C. M., Preston, M., Klentz, B., & Steblay, N. M. (1983). Fifteen years of foot-in-the-door research: A meta-analysis. *Personality and Social Psychology Bulletin, 9*, 181–186.

Becker, S. W., & Eagly, A. H. (2004). The heroism of women and men. *American Psychologist, 59*, 163–178.

Bellah, R. N., Madsen, R., Sullivan, W. M., Swidler, A., & Tipton, S. M. (1985). *Habits of the heart: Individualism and commitment in American life.* Berkeley: University of California Press.

Bem, S .L. (1981). Gender schema theory: A cognitive account of sex typing. *Psychological Review, 88*, 354–364.

Bengston, V. (1985). Diversity and symbolism in grandparental roles. In V. Bengston & J. Robertson (Eds.), *Grandparenthood* (pp. 11–25). Beverly Hills, CA: Sage.

Benson, P. L., Karabenick, S. A., & Lerner, R. M. (1976). Pretty pleases: The effects of physical attractiveness, race, and sex on receiving help. *Journal of Experimental Social Psychology, 12*, 409–415.

Berger, J. M., Levant, R., McMillan, K. K., Kelleher, W., & Sellers, A. (2005). Impact of gender role conflict, traditional masculinity ideology, alexithymia, and age on men's attitudes toward psychological help seeking. *Psychology of Men and Masculinity, 6*, 73–78.

Bergin, C. A. C., Bergin, D. A., & French, E. (1995). Preschoolers' prosocial repertoires: Parents' perspectives. *Early Childhood Research Quarterly, 10*, 81–103.

Bergman, M. E., Day , R., Langhout, P. A., Palmieri, L. M. Cortina, & Fitzgerald, L. F. (2002). The (un)reasonableness of reporting: Antecedents and consequences of reporting sexual harassment. *Journal of Applied Psychology, 87*, 230–242.

Berkowitz, L. (1972). Social norms, feelings, and other factors affecting helping behavior and altruism. In L. Berkowitz (Ed.), *Advances in experimental social psychology* (Vol. 6, pp. 63–108). New York: Academic Press.

Berkowitz, L., & Daniels, L. R. (1963). Responsibility and dependency. *Journal of Abnormal and Social Psychology, 66*, 429–436.

Berkowitz, L., & Daniels, L. R. (1964). Affecting the salience of the social responsibility norm: Effect of past help on the responses to dependency relationships. *Journal of Abnormal and Social Psychology, 68*, 275–281.

Berkowitz, W. (1987). *Local heroes.* Lexington, MA: Lexington Books.

Beutel, A. M., & Johnson, M. K. (2004). Gender and prosocial values during adolescence: A research note. *Sociological Quarterly, 45*, 379–393.

Bickman, L. (1971). The effect of another bystander's ability to help on bystander intervention in an emergency. *Journal of Experimental Social Psychology, 7*, 367–379.

Bickman, L., & Kamzan, M. (1973). The effect of race and need on helping behavior. *Journal of Personality and Social Psychology, 89*, 73–77.

Bickman, L., Teger, A., Gabriele, T., McLaughlin, C., Berger, M., & Sunaday, E. (1973). Dormitory density and helping behavior. *Environment and Behavior, 5*, 465–490.

Bierhoff, H. W., Klein, R., & Kramp, P. (1991). Evidence for the altruistic personality from data on accident research. *Journal of Personality, 59*, 263–280.

Biller-Andorno, N. (2002). Gender imbalance in living organ donation. *Medical Health Care and Philosophy, 5*, 199–204.

Blyth, D .A., Saito, R., & Berkas, T. (1997). A quantitative study of the impact of service-learning programs. In A. S. Waterman (Ed.), *Service-learning: Applications from the research* (pp. 39–56). Mahwah, NJ: Lawrence Erlbaum Associates.

Bobo, L., & Hutchings, V. L. (1996). Perceptions of racial group competition: Extending Blumer's theory of group position to a multiracial context. *American Sociological Review, 61,* 951–972.

Boccacin, L. (2000). The importance of the "Anonymous Gift to the Unknowns." The case of blood donation. *Sociologia e Politiche Sociali, 3,* 19–35. (Abstract in English)

Boehm, C. (2000). Group selection in the upper paleolithic. *Journal of Consciousness Studies, 7,* 211–215.

Bonhote, K., Romano-Egan, J., & Cornwell, C. (1999). Altruism and creative expression in a long-term older adult psychotherapy group. *Issues in Mental Health Nursing, 20,* 603–617.

Borgida E., Conner, C., & Manteufal, L. (1992). Understanding living kidney donation: A behavioral decision-making perspective. In S. Spacapan & S. Oskamp (Eds.), *Helping and being helped* (pp. 183–212). Newbury Park, CA: Sage.

Borman, W. C. (2004). The concept of organizational citizenship. *Current Directions in Psychological Science, 13,* 238–241.

Borman, W. C., & Motowidlo, S. J. (1993). Expanding the criterion domain to include elements of contextual performance. In N. Schmitt & W. C. Borman (Eds.), *Personnel selection in organizations* (pp. 71–98). San Francisco, CA: Jossey-Bass.

Borman, W. C., & Penner, L. A. (2001). Citizenship performance: Its nature, antecedents, and motives. In B. W. Roberts & R. Hogan (Eds.), *Personality psychology in the workplace.* (pp. 45–61). Washington, DC: American Psychological Association.

Borman, W. C., Penner, L. A., Allen, T. D., & Motowidlo, S. J. (2001). Personality predictors of citizenship performance. *International Journal of Selection and Assessment, 9,* 52–69.

Boster, F. J., Mitchell, M. M., Lapinski, M. K., Cooper, H., Orrego, V. O., & Reinke, R. (1999). The impact of guilt and type of compliance-gaining message on compliance. *Communication Monographs, 66,* 168–177.

Bowlby, J. (1969). *Attachment and loss: Vol. 1. Attachment.* New York: Basic Books.

Bowlby, J. (1988). *A secure base: Parent-child attachment and healthy human development.*

Boykin, A .W. (1983). The academic performance of Afro-American children. In J. T. Spence (Ed.), *Achievement and achievement motives* (pp. 321–371). San Francisco, CA: Freeman.

Brady, H., Schlozman, K. L., & Verba S. (1999). Prospecting for participants: rational expectations and the recruitment of political activists. *American Political Science Review, 93,* 153–169.

Brann, P., & Foddy, M. (1987). Trust and the consumption of a deteriorating common resource. *Journal of Conflict Resolution, 31,* 615–630.

Breakwell, G. M. (1986). *Coping with threatened identities.* London: Methuen.

Brehm, J. W. (1966). *A theory of psychological reactance.* New York: Academic Press.

Brehm, S. S., & Brehm, J. W. (1981). *Psychological reactance: A theory of freedom and control.* New York: Academic Press.

Brewer, M. B. (1988). A dual process model of impression formation. In T. S. Srull & R. S. Wyer (Eds.), *Advances in social cognition: Vol. I: A dual process model of impression formation* (pp. 1–36). Hillsdale, NJ: Lawrence Erlbaum Associates.

Bringle, R. G., & Kremer, J. F. (1993). Evaluation of an intergenerational service-learning project for undergraduates. *Educational Gerontology, 19,* 407–416.

Brody, G. H., & Shaffer, D. R. (1982). Contributions of parents and peers to children's moral socialization. *Developmental Review, 2,* 31–75.

Broman, C. L. (1987). Race differences in professional help seeking. *American Journal of Community Psychology, 15,* 473–489.

Broman, C. L., Neighbors, H. W., & Taylor, R. J. (1989). Race differences in seeking help from social workers. *Journal of Sociology and Social Welfare, 16,* 109–123.

Brown, D. R., Gary, L., Green, A., & Milburn, N. (1992). Patterns of social affiliation as predictors of depressive symptoms among urban blacks. *Journal of Health and Social Behavior, 33,* 242–253.

Brown, R., & Zagefka, H. (2005). Ingroup affiliations and prejudice. In J. F. Dovidio, P. G. Glick, & L. Rudman (Eds.), *On the nature of prejudice: Fifty years after Allport* (pp. 54–70). Malden, MA: Blackwell.

Brown, S. L., Nesse, R. M., Vinokur, A. D., & Smith, D. M. (2003). Providing social support may be more beneficial than receiving it: Results from a prospective study of mortality. *Psychological Science, 14,* 320–327.

Bruder-Mattson, S. F., & Hovanitz, C. A. (1990). Coping and attributional styles as predictors of depression. *Journal of Clinical Psychology, 46,* 557–565.

Bryan, A. D., Hammer, J. C., & Fisher, J. D. (2000). Whose hands reach out to the homeless? Patterns of helping among high and low communally oriented individuals. *Journal of Applied Social Psychology, 30,* 877–905.

Buck, R. (1999). The biological affects: A topology. *Psychological Review, 106,* 301–336.

Buck, R. (2002). The genetics and biology of true love: Prosocial biological affects and the left hemisphere. *Psychological Review, 109,* 739–744.

Burnstein, E., Crandall, C., & Kitayama, S. (1994). Some neo-Darwinian decision rules for altruism: Weighing cues for inclusive fitness as a function of the biological importance of the decision. *Journal of Personality & Social Psychology, 67,* 773–789.

Buss, D. M. (2004). *Evolutionary psychology: The new science of the mind.* Boston: Allyn Bacon.

Byrne, D. (1971). *The attraction paradigm.* New York: Academic Press.

Cacioppo, J. T., & Berntson, G. G. (Eds.). (2002). *Foundations in social neuroscience.* Cambridge, MA: MIT Press.

Calabrese, R. L., & Schumer, H. (1986). The effects of service activities on adolescent alienation. *Adolescence, 21,* 675–687.

Caldwell, R. A., & Reinhart, M. A. (1988). The relationship of type of personality to individual differences in the use and type of social support. *Journal of Social and Clinical Psychology, 6,* 140–146.

Callero, P. L. (1985/1986). Putting the social in prosocial behavior: An interactionist approach to altruism. *Humboldt Journal of Social Relations, 13,* 15–34.

Campbell, A. (1999). Staying alive: Evolution, culture, and women's intrasexual aggression. *Behavioral & Brain Sciences, 22,* 203–252.

Campbell, D. T. (1958). Common fate, similarity, and other indices of the status of aggregates of persons as social entities. *Behavioral Science, 3,* 14–25.

Campbell, D T. (1965). Ethnocentric and other altruistic motives. In D. Levine (Ed.), *Nebraska symposium on motivation* (Vol. 13, pp. 283–311). Lincoln: University of Nebraska Press.

Campbell, D .T. (1975). On the conflicts between biological and social evolution and between psychology and moral tradition. *American Psychologist, 30,* 1103–1126.

Cancain, F. M., & Oliker, S. J. (2000). *Caring and gender.* Thousand Oaks, CA: Pine Forge Press.

Caporael, L. R. (2001). Evolutionary psychology: Toward a unifying theory and a hybrid science. *Annual Review of Psychology, 52,* 607–628.

Caprara, G. V., Barbaranelli, C., Pastorelli, C., Bandura, A., & Zimbardo, P. G. (2000). Prosocial foundations of children's academic achievement. *Psychological Science, 11,* 302–306.

Caprara, G. V. & Steca, P. (2005). Self-efficacy beliefs as determinants of prosocial behavior conducive to life satisfaction across ages. *Journal of Social and Clinical Psychology, 24,* 191–217.

Carlo, G., Eisenberg, N., & Knight, G. P. (1992). An objective measure of prosocial moral reasoning. *Journal of Research on Adolescence, 2,* 331–349.

Carlo, G., Eisenberg, N., Troyer, D., Switzer, G. E., & Speer, A. L. (1991). The altruistic personality: In what contexts is it apparent? *Journal of Personality and Social Psychology, 61,* 450–458.

Carlo, G., Koller, S. H., Eisenberg, N., Da Silva, M. S., & Frohlich, C. B. (1996). A cross-national study on the relations among prosocial moral reasoning, gender role orientations, and prosocial behaviors. *Developmental Psychology, 32,* 231–240.

Carlo, G., Okun, M. A., Knight, G. P., & de Guzman, M. R. T. (2005). The interplay of traits and motives on volunteering: Agreeableness, extraversion and prosocial value motivation. *Personality and Individual Differences, 38,* 1293–1305.

Carlo, G., Roesch, S. C., Knight, G. P., & Koller, S. H. (2001). Between- or within-culture variation? Culture group as a moderator of the relations between individual differences and resource allocation preferences. *Journal of Applied Developmental Psychology, 22,* 559–579.

Carnevale, P. J., Pruitt, D. G., & Carrington, P. I. (1982). Effects of future dependence, liking, and repeated requests for help on helping behavior. *Social Psychology Quarterly, 45,* 9–14.

Carver, C., & Scheier, M. (2004). *Perspectives on personality.* Boston: Pearson.

Caspi, A., McClay, J., Moffitt, T., Mill, J., Martin, J., Craig, I. W., Taylor, A., & Poulton, R. (2002). Role of genotype in the cycle of violence in maltreated children. *Science, 297,* 851–854.

Charng, H. W., Piliavin, J. A., & Callero, P. L. (1988). Role-identity and reasoned action in the prediction of repeated behavior. *Social Psychology Quarterly, 51,* 303–317.

Cheek, J. M., Melchior, L. A., & Carpentieri, A. M. (1986). Shyness and self concept. In L. M. Hartman, & K. R. Blankstein (Eds.), *Advances in the study of communication and affect: Vol. 2. Perception of self in emotional disorder and psychotherapy* (pp. 113–131). New York: Plenum.

Chen, X., Hui, C., & Sego, D. J. (1998). The role of organizational citizenship behavior in turnover: Conceptualization and preliminary tests of key hypotheses. *Journal of Applied Psychology, 83,* 922–931.

Cheng, P. W., & Holyoak, K. J. (1989). On the natural selection of reasoning theories. *Cognition, 33,* 285–313.

Cheuk, W. H., & Rosen, S. (1993). How efficacious, caring Samaritans cope with unexpected rejection. *Current Psychology, 12,* 99–112.

Cheuk, W. H., Wong, K. S., Swearse, B., & Rosen, S. (1997). Stress preparation, coping style, and nurses' experiences of being spurned by patients. *Journal of Social Behavior & Personality, 12,* 1055–1064.

Cialdini, R. B., Baumann, D. J., & Kenrick, D. T. (1981). Insights from sadness: A three-step model of the development of altruism as hedonism. *Developmental Review, 1,* 207–223.

Cialdini, R. B., Brown, S. L., Lewis, B. P., Luce, C., & Neuberg, S. L. (1997). Reinterpreting the empathy-altruism relationship: When one into one equals oneness. *Journal of Personality and Social Psychology, 73,* 481–494.

Cialdini, R. B., Darby, B. K., & Vincent, J. E. (1973). Transgression and altruism: A case for hedonism. *Journal of Experimental Social Psychology, 9,* 502–516.

Cialdini, R. B., & Fultz, J. (1990). Interpreting the negative mood/helping literature via mega-analysis: A contrary view. *Psychological Bulletin, 107,* 210–214.

Cialdini, R. B., & Kenrick, D. T. (1976). Altruism as hedonism: A social development perspective on the relationship of negative mood state and helping. *Journal of Personality and Social Psychology, 34,* 907–914.

Cialdini, R. B., Kenrick, D. T., & Baumann, D. J. (1982). Effects of mood on prosocial behavior in children and adults. In N. Eisenberg (Ed.), *The development of prosocial behavior* (pp. 339–359). New York: Academic Press.

Cialdini, R. B., Schaller, M., Houlihan, D., Arps, K., Fultz, J., & Beaman, A. L. (1987). Empathy-based helping: Is it selflessly or selfishly motivated? *Journal of Personality and Social Psychology, 52,* 749–758.

Cicognani, E. (1999). Chi diventerà donatore di organi? Uno studio sulle determinanti dei comportamenti di salute "altruistici." *Psicologia della Salute, 3/4,* 112–133.

Clark, L. A., & Watson, D. (1999). Temperament: A new paradigm for trait psychology. In L. A. Pervin & O. P. John (Eds.). *Handbook of personality: Theory and research* (2nd ed., pp. 399–423). New York: Guilford Press.

Clark, M. S., & Isen, A. M. (1982). Toward understanding the relationship between feeling states and social behavior. In A. H. Hastorf & A. M. Isen (Eds.), *Cognitive social psychology* (pp. 73–108). New York: Elsevier.

Clark, M. S., & Mills, J. (1993). The difference between communal and exchange relationships: What is and what is not. *Personality and Social Psychology Bulletin, 19,* 684–691.

Clark, M. S., Mills, J., & Corcoran, D. (1989). Keeping track of needs and inputs of friends and strangers. *Journal of Personality and Social Psychology, 15,* 533–542.

Clark, R. D. III. (1975). The effects of reinforcement, punishment and dependency on helping behavior. *Personality & Social Psychology Bulletin, 1,* 596–599.

Clark, R. D. III, & Word, L. E. (1972). Why don't bystanders help? Because of ambiguity? *Journal of Personality and Social Psychology, 24,* 392–400.

Clark, R. D., III, & Word, L. E. (1974). Where is the apathetic bystander? Situational characteristics of the emergency. *Journal of Personality and Social Psychology, 29,* 279–287.

Clary, E. G., & Orenstein, L. (1991). The amount and effectiveness of help: The relationship of motives and abilities to helping behavior. *Personality and Social Psychology Bulletin, 17,* 58–64.

Clary, E. G., & Snyder, M. (1991). A functional analysis of altruism and prosocial behavior: The case of volunteerism. In M. Clark (Ed.), *Review of personality and social psychology: Vol. 12. Prosocial behavior* (pp. 119–148). Newbury Park, CA: Sage.

Clary, E. G., & Snyder, M. (1999). The motivations to volunteer: Theoretical and practical considerations. *Current Directions in Psychological Science, 8,* 156–159.

Clary, E. G., Snyder, M., Ridge, R. D., Copeland, J., Stukas, A. A., Haugen, J., & Miene, P. (1998). Understanding and assessing the motivations of volunteers: A functional approach. *Journal of Personality and Social Psychology, 74,* 1516–1530.

Clary, E. G., Snyder, M., & Stukas, A. A. (1996). Volunteers' motivations: Findings from a national survey, *Nonprofit and Voluntary Sector Quarterly, 25,* 485–505.

Clotfelter, C. T. (1999). Why "amateurs"? *Law and Contemporary Problems, 62,* 1–16.

Clutton-Brock, T. (2002). Breeding together: Kin selection and mutualism in cooperative vertebrates. *Science, 296,* 69–72.

Colby, A., & Damon, M. (1992, August). *Development of extraordinary moral commitment.* Paper presented at annual meeting of American Psychological Association, Washington, DC.

Colby, A., & Kohlberg, L. (1987). *The measurement of moral judgment: Vol 1. Theoretical foundations and research validation.* Cambridge, UK: Cambridge University Press.

Colby, A., Kohlberg, L., Gibbs, J., & Lieberman, M. A. (1983). A longitudinal study of moral judgment. *Monographs of the Society for Research in Child Development, 48* (Nos.1–2, Serial No. 200).

Colman, A. M. (2003). Cooperation, psychological game theory, and limitations of rationality in social interaction. *Behavioral and Brain Science, 26,* 139–198.

Comte, A. (1875). *System of positive polity* (Vol. 1). London: Longmans, Green, & Co. (Original work published 1851)

Connell, P., & Penner, L. A. (2004, April). *The antecedents of OCB: Motives as mediators.* Paper presented at the Annual Meeting of Society for Industrial and Organizational Psychology. Chicago.

Conrad, D., & Hedin, D. (1982). The impact of experiential education on adolescent development. *Child and Youth Services, 4,* 57–76.

Conrad, D., & Hedin, D. (1989). *High school community service: A review of research and programs.* Madison, WI: National Center on Effective Secondary Schools.

Conway, L. G. III, Ryder, A. G., Tweed, R. G., & Sokol, B. W. (2001). Intranational cultural variation: Exploring further implications of collectivism in the United States. *Journal of Cross-Cultural Psychology, 32,* 681–697.

Cooper, R., & Slavin, R. E. (2004). Cooperative learning: An instructional strategy to improve intergroup relations. In W. G. Stephan & W. P. Vogt (Eds.), *Education programs for improving intergroup relations: Theory, research, and practice* (pp. 55–73). New York: Teacher's College Press.

Cosmides, L., & Tooby, J. (1992) Cognitive adaptations for social exchange. In J. H. Barkow & L. Cosmides (Eds.), *The adapted mind: Evolutionary psychology and the generation of culture* (pp. 193–228). London: Oxford University Press.

Cottrell, C. A., & Neuberg, S. L. (2005). Different emotional reactions to different groups: A sociofunctional threat-based approach to prejudice. *Journal of Personality and Social Psychology, 88,* 770–789.

Cowen, E. L. (1982). Help is where you find it. Four informal helping groups. *American Psychologist, 37,* 385–395.

Crockenberg, S. B., & Litman, C. (1990). Autonomy as competence in 2 year olds: Maternal correlates of child defiance, compliance, and self-assertion. *Developmental Psychology, 26,* 961–971.

Crocker, J., Luhtanen, R. K., Cooper, M. L., & Bouvrette, A. (2003). Contingencies of self-worth in college students: Theory and measurement. *Journal of Personality and Social Psychology, 85,* 894–908.

Crosby, F., Bromley, S., & Saxe, L. (1980). Recent unobtrusive studies of Black and White discrimination and prejudice: A literature review. *Psychological Bulletin, 87,* 546–563.

Cross, S. E., & Madson, L. (1997). Models of the self: Self-construals and gender. *Psychological Bulletin, 122,* 5–37.

Crystal Clear Creation. (n.d.). Retrieved December 20, 2005, from http//www.users.bigpond.com/rdoolan/altuists.html

Cunningham, M. R. (1985/1986). Levites and brother's keepers: A sociobiological perspective on prosocial behavior. *Humboldt Journal of Social Relations, 13,* 35–67.

Curry, R. L. (1988). Influence of kinship on helping behavior in Galapagos mockingbirds. *Behavioral Ecology and Sociobiology, 22,* 141–152.

Damrosch, L. (2005). *Jean-Jacques Rousseau: Restless genius.* Boston, MA: Houghton-Mifflin.

Darley, J. M., & Batson, C. D. (1973). From Jerusalem to Jericho: A study of situational and dispositional variables in helping behavior. *Journal of Personality and Social Psychology, 27,* 100–108.

Darley, J. M., & Latané, B. (1968). Bystander intervention in emergencies: Diffusion of responsibility. *Journal of Personality Social Psychology, 8,* 377–383.

Darwin, D. (1859). *The origin of species by means of natural selection: Or the preservation of favored races in the struggle for life.* Chicago: W. B. Conkey.

Davis, M. H. (1980). Measuring individual differences in empathy. *JSAS Catalog of Selected Documents in Psychology, 10,* 85.

Davis, M. H. (1983). Empathic concern and muscular dystrophy telethon: Empathy as a multidimensional construct. *Personality and Social Psychology Bulletin, 9,* 223–229.

Davis, M. H. (1994). *Empathy: A social psychological approach.* Madison, WI: Brown and Benchmark.

Davis, M. H., Hall, J. A., & Meyer, M. (2003). The first year: Influences on the satisfaction, involvement, and persistence of new community volunteers. *Personality and Social Psychology Bulletin, 29,* 248–260.

Davis, M. H., Luce, C., & Kraus, S. J. (1994). The heritability of characteristics associated with dispositional empathy. *Journal of Personality, 62,* 369–391.

Davis, M. H., Mitchell, K. V., Hall, J. A., Lothert, J., Snapp, T., & Meyer, M. (1999). Empathy, expectations, and situational preferences: Personality influences on the decision to participate in volunteer helping behaviors. *Journal of Personality, 67,* 469–503.

Dawes, R. M. (1980). Social dilemmas. *Annual Review of Psychology, 31,* 169–193.

Dawes, R. M., McTavish, J., & Shaklee, H. (1977). Behavior, communication, ans assumptions about people's behavior in a common dilemma situation. *Journal of Personality and Social Psychology, 35,* 1–11.

Dawes, R. M., Orbell, J. M., Simmons, R. T., & van de Kragt, A. J. C. (1986). Organizing groups for collective action. *American Political Science Review, 80,* 1171–1185.

Dawkins, R. (1976). *The selfish gene.* Oxford, England: Oxford University Press.

Deci, E. L., Koestner, R., & Ryan, R. M. (1999). A meta-analytic review of experiments examining the effects of extrinsic rewards on intrinsic motivation. *Psychological Bulletin, 125,* 627–668.

De Cremer, D. (2002). Respect and cooperation in social dilemmas: The importance of feeling included. *Personality and Social Psychology Bulletin, 28,* 1335–1341.

De Cremer, D. (2003). Why inconsistent leadership is regarded as procedurally unfair: The importance of social self-esteem concerns. *European Journal of Social Psychology, 33,* 535–550.

De Cremer, D., Snyder, M., & Dewitte, S. (2001). "The less I trust, the less I contribute (or not)?" The effects of trust, accountability, and self-monitoring in social dilemmas. *European Journal of Social Psychology, 31*, 93–107.

De Cremer, D., & Stouten, J. (2003). When do people find cooperation most justified? The effect of trust and self-other merging in social dilemmas. *Social Justice Research, 16*, 41–52.

De Cremer, D., & Tyler, T. R. (2005). Managing group behavior: The interplay between procedural fairness, sense of self, and cooperation. In M. P. Zanna (Ed.). *Advances in experimental social psychology* (Vol. 37, pp. 151–218). San Diego, CA: Elsevier Academic Press.

De Cremer, D., & van Vugt, M. (1998). Collective identity and cooperation in a public goods dilemma: A matter of trust or self-efficacy? *Current Research in Social Psychology, 3*, 1–11.

Dehart, G., Sroufe, A., & Cooper, R. (2003). *Child development: Its nature and course* (4th ed.). New York: McGraw-Hill.

DeKay, W. T., & Buss, D. M. (1992). Human nature, individual differences, and the importance of context: Perspectives from evolutionary psychology. *Current Directions in Psychological Science, 6*, 184–189.

Deluga, R. J. (1998). Leader-member exchange quality and effectiveness ratings. *Group and Organization Management, 23*, 189–216.

DePaulo, B. M., Dull, W. R., Greenberg, J. M., & Swaim, G. W. (1989). Are shy people reluctant to ask for help? *Journal of Personality and Social Psychology, 56*, 834–844.

de Quervain, D. J., Fischbacher, U., Treyer, V., Schellhammer, M., Schnyder, U., Buck, A., & Fear, E. (2004). The neural basis of altruistic punishment. *Science, 305*, 1254–1258.

Derlega, V. J., Barbee, A. P., & Winstead, B. A. (1994) Friendship, gender and social support. In B. R. Burelson, T. L. Albrecht, & I. G. Sarason (Eds.), *The communication of social support: Messages, interactions, relationships, and community.* (pp. 136–150). Newbury Park, CA: Sage.

Deutsch, F. M., & Lamberti, D. M. (1986). Does social approval increase helping? *Personality and Social Psychology Bulletin, 12*, 149–157.

de Waal, F. B. (2000). Primates—A natural heritage of conflict resolution. *Science, 289*, 586–590.

Diamond, W. D., & Kashyap, R. K. (1997). Extending models of prosocial behavior to explain university alumni contributions. *Journal of Applied Social Psychology, 27*, 915–928.

Dickson-Gómez, J. B., Knowlton, A., & Latkin, C. (2004). Values and identity: The meaning of work for injection drug users involved in volunteer HIV prevention outreach. *Substance Use and Misuse, 39*, 1259–1286.

Diekman, A. B., & Eagly, A. H. (2000). Stereotypes as dynamic constructs: Women and men of the past, present, and future. *Personality and Social Psychology Bulletin, 26*, 1171–1188.

Dilalla, L. F., & Gottesman, I. I. (Eds.) (2004). *Behavior genetics principles: Perspectives in development, personality, and psychopathology (Decade of Behavior).* Washington, DC: APA Press.

Dovidio, J. F. (1984). Helping behavior and altruism: An empirical and conceptual overview. In L. Berkowitz (Ed.), *Advances in experimental social psychology* (Vol. 17, pp. 361–427). New York: Academic Press.

Dovidio, J. F., Allen, J. L., & Schroeder, D. A. (1990). The specificity of empathy-induced helping: Evidence for altruism. *Journal of Personality and Social Psychology, 59*, 249–260.

Dovidio, J. F., & Gaertner, S. L. (1981). The effects of race, status, and ability on helping behavior. *Social Psychology Quarterly, 44*, 192–203.

Dovidio, J. F., & Gaertner, S. L. (1983). Race, normative structure, and help-seeking. In B. M. DePaulo, A. Nadler, & J. D. Fisher (Eds.), *New directions in helping* (Vol. 2, pp. 285–302). New York: Academic Press.

Dovidio, J. F., & Gaertner, S. (1993). Stereotypes and evaluative intergroup bias. In D. M. Mackie, & D. L. Hamilton (Eds.), *Affect, cognition, and stereotyping: Interactive processes in group perception* (pp. 167–193). San Diego, CA: Academic Press.

Dovidio, J. F., & Gaertner, S. L. (2004). Aversive racism. In M. P. Zanna (Ed.), *Advances in experimental social psychology* (Vol. 36, pp. 1–51). San Diego, CA: Academic Press.

Dovidio, J. F., Gaertner, S. L., & Kawakami, K. (2003). The Contact Hypothesis: The past, present, and the future. *Group Processes and Intergroup Relations, 6,* 5–21.

Dovidio, J. F., Gaertner, S. L., Kawakami, K., & Hodson, G. (2002). Why can't we just get along? Interpersonal biases and interracial distrust. *Cultural Diversity and Ethnic Minority Psychology, 8,* 88–102.

Dovidio, J. F., Gaertner, S. L., Validzic, A., Matoka, A., Johnson, B., & Frazier, S. (1997). Extending the benefits of recategorization: Evaluations, self-disclosure, and helping. *Journal of Experimental Social Psychology, 33,* 401–420.

Dovidio, J. F., Glick, P., & Rudman, L. A. (Eds.). (2005). *On the nature of prejudice: Fifty years after Allport.* Malden, MA: Blackwell.

Dovidio, J. F., Kawakami, K., & Beach, K. R. (2001). Implicit and explicit attitudes: Examination of the relationship between measures of intergroup bias. In R. Brown & S. L. Gaertner (Eds.), *Blackwell handbook of social psychology, Vol. 4, Intergroup relations* (pp. 175–197). Oxford, UK: Blackwell.

Dovidio, J. F., Mann, J. A., & Gaertner, S. L. (1989). Resistance to affirmative action: The implications of aversive racism. In F. A. Blanchard & F. J. Crosby (Eds.), *Affirmative action in perspective* (pp. 83–103). New York: Springer-Verlag.

Dovidio, J. F., & Penner, L. A. (2001). Helping and altruism. In G. Fletcher & M. S. Clark (Eds.), *Blackwell handbook of social psychology, Vol. 2, Interpersonal processes* (pp. 162–195). Oxford, UK: Blackwell.

Dovidio J. F., Piliavin, J. A., Gaertner, S. L., Schroeder, D. A, & Clark, R. D. III. (1991). The Arousal: Cost-Reward Model and the process of intervention: A review of the evidence. In M. S. Clark (Ed.), *Review of personality and social psychology: Vol. 12. Prosocial behavior* (pp. 86–118). Newbury Park, CA: Sage.

Dovidio, J. F., Schroeder, D. A., Allen, J., & Sibicky, M. E. (1989, May). *Empathy, egoism, and altruism.* Paper presented at the International Conference on Prosocial Behavior, Nags Head, NC.

Dozier, J. B., & Miceli, M. P. (1985). Potential predictors of whistle-blowing: A prosocial behavior perspective. *Academy of Management Review, 10,* 823–836.

Drake, A. W., Finkelstein, S. N., & Sapolsky, H. M. (1982). *The American blood supply.* Cambridge, MA: MIT Press.

Dunbar, R. I. (1999). Culture, honesty and the free-rider problem. In R. I. Dunbar, C. Knight, & C. Power (Eds.), *The evolution of culture* (pp. 194–213). Edinburgh: Edinburgh University Press.

Dutton, D. G., & Aron, A. P. (1974). Some evidence for heightened sexual attraction under conditions of high anxiety. *Journal of Personality and Social Psychology, 30,* 510–517.

Dutton, D. G., & Aron, A. P. (1989). Romantic attraction and generalized liking for others who are sources of conflict-based arousal. *Canadian Journal of Behavioural Science, 21,* 246–257.

Dutton, D. G., & Lake, R. A. (1973). Threat of own prejudice and reverse discrimination in interracial situations. *Journal of Personality and Social Psychology, 28,* 94–100.

Dutton, D. G., & Lennox, V. L. (1974). Effect of prior "token" compliance on subsequent interracial behavior. *Journal of Personality and Social Psychology, 29,* 65–71.

Dynes, R. R., & Quarantelli, E. L. (1980). Helping behavior in large-scale disasters. In D. H. Smith, & J. Macaulay, (Eds.), *Participation in social and political activities* (pp. 339–354). San Francisco, CA: Jossey-Bass.

Eagly, A. H., & Crowley, M. (1986). Gender and helping behavior: A meta-analytic review of the social psychological literature. *Psychological Bulletin, 100,* 283–308.

Easterbrook, J. A. (1959). The effect of emotion on cue utilization and the organization of behavior. *Psychological Review, 66,* 183–201.

Eccles, J. P. (1991). Gender role socialization. In R. Baron & W. G. Graziano (Eds.), *Social psychology* (pp. 160–191). Fort Worth, TX: Holt, Rinehart, & Winston.

Edelmann, R. J., Childs, J., Harvey, S., Kellock, I., & Strain-Clark, C. (1984). The effect of embarrassment on helping. *Journal of Social Psychology, 124,* 253–254.

Edelmann, R. J., Evans, G., Pegg, I., & Tremain, M. (1983). Responses to physical stigma. *Perceptual and Motor Skills, 57,* 294.

Eek, D., & Biel, A. (2003). The interplay between greed, efficiency, and fairness in public-goods dilemmas. *Social Justice Research, 16,* 195–215.

Eisenberg, N. (1982). The development of reasoning regarding prosocial behavior. In N. Eisenberg (Ed.), *The development of prosocial behavior* (pp. 219–249). New York: Academic Press.

Eisenberg, N. (1986). *Altruistic emotion, cognition and behavior.* Hillsdale, NJ: Lawrence Erlbaum Associates.

Eisenberg, N. (1992). *The caring child.* Cambridge, MA: Harvard University Press.

Eisenberg, N., & Fabes, R. (1990). Empathy: Conceptualization, measurement and relation to prosocial behavior. *Motivation and Emotion, 14,* 131–149.

Eisenberg, N., & Fabes, R. A. (1991). Prosocial behavior and empathy: A multimethod developmental perspective. In M. S. Clark (Ed.), *Review of personality and social psychology: Vol. 12. Prosocial behavior* (pp. 34–61). Newbury Park, CA: Sage.

Eisenberg, N., Fabes, R. A., Guthrie, I. K., & Reiser, M. (2000). Dispositional emotionality and regulation: Their role in predicting quality of social functioning. *Journal of Personality and Social Psychology, 78,* 136–157.

Eisenberg, N., Fabes, R., & Miller, P. A. (1990). Preschoolers' vicarious emotional responding and their situational and dispositional prosocial behavior. *Merrill-Palmer Quarterly, 36,* 507–529.

Eisenberg, N., Guthrie, I. K., Cumberland, A., Murphy, B. C., Shepard, S. A, Zhou, Q., & Carlo, G. (2002). Prosocial development in early adulthood: A longitudinal study. *Journal of Personality and Social Psychology, 82,* 993–1006.

Eisenberg, N., & Lennon, R. (1983). Sex differences in empathy and related capacities. *Psychological Bulletin, 94,* 100–131.

Eisenberg, N., & Miller, P. (1987). The relation of empathy to prosocial and related behaviors. *Psychological Bulletin, 101,* 91–119.

Eisenberg, N., Miller, P., McNally, S., & Shea, C. (1991). Prosocial development in adolescence: A longitudinal study. *Developmental Psychology, 27,* 849–857.

Eisenberg, N., & Morris, A. S. (2001). The origins and social significance of empathy-related responding: A review of empathy and moral development: Implications for caring and justice by M. L. Hoffman. *Social Justice Research, 14,* 95–120.

Eisenberg, N., Shell, R., Pasternack, J., Lennon, R., Beller, R., & Mathy, R. M. (1987). Prosocial development in middle childhood: A longitudinal study. *Developmental Psychology, 23,* 712–718.

Eisenberg-Berg, N. (1979). Development of children's prosocial moral judgment. *Developmental Psychology, 15,* 128–137.

Eisenberg-Berg, N., & Neal, C. (1981). Effects of identity of the story character and cost of helping on children's moral judgment. *Personality and Social Psychology Bulletin, 7,* 17–23.

Eisenberg-Berg, N., & Roth, K. (1980). The development of children's prosocial moral judgment: A longitudinal follow-up. *Developmental Psychology, 16,* 375–376.

Elbaum, B., Vaughn, S., Hughes, M., & Moody, S. W. (1999). Grouping practices and reading outcomes for students with disabilities. *Exceptional Children, 65,* 399–415.

Ellison, C. G. (1991). Religious involvement and subjective well-being. *Journal of Health and Social Behavior, 32,* 80–99.

Enzle, M. E., & Harvey, M. D. (1979). Recipient mood states and helping behavior. *Journal of Experimental Social Psychology, 15,* 170–182.

Epstein, Y. M., & Hornstein, H. A. (1969). Penalty and interpersonal attraction as factors influencing the decision to help another person. *Journal of Experimental Social Psychology, 5,* 272–282.

Erdoes, R., & Ortiz, A. (Eds.). (1984). *American Indian myths and legends* (pp. 252–253). New York: Pantheon Books.

Esses, V. M., Dovidio, J. F., Jackson, L. M., & Armstrong, T. L. (2001). The immigration dilemma: The role of perceived group competition, ethnic prejudice, and national identity. *Journal of Social Issues, 57,* 389–412.

Essock-Vitale, S. M., & McGuire, M. T. (1980). Predictions derived from the theories of kin selection and reciprocation assessed by anthropological data. *Ethology and Sociobiology, 1,* 233–243.

Euler, H. A., & Weitzel, B. (1996). Discriminative grandparental solicitude as reproductive strategy. *Human Nature, 7,* 39–59.

Eysenck, M. V. (1977). *Human memory: Theory, research, and individual differences.* Oxford, UK: Pergamon Press.

Fabes, R. A., Eisenberg, N., & Eisenbud, L. (1993). Behavioral and physiological correlates of children's reactions to others in distress. *Developmental Psychology, 29,* 655–664.

Fabes, R. A., Eisenberg, N., & Miller, P. A. (1990). Maternal correlates of children's vicarious emotional responsiveness. *Developmental Psychology, 26,* 639–648.

Fabes, R. A., Fultz, J., Eisenberg, N., May-Plumlee, T., & Christopher, F. S. (1989). Effects of rewards on children's prosocial motivation: A socialization study. *Developmental Psychology, 25,* 509–515.

Fehr, E., & Gachter, S. (2002). Altruistic punishment in humans. *Nature, 415,* 137–140.

Fehr, E., & Henrich, J. (2003). On the evolutionary foundations of human altruism. In P. Hammerstein (Ed.), *Genetic and cultural evolution of cooperation* (pp. 55–82). Cambridge, MA: MIT Press.

Feldman, N. S., & Ruble, D. N. (1981). The development of person perception: Cognitive versus social factors. In S. S. Brehm, S. M. Kassin, & F. X. Gibbons (Eds.), *Developmental social psychology* (pp. 191–206). New York: Oxford University Press.

Feldman, R. (1968). Response to a compatriot and foreigner who seek assistance. *Journal of Personality and Social Psychology, 10,* 202–214.

Fendrich, J. M. (1993). *Ideal citizens: The legacy of the civil rights movement.* Albany: State University of New York Press.

Ferguson, E. (2004). Conscientiousness, emotional stability, perceived control and the frequency, recency, rate and years of blood donor behaviour. *British Journal of Health Psychology, 9,* 293–314.

Ferguson, E., & Bibby, P. A. (2002). Predicting future blood donor returns: Past behavior, intentions, and observer effects. *Health Psychology, 21,* 513–518.

Ferree, G., Barry, J., & Manno, B. (1998). *The national survey of philanthropy and civic renewal.* Washington, DC: National Commission on Philanthropy and Civic Renewal.

Festinger, L. (1954). A theory of social comparison processes. *Human Relations, 7,* 117–140.

Festinger, L. (1957). *A theory of cognitive dissonance.* Palo Alto, CA: Stanford University Press.

Finkelstein, M. A., & Penner, L. A. (2004). Predicting organizational citizenship behavior: Integrating the functional and role identity approaches. *Social Behavior and Personality, 32,* 383–398.

Finkelstein, M. A., Penner, L. A. & Brannick, M. T. (2005) Motive, role identity, and prosocial personality as predictors of volunteer activity. *Social Behavior and Personality, 33,* 403–418.

Firestone, I. J., Lichtman, C. M., & Colamosca, J. V. (1975). Leader effectiveness and leadership conferral as determinants of helping in a medical emergency. *Journal of Personality & Social Psychology, 31,* 343–348.

Fisher, J. D., Nadler, A., & Whitcher-Alagna, S. (1982). Recipient reactions to aid. *Psychological Bulletin, 91,* 27–54.

Fisher, J. D., Nadler, A., & Whitcher-Alagna, S. (1983). Four conceptualizations of reactions to aid. In J. D. Fisher, A. Nadler, & B. M. DePaulo (Eds.), *New directions in helping: Vol. 1. Recipient reactions to aid* (pp. 51–84). San Diego, CA: Academic Press.

Fisher, R. J., & Ackerman, D. (1998). The effects of recognition and group need on volunteerism: A social norm perspective. *Journal of Consumer Research, 25,* 262–275.

Fiske, A. P. (1991). The cultural relativity of selfish individualism: Anthropological evidence that humans are inherently sociable. In M. S. Clark (Ed.), *Review of personality and social psychology: Vol. 12. Prosocial behavior* (pp. 176–214). Newbury Park, CA: Sage.

Fiske, S. T., Cuddy, A. J. C., Glick, P., & Xu, J. (2002). A model of (often mixed) stereotype content: Competence and warmth respectively follow from perceived status and competition. *Journal of Personality and Social Psychology, 82,* 878–902.

Fiske, S. T., Lin, M., & Neuberg, S. L. (1999). The continuum model: Ten years later. In S. Chaiken & Y. Trope (Eds.), *Dual process theories in social psychology* (pp. 231–254). New York: Guilford.

Fiske, S. T., Xu, J., Cuddy, A. C., & Glick, P. (1999). (Dis)respecting versus (dis)liking: Status and interdependence predict ambivalent stereotypes of competence and warmth. *Journal of Social Issues, 55,* 473–491.

Flavell, J. H. (1985). *Cognitive development.* Englewood Cliffs, NJ: Prentice Hall.

Fletcher, T. D., & Major, D. A. (2004). Medical students' motivations to volunteer: An examination of the nature of gender differences. *Sex Roles, 51,* 109–114.

Flippen, A. R., Hornstein, H. A., Siegal, W. E., & Weitzman, E. A. (1996). A comparison of similarity and interdependence as triggers for in-group formation. *Personality and Social Psychology Bulletin, 22,* 882–893.

Foss, R. (1983). Community norms and blood donation. *Journal of Applied Social Psychology, 13,* 281–291.

Fox, J. W. (1984). Sex, marital status and age as social selection factors in recent psychiatric treatment. *Journal of Health and Social Behavior, 25,* 394–405.

Freedman, J. L., & Fraser, S. C. (1966). Compliance without pressure: The foot in the door technique. *Journal of Personality and Social Psychology, 4,* 195–202.

Freeman, R. (1997). Working for nothing: the supply of volunteer labor. *Journal of Labor Economics, 15,* 140–167.

Frey, D. L., & Gaertner, S. L. (1986). Helping and the avoidance of inappropriate interracial behavior: A strategy that perpetuates a nonprejudiced self-image. *Journal of Personality and Social Psychology, 50,* 1083–1090.

Friedland, R. P., Fritsch, T., Smyth, K. A., Koss, E., Lerner, A. J., Chen, C. H., Petot, G. J., & Debanne, S. M. (2001). Patients with Alzheimer's disease have reduced activities in midlife compared with healthy control-group members. *Proceedings of the National Academy of Sciences, USA, 98,* 3440–3445.

Friedrich, L. K., & Stein, A. H. (1975). Prosocial television and young children: The effects of verbal labeling and role playing on learning and behavior. *Child Development, 46,* 27–38.

Friedrich-Cofer, L. K., Huston-Stein, A., Kipnis, D. M., Susman, E. J., & Clewett, A. S. (1979). Environmental enhancement of prosocial television content: Effects of interpersonal behavior, imaginative play, and self-regulation in a natural setting. *Developmental Psychology, 15,* 637–646.

Frieze, I. H. (1979). Perceptions of battered wives. In I. H. Frieze, D. Bar-Tal, & J. S. Carroll (Eds.), *Attribution theory: Applications to social problems* (pp. 79–108). San Francisco, CA: Jossey-Bass.

Fritzsche, B. A., Finkelstein, M. A., & Penner, L. A. (2000). To help or not to help? Capturing individuals' decision policies. *Social Behavior and Personality, 28,* 561–578.

Froming, W. J., Allen, L., & Jensen, R. (1985). Altruism, role-taking, and self-awareness: The acquisition of norms governing altruistic behavior. *Child Development, 56,* 1223–1228.

Frontline. (2001). Inside the tobacco deal. Retrieved December 30, 2005, from http://www.pbs.org/wgbh/pages/frontline/shows/settlement/timelines/wigand.html

Fultz, J., Batson, C. D., Fortenbach, V. A., McCarthy, P. M., & Varney, L. L. (1986). Social evaluation and the empathy-altruism hypothesis. *Journal of Personality and Social Psychology, 50,* 761–769.

Fultz, J., Schaller, M., & Cialdini, R. B. (1988). Empathy, sadness, and distress: Three related but distinct vicarious affective responses to another's suffering. *Personality and Social Psychology Bulletin, 14*, 312–325.

Furnham, A. (1995). The just world, charitable giving, and attitudes to disability. *Personality and Individual Differences, 19*, 577–583.

Gaertner, S. L., & Bickman, L. (1971). Effects of race on the elicitation of helping behavior. *Journal of Personality and Social Psychology, 20*, 218–222.

Gaertner, S. L., & Dovidio, J. F. (1977). The subtlety of white racism, arousal, and helping behavior. *Journal of Personality and Social Psychology, 35*, 691–707.

Gaertner, S. L., & Dovidio, J. F. (1986). The aversive form of racism. In J. F. Dovidio & S. L. Gaertner (Eds.), *Prejudice, discrimination, and racism* (pp. 61–90). Orlando, FL: Academic Press.

Gaertner, S. L., & Dovidio, J. F. (2000). *Reducing intergroup bias: The Common Ingroup Identity Model*. Philadelphia, PA: Psychology Press.

Gaertner, S. L., Dovidio, J. F., Anastasio, P. A., Bachman, B. A., & Rust, M. C. (1993). The common ingroup identity model: Recategorization and the reduction of intergroup bias. In W. Stroebe & M. Hewstone (Eds.), *European review of social psychology* (Vol. 4, pp. 1–26). New York: John Wiley & Sons.

Gaertner, S. L., Dovidio, J. F., Rust, M. C., Nier, J., Banker, B., Ward, C. M., Mottola, G. R., & Houlette, M. (1999). Reducing intergroup bias: Elements of intergroup cooperation. *Journal of Personality and Social Psychology, 76*, 388–402.

Gaertner, S. L., Mann, J. A., Dovidio, J. F., Murrell, A. J., & Pomare, M. (1990). How does cooperation reduce intergroup bias? *Journal of Personality and Social Psychology, 59*, 692–704.

Garcia, S. M., Weaver, K., Moskowitz, G. B., & Darley, J. M. (2002). Crowded minds: The implicit bystander effect. *Journal of Personality and Social Psychology, 83*, 843–853.

Gardner, W. E. (1978). Compeer assistance through tutoring and group guidance activities. *Urban Review, 10*, 45–54.

Garvey, C. (1990). *Play*. Cambridge, MA: Harvard University Press.

Gaulin, S. J. C., McBurney, D. H., & Brakeman-Wartell, S. L. (1997). Matrilateral biases in the investment of aunts and uncles: A consequence and measure of paternity uncertainty. *Human Nature, 8*, 139–151.

Gecas, V. (2000). Value identities, self-motives, and social movements. In S. Stryker & T. J. Owens (Eds.), *Self, identity, and social movements* (pp. 93–109). Minneapolis: University of Minnesota Press.

Gecas, V., & Burke, P. J. (1995). Self and identity. In K. S. Cook, G. A. Fine, & J. S. House (Eds.), *Sociological perspectives on social psychology* (pp. 41–67). Boston: Allyn and Bacon.

Gelfand, D. M., & Hartmann, D. P. (1982). Response consequences and attributions: Two contributors to prosocial behavior. In N. Eisenberg (Ed.), *The development of prosocial behavior* (pp. 167–196). New York: Academic Press.

George, J. M. (1991). The effects of positive mood on prosocial behaviors at work. *Journal of Applied Psychology, 76*, 497–513.

George, J. M., & Bettenhausen, K. (1990). Understanding prosocial behavior, sales performance, and turnover: A group-level analysis in a service context. *Journal of Applied Psychology, 75*, 698–709.

Gergen, K. J., Ellsworth, P., Maslach, C., & Seipel, M. (1975). Obligation, donor resources, and reactions to aid in three cultures. *Journal of Personality and Social Psychology, 31*, 390–400.

Gergen, K. J., Morse, S. J., & Gergen, M. M. (1980). Behavior exchange in cross-cultural perspective. In H. C. Triandis, & R. W. Brislin (Eds.), *Handbook of cross-cultural psychology: Vol. 15. Social psychology* (pp. 121–153). Boston: Allyn and Bacon.

Ghiselin, M .T. (1974). *The economy of nature and the evolution of sex*. Berkeley: University of California Press.

Gibbons, F. X. (1990). Self-attention and behavior: A review and theoretical update. In M. P. Zanna (Ed.), *Advances in experimental social psychology* (Vol. 23, pp. 249–303). San Diego, CA: Academic Press.

Gilbert, D. T., Fiske, S .T., & Lindzey, G. (1998). *Handbook of social psychology* (4th ed.). New York: McGraw-Hill.

Gilbert, D. T., & Silvera, D. H. (1996). Overhelping. *Journal of Personality and Social Psychology, 70*, 678–690.

Gilbert, D. T., Fiske, S. T., & Lindzey, G. (Eds.). (1998). *The handbook of social psychology* (Vol. 2, 4th ed.) New York: McGraw-Hill.

Giles, M., & Cairns, E. (1995). Blood donation and Ajzen's theory of planned behaviour: An examination of perceived behavioural control. *British Journal of Social Psychology, 34*, 173–188.

Giles, D. E., Jr., & Eyler, J. (1994). The impact of a college community service laboratory on students' personal, social, and cognitive outcomes. *Journal of Adolescence, 17*, 327–339.

Giles, D. E., Jr., & Eyler, J. (1998). A service learning research agenda for the next five years. *New Directions for Teaching and Learning, 73*, 65–72.

Gillath, O., Shaver, P. R., & Mikulincer, M. (2005). An attachment-theoretical approach to compassion and altruism. In P. Gilbert (Ed.), *Compassion: Its nature and use in psychotherapy* (pp. 121–147). London: Brunner-Routledge.

Gilligan, C. (1982). *In a different voice.* Cambridge, MA: Harvard University Press.

Gintis, H., Bowles, S., Boyd, R., & Fehr, E. (2003). Explaining altruistic behavior in humans. *Evolution and Human Behavior, 24*, 153–172.

Glassman, R. B., Packel, E. W., & Brown, D. L. (1986). Green beards and kindred spirits: A preliminary mathematical model of altruism toward nonkin who bear similarities to the giver. *Ethology and Sociobiology, 7*, 107–115.

Goldberg, L. R. (1993). The structure of phenotypic personality traits. *American Psychologist, 48*, 26–34.

Golding, J. M., & Burnam, M. A. (1990). Stress and social support as predictors of depressive symptoms in Mexican-Americans and Non-Hispanic Whites. *Journal of Social and Clinical Psychology, 9*, 268–287.

Gopnik, A., & Meltzoff, A. N. (1997). *Words, thoughts, and theories.* Cambridge, MA: MIT Press.

Goranson, R., & Berkowitz, L. (1966). Reciprocity and responsibility reactions to prior help. *Journal of Personality and Social Psychology, 3*, 227–232.

Gouldner, A. (1960). The norm of reciprocity: A preliminary statement. *American Sociological Review, 25*, 161–178.

Gourevitch, P. (1999). *We wish to inform you that tomorrow we will be killed with our families: Stories from Rwanda.* New York: Picador.

Graham J. W. (1986). Principled organizational dissent: A theoretical essay. *Research in Organizational Behavior, 8*, 1–52.

Gray, J. R. (2002). Does a prosocial-selfish distinction help explain the biological affects? Comment on Buck 1999. *Psychological Review, 109*, 729–738.

Graziano W. G., & Eisenberg, N. (1997). Agreeableness: A dimension of personality. In R. Hogan, R. Johnson, & S. Briggs (Eds.), *Handbook of personality psychology* (pp. 795–824). San Diego, CA: Academic Press.

Graziano, W. G., & Tobin, R. M. (2002). Agreeableness: Dimension of personality or social desirability artifact? *Journal of Personality, 70*, 695–727.

Greenberg, J., Solomon, S., & Pyszczynski, T. (1997). Terror management theory of self-esteem and cultural worldviews: Empirical assessments and conceptual refinements. In M. P. Zanna (Ed.), *Advances in experimental social psychology* (Vol. 29, pp. 61–139). San Diego: Academic Press.

Greenberger, D. B., Miceli, M. P., & Cohen, D .J. (1987). Oppositionists and group norms: The reciprocal influence of whistle-blowers and co-workers. *Journal of Business Ethics, 6*, 527–542.

Greenwald, A. G., Banaji, M. R., Rudman, L. A., Farnham, S. D., Nosek, B. A., & Mellott, D. S. (2002). A unified theory of implicit attitudes, stereotypes, self-esteem, and self-concept. *Psychological Review, 109,* 3–25.

Greitmeyer, T., & Rudolph, U. (2003). Help giving and aggression from an attributional perspective: Why and when we help or retaliate. *Journal of Applied Social Psychology, 33,* 1069–1087.

Griffin, A. S., & West, S. A. (2003). Kin Discrimination and the Benefit of Helping in Cooperatively Breeding Vertebrates. *Science, 302,* 634–636.

Grube, J. A., & Piliavin, J. A. (2000). Role identity, organizational experiences and volunteer performance. *Personality and Social Psychology Bulletin, 26,* 1108–1119.

Grusec, J. E. (1982). The socialization of altruism. In N. Eisenberg (Ed.), *The development of prosocial behavior* (pp. 139–166). New York: Academic Press.

Grusec, J. E. (1991a). The socialization of empathy. In M. S. Clark (Ed.), *Review of personality and social psychology: Vol. 12. Prosocial behavior* (pp. 9–33). Newbury Park, CA: Sage.

Grusec, J. E. (1991b). Socialization of concern for others in the home. *Developmental Psychology, 27,* 338–342.

Grusec J. E, Davidov, M., & Lundell, L. (2002). Prosocial and helping behavior. In P. K. Smith C. H. Hart (Eds.) *Blackwell handbook of childhood social development: Blackwell handbooks of developmental psychology* (pp. 457–474). Malden, MA: Blackwell.

Grusec, J. E., & Goodnow, J. J. (1994). Impact of parental discipline methods on the child's internalization of values. *Developmental Psychology, 30,* 4–19.

Grusec, J. E., Kuczynski, L., Rushton, J. P., & Simutis, Z. M. (1978). Modeling, direct instructions, and attributions: Effects of altruism. *Developmental Psychology, 14,* 51–57.

Grusec, J. E., & Lytton, H. (1988). *Social development: History, theory, and research.* New York: Springer-Verlag.

Grusec, J. E., & Redler, E. (1980). Attribution, reinforcement, and altruism: A developmental analysis. *Developmental Psychology, 16,* 525–534.

Grusec, J. E., Saas-Kortsaak, P., & Simutis, Z. M. (1978). The role of example and moral exhortation in the training of altruism. *Child Development, 49,* 920–923.

Gueguen, N., & De Gail, M. (2003). The effect of smiling on helping behavior: Smiling and Good Samaritan behavior. *Communication Reports, 16,* 133–140.

Haidt, J., & Rodin, J. (1999). Control and efficacy as interdisciplinary bridges. *Review of General Psychology, 3,* 317–337.

Hamilton, S. F., & Zeldin, R. S. (1987). Learning civics in the community. *Curriculum Inquiry, 17,* 407–420.

Hamilton, W. D. (1964). The genetic evolution of social behavior. *Journal of Theoretical Biology, 7,* 1–52.

Hardin, G. (1968). The tragedy of the commons. *Science, 162,* 1243–1248.

Hardin, R. (2002). *Trust and trustworthiness.* New York: Russell Sage Foundation.

Harmon-Jones, E., Peterson, H., & Vaughn, K. (2003). The dissonance-inducing effects of inconsistency between experienced empathy and knowledge of past failures to help: Support for the action-based model of dissonance. *Basic and Applied Social Psychology, 25,* 69–78.

Harrell, W. A. (1978). Physical attractiveness, self-disclosure, and helping behavior. *Journal of Social Psychology, 104,* 15–17.

Harris, M. B. (1977). Effects of altruism on mood. *Journal of Social Psychology, 91,* 37–41.

Harris, M. B., Benson, S. M., & Hall, C. L. (1975). The effects of confession on altruism. *Journal of Social Psychology, 102,* 197–208.

Hart, D., Atkins, R., & Donnelly, T. (2004). *Psychological and socio-structural influences on involvement in volunteering.* Unpublished manuscript, Rutgers University.

Harter, S. (1986). Processes underlying the construct, maintenance, and enhancement of the self-concept in children. In J. Suls, & A. Greenwald (Eds.), *Psychological perspectives on the self* (Vol. 3, pp. 137–181). Hillsdale, NJ: Lawrence Erlbaum Associates.

Hartung, J. (1985). Matrilineal inheritance: New theory and analysis. *Behavioral and Brain Sciences, 8,* 661–688.

Hatfield, E., & Sprecher, S. (1983). Equity theory and recipients' reactions to aid. In J. Fisher, A. Nadler, & B. M. DePaulo (Eds.), *New directions in helping: Vol 1. Recipient's reaction to aid* (pp. 113–143). New York: Academic Press.

Hayes, R. B., Catania, J. A., McKusick, L., & Coates, T. J. (1990). Help-seeking for AIDS-related concerns: A comparison of gay men with various HIV diagnoses. *American Journal of Community Psychology, 18,* 743–755.

Hearold, S. (1986). A synthesis of 1043 effects of television on social behavior. In G. Comstock (Ed.), *Public communications and behavior* (Vol. I, pp. 65–133). New York: Academic Press.

Hebl, M. R., & Mannix, L. M. (2003). The weight of obesity in evaluating others: A mere proximity effect. *Personality and Social Psychology Bulletin, 29,* 28–38.

Hedge, A., & Yousif, Y. H. (1992). Effects of urban size, urgency, and cost of helpfulness: A cross-cultural comparison between the United Kingdom and the Sudan. *Journal of Cross-Cultural Psychology, 23,* 107–115.

Heider, F. (1958). *The psychology of interpersonal relationships.* New York: Wiley.

Helwig, C. C. (2004). Integrating—and respecting—the right and the good in moral development. *Journal of Applied Developmental Psychology, 25,* 619–624.

Henry, P. J., Reyna, C., & Weiner, B. (2004). Hate welfare but help the poor: How the attributional content of stereotypes explains the paradox of reactions to the destitute in America. *Journal of Applied Social Psychology, 34,* 34–58.

Higgins, E. T., & Spiegel, S. (2004). Promotion and prevention strategies for self-regulation: A motivated cognition approach. In R. F. Baumeister & K. D. Vohs (Eds.), *Handbook of self-regulation: Research, theory, and applications* (pp. 171–187). New York: Guilford Press.

Hinde, R. A., & Groebel, J. (1991). *Cooperation and prosocial behavior.* Cambridge: Cambridge University Press.

Hitlin, S. (2003). Values as the core of personal identity: Drawing links between two theories of self. *Social Psychology Quarterly, 66,* 118–137.

Hobbes, T. (1994). *Leviathan* (E. M. Curley, Ed.). Indianapolis, IN: Hackett. (Original work published 1651/1668)

Hodgkinson, V. A., & Murray, W. (1996). 1986–1996. *Giving and volunteering in the United States.* Washington, DC: Independent Sector.

Hodgkinson, V. A., & Weitzman, M. S. (1990). *Giving and volunteering in the United States: Findings from a national survey.* Washington, DC: Independent Sector.

Hodgkinson, V. A., & Weitzman, M. S. (With S. M. Noga & H. A. Gorski). (1992). *Volunteering and giving among American teenagers 12 to 17 years of age.* Washington, DC: Independent Sector.

Hoefnagels, C., & Zwikker, M. (2001). The bystander dilemma and child abuse: Extending the Latané and Darley model to domestic violence. *Journal of Applied Social Psychology, 31,* 1158–1183.

Hoffman, M. L. (1970). Conscience, personality and socialization techniques. *Human Development, 13,* 90–126.

Hoffman, M. L. (1977). Sex differences in empathy and related behaviors. *Psychological Bulletin, 34,* 712–722.

Hoffman, M. L. (1978). Physiological and biological perspectives on altruism. *International Journal of Behavioral Development, 1,* 323–339.

Hoffman, M. L. (1981). Is altruism part of human nature? *Journal of Personality and Social Psychology, 40,* 121–137.

Hoffman, M. L. (1984). The measurement of empathy. In C. E. Izard, J. Kagan, & R. B. Zajonc (Eds.), *Emotions, cognitions, and behavior* (pp. 103–131). Cambridge, UK: Cambridge University Press.

Hoffman, M. L. (1990). Empathy and justice motivation. *Motivation and Emotion, 14,* 151–172.

Hoffman, M. L. (1994). Discipline and internalization. *Developmental Psychology, 30*, 26–28.

Hoffman, M. L. (2000). *Empathy and moral development: Implications for caring and justice.* New York: Cambridge University Press.

Holmes, J. G., Miller, D. T., & Lerner, M. J. (2002). Committing altruism under the cloak of self-interest: The exchange fiction. *Journal of Experimental Social Psychology, 38,* 144–151.

Hoover, C. W., Wood, E. E., & Knowles, E. S. (1983). Forms of social awareness and helping. *Journal of Experimental Social Psychology, 18,* 577–590.

Hopfensperger, J. (1988, October 5). He lives to give. *Minneapolis Star Tribune,* 1B, 7B.

Hornstein, H. A. (1970). The influence of social models on helping behavior. In J. Macaulay, & L. Berkowitz (Eds.), *Altruism and helping behavior* (pp. 29–42). New York: Academic Press.

Hornstein, H. A. (1976). *Cruelty and kindness: A new look at aggression and altruism.* Englewood Cliffs, NJ: Prentice Hall.

Hornstein, H. A. (1982). Promotive tension: Theory and research. In V. J. Derlega & J. Grzelak (Eds.), *Cooperation and helping behavior: Theories and research* (pp. 229–248). New York: Academic Press.

Hume, R. E. (1959). *The world's living religions.* New York: Scribner.

Humphrey, G. (1923). The conditioned reflex and elementary social reaction. *Journal of Abnormal and Social psychology, 17,* 113–119.

Hunt, M. (1990). *The compassionate beast.* New York: William Morrow.

Huston, T. L., Ruggiero, M, Conner, R., & Geis, G. (1981). Bystander intervention into crime: A study based on naturally occurring episodes. *Social Psychology Quarterly, 44,* 14–23.

Independent Sector. (2002). *Giving and volunteering in the United States.* Washington, DC: Author.

Insko, C. A., Kirchner, J. L., Pinter, B., Efaw, J., & Wildschut, T. (2005). Interindividual–intergroup discontinuity as a function of trust and categorization: The paradox of expected cooperation. *Journal of Personality and Social Psychology, 88,* 365–385.

Insko, C. A., & Schopler, J. (1998). Differential distrust of groups and of individuals. In C. Sedikides, J. Schopler, & C. A. Insko (Eds.), Intergroup cognition and intergroup behavior (pp. 75–107). Hillsdale, NJ: Lawrence Erlbaum Associates.

Insko, C. A., Schopler, J., Drigotas, S. M., Graetz, K. A., Kennedy, J., Cox, C., & Bornstein, G. (1993). The role of communication in interindividual-intergroup discontinuity. *Journal of Conflict Resolution, 37,* 108–138.

Insko, C. A., Schopler, J., Graetz, K. A., & Drigotas, S. M., Currey, D. P., & Smith, S. L. (1994). Interindividual–intergroup discontinuity in the prisoner's dilemma game. *Journal of Conflict Resolution, 38,* 87–116.

Isen, A. M. (1970). Success, failure, attention, and reaction to others: The warm glow of success. *Journal of Personality and Social Psychology, 15,* 294–301.

Isen, A. M. (1993). Positive affect and decision making. In M. Lewis & M. Haviland (Eds.), *Handbook of emotion* (pp. 261–267). New York: Guilford.

Isen, A. M., Clark, M., & Schwartz, M. (1976). Duration of the effect of good mood on helping: "Footprints in the sands of time." *Journal of Personality and Social Psychology, 34,* 385–393.

Isen, A. M., & Levin, P. F. (1972). Effect of feeling good on helping: Cookies and kindness. *Journal of Personality and Social Psychology, 21,* 384–388.

Isen, A. M., Shalker, T. E., Clark, M., & Karp, L. (1978). Affect, accessibility of material in memory, and behavior. *Journal of Personality and Social Psychology, 36,* 1–12.

Israel, A. C. (1978). Some thoughts on the correspondence between saying and doing. *Journal of Applied Behavior Analysis, 11,* 271–276.

Israel, A. C., & Brown, M. S. (1979). Effects of directiveness of instructions and surveillance on the production and persistence of children's donations. *Journal of Experimental Child Psychology, 27,* 250–261.

Janoski, T., & Wilson, J. (1995). Pathways to voluntarism, *Social Forces, 71,* 271–292.

Janssens, J. M. A. M., & Dekovic, M. (1997). Child rearing, moral reasoning, and prosocial behavior. *International Journal of Behavioral Development, 20,* 509–527.

Johnson, D. E., Erez, A., Kiker, D. S., & Motowidlo, S. J. (2002). Liking and attributions of motives on relationship between a ratee's reputation and helpful behaviors. *Journal of Applied Psychology, 87,* 808–815.

Johnson, D. W., & Johnson, R. T. (2000). The three Cs of reducing prejudice and discrimination. In S. Oskamp (Ed.), *Reducing prejudice and discrimination* (pp. 239–268). Hillsdale, NJ: Lawrence Erlbaum Associates.

Johnson F. L., & Aries, E. J. (1983). Conversational patterns among same-sex pairs of late adolescent close friends. *Journal of Genetic Psychology, 142,* 225–238.

Johnson, M. K., Beebe, T., Mortimer, J. T., & Snyder, M. (1998). Volunteerism in adolescence: A process perspective. *Journal of Research on Adolescence, 8,* 309–332.

Johnson, R. C., Danko, G. P., Darvill, T. J., Bochner, S., Bowers, J. K., Huang, Y. H., Park, J. Y., Pecjak, V., Rahim, A. R. A., & Pennington, D. (1989). Cross-cultural assessment of altruism and its correlates. *Personality and Individual Differences, 8,* 855–868.

Jonas, E., Schimel, J., Greenberg, J., & Pyszczynski, T. (2002). The Scrooge effect: Evidence that mortality salience increases prosocial attitudes and behavior. *Personality and Social Psychology Bulletin, 28,* 1342–1353.

Jos, P. H., Tompkins, M. E., & Hays, S. W. (1989, November/December). In praise of difficult people: A portrait of the committed whistleblower. *Public Administration Review,* pp. 552–561.

Kahn, A., & Tice, T. E. (1973). Returning a favor and retaliating harm: The effects of stated intention and actual behavior. *Journal of Experimental Social Psychology, 9,* 43–56.

Katz, D. (1964). The motivational basis of organizational behavior. *Behavioral Science, 9,* 131–143.

Kayal, P. (1993). *Bearing witness: Gay men's health crisis and the politics of AIDS.* Boulder, CO: Westview Press.

Kelley, H. H. (1967). Attribution theory in social psychology. In D. Levine (Ed.), *Nebraska Symposium on Motivation, 15,* 192–238.

Kelley, H. H. (1973). The process of causal attributions. *American Psychologist, 28,* 107–128.

Kelley, H. H., Holmes, J. G., Kerr, N. L., Reis, H. T., Rusbult, C. E., & van Lange, P .A. M. (2003). *An atlas of interpersonal situations.* Cambridge: Cambridge University Press.

Kelley, H. H., & Thibaut, J. W. (1978). *Interpersonal relations: A theory of interdependence.* New York: Wiley.

Kelley, K., & Byrne, D. (1976). Attraction and altruism: With a little help from my friends. *Journal of Research in Personality, 10,* 59–68.

Keltner, D., Gruenfeld, D. H., & Anderson, C. (2003). Power, approach, and inhibition. *Psychological Review, 110,* 265–284.

Kendrick, J. R., Jr. (1996). Outcomes of service-learning in an introduction to sociology course. *Michigan Journal of Community Service Learning, 3,* 72–81.

Kenworthy, J. B., Turner R. N., Hewstone, M., & Voci, A. (2005). Intergroup contact: When does it work and why? In J. F. Dovidio, P. G. Glick, & L. Rudman (Eds.), *On the nature of prejudice: Fifty years after Allport* (pp. 1–15). Malden, MA: Blackwell.

Kerr, N. L. (1995). Norms in social dilemmas. In D .A. Schroeder (Ed.), *Social dilemmas: Perspectives on individuals and groups* (pp. 31–48). Westport, CT: Praeger.

Kerr, N. L. (1999). Anonymity and social control in social dilemmas. In M. Foddy, M. Smithson, M. Hogg, & S. Schneider (Eds.), *Resolving social dilemmas: Dynamic, structural, and intergroup aspects* (pp. 103–119). Philadelphia, PA: Psychology Press.

Kerr, N. L., Garst, J., Lewandowski, D. A., & Harris, S. E. (1997). That still, small voice: Commitment to cooperate as an internalized versus a social norm. *Personality and Social Psychology Bulletin, 23,* 1300–1311.

Kerr, N. L., & MacCoun, R. J. (1985). Role expectations in social dilemmas: Sex roles and task motivation in groups. *Journal of Personality and Social Psychology, 49,* 1547–1556.

Kestenbaum, J., Farber, E., & Sroufe, L. A. (1989). Individual differences in empathy among preschoolers: Relation to attachment history. In N. Eisenberg (Ed.), *Empathy and related emotional responses: No. 44. New directions for child development* (pp. 51–56). San Francisco, CA: Jossey-Bass.

Kidder, D. L. (2002). The influence of gender on the performance of organizational citizenship behaviors. *Journal of Management, 28,* 629–648.

Kim, H., Hisata, M., Kai, I., & Lee, S.-K. (2000). Social support exchange and quality of life among the Korean elderly. *Journal of Cross-Cultural Gerontology, 15,* 331–347.

King, E. B., George, J. M., & Hebl, M. R (2005). Linking personality to helping behaviors at work: An interactional perspective. *Journal of Personality, 73,* 585–608.

Kleinke, C. L. (1977). Effects of dress on compliance to requests in a field setting. *Journal of Social Psychology, 101,* 223–224.

Kohlberg, L. (1963). The development of children's orientations toward a moral order: I Sequence in the development of moral thought. *Vita Humana, 6,* 11–33.

Kohlberg, L. (1985). *The psychology of moral development.* San Francisco, CA: Harper & Row.

Kohn, A. (1986). *No contest: The case against competition.* Boston: Houghton Mifflin.

Kohn, A. (1990). *The brighter side of human nature.* New York: Basic Books.

Komorita, S. S., & Parks, C. D. (1994). *Social dilemmas.* Madison, WI: Brown and Benchmark.

Konovsky, M. A., & Organ, D. W. (1996). Dispositional and contextual determinants of organizational citizenship behavior. *Journal of Organizational Behavior, 17,* 253–266.

Korchmaros, J. D., & Kenny, D. A. (2001). Emotional closeness as a mediator of the effect of genetic relatedness on altruism. *Psychological Science, 12,* 262–265.

Korte, C. (1969). Group effects on help-giving in an emergency. *Proceedings of the 77th Annual Convention of the American Psychological Association, 4,* 383–384.

Kramer, R. M. (1999). Trust and distrust in organizations: Emerging perspectives, enduring questions. *Annual Review of Psychology, 50,* 569–598.

Kramer, R. M. & Brewer, M. B. (1984). Effects of group identity on resource use in a simulated commons dilemma. *Journal of Personality and Social Psychology, 46,* 1044–1057.

Krebs, D. (1982). Psychological approaches to altruism: An evaluation. *Ethics, 92,* 447–458.

Krebs, D. (1987). The challenge of altruism in biology and psychology. In C. Crawford, M. Smith, & D. Krebs (Eds.), *Sociobiology and psychology: Ideas, issues, and applications* (pp. 81–118). Hillsdale, NJ: Lawrence Erlbaum Associates.

Krebs, D., & Miller, D. T. (1985). Altruism and aggression. In G. Lindzey & E. Aronson (Eds.), *Handbook of social psychology* (Vol. 2, 3rd ed., pp. 1–71). New York: Random House.

Krueger, R. F., Hicks, B. M., & McGue, M. (2001). Altruism and antisocial behavior: Independent tendencies, unique personality correlates, distinct etiologies. *Psychological Science, 12,* 397–402.

Krueger, T. (2004). *The influence of an organizational citizen role identity on sustained organizational citizenship behavior.* Unpublished dissertation, University of South Florida.

Kruger, D. J. (2003). Evolution and altruism: Combining psychological mediators with naturally selected tendencies. *Evolution & Human Behavior, 24,* 118–125.

Krupat, E., & Guild, W. (1980). Defining the city: The use of objective and subjective measures for community description. *Journal of Social Issues, 36*(3), 9–28.

Kuhlman, D. M., & Marshello, A. (1975). Individual differences in game motivation as moderators of preprogrammed strategic effects in prisoner's dilemma. *Journal of Personality and Social Psychology, 32,* 922–931.

Kunz, P. R., & Woolcott, M. (1976). Season's greetings: From my status to yours. *Social Science Research, 5,* 269–278.

Ladd, G. W., Lange, G., & Stremmel, A. (1983). Personal and situational influences on children's helping behavior: Factors that mediate compliant helping. *Child Development, 54,* 488–510.

Laham, S., Gonsalkorale, K., & von Hippel, W. (2005). Darwinian grand parenting: Preferential investment in more certain kin *Personality and Social Psychology Bulletin, 31*, 63–72.

Lam, P. (2002). As the flocks gather: How religion affects voluntary association participation. *Journal of the Scientific Study of Religion, 41*, 405–422.

Lamb, S., & Zakhireh, B. (1997). Toddlers' attention to the distress of peers in a day care setting. *Early Education and Development, 8*, 105–118.

Langer, E. J. (1989). *Mindfulness*. Reading, MA: Addison-Wesley.

Langer, E. J., & Rodin, J. (1976). The effects of choice and enhanced personal responsibility for the aged: A field experiment in an institutional setting. *Journal of Personality and Social Psychology, 34*, 191–198.

Latané, B., & Darley, J. M. (1970). *The unresponsive bystander: Why doesn't he help?* New York: Appleton-Century-Crofts.

Latané, B., & Nida, S. (1981). Ten years of research on group size and helping. *Psychological Bulletin, 89*, 308–324.

Latané, B., Nida, S. A., & Wilson, D. W. (1981). The effects of group size on helping behavior. In J. P. Rushton & R. M. Sorrentino (Eds.), *Altruism and helping behavior: Social, personality, and developmental perspectives* (pp. 287–313). Hillsdale, NJ: Lawrence Erlbaum Associates.

Latting, J. (1990). Motivational differences between Black and White volunteers. *Nonprofit and Voluntary Sector Quarterly, 19*, 121–136.

Lavin, J. (2005). *Management secrets of the New England Patriots*. Stamford, CT: Pointer Press.

Lee, F. (2002) The social costs of seeking help. *Journal of Applied Behavioral Science, 38*, 17–35.

Lee, J. A., & Holden, S. J. S. (1999). Understanding the determinants of environmentally-conscious behavior. *Psychology and Marketing, 16*, 373–392.

Lee, J. A., & Murningham, J. K. (2001). The empathy-prospect model and the choice to help. *Journal of Applied Social Psychology, 31*, 816–839.

Lee, L. (1997). *Change of self-concept in the first year of college life: The effect of gender and community involvement*. Unpublished PhD dissertation, University of Wisconsin.

Lee, L., Piliavin, J. A., & Call, V. R. A. (1999). Giving money, time, and blood: Similarities and differences. *Social Psychology Quarterly, 62*, 276–290.

Leek, M., & Smith, P. K. (1989). Phenotypic matching, human altruism, and mate selection. *Behavioral and Brain Sciences, 12*, 534–535.

Leek, M., & Smith, P. K. (1991). Cooperation and conflict in three-generation families. In P. K. Smith (Ed.), *The psychology of grandparenthood: An international perspective* (pp. 177–194). London: Routledge.

Lepper, M. (1981). Intrinsic and extrinsic motivation in children: The detrimental effects of superfluous social controls. In W. A. Collins (Ed.), *Minnesota Symposium on Child Psychology* (Vol. 14, pp. 115–214). Hillsdale, NJ: Lawrence Erlbaum Associates.

Lerner, M. J. (1980). *The belief in a just world: A fundamental delusion*. New York: Plenum.

Levin, P. F., & Isen, A. M. (1975). Further studies on the effect of good mood on helping. *Sociometry, 38*, 141–147.

Levine, J. M., & Moreland, R. L. (1994). Group socialization: Theory and research. In W. Stroebe & M. Hewstone (Eds.), *European review of social psychology* (Vol. 5, pp. 305–336). Chichester, England: Wiley.

Levine, M., Cassidy, C., Brazier, G., & Reicher, S. D. (2002). Self-categorization and non-intervention: Two experimental studies. *Journal of Applied Social Psychology, 32*, 1452–1463.

Levine, M., Prosser, A., Evans, D., & Reicher, S. D. (2005). Identity and emergency helping: How social group membership and inclusiveness of group boundaries shape helping behavior. *Personality and Social Psychology Bulletin, 31*, 443–453.

Levine, R. V., Martinez, T. S., Brase, G., & Sorenson, K. (1994). Helping in 36 U. S. cities. *Journal of Personality and Social Psychology, 67*, 69–82.

Lewin, K. (1936). *Principles of topological psychology*. New York: McGraw-Hill.
Leyens, J.-P., Cortes, B., Demopulin, S., & Dovidio, J. F., Fiske, S. T., Gaunt, R., Paladino, M.-P., Rodriquez-Perez, A., Rodriguez-Torres, R., Vaes, J. (2003). Emotional prejudice, essentialism, and nationalism: The 2002 Tajfel Lecture. *European Journal of Social Psychology, 33*, 703–718.
Li, Y., & Ferraro, K. F. (2005). Volunteering and depression in later life: Social benefit or selection processes? *Journal of Health and Social Behavior, 46*, 68–84.
Lieberman, M. A., & Tobin, S. S. (1983). *The experience of old age: Stress, coping and survival*. New York: Basic Books.
Liebert, R. M., & Sprafkin, J. (1988). *The early window: The effects of television on children and youth*. New York: Pergamon.
Liew, J., Eisenberg, N., Losoya, S. H., Fabes, R. A., Guthrie, I. K., & Murphy, B. C. (2003). Children's physiological indices of empathy and their socioemotional adjustment: Does caregivers' expressivity matter? *Journal of Family Psychology, 17*, 584–597.
Ligout, S., Sebe, F., & Porter, R. H. (2004). Vocal discrimination of kin and non-kin agemates among lambs. *Behaviour, 141*, 355–369.
Lindzey, G. (Ed.). (1954). *Handbook of social psychology*. Cambridge, MA: Addison-Wesley.
Lindzey, G., & Aronson, E. (Eds.). (1985). *Handbook of social psychology* (3rd ed.). New York: Random House.
Lipscomb, T. J., McAllister, H. A., & Bregman, N. J. (1985). A developmental inquiry into the effects of multiple models on children's generosity. *Merrill-Palmer Quarterly, 31*, 335–344.
London, P. (1970). The rescuers: Motivational hypotheses about Christians who saved Jews from the Nazis. In J. Macaulay, & L. Berkowitz (Eds.), *Altruism and helping behavior* (pp. 241–250). New York: Academic Press.
Lopes, P. N., Salovey, P., Côté, S., Beers, M., & Petty, R. E. (2005). Emotion regulation abilities and the quality of social interaction. *Emotion, 5*, 113–118.
Lott, A. J., & Lott, B. E. (1965). Group cohesiveness as interpersonal attraction: A review of relationships with antecedent and consequent variables. *Psychological Bulletin, 64*, 259–309.
Loy, P. H., & Stewart, L. P. (1984). The extent and effects of sexual harassment of working women. *Sociological Focus, 17*, 31–43.
Luoh, M.-C., & Herzog, A. R. (2002). Individual consequences of volunteer and paid work in old age: health and mortality. *Journal of Health and Social Behavior, 43*, 490–509.
Ma, H.-K. (1985). Cross-cultural study of altruism. *Psychological Reports, 57*, 337–338.
Macaulay, J. R. (1970). A shill for charity. In J. Macaulay, & L. Berkowitz, (Eds.), *Altruism and helping behavior* (pp. 43–60). New York: Academic Press.
Macaulay, J. R., & Berkowitz, L. (Eds). (1970). *Altruism and helping behavior*. New York: Academic Press.
MacDonald, K. (1984). An ethological-social learning theory of the development of altruism: Implications for human sociobiology. *Ethology and Sociobiology, 5*, 97–109.
Machiavelli, N., (2003). *The Prince* (G. Bull, Trans.). London: Penguin Books. (Original work published 1513)
Mackie, D. M., Devos, T., & Smith, E. R. (2000). Intergroup emotions: Explaining offensive action tendencies in an intergroup context. *Journal of Personality and Social Psychology, 79*, 602–616.
Mackie, D. M., & Smith, E. R. (Eds.). (2000). *From prejudice to intergroup emotions: Differentiated reactions to social groups*. New York: Psychology Press.
MacLean, P. D. (1973). *A triune concept of the brain and behavior*. Toronto, Canada: University of Toronto Press.
MacLean P. D. (1985). Evolutionary psychiatry and the triune brain. *Psychological Brain, 15*, 219–221.
Mails, T. E. (1988). *Secret Native American pathways: A guide to inner peace*. Tulsa, OK: Council Oaks Books.

Main, M., & Weston, D. R. (1981). The quality of the toddler's relationship to mother and to father: Related to conflict behavior and the readiness to establish new relationships. *Child Development, 52,* 932–940.

Maner, J. K., Luce, C. L., Neuberg, S. L., Cialdini, R. B., Brown, S., & Sagarin, B. J. (2002). The effects of perspective taking on motivations for helping: Still no evidence for altruism. *Personality and Social Psychology Bulletin, 28,* 1601–1610.

Manucia, G. K., Baumann, D. J., & Cialdini, R. B. (1984). Mood influences in helping: Direct effects or side effects? *Journal of Personality and Social Psychology, 46,* 357–364.

Markey, P. M. (2000). Bystander intervention in computer-mediated communication. *Computers in Human Behavior, 16,* 183–188.

Markus, G. B., Howard, J. P. F., & King, D. C. (1993). Integrating community service and classroom instruction enhances learning: Results from an experiment. *Educational Evaluation and Policy Analysis, 15,* 410–419.

Marta, E., Manzi, C., & Vignoles, V. L. (2005, July). *Identity and the theory of planned behaviour: Predicting maintenance of volunteering behaviour after three years.* Poster presented at the meetings of the European Association of Experimental Social Psychology, Wurzburg, Germany.

Martichuski, D. K., & Bell, P. A. (1991). Reward, punishment, privatization, and moral suasion in a commons dilemma. *Journal of Applied Social Psychology, 21,* 1356–1369.

Martin, G. B., & Clark, R. D. III. (1982). Distress crying in infants: Species and peer specificity. *Developmental Psychology, 18,* 3–9.

Marwell, G., Aiken, M. T., & Demerath, N. J. II. (1987). The persistence of political attitudes among 1960's political activists. *Public Opinion Quarterly, 51,* 359–375.

Marx, K., & Engels, F. (1998). *The communist manifesto.* London: Verso. (Original work published 1848)

Mathews, K. E., & Canon, L. K. (1975). Environmental noise level as a determinant of helping behavior. *Journal of Personality and Social Psychology, 32,* 571–577.

Matthews, K. A., Batson, C. D., Horn, J., & Rosenman, R. H. (1981). "Principles in his nature which interest him in the fortune of others ...": The heritability of empathic concern for others. *Journal of Personality, 49,* 237–247.

Mattis, J. S., Beckham, W. P., Saunders, B. A., Williams, J. E., McAllister, D., Myers, V., Knight, D., Rencher, D., & Dixon, C. (2004). Who will volunteer? Religiosity, everyday racism, and social participation among African American men. *Journal of Adult Development, 11,* 261–272.

McAdam, D. (1988). *Freedom summer.* New York: Oxford University Press.

McAndrew, F. T. (2002). New evolutionary perspectives on altruism: Multilevel-selection and costly-signaling theories. *Current Directions in Psychological. Science, 11,* 79–82.

McCall, G. J., & Simmons J. L. (1978). *Identities and interactions.* New York: The Free Press.

McClintock, C. G. (1978). Social values: Their definition, measurement and development. *Journal of Research and Development in Education, 12,* 121–137.

McCombie, R. P. (1991). Blood donation patterns of undergraduate students: Family and friendship correlates. *Journal of Community Psychology, 19,* 161–165.

McCrae, R. R., & Costa, P. T., Jr. (1999). A five-factor theory of personality. In L. A. Pervin & O. P. John (Ed.), *Handbook of personality: Theory and research* (2nd ed., pp. 139–153). New York: Guilford.

McCullough, M. (2001). Forgiveness: Who does it and how do they do it? *Current Directions in Psychological Science, 10,* 194–197.

McCullough, M. E., Worthington, E. L., Jr., & Rachal, K. C. (1997). Interpersonal forgiving in close relationships. *Journal of Personality and Social Psychology, 73,* 321–336.

McDougall, W. (1936). *Social psychology* (23rd ed.). London: Methuen. (Original work published 1908)

McGovern, L. P. (1976). Dispositional social anxiety and helping behavior under three conditions. *Journal of Personality, 44,* 84–97.

McGovern, L. P., Ditzian, J. L., & Taylor, S. P. (1975). The effect of one positive reinforcement on helping behavior. *Bulletin of the Psychonomics Society, 5,* 421–423.

McGuire, A. M. (1994). Helping behaviors in the natural environment: Dimensions and correlates of helping. *Personality and Social Psychology Bulletin, 20,* 45–56.

McMillen, D. L., Sanders, D. Y., & Solomon, G. S. (1977). Self-esteem, attentiveness, and helping behavior. *Personality and Social Psychology Bulletin, 3,* 257–261.

McPherson, J., & Rotolo, T. (1996). Diversity and change in voluntary groups. *American Sociological Review, 61,* 179–202.

Medvene, L. (1992). Self-help groups, peer helping, and social comparison. In S. Spacapan, & S. Oskamp (Eds.), *Helping and being helped: Naturalistic studies* (pp. 49–82). Newbury Park, CA: Sage.

Meltzoff, A. N. (2002). Elements of a developmental theory of imitation. In A. N. Meltzoff, N. Andrew, & W. Prinz (Eds.), *The imitative mind: Development, evolution, and brain bases* (pp. 19–41). New York: Cambridge University Press.

Messick, D. M. (1973). To join or not to join: An approach to the unionization decision. *Organizational Behavior and Human Decision Processes, 10,* 145–156.

Messick, D. M., & Brewer, M. B (1983). Solving social dilemmas. In L. Wheeler & P. R. Shaver (Eds.), *Review of personality and social psychology* (Vol. 4, pp. 11–44). Beverly Hills, CA: Sage.

Messick, D. M., Wilke, H., Brewer, M. B., Kramer, R. M., & Zemke, P. E., & Lui, L. (1983). Individual adaptations and structural change as solutions to social dilemmas. *Journal of Personality and Social Psychology, 44,* 294–309.

Meyer, J. P. (1997). Organizational commitment. *International Review of Industrial and Organizational Psychology, 12,* 175–219.

Miceli, M. P., Roach, B. L., & Near, J. P. (1988). The motivations of anonymous whistle-blowers: The case of federal employers. *Public Personnel Management, 17,* 281–296.

Mickler, S. E., & Rosen, S. (1994). Burnout in spurned medical caregivers and the impact of job expectancy training. *Journal of Applied Social Psychology, 24,* 2110–2131.

Midlarsky, E. (1985/1986). Helping during the Holocaust: The role of political, theological and socioeconomic identification. *Humboldt Journal of Social Relations, 13,* 85–305.

Midlarsky, E. (1991). Helping as coping. In M. S. Clark (Ed.), *Prosocial behavior: Vol. 12. Review of personality and social psychology* (pp. 238–264). Newbury Park, CA: Sage.

Midlarsky, E., & Hannah, M. E. (1985). Competence, reticence, and helping by children and adolescents. *Developmental Psychology, 21,* 534–541.

Midlarsky, E., & Hannah, M. E. (1989). The generous elderly. *Psychology and Aging, 4,* 346–351.

Midlarsky, E., Jones, S., & Corley, R. (2005). Personality correlates of heroic rescue during the holocaust. *Journal of Personality, 73,* 907–934.

Midlarsky, E., & Kahana, E. (1994). *Altruism in later life.* Thousand Oaks, CA: Sage Publications.

Midlarsky, E., Kahana, E., Corley, R., Nemeroff, R., & Schonbar, R. A. (1999). Altruistic moral judgment among older adults. *International Journal of Aging and Human Development, 49,* 27–41.

Midlarsky, E., & Midlarsky, M. (1973). Some determinants of aiding under experimentally-induced stress. *Journal of Personality, 41,* 305–327.

Mikolay, D., Dovidio, J. F. Ellyson, S. L. Maggiano, N. A., & Keating, C. F. (1989, March). *Androgyny as a mediating variable in helping behavior.* Paper presented at annual meeting of Eastern Psychological Association, Boston.

Mikulincer, M., & Shaver, P. R. (2001). Attachment theory and intergroup bias: Evidence that priming the secure base schema attenuates negative reactions to out-groups. *Journal of Personality and Social Psychology, 81,* 97–115.

Mikulincer, M., & Shaver, P. R. (2003). The Attachment behavioral system in adulthood: activation, psychodynamics, and interpersonal processes. In M. P. Zanna (Ed.), *Advances in Experimental Social Psychology* (Vol. 35, pp. 53–152). New York: Academic Press.

Mikulincer, M., & Shaver, P. R. (2005). Attachment security, compassion, and altruism. *Current Directions in Psychological Science, 14,* 34–38.

Mikulincer, M., Shaver, P. R., Gillath, O., & Nitzberg, R. E. (2004). *Attachment, caregiving, and altruism: Boosting attachment security increases compassion and helping.* Manuscript submitted for publication.

Milgram, S. (1970). The experience of living in cities. *Science, 167,* 1461–1468.

Miller, D. T. (1977). Altruism and threat to belief in a just world. *Journal of Experimental Social Psychology, 13,* 113–124.

Miller, J. (1994a). Linking traditional and service-learning courses: Outcome evaluations utilizing two pedagogically distinct models. *Michigan Journal of Community Service Learning, 1,* 29–36.

Miller, J. (1994b). Cultural diversity in the morality of caring: Individually-oriented versus duty-based interpersonal moral codes. *Journal of Comparative Science, 28,* 3–39.

Miller, J. G., & Bersoff, D. M. (1994). Cultural influences on the moral status of reciprocity and the discounting of endogenous motivation. *Personality and Social Psychology Bulletin, 20,* 592–602.

Miller, M. L., Moen, P., & Dempster-McClain, D. (1991). Motherhood, multiple roles, and maternal well-being: An event history analysis of women's roles and resilience. *American Sociological Review, 54,* 635–647.

Miller, N., & Brewer, M. B. (1986). Categorization effects on ingroup and outgroup perception. In J. F. Dovidio & S. L. Gaertner (Eds.), *Prejudice, discrimination, and racism* (pp. 209–230). Orlando, FL: Academic Press.

Miller, P. A., Eisenberg, N., Fabes, R. A., & Shell, R. (1996). Relations among moral reasoning and vicarious emotion to young children's prosocial behavior toward peers and adults. *Developmental Psychology, 32,* 210–219.

Miller, W. R. (1985). Motivation for treatment: A review with a special emphasis on alcoholism. *Psychological Bulletin, 98,* 84–107.

Mitchell, M. M., Brown, K. M., Morris-Villagran, M., & Villagran, P. D. (2001). The effects of anger, sadness, and happiness on persuasive processing: A test of the negative state relief model. *Communication Monographs, 68,* 347–359.

Moen, P., Dempster-McClain, D., & Williams, R. M., Jr. (1992). Successful aging: A life-course perspective on women's multiple roles and health. *American Journal of Sociology, 97,* 1612–1638.

Moghaddam, F. M., Taylor, D. M., & Wright, S. C. (1993). *Social psychology in cross-cultural perspective.* New York: W. H. Freeman.

Moore, B. S., & Eisenberg, N. (1984). The development of altruism. *Annals of Child Development, 1,* 107–174.

Moore, C., Baresi, J., & Thompson, C. (1998). The cognitive basis of future-oriented prosocial behavior. *Social Development, 7,* 198–218.

Moore, C. W., & Allen J. P., (1996). The effects of volunteering on the young volunteer. *Journal of Primary Prevention, 17,* 231–258.

Moore, J. (1984). The evolution of reciprocal sharing. *Ethology and Sociobiology, 5,* 4–14.

Moorman, R. H., Niehoff, B. P., & Organ, D. W. (1993). Treating employees fairly and organizational citizenship behavior: Sorting the effects of job satisfaction, organizational commitment, and procedural justice. *Employee Responsibilities and Rights Journal, 6,* 209–225.

Morgan, C. J. (1985). Natural selection for altruism in structured populations. *Ethology and Sociobiology, 6,* 211–218.

Moriarty, T. (1975). Crime, commitment, and the responsive bystander: Two field experiments. *Journal of Personality and Social Psychology, 31,* 370–376.

Morrow-Howell, N., Hinterlong, J., Rozario, P. A., & Tang, F. (2003). Effects of volunteering on the well-being of older adults. *Journals of Gerontology: Series B: Psychological Sciences and Social Sciences, 58B,* S137–S145.

Moss, M. K., & Page, R. A. (1972). Reinforcement and helping behavior. *Journal of Applied Social Psychology, 2,* 360–371.

Mueller, C. W., & Donnerstein, E. (1981). Film-facilitated arousal and prosocial behavior. *Journal of Experimental Social Psychology, 17,* 31–41.

Mueller, C. W., Donnerstein, E., & Hallam, J. (1983). Violent films and prosocial behavior. *Personality and Social Psychology Bulletin, 9*, 83–89.

Mullen, B., Brown, R. J., & Smith, C. (1992). Ingroup bias as a function of salience, relevance, and status: An integration. *European Journal of Social Psychology, 22*, 103–122.

Munekata, H., & Ninomiya, K. (1985). The development of prosocial moral judgments. *Japanese Journal of Educational Psychology, 33*, 157–164.

Murchison, C A. (Ed.). (1935). *Handbook of social psychology*. Worchester, MA: Clark University Press.

Murphy, D. E. (2002). *September 11: An oral history*. New York: Doubleday.

Musick, M. A., Herzog, A. R., & House, J. S. (1999). Volunteering and mortality among older adults: Findings from a national sample. *Journals of Gerontology: Series B: Psychological Sciences and Social Sciences, 54B*, S173–S180.

Musick, M. A., Wilson, J., & Bynum, W. B., Jr. (2000). Race and formal volunteering: The differential effects of class and religion. *Social Forces, 78*, 1539–1571.

Mustillo, S., Wilson, J., & Lynch, S. M. (2004). Legacy volunteering: A test of two theories of intergenerational transmission. *Journal of Marriage and Family, 66*, 530–541.

Myers-Lipton, S. J. (1996a). Effect of a comprehensive service-learning program on college students' civic responsibility. *Teaching Sociology, 26*, 243–258.

Myers-Lipton, S. J. (1996b). Effects of service-learning on college students' attitudes toward an international understanding. *Journal of College Student Development, 37*, 659–668.

Nadler, A. (1987). Determinants of help seeking behavior: The effects of helper's similarity, task centrality and recipient's self esteem. *European Journal of Social Psychology, 17*, 57–67.

Nadler, A. (1991). Help-seeking behavior: Psychological costs and instrumental benefits. In M. S. Clark (Ed.), *Review of personality and social psychology: Vol. 12. Prosocial behavior* (pp. 290–311). Newbury Park, CA: Sage.

Nadler, A. (2002). Inter-group helping relations as power relations: Maintaining or challenging social dominance between groups through helping. *Journal of Social Issues, 58*, 487–502.

Nadler, A. (2005, July). *Intergroup helping relations as status maintenance mechanisms*. Paper presented at the meeting of the European Association for Experimental Social Psychology, Wurzbug, Germany.

Nadler, A., & Fisher, J. D. (1986). The role of threat to self-esteem and perceived control in recipient reaction to help: Theory development and empirical validation. In L. Berkowitz (Ed.), *Advances in experimental social psychology* (Vol. 19, pp. 81–122). San Diego, CA: Academic Press.

Nadler, A., & Halabi, S. (in press). Intergroup helping as status relations: Effects of status stability, identification, and type of help on receptivity to high status group's help. *Journal of Personality and Social Psychology*.

National Centre for Volunteering Research. (2002). *1997 National survey of volunteering in the U.K.* London England: East London University.

Nestmann, F. (1991). Role-related helping: Natural helpers in the service sector. In L. Montada, & H. W. Bierhoff (Eds.), *Altruism in social systems* (pp. 224–249). Lewiston, NY: Hogrefe and Huber.

Neuberg, S. L., Smith, D. M., Hoffman, J. C., & Russell, F. J. (1994). When we observe stigmatized and normal people interacting: Stigma by association. *Personality and Social Psychology Bulletin, 20*, 196–209.

Newman, R. S., & Goldin, L. (1990). Children's reluctance to seek help with schoolwork. *Journal of Educational Psychology, 82*, 92–100.

Newman, S., Vasudev, J., & Onawola, R. (1985). Older volunteers' perceptions of impacts of volunteering on their psychological well-being. *Journal of Applied Gerontology, 4*, 1234–1127.

Newmann, B. H. (1997). Donor reactions and injuries from whole blood donation (review). *Transfusion Medicine Review, 11*, 64–75.

Newmann, B. H., Pichette, D., & Dzaka, E. (2003). Adverse effects in blood donors after whole-blood donation: A study of 1000 blood donors interviewed 3 weeks after whole-blood donation. *Transfusion, 43,* 598–603.

Newmann, F. A., & Rutter, R. A. (1983). *The effects of high school community service programs on students' social development: Final report.* Wisconsin Center for Educational Research.

Neyer, F. J., & Lang, F. R. (2003). Blood is thicker than water: Kinship orientation across adulthood. *Journal of Personality & Social Psychology, 84,* 310–321.

Nier, J. A., Gaertner, S. L., Dovidio, J. F., Banker, B. S., & Ward, C. M. (2001). Changing interracial evaluations and behavior: The effects of a common group identity. *Group Processes and Intergroup Relations, 4,* 299–316.

Nilsson Sojka, B., & Sojka, P. (2003). The blood donation experience: Perceived physical, psychological and social impact of blood donation on the donor. *Vox Sanguinis, 84,* 120–128.

Nisbett, R. E. (1980). The trait construct in lay and professional psychology. In L. Festinger (Ed.), *Retrospections in social psychology* (pp. 109–130). New York: Oxford.

Nisbett, R. E., & Schachter, S. (1966). The cognitive manipulation of pain. *Journal of Experimental Social Psychology, 2,* 227–236.

North, A. C., Tarrant, M., & Hargreaves, D. J. (2004). Effects of music on helping behavior: A field study. *Environment & Behavior, 36,* 266–275.

Nowak, M. A., & Sigmund, K. (1998). Evolution of indirect reciprocity by image scoring. *Nature, 393,* 573–577.

Öhman, A., & Dimberg, U. (1978). Facial expressions as conditional stimuli for electrodermal responses: A case of "preparedness"? *Journal of Personality and Social Psychology, 36,* 1251–1258.

Öhman, A., & Mineka, S. (2001). Fears, phobias, and preparedness: Toward an evolved module of fear and fear learning. *Psychological Review, 108,* 483–522.

Öhman, A., & Mineka, S. (2003). The malicious serpent: Snakes as a prototypical stimulus for an evolved module of fear. *Current Directions in Psychological Science, 12,* 5–9.

Oliner, S. P., & Oliner, P. M. (1988). *The altruistic personality: Rescuers of Jews in Nazi Europe.* New York: Free Press.

Olson, M. (1965). *The logic of collective action: Public goods and the theory of groups.* Cambridge, MA: Harvard University Press.

Olsson, A., Ebert, J. P., Banaji, M. R., & Phelps, E. A. (2005). The role of social groups in the persistence of learned fear. *Science, 309,* 785–787.

Oman, D., Thoresen, C. E., & McMahon, K. (1999). Volunteerism and mortality among the community-dwelling elderly. *Journal of Health Psychology, 4,* 301–316.

Omoto, A. M., & Snyder, M. (1995). Sustained helping without obligation: Motivation, longevity of service, and perceived attitude change among AIDS volunteers. *Journal of Personality and Social Psychology, 68,* 671–686.

Omoto, A. M., & Snyder, M. (2002). Considerations of community: The context and process of volunteerism. *American Behavioral Scientist, 45,* 846–867.

Orbell, J., & Dawes, R. M. (1981). Social dilemmas. In G. Stephenson & J. H. Davis (Eds.), *Progress in applied social psychology* (pp. 37–65). Chichester: Wiley.

Orbell, J. M., van de Kragt, A. J. C., & Dawes, R. M. (1991). Covenants with the sword: The role of promises in social dilemma circumstances. In K. Koford & J. Miller (Eds.), *Social norms and economics institutions* (pp. 117–133). Ann Arbor, MI: University of Michigan Press.

Organ, D. W. (1988). *Organizational citizenship behavior: The good soldier syndrome.* Lexington, MA: Lexington Books.

Organ, D. W. (1990). The motivational basis of organizational citizenship behavior. *Research in Organizational Behavior, 12,* 43–72.

Organ, D. W. (1997). Organizational citizenship behavior: It's construct clean-up time. *Human Performance, 10,* 85–97.

Organ, D. W., & Konovsky, M. A. (1989). Cognitive versus affective determinants of organizational citizenship behavior. *Journal of Applied Psychology, 74,* 157–164.

Organ, D. W., & Ryan, K. (1995). A meta-analytic review of attitudinal and dispositional predictors of organizational citizenship behavior. *Personnel Psychology, 48,* 775–802.

Orr, J. M., Sackett, P. R., & Mercer, M. (1989). The role of prescribed and nonprescribed behaviors in estimating the dollar value of performance. *Journal of Applied Psychology, 74,* 34–40.

Osguthorpe, R. T., & Scruggs, T. E. (1986). Special education students as tutors: A review and analysis. *Remedial and Special Education, 7,* 15–25.

Ostrom, E. (2003). Toward a behavioral theory linking trust, reciprocity, and reputation. In E. Ostrom & J. Walker (Eds.), *Trust and reciprocity: Interdisciplinary lessons from experimental research* (pp. 19–79). New York: Russell Sage Foundation.

Ostrom, E., Gardner, R., & Walker, J. (1994). *Rules, games, and common-pool resources.* Ann Arbor: University of Michigan Press.

Otten, C. A., Penner, L. A., & Altabe, M. N. (1991). An examination of therapists' and college students' willingness to help a psychologically distressed person. *Journal of Social and Clinical Psychology, 10,* 102–120.

Otten, C. A., Penner, L. A., & Waugh, G. (1988). That's what friends are for: The determinants of psychological helping. *Journal of Social and Clinical Psychology, 7,* 34–41.

Otten, S., & Moskowitz, G. B. (2000). Evidence for implicit evaluative in-group bias: Affect-based spontaneous trait inference in a minimal group paradigm. *Journal of Experimental Social Psychology, 36,* 77–89.

Pakaslahti, L., Karjalainen, A., & Keltikangas-Järvinen, L. (2002). Relationships between adolescent prosocial problem-solving strategies, prosocial behaviour, and social acceptance. *International Journal of Behavioral Development, 26,* 137–144.

Park, B., & Rothbart, M. (1982). Perception of out-group homogeneity and levels of social categorization: Memory for the subordinate attributes of in-group and out-group members. *Journal of Personality and Social Psychology, 42,* 1051–1068.

Paulhus, D. L., & Van Selst, M. (1990). The Spheres of Control Scale: 10 Yrs of research. *Personality and Individual Differences, 11,* 1029–1036.

Pearce, P. L., & Amato, P. R. (1980). A taxonomy of helping: A multidimensional scaling analysis. *Social Psychology Quarterly, 43,* 363–371.

Penner, L. A. (2002). Dispositional and organizational influences on sustained volunteerism: An interactionist perspective. *Journal of Social Issues, 58,* 447–467.

Penner, L. A. (2004). Volunteerism and social problems: Making things better or worse? *Journal of Social Issues, 60,* 645–666.

Penner, L. A., Brannick, M. T., Webb, S., & Connell, P. (2005). The effects of the September 11, 2001 attacks on volunteering: An archival analysis. *Journal of Applied Social Psychology, 35,* 1333–1360.

Penner, L. A., Dertke, M. C., & Achenbach, C. J. (1973). The flash system: A field study of altruism. *Journal of Applied Social Psychology, 3,* 362–373.

Penner, L. A., Dovidio, J. F, Piliavin, J. A., & Schroeder, D. A. (2005). Prosocial behavior: Multilevel perspectives. *Annual Review of Psychology, 56,* 365–392.

Penner, L. A., & Finkelstein, M. A. (1998). Dispositional and structural determinants of volunteerism. *Journal of Personality and Social Psychology, 74,* 525–537.

Penner, L. A., & Fritzsche, B. A. (1993). Magic Johnson and reactions to people with AIDS: A natural experimental. *Journal of Applied Social Psychology, 23,* 1035–1050.

Penner, L. A., Fritzsche, B. A., Craiger, J. P., & Freifeld, T. R. (1995). Measuring the prosocial personality. In J. Butcher & C. D. Spielberger (Eds.) *Advances in personality assessment* (Vol. 10, pp. 147–163). Hillsdale, NJ: Lawrence Erlbaum Associates.

Penner, L. A., Midili, A. R., & Kegelmeyer, J. (1997). Beyond job attitudes: A personality and social psychology perspective on the causes of organizational citizenship behavior. *Human Performance, 10,* 111–131.

Perlow, L., & Weeks, J. (2002). Who's helping whom? Layers of culture and workplace behavior. *Journal of Organizational Behavior, 23,* 345–361.

Persson, G. E. B. (2005). Developmental perspectives on prosocial and aggressive motives in preschoolers' peer interactions. *International Journal of Behavioral Development, 29,* 80–91.

Pettigrew, T. F. (1998). Intergroup contact theory. *Annual Review of Psychology, 49,* 65–85.

Pettigrew, T. F., & Tropp, L. R. (2000). Does intergroup contact reduce prejudice? Recent meta-analytic findings. In S. Oskamp (Ed.), *Reducing prejudice and discrimination* (pp. 93–114). Mahwah, NJ: Lawrence Erlbaum Associates.

Phelps, E. A., O'Connor, K. J., Cunningham, W. A., Funayama, E. S., Gatenby, J. C., Gore, J. C., & Banaji, M. R. (2000). Performance on indirect measures of race evaluation predicts amygdala activation. *Journal of Cognitive Neuroscience, 12,* 729–738.

Piaget, J. (1965). *The moral judgment of the child.* New York: Free Press. (Original work published 1932)

Piaget, J., & Inhelder, B. (1971). *Mental imagery in the child.* New York: Basic Books.

Piliavin, I. M., Gartner, R. I., Thornton, C., & Matsueda, R .L. (1986). Crime, deterrence, and rational choice. *American Sociological Review, 51,* 101–119.

Piliavin, I. M., Piliavin, J. A., & Rodin, J. (1975). Costs, diffusion, and the stigmatized victim. *Journal of Personality and Social Psychology, 32,* 429–438.

Piliavin, I. M., Rodin, J., & Piliavin, J. A. (1969). Good Samaritanism: An underground phenomenon? *Journal of Personality and Social Psychology, 13,* 289–299.

Piliavin. J. A. (2004, October). *Positive consequences of volunteering across the lifespan.* Paper presented at the International Positive Psychology Summit, Washington, D.C.

Piliavin, J. A. (2005a, July). *Lifelong voluntary participation, well-being, and health.* Paper presented at the biannual meetings of the European Association of Experimental Social Psychology, Wurzburg, Germany.

Piliavin, J. A. (2005b, August). *Health benefits of volunteering in the Wisconsin Longitudinal Study.* Paper presented at the 100th annual meeting of the American Sociological Association, Philadelphia, PA.

Piliavin, J. A., & Callero, P. L. (1991). *Giving blood: The development of an altruistic identity.* Baltimore, MD: Johns Hopkins University Press.

Piliavin, J. A., Callero, P. L., & Grube, J. E. (2002). Role as resource for action in public service. *Journal of Social Issues, 58,* 469–486.

Piliavin, J. A., & Charng, H. W. (1990). Altruism: A review of recent theory and research. *Annual Review of Sociology, 16,* 27–65.

Piliavin, J. A., Dovidio, J. F., Gaertner, S. L., & Clark, R. D. III. (1981). *Emergency intervention.* New York: Academic Press.

Piliavin, J. A., & Grube, J. E. (2001, July). *Identity and the courage of one's convictions.* Paper presented at the meeting of the British Psychological Association, Sussex, England.

Piliavin, J. A., & Libby. D. (1985/1986). Personal norms, perceived social norms, and blood donation. *Humbolt Journal of Social Relations, 13,* 159–194.

Piliavin, J. A., & Piliavin, I. M. (1972). The effects of blood on reactions to a victim. *Journal of Personality and Social Psychology, 23,* 253–261.

Piliavin, J. A., Piliavin, I. M., & Broll, L. (1976). Time of arrival at an emergency and likelihood of helping. *Personality and Social Psychology Bulletin, 2,* 273–276.

Piliavin, J. A., & Unger, R. K. (1985). The helpful but helpless female: Myth or reality? In V. O. O'Leary, R. K. Unger, & B. S. Wallston (Eds.), *Women, gender, and social psychology* (pp. 149–186). Hillsdale, NJ: Lawrence Erlbaum Associates.

Platt, J. (1973). Social traps. *American Psychologist, 28,* 641–651.

Plomin, R., & Caspi, A. (1999). Behavioral genetics and personality. In L. A. Pervin & O. P. John (Eds.), *Handbook of personality: Theory and research* (2nd ed., pp. 251–276). New York: Guilford Press.

Podsakoff, P. M., Ahearne, M., & MacKenzie, S. B. (1997). Organizational citizenship behavior and the quantity and quality of work group performance. *Journal of Applied Psychology, 82,* 262–270.

Podsakoff, P. M., & MacKenzie, S. B. (1994). Organizational citizenship behaviors and sales unit effectiveness. *Journal of Marketing Research, 31,* 351–363.

Podsakoff, P. M., MacKenzie, S. B., Paine, J. B., & Bachrach, D. G. (2000). Organizational citizenship behaviors: A critical review of the theoretical and empirical literature and suggestions for future research. *Journal of Management, 26,* 513–563.

Pomazal, R. S., & Clore, G. L. (1973). Helping on the highway: The effects of dependency and sex. *Journal of Applied Social Psychology, 3*, 160–164.

Porter, R. H. (1987). Kin recognition: Functions and mediating mechanisms. In C. Crawford, M. Smith, & D. Krebs (Eds.), *Sociobiology and psychology* (pp. 175–204). Hillsdale, NJ: Lawrence Erlbaum Associates.

Porter, R. H., Boyle, C., Hardister, T., & Balogh, R. D. (1989). Salience of neonates' facial features for recognition by family members. *Ethology and Sociobiology, 10*, 325–330.

Porter, R. H., Cernoch, J. M., & Balogh, R. D. (1984). Recognition of neonates by facial-visual characteristics. *Pediatrics, 74*, 501–504.

Porter, R. H., Cernoch, J. M., & Balogh, R. D. (1985). Odor signatures and kin recognition. *Physiology and Behavior, 34*, 445–448.

Porter, R. H., Cernoch, J. M., & McLaughlin, F. J. (1983) Maternal recognition of neonates through olfactory cues. *Physiology and Behavior, 30*, 151–154.

Poundstone, W. (1993). *Prisoner's dilemma.* New York: Anchor.

Pratt, M., W., Hunsberger, B., Pancer, S. M., & Alisat, S. (2003). A longitudinal analysis of personal values socialization: Correlates of a moral self-ideal in late adolescence. *Social Development, 12*, 563–585.

Preston, S. D., & de Waal, F. B. M. (2002). Empathy: Its ultimate and proximate bases. *Behavioral and Brain Sciences, 25*, 1–72.

Pryor, J. B., Reeder, G. D., & McManus, J. A. (1991) Fear and loathing in the workplace: Reactions to AIDS infected co-workers. *Personality and Social Psychology Bulletin, 17*, 133–139.

Putnam, R. D. (2002). *Bowling alone: The collapse and revival of the American community.* New York: Touchstone Books.

Rabow, J., Newcomb, M. D., Monto, M. A., & Hernandez, A. C. R. (1990). Altruism in drunk driving situations: Personal and situational factors in helping. *Social Psychology Quarterly, 53*, 199–213.

Radke-Yarrow, M. R., & Zahn-Waxler, C. J. (1984). Roots, motives, and patterns in children's prosocial behavior. In E. Staub, D. Bar-Tal, J. Karylowski, & J. Reykowski (Eds.), *Origins and maintenance of prosocial behaviors* (pp. 81–100). New York: Plenum.

Radke-Yarrow, M. R., Zahn-Waxler, C. J., & Chapman, M. (1983). Children's prosocial dispositions and behavior. In E. M. Hetherington (Ed.), *Handbook of child psychology, Vol. 4, Socialization, personality, and social development* (pp. 469–546). New York: Harper and Row.

Rand, A. (1964). *The virtue of selfishness.* New York: New American Library.

Rapoport, A., & Eshed-Levy, D. (1989). Provision of step-level public goods: Effects of greed and fear of being gypped. *Organizational Behavior and Human Decision Processes, 44*, 325–344.

Raven, B. H., & Rubin, J. Z. (1983). *Social psychology* (2nd ed.). New York: Wiley.

Raviv, A., Bar-Tal, D., & Lewis-Levin, T. (1980). Motivations for donation behavior by boys of three different ages. *Child Development, 51*, 610–613.

Reddy, R. D. (1980). Individual philanthropy and giving behavior. In D. H. Smith & J. Macaulay (Eds.), *Participation in social and political activities* (pp. 370–399). San Francisco, CA: Jossey-Bass.

Reed, P., & Selbee, L. (2000). *Distinguishing characteristics of volunteers in Canada.* Ottawa, Canada: Statistics Canada.

Regan, D. T. (1971). Effect of a favor on liking and compliance. *Journal of Experimental Social Psychology, 7*, 627–639.

Regan, D. T., Williams, M., & Sparling, S. (1972). Voluntary expiation of guilt: A field experiment. *Journal of Personality and Social Psychology, 24*, 42–45.

Reitschlin, J. (1998). Voluntary association membership and psychological distress. *Journal of Health and Social Behavior, 39*, 348–355.

Ridley, M. (2003). *Nature via nurture.* New York: Harper Academic.

Ridley, M., & Dawkins, R. (1984). The natural selection of altruism. In J. Rushton & R. Sorrentino (Eds.), *Altruism and helping behavior: Social, personality, and developmental perspectives* (pp. 19–39). Hillsdale, NJ: Lawrence Erlbaum Associates.

Rind, B., & Strohmetz, D. (1999). Effect on restaurant tipping of a helpful message written on the back of customer's checks. *Journal of Applied Social Psychology, 29,* 139–144.

Rioux, S. M., & Penner, L. A. (2001). The causes of organizational citizenship behavior: A motivational analysis. *Journal of Applied Psychology, 86,* 1306–1314.

Ripley, J. S., & Worthington, E. L., Jr. (2002). Hope-focused and forgiveness-based group interventions to promote marital enrichment. *Journal of Counseling and Development, 80,* 452–463.

Robinson, J. L., Zahn-Waxler, C. J., & Emde, R. N. (2001). Relationship context as a moderator of sources of individual differences in empathic development. In R. Emde & J. Hewitt (Eds.), *Infancy to early childhood: Genetic and environmental influences on developmental change* (pp. 257–268). London: Oxford University Press.

Rodin, J., & Langer, E. J. (1977). Long-term effects of a control-relevant intervention with the institutionalized aged. *Journal of Personality and Social Psychology, 35,* 897–902.

Rokeach, M., & Mezei, L. (1966). Race and shared belief as factors in social choice. *Science, 151,* 167–172.

Rosen, S., Mickler, S. E., & Collins, J. E. (1987). Reactions of would-be helpers whose offer of help is spurned. *Journal of Personality and Social Psychology, 53,* 288–297.

Rosen, S., Mickler, S. E., & Spiers, C. (1985/1986). The spurned philanthropist. *Humboldt Journal of Social Relations, 13,* 145–158.

Rosenberg, M., & McCullough, B. C. (1981). Mattering: Inferred significance and mental health among adolescents. *Community and Mental Health, 2,* 163–182.

Rosenhan, D. L. (1969). Some origins of concern for others. In P. H. Mussen, J. Langer, & M. Covington (Eds.), *Trends and issues in developmental psychology* (pp. 134–153). New York: Holt, Rinehart & Winston.

Rosenhan, D. L. (1970). The natural socialization of altruistic autonomy. In J. Macaulay, & L. Berkowitz (Eds.), *Altruism and helping behavior* (pp. 251–268). New York: Academic Press.

Rosenthal, S., Feiring, C., & Lewis, M. (1998). Political volunteering from late adolescence to young adulthood: patterns and predictions. *Journal of Social Issues 54,* 471–493.

Ross, L., & Nisbett, R. E. (1991). *The person and the situation: Perspectives on social psychology.* New York: McGraw-Hill.

Ross, S. R., Rausch, M. K., & Canada, K. E. (2003). Competition and cooperation in the five-factor model: Individual differences in achievement motivation. *Journal of Psychology: Interdisciplinary and Applied, 137,* 323–337.

Rothstein, S. I., & Pierotti, R. (1988). Distinctions among reciprocal altruism, kin selection, and cooperation and a model for the initial evolution of beneficent behavior. *Ethology and Sociobiology, 9,* 189–209.

Rotter, J. B. (1967). A new scale for the measurement of interpersonal trust. *Journal of Personality, 35,* 651–665.

Ruble, D. N., & Rholes, W. S. (1983). The development of children's perceptions and attributions about their social world. In J. H. Harvey, W. Ickes, & R. F. Kidd (Eds.), *New directions in attribution research* (Vol. 3, pp. 3–36). Hillsdale, NJ: Lawrence Erlbaum Associates.

Rusbult, C. E., & van Lange, P. A. M. (1996). Interdependence processes. In E. T. Higgins & A. Kruglanski (Eds.), *Social psychology: Handbook of basic principles* (pp. 564–596). New York: Guilford.

Rushton, J. P. (1975). Generosity in children: Immediate and long term effects of modeling, preaching, and moral judgment. *Journal of Personality and Social Psychology, 31,* 459–466.

Rushton, J. P. (1982). Social learning theory and the development of prosocial behavior. In N. Eisenberg (Ed.), *The development of prosocial behavior* (pp. 77–105). New York: Academic Press.

Rushton, J. P. (1984). The altruistic personality: Evidence from laboratory, naturalistic and self-report perspectives. In E. Staub, D. Bar-Tal, J. Karylowski, & J. Reykowski (Eds.), *Development and maintenance of prosocial behavior* (pp. 271–290). New York: Plenum.

Rushton, J. P., & Campbell, A. C. (1977). Modeling, vicarious reinforcement and extraversion on blood donating in adults: Immediate and long term effects. *European Journal of Social Psychology, 7,* 297–306.

Rushton, J. P., Fulker, D. W., Neale, M. C., Nias, D. K. B., & Eysenck, H. J. (1986). Altruism and aggression: The heritability of individual differences. *Journal of Personality and Social Psychology, 50,* 1192–1198.

Rushton, J. P., Russell, R. J. H., & Wells, P. A. (1984). Genetic similarity theory: Beyond kin selection altruism. *Behavioral Genetics, 14,* 179–193.

Rushton, J. P., & Teachman, G. (1978). The effects of positive reinforcement, attributions, and punishment on model induced altruism in children. *Personality and Social Psychology Bulletin, 4,* 322–325.

Sagi, A., & Hoffman, M. L. (1976). Empathic distress in the newborn. *Developmental Psychology, 12,* 175–176.

Salamon, J. (2003). *Rambam's ladder: A meditation on generosity and why it is necessary to give.* New York: Workman.

Salmon, C. A., & Daly, M. (1996). On the importance of kin relations to Canadian women and men. *Ethology and Sociobiology, 17,* 289–297.

Salovey, P., Mayer, J. D., & Rosenhan, D. L. (1991). Mood and helping: Mood as a motivator of helping and helping as a regulator of mood. In M. S. Clark (Ed.), *Review of personality and social psychology: Vol. 12. Prosocial behavior* (pp. 215–237). Newbury Park, CA: Sage.

Sampson, R. J., & Laub, J. H. (2002). Life-course desisters? Trajectories of crime among delinquent boys followed to age 70. *Criminology, 41,* 555–592.

Samuelson, C. D., & Messick, D. M. (1986a). Alternative structural solutions to resource dilemmas. *Organizational behavior and human decision processes, 37,* 139–155.

Samuelson, C. D., & Messick, D. M. (1986b). Inequities in access to and use of shared resources in social dilemmas. *Journal of Personality and Social Psychology, 51,* 960–967.

Samuelson, C. D., Messick, D. M., Rutte, C. G., & Wilke, H. (1984). Individual and structural solutions to resource dilemmas in two cultures. *Journal of Personality and Social Psychology, 47,* 94–104.

Saucier, D. A., Miller, C. T., & Doucet, N. (2005). Differences in helping Whites and Blacks: A meta-analysis. *Personality and Social Psychology Review, 9,* 2–16.

Sauer, L. A., & France, C. R. (1999). Caffeine attenuates vasovagal reactions in female first-time blood donors. *Health Psychology, 18,* 403–409.

Sax, L. J., & Astin, A. W. (1997). The benefits of service: Evidence from undergraduates. *Educational Record, 78,* 25–32.

Schachter, S., & Singer, J. E. (1962). Cognitive, social, and physiological determinants of emotional state. *Psychological Review, 69,* 379–399.

Schaller, M., & Cialdini, R. B. (1988). The economics of empathic helping: Support for a mood management motive. *Journal of Experimental Social Psychology, 24,* 163–181.

Schmidt, G., & Weiner, B. (1988). An attribution-effect-action theory of behavior: Replications of judgments of help-giving. *Personality and Social Psychology Bulletin, 14,* 610–621.

Schmitt, D. R., & Marwell, G. (1972). Withdrawal and reward reallocation as responses to inequity. *Journal of Experimental Social Psychology, 8,* 207–221.

Schneider, K. T., Swan, S., & Fitzgerald, S. R. (1997). Job-related and psychological effects of sexual harassment in the workplace: Empirical evidence from two organizations. *Journal of Applied Psychology, 82,* 401–415.

Schopler, J., & Insko, C. A. (1992). The discontinuity effect in interpersonal and intergroup relations: Generality and mediation. In W. Stroebe & M. Hewstone (Eds.), *European review of social psychology* (Vol. 3, pp. 121–151). Chichester, UK: Wiley.

Schopler, J., Insko, C. A., Drigotas, S. M., Wieselquist, J., Pemberton, M., & Cox, C. (1995). The role of identifiability in the reduction of interindividual-intergroup discontinuity. *Journal of Experimental Social Psychology, 31,* 553–574.

Schopler, J., Insko, C. A., Graetz, K. A., Drigotas, S. M., Smith, V. A., & Dahl, K. A. (1993). Individual-group discontinuity: Further evidence for mediation by fear and greed. *Personality and Social Psychology Bulletin, 19*, 419–431.

Schopler, J., Insko, C. A., Wieselquist, J., Pemberton, M., Witcher, B., Kozar, R., Roddenberry, C., & Wildschut, T. (2001). When groups are more competitive than individuals: The domain of the discontinuity effect. *Journal of Personality and Social Psychology, 80*, 632–644.

Schreiber, G. B., Sharma, U. K., Wright, D. J., Glynn, S. A., Ownby, H. E., Tu, Y., Garratty, G., Piliavin, J., Zuck, T., & Gilcher, R. (2005). First year donation patterns predict long-term commitment for first-time donors. *Vox Sanguinis, 88*, 114–121.

Schroeder, D. A. (Ed.). (1995). *Social dilemmas: Perspectives on individuals and groups.* Westport, CT: Praeger.

Schroeder, D. A., Dovidio, J. F., Sibicky, M. E., Matthews, L. L., & Allen, J. L. (1988). Empathic concern and helping behavior: Egoism or altruism? *Journal of Experimental Social Psychology, 24*, 333–353.

Schroeder, D. A., Jensen, T. D., Reed, A., Sullivan, D., & Schwab, M. (1983). The actions of others as determinants of behavior in social trap situations. *Journal of Experimental Social Psychology, 19*, 522–539.

Schroeder, D. A., Penner, L. A., Dovidio, J. F., & Piliavin, J. A. (1995). *The psychology of helping and altruism.* New York: McGraw-Hill.

Schroeder, D. A., Sibicky, M. E., & Irwin, M. E. (1995). A framework for understanding decisions in social dilemmas. In D. A. Schroeder (Ed.), *Social dilemmas: Perspectives on individuals and groups* (pp. 183–199). Westport, CT: Praeger.

Schroeder, D. A., Steel, J. E., Woodell, A. J., & Bembenek, A. F. (2003). Justice within social dilemmas. *Personality and Social Psychology Review, 7*, 374–387.

Schultz, R., Williamson, G. M., Morycz, R. K., & Biegel, D. E. (1991). Costs and benefits of providing care to Alzheimer's patients. In S. Spacapan & S. Oskamp (Eds.), *Helping and being helped: Naturalistic studies* (pp. 153–181). Newbury Park, CA: Sage.

Schwartz, S. H. (1977). Normative influences on altruism. In L. Berkowitz (Ed.), *Advances in experimental social psychology* (Vol. 10, pp. 222–280) New York: Academic Press.

Schwartz, S. H. (1994). Are there universal aspects in the structure and content of human values? *Journal of Social Issues, 50*, 19–45.

Schwartz, S. H., & Howard, J. A. (1981). A normative decision-making model of altruism. In J. P. Rushton, & R. M. Sorrentino (Eds.), *Altruism and helping behavior: Social, personality, and developmental perspectives* (pp 189–211). Hillsdale, NJ: Lawrence Erlbaum Associates.

Schwartz, S. H., & Howard, J. A. (1982). Helping and cooperation: A self-based motivational model. In V. J. Derlega & J. Grzelak (Eds.), *Cooperation and helping behavior: Theories and research* (pp. 327–353). New York: Academic Press.

Schwartz, S. H., & Howard, J. A. (1984). Internalized values as motivators of altruism. In E. Staub, D. Bar-Tal, J. Karylowski, & J. Reykowski (Eds.), *Development and maintenance of prosocial behavior* (pp. 229–255). New York: Plenum.

Scruggs, T. E., Mastropieri, M. A., & Richter, L. (1985). Peer tutoring with behaviorally disordered students: Social and academic benefits. *Behavioral Disorders, 10*, 283–294.

Segal, N. L. (1984) Cooperation, competition, and altruism within twin sets: A reappraisal. *Ethology and Sociobiology, 5*, 163–177.

Segal, N. L. (1991, April). *Cooperation and competition in adolescent MZ and DZ twins during the Prisoners' Dilemma Game.* Paper presented at meeting of the Society for Research in Child Development, Seattle, WA.

Segal, N. L. (1993). Twin sibling, and adoption methods: test of evolutionary hypotheses. *American Psychologist, 48*, 943–956.

Selman, R. L. (1980). *The growth of interpersonal understanding.* Orlando, FL: Academic Press.

Sen, B. (2004). Adolescent propensity for depressed mood and help seeking: Race and gender Differences. *Journal of Mental Health Policy and Economics, 7*, 133–145.

Settoon, R. P., Bennett, N., & Liden, R. C. (1996). Social exchange in organizations: Perceived organizational support, leader-member exchange, and employee reciprocity. *Journal of Applied Psychology, 81*, 219–227.

Shell, R., & Eisenberg, N. (1992). A developmental model of recipient's reactions to aid. *Psychological Bulletin, 111*, 413–433.

Sherif, M. (1966). *Group conflict and cooperation: Their social psychology.* London: Routledge and Kegan Paul.

Sherif, M., Harvey, O. J., White, B. J., Hood, W. R., & Sherif, C. W. (1961). *Intergroup conflict and cooperation. The Robbers Cave experiment.* Norman: University of Oklahoma Book Exchange.

Sherman, P. W. (1981). Kinship demography, and Belding's ground squirrel nepotism. *Behavioral Ecology and Sociology, 8*, 604–606.

Sherman, P. W. (1985). Alarm calls of Belding's ground squirrels to aerial predators: Nepotism or self-preservation? *Behavioral Ecology and Sociobiology, 17*, 313–323.

Sheu, H. B., & Sedlacek, W. E. (2004). An exploratory study of help-seeking attitudes and coping strategies among college students by race and gender. *Measurement and Evaluation in Counseling and Development, 37*, 130–143.

Shotland, R. L., & Heinold, W. D. (1985). Bystander response to arterial bleeding: Helping skills, the decision-making process, and differentiating the helping response. *Journal of Personality and Social Psychology, 49*, 347–356.

Shotland, R. L., & Huston, T. L. (1979). Emergencies: What are they and how do they influence bystanders to intervene? *Journal of Personality and Social Psychology, 37*, 1822–1834.

Shotland, R. L. & Straw, M. (1976). Bystander response to an assault: When a man attacks a woman. *Journal of Personality and Social Psychology, 34*, 990–999.

Sibicky, M. E., Schroeder, D. A., & Dovidio, J. F. (1995). Empathy and helping: Considering the consequences of intervention. *Basic and Applied Social Psychology, 16*, 435–453.

Sidanius, J., & Pratto, F. (1999). *Social dominance: An intergroup theory of social hierarchy and oppression.* New York: Cambridge University Press.

Sieber, S. D. (1974). Toward a theory of role accumulation. *American Sociological Review, 39*, 567–578.

Simner, M. L. (1971). Newborn's response to the cry of another infant. *Developmental Psychology, 5*, 136–150.

Simon, B., Stürmer, S., & Steffens, K. (2000). Helping individuals or group members? The role of individual and collective identification in AIDS volunteerism. *Personality and Social Psychology Bulletin, 26*, 497–506.

Simpson, B. (2004). Social values, subjective transformations, and cooperation in social dilemmas. *Social Psychology Quarterly, 67*, 385–395.

Skarlicki, D. P., & Latham, G. P. (1996). Increasing citizenship behavior within a labor union: A test of organizational justice theory. *Journal of Applied Psychology, 81*, 161–169.

Skitka, L. J. (1999). Ideological and attributional boundaries on public compassion: Reactions to individuals and communities affected by a natural disaster. *Personality & Social Psychology Bulletin, 25*, 793–808.

Smith, A. (1933). *The wealth of nations.* New York: E. P. Dutton. (Original work published 1776)

Smith, C. A., Organ, D. W., & Near, J. P. (1983). Organizational citizenship behavior: Its nature and antecedents. *Journal of Applied Psychology, 68*, 653–663.

Smith, C. L., Gelfand, D. M., Hartmann, D. P., & Partlow, M. E. P. (1979). Children's causal attributions regarding help giving. *Child Development, 50*, 203–210.

Smith, D. (1994). Determinants of voluntary association participation and volunteering. *Nonprofit and Voluntary Sector Quarterly, 23*, 243–263.

Smith, K. D., Keating, J. P., & Stotland, E. (1989). Altruism reconsidered: The effect of denying feedback on a victim's status to empathic witnesses. *Journal of Personality and Social Psychology, 57*, 641–650.

Smith, R. E., Smythe, L., & Lien, D. (1972). Inhibition of helping behavior by a similar or dissimilar nonreactive fellow bystander. *Journal of Personality and Social Psychology, 23,* 414–419.

Snyder, M. (1992). Of persons and situations, of personality and social psychology. *Psychological Inquiry, 3,* 94–98.

Snyder, M., Clary, E. G., & Stukas, A. A. (2000). The functional approach to volunteerism. In G . R. Maio & J. M. Olson (Eds.), *Why we evaluate. Functions of attitudes* (pp. 365–393). Mahwah, NJ: Lawrence Erlbaum Associates.

Snyder, M., & Ickes, W. (1985). Personality and social behavior. In G. Lindzey & E. Aronson (Eds.), *Handbook of social psychology* (3rd ed., Vol. 2, pp. 883–947). New York: Random House.

Snyder, M., & Omoto, A. M. (2001). Basic research and practical problems: Volunteerism and the psychology of individual and collective action. In W. Wosinska & R. B. Cialdini (Eds.), *The practice of social influence in multiple cultures* (pp. 287–307). Mahwah, NJ: Lawrence Erlbaum Associates.

Snyder, M., Omoto, A. M., & Crain, A. L. (1999). Punished for their good deeds: Stigmatization of AIDS volunteers. *American Behavioral Scientist, 42,* 1175–1192.

Sober, E. (1988). What is evolutionary altruism? *Journal of Philosophy* [Special issue: M. Matthen, & B. Linsky (Eds.), *Philosophy and Biology, 14,* 75–100.

Sober, E. (1992). The evolution of altruism: Correlation, cost and benefit. *Biology and Philosophy, 7,* 177–188.

Sober, E. (2002). The ABCs of altruism. In S. G. Post & L. G. Underwood (Eds.), *Altruism & altruistic love: Science, philosophy, & religion in dialogue* (pp. 17–28). London: Oxford University Press.

Sober, E., & Wilson, D. S. (1998). *Unto others: The evolution and psychology of unselfish behavior.* Cambridge, MA: Harvard University Press.

Staub, E. (1971). Helping a person in distress: The influence of implicit and explicit "rules" of conduct on children and adults. *Journal of Personality and Social Psychology, 17,* 137–144.

Staub, E. (1974). Helping a distressed person: Social, personality, and stimulus determinants. In L. Berkowitz (Ed.), *Advances in experimental social psychology* (Vol. 7, pp. 293–341). New York: Academic Press.

Staub, E. (1981). *Positive social behavior and morality (Vol. 1): Social and personal influences.* New York: Academic Press.

Staub, E. (1993). Notes on cultures of violence, cultures of caring and peace, and the fulfillment of basic human needs. *Political Psychology, 24,* 1–21.

Staub, E. (1996). Altruism and aggression: Origins and cures. In R. S. Feldman (Ed.). *Psychology of adversity* (pp. 115–144). Amherst: University of Massachusetts Press.

Staub, E. (2004). Justice, healing, and reconciliation: How the people's courts in Rwanda can promote them. *Peace and Conflict: Journal of Peace Psychology, 10,* 25–32.

Steblay, N. M. (1987). Helping behavior in rural and urban environments: A meta-analysis. *Psychological Bulletin, 102,* 346–356.

Steele, C. (1992). Race and the schooling of Black Americans. *The Atlantic, 269* (4), 68–78.

Stein, D. D., Hardyck, J. A., & Smith, M. B. (1965). Race *and* belief: An open and shut case. *Journal of Personality and Social Psychology, 1,* 281–289.

Sterling, B., & Gaertner, S. L. (1984). The attribution of arousal and emergency helping: A bidirectional process. *Journal of Experimental Social Psychology, 20,* 286–296.

St. John, C., & Fuchs, J. (2002). The heartland responds to terror: Volunteering after the bombing of the Murrah federal building. *Social Science Quarterly, 83,* 397–415.

Stone, V. E., Cosmides, L., Tooby, J., Kroll, N., & Knight, R. T. (2002). Selective impairment of reasoning about social exchange in a patient with bilateral limbic system damage. *Proceedings of the National Academy of USA, 99,* 11531–11536.

Strauss, J. S. (1992). Need for integrating environmental and biological factors in psychiatry. *American Journal of Psychiatry, 149,* 147.

Stryker, S. (1980). *Symbolic interactionism: A social structural version.* Menlo Park, CA: Benjamin/Cummings.

Stukas, A. A., Clary, E. G., & Snyder, M. (1999a) The effects of "mandatory volunteerism" on intentions to volunteer. *Psychological Science, 10,* 59–64.

Stukas, A. A., Clary, E. G., Snyder, M. (1999b). Service learning: Who benefits and why. *Social Policy Report: Society for Research in Child Development, 8,* 1–19.

Stürmer, S., Snyder, M., & Omoto, A. M. (2005). Prosocial emotions and helping: The moderating role of group membership. *Journal of Personality and Social Psychology, 88,* 532–546.

Sundeen, R., & Raskoff, S. (1995). Teenage volunteers and their values. *Nonprofit and Voluntary Sector Quarterly, 24,* 337–357.

Swinyard, W. R., & Ray, M. L. (1979). Effects of praise and small requests on receptivity to direct-mail appeals. *Journal of Social Psychology, 108,* 177–184.

Switzer, G. E., Dew, M. A., Butterworth, V. A., Simmons, R. G., & Schimmel, M. (1997). Understanding donors' motivations: A study of unrelated bone marrow donors. *Social Science and Medicine, 45,* 137–147.

Tajfel, H. (1969). Cognitive aspects of prejudice. *Journal of Social Issues, 25*(4), 79–97.

Tajfel, H., & Turner, J. C. (1979). An integrative theory of intergroup conflict. In W. G. Austin & S. Worchel (Eds.), *The social psychology of intergroup relations* (pp. 33–47). Monterey, CA: Brooks/Cole.

Takeuchi, D. T., Leaf, P. J., & Kuo, H. S. (1988). Ethnic differences in the perception of barriers to help-seeking. *Social Psychiatry and Psychiatric Epidemiology, 23,* 273–280.

Taormina, R. J., Messick, D. M., Iwaki, S., & Wilke, H. (1988). Cross-cultural perspectives on foreign aid deservingness decisions. *Journal of Cross-Cultural Psychology, 19,* 387–412.

Taylor, C. J. (1998). Factors affecting behavior toward people with disabilities. *Journal of Social Psychology, 138,* 766–771.

Taylor, S. E., & Lobel, M. (1989). Social comparison activity under threat: Downward comparison. *Psychological Review, 96,* 569–575.

Tesser, A. (1999). Toward a self-evaluation maintenance model of social behavior. In R. F. Baumeister (Ed.), *The self in social psychology* (pp. 446–460). New York: Psychology Press.

Thibaut, J. W., & Kelley, H. H. (1959). *The social psychology of groups.* New York: Wiley.

Thibaut, J. W., & Walker, L. (1975). *Procedural justice: A psychological analysis.* Hillsdale, NJ: Lawrence Erlbaum Associates.

Thoits, P. A. (1986). Social support and psychological well-being: Theoretical possibilities. In I. G. Sarason & B. R. Sarason (Eds.), *Social support: Theory, research, and application* (pp. 51–72). Dordrecht, the Netherlands: Martinus Nijhoff.

Thoits, P. A. (1992). Multiple identities: Examining gender and marital status differences in distress. *Social Psychology Quarterly, 55,* 236–256.

Thoits, P. A. (1995). Identity-relevant events and psychological symptoms: A cautionary tale. *Journal of Health and Social Behavior, 36,* 72–82.

Thoits, P. A., & Hewitt, L. N. (2001). Volunteer work and well-being. *Journal of Health and Social Behavior, 42,* 115–131.

Thomas, G. C., & Batson, C. D. (1981). Effect of helping under normative pressure on self-perceived altruism. *Social Psychology Quarterly , 44,* 127–131.

Thomas, G. C., Batson, C. D., & Coke, J. S. (1980). Do good Samaritans discourage helpfulness?: Self-perceived altruism after exposure to highly helpful others. *Journal of Personality and Social Psychology, 40,* 194–200.

Thompson, R. A. (1987). Empathy and emotional understanding: The early development of empathy. In N. Eisenberg & J. Strayer (Eds.), *Empathy and its development* (pp. 119–146). Cambridge: Cambridge University Press.

Tietjan, A. (1986). Prosocial reasoning among children and adults in a Papua New Guinea society. *Developmental Psychology, 22,* 861–868.

Tillman, P. (1998). *In search of moderators of the relationship between predictors and organizational citizenship behavior and organizational citizenship behaviors: The case of motives.* Unpublished master's thesis, University of South Florida.

Toch, H. (2000). Altruistic activity as correctional treatment. *International Journal of Offender Therapy and Comparative Criminology, 44,* 270–278.

Toffler, A. (1964, March). Ayn Rand: A candid conversation with the "Fountainhead" of "Objectivisim." *Playboy, 11,* 30–34.

Toi, M., & Batson, C. D. (1982). More evidence that empathy is a source of altruistic motivation. *Journal of Personality & Social Psychology, 43,* 281–292.

Tooby, J., & Cosmides, L. (1992). The psychological foundations of culture. In J. Barkow & L. Cosmides (Eds.), *The adapted mind: Evolutionary psychology and the generation of culture* (pp. 19–136). London: Oxford University Press.

Trivers, R. (1971). The evolution of reciprocal altruism. *Quarterly Review of Biology, 46,* 35–57.

Turner, J. C., Hogg, M. A., Oakes, P. J., Reicher, S. D., & Wetherell, M. S. (1987). *Rediscovering the social group: A self-categorization theory.* Oxford, UK: Basil Blackwell.

Turner, M. E., & Pratkanis, A. R. (1994). Affirmative action as help: A review of recipient reactions to preferential selection and affirmative action. *Basic and Applied Social Psychology, 15,* 43–69.

Turner, R. H. (1978). The role and the person. *American Journal of Sociology, 84,* 1–23.

Tyler, A. F. (1962). *Freedom's ferment.* New York: Harper Torchbooks.

Tyler, T. R., & Blader, S. L. (2000). *Cooperation in groups: Procedural justice, social identity, and behavioral engagement.* New York: Psychology Press.

Tyler, T. R., & Blader, S. L. (2003). The Group Engagement Model: Procedural justice, social identity, and cooperative behavior. *Personality and Social Psychology Review, 7,* 349–361.

Uggen, C., & Janikula, J. (1999). Volunteerism and arrest in the transition to adulthood. *Social Forces, 78,* 331–362.

Unger, L. S., & Thumuluri, L. K. (1997). Trait empathy and continuous helping: The case of voluntarism. *Journal of Social Behavior and Personality, 12,* 785–800.

U.S. Department of Energy. (2003, August). *International gross domestic product information.* Retrieved August 12, 2004, from www.eia.doe.gov

U.S. Department of Labor. (2005, December). *Volunteering in the United States, 2005.* Retrieved on December 30, 2005, from www.bls.gov/news.release/volume.nr0.htm

Uslaner, E. (2002). Religious and civic engagement in Canada and the United States. *Journal of the Scientific Study of Religion, 41,* 239–254.

Utne, M. K., & Kidd, R. F. (1980). Equity and attribution. In G. Mikula (Ed.), *Justice and social interaction* (pp. 63–93). New York: Springer-Verlag.

Vadeboncoeur, J. A., Rahm, J. A., Aguilera, D., & LeCompte, M. D. (1996). Building democratic character through community experiences in teacher education. *Education and Urban Society, 28,* 189–207.

Vaes, J., Paladino, M.-P., & Leyens, J.-P. (2002). The lost e-mail: Prosocial reactions induced by uniquely human emotions. *British Journal of Social Psychology, 41,* 521–534.

Valiente, C., Eisenberg, N., Fabes, R. A., Shepard, S. A., Cumberland, A., & Losoya, S. H. (2004). Prediction of children's empathy-related responding from their effortful control and parents' expressivity. *Developmental Psychology, 40,* 911–926.

van de Kragt, A. J. C., Orbell, J. M., & Dawes, R. M. (1983). The minimal contributing set as a solution to public goods problems. *American Political Science Review, 77,* 112–122.

van Dijk, E., & Wilke, H. (1995). Coordination rules in asymmetric social dilemmas: A comparison between public good dilemmas and resource dilemmas. *Journal of Experimental Social Psychology, 31,* 1–27.

van Dijk, E., & Wilke, H. (2000). Decision-induced focusing in social dilemmas: Give-some, keep-some, take-some, and leave-some dilemmas. *Journal of Personality & Social Psychology, 78,* 92–104.

van Dijk, E., Wilke, H. A. M., Wilke, M., & Metman, L. (1999). What information do we use in social dilemmas? Environmental uncertainty and the employment of coordination rules. *Journal of Experimental Social Psychology, 35,* 109–135.

van Dijk, E., Wilke, H., & Wit, A. P. (2003). Preference for leadership in social dilemmas: Public goods dilemmas versus common resource dilemmas. *Journal of Experimental Social Psychology, 39,* 170–176.

VanDyne, L., Cummings, L. L., & Parks, J. M. (1995). Extra-role behaviors: In pursuit of construct and definitional clarity (a bridge over muddied waters). *Research in Organizational Behavior, 17,* 215–285.

van Lange, P. A. M. (1999). The pursuit of joint outcomes and equality in outcomes: An integrative model of social value orientation. *Journal of Personality and Social Psychology, 77,* 337–349.

van Lange, P. A. M., & De Dreu, C. K. (2001). Social interaction: Cooperation and competition. In M. Hewstone & W. Stroebe (Eds.), *Introduction to social psychology* (pp. 341–369). Oxford: Blackwell.

van Lange, P. A. M., & Kuhlman, D. M. (1994). Social value orientation and impressions of a partners' honesty and intelligence: A test of the might versus morality effect. *Journal of Personality and Social Psychology, 67,* 126–141.

van Lange, P. A. M., Otten, W., DeBruin, E. M. N., & Joireman, J. A. (1997). Development of prosocial individualistic, and competitive orientations: Theory and preliminary evidence. *Journal of Personality and Social Psychology, 73,* 733–746.

van Lange, P., van Vugt, M., & Bekkers, R. (2005, July). *From experimental games to prosocial behavior.* Paper presented at the 14th General Meeting of the European Association of Experimental Social Psychology, Wurzburg, Germany.

van Lange, P. A. M., & Visser, K. (1999). Locomotion in social dilemmas: How we adapt to cooperative, tit-for-tat, and noncooperative partners. *Journal of Personality and Social Psychology, 77,* 762–773.

van Lange, P. A. M., van Vugt, M., & De Cremer, D. (2000). Choosing between personal comfort and the environment: Solution to the transportation dilemma. In M. van Vugt, M. Snyder, T. R. Tyler, & A. Biel (Eds.), *Cooperation in modern society: Promoting the welfare of communities, states and organizations* (pp. 45–63). New York: Routledge.

van Vugt, M., & Hart, C. M. (2004). Social identity as social glue: The origins of group loyalty. *Journal of Personality and Social Psychology, 86,* 585–98.

van Vugt, M., & van Lange, P. A. M. (in press). Psychological adaptations for prosocial behavior: The altruism puzzle. In M. Schaller, J. Simpson, & D. Kenrick (Eds.), *Evolution and social psychology.* New York: Psychology Press.

van Willigen, M. (1998, August). *Doing good, feeling better: The effect of voluntary association membership on individual well-being.* Paper presented at the annual meeting of the Society for the Study of Social Problems, Chicago.

Vaughan, K. B., & Lanzetta, J. T. (1980). Vicarious instigation and conditioning of facial expressive and autonomic responses to a model's expressive display of pain. *Journal of Personality and Social Psychology, 38,* 909–923.

Vecina, M. L. (2001). *Psychosocial factors that influence the duration of volunteering.* Unpublished dissertation, Universidad Complutense de Madrid.

Verkuyten, M., & Hagendoorn, L. (1998). Prejudice and self-categorization: The variable role of authoritarianism and in-group stereotypes. *Personality and Social Psychology Bulletin, 24,* 99–110.

Veroff, J. B. (1981). The dynamics of help-seeking in men and women: A national survey study. *Psychiatry, 44,* 189–200.

Vigoda, E. (1999). Good organizational citizenship: Characteristics and predictors of voluntary behavior in the workplace. *Megamot, 39,* 535–561.

Vine, I. (1983). Sociobiology and social psychology—Rivalry or symbiosis? *British Journal of Social Psychology, 22,* 1–11.

Volunteer Australia. (2003). Retrieved December 28, 2005, from www.volunteeringaustralia.org

von Neumann, J., & Morgenstern, O. (1944). *Theory of games and economic behavior.* Princeton, NJ: Princeton University Press.

Wagner, S. L., & Rush, M. C. (2000). Altruistic organizational citizenship behavior: Context, disposition, and age. *Journal of Social Psychology, 140,* 379–391.

Walster, E., Walster, G. W., & Berscheid, E. (1978). *Equity: Theory and research.* Boston, MA: Allyn & Bacon.

Walton, M. D., Sachs, D., Ellington, R., Hazlewood, A., Griffin, S., & Bass, D. (1988). Physical stigma and the pregnancy role: Receiving help from strangers. *Sex Roles, 18,* 323–331.

Walz, S. M., & Niehoff, B. P. (1996, August). *Organizational citizenship behaviors and their effect on organizational effectiveness in limited-menu restaurants.* Paper presented at the meeting of the Academy of Management, Cincinnati, OH.

Wang, X. T. (2002). Risk as reproductive variance. *Evolution and Behavior, 23,* 35–57.

Warburton, J., & Smith, J. (2003). Out of the generosity of your heart: Are we creating active citizens through compulsory volunteer programmes for young people in Australia? *Social Policy and Administration, 37,* 772–786.

Warburton, J., & Terry, D. J. (2000). Volunteer decision making by older people: A test of a revised theory of reasoned action. *Basic and Applied Social Psychology, 22,* 245–257.

Watson, D., Wiese, D., Vaidya, J., & Tellegen, A. (1999). The two general activation systems of affect: Structural findings, evolutionary considerations, and psychobiological evidence. *Journal of Personality and Social Psychology, 76,* 820–838.

Watson, J. B. (1913). *Psychology from the standpoint of a behaviorist.* Philadelphia, PA: Lippincott.

Wayne, S. J., & Green, S. A. (1993). The effects of leader-member exchange on employee citizenship and impression management behavior. *Human Relations, 46,* 1431–1440.

Weber, J. M., Kopelman, S., & Messick, D. M. (2004). A conceptual review of decision making in social dilemmas: Applying a logic of appropriateness. *Personality and Social Psychology Review, 8,* 281–307.

Webley, P., & Lea, S. E. G. (1993). The partial unacceptability of money in repayment for neighborly help. *Human Relations, 46,* 65–76.

Wegner, D. M., & Crano, W. D. (1975). Racial factors in helping behavior: An unobtrusive field experiment. *Journal of Personality & Social Psychology, 32,* 901–905.

Weiner, B. (1980). A cognitive (attribution)-emotion-action model of motivated behavior: An analysis of judgments of help-giving. *Journal of Personality and Social Psychology, 39,* 186–200.

Weiner, B. (1986). *An attributional theory of motivation and emotion.* New York: Springer-Verlag.

Weiner, B., Perry, R. P., & Magnusson, J. (1988). An attributional analysis of reactions to stigmas. *Journal of Personality and Social Psychology, 55,* 738–748.

Weiss, H. M., & Knight, P. A. (1980). The utility of humility: Self-esteem, information search and problem solving efficiency. *Organizational Behavior and Human Performance, 25,* 216–223.

Weiss, R. F., Boyer, J. L., Lombardo, J. P., & Stich, M. H. (1973). Altruistic drive and altruistic reinforcement. *Journal of Personality and Social Psychology, 25,* 390–400.

Weiss, R. F., Buchanan, W., Altstatt, L., & Lombardo, J. P. (1971). Altruism is rewarding. *Science, 11,* 1262–1263.

Wellman, H. M., Cross, D., & Watson, J. (2001). Meta-analysis of theory-of-mind development: The truth about false belief. *Child Development, 72,* 655–684.

West, S. G., Whitney, G., & Schnedler, R. (1975). Helping a motorist in distress: The effects of sex, race, and neighborhood. *Journal of Personality and Social Psychology, 31,* 691–698.

Whatley, M. A., Webster, J. M., Smith, R. H., & Rhodes, A. (1999). The effect of a favor on public and private compliance: How internalized is the norm of reciprocity? *Basic and Applied Social Psychology, 21,* 251–259.

Wheeler, J. A., Gorey, K. M., & Greenblatt, B. (1998). The beneficial effects of volunteering for older volunteers and the people they serve: A meta-analysis. *International Journal of Aging and Human Development, 47,* 69–79.

Whiting, B. B., & Edwards, C. P. (1988). *Children of different worlds: The formation of social behavior.* Cambridge, MA: Harvard University Press.

Whiting, B. B., & Whiting, J. J. M. (1975). *Children of six cultures.* Cambridge, MA: Harvard University Press.

Wicklund, R. A. (1975). Objective self-awareness. In L. Berkowitz (Ed.), *Advances in experimental social psychology* (Vol. 8, pp. 233–275). San Diego, CA: Academic Press.

Wildschut, T., Insko, C. A., & Gaertner, L. (2002). Intragroup social influence and intergroup competition. *Journal of Personality & Social Psychology, 82,* 975–992.

Wildschut, T., Pinter, B., Vevea, J. L., Insko, C. A., & Schopler, J. (2003). Beyond the group mind: A quantitative review of the interindividual-intergroup discontinuity effect. *Psychological Bulletin, 129,* 698–722.

Williams, G. C. (1966). *Adaptation and natural selection.* Princeton, NJ: Princeton University Press.

Williams, J., & Best, D. L. (1990). *Measuring sex stereotype: A multinational study.* Newbury Park, CA: Sage.

Williams, K. D., Jackson, J. M., & Karau, S. J. (1995). Collective hedonism: A social loafing analysis of social dilemmas. In D. A. Schroeder (Ed.), *Social dilemmas: Perspectives on individuals and groups* (pp. 117–141). Westport, CT: Praeger.

Williams, L. J., & Anderson, S. E. (1991). Job satisfaction and organizational commitment as predictors of organizational citizenship and in-role behaviors. *Journal of Management, 91,* 601–617.

Williams, R. (1991). The impact of field education on student development: Research findings. *Journal of Cooperative Education, 27,* 29–45.

Williamson, G. M., & Clark, M. S. (1989). Effects of providing help to another and of relationship type on the provider's mood and self-evaluation. *Journal of Personality and Social Psychology, 56,* 722–734.

Williamson, G. M., & Clark, M. S. (1992). Impact of desired relationship on affective reactions to choosing and being required to help. *Personality and Social Psychology Bulletin, 18,* 10–18.

Williamson, G. M., Clark, M. S., Pegalis, L. J., & Behan, A. (1996). Affective consequences of refusing to help in communal and exchange relationships. *Personality and Social Psychology Bulletin, 22,* 34–47.

Wills, T. A. (1983). Social comparison in coping and help seeking. In B. M. DePaulo, A. Nadler, & J. D. Fisher (Eds.), *New directions in helping: Vol. 2. Help seeking* (pp. 109–142). New York: Academic Press.

Wills, T. A. (1992). The helping process in the context of personal relationships. In S. Spacapan & S. Oskamp (Eds.), *Helping and being helped: Naturalistic studies* (pp. 17–48). Newbury Park, CA: Sage.

Wills, T. A., & DePaulo, B. M. (1991). Interpersonal analysis of the help-seeking process. In C. R. Snyder & D. R. Forsyth (Eds.), *Handbook of social and clinical psychology* (pp. 350–375). New York: Pergamon.

Wilson, D. W., & Kahn, A. (1975). Rewards, costs, and sex differences in helping behavior. *Psychological Reports, 36,* 31–34.

Wilson, J. (2000). Volunteering. *Annual Review of Sociology, 26,* 215–240.

Wilson, J., & Musick, M. A. (1997a). Work and volunteering: The long arm of the job. *Social Forces, 76,* 251–272.

Wilson, J., & Musick, M. A. (1997b). Who cares?: Toward an integrated theory of volunteer work. *American Sociological Review, 62,* 694–713.

Wilson, J., & Musick, M. A. (2000). The effects of volunteering on the volunteer. *Law and Contemporary Problems, 62,* 141–167

Wilson, J., & Musick, M. A. (2003). Doing well by doing good: Volunteering and occupational achievement among American women. *Sociological Quarterly, 44,* 433–451.

Wilson, J. P. (1976). Motivation, modeling, and altruism: A person x situation analysis. *Journal of Personality and Social Psychology, 34,* 1078–1086.

Wilson, T. D. (2002). *Strangers to ourselves: Discovering the adaptive unconscious.* Cambridge, MA: Harvard University Press.

Winter, S. (1996). Paired reading: Three questions. *Educational Psychology in Practice, 12,* 182–189.

Wispé, L. G. (Ed.). (1978). *Altruism, sympathy, and helping.* New York: Academic Press.

Wit, A. P., & Kerr, N. L. (2002). "Me versus just us versus us all" categorization and cooperation in nested social dilemmas. *Journal of Personality & Social Psychology, 83,* 616–637.

Wolcott, I. H. (1986). Seeking help for marital problems before separation. *Australian Journal of Sex, Marriage and Family, 7,* 154–164.

Wood, W., & Eagly, A. H. (2002). A cross-cultural analysis of the behavior of women and men: Implications for the origins of sex differences. *Psychological Bulletin, 128,* 699–727.

Worchel, S. W., Wong, F. Y., & Scheltema, K. E. (1989). Improving intergroup relations: Comparative effects of anticipated cooperation and helping on attraction for an aid-giver. *Social Psychology Quarterly, 52,* 213–219.

Wuthnow, R. (1991). *Acts of compassion: Caring for others and helping ourselves.* Princeton, NJ: Princeton University Press.

Yakimovich, D., & Saltz, E. (1971). Helping behavior: The cry for help. *Psychonomic Science, 23,* 390–400.

Yamagishi, T. (1986). The provision of a sanctioning system as a public good. *Journal of Personality and Social Psychology, 51,* 110–116.

Yates, M., & Youniss, J. (1996a). Community service and political-moral identity in adolescents. *Journal of Research on Adolescence, 6,* 271–284.

Yates, M., & Youniss, J. (1996b). A developmental perspective on community service in adolescence. *Social Development, 5,* 85–11.

Yates, M., & Youniss, J. (1998). Community service and political identity development in adolescence. *Journal of Social Issues, 54,* 495–512.

Yinon, Y., & Landau, M. O. (1987). On the reinforcing value of helping behavior in a positive mood. *Motivation and Emotion, 11,* 83–93.

Yogev, A., & Ronen, R. (1982). Cross-age tutoring: Effects on tutors' attributes. *Journal of Educational Research, 75,* 261–268.

Yousif, Y. H., & Korte, C. (1995). Urbanization, culture, and helpfulness: Cross-cultural studies in England and the Sudan. *Journal of Cross-Cultural Psychology, 26,* 474–489.

Yzerbyt, V., Rocher, S., & Schadron, G. (1997). Stereotypes as explanations: A subjective essentialistic view of group perception. In R. Spears, & P. J. Oakes (Eds), *The social psychology of stereotyping and group life* (pp. 20–50). Malden, MA: Blackwell.

Zahn-Waxler, C. J., Radke-Yarrow, M. R., Wagner, E., & Chapman, M. (1992). Development of concern for others. *Developmental Psychology, 28,* 126–136.

Zahn-Waxler, C. J., Robinson, J. L., & Emde, R. N. (1992). The development of empathy in twins. *Developmental Psychology, 28,* 1038–1047.

Zahn-Waxler, C. J., Schiro, K., Robinson, J. L., Emde, R. N., & Schmitz, S. (2001). Empathy and prosocial patterns in young MZ and DZ twins: Development and genetic and environmental influences. In R. Emde & J Hewitt (Eds.), *Infancy to early childhood: Genetic and environmental influences on developmental change* (pp. 141–162). London: Oxford University Press.

Zajonc, R. B. (1980). Feeling and thinking: Preferences need no inferences. *American Psychologist, 35,* 151–175.

Zillman, D. (1983). Transfer of excitation in emotional behavior. In J. T. Cacioppo & R. E. Petty (Eds.), *Social psychophysiology: A sourcebook* (pp. 215–240). New York: Guilford.

Zimbardo, P. G. (1977). *Shyness: What it is, what to do about it.* Reading, MA: Addison-Wesley.

Zimmerman, D., Donnelly, S., Miller, J., Stewart, D., & Albert, S. E. (2000). Gender disparity in living renal transplant donation. *American Journal of Kidney Disease, 36,* 534–540.

Zuckerman, M. (1975). Belief in a just world and altruistic behavior. *Journal of Personality and Social Psychology, 31,* 972–976.

Zuckerman, M., & Reis, H. T. (1978). Comparison of three models for predicting altruistic behavior. *Journal of Personality & Social Psychology, 36,* 498–510.

Author Index

A

Abrahams, R. D., 8, 9
Achenbach, C. J., 219
Ackerman, D., 90
Adams, J. S., 113, 168
Adelman, M. B., 149
Aguilera, D., 243
Ahammer, I. M., 204
Ahearne, M., 167
Ahmad, N., 284, 311
Aiken, M. T., 228, 245
Ainsworth, M. D. S., 205
Ajzen, I., 164
Akert, R. M., 25
Albert, S. E.,216
Albrecht, T. L., 149
Alcock, J., 44
Alisat, S., 193
Allen, B. C., 93
Allen, H., 88, 109
Allen, J. L., 136, 139
Allen, J. P., 244, 245, 247
Allen, L., 183
Allen, T. D., 169, 234, 235
Allport, G. W., 297, 303, 343
Altabe, M. N., 233
Altstatt, L., 241
Amato, P. R., 23, 24
American Nurses Association, 173
Anastasio, P. A., 299

Anderson, C., 120
Anderson, C. A., 204
Anderson, S. E., 93, 168
Applebaum, L. D., 115
Archer, R. L., 115
Argyle, M., 27, 270
Aries, E. J., 219
Arlitt, A. H., 59
Armitage, C. J., 164
Armstrong, T. L., 344
Arnold, E., 229
Aron, A., 119, 129
Aronfreed, J., 63, 199
Aronson, E., 25, 307, 309
Ashton, M., 227
Astin, A. W., 243, 246
Atkins, R., 153, 156
Ausubel, N., 13, 14
Avalos, J., 246
Axelrod, R., 277, 281

B

Bachman, B. A., 299
Bachrach, D. G., 167
Baden, J. A., 17, 275
Balogh, R. D., 54
Banaji, M. R., 294
Bandura, A., 110, 193, 203, 231
Banker, B. S., 94
Barbaranelli, C., 193

391

Barbee, A. P., 258, 259, 261
Baron, R. A., 79, 91
Barrett, D. W., 117
Barrett, L., 40
Barry, J., 154
Bar-Tal, D., 182, 185, 186, 187, 189, 192,
    197, 344
Bartholomew, K., 236
Barton, E. J., 207
Batson, C. D., 25, 26, 28, 56, 58, 65, 86, 89,
    119, 120, 131, 132, 133, 134, 135,
    136, 137, 138, 140, 211, 230, 237,
    283, 284, 309, 310, 311, 325, 326,
    335, 337
Baumann, D. J., 123, 125, 172
Beach, K. R., 338
Beaman, A. L., 212
Becker, S. W., 215, 216, 218
Beebe, T., 244, 247
Beers, M., 235
Behan, A., 111
Bekkers, R., 285
Bell, P. A., 279
Bellah, R. N., 153, 154
Bem, S. L., 219
Bembenek, A. F., 12, 345
Bengston, V., 213
Bennett, N., 169
Benson, P. L., 92, 96
Benson, S. M., 124
Berger, J. M., 258, 259
Bergin, C. A. C., 106
Bergin, D. A., 106
Bergman, M. E., 172
Berkas, T., 243
Berkowitz, L., 25, 111, 112, 115, 231, 233
Berkowitz, W., 147
Berntson, G. G., 338
Berscheid, E., 111, 168
Bersoff, D. M., 320, 329
Best, D. L., 218
Bettenhausen, K., 167
Beutel, A. M., 216
Bibby, P. A., 163
Bickman, L., 78, 83, 97
Biegel, D. E., 252
Biel, A., 289
Bierhoff, H. W., 114, 234
Biller-Andorno, N., 216
Blader, S. L., 300, 345
Blyth, D. A., 243
Bobo, L., 344

Boccacin, L., 164
Boehm, C., 51
Bonhote, K., 123
Borgida E., 45, 82, 149
Borman, W. C., 166, 167, 169, 234, 342
Boster, F. J., 126
Bouvrette, A., 123
Bowlby, J., 205, 236
Bowles, S., 277
Boyd, R., 277
Boyer, J. L., 241
Boykin, A. W., 8
Boyle, C., 54
Bradley, L. M., 93
Brady, H., 155
Brakeman-Wartell, S. L., 48
Brann, P., 282
Brannick, M. T., 93, 150, 161
Brase, G., 83
Brazier, G., 95
Breakwell, G. M., 172
Bregman, N. J., 203
Brehm, J. W., 203, 245, 254
Brehm, S. S., 203, 245, 259
Brewer, M. B., 274, 283, 294, 304
Bringle, R. G., 243
Brody, G. H., 202
Broll, L., 70, 120
Broman, C. L., 259
Bromley, S., 98
Brown, D. L., 54
Brown, D. R., 248
Brown, K. M., 122
Brown, M. S., 207
Brown, R. J., 299
Brown, S. L., 26, 92, 340
Bruder-Mattson, S. F., 259
Bryan, A. D., 93
Buchanan, W., 241
Buck, R., 57, 311, 342
Burke, P. J., 248
Burnam, M. A., 259
Burnstein, E., 45, 47
Buss, D. M., 36, 42, 49, 51, 52
Butterworth, V. A., 105
Bynum, W. B., Jr., 155
Byrne, D., 91, 92, 109

C

Cacioppo, J. T., 338
Cairns, E., 164

Calabrese, R. L., 247
Caldwell, R. A., 260
Call, V. R. A., 155, 206
Callero, P. L., 107, 149, 154, 158, 159, 162, 163, 164, 173, 206, 212, 213, 241
Campbell, A., 220
Campbell, A. C., 211
Campbell, D. T., 8, 296, 298
Canada, K. E., 228
Cancain, F. M., 216
Canon, L. K., 83
Caporael, L. R., 49
Caprara, G. V., 193, 210
Carlo, G., 190, 193, 216, 228, 234, 341
Carnevale, P. J., 112
Carpentieri, A. M., 260
Carrington, P. I., 112
Carver, C., 235
Caspi, A., 37, 340
Cassidy, C., 95
Catania, J. A., 263
Cernoch, J. M., 54
Chapman, M., 61, 106, 193, 196
Charng, H. W., 213
Cheek, J. M., 260
Chen, X., 167
Cheng, P. W., 51
Cheuk, W. H., 240
Childs, J., 89
Christopher, F. S., 200
Cialdini, R. B., 26, 92, 119, 123, 124, 125, 130, 132, 136, 137, 138, 182, 183, 184, 185, 186, 187, 189, 310
Cicognani, E., 235
Clark, L. A., 36
Clark, M., 91
Clark, M. S., 93, 111, 123, 142. 241, 261
Clark, R. D., III, 21, 59, 72, 75, 81, 85, 86, 115, 120, 130
Clary, E. G., 154, 156, 157, 169, 238, 243, 245, 251
Clewett, A. S., 205
Clore, G. L., 216
Clotfelter, C. T., 148
Clutton-Brock, T., 42
Coates, T. J., 263
Cohen, D. J., 173
Coke J. S., 211
Colamosca, J. V., 79
Colby, A., 186, 188, 189, 231, 233
Cole, C. M., 212
Collins, J. E., 240

Colman, A. M., 293
Comte, A., 25
Connell, P., 93, 150, 169, 170, 235, 238
Conner, C., 45, 82, 149, 216
Connor, M., 164
Conrad, D., 247
Conway, L. G., III, 96
Cooper, M. L., 123
Cooper, R., 36, 306
Corcoran, D., 142
Corley, R., 106, 210, 232
Cornwell, C., 123
Cosmides, L., 50, 51
Costa, P. T., Jr., 228
Côté, S., 235
Cottrell, C. A., 325
Cowen, E. L., 175, 176
Craiger, J. P., 156, 228
Crain, A. L., 90
Crandall, C., 45, 47
Crano, W. D., 96
Crockenberg, S. B., 202
Crocker, J., 123
Crosby, F., 98, 99
Cross, D., 196
Cross, S. E., 218
Crowley, M., 214, 215, 217, 219
Crystal Clear Creation, 41
Cuddy, A. J. C., 119, 325
Cummings, L. L., 171
Cunningham, M. R., 56, 118
Curry, R. L., 44

D

Da Silva, M. S., 193
Daly, M., 48
Damon, M., 231, 233
Damrosch, L., 16
Daniels, L. R., 112, 115, 231, 233
Darby, B. K., 123
Darley, J. M., 20, 28, 29, 68, 69, 71, 72, 76, 77, 78, 80, 81, 82, 85, 86, 88, 100, 103, 109, 310, 335, 336
Darwin, C., 33, 39, 40, 42
Davidov, M., 181
Davis, M. H., 56, 58, 107, 136, 156, 159, 196, 232, 238, 335
Dawes, R. M., 271, 272, 274, 275, 280, 281, 284, 285
Dawkins, R., 8, 26, 39, 40, 42
De Cremer, D., 282, 283, 291, 300, 302, 339, 345

De Dreu, C. K., 288, 289
de Guzman, M. R. T., 228
de Quervain, D. J., 51, 278
de Waal, F. B. M., 57, 341
DeBruin, E. M. N., 285
Deci, E. L., 245
DeGail, M., 90
Dehart, G., 36
DeKay, W. T., 36
Dekovic, M., 192
Deluga, R. J., 169
Demerath, N. J., II, 228, 245
Dempster-McClain, D., 247, 249
DePaulo, B. M., 260, 261
Derlega, V. J., 258, 259, 261
Dertke, M. C., 219
Deutsch, F. M., 90
Devos, T., 120
Dew, M. A., 105
Dewitte, S., 282
Diamond, W. D., 112
Diaz-Loving, R., 136
Dickson-Gómez, J. B., 107
Diekman, A. B., 218
Dilalla, L. F., 38
Dimberg, U., 63
Ditzian, J. L., 90
Donnelly, S., 216
Donnelly, T., 153, 156
Donnerstein, E., 129
Doucet, N., 97, 98
Douglas, N.,227
Dovidio J. F., 20, 21, 56, 65, 72, 85, 86, 91,
      92, 93, 94, 97, 100, 102, 103, 107,
      119, 120, 122, 126, 127, 128, 129,
      136, 138, 139, 149, 152, 219, 225,
      227, 231, 297, 299, 300, 303, 304,
      309, 335, 338, 344, 346
Dozier, J. B., 82
Drake, A. W., 162
Dull, W. R., 261
Dunbar, R. I., 40, 51
Dutton, D. G., 97, 98, 119, 129
Dynes, R. R., 152
Dzaka, E., 162

E

Eagly, A. H., 214, 215, 216, 218, 219, 335,
      342
Easterbrook, J. A., 121, 129
Ebert, J. P., 294

Eccles, J. P., 217
Edelmann, R. J., 89, 96
Edwards, C. P., 206
Eek, D., 284
Efaw, J., 281
Eisenberg, N., 56, 63, 118, 126, 127, 189,
      190, 191, 192, 193, 197, 199, 200,
      202, 203, 205, 207, 209, 218, 227,
      233, 234, 235, 256, 259, 340
Eisenberg-Berg, N., 190
Eisenbud, L., 202
Elbaum, B., 246
Ellison, C. G., 248
Ellsworth, P., 346
Ellyson, S. L., 219
Emde, R. N., 58, 59
Engels, F., 17
Enzle, M. E., 117
Epstein, Y. M., 85
Erdoes, R., 8, 11
Erez, A., 90
Eshed-Levy, D., 284
Esses, V. M., 344
Essock-Vitale, S. M., 45
Euler, H. A., 48
Evans, D., 94
Evans, G., 96
Eyler, J., 243
Eysenck, H. J., 58
Eysenck, M. V., 129

F

Fabes, R. A., 56, 118, 126, 127, 192, 197,
      200, 201, 2002, 2005, 218, 340
Farber, E., 205
Fehr, E., 277, 278, 281, 282
Feiring, C., 154
Feldman, N. S., 197
Feldman, R., 96
Fendrich, J. M., 245
Ferguson, E. ,163
Ferraro, K. F., 251
Ferree, G., 154
Festinger, L., 76, 240, 304
Finkelstein, M. A., 105, 157, 159, 161, 168,
      169, 170, 234
Finkelstein, S. N., 162
Firestone, I. J., 79
Fisher, J. D., 93, 253, 254, 255, 260, 346
Fisher, R. J., 90
Fiske, A. P., 184, 199

Fiske, S. T., 119, 294, 309, 325
Fitzgerald, S. R., 172
Flavell, J. H., 195
Fletcher, T. D., 216
Flippen, A. R., 93
Foddy, M., 282
Fortenbach, V. A., 136
Foss, R., 84
Foushee, H. C., 136
Fox, J. W., 260
France, C. R., 163
Fraser, S. C., 212
Freedman, J. L., 211
Freeman, R., 153
Freifeld, T. R., 156, 228
French, E., 106
Frey, D. L., 97, 116
Friedland, R. P., 248
Friedrich, L. K., 205, 245
Friedrich-Cofer, L. K., 205
Frieze, I. H., 260
Fritzsche, B. A., 105, 156, 228, 234
Frohlich, C. B., 193
Froming, W. J., 183
Frontline, 174
Fuchs, J., 152
Fulker, D. W., 58
Fultz, J., 89, 132, 136, 137, 200, 211, 310
Furnham, A., 115

G

Gachter, S., 278, 281, 282
Gaertner, L., 299
Gaertner, S. L., 21, 72, 85, 86, 91, 93, 94,
   97, 102, 116, 120, 127, 128, 129,
   231, 297, 299, 300, 304, 310, 338,
   344, 346
Garcia, S. M., 78, 336
Gardner, R., 274, 289
Gardner, W. E., 247
Garst, J., 281, 344
Gartner, R. I., 242
Garvey, C., 111
Gary, L., 248
Gaulin, S. J. C., 48
Gecas, V., 248
Geis, G., 216
Gelfand, D., 200
George, J. M., 114, 167, 228
Gergen, K. J., 298, 346
Gergen, M. M., 298, 346

Ghiselin, M. T., 40
Gibbons, F. X., 118
Gibbs, J., 188
Gilbert, D. T., 309, 334
Giles, D. E., Jr., 243
Giles, M., 164
Gillath, O., 236, 237, 238
Gilligan, C., 198
Gintis, H., 277
Glassman, R. B., 54
Glick, P., 119, 303, 325
Goldberg, L. R., 7
Goldin, L., 259
Golding, J. M., 259
Gollwitzer, P. M., 136
Gonsalkorale, K., 48
Goodnow, J. J., 202, 203
Gopnik, A., 196
Goranson, R., 112
Gorey, K. M., 248
Gottesman, I. I., 38
Gouldner, A., 19, 111
Gourevitch, P., 4
Graham, J. W., 171
Gray, J. R., 311
Graziano, W. G., 227, 228, 234, 235
Green, A., 248
Green, S. A., 169
Greenberg, J., 150
Greenberg, J. M., 261
Greenberger, D. B., 173
Greenblatt, B., 248
Greenwald, A. G., 107
Greitmeyer, T., 116
Griffin, A. S., 42
Groebel, J., 5
Grube, J. A., 158, 159, 160, 168, 173, 251, 339
Gruenfeld, D. H., 119
Grusec J. E., 108, 109, 181, 198, 199, 200, 201,
   202, 203, 205, 207, 208, 209, 347
Gueguen, N., 90
Guild, W., 84
Guthrie, I. K., 340

H

Hagendoorn, L., 302
Haidt, J., 251
Halabi, S., 257, 298
Hall, C. L., 124
Hall, J. A., 107, 159, 238
Hallam, J., 129

Hamilton, S. F., 243
Hamilton, W. D., 42
Hammer, J. C., 93
Hannah, M. E., 89, 213
Hardin, G., 271, 272, 274
Hardin, R., 281
Hardister, T., 54
Hardyck, J. A., 96
Hargreaves, D. J., 70
Harmon-Jones, E., 120
Harrell, W. A., 91
Harris, M. B., 124, 241
Harris, S. E., 281, 344
Hart, C. M., 283, 336
Hart, D., 153, 156, 157
Harter, S., 259
Hartmann, D. P., 200
Hartung, J., 48
Harvey, M. D., 117
Harvey, O. J., 296
Harvey, S., 89
Hatfield, E., 254
Hayes, R. B., 263
Hays, S. W., 173
Hearold, S., 205
Hebl, M. R., 90, 228
Hedge, A., 82
Hedin, D., 247
Heider, F., 197, 208
Heinold, W. D., 80
Helmes, E., 227
Henrich, J., 277
Henry, P. J., 116
Hernandez, A. C. R., 82
Herrling, S., 244
Herzog, A. R., 248, 251
Hewitt, L. N., 250, 340
Hewstone, M., 344
Hicks, B. M., 340
Higgins, E. T., 111
Hinde, R. A., 5
Hinterlong, J., 248
Hisata, M., 210
Hitlin, S., 239
Hobbes, T., 15, 16, 28
Hodgkinson, V., 154, 241
Hodson, G., 338
Hoefnagels, C., 82
Hoffman, J. C., 57, 90
Hoffman, M. L., 56, 59, 60, 109, 118, 127, 202, 203, 230
Hogg, M. A., 93, 295

Hoggson, N., 244
Holden, S. J. S., 136
Holmes, J. G., 112, 113
Holyoak, K. J., 51
Hood, W. R., 296
Hoover, C. W., 118
Hopfensperger, J., 3
Horn, J., 58
Hornstein, H. A., 85, 93, 110, 119, 211
Horowitz, L. M., 236
House, J. S., 251
Hovanitz, C. A., 259
Howard, J. A., 110, 117, 118
Howard, J. P. F., 243
Hughes, M., 246
Hui, C., 167
Hume, R. E., 11, 12
Humphrey, G., 59
Hunsberger, B., 193
Hunt, M., 29, 229, 231
Huston, T. L., 71, 216, 217
Huston-Stein, A., 205
Hutchings, V. L., 344

I

Ickes, W., 227
Independent Sector, 148, 152, 153, 154, 155, 157, 216, 225
Inhelder, B., 196
Insko, C. A., 297, 298, 301, 302
Irwin, M. E., 292, 303
Isen, A. M., 70, 89, 91
Israel, A. C., 207
Iwaki, S., 346

J

Jackson, J. M., 279
Jackson, L. M., 344
Janikula, J., 245
Janoski, T., 154
Janssens, J. M. A. M., 192
Jensen, R., 183
Jensen, T. D., 279
Johnson, D. E., 90
Johnson, D. W., 306
Johnson, F. L., 219
Johnson, M. K., 216, 244, 247
Johnson, R. C., 306
Johnson, R. T., 215
Joireman, J. A., 285

Jonas, E., 150
Jones, S., 232
Jos, P. H., 173

K

Kahana, E., 106, 210, 249, 250
Kahn, A., 90, 112
Kai, I., 210
Kamzan, M., 97
Karabenick, S. A., 92
Karau, S. J., 279
Karjalainen, A., 216
Karp, L., 91
Kashyap, R. K., 112
Katz, D., 166
Kawakami, K., 297, 338, 349
Kayal, P., 146
Keating, C. F., 219
Keating, J. P., 90, 137
Kegelmeyer, J. ,156
Kelleher, W., 258
Kelley, H. H., 208, 288
Kelley, K., 91, 109
Kellock, I., 89
Keltikangas-Järvinen, L., 216
Keltner, D., 119
Kendrick, J. R., Jr., 243
Kenny, D. A., 48
Kenrick, D. T., 123, 182, 183, 184
Kenworthy, J. B., 344
Kerr, N. L., 279, 281, 300, 301, 344
Kestenbaum, J., 205
Kidd, R. F., 90
Kidder, D. L., 219
Kiker, D. S., 90
Kim, H., 210
King, D. C., 243
King, E. B., 228
Kipnis, D. M., 205
Kirchner, J. L., 281
Kitayama, S., 45, 47
Klein, R., 114, 234
Kleinke, C. L., 91
Klentz, B., 212
Knight, G. P., 190, 216, 228
Knight, P. A., 260
Knight, R. T., 51
Knowles, E. S., 118
Knowlton, A., 107
Koestner, R., 245
Kohlberg, L., 186, 188, 189

Kohn, A., 27, 270
Komorita, S. S., 271, 274, 275, 276, 285
Konovsky, M. A., 168
Kopelman S., 271
Korchmaros, J. D., 48
Korte, C., 76, 82
Kramer, R. M., 281
Kramp, P., 114, 234
Kraus, S. J., 58
Krebs, D., 25, 49, 309
Kremer, J. F., 243
Kroll, N., 51
Krueger, R. F., 340
Krueger, T., 170
Kruger, D. J., 48
Krupat, E., 84
Kuczynski, L., 207
Kuhlman, D. M., 285, 288
Kunz, P. R., 112
Kuo, H. S., 259
Kuperminc, G. P., 244

L

Ladd, G. W., 89
Laham, S., 168, 169
Lake, R. A., 97
Lam, P., 155
Lamb, S., 106
Lamberti, D. M., 90
Landau, M. O., 123, 241
Lang, F. R., 48
Lange, G., 89
Langer, E. J., 251, 260
Lanzetta, J. T., 127
Latané, B., 20, 28, 29, 68, 69, 71, 72, 74, 76, 77, 80, 81, 82, 85, 88, 100, 103, 109, 279, 335
Latham, G. P., 48, 168, 169
Latkin, C., 107
Latting, J., 154
Laub, J. H., 242
Lavin, J., 5
Lea, S. E. G., 263
Leaf, P. J., 259
Leahy, R. L., 195
LeCompte, M. D., 243
Lee, F., 262
Lee, J. A., 100, 136
Lee, L., 155, 160, 206, 247
Lee, S.-K., 210
Leek, M., 54

Leiser, T., 185
Lennox, V. L., 98
Lepper, M., 201
Lerner, M. J., 111, 112, 114, 337
Lerner, R. M., 92
Levant, R., 258
Levin, P. F., 70, 91
Levine, J. M., 270
Levine, M. ,94, 95, 300
Levine, R. V., 83, 84
Lewandowski, D. A., 281, 344
Lewin, K., 225
Lewis, B. P., 26, 92
Lewis, M., 154
Lewis-Levin, T., 192
Leyens J.-P., 93, 301
Li, Y., 251
Libby. D., 84
Lichtman, C. M., 79
Liden, R. C., 169
Lieberman, M. A., 188, 260
Liebert, R. M., 204
Lien, D., 76
Liew, J., 63
Ligout, S., 54
Lin, M., 294
Lindzey, G., 309
Lipscomb, T. J., 203
Litman, C., 202
Lobel, M., 263
Lombardo, J. P., 241
London, P., 206, 230
Lopes, P. N., 235
Lott, A. J., 304
Lott, B. E., 304
Loy, P. H., 172
Luce, C., 26, 58, 92
Luhtanen, R. K., 123
Lundell, L., 181
Luoh, M-C., 248
Lycett, J., 40
Lynch, S. M., 155
Lytton, H., 202

M

Ma, H.-K., 117
Macaulay, J. R., 25, 211
MacCoun, R. J., 279
MacDonald, K., 56
Machiavelli, N., 15, 28
MacKenzie, S. B., 167

Mackie, D. M., 119, 120
MacLean, P. D., 56
Madsen, R., 153
Madson, L., 218
Maggiano, N. A., 219
Magnusson, J., 116, 324
Mails, T. E., 12
Main, M., 205
Major, D. A., 216
Maner, J. K., 136, 138
Mann, J. A., 97, 304
Mannix, L. M., 90
Manno, B., 154
Manteufal, L., 82, 149
Manucia, G. K., 125, 136
Manzi, C., 161
Markey, P. M., 82
Markus, G. B., 243
Marshello, A., 285
Marta, E., 161
Martichuski, D. K., 279
Martin, G. B., 59
Martinez, T. S., 83
Marwell, G., 113, 228, 245
Marx, K., 16, 17
Maslach, C., 346
Mastropieri, M. A., 246
Mathews, K. E., 83
Matsueda, R. L., 242
Matthews, K. A., 58
Matthews, L. L., 136
Mattis, J. S., 155
Mayer, J. D., 70, 122
May-Plumlee, T., 200
McAdam, D., 245
McAllister, H. A., 203
McAndrew, F. T., 52
McBurney, D. H., 48
McCall, G. J., 213
McCarthy, P. M., 136
McClintock, C. G., 285
McCombie, R. P., 162
McCrae, R. R., 228
McCullough, B. C., 250, 251,
McCullough, M., 343
McDougall, W., 18, 19, 309
McGovern, L. P., 89, 90
McGue, M., 340
McGuire, A. M., 23, 106
McGuire, M. T., 45
McKusick, L., 263
McLaughlin, F. J., 54

McMahon, K., 249
McManus, J. A., 263
McMillan, K. K., 258
McMillen, D. L., 70
McNally, S., 192
McPherson, J., 152
McTavish, J., 280
Medvene, L., 263, 264
Melchior, L. A., 260
Meltzoff, A. N., 38, 196
Mercer, M., 167
Messick, D. M., 271, 279, 291, 346
Metman, L., 344
Meyer, J. P., 168
Meyer, M. ,107, 159, 238
Mezei, L., 96
Miceli, M. P., 82, 173
Mickler, S. E., 240
Midili, A. R., 156
Midlarsky, E., 89, 106, 210, 213, 230, 232,
    249, 250, 251, 341
Midlarsky, M., 89
Mikolay, D., 219
Mikulincer, M., 235, 237, 238
Milburn, N., 248
Milgram, S., 83
Miller, C. T., 97, 98
Miller, D. T., 112, 114, 309, 329
Miller, J., 192, 198, 216, 243
Miller, J. G., 320
Miller, M. L., 247
Miller, N., 304
Miller, P. A., 56, 127, 192, 197, 205, 233
Miller, W. R., 260
Mills, J., 142, 261
Mineka, S., 63
Mitchell, M. M., 122
Moen, P., 247, 249
Moghaddam, F. M., 95
Monto, M. A., 82
Moody, S. W., 246
Moore, B. S., 199, 205, 207, 209, 247
Moore, C., 197
Moore, C. W., 244, 245, 247
Moore, J., 50
Moorman, R. H., 168
Moran, T., 283
Moreland, R. L., 270
Morgan, C. J., 53, 298
Morgenstern, O., 272
Moriarty, T., 79
Morris, A. S., 56

Morris-Villagran, M., 122
Morrow-Howell, N., 248
Morse, S. J., 298
Mortimer, J. T., 244, 247
Morycz, R. K., 252
Moskowitz, G. B., 78, 295, 336
Moss, M. K., 108
Motowidlo, S. J., 90, 166, 169, 234
Mueller, C. W., 129
Mullen, B., 299
Munekata, H., 193
Murchison, C A., 309
Murningham, J. K., 100
Murphy, D. E., 1
Murray, J. P., 204
Murrell, A. J., 304
Musick, M. A., 153, 155, 157, 242, 246, 251
Mustillo, S., 155
Myers-Lipton, S. J., 243

N

Nadler, A., 27, 253, 254, 255, 256, 257, 258,
    260, 261, 263, 298, 342, 346
National Centre for Volunteering Re-
    search, 149, 153, 157
Neal, C., 190
Neale, M. C., 58
Neighbors, H. W., 259
Nemeroff, R., 106, 210
Nesse, R. M., 340
Nestmann, F., 175, 176
Neuberg, S. L., 26, 90, 92, 294, 325
Newcomb, M. D., 82
Newman, R. S., 259
Newman, S., 241
Newmann, B. H., 162
Newmann, F. A., 247
Neyer, F. J., 48
Nias, D. K. B., 58
Nida, S., 74, 279
Niehoff, B. P., 168
Nier, J. A., 94, 300
Nilsson Sojka, B., 162, 241
Ninomiya, K., 193
Nisbett, R. E., 107, 129, 226
Nitzberg, R. E., 237, 238.
North, A. C., 70
Nowak, M. A., 278

O

Oakes, P. J., 93, 295

Öhman, A., 63
Okun, M. A., 228
Oleson, K. C., 56, 131, 135
Oliker, S. J., 216
Oliner, P. M., 206, 228, 229, 230, 231, 234
Oliner, S. P., 206, 228, 229, 230, 231, 234
Olson, M., 279
Olsson, A., 294
Oman, D., 249, 251
Omoto, A. M., 90, 95, 149, 156, 157, 158,
    163, 169, 225, 238, 252
Onawola, R., 241
O'Quin, K., 89
Orbell, J. M., 274, 275, 281, 284
Orenstein, L., 154, 157
Organ, D. W., 165, 167, 168, 169
Orr, J. M., 167
Ortiz, A., 8, 11
Osguthorpe, R. T., 246, 247
Ostrom, E., 274, 280, 294
Otten, C. A., 78, 101, 216, 233
Otten, S., 295
Otten, W., 285

P

Packel, E. W., 54
Paduano, A., 211
Page, R. A., 108
Paine, J. B., 167
Pakaslahti, L., 216
Paladino, M.-P., 93
Pancer, S. M., 193
Park, B., 295
Parks, C. D., 271, 274, 275, 276, 285, 343
Parks, J. M., 171
Partlow, M. E. P., 200
Pascal, V., 63
Pastorelli, C., 193
Patnoe, S., 207
Paulhus, D. L., 231
Paunonen, S. V., 227
Pearce, P. L., 23, 24
Pegalis, L. J., 111
Pegg, I., 96
Penner, L. A., 65, 78, 93, 105, 107, 150,
    151, 152, 155, 156, 157, 159, 167,
    168, 170, 216, 219, 227, 228, 233,
    234, 235, 238, 239, 269, 309, 310,
    335, 339
Perlow, L., 90
Perry, R. P., 116, 324

Persson, G. E. B., 216
Peterson, H., 120
Pettigrew, T. F., 297, 303, 344
Petty, R. E., 235
Phelps, E. A., 338
Philliber, S., 244
Piaget, J., 195, 196
Pichette, D., 162
Pierotti, R., 50
Piliavin, I. M., 23, 70, 89, 96, 100, 120
Piliavin, J. A., 21, 22, 23, 70, 84, 85, 86, 96,
    100, 101, 103, 107, 120, 126, 128,
    130, 141, 142, 149, 154, 155, 158,
    159, 160, 162, 163, 164, 168, 173,
    201, 205, 206, 212, 213, 214, 215,
    217, 219, 226, 239, 241, 142, 251,
    152, 310, 339
Pinter, B., 281, 297
Platt, J., 291
Plomin, R., 37
Podsakoff, P. M., 167
Pomare, M., 304
Pomazal, R. S., 216
Porter, R. H., 54
Poundstone, W., 272
Pratkanis, A. R., 255
Pratt, M. W., 193
Pratto, F., 295
Preston, M., 212
Preston, S. D., 57
Prosser, A., 94
Pruitt, D. G. ,112
Pryor, J. B., 263
Putnam, R. D., 152, 153
Pyszczynski, T., 150

Q

Quarantelli, E. L., 152

R

Rabow, J., 82
Rachal, K. C., 343
Radke-Yarrow, M. R., 61, 62, 106, 193, 196
Rahm, J., 243
Rand, A., 17, 18, 28
Rapoport, A., 284
Raskoff, S., 154, 155
Rausch, M. K., 228
Raven, B. H., 270
Raviv, A., 185, 187, 192, 197

Ray, M. L., 211
Reddy, R. D., 90, 107, 111
Redler, E., 198, 208, 209
Reed, A., 279
Reed, P., 149, 153, 155, 157
Reeder, G. D., 263
Regan, D. T., 113, 122
Reicher, S. D., 93, 94, 95, 295
Reinhart, M. A., 260
Reis, H. T., 79
Reiser, M., 340
Reitschlin, J., 248
Reyna, C., 116
Rhodes, A., 111
Rholes, W. S., 197
Richter, L., 246
Ridley, M., 39, 40
Rind, B., 112
Rioux, S. M., 169, 170, 238, 239
Ripley, J. S., 341
Roach, B. L., 82
Robinson, J. L., 58, 59
Rocher, S., 298
Rodin, J., 96, 100, 102, 251, 260
Roesch, S. C., 216
Rokeach, M., 96
Romano-Egan, J., 123
Ronen, R., 243, 247
Rosen, S., 240
Rosenberg, M., 250, 251
Rosenhan, D. L., 70, 206, 230
Rosenman, R. H., 58, 122
Rosenthal, S., 154
Ross, L., 107
Ross, S. R., 228
Roth, K., 190
Rothbart, M., 295
Rothstein, S. I., 50
Rotolo, T., 152
Rotter, J. B., 282
Rozario, P. A., 248
Rubin, J. Z., 270
Ruble, D. N., 197
Rudman, L. A., 303
Rudolph, U., 116
Ruggiero, M., 216
Rusbult, C. E., 288
Rush, M.C., 168
Rushton, J. P., 54, 58, 199, 200, 203, 204,
    207, 211, 226, 234
Russell, F. J., 54
Russell, R. J. H., 54, 90

Rust, M. C., 299
Rutte, C. G., 291
Rutter, R. A., 247
Ryan, K., 167, 168
Ryan, R. M., 245
Ryder, A. G., 96

S

Saas-Kortsaak, P., 207
Sackett, P. R., 167
Sagi, A., 59, 127
Saito, R., 243
Salamon, J., 13
Salmon, C. A., 48
Salovey, P., 70, 122, 235
Saltz, E., 72
Sampson, R. J., 242
Samuelson, C. D., 291
Sanders, D. Y., 70
Sapolsky, H. M., 162
Sargeant, L. D., 93
Saucier, D. A., 97, 98
Sauer, L. A., 163
Sax, L. J., 243, 246
Saxe, L., 98
Schachter, S., 119, 129
Schadron, G., 298
Schaller, M., 124, 132, 137, 138
Scheier, M., 235
Scheltema, K. E., 298
Schimel, J., 150
Schimmel, M., 105
Schiro, K., 59
Schlozman, K. L., 155
Schmidt, G., 121
Schmitt, D. R., 113
Schmitz, S., 59
Schnedler, R., 96
Schneider, K. T., 172
Schoenrade, P. A., 211
Schonbar, R. A., 106, 210
Schopler, J., 297, 298, 299, 301, 302
Schreiber, G. B., 163
Schroeder, D. A., 12, 86, 136, 138, 139,
    272, 279, 292, 303, 310, 345
Schultz, R., 252
Schumer, H., 247
Schwab, M., 279
Schwartz, M., 91
Schwartz, S. H., 79, 102, 110, 117, 118, 239
Scruggs, T. E., 246, 247

Sebe, F., 54
Sedlacek, W. E., 258, 259
Segal, N. L., 49, 54
Sego, D. J., 167
Seipel, M., 346
Selbee, L., 153, 155, 157
Sellers, A., 258
Selman, R. L., 197
Sen, B., 258, 259
Settoon, R. P., 169
Shaffer, D. R., 202
Shaklee, H., 280
Shalker, T. E., 91
Shaver, P. R., 236, 237, 238
Shea, C., 192
Shell, R., 192, 256, 259
Sherif, C. W., 296
Sherif, M., 296, 303, 304, 344
Sherman, P. W., 44
Sheu, H. B., 258, 259
Shotland, R. L., 71, 80, 85
Sibicky, M. E., 136, 139, 303, 321
Sidanius, J., 295
Sieber, S. D., 247
Siegal, W. E., 93
Sigmund, K., 278
Silvera, D. H., 334
Simmons J. L., 213
Simmons, R. G., 105
Simmons, R. T., 284
Simner, M. L., 59, 127
Simon, B., 95
Simpson, B., 290, 292
Simutis, Z. M., 207
Singer, J. E., 119
Skarlicki, D. P., 168, 169
Skitka, L. J., 116
Slavin, R. E., 306
Smith, A., 18
Smith, C., 299
Smith, C. A., 166
Smith, C. L., 200
Smith, D., 153
Smith, D. M., 90, 340
Smith, E. R., 119, 120
Smith, J., 110
Smith, K. D., 90, 137
Smith, M. B., 96
Smith, P. K., 54
Smith, R. E., 76
Smith, R. H., 111
Smythe, L., 76

Snyder, M., 90, 95, 107, 149, 154, 156, 157,
    158, 163, 169, 225, 227, 238, 243,
    244, 245, 247, 251, 252, 282, 347
Sober, E., 8, 26, 51, 141
Sojka, P., 162, 241
Sokol, B. W., 96
Solomon, G. S., 70
Solomon, S., 150
Sorenson, K., 83
Sparling, S., 122
Speer, A. L., 234
Spiegel, S., 111
Spiers, C., 240
Sprafkin, J., 204
Sprecher, S., 254
Sroufe, A., 36
Sroufe, L. A., 36, 205
St. John, C., 152
Staub, E., 74, 79, 80, 89, 108, 115, 207, 233,
    337, 341
Steblay, N. M., 82, 84, 212
Steca, P., 210
Steel, J. E., 12, 345
Steele, C., 254
Steffens, K., 95
Stein, A. H., 205
Stein, D. D., 96
Sterling, B., 129
Stewart, D., 216
Stewart, L. P., 172
Stich, M. H., 241
Stone, V. E., 51
Stotland, E., 90, 137
Stouten, J., 283
Strain-Clark, C., 89
Strauss, J. S., 43
Straw, M., 85
Stremmel, A., 89
Strohmetz, D., 112
Stryker, S., 213
Stukas, A. A., 154, 156, 243, 245
Stürmer, S., 95
Sullivan, D., 279
Sullivan, W. M., 153
Sundeen, R., 154, 155
Susman, E. J., 205
Swaim, G. W., 261
Swan, S., 172
Swearse, B., 240
Swidler, A., 153
Swinyard, W. R., 211
Switzer, G. E., 105, 234

T

Tajfel, H., 93, 283, 295
Takeuchi, D. T., 259
Tang, F., 248
Taormina, R. J., 346
Tarrant, M., 70
Taylor, C. J., 101
Taylor, D. M., 95
Taylor, R. J., 259
Taylor, S. E., 263
Taylor, S. P., 90
Teachman, G., 200
Tellegen, A., 122
Terry, D. J., 110
Tesser, A., 254
Thibaut, J. W., 168, 288
Thoits, P. A., 247, 250, 340
Thomas G. C., 211
Thompson, C., 197
Thompson, R. A., 59
Thoresen, C. E., 249
Thornton, C., 242
Thumuluri, L. K., 234
Tice, T. E., 112
Tietjan, A., 193
Tillman, P., 234
Tipton, S. M., 153
Tobin, R. M., 228, 260
Tobin, S. S., 260
Toch, H., 123
Toffler, A., 18
Toi, M., 135
Tompkins, M. E., 173
Tooby, J., 50, 51
Tremain, M., 96
Trivers, R., 49, 51
Tropp, L. R., 303, 344
Troyer, D., 234
Turner, J. C., 93, 283, 295
Turner, M. E., 255
Turner, R. H., 213
Turner, R. N., 344
Tweed, R. G., 96
Tyler, A. F., 17
Tyler, T. R., 399, 345

U

Uggen, C., 245
Unger, L. S., 234
Unger, R. K., 214, 215, 217, 219

United States Department of Energy, 147
United States Department of Labor, 150, 155
Uslaner, E., 155
Utne, M. K., 90

V

Vadeboncoeur, J. A., 243
Vaes, J., 93
Vaidya, J., 122
Valiente, C., 63
van de Kragt, A. J. C., 275, 281, 284
van Dijk, E., 278, 291, 344
van Lange, P. A. M., 276, 285, 286, 287, 288, 289, 302, 347
Van Selst, M., 231
van Vugt, M., 276, 283, 285, 302, 339
van Willigen, M., 248
Vanderplas, M., 89
VanDyne, L., 171, 172
Varney, L. L., 136
Vasudev, J., 244
Vaughan, K. B., 127
Vaughn, K., 120
Vaughn, S., 246
Vecina, M. L., 159
Verba, S., 155
Verkuyten, M., 302
Veroff, J. B., 260
Vevea, J. L., 297
Vignoles, B. L., 161
Vigoda, E., 168
Villagran, P. D., 122
Vincent, J. E., 123, 125
Vine, I., 51
Vinokur, A. D., 340
Visser, K., 288
Voci, A., 344
Volunteering Australia, 149, 153
von Hippel, W., 48
von Neumann, J., 272

W

Wagner, E., 61, 106, 196
Wagner, S. L., 168
Walker, J., 274, 280
Walker, L., 168
Walster, E., 111, 113, 168
Walster, G. W., 111, 168
Walton, M. D., 96, 102

Walz, S. M., 167
Wang, X. T., 48
Warburton, J., 110
Ward, C. M., 94
Watson, D., 36, 122
Watson, J., 196
Watson, J. B., 19
Waugh, G., 78, 216
Wayne, S. J., 169
Weaver, K., 78, 336
Webb, S., 150
Weber, J. M., 271, 274, 293
Webley, P., 263
Webster, J. M., 111
Weeks, J., 90
Wegner, D. M., 96
Weiner, B., 116, 121, 324
Weiss, H. M., 260
Weiss, R. F., 241
Weitzel, B., 48
Weitzman, E. A., 93
Weitzman, M. S., 154, 241
Wellman, H. M., 196
Wells, P. A., 54
West, S. A., 42
West, S. G., 96
Weston, D. R., 205
Wetherell, M. S., 93
Whatley, M. A., 111, 112
Wheeler, J. A., 248
Whitcher-Alagna, S., 253, 254, 255
White, B. J., 296
Whiting, B. B., 198, 206
Whiting, J. J. M., 198, 206
Whitney, G., 96
Wicklund, R. A., 118
Wiese, D., 122
Wildschut, T., 281, 297, 298, 299
Wilke, H. A. M., 278, 291, 344, 346
Wilke, M., 344
Williams, G. C., 52
Williams, J., 218
Williams, K. D., 279
Williams, L. J., 93, 168
Williams, M., 122
Williams, R., 243
Williams, R. M., 249
Williamson, G. M., 93, 111, 123, 240, 252
Wills, T. A., 260, 261, 263, 264
Wilson, D. S., 8, 26, 51

Wilson, D. W., 74, 90
Wilson, J., 148, 152, 153, 154, 155, 157,
    242, 246
Wilson, J. P., 74
Wilson, T. D., 25, 107
Winstead, B. A., 258
Winter, S., 247
Wispé, L. G., 25
Wit, A. P., 291, 300, 301
Witzel, B., 48
Wolcott, I. H., 261
Wong, F. Y., 298
Wong, K. S., 240
Wood, E. E., 118
Woodell, A. J., 12, 345
Woolcott, M., 112
Worchel, S. W., 298
Word, L. E., 72, 75, 81, 130
Worthington, E. L., Jr., 341, 343
Wright, S. C., 95
Wuthnow, R., 154, 241

X

Xu, J., 119, 325

Y

Yakimovich, D., 72
Yamagishi, T., 282, 291
Yates, M., 243
Yinon, Y., 123, 241
Yogev, A., 243, 247
Youniss, J., 243
Yousif, Y. H., 82
Yzerbyt, V., 298

Z

Zagefka, H., 299
Zahn-Waxler, C. J., 58, 59, 61, 62, 106, 193,
    196
Zajonc, R. B., 320
Zakhireh, B., 106
Zeldin, R. S., 243
Zillman, D., 129
Zimbardo, P. G., 193, 260
Zimmerman, D., 216
Zuckerman, M., 79, 114
Zwikker, M., 82

Subject Index

A

Academic problems, seeking help for, 261, 263–264
Affective models, 321–327
Age differences
  in help seeking, 259–260
  in helping, 30–31, 59–63
AIDS, 23, 140, 146, 157–158, 234, 252, 263
Alcoholism, 262, 264
Altruism, definition of, 24–26, 35
  see also Empathy-altruism model
Altruistic genes, 53
Altruistic punishment, 278, 281–282
Arousal: Cost-Reward Model, 100–103, 105, 126–131, 310
Attachment theory, 236–238
Attraction, 91–92, 95, 304
Attributions, 121, 127–129, 197–198, 211–213, 254–255, 292–293, 324–325, 331
Aversive racism, 97–100

B

Behavioral genetics, 37–38, 64, 336, 340
Behaviorism, 140
Biological factors, 34, 38, 64, 182, 223, 311–312

Blood donors / C

Blood donors, 3, 162–164, 178, 228, 241–242, 315
Bystander inhibition, 19–20, 72–79, 224–225, 268, 309–310
Bystander intervention, Latané-Darley decision model, 19–20, 28, 29, 68–85, 103, 310, 335

C

Charitable activities, 150–155
Cheating, 50–51, 55
Civil rights activists, 228, 230, 245
Classical conditioning, 63, 329
Cognitive development, 195–199
Cognitive dissonance, 240, 304
Cognitive empathy, 196–197
Cognitive learning models, 184–187
Commons dilemma, 271–272
Collectivist cultures, 95–96
Common ingroup identity, 299–301, 304–305, 318, 346
Communal relationships, 262–263
Communication, 279–281
  see also Spontaneous communication, Verbal communication
Community activism, 144–148, 176–177, 245, 268, 314

Contact Hypothesis, 296–297, 303–304, 343–344
Cooperation, definition of, 27–28, 270
Cost-reward analyses, 86–103, 217, 266, 278–279, 298, 310, 313, 318, 326, 331–333, 338, 348
    see also Arousal: cost-reward model
Crisis hotlines, 144
Cross-cultural studies, 37, 49–50, 95–96, 198–199, 214, 312, 325, 329
Cross-racial helping, 96–97
Cross-species studies, 38–39, 64, 312
Cultural factors (*see* Cross-cultural studies)

D

Decision-making models
    in help giving, 68–103
    in help seeking, 253–258
Demographic variables, 82–86, 152–154, 258–260, 314
Developmental issues, 30–31, 59–63, 118–119, 180–214, 258–260, 315–316, 340
Diffusion of responsibility, 76–77
Disasters, 1–3, 150–152
Discipline, parental, 230
Dispositional empathy, 232–234
Distress cues, 74–76

E

Educational level, 153
Egoistic motivation, 314, 325–326, 344
Emotions, 57, 63, 89, 119–121, 320
    see also Moods
Empathic arousal, 118–119, 126–127, 139, 142–143, 313, 320
Empathic concern, 132, 134–136, 314, 325
Empathy, 55–64, 157–158, 177, 191, 202, 228, 231–234, 301, 310, 316, 324, 326. 332, 335, 337, 339, 347
    heritability of, 58–59
Empathy-altruism model, 131–140, 311
Empathy-specific punishment, 137
Empathy-specific reward, 137
Equity theory, 113–115, 169, 254
Ethnic differences, 154–155. 259
Evolutionary altruism, 141–142
Evolutionary theory, 29, 33, 40–55, 64, 276–278, 312, 323, 334, 336, 339

Exchange relationships, 262–263
Extensivity, 231, 234

F

Fear, 284–285
Feelings (*see* Emotions)
First-aid training, 80
Foot-in-the-door technique, 212
Forgiveness, 239, 341–343
Functional analysis technique, 156–158, 169–170, 238, 239, 315, 334, 347

G

Gay Men's Health Crisis, 146–147
Gender, definition of, 217–218
    see also Sex differences
Gender roles, 214–219, 260, 315–316, 331, 335
Genetic factors, 26, 35–38, 42–59, 276–278, 310–311, 321, 323, 329, 339–340, 342
Good Samaritan parable, 86–88
Greed, 284–285
Group identity, 93–96
Group selection theory, 51–52
Guilt feelings, 92, 122–123

H

Handbook of Social Psychology, 309–310
Help-seeking behaviors, 252–264
Help-seeking paradox, 263
Help providers, consequences for, 239–252
Heroism, 1, 4, 147, 216, 220, 229–232, 342–343
Holocaust, 228–232
Human Genome Project, 35

I

Image-reparation hypothesis, 122–124
Impulsive helping, 129–130, 333
Individual differences, 31, 156–158, 166, 169, 177–178, 223–239, 285–290, 302–303, 414, 316, 318, 324, 329
Individualist cultures, 95–96
Infant studies,of empathy, 38, 59–60
Informal helping, 148–149, 174–176
Informational social influence, 71–74, 76, 78–79

Instincts, 18, 19, 309
Instrumental conditioning (*see* Operant conditioning)
Integrated Model of Cooperation, 292–294
Interactionism (person-situation), 225–226, 235–236, 316
Interindividual-intergroup discontinuity effect, 297

J

Jews in Nazi Germany, 228–232
Just-world hypothesis, 111–114, 337

K

Kin selection theory, 43–49, 53–54, 276–277, 312, 322–323, 328–329
Kitty Genovese incident, 18–19, 66, 67–68, 76, 77, 81, 88, 101, 103, 309–310, 333

L

Learned helpfulness, 198–110, 312, 328–329

M

Macro-level analysis, 32, 311, 335–336, 343, 345–346
Maturational changes, 329–330
see also Developmental issues
Meso-level analysis, 32, 310, 335, 343, 346
Micro-level analysis, 32, 311, 335–336, 339, 346
Misattribution paradigm, 129
Modeling, 154, 157, 160–161, 203–206, 210–211, 315
see also Observational learning
Moods, 69–70, 122–126, 330
see also Emotions
Moral reasoning, 186–189, 202, 315, 337
Mothers Against Drunk Driving, 147–148
Motivation, 29–30, 36, 65, 107–108

N

Nature-nurture issues (*see* Genetic factors)
Nazis, 228–232
Negative reinforcement (*see* Reinforcement)

Negative-state relief model, 123–126, 130–131
Neural imaging, 338–339
Norms,
    personal, 110, 117–118, 160–161, 313, 330
    social, 110–113, 115–117, 167–168, 313, 316, 330, 344

O

Observational learning 203–211, 315, 328–329, 330
see also Modeling
Operant conditioning, 108, 241, 329
Organizational Citizenship Behavior, 165–170, 173–175, 177–178, 219, 228, 234, 314, 342
Other-orientated empathy, 234

P

Personality variables
    definition of, 225–226
    in help giving, 225–236, 314, 316, 331, 339
    in help seeking, 260–261
    see also Interactionism
Principled Organizational Dissent, 145, 165, 171–174, 177, 314
Prisoner's dilemma, 272–274, 290, 297–299, 302
Prosocial behavior, definition of, 21–22
Prosocial moral reasoning, 189–193
Prosocial personality type, 227–229, 234–235
Public goods (give-some) dilemmas, 275, 282, 293

R

Racial differences
    in help seeking, 259
    in helping, 96–100, 154–155
Racial prejudice, 97–100, 338
Reactance theory, 203, 245, 254
Reciprocity, 49–51, 111–113, 167, 277–278, 297–298, 312, 317, 318, 322–324, 328–329, 344
Reginald Denny incident, 66–67, 105
Reinforcement, 199–203, 291, 315, 326
Religion, 8–14, 155

Rewards, (*see* Cost-reward analyses)
Robber's Cave study, 296, 303–304, 344
Role Identity Model, 159–164, 170, 173
Rural-urban differences, 84–85

S

Self-efficacy, 231, 248, 250, 251, 260, 316, 320
Self-esteem, 234, 246, 248, 251, 253–258, 260, 263, 317
Self-help groups, 255, 262
Self-other merging, 138–139
Service learning, 242–245
Sex differences
    in help giving, 153, 214–220, 331
    in help seeking, 258–259
Shyness, 260–261
Similarity
    in help giving, 53–54, 76, 92, 93–94, 96–97
    in help seeking, 262–264
Situational variables
    in help giving, 74–76, 79–80, 312, 314, 318, 320–321, 324, 330, 340
    in help seeking, 261–265
    see also Interactionism
Social comparison theory, 76
Social Darwinism, 39
Social dilemmas, 6, 271–294, 324, 344
Social Identity Theory, 257, 294–295, 299–301, 342
Social influence hypothesis, 72–79, 279–283, 298–299, 318
Socialization
    in adulthood, 152–154, 210–213, 223, 316, 331, 341

    in childhood, 181–184, 221–223, 325, 329, 341
Socialization model, 182–184, 187
Social learning, 181, 199–210, 221, 315
Social roles, 211–213
Social support, 149, 251, 258–259, 262
Social value orientation, 285–290, 302–303, 305, 318
Socioeconomic status, 153–155
Spontaneous communication, 322–323, 342
Status, 256–257, 264, 298, 306, 342, 345–346
Stimulus overload, 83–84
Structural solutions, 290–291, 345
Survival of the fittest, 33–34, 40

T

Take-some dilemmas, 274–275
Talmudic writings, 13
Taoism, 11
Temperaments, 36
Threat to Self-Esteem Model, 253–258, 346
Tit-for-tat, 277
Trust, 1, 282–283, 302, 347
Trustworthiness, 282–283, 302, 347
Twin studies, 58–59

V

Verbal communication, 206–210, 279–281, 315, 318
Volunteer Process Model, 158–159, 163
Volunteerism, 2–3, 30, 144–145, 148–164, 178, 213, 225, 239, 242–252, 266, 268, 314, 326, 332